THE HUMAN SUSTAINABLE CITY

T0330969

The Human Sustainable City
Challenges and Perspectives from the Habitat Agenda

Edited by

LUIGI FUSCO GIRARD
University of Naples 'Federico II'

BRUNO FORTE
Pontifical Theological Faculty of Southern Italy – Naples

MARIA CERRETA
University of Naples 'Federico II'

PASQUALE DE TORO
University of Naples 'Federico II'

FABIANA FORTE
Second University of Naples

Taylor & Francis Group

LONDON AND NEW YORK

First published 2003 by Ashgate Publishing

Reissued 2019 by Routledge
2 Park Square, Milton Park, Abingdon, Oxon, OX14 4RN
52 Vanderbilt Avenue, New York, NY 10017

Routledge is an imprint of the Taylor & Francis Group, an informa business

Publisher's Note
The publisher has gone to great lengths to ensure the quality of this reprint but points out that some imperfections in the original copies may be apparent.

Disclaimer
The publisher has made every effort to trace copyright holders and welcomes correspondence from those they have been unable to contact.

A Library of Congress record exists under LC control number:

ISBN 13: 978-1-138-70818-1 (hbk)
ISBN 13: 978-1-138-70815-0 (pbk)
ISBN 13: 978-1-315-19856-9 (ebk)

Contents

List of Contributors

Mejbahuddin Ahmed, Khulna University, Bangladesh.

Pilar García Almirall, Universitat Politécnica de Catalunya, Barcelona, Spain.

Olga Belous, Klaipeda University, Lithuania.

Bohuslav Blazek, Foundation EcoTerra, Prague, Czech Republic.

Malcolm C. Burns, Universitat Politécnica de Catalunya, Barcelona, Spain.

J. Baird Callicott, University of North Texas, Denton, USA.

Evgenia Dimitrakopoulou, National Technical University of Athens, Greece.

Nanne Engelbrektsson, Göteborg University, Sweden.

Jürgen Eppinger, Municipality of Hanover, Germany.

Maria Giaoutzi, National Technical University of Athens, Greece.

Alan Gilbert, University College London, United Kingdom.

Peter Hall, University College London, United Kingdom.

David Harvey, Johns Hopkins University, Baltimore, USA.

Guang-Jun Jin, Shenhen Graduate School – HIT, China.

Üner Kirdar, United Nations Development Programme, New York, USA.

Anil Laul, Anangpur Building Centre, India.

Joan Martinez-Alier, Universitat Autònoma de Barcelona, Spain.

Charlton D. McIlwain, Oklahoma City University, Norman, USA.

Francesca Medda, London School of Economics, United Kingdom.

Ignazio Musu, University of Venice, Italy.

Peter Nijkamp, Free University, Amsterdam, The Netherlands.

Christian Ost, Brussels Business School, Belgium.

Hassan Radoine, University of Pennsylvania, USA.

Keith Richardson, Economic Partnerships, Morpeth, United Kingdom.

Nicole Rijkens-Klomp, University of Maastricht, The Netherlands.

Josep Roca Cladera, Universitat Politécnica de Catalunya, Barcelona, Spain.

Jan Rosvall, Göteborg University, Sweden.

Jan Rotmans, University of Maastricht, The Netherlands.

Leonie Sandercock, University of British Columbia, Vancouver, Canada.

Sarbjeet Singh Sandhu, Chandigarh Administration, India.

Denise L. Scannell, University of Oklahoma, Norman, USA.

Jack W. Scannell, Environmental Coalition of South Seattle, USA.

Kirtee Shah, Habitat International Coalition, Ahmedabad, India.

Marjolein B.A. van Asselt, University of Maastricht, The Netherlands.

Martin van de Lindt, University of Maastricht, The Netherlands.

Nicholas You, UN-Habitat, Nairobi, Kenya.

Stefano Zamagni, University of Bologna, Italy.

Cong-xia Zhao, Harbin University of Civil Engineering and Architecture, China.

Preface

The dawn of a new millennium bids us to reflect upon our civilization, its mission, and the future of humanity as well as that of our entire planet.

If humanity is to survive and avoid new catastrophes, a global political order must be accompanied by mutual respect among the many spheres of civilization and cultures. It must also be joined with a sincere effort to find fundamental shared values and moral imperatives, and to transform them into the very foundations for coexistence in a globally interdependent world.

If we examine the problems the world faces today – economic, social, environmental as well as civilization's more general issues – whether we like it or not, we will always question if a specific course of action is more or less suitable, and if it is appropriate in terms of long-term responsibility towards our planet.

I believe that the most important political matters of our time regard the moral order and its sources, human rights and its relative sources of legitimization, human responsibility and a penetrating vision of what nothing, and no one, can mask in a shroud of noble words.

I am deeply convinced that the debate on civilization and the challenges that it must face also and necessarily includes the debate on the environment in which we live and to which we belong.

The countries which emerged from the collapse of the totalitarian regimes in the last decade are not alone in combating senseless interventions upon the environment, although it is in these countries that we find unsound urban systems with concentrations exceeding any acceptable limit. Even the jewels of European architecture and history, such as the capital of the Czech Republic, Prague, bear the sad traces of megalomaniacal and out-of-scale urban planning with no respect for the environmental context.

Today as well, we unfortunately witness crass disrespect towards what was built by past generations.

In many places, settlements are losing their human dimension. In the enormous urban agglomerations, people are alone; they lose their awareness of both belonging to civil society as well as its very continuity. The result of this is individual frustration, the growth of illegality, crime and a series of other negative social and psychological phenomena.

Anonymous bedroom districts with huge, starkly ugly apartment blocks, which disfigure the landscape and human settlements in general, cannot, unfortunately, be simply eliminated. They are the cumbersome legacy with which we, and future generations, must grapple.

Thus, I believe that it is a very encouraging sign to ponder the possible destiny of our environment and to discuss the manifold issues on a highly specialized level – as the different authors of this volume have done – in order to prevent further devastation of our common cultural heritage. We must, in fact, help preserve one of the most precious and beautiful gifts that we have inherited from past generations – our environment, in harmonious symbiosis with humankind and its cultural heritage.

Moreover, I must emphasize the key role of civil society, the means by which humanity can give the best of itself. Human beings feel the need to connect with one another and, at times, help each other out, as well as to serve the public good even when not gaining immediate profit, but aware of having done some good for future generations. This need and potential is innate to humankind. It seems to me that the more space is opened for civil society and the more it develops, the greater is the activation of this potential – often dormant in society and in every individual. Naturally, with incalculable positive effects on the life not only of the individual but of society as a whole.

Civil society is an organism with an intricate, fragile structure, which, in some cases, is even mysterious. Its growth requires decades, if not centuries. It follows that, after years of virtual non-existence, civil society cannot be restored by top-down operations or by statute. The reconstruction of its three pillars – private voluntary associations, state decentralization, and the delegation of political power to independent bodies – necessarily requires patience.

Civil society produces authentic pluralism; the more its various components are heard and allowed to flourish, the more stable its political order will be. Civil society also safeguards its citizens from the excessive impact of change at the centre of political power.

But the most important aspect of civil society is that it allows people to fulfil themselves. Human beings are not only manufacturers of goods and profits, or mere consumers. They are also – and this could be their most deeply authentic quality – creatures who seek to live with others, who aspire to different forms of coexistence and cooperation, who endeavour to influence what happens around them and who desire to be appreciated.

Civil society is one of the fundamental means by which human nature can reveal the full extent of its potential. Enemies of civil society know this and that is why they are opposed to it.

I believe that civil society builds itself from the bottom up – authentically. The state that truly supports civil society is not a state that artificially creates it from the top down, but rather, it is a state that creates favourable conditions for society's autonomous, natural, and authentic structuring.

The many forms of human association are simply the fundamental and elementary self-fulfilment of individuals as social beings, *zoon politikon*. This means that people unite, in various places, based on shared interests and common goals and act together. This is the essential form of participation in public life and the first sphere in which people voluntarily, with their personal needs, move beyond the context of private life.

The second sphere is very similar; and is defined as the non-profit sector.

The third sphere of society's self-structuring, participation in public life, is the realm of autonomy. In fact, autonomy is an essential tool for civil society. It is a meaningful space where citizens participate in public life as a community of human beings, where each individual can manifest and fulfil his/her own interest towards community, society – the *polis*.

Václav Havel

Introduction

Luigi Fusco Girard

The Human Sustainable City in the Era of Globalization and Urbanization

Different Cities and Common Problems

In an increasingly interdependent world, globalization is an economic/ financial process affecting not only consumption and modes of production, but also lifestyles, ways of thinking and acting. It is the engine of change of our times (Sen, 1997, 1999; Stiglitz, 2002).

The era of globalization is also one of urbanization and the devolution of powers to local authorities. Globalization, along with processes of urbanization and decentralization, highlights the central role of cities. They are that part of space where the global economics of flows originates and ends. And so cities throughout the world find themselves facing new problems and new challenges.

Indeed, the city is the specific physical and territorial context where the great challenges of our times are played out, in particular, the challenges of economic development, of justice, of peaceful co-existence and of safeguarding the environment. It is the form of shared organization of human life, of human relations and coordination through economic, social and political exchange; it is the reflection of values and culture.

The city is also a place of innovation. It is the engine of a country's economic development, but it is also the laboratory where tomorrow's human beings and society are shaped.

The city is that 'part' of a country which 'contains' its most distinctive characteristics, be they cultural, social, economic or other. But, above all, the city – where the fabric of relationships linking all subjects is most evident – is the place which sees the birth of human rights in relation to other humans, integrating those rights founded upon autonomy and freedom.

The city becomes the place where human dignity – one's capacity to form relationships with other individuals – is achieved or is not. It is the place where interpersonal bonds, or the conflicts between human beings – and between human beings and the environment – are expressed and consolidated.

Mumford (1961) underlined the fact that the city first took form 'as the home of a god' – a place where eternal values were represented. What, today, are the new, fundamental values?

The city is the place that compounds the culture of modernity, which is characterized by ever-growing individualism. While engendering economic 'integration', it 'disintegrates' on the social and community levels, eventually crushing inter-personal relationships and thus reducing them to an exchange between monetary equivalents (Zamagni, 1998, 1999).

Indeed, it is in the city where the most intense communicative processes come into being that the relational crisis – the most insidious form of poverty – is greatest. But it is also in the city that the need to build new kinds of relations emerges, such as relations between subjects, between institutions, between cultures, between races, between religions, etc., because this is where interdependence is greatest. Thus, the demand for new institutions, which can foster horizontal communication, dialogue, active involvement and participation, in order to sustain a new pact for communal living, springs from the city.

The globalized world, that emerged from the collapse of the East-West bipolar configuration in 1989, has seen the growth of a pluralistic order including eight main cultural areas (Christian, Islamic, Confucian, Hindu, American, Japanese, European and African), each with its own model of civilization (Huntington, 1997). Each of these areas is marked by specific values and priorities – the expression of particular identities.

Each culture is reflected in its cities, which have always been recognized as 'poles' of civilization and are therefore characterized by their own identity and specific nature, albeit within the framework of their profound variety (Taylor, 1992).

Different cultures influence the definition and realization of 'human' development in different ways. For example, the European city expresses the balance between private and general interests, the centrality of its squares, where civil and religious monuments are located, in an overall system embodying the concept of 'space on a human scale' (Benevolo, 1993). In the Islamic city, on the other hand, we note strong interdependence between the various components and religious sites, characterized by the spatial presence of the spiritual dimension. This cultural plurality and diversity are sources of great richness. Certainly, each cultural area has its own specific problems. For example, in China we find strong evidence of accelerated urbanization requiring the rapid growth of new cities. In Europe, on the other hand, the main problem is recovery and rehabilitation rather than new expansion. Indeed, in the European city, the population growth rates are extremely low (reaching, in the period 1995-2000, zero per cent in Madrid, 0.04 per cent in Berlin and 0.09 per cent in Vienna) and the population is rapidly ageing. But at the same time, we are witnessing a movement towards new inflows of people from the East and from the South, mainly directed to often badly decayed suburbs, leading to a demand – growing over time – for additional housing and services.

The scarcity of available urban land will lead to the search for increasingly integrated uses, limiting sprawl and posing problems of 'sustainable urbanization'.

Contrary to Europe, the Asian city may be defined as one of accelerated development, since it displays very marked urbanization dynamics (with rates, from 1995-2000, of 9.8 per cent at Wenzhou and 9.49 per cent at Songnam) and the highest rates of economic development (between six per cent and eight per cent). And here we find a corresponding increase in negative environmental impacts (Piccinato, 2002).

The Latin-American city, on the other hand, is marked by tremendous differences between rich and poor. Saõ Paulo, for example, contains more than seven per cent of Brazil's population and contributes 37 per cent to the national GDP, but a multitude of its poor continue to live in *favelas*. Again, the African city, which records the highest urbanization rates (for example, 10.08 per cent at Tabora, 6.32 per cent at Onagadougou, 5.33 per cent at Lagos) is the poorest, marked by the explosion of the informal economy.

One element which is common among these diverse and heterogeneous situations is the process of growing polarization. The world is becoming increasingly globalized and urbanized but, at the same time, we are witnessing growing disparities – spreading pockets of urban poverty from St. Petersburg to Johannesburg, from New York to Rio de Janeiro and Nairobi. Another common characteristic is the rise of pollution levels and ecological risks.

A third process common to all the world's cities is the standardization/homogenization of urban models which globalization has extended to all the new neighbourhoods, causing loss of urban cultural identity. To counter this trend and in particular to better compete in the world market for new economic activities, in many cities, we note a search for identity through the recovery of cultural heritage, the discovery of history and culture as factors in new development, and the implementation of integrated programs for the conservation of the cultural heritage of historic centres and cities (in order to attract exogenous resources in global competition). This phenomenon may be observed not only on the Latin-American continent (take, for example, the historic centres of Olinda, Havana or Mexico City) but also in Africa (the Medina of Tunis and Fez, the historic city of Zanzibar, etc.), and even in Europe, America and Asia, with the search for new, increasingly integrated strategies.

The Main Urban Challenges

The new millennium has presented new challenges for humankind. In particular, the challenge of ecology, of development with justice and of rebuilding our ability to live together, i.e. relating.

These three different challenges boil down to the common issue of increasing poverty, in other words the poverty of our man-made, natural, human and social capital (Serageldin, 1996). The growth of poverty, moreover, goes hand in hand with the development of globalization, so that the possibility of constructing a more human world will depend on our capacity to identify adequate responses.

These three great challenges are interwoven and take on different forms and combinations in each city. In an increasingly globalized and urbanized world, the struggle against poverty and the ecological crisis, focused on reconstructing community and creating relationships, is mostly played out in the city.

The battle against the fragmented or 'dual' city thus becomes a fight for the 'integrated' city, where economic development is pursued within a broader perspective of social and environmental justice. We must therefore improve the quality of human life beginning with slum dwellers or 'run-down' neighbourhoods, integrating them into the dynamics of urban development.

The struggle to reduce the scope of the ecological crisis is also played out in the city, which is the greatest source of air, water, noise and soil pollution. The degree of success in facing these complex issues depends, in turn, on the capacity for reconstructing new communities – that is for reproducing the most important form of capital: 'social capital'.

Urbanization to be Humanized

Growing globalization and urbanization processes make the implementation of strategies for the 'human sustainable city' more and more difficult. Urbanization is increasing exponentially.

In 2000, approximately 47 per cent of the world population lived in the cities. In 2020, it is estimated that this rate will have increased to 56 per cent. Every day, 170,000 people move to cities, and they require about 30,000 new housing units per day. In short, we will find ourselves facing alarming growth of slums and deteriorated neighbourhoods unless the cities improve their ability to respond to these issues.

This means that the cities will become new frontier zones, where players with completely different interests will meet and confront each other, where lacerating conflicts and social tensions may be born, and where the contradictions of globalization will concentrate (Scandurra, 1999).

But cities can also be seen as places where these conflicts can be resolved, where new development and 'human ecology' strategies can be born, new coalitions between civil society, public institutions and economic subjects can come to the fore, and thus the starting point for a new policy and a more vital democracy. Redistributive strategies for innovative development based on the promotion of equal opportunities for development and the redistribution of benefits, can transform the city from an *engine of economic growth* into *an engine of social change* (UNCHS, 2001b).

Thus, in spite of the difficulties caused by globalization and urbanization, we believe that the city can play a leading role in both promoting and countering the goals of human sustainable development. The city devours natural/environmental resources, discharging its waste beyond its physical limits. Moreover, with globalization cities tend to adopt business strategies aimed at increasingly intense competitiveness. Many examples have proven that economic development has not brought about a redistribution of opportunity but has rather caused the expansion of poor neighbourhoods.[1]

It therefore becomes ever more urgent to identify new 'inclusive' development strategies (Kirdar, Harvey, You, Shah, Richardson, Sandercock, this volume). From this viewpoint, the city could become the place where economic/financial globalization can be rendered more 'human' and where it is possible to produce wealth and, at the same time, reduce inequalities. This will come about only if we manage to conceive of new scenarios for citizen participation in economic and democratic life through actions and projects which, starting from the collective elaboration of a shared vision, can activate civic networks – a connecting fabric of relationships and shared citizenship.

Ultimately, this would mean that cities, having formed new internal networks and by participating in new external ones, might counterbalance 'top-down globalization' governed by economy and finance with 'bottom-up' social, civil and cultural globalization, enhancing specific identities (Castells, 1998).

The Processes of Globalization and the New Ethical Challenge

Globalization and the Global City

With globalization, a new geography of centrality and marginality emerges (Sassen, 2002). It is an urban and economic geography which cuts across national borders and the North-South divide, and includes cities such as New York, London, Tokyo, Paris, Frankfurt, Amsterdam, Sydney, Los Angeles, Hong Kong, but also Saõ Paulo, Buenos Aires, Bangkok, Mexico City. Some cities take on a strong, leading role, whereas others are in decline. There is a growing divergence between the concentration of resources and the concentration of activities. While increasing quantities of resources and investment are concentrated in some areas, many cities/regions are excluded and become increasingly peripheral.

New York, London and Tokyo are the clearest examples of global cities by reason of their worldwide network of commercial and financial contacts. Montreal, Toronto, Chicago, Saõ Paulo, Rio de Janeiro and Singapore are also 'driving forces' of the new capitalism centred on the city. But they are also places where millions of poor and unemployed are concentrated (like in the *favelas* of Rio or Saõ Paulo, in the slums of the Bronx, etc.). Globalization is spawning a 'fragmented' city, marked by growing social and spatial inequalities, where an ever richer and more protected élite is in stark contrast with an increasingly less-protected majority. Life for this majority is mostly ruled by the informal economy, low-cost production, 'flexible' work organization with no contractual protection or welfare provisions.

Thus, on the one hand, the global cities produce huge economic and financial capital added values while, on the other, they generate loss of social and ecological wealth.

Cities are places which draw together both great transnational powers as well as many examples of marginalization. Multinational corporations see the cities as control centres and places for specialized services, where profits are maximized and power is concentrated (Sassen, 1994). The underprivileged see the city as the place where they can assert their rights for housing, work, services, etc.: the right to existence (UNCHS, 2001b). Therefore, the city in the era of globalization sees growth in the number of rich, who become increasingly richer, and of the poor who become increasingly poorer. The distance between these two worlds is much greater than the physical and spatial distance of their respective urban areas.

Globalization and the Growth of Inequalities

Globalization is engendering a series of significant benefits, but very often they are unevenly distributed and monopolized only by an élite which already possesses specialized know-how as well as specific operational and financial capabilities.

The combined effect of the financialization of the economy and of reengineering strategies is the slump in employment levels in the formal sector and increase in precarious employment in the informal sectors. It can be said that globalization processes, intermingling with the diffusion of new information and communication technologies, are driven by three great 'forces': the competitive market, liberalization and privatization.

The free-market mechanism certainly makes for greater efficiency. However, the free market is not the cure-all for the ills of the twenty-first century. The market is not 'inclusive' but rather 'exclusive'. Moreover, it does not function when there is a need to produce certain types of goods or services such as housing for the poor or welfare services for low-income groups.

Moreover, the free market tends to externalize some costs, shifting them onto subjects who are in no way involved in the processes of exchange, including future generations. Neither does it provide any form of protection against the formation of oligopolies and new monopolies. The strong players on the globalization stage are the great multinationals, whose only aim is to maximize profits using new technologies to their best advantage. Indeed, the liberalized market creates neither long-term sustainable development nor social cohesion – i.e. a sense of community – nor forms of relating.

And finally, the free market is unable to assess what is relevant for future generations. It exploits resources without guaranteeing their conservation over time.

Therefore, we need new public policies that can achieve greater security and equity as well as public control over choices of power-wielding subjects in order to avoid the undesirable effects of growing globalization focussing only on the market and enterprise and disregarding the person (Camagni, 2000).

Certainly globalization has produced considerable economic wealth. It has proved to be the true engine of growth over the last decade, but it has caused a patchy distribution of benefits. Indeed, in some countries, average income has decreased, whereas social costs have spiralled (for example, as a result of the pressure of structural adjustment programs) with the privatization of goods and public services, increased taxation pressure and the public spending cuts (Stiglitz, 2002). No less than 60 countries are worse off now than they were in 1980. In Europe we have witnessed an increase in social exclusion and the decay of many suburbs. In the United States, spatial segregation and discrimination have increased. In Latin America, no less than 30 per cent of the population is made up of the urban poor. Over the past few years, inequalities have been decidedly increasing a fact which is also demonstrated by some well-known indicators (UNDP, 2001).

We may conclude that globalization has an economic dimension which is generally positive and a social dimension which, taken overall, is negative. At the same time, the progressive growth of marginality, of poverty and of inequality highlights the failure of the free market to redistribute opportunity and the failure of global governance to meet the challenges of these processes.

The Great Ethical Challenge of the Twenty-First Century: The Reduction of Poverty

Today the poor are already the majority of the world's population. The reduction of poverty and inequality stands out as the great ethical challenge of the twenty-first century.

Economic development is essential for increasing the wealth available to combat poverty. But it is by no means sufficient. Economic development is not an end to itself; it is merely a means of achieving human development in all its various dimensions, not only the economic one. The effect of economic development in terms of poverty reduction depends not only on the rate, but also on the 'type', of development. Economic development could, in turn, generate a greater number of poor and underprivileged, because it could require increasingly less work. It could damage the environmental/natural resources which should be available for future generations. It could destroy the cultural heritage, the history and the very identity of people. Economic growth, in and of itself, does not in any way guarantee redistribution and equity.

This is why we need to 'humanize' the economic development which globalization has made possible to reduce the conflict between the economic and social dimensions of globalization. The refocusing of globalization towards the benefit of the poor and the environment has become the great challenge of our time.

Europe, drawing on its unique culture and the experience of the welfare state, is in a position to propose new, original and effective combinations between economic development and solidarity.

Worldwide, lack of housing affects about 100 million people, while more than one billion people live in 'indecent' housing in Calcutta, Bombay, Mexico City, Lagos, New Delhi, etc. The more densely populated these urban-metropolitan areas, the more evident are these phenomena of marginality. Bangalore is perhaps the clearest example of a new urban economy which has become integrated into the globalized economy, but which has also destroyed its traditional economy.

Highly urbanized poverty is concentrated in environmentally deteriorated areas which become even less liveable (Laul, this volume) and the magnitude of the problem is becoming increasingly evident. Today, almost half of the world's population lives in the cities. It is estimated that by 2015 about one billion people will have moved to the cities. And 93 per cent of this number will move to the cities of the less developed countries. Europe too will be involved – albeit to a lesser extent – in this new migratory flow.

This number of one billion poses problems regarding urban management/governance of mind-boggling complexity, as demand for goods/services will grow much faster than response capacity. The probable consequence of these two velocities will be the rapid expansion of *bidonvilles*, *slums*, *favelas*, the most visible expressions of urban poverty.

The *Millennium Declaration* on 'Cities without Slums' set the goal of improving the standard of living for at least 100 million people by 2020. Yet this is only ten per cent of today's poor, a number that will increase over the next few years, doubling in 2025 to reach two billion.

We must act upon the processes and not upon the results, which means that we must prevent, as far as possible, the growth of new informal settlements by envisioning new strategies focused first and foremost on encouraging populations to remain in rural areas.

The efficiency-oriented strategies of the city-enterprise for competing in the globalized world have proven unable to reduce slums. We need new 'inclusive' strategies that modify the methods of urban management/ government.

From the City as 'Engine of Development' to the City as an 'Agent of Social Change'

In the 1990s, cities were considered 'engines of economic development' – places where capital was accumulated and re-invested. They became the most important centres for the provision of services, especially specialized ones. Globalization obliges cities to participate in 'global' competition, encouraging them to organize themselves as a single, collective player.

The competition resulting from globalization is stimulating the birth of a form of urban management marked increasingly by an 'entrepreneurial' approach, which regards the city as a product for exchange with the rest of the world ('marketing approach'), to be made available to the best buyer on the global market. The city must be made increasingly 'attractive' in the eyes of the economic subjects of globalization in order to attract outside investments.

Once the city becomes the centre of a region's or country's economic activities, the question arises regarding how to apply business' economic rationality to urban management in order to improve its efficiency/ functionality.

In globalization, all players compete: individuals, enterprises, cities. The cities are not 'islands' in the midst of a calm sea; they are part of an economic and spatial network dominated by competitive forces. Cities compete to attract resources, activities, investments, people. Therefore, to win out, they must operate on two fronts: (a) minimizing costs; (b) maximizing quality. So, private enterprise decides to reorganize, moving where manpower and production cost less and thus improves its performance.

In this sense, the city focuses on the possibility of maximizing quality and reducing inefficiency. Its quality is that of its physical spaces, its private spaces and services and – in more general terms – its natural capital, its human resources, its man-made capital, and its social capital. In practical terms, cities are placed in a global 'force field' which demands new 'energies' of the cities themselves. In particular, the metropolitan cities become the new 'arenas' of global competition, where, to emerge as a winner, it is necessary to produce quality (Nijkamp and Wouter, 2001).

Indeed, the global city – the city of international airports, of efficient infrastructure networks and business districts, of luxury hotels, the headquarters of specialized services and finance – invests in continuous improvement because it is fully aware that an area 'lacking quality' is not only more difficult to live in but will never attract investment.

But these development policies are not necessarily beneficial for the weaker social classes. Often they accentuate intra-urban disparities, under the strong pressure of land value: urban poverty grows with globalization, while social capital is reduced.

The city becomes the place where the 'informal' economy concentrates and grows. Indeed, in many urban realities the informal economy offers the greatest amount of employment opportunities. On the other hand, it has also been reported that, where informal employment is highest, the average income level is lowest, and vice versa.

With 'city marketing', public institutions open to the private sector. Citizens become 'customers'; public sector production decreases in relation to private production. Efficiency becomes the key criterion. Attention focuses on product and process innovation, with the goal of improving the city's 'position' on the market and to offer quality assurance. In stimulating economic growth and improving comparative advantages in the 'city market' little attention is paid to rearranging the spatial distribution of opportunities in order to mitigate the undesirable consequences of the process.

One consequence of this business approach is that the provision of urban housing and services is shifting from the public sphere to the market, thus excluding those with insufficient purchasing power. Moreover, as transport services, utilities, security, etc., are privatized, social polarization increases further.

Urban marketing attempts to present a city's image externally and abroad as well as to improve its offer by privatizing and marketing public services. Urban marketing is increasingly seen as the overall valorization of existing and potential resources, which permit – when carefully combined and coordinated – the production of new added value and the attraction of new outside resources (investments, financial flows, professional skills, etc.). This type of strategic business management increases cities' competition including strategic alliances between cities in light of possible synergies and better cooperation with their surrounding area (combining cooperation and competition).

Another essential characteristic is the promotion of continuing innovation, again according to a business logic, seeking the renewal/re-qualification of urban 'products' and services, stimulating research (universities, laboratories, etc.), transforming know-how into local economic development. Certainly what the city produces is very different from what enterprise produces, because the city produces public goods, merit goods, intangible assets, etc., including, for example, monumental/ cultural and environmental heritage.

This business-oriented approach to urban government is, therefore, effective for better competition on the global market, but it is not sufficient. In fact, urban marketing policies, which rely only on the free market to resolve urban issues, ignore their structural limits in terms of the improvement of everyone's life (including that of the underprivileged), due to the presence of external effects and public assets. They guarantee efficiency and competitiveness, but they involve increasing social costs. They should be open to richer strategies, to positive-sum promotional strategies which also involve civil society through new partnerships with the business world. Therefore it is necessary to abandon an approach to the city as 'an engine of development' and move towards one that considers the city as an 'agent of social change' to redistribute the benefits of development (Hall and Pfeiffer, 2000).

Indeed, social inequalities inhibit urban economic development. They reduce the possibilities for productive investments on the part of the poor more than they increase these possibilities for the rich, as recent econometric studies have demonstrated (Aghion and Willanson, 1998). In other words, an urban strategy which is 'attentive' to the world of enterprise, oriented towards project implementation, marked by flexibility and the desire for innovation, should also seek to promote cooperation between the various players (to improve the ability to compete with other cities) and civil society; that is, it should be concerned not only with the export market (whether regional or international) or that of the local enterprise, but also with citizens and their welfare.

The Habitat Agenda: New Principles for New Practices

The New Approach of the Habitat Agenda to Urban Sustainability

The *Istanbul Declaration* outlined new strategies for the city of the twenty-first century, including a set of common principles for the promotion of sustainable development.

The Habitat Agenda effectively acknowledges that the neoliberalist 'laissez-faire' approach, based on a reduction in control, on deregulation, an so on, is not adequate enough to ensure sustainable governance of the city. As stressed earlier, the 'business-oriented' approach to the city does not consider the failure of the market to account for externalities and for several assets that the market has no interest in producing (merit goods, shelter for the poor, some public urban services, etc.). Indeed, the Habitat Agenda sees the city as an 'engine of development' but also as an 'engine of social change' (Hall and Pfeiffer, 2000; UNCHS, 2001b; Wakely and You, 2001). To this end, it recommends a form of public intervention based on equalization and redistribution, in order to avoid the usual waste of resources, focusing instead on a redistribution-oriented policy of integrated economic development. Indeed, the Habitat Agenda places particular emphasis on the culture of human rights. This means, among other things, that public services should cover all urban areas, thus reducing the differentials linked to poverty within the city.

The relevant points of the *Istanbul Declaration* (UNCHS, 1996) may be summarized as follows:

- Quality of life is dependent on the physical conditions of the natural/built environment, and on cultural, economic and social factors.
- It is necessary to achieve lasting improvement of the physical environment by promoting its rehabilitation, renewal, maintenance and through appropriate management of the existing housing stock.
- It is necessary to promote the conservation and rehabilitation of buildings, monuments and spaces of historic, cultural and natural value.
- It is necessary to improve the efficiency of the housing markets.
- Policies dealing with housing must guarantee the maintenance and management of the existing housing resources.
- It is necessary to develop new urban management strategies.
- It is necessary to increase efforts in renewal, rehabilitation, improvement and increase of the urban built stock.
- An attempt should be made to identify sustainable forms of land use in urban planning. The Earth is a source of energy, water and food for numerous biological systems over and above all human beings. Urban centres must develop in harmony with the natural environment. There is a need for new methods of designing and urban management. There is a fundamental requirement to promote new urban patterns that reduce the demand for transport and the consumption of energy, while preserving adequate urban density.
- Green urban areas are essential for biological and hydro-geological balance, as well as for economic development. They contribute to the natural absorption of rainwater, helping to save water. At the same time, they help reduce air pollution and create a suitable micro-climate.
- It is necessary to encourage the participation of associations and voluntary organizations and encourage the third sector.
- Careful energy management must be ensured: transport, industrial production and household uses are the three main sources of fossil fuel consumption.
- Historic and heritage sites of cultural, scientific, symbolic and spiritual value are important expressions of the culture, identity and religion of any society. Their role must be recognized: they are important factors

in ensuring the stability of a society and represent community pride. Access to culture and the cultural dimension of development is fundamental.

- It is necessary to document historic and cultural value and broaden the knowledge and understanding of it; it is important to be aware that these values contribute to a place's cultural and economic development. The maintenance of built stock and natural capital is an important part of the implementation of sustainability strategies.

Decentralized and participatory urban management should be implemented also involving the third sector.

The General Principles of the Habitat Agenda

To succeed in humanizing development, cities should transform themselves from engines of economic growth to new engines of social change, capable of promoting not only development but also social justice and environmental sustainability. How can they achieve this?

The Habitat Agenda provides a comprehensive set of criteria, incentives and rules for drawing up an integrated action plan for the provision of sustainable shelter and the global sustainability of the city, where housing strategies, city planning and management and governance arrangements are closely inter-linked (Beguinot, 1998). In effect, the Habitat Agenda closely links the sustainable development of human settlements to respect for human rights, starting from the right to adequate housing. Certainly, its roots are to be found in Agenda 21 (see Habitat Agenda, §§ 29, 103, 136, 138, 211, 213), which is focused on an action plan combining the goals of economic development with those of environmental protection. While Local Agenda 21 outlines the process for drawing up a pact for the environment, the Habitat Agenda has a broader perspective, even more explicitly including goals of redistribution and social justice.

The Habitat Agenda highlights the goal of reducing social exclusion, i.e. poverty – increasingly an urban phenomenon – even before focusing on the needs of future generations. It also targets city planning and economic development more than environmental protection. Indeed, the Agenda aims at helping to create not only a more efficient and productive city in terms of global competition, but also a more 'inclusive' one. This means a city freed both from decayed inner city districts and from suburban slums, which today are constantly expanding and constitute a blatant negation of human rights. The Habitat Agenda is clearly inspired by the criteria of human development and is thus founded on the culture of human rights.

The principle of decentralization, involving the transfer of responsibility to local government bodies and municipalities, is a leitmotif found throughout the various chapters of the Habitat Agenda (see, for example,

§ 177). It recognizes the strategy of sustainability as a guideline for tackling the problems of housing, land use, energy and transport, the conservation of the natural and built environment, the improvement of the urban economic base with an approach open to participatory governance, to forms of self-government for the cities.[2]

The goals of the Habitat Agenda (as set out in Chapter II) may be summarized as follows:

- Guarantee for all people equal access to housing and services (above all health, education and environmental resources).
- Eradicate poverty.
- Improve the quality of physical space in the cities and settlements.
- Strengthen the family as the basic unit of society.
- Promote the rights and responsibilities of citizens.
- Promote partnership/participation.
- Enhance solidarity with those belonging to disadvantaged and vulnerable groups.
- Improve the availability of financial resources.
- Protect the environment and improve health-care and sanitation.

We may say that the Habitat Agenda expresses, today, the principles, objectives and organizational rules for any type of development program geared to 'citizen-friendly' settlements (Various Authors, 2002).

The Reasons for the Success in the Implementation of the Habitat Agenda

While acknowledging that there are no preordained formulas, since each city is a unique case, we can identify a number of key elements for success and, thus, draw from the identification and evaluation of 'best practices' some guidelines and recommendations for planning the future.

As You stresses (in this volume) the Best Practices and Local Leadership Programme (BLP) of UN-Habitat, based in Nairobi, has been analyzing best practices since 1996 creating a database containing over 1,600 cases.[3] These best practices represent concrete experiences of success in humanizing urban life, integrating different interests and values.

Ex-post evaluation of the best practices conducted since 1996 warrants the conclusion that the most significant successes in promoting development and reducing various forms of poverty were achieved by those cities that chose to focus on six different, but interlinked, plans (Nijkamp et al., 1993; Wakely and You, 2001; Various Authors, 2001; Allen and You, 2002):

- The improvement of *ecoware*, that is of the quality of the natural/built environment by means of urban ecological management, cutting the consumption of energy, materials, etc. In this regard, environmental efficiency should be significantly improved (von Weizsäcker et al., 1998).
- Improvement of *hardware*, that is of the system of communications, transport and man-made capital (residential, infrastructural, etc).
- Improvement of *finware*, that is of the organization of financial support systems (loans and capital) integrating those already existing to combine economies of scale with purpose-oriented economies (productivity, quality, diversity).
- Improvement of *orgware*, i.e. the set of institutions for the organization of human life in the city to promote communication, coordination and capacity for cooperative actions.
- Improvement of *civicware*, that is of civil/social infrastructure.
- Improvement of *software*, including not only business skills, professional know-how and innovation, but also a cultural mindset and the immaterial energy necessary for urban development.

In order to design a sustainable and human development project for the city, it is therefore necessary to act simultaneously on all these different levels, with opportune combinations, learning lessons from the best practices already implemented in various world regions (for example, Chattanooga, Santo Andrè, Santiago de Compostela, etc.).

Ecological Infrastructure: Ecoware

Cities occupy two per cent of the world's surface. But they require 75 per cent of world resources to 'function' as is shown by their 'ecological footprint'. For example, the city of London, which covers 627,000 hectares, requires about 80 million hectares to sustain its linear metabolism (according to the cycle: extraction and use of natural resources, waste production and transfer to the natural system).

Thus, urban economies must improve their productivity in the context of global competition, by acknowledging the limits of:

- the natural system's carrying capacity, i.e. the ecosystem's resilience;
- the capacity of replacing natural capital with man-made capital;
- the application of technologies to 'repair' environmental resources which, if damaged, are often permanently compromised.

The challenge of sustainable development is the challenge of developing an urban economy which: (1) relies less on fossil fuels; (2) reduces the exploitation of natural and environmental resources (minerals, forests, the land); (3) restructures its transport system; (4) restructures its public services and amenities (e.g. city parks and gardens); (5) reviews its production processes in the direction of more efficient use of natural resources; (6) redesigns its production processes to reduce/recycle waste and regenerate products at the end of their useful life.

The two basic principles of sustainable development (Daly, 1991) namely (1) that harvest rates should equal regeneration rates and (2) that waste emission rates should equal the natural assimilative capacities of the ecosystems into which the wastes are emitted, must, ultimately, be harmonized with the criteria of economic and social sustainability.

The problem of waste management is an increasingly difficult urban issue. Elevated living standards multiplies the amount of urban waste even where population figures remain stable. We might cite, for example, the case of Rio de Janeiro, where in 1994 municipal solid waste was 6,200 tons per day, while in 1997 it had escalated to almost 8,050 tons per day, though the population had remained constant (UNCHS, 2001b).

We need efficient infrastructure and plants for the recovery of certain materials (paper, metal, glass, plastic, etc.), for recycling and for energy saving.

Planning *ecoware* means, above all, attempting to safeguard a territory providing ecological support to the city, extensive enough to sustain the functioning of its economic system. It also means identifying the most sustainable form for the use of a very scarce resource such as the territory.

Thus, urban planning is increasingly 'forced' to search out the most efficient method of land use by identifying the most sustainable degree of multi-functionality in space and time (Rodenburg et al., 2002). It is no longer a question of choosing one function over others, but of identifying the level of multi-functional concentration which maximizes synergies, beyond which we begin to note diseconomies and social and environmental costs. The search for this sustainable degree of functional interaction implies the use of adequate evaluation tools (Borri et al., 1997; van den Bergh et al., 1997).

Moreover, urban-territorial integrated planning must always incorporate an energy plan pinpointing homogeneous energetic areas and renewable/alternative sources, as well as a plan of the energy transportation networks. It has been noted that an increase in energy efficiency will have far-reaching environmental and occupational consequences (Eppinger, this volume). The adoption of the ISO 14001 standard or EMAS I and II is certainly a step in the right direction, as has been shown by many experiences in various urban contexts (Belous, Musu, Richardson, this volume). All the initiatives that contribute to the 'de-carbonization' of urban economy through the substitution of oil with renewable energy sources promote *ecoware*. Renewable energy allows win-win strategies because it contributes to economic development by simultaneously conserving biodiversity and ecological quality. For example, the more hydrogen is consumed the more it becomes available in a cyclical process.

Hardware: Transport System and Housing

Hardware includes the infrastructure system (including mobility systems), equipment and built stock. In order to promote a sustainable system of mobility/transport, to make the city more eco-efficient (reducing the urban ecological footprint) and more equitable (reducing accessibility differentials), an attempt has been made to improve:

* efficiency in land use by locating housing in easily accessible areas that are well connected to employment and services;
* the efficiency of public transport between the city and its suburbs;
* availability of alternative modes of transport, through organizational or technological alternatives to the private car;
* the network of pedestrian walkways and car parks;
* equitable access.

The concept of the 'urban village' where it is possible to minimize commuting, the use of cars and travelling time between home and work, a place with high-quality public spaces, where micro-communities can be recreated, is an example of integrated transport-residence-work organization model (Dimitrakopulou and Giaoutzi, Martinez-Alier, Hall, this volume). The rehabilitation of the built stock for social, cultural, and above all residential purposes is another important line of action.

In developing countries, in particular, improvement in *hardware* means the construction of new housing. For example, 40 per cent to 70 per cent of the population of most African cities lives in slums (UNCHS, 2001a). Thus the building industry becomes the fulcrum of development policies, since, because of its interdependence with all other economic sectors, it is characterized by higher multiplication effects in terms of employment and income.

The Financing Node: Finware

Cities need new resources to implement any sustainable development strategy. Naturally, development is first and foremost dependent on upgrading the urban economy, which in turn requires scientific and technological innovation centres, development incubators, etc., as well as local tax reforms for greater effectiveness. New funding mechanisms are also needed; some have already been developed. In particular, financial resources for housing available through traditional channels are usually accessible to the medium or medium-high income brackets, but not to the low income bracket or the poor who cannot provide the guarantees normally requested (Fusco Girard and Forte, 2000). Indeed, the poor are unable to pay high mortgage instalments because of their income status as well as the high interest rates. Thus, the only possibility open to them is building their own home, a solution which however requires a very long time period. A possible alternative would be different credit systems; one that has often been proposed is micro-financing for housing. This is a flexible credit tool, adaptable to the changes in the income of the poor families and to various construction methods. This form of short-term credit has been tried out with success also in Brazil, Mexico, Chile, South Africa, etc.

Starting with the Grameen Bank, which began to operate in Bangladesh as far back as 1976, we have seen an increase in the number of so-called 'ethical banks' which finance projects of economic solidarity.

This is certainly one possible way of improving access to financing, although it is not sufficient in and of itself. For example, in Ho Chi Minh City, the results of micro-financing were negative because five years after the system's adoption, slums had increased. It would seem that, in order to fight social exclusion, this approach must be integrated, so that it is not applied only to ten per cent of available resources, while the remaining 90 per cent is managed according to the traditional channels and processes of large financing bodies.

A radically different approach, while still having its starting point in the informal sector of the economy, was put forward by Hernando De Soto (2000) for developing countries. It is oriented towards enabling the poor to build their own houses, without receiving them from the public sector. This approach recommends 'regularizing' the property market of the unauthorized settlements and slums in the developing countries. Since they are illegal, they are not 'recognized' by public agencies and, therefore, they do not contribute in any way, with the activities performed there, to the taxable base of the city.

De Soto has estimated a market value of about 9.3 trillion dollars for unlicensed property units alone. This is, quite clearly, an extremely high real estate value which, in actual fact, does not exist, since it is excluded from services and utilities, it is not assessed for tax purposes and above all cannot be used as a personal property guarantee on loans. Consequently, extensive property assets are cut off from investment opportunities and the urban planning system is highly distorted, as is the system of property values. As a result, levels of poverty increase.

De Soto's proposal is that we should bring the millions of residential units belonging to the spontaneous neighbourhoods into the formal economic system, legalizing them and recognizing the property rights pertaining to them. The point is to 'extract' financial resources for development not from the circuit involving the percentage of the population which already possesses wealth, but from what is used by the remainder, introducing it into the market economy. Unit value will clearly be very low, but it will be applied to a great number of properties. If public institutions promote the formalization of the informal market, all sectors of society can be involved, generating capital gains for the poor as well. They too, in their turn, will be able to produce capital, becoming in the true sense of the word the new 'engine' of development.

Local taxation improvement is a key tool for generating new public resources, as it has been experimented in Patna (HSMI, 2000). A 'new taxation' on activities damaging the environment (see, for examples, the cases of Denmark, Germany and Sweden) are oriented in this direction.

Towards New Local Institutions: Orgware

The city is a complex system, whose government requires a systemic approach, through the improvement of its institutional infrastructure (Kirdar, this volume).

Institutions are the rules to coordinate multiple, heterogeneous and conflictual interests and values, balancing them in order to promote general interest in the organization of human life.

Successful cities are those which have adopted institutional arrangements targeting several fronts in an integrated manner. The integrated approach has always proven very effective (Rijkens et al., Engelbrektsson and Rosvall, this volume).

The Local Agenda 21 processes launched in a growing number of cities throughout the world have contributed to the spread of this approach (Shah, Belous, Musu, Richardson, this volume). The now consolidated experiment of the 'participatory budget' in Porto Alegre, which involves directly and indirectly about 100,000 people every year, with the two plenary assemblies and the various committees, forums, hearings, etc., offers a concrete example of actions identification through organizational-institutional innovation, and it has by now been adopted by many local government bodies in Europe as well. Following this experience, it should be opportune to introduce participatory budget in Local Agenda 21 processes and the 'ethical account' approach (Pruzan, 1997).

The 'enabling' approach, which replaces direct production, is strongly pluralistic, but in order to achieve it, local governments must possess strong capacities for coordination, concerted action, cooperation, co-management, co-designing, in a new framework of different players/sectors.

It is also necessary to re-launch programming/planning policy, replacing the neo-liberalist approach, focused on short-term management, with a strategic vision over the medium and long term. In order to re-launch planning (Hall, this volume) and the enabling strategy, the role of institutions must be upgraded and increased, in particular regarding control/monitoring/evaluation of the results obtained (Fusco Girard and Njikamp, 1997), as well as preliminary assessment of projects/plans/ programs (Amhed, this volume). A need is felt for indicators which help in understanding, analyzing, comparing, evaluating and constructing choices, that can express adequately welfare changes and indicate the differentials between one area and another (Nijkamp and Medda, Roca Cladera et al., Ost, this volume). Urban planning is too often more interested only in market values than in combining non-use values, use-values and market values.

Civil/Social Infrastructure: Civicware

In the era of globalization, cities are experiencing progressive social fragmentation and a loss of collective consciousness, that is of social capital. At the same time, as the city consumes social capital, it has a growing need for it as a strategic element in its development (Harvey, Sandercock, Blazek, this volume).

Today, the challenge facing the community may be summarized as the challenge to reproduce social capital at a rate at least equal to its rate of consumption. Social capital expresses the 'relational environment', which orients people in the direction of responsible choices, public spirit, general interest, common good and legality. Social capital is the basic ingredient of civil society. The stronger civil society grows, the more effective are its urban institutions. The world of non-profit associations, civil and religious associations and charities, and in more general terms the system of civil economy, produces relational and social values because it assumes the requirement to heed the needs of others and the common interest as a general imperative. The community 'binds together' its components; it gives them a capacity for interdependence, for cohesion, because each is aware of forming part of a system: each knows how to behave and what he or she may expect from others. Social capital profoundly modifies the choices of the single individual; it allows sharing of knowledge which, in turn, helps to construct efficient choices by all and not by just a few; it allows the coordination and promotion of synergies, the construction of collective choices. Through social capital, trust is activated and citizenship is constructed in the city.

The Improvement of Urban Software: Cultural Formation

The challenge of improving urban *software* means first and foremost improving entrepreneurship and professional skills: there is a need for excellence in know-how to sustain continuous innovation. But creative, scientific and professional knowledge must be coupled with critical knowledge, that can identify priorities, distinguish what is important from what is only apparently so. In many cases, an overwhelming amount of information and knowledge is available, but what is lacking is the ability to sort it and arrange it critically. Lack of critical knowledge is perhaps the most insidious form of poverty.

Urban *software* aims at providing the cultural basis for sustainability (Scannell et al., Shah, this volume). The culture of sustainability opens to multiple dimensions of life. It attempts to strike a balance between instrumental and intrinsic values (Callicott, this volume), between present and future generations, between private interests and the general interest. It also recognizes the importance of gratuity and gift. As such, it is the exact antithesis of the culture of economic and financial globalization, founded on exchange between monetary equivalents.

We need to disseminate a new urban culture of sustainability, which must be promoted by making all the stakeholders aware both of the intrinsic value of ecosystems, which, with their autopoietic activity, sustain human life, as well as of the profound links between Humans and Nature, overcoming the culture of 'separation': between people and the environment; between the individual and the community.

In short, the culture of sustainability means becoming aware of the 'complex social value' of resources (Fusco Girard, 1987) and not only of their market value. It also entails awareness of the fact that there is a common heritage of resources (natural, cultural, etc.) available to all, which cannot be appropriated for individual purposes without damaging the rights of other human beings. The culture of sustainability is the culture of co-evolution, co-existence, coordination, cooperation: of developing the capacity to live together.

The Fight against Urban Poverty: Some Good Practices

The Reduction of Urban Poverty in the 'Informal Settlements': Some Examples

'Informal settlements' have multiplied with the diffusion of liberalization policies and the reduction of financial support for subsidized housing programs. These settlements involve very high human and environmental costs, with soaring rates of morbidity, illegality, violence, etc.

Saõ Paulo, Nairobi and Istanbul are three cities participating in globalization processes with markedly different roles and characteristics, but having one common problem: the rapid spread of informal neighbourhoods and slums, with all the attendant consequences: environmental decay, social inequity and conflict. These cities have tied the construction of new housing to the creation of new employment and the provision of services, managing to send concrete 'signals of hope' even when starting from very difficult situations.

In the metropolitan area of Saõ Paulo (which today counts a population of approximately 17.8 million, 65 per cent of whom live in substandard housing) between the late 1980s and the early 1990s, in collaboration with the Catholic University, a process of rehabilitation was launched based on the self-organization of the most vulnerable social groups. The starting point was setting up associations and cooperatives which were tasked with constructing new housing units in the slum areas according to a set of rules issued by the city authorities.

This approach has achieved up to 50 per cent savings in construction costs (as compared to housing projects undertaken by public bodies) and, consequently, has made it possible to double the quantity produced. At the same time, in particular in Santo André, 'social incubators' were set up. Their role was to support association/community networks on issues such as access to credit, promotion of entrepreneurship, technical assistance, professional training and new tools for negotiated actions. Waste collection and recycling (plastic, glass, paper, rubber) activity has produced new forms of employment as well as improving the environment. The 'participatory budget' was introduced to develop active citizenship. Indeed, the overall strategy was also aimed at reducing this intangible form of poverty (Daniel and Avamileno, 2002).

Nairobi may be considered a global city because it is the seat of a very large number of international organizations. Between 1995 and 2000 its population grew by about 4.9 per cent per year. Some 65 per cent of its inhabitants live below the poverty threshold, a fact reflected in the rapid expansion of its *bidonvilles* (where 60 per cent of the population lives). Here the dignity of the human person is totally neglected. Kibera, Kasarani, Dagoretti, Mathare and Korogocho are but a few of these informal settlements marked by extremely high density (about 42,000 inhabitants per sq km) with small housing units of one or two rooms, lacking any infrastructure and sanitation.

For example, in Mathare, a rehabilitation program has been undertaken with the participation of the German Federal Republic and the Catholic Church of Nairobi, covering about 32,000 people, based on a 99-year lease agreement. Thanks to the involvement of non-profit organizations in construction and maintenance work, costs have been significantly reduced, and health and education facilities and services have been guaranteed. Over 100 stalls were set up for the sale of foodstuffs and the production of soap, candles, generating jobs and income. In the rehabilitation project at Korogocho emphasis was also placed on self-organization skills. The third sector is the driving force of several development initiatives aimed at fighting desperation and constructing hope (Sandercock, this volume).

Istanbul, the most westerly of the Middle Eastern cities, a bridge connecting Europe and Asia, plays an important role as a link between the system of Islamic cities (Cairo, Teheran, Lahore, etc.) and the global ones. It has a population of about ten million, which is increasing at an annual rate of 3.56 per cent. The approximately 350,000 new inhabitants per year who move to the city often find housing in self-built units, thus expanding the already existing informal settlements.

To handle the housing problem at a pace consistent with the growth in demand, action has been taken to improve the relationship between public institutions, private subjects and the development cooperation sector. The metropolitan city authority acquires outlying land plots at low cost and, subsequently, hands them over to a joint venture which constructs the new settlement in just over two years. For example, at Ikitelli, a development project is nearing completion on a free area of a new city: it includes some 20,000 housing units for the medium-low income bracket. Unit cost is on an average 20 per cent less than 'standard' cost.

All these pilot experiences attempt to meet the challenge of also extending opportunity to those excluded from the new processes, linking the improvement of outlying districts to employment (micro-enterprises, youth cooperatives, etc.) and new services (sources, in their turn, of new job opportunities).

A common element in these experiments and a key factor in their success was the presence (in particular in the metropolitan area of Saõ Paulo and Nairobi) of associations, volunteer groups, cooperative enterprises and non-profit associations. Without their contribution, it would have been impossible to supply those goods and services which the market has no interest in providing and which public agencies are unable to offer due to an increasing lack of resources. On the other hand, we must remember that the non-profit sector, in its turn, spurs the creation not only of services and new job opportunities, but also of relational values and cooperative capacity.

The Conservation of the Cultural and Environmental Heritage in the Struggle against Poverty

New urban strategies of an inclusive type, aiming at meeting the challenge of justice, ecology and peaceful coexistence, are important for both informal settlements and historic centres. Environmental decay and poverty form a loop: one feeds the other and vice versa.

Generally, the poor live in the most environmentally decayed areas. The most polluting industries are sited in the areas marked by lower (or the lowest) income levels. Rehabilitation of the urban and extra-urban environment thus greatly improves the conditions of life of the poor. It has a positive impact on their health, access to services, productivity of labour and other activities, and employment opportunities.

All too often, little attention has been paid to the relationship between employment/work and environmental conservation. Actually, there is a close interdependence between sustainability, conservation and employment. Indeed, work plays a critical role in the implementation of sustainable human development (Frey, 2000).

Development is 'sustainable' if it is founded on the flow of wealth from capital and not on the consumption of capital stock, i.e., if at the end of the cycle, the original capital is preserved (be it natural, man-made, social or human).

Conservation of these forms of capital over time is, indeed, the key element for guaranteeing that future generations will be able to exploit at least the same opportunities that the current generation enjoys. In other words, the conservation of capital guarantees a process of 'circular' production. A 'circular' process is a 'self-sustaining' one.

Therefore, the conservation of different forms of capital, which guarantees their 'permanence' over time, becomes the primary criterion for sustainability: each generation hands down to future generations capital which is at least equivalent to that which it has available today.

This concept implies careful and continuous conservation/maintenance/management over time of natural, man-made, human and social capital. This, in turn, involves employment and work: in maintenance, in the management/reproduction of natural capital (parks, forests. etc.); in the maintenance/management/reproduction of man-made capital (above all cultural); in training, knowledge, know-how and research, that is in human capital and in the formation of social capital (associative/civil/social economics, etc.).

In effect, a large portion of our cultural heritage is composed of sites which, still today, play a religious and spiritual role in the daily life of the city: cathedrals, monasteries, churches, mosques, *medinas, madrasses,* etc., are located in the most central and significant places.

This cultural capital, insofar as it is the expression of the collective memory of a community, contributes to the reconstruction of the sense of belonging to a territory, to the rediscovery of common cultural roots and thus to the reproduction or self-production of social capital, whose lack has a critical impact on development (Fusco Girard and Forte, 2000).

The capitalist economic system, in fact, relies on a number of implicit values, such as trust, respect, reciprocity, etc., but at the same time tends to use up these very values. The challenge of cultural sustainability is to reproduce these values at a rate which is at least equivalent to their consumption.

The system of civil economy is able to reproduce these values (Zamagni and Bruni, 2003). If the conservation of this heritage is implemented carefully and integrated with the proper kind of management processes, and also involves the third sector, it contributes to the reproduction of social capital and becomes 'a driving force for cultural identity'.

The conservation of this heritage may also be a catalyst in a new process of economic development because it helps the city 'attract' investments and stimulates the regeneration of economic activities.

Finally, the conservation of heritage may also become an 'engine of social change' since it creates considerable employment opportunities and can be joined with the provision of many social services. More than other activities, it satisfies the right to work, to services, to housing. In this sense, it permits the coupling of economic and cultural development with the fight for the reduction of poverty.

Some clear examples of this approach are the rehabilitation of the Medina of Fez, of the historic centre of St. Petersburg, Seville and many other cities throughout the world.[4] The new project for the Medina of Fez (Radoine, this volume) is centred on the recognition of the cultural value of the neighbourhood and the struggle against the poverty of its residents. Indeed, 36 per cent of the inhabitants of the Medina (about 52,000 people) live in poverty and more than half the houses are in extremely poor condition. This project aims at creating 10,000 new job opportunities over the next few years, and improving accommodation standards as well as social and cultural services.

St. Petersburg possesses a unique cultural heritage, which is gradually being introduced into a perspective of economic development: Nevsky Prospect, the Hermitage, the complex of historical buildings, etc., represent a variety of architectural styles of great interest. The new action plan for the city aims at attracting businesses and investment, attempting to set up a form of public/private partnership based on a 'contract' between the various private players/public bodies. One strategic objective is the enhancement of cultural heritage for international fruition, a process which will contribute to remedying growing unemployment.

In Seville, the rehabilitation of the historic centre has been carried forward through a highly integrated approach, covering the cultural, religious, industrial and residential heritage. In the zone of San Louis Alameda de Hercules many new enterprises have been set up, new co-operative associations of artisans and shopkeepers have emerged and new arrangements have been made with existing businesses in order to provide new jobs for the unemployed.

Similar initiatives are emerging in Santiago de Compostela (which received in 2002 the International Dubai Award as a best practice in improving the living environment), Salamanca, in the historic centre of Bergen, Götheborg (Rosvall and Engelbrektsson, this volume), Prague, Lübeck, Edinburgh, Warsaw, etc., in Latin America (Olinda, Ouro Preto, etc.), as well as in other cities in North America and China (Guang-Jun Jin and Cong-xia Zhao, this volume).

It should be noted that rehabilitation of the historic and cultural heritage comes about as a result of the improvement of use values. By variously combining many space/time functions, centrality is reproduced, and this new capacity of attraction spurs an increase in exchange value (Ost, this volume). However, this type of economic-property enhancement may conflict with the objective of social protection, in view of the limited financial resources of the inhabitants, their age, etc. So an attempt is made to manage this conflict through suitable governance tools, based on case-by-case negotiations, and combining all types of incentives alongside the traditional tools of 'soft' loans and interest subsidies.

The establishment of new cultural, scientific, commercial and social operations, with their positive impact on employment, adds to the social value of these recovery and rehabilitation projects, by linking the struggle against poverty to environmental reclamation.

The rehabilitation of informal settlements, often to be found in peripheral zones, and of the historic centres targets places that suffer the greatest problems as regards pacific coexistence, environmental decay and social justice.

The indicators of this rehabilitation process are thus those which best record the concrete capacity of a city to create more inclusive – hence more sustainable – development strategies, linking the production of new goods and services to the promotion of citizenship.

These examples illustrate that it is really possible to integrate economic, environmental and social goals. In particular, they show that the promotion of physical, environmental, social quality is convenient for economic development. This conclusion is very important in a world characterized by economic culture, because it can communicate that values of beauty, justice and solidarity can produce benefits in economic dimensions as well, truly contributing to improving living conditions.

The Centrality of Intangible Assets for the Promotion of the Human Sustainable City Project

Social Capital and its Promotion

The human sustainable city is marked by a consistent 'middle' sector, between public and private, made up of civil networks founded on trust and which, in turn, produce trust. This social capital constructs integration and systemic behaviour, that help the city to function as a 'human body'.

Social capital is, moreover, able to construct self-government and self-organization skills: that is self-sustainability. Through economic development it contributes to the reduction of poverty and to ecological sustainability. Social capital is a product of, and in turn produces, human capital, reflecting the perception of rights and obligations.

Social capital increases the benefits accruing from investments in man-made capital and in human capital. In other words, it is able to 'shape' the process of production and economic development, reducing costs and times. In general terms, we may say that social capital increases the productivity of human, man-made and natural capital. In particular, social capital helps us to perceive and draw up positive-sum instead of zero-sum strategies: that is, cooperative strategies.

The starting point for the formation of social capital is the family. At this level, social capital may be defined as the set of relationships between parents and their children. The human capital possessed by the parents is transmitted to their children, hence to future generations. If social capital is weakened within the family, the human capital invested in each successive generation will inevitably be reduced.

The second level on which social capital is formed is the community: strong families and stable communities multiply social capital. It is possible to attempt to produce social capital by means of specific processes, such as the 'city contracts' or 'neighbourhood contracts' or the processes of Local Agenda 21. Through the new city contacts, an attempt is made to promote integrative intervention strategies which stimulate participatory processes, with approaches negotiated between the various social partners (as for example in Belgium) for identifying a shared vision of future.

In Italy, with the so-called Neighbourhood Contracts, a similar participation process is being stimulated.

In Turkey, on the outskirts of Ankara, the largest experiment in co-operative construction hitherto undertaken has taken shape. This is the 'satellite' town of Batikent, which has about 250,000 inhabitants, with an average density of about 250 inhabitants per hectare. Here, commercial and social entities also are run with cooperation and participation arrangements. Indeed, the aim is to promote response to the demand for housing, but at the same time enhance public spirit and the capacity for self-governance.

In conclusion, social capital makes it possible to improve not only market, but also social exchange – which does not pass through market channels – and hence the quality of life. Therefore, social capital is able to promote not only increased productivity, but also to construct redistribution strategies. Without social capital these strategies are very difficult to implement and do not receive the necessary democratic consensus. Without this form of capital there can be no development of the economy, no good governance, and no widespread democracy.

Social capital is fundamental for strengthening urban governance, which relies on direct democratic participation as well as democratic representation. Indeed, governance must strike a balance and identify trade-offs between multiple, heterogeneous and conflicting needs and objectives. These trade-offs imply, in turn, sufficient critical knowledge and capacity for evaluation.

Finally, without social capital, we cannot activate any form of negotiation, cooperation or partnership. Social capital is the most important form of 'capital'. But it depends on culture.

From Social Capital to Human Capital: Culture and Choices

The most significant experiences undertaken since the early 1990s have aimed at enhancing not only *ecoware* and *hardware*, but also *civicware* and hence *software*. The most outstanding examples are those that have succeeded in connecting the six different levels we have outlined above, in a virtuous circle of interdependence. They show that an 'alternative' city is possible, that new signs of change and hope can be created even in the most difficult contexts.

A human sustainable city can come into being if there is an ability to achieve the general interest or the common good in its development. The pursuit of this objective is the fundamental ethical construct which should guide the choices of every subject.

These choices, in the short, medium and long term, affect the future of the city and all its elements. In other words, there can be no prospect for human development unless we face the thorny problem of the choices to be made by each actor. Each choice is marked by a conflict between the individual good and the common good (Harvey, this volume). It is reduced (or better still dissolves) insofar as in each choice we are able to creatively devise new forms of mediation.

This depends, in turn, on culture, that is on know-how, knowledge and values and the priority we assign to the latter, allowing us to compare multiple, heterogeneous and conflicting needs/goals.

A culture marked by relations between human beings/human beings and human beings/nature is 'intrinsically' oriented towards integration and inclusion, and then to the common good and produces life styles coherent with the construction of a 'people-friendly' city, as well as a vision of well-being marked by material and intangible components, by having and being more. It is also open to question on sense/meaning.

A great danger to humanization is posed by the bio-ecological culture which reduces the human being to a marginal position in the ecosystem, combined with total faith in technology (thus there are no limits to manipulations) and with an economy-driven culture based on maximum profit, to be obtained always and at whatever the cost.

The image of the human being as prisoner of new technologies, with no true links to his/her fellow beings other than utilitarian/mechanistic relationships, is the image of a mono-dimensional being (Marcuse, 1964), the very antithesis of the Humanist ideal.

Promoting humanization means rejecting the image of the mono-dimensional human being in the name of the idea of an 'integral and plural' human being linked to other human beings and to the Earth, free in his/her ability for self-determination, in his/her uniqueness and irreproducibility, and marked by an intrinsic value which makes him/her inviolable and never instrumental: the human being seen as *a person*.

The ability to reconstruct integration in an era of fragmentation and division should be the first characteristic of 'New Humanism'.[5] It was the hallmark of Renaissance Humanism, which integrated art and science, universal principles and techniques, experience and reason, idealism and realism, analysis and intuition, the ancient and the modern world, and the natural and the transcendental.

New Humanism should propose the image of a person who is able to build relationships with others, with future generations and with nature: an integral person in whom we see the melding of all dimensions from the material to the spiritual. Relational capacity is the fundamental aspect of humanity. It can be implemented in the city, beginning with the diffusion of the knowledge and understanding of best practices.

Spiritual Capital

The culture of giving is an essential component for the humanization of urban development. The gift implies opening towards and attention to our fellow citizens, to reciprocal care, which provides an additional input of energy that triggers change, paving the way for a never-ending chain reaction of solidarity, which will also embrace future generations.

The culture of relations and giving is a typical product of the non-profit sector, of voluntary initiatives, of co-operation and associations, of the so-called third sector. It provides the spiritual energy necessary to sustain a true project for human development.

Indeed there does exist a form of interdependence between social, cultural and spiritual capital. All the most significant experiences highlight the fact that the value of solidarity has become manifest in the form of concrete actions thanks to the presence of individuals belonging to civil and religious movements/associations, marked by strong spiritual capital. The latter has made it possible to achieve integration and inclusion between diverse aspects and dimensions, even in the most fragmentary and conflicting situations.

Words such as 'spirituality', 'spiritual vision' and 'spiritual development' are to be found ever more frequently over the past few years in official documents addressing the issue of sustainability. But we need to focus more accurately on the meaning of these words, recognizing the fact that one of the reasons for the difficulty in implementing sustainable development is linked to this dimension.

In the Report of the People's Republic of China (Ministry of Foreign Affairs, 2001) regarding the development of human settlements between 1996 and 2001, we find that 'only from the integration of material forms of construction with spiritual progress can communities emerge and become living environments of advanced civilization' (§ 6.2.6).

This emphasis on the importance of the spiritual dimension of development is, moreover, perfectly in line with the most recent final documents drawn up by various agencies of the United Nations. We may for instance recall that, in 1992, Agenda 21 highlighted the importance of 'social, economic and spiritual development', pointing out that 'individuals should be allowed to develop to their full potential, including healthy physical, mental and spiritual development'.[6] (§§ 6.3 and 6.23) (UNCED, 1992).

The Declaration of the Beijing Fourth World Conference on Women recognizes that 'religion, spirituality and belief play a central role in the lives of millions of women and men, in the way they live and in the aspirations they have for the future' (chapter 2, § 24) (FWCW, 1995).

In the Habitat Agenda the governments agree on the requirement to 'achieve a world of greater stability and peace, built on ethical and spiritual vision' (chapter 1, § 4) (UNCHS,1996). This principle is repeated in paragraphs 25 and 27 regarding personal, social, cultural and spiritual development, also in reference to assist the preservation of World Heritage Sites, protected by UNESCO, also through international cooperation. In paragraphs 42 and 152, particular recognition is given to cultural and spiritual values with reference to the cultural heritage to be preserved and the values to be respected in the implementation of development strategies.

The Earth Charter in Principle 1/b of the General Principles affirms 'faith in the inherent dignity of all human beings and in the intellectual, artistic, ethical, and spiritual potential of humanity' (Earth Council, 2000). Principle 12 expresses the pledge to 'uphold the right of all, without discrimination, to a natural and social environment supportive of human dignity, bodily health, and spiritual well-being, with special attention to the rights of indigenous peoples and minorities'. Principle 14/d recognizes the 'importance of moral and spiritual education for sustainable living'.

Article 10 of the *Naples Declaration* (this volume), stresses the importance of the spiritual dimension as a foundation for the values of solidarity and justice.

The Contribution of Religions and of the Christian Religion

The wisdom and values affirmed by each religion may contribute to the fight against the de-humanization of reality, giving depth to the spiritual dimension.

The various religions may help promote a form of development founded on the centrality of the human being. They acknowledge the interrelatedness of each one of us and advocate an idea of the common good that is often extended to include Nature/Creation, thus re-orienting human actions. Some religions offer the vision of the ideal city. In the Bible, Jerusalem is the City of Man 'which descends from heaven' (Apocalypse, 21,2): it is the reflection of the City of God towards which, in a spiritual sense, the Tribes of Israel move. In this sense, it becomes the transcendental target of humanity, the perfect city of light and words, the exact opposite of Babylon.

The dialogue between scientists and religious communities may produce fruitful synergy contributing to the diffusion of humanistic, religious and civil values in contemporary culture, which is increasingly attuned to economic values. The dialogue between the great religions of the world (Christianity, Buddhism, Hinduism, Judaism and Islam) which met together at Assisi in 1986, bears witness to their contribution to the protection of the ecosystem and respect for each other (Addison Posey, 1999; Golser, 2001).

The different religions tend to recognize that the natural world has an 'intrinsic value' – not dependent on its capacity to satisfy human needs. Human beings clearly play a special role in the ecosystem and have a unique responsibility regarding the use they make of Nature. Some uses are legitimate, whereas others often cause irreversible damage. Today, religions should collaborate ever more closely on the themes of re-establishing peace and justice and safeguarding creation, promoting the construction of a world ethics based on a great spiritual capital.

The Christian religion, focused on the primacy and dignity of the human being, on solidarity and promotion of the 'integral human being', is open to dialogue with the other religious and cultural traditions.

With the Vatican Council II, the Catholic Church stressed the centrality of human rights, laying the cornerstone of that which was later defined 'human development'.

The Encyclical *Populorum Progressio* (1967) – on the development of peoples – focused on the concept of the 'integral development of mankind', as a new name for peace, to be constructed through justice, and it was in fact the forerunner of many elements of sustainable development. 'Integral development' is marked by inclusion and relational capacity. It expresses opening towards one's fellow beings, towards the manifold dimensions of life, towards creation. It is the essential element of humanity.

Subsequently, with the Encyclicals *Sollecitudo Rei Socialis* (1987) and *Centesimus Annus* (1991), we see the emergence of a framework which in the Summit of Rio de Janeiro (1992) led to the drafting of Agenda 21. More recently, in the last Consultation of the Council of European Episcopal Conferences (2002) the Catholic Church stressed yet again the importance of actions promoting a 'change of values in society', that is advocating a culture that recognizes 'the primacy of spiritual activities'.

The 'cultural project' of the Italian Episcopal Conference (CEI) is also moving in this direction to promote a new way of thinking by people, oriented by different priorities.

Towards a Human Sustainable City Project

The Habitat Agenda offers a general framework for a new project for the city. Globalization, which has been the engine for change over the last decade, has been matched by an inverse process of decentralization which has seen the cities as leading players. The cities are becoming increasingly aware of their role as real 'agents of change' to the same or even a greater degree than nations. Indeed, it was the cities that best implemented the objectives of sustainable development agreed upon at Rio in 1992, with a number of good practices. In particular, we refer to the bottom-up approach for humanizing globalization, starting from localism, from the cities and city networks, by strengthening relations between public institutions, the market and a vital civil society.

The human sustainable city produces new economic wealth in a more inclusive way. It is able to give more to many people while taking less from ecological world (resources, energy, etc.).

The human sustainable city champions the rights of all, including the disadvantaged, and curbs growing inequalities by promoting integration. Similarly to individual human beings, the 'people-friendly city' (Lazzati, 1984) builds integration, combining material and non-material needs, utility, desires and hopes. The city where human beings are connected by a dense communicational/relational fabric behaves as a single unit. And like every human body, it has a centre that unifies multiple activities and functions. Thus the human sustainable city is the city which manages to integrate production, residence, consumption, mobility and leisure time in a single vital pulsing unit.

The human sustainable city can receive new inhabitants without increasing slums and 'districts in crisis'. It recognizes the centrality of the human being, rather than the car, the industrial plant or the urban green.

This image of the city that integrates its different parts and arranges them in systemic ways is to be found in many religious traditions. For example, in the Bible, the city is bride, mother, widow, harlot; it is a 'person', the subject of feelings of love and hate. We address it using 'thou' because its acts as a collective individual (Riva, 1998).

In the Islamic and Hindu religions the human city expresses, on a large scale, the vital integration of functions which is found at individual level in the human body. Indeed, the city is able to reflect, in its core, a transcendental dimension (Nasr, 2000).

The Centrality of the Project of Change

Today the city is held together by relationships of exchange (i.e. by interests) and by 'vertical' mass-media communication.

To achieve a more human city we should reduce the growing

inequalities within it and promote horizontal communication and cultural change, in order to revise the priority list of values upon which we base our choices. This responsibility falls not only on the public institution, but on all of us. Each one of us can promote relational and cultural values every day in his/her work place, by proposing a vision of man, of organizations, of neighbourhoods, of cities, and thus contributing to build the 'good life'.

We must all become 'architects' of a new concrete Utopia in our society/city. Renaissance Humanism inspired Utopia. Campanella, Bacon, Thomas More all stressed the role of Utopia. Leon Battista Alberti, Filarete, and others proposed visions of cities in the space of the Renaissance, anticipating Fourier's phalanstery. According to Marcuse, a Utopian vision inspires us to build a better future.

We need new enthusiasm and unbounded energy to help us act first and foremost in the cultural sphere, launching an essentially cultural project founded on human rights, shared values and social responsibility (Pruzan, 1997).

The Habitat Agenda provides the basic guidelines for this project for a sustainable and human city. In particular, it stresses the cultural dimension of sustainable development and the role of the conservation of cultural heritage (§§ 42 and 152).

The best practices monitored in the Habitat Agenda help to open – through concrete experiences – a dialogue between 'expert knowledge' and 'common knowledge'. They communicate that ethical investment is effective in economic terms (as, for example, micro-credit experiences); that promotion of social quality attracts new economic activities; that conservation of ecological heritage is the pre-requisite for economic development.

The rehabilitation of historic centres contributes to the urban economic base, but also to imparting a soul to urban development, to humanizing it, placing it in a dialectical relationship between past and present, private and public spaces, beauty and function. It gives strength to memory, to collective memory and builds resistance against a culture that only recognizes the present. Conservation aims not merely at promoting tourist development, but also at vitalizing the city's cultural and spiritual development (Fusco Girard and Forte, 2000).

The conservation of cultural heritage helps secure one's roots: without memory there can be no future; there is only inhumanity. Rehabilitation of this heritage increases the feeling of belonging to a territory, and helps people rediscover the base for common values; ultimately, it produces citizenship. Insofar as the rehabilitation of the historic centre integrates different parts and functions, forming a single unit that links together various functions and dimensions, it also conveys the 'spirit of the city' (La Pira, 1957) – its particular identity.

The Structure of the Book

The papers selected for this volume, arranged in three parts, develop, either directly or indirectly, the points illustrated above. They highlight the fact that we must face the challenges of globalization and increasing urbanization: in particular those regarding development, justice, ecology and peaceful relations/coexistence.

Justice is the ultimate ethical challenge of this new century. It is not Utopian to attempt to promote a more equitable distribution of opportunities in the era of globalization. There are signs of hope which need to be identified, disseminated and, as far as possible, multiplied through adequate projects. There is also a need for new public intervention strategies, able to compensate for the shortcomings of the free market, which tends to replicate social polarization and environmental degradation. The improvement of civil society is crucial for implementing new strategies of sustainable human development.

The various papers place the 'integral' human being, rather than the enterprise or the 'green', at the centre of development, and this is clearly a choice of priority. Considering humanity in all its dimensions (social, economic, ecological, political, cultural, spiritual) means rediscovering Humanism as a new guiding principle for development, a principle counteracting the de-humanizing effect of trade and financial globalization which reduces all values to economic/efficiency criteria.

This Humanism is the thread that links and unifies all the various papers, all sharing the common goal of building a more desirable future of communal living, hence of the city.

This Humanistic vision engenders integration/relations between those who are included and those who are excluded, between rich and poor, and promotes cooperation between public, private and social players.

A further element tying together many of the articles in this book is the need to promote a 'culture of relations' between human beings and their environmental context; a culture that builds dialogue, reciprocity, solidarity, thus a human city. Such a culture, poised against the progressive decline of human relations, fosters a shared vision of the general interest, active citizenship, dissemination of information, ongoing assessment of choices. A city that incorporates this culture will attract activities, investments and development more than any other, winning in the field of global competition.

The culture of relational capacity also fosters participatory democracy alongside representative democracy, giving new life to public action, which should not only aim at efficiency/productivity, but also at promoting social cohesion, that is civil society.

Building a city requires rational processes and technologies. But since a city is not made of bricks, cement and asphalt alone, it also requires trust, the possibility of creating relationships and solidarity between its citizens. It requires change not only regarding the city's *hardware, ecoware, finware* and *orgware*, but also its *software* and *civicware*.

The papers develop technical reflections and describe experiences, alternating the construction of future scenarios (related to the urban common good and the tools for implementing it) with an analysis of the 'status quo'. They pose many questions and give some answers, describe successes and explain failures, always giving depth and concrete form to the ideas outlined in this Introduction. The struggle against poverty in its various forms (economic, social, environmental) is a thread linking many papers and affects all the cities, from Nairobi to Saõ Paulo, from Patna to Porto Alegre, from Bangalore to Chengdu.

Although updated and integrated, the various papers were initially presented at an International Meeting entitled: 'The Human Being and City. Towards a Human and Sustainable Development' (University for a New Humanism), held in Naples during the Catholic Church's Jubilee Year 2000. Coherently with the vision of the Jubilee as a time to stop and reflect upon *where we are going, what we are doing and what we can do* to envision a project that respects the dignity of the individual and the value of the environment and promotes justice and solidarity, the various authors express their views on the most critical issues for humanizing the city.

One of these points is rebuilding a network of relationships to create a 'people-friendly city' (Lazzati, 1984), an element recognized as central by the Christian tradition.

In the Christian Humanist tradition, human beings realize their potential through relating with others and they are themselves insofar as they reconcile the manifold dimensions of life in their own consciences.

Moreover, Mounier and Maritain's concept of communal and personal Humanism has always stressed this integration which today must be extended further to include Nature/Creation.

This volume is divided into three sections. They highlight the importance of moving from values and principles to good practices, and based on the latter, improving the project for the future of the city: a project for an authentically human and sustainable urban development, founded on environment, inclusion and integration.

In the conclusion, it is stressed the centrality of the ethical challenge in our especially complex and dramatic times.

Finally, this ethical – and spiritual – dimension is highlighted by the *Naples Declaration* (this volume) signed by University professors from 25 countries (Argentina, Austria, Bangladesh, Belgium, Bulgaria, China, Chile, Czech Republic, Germany, Greece, India, Italy, Kenya, Lithuania, Poland, Russia, Singapore, Slovakia, Spain, South Africa, Sweden, The Netherlands, United Kingdom, United States of America, Ukraine).

The Declaration sets the principles for shifting from industrial and financial globalization to the globalization of cities and city networks, that is of the rights of citizenship and widespread democracy.

These principles are not a dream, they have 'come true' in a number of cities worldwide. We need to broaden our knowledge of these experiences and to analyze them so that we can translate them into new projects for sustainable human development in our specific urban contexts.

Notes

1   Saõ Paulo, the wealthiest city in Brazil provides a very interesting example regarding its economic output. In just a few years it has become a global city, attracting increasing amounts of foreign investment, since it has adopted all types of innovation with extraordinary speed. However, the high number of unemployed (3.9 million in the metropolitan area in 1993), lack of housing (3.9 million units) and the spread of the *favelas* show that economic development does not necessarily proceed hand in hand with the promotion of better opportunities for all.
2   The 'Declaration on Cities and other Human Settlements in the New Millennium' following the General Assembly of the United Nations held in June 2001 in New York, confirmed the objectives, principles and strategies of the Habitat Agenda, highlighting the most significant practical experiments undertaken and also the obstacles encountered (see sub-paragraphs B and C, §§ 7-28).
3   For partial consultation of the database, visit the site: www.bestpractices.org.
4   The conservation of natural capital damaged by industrial activities in Hamilton (Canada), Swansea (Wales) and Chattanooga (USA) was an opportunity for producing new use-values and market values, new jobs, and for reproducing non-use values.
5   The birth of a 'New Humanism' was mentioned as early as 1965 in the Constitution *Gaudium et Spes* of Vatican Council II on the 'Church in the Contemporary World' (see § 55, Rome, 1965).
6   The final Declaration of the Copenhagen Summit on Social Development also acknowledges that 'our societies must respond more effectively to the material and spiritual needs of individuals, their families and the communities in which they live' (§ 3).

References

Addison Posey, D. (1999), *Cultural and Spiritual Values of Biodiversity*, UNEP and IT (International Technology Publishers), Nairobi.

Aghion, P. and Williamson, J. (1998), *Growth, Inequality and Globalization*, Cambridge University Press, Cambridge.

Allen, A. and You, N. (2002), *Sustainable Urbanisation. Bridging the Green and Brown Agendas*, University College London Press, London.

Beguinot, C. (1998), 'Saggio introduttivo', in A. Notarangelo and B. Petrella (eds), *La città nel XXI secolo tra recupero innovazione cooperazione*, Giannini, Naples.

Benevolo, L. (1993), *Le città nella storia d'Europa*, Laterza, Bari.

Borri, D., Khakee, A. and Lacirignola, C. (1997), *Evaluating Theory, Practice and Urban Rural Interplay in Planning*, Kluwer, Dordrecht.

Camagni, R. (2000), 'Processi di globalizzazione e sostenibilità urbana. Nuova governance urbana e nuovi strumenti per l'infrastrutturazione finanziaria', in L. Fusco Girard and B. Forte (eds), *Città sostenibile e sviluppo umano*, Angeli, Milan, pp. 296-322.

Castells, M. (1998), *End of Millennium*, Blackwell Publishers, Oxford.

Daly, H.E. (1991), 'Elements of Environmental Economics', in R. Costanza (ed.), *Ecological Economics*, Columbia University Press, New York.

Daniel, C. and Avamileno, J. (2002), *Santo André mais ugual. Programa integrado de inclusão social*, Prefectura de Santo André, Santo André.

de Soto, H. (2000), *The Mystery of Capital*, Basic Book, New York.

Earth Council (2000), *The Earth Charter*, The Hague.

Frey, L. (2000), 'Sviluppo umano e sostenibile: aspetti relativi al lavoro', in L. Fusco Girard and B. Forte (eds), *Città sostenibile e sviluppo umano*, Angeli, Milan, pp. 169-92.

Fusco Girard, L. (1987), *Risorse architettoniche e culturali: valutazioni e strategie di conservazione*, Angeli, Milan.

Fusco Girard, L. and Forte, B. (2000), *Città sostenibile e sviluppo umano*, Angeli, Milan.

Fusco Girard, L. and Nijkamp, P. (1997), *Le valutazioni per lo sviluppo sostenibile della città e del territorio*, Angeli, Milan.

FWCW (Fourth World Conference on Women) (1995), *Report of the Conference*, Beijing.

Golser, K. (2001), 'Ethical Dimensions of Sustainable Development', in Pontifical Council for Justice and Peace, *Agenda for Rio+10*, Rome.

Hall, P. and Pfeiffer, U. (2000), *Urban Future 21. A Global Agenda for Twenty-first Century Cities*, E. and F.N. Spon, London.

HSMI (2000), *Property Tax Assessment and Municipal Finances. Patna Experience*, New Delhi.

Huntington, S.P. (1997), *Lo scontro delle civiltà*, Garzanti, Milan.

John Paul II (1987), Encyclical *Sollicitudo Rei Socialis*.

John Paul II (1991), Encyclical *Centesimus Annus*.

La Pira, G. (1957), 'Le città sono vive', in F. Montanari (ed.), La Scuola, Brescia.

Lazzati, G. (1984), *La città dell'uomo*, Ave, Rome.

Marcuse, H. (1964), *One-dimensional Man. Studies in the Ideology of Advanced Industrial Society*, Beacon Press, Boston.

Ministry of Foreign Affairs, People's Republic of China, (2001), *Report on the Development of Human Settlements*, Architecture and Building Press, Beijing.

Mumford, L. (1961), *The City in History*, Harcourt, Brace and Jovanovich, New York.

Nasr, S.H. (2000), 'The Spirit of the Cities', in I. Serageldin, E. Shluger and J.M. Brown (eds), *Historic Cities and Sacred Cities*, The World Bank, Washington.

Nijkamp, P. and Wouter, J. (2001), *The City in the Information and Communication Technology Age: A Comparative Study on Path Dependency*, Free University, Amsterdam.

Nijkamp, P., Oirschot, G. and Oosterman, A. (1993), *Regional Development and Engineering Creativity: An Instrumental Comparison of Science Parks in a Knowledge Society*, Free University, Amsterdam.

Paul VI (1967), Encyclical *Populorum Progressio*.

Piccinato, G. (2002), *Un mondo di città*, Edizioni di Comunità, Turin.

Pruzan, P. (1997), *Planning with Multiple Criteria*, Copenhagen Business School Press, Copenhagen.

Riva, F. (1998), 'L'uomo biblico e la città', *Città dell'uomo*, vol. 7/8.

Rodenburg, C.A, Vreeker, R. and Nijkamp, P. (2002), *The Economics of Multi-functional Land Use*, Free University, Amsterdam.

Sassen, S. (1994), *Cities in a World Economy*, Pine Forge Press, London.

Sassen, S. (ed.) (2002), *Global Networks Linked Cities*, Routledge, London.

Scandurra, E. (1999), *La città che non c'è. La pianificazione al tramonto*, Dedalo, Bari.

Sen, A. (1997), *Resources, Values and Development*, Harvard University Press, Cambridge.

Sen, A. (1999), *Development as Freedom*, Alfred A. Knopf, New York.

Serageldin, I. (1996), *Sustainability and Wealth of Nations*, The World Bank, Washington.

Stiglitz, J.E. (2002), *La globalizzazione e i suoi oppositori*, Einaudi, Turin.

Taylor, C. (1992), *The Politics of Recognition*, Princeton University Press, Princeton.

UNCED (United Nations Commission on Environment and Development) (1992), *Agenda 21 and Rio Declaration*, Rio de Janeiro.

UNCHS (United Nations Centre for Human Settlements) (1996), *The Habitat Agenda and Istanbul Declaration*, Istanbul.

UNDP (United Nations Development Programme) (2001), *Human Development Report 2001*, Oxford University Press, New York.

UNCHS (United Nations Centre for Human Settlements) (2001a), *The State of the World's Cities 2001*, UNCHS (Habitat), Nairobi.

UNCHS (United Nations Centre for Human Settlements) (2001b), *Cities in a Globalizing World. Global Report on Human Settlements 2001*, UNCHS (Habitat), Nairobi.

van den Bergh, J.C.J.M., Button, K.J., Nijkamp, P. and Pepping, G.C. (1997), *Meta-analysis in Environmental Economics*, Kluwer, Dordrecht.

Various Authors (2001), *The Future is Now*, International Institute for Environment and Development, London.

Various Authors (2002), *Habitat Agenda/Agenda Habitat. Verso la sostenibilità urbana e territoriale*, Angeli, Milan.

von Weizsäcker, E.U., Lovins, A.B. and Lovins, L.H. (1998), *Factor Four: Doubling Wealth, Halving Resource Use*, Earthscan, London.

Wakely, P. and You, N. (2001), *Implementing Habitat Agenda: In Search of Urban Sustainability*, University College London Press, London.

Zamagni, S. (1998), *Non profit come economia civile*, Il Mulino, Bologna.

Zamagni, S. (1999), 'Social Paradoxes of Growth and Civil Economy', in G. Gandolfo and F. Marzano (eds), *Economic Theory and Social Justice*, London, MacMillan, pp. 212-37.

Zamagni, S. and Bruni, L. (2003), 'Un'economia civile per città felici', in L. Fusco Girard, B. Forte, M. Cerreta, P. De Toro and F. Forte (eds), *L'uomo e la città. Verso uno sviluppo umano e sostenibile*, Angeli, Milan.

PART I
AN ENVIRONMENTAL APPROACH

Introduction to Part I

Pasquale De Toro

An Increasingly Urban World

On 6-8 June 2001 a Special Session of the UN General Assembly was held in New York for an *Overall Review and Appraisal of the Implementation of the Habitat Agenda*. It is also known as *Istanbul +5*, coming as it did five years after the Second Conference on Human Settlements (Habitat II), held in Istanbul from 3 to 14 June 1996, which adopted the Habitat Agenda (UNCHS, 1996), comprising a set of actions with the goal of achieving the two fundamental objectives set by the Conference: *adequate shelter for all* and *sustainable human settlement development in a urbanizing world.*

The *Habitat +5* meeting drew up the *Declaration on Cities and Other Human Settlements in the New Millennium*, which reviews the degree of implementation of the Habitat Agenda worldwide, progress made, obstacles and emerging issues, and comes to the conclusion that the Agenda is not only still viable today, but must act as a cornerstone for the sustainable development of human settlements in coming years. Indeed, today we find ourselves at a crossroads in human history, at a time when the 'urban issue' is paramount. Almost half of the total world population of six billion people lives in cities, a rate that is set to increase in the near future. The world is facing unprecedented growth in urban population, especially in developing countries.

This introduction, while not claiming to provide a comprehensive account of the health of the world's cities from an environmental point of view, seeks to highlight some fundamental aspects, with a view to understanding at what level of sustainability/unsustainability we are living and acting today, especially in urban settings, as well as what actions can be undertaken to achieve a more sustainable future.

First and foremost, we need to understand the size of the *urbanizing world* in which we are living. The current world population exceeds six billion inhabitants, a figure that is all the more staggering if compared to the number at the turn of the twentieth century – 1.6 billion, which increased swiftly to two billion in 1927, three billion in 1960, four billion in 1974, five billion in 1987 and six billion in 1999 (UNDP, 2002). Moreover, the world's population is increasingly made up of city dwellers: around the year 1000 AD, the city with the largest population in the world was Cordoba, with 450,000 people, in 1800 it was Peking, with 1.1 million people, in 1900 London, with 6.5 million, in 2000 Tokyo with 26.4 million (a far cry from its 1.5 million population in 1900). Nowadays, megacities, i.e. those exceeding the ten million people mark, number no less than 19 (including, among others, Mexico City, Bombay, Saõ Paolo, New York, Beijing), while in 1900, the cities with more than one million inhabitants were just 16. Finally, whereas today about half the world's population are city dwellers, in 1900, a mere 10 per cent of the total population lived in cities (UNDP, 2002; UNCHS, 2001).

The trend towards urbanization is also set to continue in the coming years: according to UN forecasts, three global population scenarios could take shape by the year 2050: a conservative estimate setting total population at 7.7 billion, a medium one at 9.3 billion, and a maximum growth scenario forecasting a staggering 11.2 billion (UNDP, 1997). Against these growth forecasts, it is expected that by 2030, about 60 per cent of the global population (which could exceed eight billion) will live in cities. This figure is all the more telling if we consider that as late as 1950 only 29.7 per cent of the world's inhabitants lived in cities, and that over the following 50 years, i.e. by the year 2000, urban population had reached 47.4 per cent of the total.

Never before in the history of humankind had urban areas reached such an impressive extension and encroached to such an extent upon rural areas. To make just a few comparisons, it took Jericho, the oldest city in the world, 7,000 years to change from a small village to a 'city' about 3,000 people strong. Ancient Athens numbered between 215,000 and 300,000 people, when, in 432 BC, it reached the maximum population which could be supported by the surrounding countryside. Rome, the only ancient city to register a large population by modern standards, presumably ranged between 750,000 and 1,250,000 inhabitants between the late Republican period and the fourth century AD. We need to wait for the development of Constantinople in the Middle Ages and Beijing in the early modern period to find two cities able to rival ancient Rome (Hall, 2001).

Today, with about 50 per cent of world population living in urban areas, the attendant environmental problems, especially in developing countries, are unprecedented. According to some estimates, 1.1 billion people breathe heavily polluted air, 220 million do not have access to potable water, 420 million do not have access to basic sanitation and at least 600 million lack adequate housing. Moreover, over the coming years, the trend towards urbanization will indeed be especially marked in developing countries: by the year 2030, about 57 per cent of their population will live in cities, against 17.8 per cent in 1950 and 40.5 per cent in 2000. While at the end of 2000, three of the ten largest cities in the world belonged to developed countries (Tokyo, New York and Los Angeles), by 2015 only Tokyo will remain in the 'top ten' and will still top the list with its estimated 27.2 million inhabitants as the largest city in the world, while the other nine will all belong to less developed or developing countries: the first six will include Dacca, Mumbai (Bombay), Saõ Paolo, Delhi and Mexico City, each exceeding 20 million inhabitants. Moreover, in 2015 there will be no less than 21 mega cities with over 10 million inhabitants and 58 cities with over 5 million (there were 40 in 2001), 48 of which in developing countries (UNDP, 2002).

Against this scenario, issues of water and energy supply, waste disposal, transport, and lack of infrastructure and housing, will deeply affect the development of cities and the quality of urban life. Unless appropriate sustainable development policies are adopted, we will find ourselves travelling along a road leading to increasing 'urban poverty' a term that defines not only a lack of material goods, but has 'a broader meaning of cumulative deprivation, characterized by squalid living conditions; risk to life and health for poor sanitation, air pollution, crime and violence, traffic accidents, and natural disasters; and the breakdown of traditional family and community safety nets' (World Bank, 2000, p. 3). Indeed, relentless urbanization is producing a growing number of informal settlements (which harbour 30 to 60 per cent of the urban population in developing countries), ranging from the slums of India to the *favelas* of Rio de Janeiro, where all aspects of urban poverty are exacerbated, offering stark evidence of the fact that, due to the failure of recent urban policies, increasing urbanization not only imports poverty from rural areas, but helps create it in the cities themselves.

The cities, especially those in developing countries, show, paralleling their fast-paced population growth, an increase in 'critical areas': unemployment, environmental deterioration, lack of urban services, decay of existing infrastructure, lack of access to land and financing, lack of *adequate shelter for all*. Indeed, it is estimated that over one billion people live in seriously substandard housing, often in slums and squatter settlements. Moreover, in many countries, what is rated as decent housing[1] is totally inadequate by our standards.

> The global housing stock in cities amounts to 700-720 million units of all types. It is estimated that 20 to 40 million urban households are homeless. A significant number of those housed, however, cannot be regarded as living in adequate shelter. Worldwide, 18 percent of all urban housing units (some 125 million units) are non-permanent structures, and 25 percent (175 million units) do not conform to building regulations. Most deficient housing units are found in the cities of the developing countries, with more than half of all less-then-adequate housing units located in the Asia and Pacific regions (UNCHS, 2001, p. 30).

And if so many housing units are substandard, we often find whole neighbourhoods that are considered to be 'less than adequate'. This is not only due to the lack of basic services, but, to a greater extent, serious environmental deterioration and pollution. If it is true that we are living in an era marked by a deep global-scale 'ecological crisis' (greenhouse effect, the Ozone hole, desertification, etc.), it is equally true that this crisis has an urban dimension. Indeed, cities are not only places where critical environmental effects are produced but also places where those effects are most strongly felt, and this is even more true in the cities in developing countries. To quote a few examples, motor vehicle traffic accounts for 70-80 per cent of total emissions in cities in developing countries; also, forecasts indicate a 60 per cent increase in CO_2 emissions in the atmosphere between 1997 and 2010, 65 per cent of which coming from developing countries.

Rapid urbanization and the environmental crisis are the two sides of the same coin: the greatest environmental problems affecting city districts or even whole cities are air and water pollution, waste collection and management (including toxic waste), and noise pollution (UNCHS, 1997). In particular, air pollution is mostly due to the use of fossil fuels for industrial production purposes, for electrical power generation, for household heating and as fuel for motor vehicles. In general terms, air pollution is marked by sulphur dioxide and other suspended particles, lead, ozone and carbon monoxide. Water pollution is caused by urban sewage and industrial wastewater, which are discharged into the rivers of many cities or into nearby lakes and seas. Moreover, groundwater pollution is linked to poor landfill management, which allows pollutants to filter into the soil, or to the pesticides used in agriculture which also penetrate the soil. The problems associated with waste are linked not only to the growing volumes of municipal solid waste (often handled without appropriate recycling procedures), but also to the storage of toxic waste, often highly flammable and liable to explode on contact with water or other chemical substances, and in most cases also carcinogenic. Finally, noise pollution is mostly associated with industrial activities, construction, airport and road traffic: hundreds of millions of people live in areas where the threshold of 70 dB(A) is exceeded by far, with all the attendant effects on physical and mental health.

The growth of cities, aside from causing serious urban pollution problems, has also led to an increase in their 'ecological footprint' – that is their consumption of resources and the increased demand for waste assimilation placed on natural ecosystems. The ecological footprint is calculated as the land area necessary to sustain current levels of resource consumption, support, and waste discharge by a given population (Wackernagel and Rees, 1996). Indeed, the steady advance of urbanization contributes to an increase in the impact of urban areas on natural resources – both renewable and non-renewable – that are crucial for the life of the city itself, such as drinking water, agricultural and forestry products, fossil fuels, etc. Although admittedly each city's ecological footprint varies according to its consumption models and waste management systems, it has been calculated that the land area needed to support a city is not less than ten times its built extension (Rees, 1992). For cities in developed countries, the imprint is greater: for instance, it has been calculated that the ecological footprint of the 29 largest cities in Europe and the Baltic is between 565 and 1,130 times larger than the area of the cities themselves (Folke et al., 1997), and even that London's ecological footprint is close to the whole productive territory of England (Chambers et al, 2000). Moreover, ecological footprint analysis does not refer solely to the current consumption of a community but also to its foreseeable demands, which can then be compared to the availability of resources, also identifying probable deficits. The ecological footprint concept thus provides a precious support for sustainable planning, and enables researchers to monitor, over time, the changes in the sustainability/unsustainability conditions of a city or even of a whole region or country.

Towards a Sustainable Future?

The aim of the sustainable development of the cities, which implies a reduction of their ecological footprint, can and must be achieved: sound environmental management can directly improve people's welfare while also supporting economic growth. At the same time, appropriate urban policies can promote and finance environmental improvements and the protection of ecosystems well beyond the boundaries of cities (UNCHS, 2001). The reduction of a city's ecological footprint implies a number of measures, of which 'most are linked to one of the following:

- Increasing biomass production within the city or its immediate surroundings (e.g. crops, fish, trees).
- Reduced waste or increased use of waste as an input into production (e.g. organic waste used for compost; waste water used for urban agriculture; improved performance on reclamation and recycling of material).
- Increased efficiency in the use of resources imported into the city (e.g. fresh water, fossil fuels and other mineral resources UNCHS, 1997, p. 409).

In terms of the latter point, it is estimated that production efficiency can be improved at least of a 'Factor Four': this means it is possible to achieve a fourfold increase in resource productivity or, alternatively, that the welfare of world population can be doubled while halving its consumption of natural resources. This 'efficiency revolution' is already feasible to a large extent in both rich and poor countries, and is also economically effective (von Weizsäcker et al., 1998). Some signs of change, which seem to point the way to a more sustainable future management of cities and territories, may already be detected, encouraging us to hope that in the near future we may witness a 'new industrial revolution' founded on Ecoefficiency. For instance, it might be possible to minimize power and material consumption in production processes, in turn reducing waste production (McDonough and Braungart, 1998).

On the other hand, greater awareness of environmental issues has, over past 15 years, spurred a noticeable increase in solar and wind power generation: during the 1990s, coal consumption increased by 1.2 per cent per year and oil consumption by 1.4 per cent, but over the same decade, solar cell sales increased by 17 per cent per year and wind power generation rose by 26 per cent (Brown et al., 1999). Moreover, hydro-electrical, geothermal and biomass power generation rose more slowly, between 1 and 4 per cent per year, but still showing a consistent trend (Brown et al., 2001).

Nowadays solar cells may also be incorporated in rooftiles and glass walls, enabling buildings to generate their own power. Moreover, semiconductor research has led to the development of thermo-photovoltaic (TPV) cells which convert heat generated by the industrial process into electrical power. To complete the picture, progress in electronic microcircuit technology has made it possible to produce the compact fluorescent lightbulb (CFL), which consumes one quarter the electricity required by incandescent light bulbs and lasts ten times longer.

Also, thanks to the decrease in the costs of wind and sun-generated electricity, over the next few years the production of hydrogen by means of water electrolysis will become cost-effective, and fuel cells will turn hydrogen into electricity, both by means of small power generators supplying electricity to housing and office buildings and in cars, as an alternative power source instead of petrol. Liquid hydrogen may on the other hand replace kerosene which nowadays is the fuel used by most commercial jet aircraft. Moreover, we should bear in mind that the current economic system based on fossil fuels favours those countries that have domestic oil deposits (especially the Middle East but also the US and the Russian Federation) while penalizing all the others, who are forced to depend on producer countries. An economy based on renewable energy sources, such as sun and wind, and especially on hydrogen, would benefit from much more abundant and evenly distributed resources. In this way, although some countries might still be able to export electrical power or hydrogen obtained from renewable sources, it is highly unlikely that other countries would come to rely heavily on imports for their energy requirements, as is the case today with oil. We should also consider that in developing countries, where millions of hectares of forests are felled each year, 55 per cent of the felled wood is directly used for fuel, a quota that would decrease drastically if new energy sources were made available.

In terms of the housing sector, the so-called 'passive house' has already been created, i.e. a house that has solar energy as its only power source. Thanks to effective window and wall insulation, this house uses up only 5 per cent of the heating energy and 10 per cent of the electrical power required for a standard housing unit. In other cases, 'superwindows' have been constructed. They consist of thin layers of glass produced with advanced technology which let in visible light but reflect infrareds. This way, housing comfort is increased while cutting energy consumption (hence fuel consumption) for heating or air conditioning. Buildings can even be planned so as to be 'zero net energy' depending exclusively on passive solar power and the body heat of their dwellers. Moreover, sustainable housing is already produced with recyclable materials and equipped with systems that collect rainwater for sanitation purposes as well as a waste recycling plant.

Finally, in terms of urban and territorial planning, environmental concerns have recently been taken into account in planning instruments for both large scale planning and zoning purposes following a number of approaches. Environmental, or rather ecological planning, advocates a holistic, multidisciplinary approach, which brings together a variety of concerns: social and economic, historical and cultural, urban and infrastructural, landscape, issues of nature protection, as well as geomorphological and hydrological features. Landscape ecology, on the other hand, has helped us read the territory through the study of its 'mosaics' helping us to understand how different configurations produce decisive effects on ecological processes and the landscape itself, seen as a set of ecosystems (Forman, 1995).

An ecological understanding of the territory and awareness of the natural processes that take place within it are nowadays accepted components of planning processes, including urban planning, thus effectively linking the city, the territory and the environment in a unitary perspective. In particular, among those territorial strategies that are more sensitive to the issues of sustainable development, great prominence has been given to the policies regarding the city's 'ecological regeneration' based on concepts of 'environmental compensation' and 'ecological-environmental potential'. These concepts attempt to articulate the underlying link between any project of urban change and the qualitative improvement of the three fundamental environmental resources (air, water and soil) in order to ensure natural regeneration and self-regeneration of those selfsame resources (Oliva, 1999). This approach has increasingly focused on the protection of all the key factors that are essential for human, animal and plant life in the city and territory (Fusco Girard and Nijkamp, 1997). This implies great attention not only to agricultural and natural resources, but also to the networks and corridors of ecological connection between urban and territorial green areas, in order to offset negative impacts, in terms of the reduction of biodiversity, fragmenting and increased artificiality of the natural environment as a consequence of human settlement processes (Galuzzi, 1999). Sustainable planning experiences therefore focus on ecological-environmental resources, placing great emphasis, for instance, on the protection and expansion of green areas, the environmental and ecological compatibility of the infrastructure system, soil reclamation (recovering abandoned areas and ruling out new forms of urban expansion), traffic problems (favouring energy saving and non-polluting forms of public transport), waste collection and disposal (by implementing re-use and re-cycling strategies), the control of all forms of pollution (water, air, soil and noise pollution).

Thus, sustainable development, as was recently re-affirmed at the World Summit held in Johannesburg from 26 August to 4 September 2002, ten years after the Rio de Janeiro Summit, is no longer a Utopian dream, but rather, despite very real difficulties and the sectoral interests which all too often push in the opposite direction, can and must be effectively achieved in the near future.

Some Perspectives for the Implementation of the Habitat Agenda

In this part of the volume we have gathered together a series of papers which, albeit from different perspectives, attempt to provide the content as well as an operational framework for the notion of 'sustainable urban development'.

Peter Hall stresses the fact that sustainable urban development should constitute the main guideline for urban policy and governance, in full awareness of the fact that 'sustainability' is a multidimensional concept requiring integration between economic, social and environmental objectives. More efficient use of resources may contribute decisively to the protection of the environment and economic development, and while today we may already envisage a revolution in efficiency based on the 'Factor Four', we feel that in order to achieve sustainable development by the end of the twenty-first century we must aim for no less than a 'Factor Ten'. Although we cannot be certain of the results it will effectively be able to achieve urban planning can play a primary role insofar as the form and organization of the city itself can either contribute, or run counter, to the quest for sustainable development, also in view of the strong implications for the mobility system. The essay begins with a review of the arguments which, from the viewpoint of sustainability, oppose decentralization to the compact city, highlighting the pros and cons of both solutions. It then points out that it is necessary to intervene on transport systems (which in the near future will be enriched by the arrival of the 'eco-car') as well as on the improvement of the urban environment, with planning process that must, however, be rooted in the people's freedom of choice between the different alternatives which will be put before them.

If the goal of sustainable urban development is a formidable challenge for the cities of the developed countries, it is all the more so for the cities – with mushrooming population – of the developing ones. In his essay, Alan Gilbert attempts to examine whether growing urbanization in a globalized world can be made more sustainable. He stresses the fact that urban sustainability does not involve only the improvement of the physical environment but also the fight against poverty, especially in developing countries which lack infrastructure and basic services, first and foremost access to potable water. This fight should lead to a different and improved form of urban management which globalization, which is producing greater competition between cities and regions, is unable to offer; thus, it would seem that the market on its own (we may mention the privatization of public services) is unable to provide services and infrastructures for the poor. It is, on the other hand, felt that the future improvement in living standards throughout the world and the conservation of the environment depend on 'policy' in a broad sense at global level – that is policy seen as a concrete opportunity to achieve sustainable development also in view of the possibilities offered by new forms of technology.

Joan Martinez-Alier comes back to the relationship between urban sustainability and transport systems, noting that the century that just ended was marked by vehicles powered by the internal combustion engine whereas the new century could well see the triumph of the eco-car powered by hydrogen. This paper highlights the fact that the growth of world population is producing enormous urban conurbations, increasingly energy-devouring, hence less and less sustainable from an ecological point of view. Thus we must face the key problem of assessing the ecological sustainability/unsustainability of the city. In particular, the author compares ecological footprint analysis with other environmental indicators at various area levels (municipal, provincial, regional), attempting to integrate them with economic and cultural aspects. He furthermore stresses the requirement for integration between economy and ecology, considering both monetary value and physical and social indicators within a multicriteria evaluation structure, as suggested by 'ecological economics', a multidisciplinary approach which assesses the reactions and conflicts between the economic system and the environment.

Therefore, before choosing any environmental conservation strategy, whether natural or urban, we must face the question of the evaluation of possible alternative options for human intervention and, therefore, of the attribution of values to the environment itself. We conserve and enhance the environment because we assign a value to it, which is not merely economic but also a value in itself, that is an 'intrinsic' value. J. Baird Callicott's essay indeed tells us that nature's intrinsic value is a fundamental ethical question since it recognizes that the present environmental crisis raises a pressing moral question. In particular, he reviews the different approaches which, starting from recognition of value in themselves only for human beings, have reached the point of offering valid justifications for the attribution of an intrinsic value firstly to sentient beings only and subsequently to all animals, to all living creatures, up to the species, the biotic communities, the ecosystems. Finally, he indicates how the theoretical construction of the intrinsic value of Nature can also be applied to urban environments.

The question as to whether or not ethics can offer a way out of the present ecological crisis opens the essay by Stefano Zamagni, who also analyses the relationship between man and the environment as essentially a moral problem. However, if ethics appear unable to offer concrete solutions for the achievement of sustainable development, traditional economic theory seems equally inadequate in this sphere. This essay examines the way in which economists have attempted to go beyond the traditional approach by embedding the environmental question in economic theory. And they do this fully aware of the fact that present growth in the production of goods and services is often incompatible with safeguarding the natural and urban environment. Indeed, the pursuit of sustainable development and the fight against poverty are two sides of the same coin and we have a moral obligation towards present and future generations. Thus it is that any intervention strategies and plans that do not take into account both the target of poverty reduction and that of improving the quality of the environment are destined to fail. To overcome the current obstacles to sustainability he proposes the creation of a World Organization for the Environment, so as to move beyond unilateral measures and enforce international treaties.

The questions of a general nature dealt with in the contributions mentioned above are followed by the concrete experiences of sustainable cities, neighbourhoods and dwellings described in the successive papers. Anil Laul deals with the problem of the lack of housing and the growth of spontaneous neighbourhoods in developing countries, and in particular in India. The author then goes on to identify the strategies to be implemented for the birth of a 'sustainable city'. To this end, he feels it is essential to develop innovative approaches covering the access to land and credit, land management, road networks, water supply, sewer networks and waste water re-cycling plants, new technologies, the use of building materials, the conservation of the cultural heritage. Moreover, he attributes great importance to educational and training schemes which should create a new generation of planners and architects able to handle the problems of sustainability through a holistic and not sectoral approach.

Sarbjeet Singh Sandhu puts forward the example of the city of Chandigarh, which was planned immediately after India's independence in 1947 and was intended as a model for the country and the whole world. This project made implicit reference to some notions of sustainability, both in the characteristics of the city's site and in its urban form, organization and building types. Although it has experienced a substantial population growth, the city still even today offers a good quality of life and urban infrastructure, despite some problems with environmental pollution and traffic congestion.

Jürgen Eppinger tells us of his experience of the residential neighbourhood of Kronsberg in Hanover, built beginning in 1993, after the urban and landscape planning competition for EXPO 2000. This neighbourhood is marked by many elements of sustainable urban planning, as regards public transport, housing density and building height, the road network and the quality of outdoor areas. Above all it is marked by elements of 'ecological optimization' such as: the careful use of energy (use of wind and solar energy and construction of buildings with a low energy consumption coefficient), the management of rain water, waste and soil, reforestation of the surrounding territory and the creation of tree-lined avenues and public parks. This is an example which could well serve as a stimulus for other cases in which, albeit with specific requirements, there is a wish to apply the principles of sustainable planning, ranging from the regional scale to that of a single building.

And finally Eugenia Dimitrakopoulou and Maria Giaoutzi deal with the question of sustainable mobility, bearing in mind that the transport sector has a strong impact on the environment, in terms of air quality, energy consumption, land use, waste production, and health impact, etc., both at local and global levels. In particular, this essay outlines an evaluation approach to the strategic analysis of sustainable mobility based on 'Backcasting Scenario Building', which can support the evaluation of a set of transport policies. In the light of the goals of economic efficiency, regional development and environmental protection, three possible future scenarios were drawn up, referring to the year 2020, fully aware that sustainable development may be achieved only by combining transport policies with other policies such as those regarding land use, development, taxation and technology.

Conclusions

All the contributions in this part of the volume focus on innovative approaches to 'sustainable urban development' whether by identifying the problems or offering appropriate solutions with particular regard to urban and territorial planning. On the other hand, the themes addressed in this part of the book (from the organization of the form and structure of the city to urban mobility, from the battle against poverty to the need to integrate economy and ecology, from the objective of providing suitable housing for everyone to the creation of new quarters based on the sustainable use of natural and energy resources) are all key aspects of urban sustainability as was shown also in the recent World Summit on *Sustainable Development* of Johannesburg and, above all, in the Habitat Agenda.

In the *Plan of Implementation* approved at the end of the Johannesburg Summit, explicit reference is made to the issue of urbanization, establishing the objective of achieving 'by 2002, a significant improvement in the lives of at least 100 million slum dwellers, as proposed in the *Cities without slum initiative*' but it is the Habitat Agenda which is the main document for the improvement of human settlements in the metropolitan areas, cities and countries of the whole world.

Reference to the goals and principles of the Habitat Agenda is made, both explicitly and implicitly, in all the papers selected for this part of the volume. Among the most important themes addressed which are contained in Chapter 4 of the Habitat Agenda (*Global Action Plan: Strategies for Implementation*) we should stress the following which refer especially to the objective of achieving *sustainable human settlement development in an urbanizing world*:

- sustainable land use (The Habitat Agenda, §§ 109-114);
- social development: eradication of poverty, creation of productive employment and social integration (§§ 115-124);
- population and sustainable human settlements development (§§ 125-127);
- environmentally sustainable, healthy and liveable human settlements (§§ 128-144);
- sustainable energy use (§§ 145-146);
- sustainable transport and communication systems (§§ 147-151).

As may be seen, these issues are also found in the processes of Local Agenda 21 (UNCED, 1992; United Nations, 2001), so much so that it is not always possible to trace a clear boundary between the objectives of Agenda 21 (representing a true pact for the environment) and those of the Habitat Agenda (that is a pact for the built environment, with its implications for social justice). Both these Agendas take unto themselves, albeit from differing perspectives, the objectives of sustainability and both should be considered *working agendas for the twenty-first century* because, if implemented, they will be able to offer solutions to the environmental and urban crises marking our age.

Note

1 Adequate shelter means more than a roof over one's head. It also means adequate privacy; adequate space; physical accessibility; adequate security; security of tenure; structural stability and durability; adequate lighting, heating and ventilation; adequate basic infrastructure, such as water supply, sanitation and waste management facilities; suitable environmental quality and health-related factors; and adequate and accessible location with regard to work and basic facilities: all of which should be available at an affordable cost (The Habitat Agenda, § 60).

References

Brown, L.R., Flavin, C. and French, H. (eds) (1999), *State of the World '99*, Worldwath Institue, Washington.

Brown, L.R., Flavin, C. and French, H. (eds) (2001), *State of the World '01*, Worldwath Institue, Washington.

Chambers, N., Simmons, C. and Wackernagel, M. (2000), *Sharing Nature's Interest. Ecological Footprints as an Indicator of Sustainability*, Earthscan.

Folke, C., Jansson, A., Larsson, J. and Costanza, R. (1997), 'Ecosystem Appropriation by Cities', *Ambio*, vol. 26, pp. 167-172.

Forman, R.T.T. (1995), *Land Mosaics: The Ecology of Landscapes and Regions*, Cambridge University Press, Cambridge.

Fusco Girard, L. and Nijkamp, P. (1997), *Le valutazioni per lo sviluppo sostenibile della città e del territorio*, Angeli, Milan.

Galuzzi, P. (1999), 'A Vademecum for the Ecological Urban Planning', *Urbanistica*, vol. 112, pp. 73-74.

Hall, P. (2001), 'Megacities, World Cities and Global Cities', *Urbanistica*, vol. 116, pp. 21-28.

McDonuogh, W. and Braungart (1998), 'The Next Industrial Revolution', *Atlantic Monthly*, October.

Oliva, F. (1999), 'Integrating Urban Planning and Ecology', *Urbanistica*, vol. 112, p. 72.

Rees, W.E. (1992), 'Ecological Footprint and Appropriated Carrying Capacity: What Urban Economics Leave Out', *Environment and Urbanization*, vol. 4, pp. 121-30.

UNCED (United Nations Commission on Environment and Development) (1992), *Agenda 21 and Rio Declaration*, Rio de Janeiro.

UNCHS (United Nations Centre for Human Settlements) (1996), *The Habitat Agenda and Istanbul Declaration*, Istanbul.

UNCHS (United Nations Centre for Human Settlements - Habitat) (1997), *An Urbanizing World: Global Report on Human Settlements 1996*, Oxford University Press, Oxford.

UNCHS (United Nations Centre for Human Settlements - Habitat) (2001), *The State of World Cities 2001*, Nairobi.

UNDP (United Nations Population Division) (1997), *World Urbanization Prospects: The 1996 Revision*, New York.

UNDP (United Nations Population Division) (2002), *World Urbanization Prospects: The 2001 Revision*, New York.

United Nations - Economic and Social Council (2001), 'Implementing Agenda 21', Report of the Secretary-General, Commission on Sustainable Development acting as the preparatory committee for the Word Summit on Sustainable Development, New York.

von Weizsäcker, E.U., Lovins, A.B. and Lovins L. H. (1998), *Factor Four: Doubling Wealth, Halving Resource Use*, Earthscan, London.

Wackernagel M. and Rees, W.E. (1996), *Our Ecological Footprint. Reducing Human Impact on Earth*, New Society Publishers, Gabriola Island.

World Bank (2000), *Cities in Transition: A Strategic View of Urban and Local Government Issues*, Washington.

Chapter 1

The Sustainable City in an Age of Globalization

Peter Hall

Introduction

In this paper I want to argue that cities at the millennium are faced with twin challenges: first, to remain competitive by encouraging older industries to remain viable, encouraging innovation and creativity, and attracting inward investment; secondly, to become models of high quality of life, particularly as best-practice cases of sustainable urban development. These are stark challenges, and they may seem to conflict with each other. Nowhere are these challenges so stark, or the contradictions so apparent, as here in Europe, first because European cities are faced with major economic challenges from cities in the dynamic middle-income world, and second because so many of them are already among the world's leaders in the competition for sustainable life quality. So I will try to ask how European cities can square the circle: how they can develop their own special varieties of sustainable development, and how they can then use these to assert their competitive position in the global marketplace.

To do this, I want to draw quite heavily on a book that I co-authored for the World Commission on 21st-century urbanization: *Urban Future 21* (Hall and Pfeiffer, 2000). It deals with cities worldwide, all kinds of cities, with a heavy emphasis on the cities of the developing world. But it does specifically address what it calls the mature city coping with ageing, of which our European cities provide an archetype.

Early on in the book, we state a basic principle, that there is now a consensus: *sustainable (urban) development should be the guiding principle for urban policy and governance.* But sustainability is now seen universally as having different dimensions.[1] This means searching for a policy that will simultaneously and successfully achieve rapid economic growth and also redistribute incomes; a struggle to reduce social inequalities, to promote social and political integration, and the achieve the protection of the environment.

Building a basic consensus around the general principle has been an important step, achieved slowly over the past decade. Defining it further, and making it work out in everyday decisions, will prove much harder to achieve. The task is hugely compounded by the fact that there are interrelationships between different strategies. Economic and social goals used often to be seen as quite separate, but can be reconciled through the pursuit of more efficient production coupled with targeted initiatives to alleviate poverty. Environmental tasks used to be seen as a burden on development, but since the early 1980s we have accepted the accumulated evidence that environmental degradation is itself a major barrier to development. Thus, in recent years it has become possible to see economic development, equity and environmental protection as aspects of the same task.

Thus – this is the important point – strategies can serve multiple ends: a better-quality physical and social environment can actually help a city generate new economic growth. For this and other reasons, we need to integrate environmental concerns into our economic decision-making: using new technology to reduce resource use, incorporating environmental concerns into our economic accounting, and increasing incentives to secure more efficient resource use in both production and consumption. That way, we can improve our consumption standards and our environmental standards all at once. But it will not always be easy: the most severe trade-offs arise between social and ecological objectives, where helping poor people may compromise the environment.

However, we believe that it is possible to reconcile these objectives – even in poor cities, let alone rich ones. The 'Factor Four' concept, developed by the Wuppertal Institute and the Rocky Mountain Institute, is revolutionary: it says that it is perfectly possible to produce twice as much as now with half the resource input (von Weizsäcker et al., 1998). Factor Four points to changes already visible. In the long run, if we are to reach sustainable development by the end of the twenty-first century, we may need something more like a Factor Ten, providing a growing world population with an increasing standard of living.

It may seem utopian. But some aspects of this revolution are already profitably available, at negative cost; other aspects can also be made profitable. The revolution in information technology has enabled computers to become continuously cheaper and smaller, while their information-processing powers are exploding. In the developing world, fewer farmers are producing an increasing amount of food for a growing number of people.

The argument is that the kinds of savings that capitalism has outstandingly achieved in other areas should now also be achievable in the environment. Just as technical and social innovation was mobilized to develop labour-saving technologies over the last two centuries, so now new incentives and new forms of social organization will be needed to mobilize energy, talent and capital for the 'greening business' and for 'greener cities'. The result will be urban systems based on renewable energy and – compared to the twentieth-century economy – services that require little or no material inputs or outputs.

By taking this route, rather remarkably, cities and nations can achieve several objectives all at once. They can (von Weizsäcker et al., 1998, pp. xxii-xxiii):

- *Live better.* Resource efficiency improves the quality of life. It is possible to see better with resource efficient lighting systems, produce better goods in efficient factories, travel more safely and comfortably in efficient vehicles, and get better nutrition from efficiently grown crops.
- *Pollute and deplete less.* Everything must go somewhere. Wasted resources pollute. Efficiency combats waste and thus reduces pollution. Resource efficiency can greatly contribute to solving such huge problems as acid rain and climatic change, deforestation, loss of soil fertility, and congested streets. By themselves, energy efficiency, plus productive and sustainable farming and forestry practices, could eliminate up to 90 per cent of today's environmental problems, at a profit, if the knowledge gap can be overcome. Efficiency can buy time in which people could learn to deal thoughtfully, sensibly and sequentially with the world's problems.
- *Make money.* Resource efficiency is profitable, or could be made profitable, by government regulations which would internalize all costs, and above all the costs of cleaning up environmental pollution. This would give businesses a positive incentive not to pollute, as otherwise their costs and prices would be higher than those of their non-polluting competitors.
- *Harness markets and enlist business.* Since resource efficiency can be made profitable, much of it can be implemented largely in the marketplace, driven by individual choice and business competition, rather than requiring governments to tell everyone how to live. However, the task of reversing perverse incentive structures remains.
- *Multiply use of scarce capital.* Resources freed by preventing waste can be used to solve other problems. With less capital buried in inefficient infrastructure, developing countries, in particular, would be in an excellent position to multiply the use of scarce capital. If a country buys equipment to make very energy-efficient lamps or windows, which are more expensive than conventional windows, it can then provide energy services with less investment than would be required to buy additional power stations.
- *Be equitable and have more employment.* Wasting resources is the other face of a distorted economy which splits society increasingly into

those who have work and those who do not. Either way, human energy and talent are being tragically misspent.

In this task, cities can do some things on their own – but only so much. They cannot compensate for national policies. Pollution control in factories or from vehicles follow largely national standards. An invigorating competition between local and central policies could strengthen motivation and provide political and administrative input. The instruments and administrative techniques are constantly improving. In all cities, there are some basic jobs to be done: efforts to reduce material input, and to increase recycling efforts to avoid waste, are a precondition for more efficient use of resources. Cities can organize the collection of paper or other reusable materials. They can run systems of deposits for environmentally harmful goods, or organize cooperation between companies to increase recycling. In particular, the rich cities, with their extremely high use of resources per head, need to intensify efforts to recycle material from paper to industrial waste or car wrecks. Cities are important in all fields where cooperation between organizations and companies is based on spatial proximity.

But the nature of the task differs subtly from one kind of city to another. In rich mature cities with their high levels of formal organization, such as we have in Europe, providing adequate infrastructure and protection of the environment for sustainable development will depend a great deal on open debate about priorities. Here the most important decisions are about land use and density. And they may appear to bring economic goals and environmental goals into sharp conflict.

Goals in Conflict? Sustainability and Urban Form

All cities are in constant flux; indeed, if they fail in dynamism they risk decay and death. They grow at the periphery and they change at the centre. And in fast-growing cities – places like Chicago and Berlin in the nineteenth century, Los Angeles in the early twentieth, or any city in the developing world today – this process can be frenetic: speculative development, driven by the perpetual optimism of the investor, leapfrogs far out into the open countryside; closer in, land that was peripheral a few decades ago is suddenly subsumed into the central business district; in the suburbs, new sub-centres mushroom almost out of nowhere.

In the coming century, this will be truer than ever. Cities must increasingly compete for highly mobile professional workers and globally-oriented business firms. As a result of securitization, financial derivatives, and the deregulation of financial intermediaries such as pension funds, insurance companies, real estate investment trusts, and banks, much of the available world's supply of investment capital is no longer very restrained by national boundaries.

This is a fact of life, and is even to be celebrated: it is part of the mechanism that generates new wealth for the people who flock into the city. But at the same time, it may generate what the economist calls negative externalities, or the lawyer calls nuisances: incompatible land uses next door to each other, such as polluting factories next to residential areas; perpetual uncertainty as to the character of a neighbourhood and the value of land; traffic congestion and traffic pollution.

These factors are more important than ever before, because they may now threaten a city's very livelihood. To maintain their economies, cities in the twenty-first century must be liveable. Growth of some sectors of the service economy, such as tourism, is absolutely dependent on liveable and attractive cities. Tourism in most nations is dependent on foreign travellers. Currently, an estimated 300 million tourists take their holidays overseas, representing the largest earner of foreign currency for many countries. In Asia, environmental issues, traffic congestion and overcrowding have been identified as serious impediments to tourism; it would be equally true of cities anywhere. To keep or enhance their share of tourists, business firms and skilled professionals, cities must be liveable.

For this reason, almost all cities in the developed world, and indeed most in the developing world, have tried to plan for their future development, and to control it: they have made plans for future development, and they have developed mechanisms for enforcing those plans through a system of zoning permits or land-use controls. Invariably, the plans have specified broad land uses, including especially changes of use, and some indication of the density of development, coupled with proposals for transportation and open space. These systems have come into being, and have been modified, over a long period, sometimes accompanied by fierce controversy. But they have become a fixed and accepted feature of urban life, with a considerable political constituency; for planning produces a degree of certainty, allowing private agents like commercial companies or individual households to make their own plans in the knowledge that their immediate environment – including their sunk investments in real estate – is secure.

But in every city there is a major complication. Urban space is quintessentially scarce, and so expensive. And, in rapidly-growing cities, it escalates in value: land, that a couple of decades earlier was suburban, becomes enveloped in the central business district; high-rise offices and hotels may be found interspersed with the informally-built shacks of the poor.

In the cities of the developed world, policy-makers have grappled for over a century with the resultant problems of land valuation and land taxation. Public policies, in the form of a new highway or a new transit line or a new zoning map, fundamentally change land values, and make fortunes for lucky landowners. In these circumstances, has the community a right or even an obligation to tax part of those gains for the community? And, in buying land compulsorily for public works, should it be required to pay values that in effect it has created?

In Europe, a century ago, nations like the Netherlands and Sweden resolved these dilemmas drastically, by buying up land for the community well in advance of demand; but even then, the pace of urban advance in cities like Amsterdam and Stockholm sometimes overwhelmed them. Other countries, like the United Kingdom half a century ago, sought to take a share of development value for the community, but these proposals brought fierce political controversy and no permanent solution. In the cities of the developing world today, of course, the challenge is far greater and the resources far fewer.

In market or mixed economies, which means most economies, planning regulations tend to work best when they are consistent with market behaviour. There are remarkably strong empirical regularities in market-based cities across countries. Urban areas develop forms that are functional for the location of industry and services, having regard to scale economies in production, lower transport costs, permissible densities for development, information-sharing and other linkages or networks across locations and agglomeration economies. Land-use regulations that ignore such market behavioural tendencies, as empirically observed and described by theory, are not likely to succeed. Policies that oppose normal human behaviour will often result in unexpected consequences and the creation of market inefficiencies.

Of course, planning sometimes has to work against trends too, when they become self-destructive and blind to the needs of the wider society. Good planning is a matter of balance. It is most effective when it seeks to shape and modify basic economic and social trends so as to make them operate more efficiently and more conveniently and more sustainably than they would do so on their own. That is a lesson taught by basic common sense, but also by the experience of twentieth-century planning history. When Ebenezer Howard proposed the garden city solution in 1898, he did so in the sure knowledge that emerging new technologies, above all electricity, would free people and the factories in which they worked from the dense nineteenth-century city (Howard, 1898). When Sven Markelius and Göran Sidenbladh designed the satellite towns around Stockholm in 1952, they did so in the knowledge that a new subway system would bring these places within a convenient travel time of the city centre, and that people living in the city's slums would flock to the new, well-designed, beautifully landscaped apartment blocks (Hall, 1998). When Jane Jacobs called for a return to traditional city street patterns in 1961, she did so from her deep personal knowledge of her neighbours' feelings about New York's Greenwich Village, where she lived (Jacobs, 1962). These ideas have stood the test of time. They provide lessons for shaping the new urban places of the twenty-first century, and for reshaping the older places that earlier eras have bequeathed to us.

As already noticed, the fundamental urban trend of the twentieth century was decentralization of people, and of the jobs they do, and of the services they use: decentralization from dense inner cities to less dense suburbs, and from larger cities to smaller ones. To this general rule, in any free market-economy society, there has scarcely been an exception. It was already observable in North America and Australasia, as well as Great Britain, from the beginning of the twentieth century; after World War II it spread to the Benelux countries and to Scandinavia, and later to all of Western Europe. In the developing world it is evident almost everywhere, from Latin America to Eastern Asia. Nor do we expect any change in the coming years.

But it is important to notice that the process and form of decentralization have varied considerably in detail. In some countries, particularly those in the Anglo-Saxon tradition, but also in Latin America, decentralization has resulted in low-to-medium-density suburbs of single-family homes with gardens, often outside the range of effective public transport. In others, particularly here in mainland Europe, it has often taken the form of satellite towns planned around new rapid transit links, with pyramids of densities: higher around the transit stations, where shops and services are also clustered, lower away from them. Further, market trends and planning in the Anglo-Saxon tradition have often combined to encourage longer-distance decentralization from larger cities to smaller towns within their general commuter orbit, as around New York and Los Angeles and London; while in other countries, such as France, virtually all of the process has been housed in direct extensions of the city itself.

These variations seem to have worked satisfactorily enough, because they conformed to basic social and cultural preferences which differ from one country to another. What is to be avoided is planning that works against such preferences, which always gives rise to tell-tale signs of failure: above all, artificial housing shortages and artificially inflated house prices, combined with idiosyncratic building forms like high-rise blocks in rural villages, which are sure indications that something has gone wrong.

In some parts of the world, both in the developed and the developing world (London, New York, Los Angeles, San Francisco, the Tokyo-Osaka corridor, Brazil's 'golden triangle', the Pearl River delta of China), decentralization has reached a new level and has produced a new form: the mega-city, a series of anything between twenty and fifty towns, physically separate but functionally networked, clustered around one or more larger central cities, and drawing enormous economic strength from a new functional division of labour (Hall, 1999). These places exist both as separate entities, in which most residents work locally and most workers are local residents, and as parts of a wider functional urban region connected by dense flows of people and information along motorways, high-speed rail lines and telecommunications cables. It is no exaggeration to say that this was the emerging urban form at the end of the twentieth century, and that it will prove pervasive in the twenty-first.

But, of course, decentralization has its critics. For it appears to contradict the basic principle of sustainability, on which all observers are agreed. It appears to generate more trips, and to use more resources – including non-renewable ones – than more compact traditional forms of urban development. Therefore, there are widespread calls everywhere – in the United Kingdom, in Germany, in Australia – for a return to the compact city. Densities should be raised, these critics say; every possible opportunity should be taken to recycle brownfield land in preference to new greenfield development; living and working should be no longer separated, but placed in close juxtaposition; further decentralization from the city should be resisted.

There is a problem with this argument, simple and beguiling as it may seem: it does not capture the full complexity of what is happening. Indeed, the experts themselves are disagreed as to prescription. While some call for compaction, others argue that decentralization produces quite sustainable results, because people and jobs re-equilibrate: both move out together, bringing a pattern of journeys shorter than before, hence more sustainable. (Two-earner households complicate this, but not entirely, because women tend to commute shorter distances than men.) But that still leaves considerable scope for different forms of decentralization: it may actually be preferable to encourage long-distance movements, as the British did with their new towns, so as to make the decentralized settlements as self-contained as possible.

In practice, even in developed economies with a broad public acceptance of planning and with a well-developed and sophisticated professional bureaucracy, achieving different planning objectives is not at all easy. For it involves difficult conflicts and trade-offs. The most efficient location for industry and warehousing, in terms of single-floor operation for efficient assembly, may involve big rural land take and access to motorway interchanges, which will absorb valuable agricultural land and may encourage commuting by car. Major commercial developments will benefit from access to central train stations, which is sustainable, but they may then impinge on low-income housing areas and on historic areas which need conservation. New highways improve access, but they may affect established communities, bringing the threat of severance and pollution. New residential areas, whether on greenfield land or recycled brownfield land, may impinge on existing areas, such as exclusive inner-city residential areas or secluded rural villages, threatening their exclusivity. Higher-density urban development may appear 'sustainable', requiring less energy for travel by car, but may leave residents exposed to higher levels of pollution, especially from noise; it also increases the need for weekend travel to the countryside or ownership of weekend houses. Protecting natural landscapes may leave them in the hands of commercial farming which does not enhance the environment, and which may even use subsidies to leave the land unproductive. Often, it is not entirely clear which course of action would be best even in terms of achieving one objective, let alone trading off as between conflicting ones.

So it is not surprising that even in countries with a highly competent professional planning bureaucracy, planning has had mixed results. In the United Kingdom, researchers have found that London's green belt actually extended commuter journeys and also created land scarcities, raising the costs of housing. Decentralization strategies – green belts, new towns, growth corridors – may also entail longer commuting times and longer paths for freight logistics. Segregation of land uses has increased the length, time and cost of journeys to work, but a return to mixed-use planning – a major policy reversal – might bring incompatible uses again in juxtaposition, with homes next to noisy bars and discotheques.

Consequently, in spite of a plethora of academic and professional studies, there is no consensus on the management of spatial development. It comes as no surprise that recently, many of these traditional beliefs of planning – separation of different land uses, green belt and urban containment strategies, decentralization to new towns – have been challenged by reports that suggest it would more sustainable to mix land uses and to encourage higher-density brownfield redevelopment within cities.

Some forms of urban growth may be more efficient (and more sustainable) than others in this regard, though there has been little systematic comparison. All involve an element of trade-off: Los Angeles type sprawl reduces access to open landscape for many inhabitants, but increases the use of private gardens and private open spaces; Berlin apartment living gives a high density of population, easy access to open space or farmland, and effective use of public transport, but is too claustrophobic for some. London's typical form of development – the suburb in the city, celebrated 60 years ago by Steen Eiler Rasmussen – allows more everyday contact with green spaces, a more open and human, less monumental, urban environment. It is rejected by a latter-day generation of architects and planners as 'not urban enough', but it is far from clear that they represent the interests and tastes of ordinary Londoners, who will express their preferences in the market.

Transport and Sustainability: The Ecocar to the Rescue?

Some say that the problem of the car and its environmental impact presents some kind of imperative: we have to find a way to reverse the century-long trend of rising car ownership. But this is questionable. Within a 15- to 20-year time span, we can be certain that the transport problem in all our cities will be completely transformed by the arrival of a successor to today's motor car, primarily for use in urban areas. We call it the 'ecocar'. Although resources (mainly renewable and the recyclable) will still be needed to construct the vehicle, it would be powered by hydrogen fuel cells. It will probably be available within ten years, but – given current turnover levels – it will not have had a major impact on the total stock of vehicles for a further ten to fifteen years. This means that the ecocar would only be in general use by the end of our time frame (2025) in mature cities and a little later (because older cars may remain longer) in dynamic and above all in hypergrowth cities. During this period, technologies to produce hydrogen with solar energy will need to be improved.

So, even if the 'technological solution' is promoted, there still remains the historic problem of transport growth (congestion) and the 'gap' between now and the time when the ecocar is in common use. The conclusion is that cities everywhere should pursue two complementary paths:

- in the short term (until about 2020) they should seek to manage traffic growth through fiscal and physical restraint, using revenues from parking charges and road pricing to support good-quality public transport and para-transit, and using the land-use planning systems to support urban forms that permit and encourage maximum use of cycling and walking for shorter trips;
- in the longer run, beyond this date, they should provide for general phasing-in of the ecocar, while recognizing that this will be more rapid in the mature cities than elsewhere, and that in hypergrowth cities it may be necessary to plan on the basis that general access to the ecocar will still be far in the future.

The important point is that these different development paths can and should be complementary. At all stages of development, whatever the available technology, the optimal system may be one that manages scarce road space optimally, by a combination of regulation (e.g. bus lanes, bus priority, high-occupancy vehicle lanes, peak-hour loading bans) and fiscal measures (e.g. road charging and parking charges) to give priority and favoured fiscal treatment to those vehicles that use road space most effectively: buses, para-transit vehicles and high-occupancy vehicles. These corridors could be managed so as to embody technological developments, in particular vehicle automation, as they become available. But they need to be seen in an even wider context. In the medium term (2020 and beyond), we can conceive of a realistic scenario, depending on technologies that are either available, or likely to become so: a system of high-speed inter-city ground transportation at speeds up to 300 or 400 kilometres an hour, linked to automated on-demand ecocar systems in the cities, and perhaps to informal means of short-distance personal transport such as collective bicycles and scooters. Such connections may in turn aid further concentration at high-order nodal points, as the experience of the Japanese Shinkansen system seems to show. And they would be used, through coordinated land-use planning, to encourage further concentrations of activity not merely in traditional downtown areas, but also in sub-centres distributed throughout the metropolitan area, including suburban sub-centres close to people's homes. These, importantly, should be reachable on foot, or bicycle or public transport.

A Model Urban Form?

Given these principles, despite the lack of agreement among experts, recent work in the UK and the USA strongly suggests that the optimum combination of policies, in terms of environmental sustainability and public acceptability, would consist not of a single solution but of what has been called a 'portfolio approach' (Hall and Ward, 1998): within the cities, medium-density urban brownfield redevelopment, combining residential and other uses, around public transport interchanges ('urban villages'), combined with similar greenfield small mixed-use units, all typically housing 20-30,000 people ('garden cities'), in linear clusters of up to about 200,000 people along public transport lines. The effect will be to create a highly polycentric pattern of development, both within and outside the city, allowing the city to grow progressively into a polycentric city region within which each part has a high degree of self-containment but each is highly networked to all the others through efficient public transport and high-quality ICT (Information and Communication Technology) links. But the effects on traffic have not been rigorously tested, and there is vigorous debate as to key elements of such a policy, including the right proportions of greenfield and brownfield development, and the precise scale of decentralization, short- versus long-distance.

Some experts go further. From California Allan Jacobs and Donald Appleyard have suggested some of the qualities of good-quality urban environments, that people will be attracted to and will enjoy living in such places: they should be liveable places, where everyone can live in relative comfort and security; they should have identity and control, in that people feel that they have some ownership and want to be involved; they should offer access to opportunity, imagination and excitement; they should give people a sense of authenticity and meaning, but not in too obvious a way; they should encourage a sense of community and participation; they should be as sustainable as possible; and they should offer a good level of environment to all (Jacobs and Appleyard, 1987).

Jacobs and Appleyard (pp. 115-6) go on to suggest what kind of an urban environment would meet those demands. They say there are five physical characteristics, all of which must be present.

The first is *liveable streets and neighbourhoods* with adequate sunshine, clean air, trees and vegetation and gardens and open space, pleasantly scaled and designed buildings, without offensive noise, and with cleanliness and physical safety. They stress that these qualities must be 'reasonable, though not excessive': sunlight standards must not result in buildings placed too far apart, or traffic safety must not produce over-wide streets and wide curves.

The second is *a certain minimum density*, which they say is about 15 dwelling units per acre (37 units per hectare) which translates to 30-60 people per acre (74-148/ha), typified by generous town houses. But, they point out, San Francisco achieves superb urban quality with 3-storey row houses above garages at densities as high as 48 units per acre (119/ha), translating to 96-192 people per acre (237-474/ha), yet offering separate entrances with direct access to the ground and either private or public open space at hand. Such densities are also characteristic of much of inner London, which also achieves great urban quality and liveability. But, they warn, at densities much more than 200 people per net residential acre – the highest planned density in Abercrombie's famous London plan – 'the concessions to less desirable living environments mount rapidly'. As well as density, there must be a certain intensity of use on the streets, and this is related to the density: both will be higher in central urban districts than in outer suburban areas.

The third necessary attribute is *integration of activities – living, working, shopping, public and spiritual and recreational activities – reasonably near each other*, though not necessarily all together everywhere. They say there is a lot to be said for 'living sanctuaries, consisting almost entirely of housing', but these should be fairly small, a few street blocks, and close to meeting places which should normally have housing in them.

Fourth, they say that *'buildings (and other objects that people place in the environment) should be arranged in such a way as to define and even enclose public space, rather than sit in space'*. Buildings along a street will do this so long as the street is not too wide in relation to them. The critical point is that the spaces, whether streets or squares, must not become too large. The spaces must also be primarily pedestrian spaces and they must be under public control.

Finally, they argue, *'many different buildings and spaces with complex arrangements and relationships are required'*. By this they mean a rather broken pattern of ownership, with small parcel sizes, producing a more public and lively city. Of course, there will need to be larger buildings, too; but these should be the exception, not the rule.

These principles, we would argue, provide an excellent guide to the design of good built urban environments. Of course, they do not cover the entire range of legitimate designs within cities; some parts, especially in the very centre and the very edge, will depart from them, and it should be no aim of the planner or urban designer to produce total uniformity across the city. But it is at least interesting, for instance, that though Jacobs and Appleyard question the Garden City ideal, their principles seem to conform pretty closely to Howard's original concept of 1898 – including his suggested density, which was right in the middle of their suggested density range. The key point is that the urban forms they recommend are not merely liveable; they are also sustainable. They provide the critical building blocks, which can then be combined into urban villages and country towns to constitute a sustainable city region.

These qualities will not come through market forces alone. As Jacobs and Appleyard argue, the problem is that commercial considerations will often suggest different arrangements – including large, monofunctional blocks or very low densities. Therefore, the planner will have to intervene on the basis that superior urban designs will be highly attractive once people can see them working. (San Francisco and inner London, cities which offer very high quality of urban life and are extremely fashionable living places with buoyant real estate markets, are examples). This will require that planners are much better educated in urban design than many of them are today.

However, we should be cautious. The principles that Jacobs and Appleyard state would be shared by the great majority of planners and urban designers anywhere in the world today, I suspect. But the urban reality across the world is very different. Could so many places and so many people prove wrong? These places differ in their atmosphere and lifestyle. They reflect cultural preferences and may not be readily transferable from one city to another: high-density apartment living in Paris, Berlin or Hong Kong may be suitable for those who care to live in those cities, but Los Angeles-type sprawl is equally acceptable to those who place a high premium on space in and around the home, even though it increases commuting costs and restricts public open space. The choice depends on historical traditions, on the surroundings and the quality of the landscape. It is a matter not only of the opportunity costs of different options, but also of different local preferences.

This is important, because in a democracy the planning system can only go so far to try to affect people's market preferences. It can and should do so wherever there are manifest and unambiguous negative externalities, and where it is clear that these are unacceptable. (Long commute times are an externality, but should be ignored if people are evidently willing to pay for them.) The most important imperative is the environmental one; but we must be quite clear about the effects, and of the results of policy changes (e.g. densification), before we embark on them.

We always have to remember that planners will not determine these questions; people and their preferences, expressed through markets and through political processes, will decide. This will not be easy, because politics may run up against markets: NIMBY (not in my back yard) politics will tend to set barriers against developments that change people's established and comfortable lifestyles, whether they are country or city people. The risk in developed countries is a kind of urban paralysis, in which it becomes almost impossible to change anything: BANANA (Build Absolutely Nothing Anywhere Near Anyone). In economies and societies characterized by rapid change, the resulting pressures may become almost impossible to manage.

Given all this, it becomes a delicate and difficult point as to how far, and in what ways, planning should intervene. Architects argue that it should seek to raise the quality of development. That is fine, as long as it does not become a device for forcing on people designs, including densities, that they do not want. In high-quality (meaning high-price) developments, the private sector will probably produce good design because people are willing to pay for it. But experience in the United Kingdom suggests that public intervention, through design guides, may be effective in the middle and lower ranges of the market. Otherwise, as the melancholy example of London Docklands reminds us, just leaving the developers free will be a recipe for mediocrity that will please no one in the slightly longer run.

In any case, the market may always be in conflict with sustainability, and increasingly so, because as people get richer they will demand more space in and around their homes, and because at least some of them will exercise their right to live in the country rather than the town. The question will remain: to what extent will planners be able to modify or even frustrate their desires, and to what extent will they be successful if they do? Recall, here, the evidence: though it is fairly clear that people living in the countryside consume on average more energy than those living at higher densities in the city, the differences are small because only about a quarter of total personal energy consumption goes on transport anyway, and we are talking about small differences; and finally, all this will be radically transformed once the ecocar arrives on the scene. So we should be very careful about narrowing the arguments about sustainable urbanism to this one dimension. If there is an argument for higher densities and particular urban forms, it is far more that these give people more choice, not less: freedom to take good public transport rather than be car-dependent, freedom for their children to walk or bike to school rather than being ferried by car. But at the end of the day, the people will choose, as they always do, whatever people would like to tell them.

Note

1 Sustainable development is development that meets the needs of the present without compromising the ability of future generations to meet their own needs (WCED, 1987, p. 8).
Sustainable development means improving the quality of human life while living within the carrying capacity of supporting ecosystems (IUCN, 1991, p. 221).
Sustainable development is development that delivers basic environmental, social and economic services to all residents of a community without threatening the viability of natural, built and social systems upon which the delivery of those systems depends (ICLEI, 1996, p. 4).

References

Hall, P. (1998), *Cities in Civilization*, Weidenfeld and Nicolson, London.
Hall, P. (1999), 'Planning for the Mega-City: A New Eastern Asian Urban Form?', in J. Brotchie, P. Newton, P. Hall P. and J. Dickey (eds), *East West Perspectives on 21st Century Urban Development: Sustainable Eastern and Western Cities in the New Millennium*, Ashgate, Aldershot, pp. 3-36.
Hall, P. and Pfeiffer, U. (2000), *Urban 21: World Report on the Urban Future 21*, Federal Ministry of Transport, Building and Housing, Berlin.
Hall, P. and Ward, C. (1998), *Sociable Cities: The Legacy of Ebenezer Howard*, Wiley, Chichester.
Howard, E. (1898), *To-morrow: A Peaceful Path to Real Reform*, Swan Sonnenschein, London [reprinted in R. LeGates and F. Stout (eds), *Early Urban Planning 1870-1940*, vol. 2, Routledge, London, 1998].
ICLEI (International Commission on Local Economic Initiatives) (1996), *The Local Agenda Planning Guide*, ICLEI, Toronto.
IUCN (International Union for Conservation of Nature) (1991), *Caring for the Earth: A Strategy for Sustainable Living*, IUCN, Gland.
Jacobs, A.B. and Appleyard, D. (1987), 'Toward an Urban Design Manifesto', *Journal of the American Planning Association*, vol. 53, pp. 112-20.
Jacobs, J. (1962), *The Death and Life of Great American Cities*, Jonathan Cape, London.
von Weizsäcker, E.U., Lovins, A.B. and Lovins, L.H. (1998), *Factor Four: Doubling Wealth, Halving Resource Use*, Earthscan, London.
WCED (World Commission on Environment and Development) (1987), *Our Common Future* (The Brundtland Report), Oxford University Press, Oxford.

Chapter 2

Is Urban Development in the Third World Sustainable?

Alan Gilbert

Introduction

The paper argues that urban growth can be sustained in most parts of the world but that the process is much less sustainable than it should be. Urban growth has tended to raise living standards across the globe or at least has been associated with a rise in quality of life indicators such as life expectancy, literacy and per capita income. Few cities are in 'crisis' and even in Africa there have been few signs of migrants wanting to return home to the countryside. While there are signs of stress in many cities, it is a major achievement to have coped with current rates of urban growth.

Nevertheless, as people move from rural impoverishment to the cities poverty is increasingly becoming an urban phenomenon. 'One in four of the world's urban population is living below the poverty line. In many cities, confronted with rapid growth, environmental problems and slow pace of economic development, it has not been possible to meet the challenges of generating sufficient employment, providing adequate housing and meeting the basic needs of the citizens' (UNCHS, 2001, p. 232). Globalization seems to be doing little to remove poverty and is bringing greater inequality. It is not doing much to improve the environment either. As such, the process of urban growth has to be made more sustainable by making it more equitable and less damaging to the environment. Unfortunately, many of the key problems continue to worsen because so few governments are taking appropriate forms of action. In part the lack of action is a consequence of the limits that globalization place on urban governance. But it is also because politicians wish to be re-elected and the trend for greater democracy and decentralization across the globe discourages firm government. The current reliance that world leaders place on the opinions of focus groups does not often produce the kind of leadership that is most needed.

My brief in this paper is so vast that I cannot possibly touch on all or even most of the issues involved. The aim is to raise a few that are soluble providing that societies are prepared to face up to the unenviable choices that answers to these questions pose. Modern society too often pretends that we can get what we want without giving anything up. If urban development in the future is to be truly sustainable, a change in that attitude is the first thing that needs to occur.

What Is Urban Sustainability?

At a trivial level urban sustainability means that cities will survive into the future. This will happen unless some global disaster hits us, such as nuclear warfare or a major rise in the level of the sea, and neither is very likely. Table 2.1 contains estimates of what the urban world will look like in the year 2030 and shows that most people will be living in urban areas in most parts of the globe. In that sense, urban growth will be sustained (Brockerhoff, 1999; Drakakis-Smith, 1995).

A more important question is whether urbanization can be made more sustainable? But before attempting to answer that question, it is important to know what it means. Unfortunately, not many of our current definitions of urban sustainability are very useful. For example, although I accept the spirit of Satterthwaite's (1997, p. 1682) statement that: 'It is not cities or urbanization that sustainable development seeks to sustain, but to meet human needs in settlements of all sizes without depleting environmental capital', I wonder how to operationalize such a concept? For a start, how are environmental capital or human needs to be measured? Even if it is possible to answer those questions it is necessary to provide morally defensible answers to difficult distributional questions. For example, what happens if we manage to raise the living standards of one-half of the world's population but not of the other half, while depleting environmental capital in one half and not depleting it in another? Is this progress or not?

Definitional questions are important for as Satterthwaite (1997, p. 1669) points out: 'The ambiguity as to what "sustainable cities" or "sustainable human settlements" means ... allows many of the large international agencies to claim that they are the leaders in promoting sustainable cities when, in reality, they have contributed much to the growth of cities where sustainable development goals are not met'. If we do not tighten our definitions of sustainable development, then politicians can avoid doing what they must do if the quality of life on the planet is to improve.

Unfortunately, there is a problem because I cannot see that developed countries will cede much to the less developed nor that the rich in developed countries will give up much to the poor. This applies both in the area of environmental protection (think of US reaction to the Kyoto protocol) and with respect to improving living conditions in the poorer countries of the world (think of the Heavily Indebted Poor Countries negotiations). We are probably not heading for disaster in the sense of an environmental catastrophe because we will take enough precautions to be able to muddle through. But, as a result of our merely muddling through, a lot of people's lives will have deteriorated in ways that could have been avoided.

Table 2.1   Urban population by major region, 1996-2030

	Percentage urban		Annual growth rate, 1990-95	
Country or area	*1996*	*2030*	*Urban*	*Rural*
World total	45.7	61.1	2.4	0.7
More developed regions[a]	75.1	83.7	0.7	-0.5
Medium developed regions	40.4	60.2	n.a.	n.a.
Less developed regions[b]	38.2	57.3	3.4	0.9
Least developed countries[c]	23.3	44.0	5.0	1.9
	Urban population		Rural population	
Country or area	*1996*	*2030*	*1996*	*2030*
World total	2,635,645	5.117,038	3,132,129	3,254,564
More developed regions	882,890	1,014,759	292,150	197,388
Medium developed regions	1,614,439	3,544,616	2,383,784	2,347,637
Less developed regions	1,752,755	4,102,279	2,839,979	3,057,176
Least developed countries	138,316	557,663	456,195	709,539

[a]   More developed regions comprise all regions of Europe and Northern America, Australia/New Zealand and Japan.
[b]   Less developed regions comprise all regions of Africa, Asia (excluding Japan) and Latin America and the Caribbean, and the regions of Melanesia, Micronesia and Polynesia.
[c]   As of 1995, the least developed countries as defined by the United Nations General Assembly, comprise 48 countries, of which 33 are in Africa, nine in Asia, one in Latin America and five in Oceania. They are also included in the less developed regions.

Source: United Nations (1998)

Urbanization, the Environment and Poverty

When the environmental question first entered the urban agenda, the major concern was over the state of the physical environment. Insofar as cities can survive only by using resources from beyond their boundaries, urban growth is bound to lead to some degree of environmental destruction. London, New York and Tokyo are sustained not only by extensive local hinterlands but also by worldwide peripheries. As cities grow larger, and particularly as they become more affluent, the 'ecological footprint' of the city becomes progressively deeper and wider (Rees, 1992). As living standards improve, a city's demands for food and resources embrace, and begin to pollute, a much wider area. According to this logic, urbanization must increase the amount of environmental destruction.

The environmental future is much worse if we remember that both the world's population and its wealth are almost certain to increase. Continued economic growth in industrialized cities is likely to cause more damage to their own and to other people's environments. Increased pollution and waste from their factories and rising numbers of cars make this inevitable. London, New York and Tokyo will continue to pollute the world much more than cities such as Calcutta. But, as per capita incomes rise in third world cities, they will contribute increasingly to environmental destruction. What is most worrying is that urban pollution is generally worst in middle-income cities particularly those which have major industrial concentrations (UNEP, 1992). Pollution is bad in such cities because governments are more interested in stimulating production than in controlling pollution.

Fortunately, economic growth may also help the environment provided that the new resources which economic growth generates are used to address environmental issues (Reed, 1992). With economic growth, governments can afford to introduce pollution controls and even implement some of them. Government regulation is helped by the fact that individual households are sufficiently affluent to contribute to the cost of waste disposal and regulatory controls. Factories can be forced to treat their waste because consumers can pay more for their products. GEMS (Great Exploration in Math and Science) data show that per capita levels of particulate matter and sulphur dioxide tend to decline over time (World Bank, 1992). At the same time, although some forms of pollution decline with economic growth, others increase. Thus, London no longer suffers badly from sulphurous smog but it has unpleasantly high levels of ozone, carbon dioxide and carbon monoxide. Different forms of energy, different forms of transport and the effect of legislation have changed the environmental problems of the city.

There is little reason to doubt that environmental destruction will continue and that cities will contribute substantially to that process. Recent debates about global commitments to pollution control do not suggest that developed countries will do much to reduce emissions. At the same time, there is every reason to hope that the damage will be containable and not destroy us all. This is not a very optimistic message but it is all that I have to offer. With respect to poverty, it is fortunate that the 'brown agenda' was added to the 'green agenda' when the environmental debate moved on from the purely physical effects of urban growth to considering the human impact of development. The health and welfare consequences of environmental pollution are obvious. Water-borne diseases are a serious problem in many Third World cities. For example, those without easy access to piped water in the metropolitan areas of southern Brazil 'were 4.8 times as likely to die from diarrhoea than those with water piped to their house' (UNCHS, 1996, p. 135). It is not only disease that is the problem. As Crane and Daniere (1996, p. 204) point out: '... the difficulty in obtaining *enough* water is at least as prejudicial as water contamination to the health of the urban poor ... the high prices that the urban poor often have to pay for water diminish the amounts they have to spend on food and thus undermine their often precarious nutritional status'.

However, despite recognition of the need to resolve the environmental problems of poor people as a way of improving their quality of life, the world at large has not moved sufficiently far towards resolving those environmental problems. At best, we do an inadequate job and sometimes make human conditions worse in the process. For example, providing informal settlements with water but not with drainage, reduces the incidence of intestinal infection but creates new conditions for disease to develop in the waste. Such an outcome is always likely when commercial agencies are trying to increase the number of subscribers. It is also encouraged by politicians under pressure from electorates to deliver on promises of new taps, drains and electricity lines. The issue, as always, comes down to political will to marshal the resources to resolve the problems of poor people.

To What Extent Can Technological Advance Save Us?

The industrial revolution brought with it the belief that technology can improve the human condition. That belief was partially vindicated during the twentieth century by the fact that over most of the globe people now live much longer. Confidence in the power of technology is also supported by evidence that the quality of infrastructure has tended to improve over time. As the World Bank (1994, p. 1) point out: 'During the past fifteen years, the share of households with access to clean water has increased by half, and power production and telephone lines per capita have doubled'. Seemingly, too, technology can help us protect the environment. Science and technology have the capacity, if used properly, to save us all. And, over the years this is precisely what has happened. The introduction of new seeds, fertilizers and pesticides may have brought many problems but they have prevented a neo-Malthusian disaster. Motorized transport may have threatened to drink the oil well dry, but technology has found new ways of discovering and exploiting the world's petroleum reserves.

Unfortunately, the positive picture presented by Figure 2.1 omits the less positive side of the picture. Many parts of the globe have participated little in the improvements. Certainly, few African cities have experienced many improvements, a consequence both of poor management and of the failure of so many African economies to grow in the period since 1970 (Nwaka, 1996; Ogu, 1996-7).

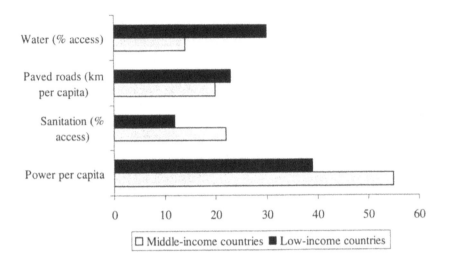

Sanitation and water data for 1975-90; power and road data for 1960-90

Source: World Bank (1994)

Figure 2.1   Growth of infrastructure provision in recent decades (percentage decennial growth rate)

Even where service delivery has apparently improved, we have to be a little suspicious of the very positive picture painted by the authorities. The fact that low-income settlements are provided with water pipes does not mean that there is always water in the pipes! This has long been a problem in poor cities around the globe but also seems to have afflicted sophisticated cities like Bogotá and Buenos Aires in recent years (Novaro and Perelman, 1994). But the major reason why we should be suspicious of global figures is that large numbers of people have benefited little even in cities where overall progress has been undeniable. To put it bluntly, those who are poor gain only limited access to infrastructure improvements (Figure 2.2).

In cities where the general level of provision is improving rapidly, many poor communities living in newer settlements lack connections to the supply network (Gilbert, 1998; Glewwe and Hall, 1992). Even when the poor receive services they also tend to bear the brunt of pollution. Water pollution is bad downstream from factories and higher income residential areas, the zones where most poor people are likely to live.

The problem with technology lies not in its potential contribution, which is vast, but with the use to which it is put. Too often technological progress occurs fastest in areas that are the most profitable. Sometimes, profitable areas have been those that have catered for a mass market, for example, cotton and later synthetic clothing and certain kinds of medicine. More typically, however, technological progress has catered for higher income groups, for example, supersonic airplanes and most 'advances' in pharmaceutical and medical practice.

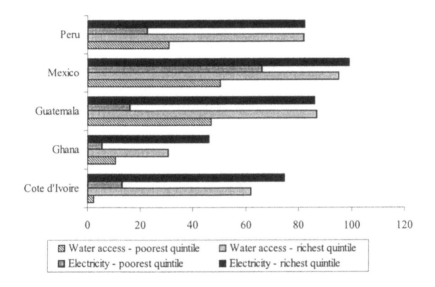

Source: World Bank (1994)

Figure 2.2   Access to infrastructure by income group in selected countries in late 1980s

The contradictory achievements of technological advance are extremely well demonstrated in the arena of transport provision. Technology has brought major improvements in our ability to move about, indeed, humans have never been so mobile. We can travel supersonically, we can travel in comfortable and reliable cars with stereo music systems, we can travel cheaply across the Atlantic and to Australia. Despite these technological advances, the transport situation within most cities has probably deteriorated over time. In Bangkok, seemingly the prototype of the congested Third World city, the average speed of a car is 13 kilometres per hour and that of a bus 9 kph (Newman and Kenworthy, 1999; Punpuing, 2001). The key problem is that rates of personal car ownership have been growing too fast. Road capacity has increased but much more slowly than the number of cars; in part because of budget constraints, in part because of the sheer increase in the numbers of vehicles, and in part because it is simply not possible to build more roads in most urban areas. The consequence of this trend is obvious: vehicle ownership and road use increase, traffic congestion and air quality worsen.

Rather than dealing politically with the basic problem, imposing more controls over the private car and developing better public transport, technological advance has been used to develop other 'solutions' (UNCHS, 2001). In Caracas, Medellín, Mexico City, Rio de Janeiro and Santiago, the authorities have taken the capital-intensive option of constructing new 'metro' transport systems (Figueroa, 1996). While 'metros' are very popular locally and help more people to get to work quickly, they do not reduce traffic congestion for long. Much more effective in terms of both cost and usage is the development of dedicated bus routes as in Curitiba and Bogotá. But unfortunately, public road transport is too often allowed to deteriorate. Rhetorical statements are made about the desirability of cycling and walking, but priority is almost always given to building metros, motorways and encouraging more people to own cars. So long as governments are reluctant to say 'no' to the private car lobby, road conditions will deteriorate. My fear is that the combination of growing private car use, economic expansion, the ethos of liberalization, distrust of the state and the failure to improve the bus system will lead to more use of an economically expensive solution; the building of a 'metro'. As such I agree totally with White and Whitney (1992, p. 36) when they say that 'The challenge for human settlements policy is not to replicate the rich country patterns in today's poor countries. The challenge is to design and manage human settlements in such a way that all the world's people may live at a decent standard based on sustainable principles'. I would add that it is also necessary to convince first world governments that their own policies are not sustainable.

Urban Management in a Globalized World

There is currently a lot of talk about urban management and how to improve it (Batley, 1996; Mattingly, 1994; Polèse and Stren, 2000; UNCRD, 1994; UNECLAC/UNCHS, 2000; World Bank, 1991, 1995, 1999). The United Nations now has its own Urban Management Programme. The assumption is that better management will lead to better living conditions. Whether it will depends upon whether government performance can be improved and on the areas towards which better performance is directed.

The question I would like to pose is whether the process of globalization is making the task of improving living conditions easier or more difficult. For a start, globalization is bringing greater competition between cities and city-regions as 'the economic systems of advanced and developing countries alike are being restructured to meet the needs of global traders and investors' (Browne, 1994, p. 1). In the process, cities are 'flinging themselves into the competitive process of attracting jobs and investment by bargaining away living standards and regulatory practices' (Peck and Tickell, 1994, p. 319). Some local and national authorities attract trans-national corporations by asking no questions about potential environmental damage or by promising to clear up the mess.

In the newly globalized world the managers of trans-national corporations expect the city authorities to provide them with the means to produce competitively. This requires that services and infrastructure are made available along with the kind of leisure and business facilities that could be expected in the developed world. These managers are not much interested in the rest of the city. As such, the danger is not only that unequal forms of post-modern development will spread across the world's markets but that they will also infiltrate the world of service delivery.

The clearest example of this danger is in the spread of privatization into the world of public utilities (Cook and Kirkpatrick, 1988; Roth, 1987; Savedoff and Spiller, 1999). While there can be little doubt that too many public agencies were not providing the poor with an adequate service, can we assume that the poor will automatically benefit from private service delivery? For a start, market efficiency does not necessarily equate with social efficiency. Why should commercial suppliers provide infrastructure to the poor? If suppliers concentrate on the commercial attractiveness of particular segments of the market, they will seek to provide increasingly sophisticated services to the better off and nothing to the poor. Providing small quantities of water to poor households across the city is not an appealing option for a commercially oriented supplier. In most developed countries, at least most poor households can afford to pay the charges for water, electricity, sewerage and telephones. In many less-developed countries, however, the situation is different; many, perhaps most, consumers cannot afford to pay much for services. For the supplier, therefore, it is not profitable to supply them.

If better urban management were motivated primarily by a wish to help the poor, to involve the poor in identifying priorities, in reducing environmental damage and generally to improve the quality of life, then the shift would be a 'good thing'. But, evidence from some, perhaps most, Third World countries suggests that privatization has really occurred because governments are looking for ways of cutting government expenditure. Remember the recipe that has been emerging from the World

Bank (1994, p. 8): 'To reform the provision of infrastructure services, this Report advocates three measures: the wider application of commercial principles to service providers, the broader use of competition, and the increased involvement of users where commercial and competitive behaviour is constrained'. I am unconvinced that this will 'produce three types of gains: reduction in subsidies, technical gains to suppliers, and gains to users'.

The problem with the market is that supplying poor households only becomes 'efficient' when account is taken of the reduced morbidity that accrues from providing a safe water supply. Even then, the benefits may be undermined if some kind of drainage and sewerage system is not provided simultaneously. In short, the market has always had problems with external economies and diseconomies. The answer is that the state should intervene by regulating the suppliers. If governments insist that every part of the city be provided with services, then commercial providers will be forced to do so. Unfortunately, in many a Third World city, it is not quite that simple.

First, governments are not that efficient as regulators. Even in Britain, the record of regulators since privatization has not been unblemished. If that is the case in Britain, how much more problematic is the issue of regulation in Bogotá or Cape Town? For, if Third World governments are quite good at imitating the laws of First World societies, they are much less good at applying and monitoring those laws. Many Third World societies are notorious for the amount of corruption and intrigue that goes on. Setting up a regulatory mechanism may merely create a new arena for bribery.

Second, even if regulators insist that private operators comply with stiff performance indicators and threaten to remove licences if the service is deficient, will that improve delivery to the poor? The answer is: sometimes. When the profit margin is too low, stringent regulation may simply persuade the supplier to cease operations (Ogu, 1996-7). We are back to the issue of effective demand. Without a subsidy, the supply will not be forthcoming. But, given current modes of thought and current economic circumstances, there is little chance of a subsidy.

Third, there is a strong ethos at the moment to cut back on the nanny state. As suggested above, the argument in much of the literature is that the state already intervenes too much. According to de Soto (1989) and Cohen (1990), private enterprise should be encouraged to operate in low-income communities. Reform and even removal of the regulations would automatically formalize the informal. Modification of the regulations would allow small-scale entrepreneurs to perform functions that are currently the preserve of other institutions. There is certainly evidence that in practice the poor are willing and able to buy services provided that suppliers are allowed to supply them.

Fourth, economic decline has forced governments to cut back on expenditure, which has left the door open to the informal sector. Given the lack of investment in public transport, private taxis and minibuses begin to carry passengers. In the absence of water pipes, private water tankers move into the *barriadas*. In Buenos Aires, the past failures of the public company led to private initiative decorating office blocks with informal solutions telephone lines. The problem is that without serious regulation this informal sector enterprise can create as many problems as it solves.

Lastly, I fear that an additional problem is being created by one of the favoured techniques of better urban management – decentralization of the administration to take government closer to the people. Decentralization of government is *de rigueur* in many countries. In Chile, municipalities were given much greater power under the Pinochet government. In Colombia, the new constitution of 1991 warmly embraced both decentralization and participation. And, in South Africa there have been strong moves towards decentralized power. Such a move was also strongly encouraged by the Washington consensus and formed part of the planned demolition of 'big' government. However, to what extent decentralization has encouraged greater efficiency and led to people being consulted more about their needs is debatable (Savedoff and Spiller, 1999). The danger with decentralization, delegation and consultation is that it may turn into political populism. By this I mean that generous promises to the people cannot be implemented. Decentralization may work well in the more sophisticated cities of Latin America (Savedoff and Spiller, 1999) but, in most parts of the developing world, local government has neither the expertise nor the resources to be effective.

The declared aims of service delivery cannot be satisfied by the methods being employed currently to provide those services. Thus privatization is incompatible with improved environmental sustainability, cost effectiveness too often incompatible with poverty reduction, reductions in taxation alien to the expansion of services. The rhetoric that has developed about social safety nets, decentralization and sustainability is designed to cover up the inability of either the modern or the post-modern state to satisfy most of the demands of society for services. This is because societies now espouse a series of mutually incompatible desires. They want more and better services, they want less pollution, they want to consume more but, critically, they want to pay less taxes and less for key public services. To paper over these mutually incompatible desires, it has been necessary to create a new mythology: that the state will create the conditions for improved service delivery by doing less and in the process will help the environment, reduce poverty and cut taxes.

What I am suggesting is that privatization, decentralization and the unleashing of market forces may produce a form of service delivery that is likely to damage the quality of life of the poor and the lack of regulatory control is like to further damage the environment. Companies will expand production, higher incomes will increase private consumption, there will be too little implementation of the green agenda and the poverty of the shantytowns will impede progress in satisfying the brown agenda. In the end, the combined forces of globalization, free enterprise and weaker government controls will lead to a situation of urban anarchy.

Will a Political Cataclysm Make Urbanization Unsustainable?

Our urban future will depend on the attitudes of the peoples who live in the cities. If they hold a positive view of their lives and their prospects, then a positive future for urban life is assured. But in the event that they should view their situation negatively, they may seek to change the economic and political system in ways that could threaten the continued growth of urban areas. While I do not think that scenario is particularly likely, it is one that has been frequently conjured up by social observers and particularly by novelists over the years. The social ills of the city were a focus of novelists of the nineteenth century such as Dickens, Hardy and Zola, as it is of many twentieth century novelists from the Third World such as Ngugi and Paton. No doubt there are exceptions but I cannot think of any. Social scientists have often echoed this negative attitude towards urbanization particularly when they have been referring to the Third World city (Hoselitz, 1957; Lerner, 1967).

Fortunately, experience has demonstrated to most social scientists that urbanization is politically sustainable. Few cities are likely to be subsumed by waves of political radical or anarchistic rural migrants. Research has revealed that the majority of the migrant population is conservative. They are more interested in making their own way in the city rather than in attempting to overthrow an admittedly rotten system (Cornelius, 1975; Portes, 1972). Political radicalism in Third World cities has always been rather thin on the ground (Gilbert and Ward, 1985; Mainwaring, 1989; Roberts, 1970; van Garderen, 1989). It is seldom in the interest of poor individuals or families to kick up a fuss. For a start, most are extremely busy earning their living and building their own self-help homes. They may also face a hostile reception for few governments are gentle in their handling of dissent, particularly in societies under authoritarian rule where repression is often extremely violent. At other times, the poor's inclination to riot is reduced by political patronage; politicians of whatever hue are adept at making promises and offering jobs and services in return for obedience (Gay, 1990; Gilbert, 1998; Mainwaring, 1989).

Nevertheless, many on the political left have been anxious to encourage the idea that political revolution is just around the corner. In the 1970s, Manuel Castells (1977) provided many radicals with theoretical justification for renewed hope in revolution. Social movements would break out in urban areas and lead to political transformation. However, despite a strenuous search for social movements during the 1970s, relatively few were in evidence. In practice, what most researchers found were urban protests against specific actions or policies rather than urban movements. People might get upset about the quality of public services or about the introduction of wage freezes but few had much awareness about the structural causes of their poverty. They wanted improvement for themselves and were not much interested in building up alliances with other neighbourhoods or with the labour movement (Evers, 1985).

A second Castells book recognized that political conservatism was the dominant feature of urban life: '... contrary to the expectations of those who believe in the myth of marginality and in spite of the fears of the world's establishment, social organization seems to be stronger than social deviance in these communities ...' (Castells, 1983, p. 175). Nevertheless, there has been plenty of protest from groups 'made up of young people, women, residential associations, church-sponsored "grass-roots" communities, and similar groups' (Portes, 1989, p. 36). The community based protests supported by the Church in Brazil, the collectives established in Chilean *campamentos*, and in the urban coalitions being built across Mexican cities were all vigorous signs that all was not well with urban life (Boran, 1989; Kowarick, 1988; Kusnetzoff, 1990; Schneider, 1995). Perhaps these were 'social movements' seeking radical forms of change, but few have managed to sustain any real political challenge. The same can be said of the outbreak of 'austerity' or IMF riots that broke out during the 1980s. According to John Walton (1989, p. 309) austerity led to 'an unprecedented wave of international protest; unprecedented in the scope and essentially singular cause of a global protest analogous to earlier national strike waves'. People have continued to protest against IMF conditionality, and particularly against fare and tariff rises, but the incidence of such riots seems to have been diminishing (Gilbert, 1998). In any case, there is no general pattern for protest is patchy and is often produced by different processes in different places (Walton, 1998).

If some believe in a turbulent urban future across most parts of the world (Gizewski and Homer-Dixon, 1995), there are others who claim that urbanization works more subtly with other forms of 'modernization' to produce democracy (Huntington, 1991). In practice there has been no simple relationship between the processes of economic development, urbanization and democratization. The rise of democracy in post-war Europe supports a positive interpretation; the rise of bureaucratic authoritarianism in Latin America after 1964 supports a negative view (O'Donnell, 1973; Skidmore and Smith, 1997; Tulchin and Brand, 1995). In South Africa, if urbanization helped destroy apartheid, it also played an important role in creating it. While economic development and democratization have ebbed and flowed, urbanization has continued in uninterrupted fashion. Economic development effectively stopped in Africa between 1970 and 1990 and in Latin America during the 1980s. Urbanization in Latin America was loosely associated with increased numbers of democratic governments during the 1960s but the 1970s produced urbanization and totalitarian rule (Hartlyn and Morley, 1986; O'Donnell, 1973).

In summary, no pattern is apparent across time or space except that there have been rather few political mobilizations sufficiently strong to slow urbanization or to threaten urban society. China and Kampuchea perhaps fall into that category but, of course, these revolutions were based essentially on rural rather than on urban support.

The Politics of Urban Sustainability

Whether the future will bring improved living conditions for the majority of the world's people and whether the environment will be damaged by human development will depend fundamentally on politics. This will not be the politics of the street nor even of the ballot box; it will be the politics of the globally powerful. As Hardoy et al. (1993, p. 201) put it: 'It is not only the achievement of the "sustainable" component of sustainable development that requires international agreements; so too does the meeting of human needs in the South. Most nations in the South cannot meet development goals, and very few are likely to meet sustainability goals, without changes in the world market and the way that development assistance is provided. A government seeking to resolve a debt crisis and reliant for most foreign exchange on the export of natural resources cannot address longer-term sustainability goals'.

It has always been true that most important decisions are made by the powerful. Within cities it is those with cars who most influence transport policy rather than those without. Within nations it is the decisions of financial managers, officials in the treasury and the central bank and top politicians that determine levels of interest rates, subsidies and government expenditure. But, increasingly, power has moved beyond the local arena to the national and beyond the national level to the global. Localities are dependent on decisions made by trans-national corporations whatever might be said about the importance of local and regional assemblies. Even national governments in the most powerful countries are no longer as autonomous as they once were. They are certainly not powerless but much more power now lies in the hands of a couple of hundred corporations that determine how we live our lives. It is the politics of technology, marketing, consumption and the market that is most likely to determine the global future.

The depressing thing about this form of politics is that it is undemocratic and often conservative. As the school of so-called 'political ecology' has demonstrated, most decisions about the environment are made by groups attempting to advance or defend their own self-interest (Bryant,

1997). Such 'powerful vested interests oppose most if not all the needed policies and priorities. Richer groups will oppose what they see as controls on their right to consume or higher costs that arise from changed pricing structures to encourage conservation and waste reduction' (Satterthwaite, 1997, p. 1685). The electoral politics of the United States determines whether the United States backs debt relief or cuts carbon emissions or allows more immigrants into the country. What is necessary for the majority of the world's population is almost entirely irrelevant.

The only hope lies in the fact that technology is changing so rapidly that it will undermine some of these powerful actors. Possibly the Internet has acted in this way, certainly in the way that it has facilitated the organization of opposition to the World Trade Organization and the Bretton Woods institutions. Whether or not that kind of action will improve the world, however, is less than certain.

Conclusion

Cities across the globe will continue to grow even if their form will undoubtedly change. Urban growth will be threatened only by some global disaster such as nuclear war or a three-inch rise in the sea level. Urban development will continue apace in Africa and Asia because it has the capacity to improve living conditions. No doubt slower population growth and greater efforts to redistribute land could modify the current balance of advantage between city and countryside and thereby slow migration. But, there is little reason to expect such a development.

The last 50 years have produced a great deal of improvement across the globe in life expectancy, education levels and in health standards. Some of the constraints on urban development have been overcome by technological advance. But if that has been the general trend, that does not mean that everyone has gained. Because the world's population has grown so much, more people than ever before live in dire poverty. Many in Africa and the Indian subcontinent would not recognize that their lives have improved a great deal.

Whether urbanization in the future will benefit those who have so far been marginalized, depends on radical changes being made in the way we run the world. Unfortunately, my view veers towards the pessimistic. Certainly, there is little chance that cities will become more equitable. The privileged may form a higher proportion of the population than today but are likely to appropriate the bulk of any improvements that occur. The poor will increase in number, will live longer and will have more consumer durables. Unfortunately, the state of their health will have improved little nor will they be much better nourished. The physical environment in most cities will have deteriorated further, not in the elite areas except in terms of traffic congestion, but certainly in the low-income areas. Private affluence and public squalor will be key features of most cities in the world, but in less developed countries, private affluence will not benefit the vast majority. Not only will efforts at economic growth and modernization have inflicted further environmental damage on Third World cities but they will also have reaped some of the harvest of environmental damage caused by rising living standards in the North. What is happening in the rain forests of the world today is symptomatic of what will be happening in the Third World in the future. At least much of the destruction will be in the countryside where the primary exports are being generated. In that sense those living in the cities will be protected from the worst. The main environmental danger is that nature will take its revenge through global warming and the floods, hurricanes and epidemics that will be unleashed by it.

References

Batley, R. (1996), 'Public-private Relationships and Performance in Service Provision', *Urban Studies*, vol. 33, pp. 723-51.

Boran, A. (1989), 'Popular Movements in Brazil: A Case Study of the Movement for the Defence of the Favelados in Sao Paulo', *Bulletin of Latin American Research*, vol. 8, pp. 83-110.

Brockerhoff, M. (1999), 'Urban Growth in Developing Countries: A Review of Projections and Predictions', *Population and Development Review*, vol. 25, pp. 757-78.

Browne, H. (1994), *For Richer; for Poorer*, Latin America Bureau, London.

Bryant, R.L. (1997), 'Beyond the Impasse: The Power of Political Ecology in Third World Environmental Research', *Area*, vol. 19, pp. 5-19.

Castells, M. (1977), *The Urban Question*, Edward Arnold, London.

Castells, M. (1983), *The City and the Grassroots*, Edward Arnold, London.

Cohen, M.A. (1990), 'Macroeconomic Adjustment and the City', *Cities*, vol. 7, pp. 49-59.

Cook, P. and Kirkpatrick, C. (1988), 'Privatisation in Less Developed Countries: An Overview', in P. Cook and C. Kirkpatrick (eds), *Privatisation in Less Developed Countries*, Harvester Wheatsheaf, London, pp. 3-44.

Cornelius, W. (1975), *Politics and the Migrant Poor in Mexico*, University of Stanford Press, Stanford.

Crane, R. and Daniere, A. (1996), 'Measuring Access to Basic Services in Global Services: Descriptive and Behavioural Approaches', *American Planning Association Journal*, vol. 62, pp. 203-21.

de Soto, H. (1989), *The Other Path*, I.B. Taurus, London [First published in Spanish in 1986].

Drakakis-Smith, D.W. (1995), 'Third World Cities: Sustainable Urban Development', *Urban Studies*, vol. 32, pp. 659-77.

Evers, T. (1985), 'Identity: The Hidden Side of New Social Movements in Latin America', in D. Slater (ed.), *New Social Movements and the State in Latin America*, Foris Publications, Amsterdam, pp. 43-71.

Figueroa, O. (1996), 'A Hundred Million Journeys a Day: The Management of Transport in Latin America's Mega-cities', in A.G. Gilbert (ed.), *The Mega-city in Latin America*, UNU Press, Tokyo, pp. 110-32.

Gay, R. (1990), 'Neighbourhood Associations and Political Change in Rio de Janeiro', *Latin American Research Review*, vol. 25, pp. 102-18.

Gilbert, A.G. (1998), *The Latin American City*, Latin America Bureau, London [expanded and revised edition].

Gilbert, A.G. and Ward, P.M. (1985), *Housing, the State and the Poor: Policy and Practice in Three Latin American Cities*, Cambridge University Press, Cambridge.

Gizewski, P. and Homer-Dixon, T. (1995), *Urban Growth and Violence: Will the Future Resemble the Past?*, AAAS and University of Toronto: Project on Environment, Population and Security.

Glewwe, P. and Hall, G. (1992), 'Poverty and Inequality During Unorthodox Adjustment: The Case of Peru, 1985-90', *Living Standards Measurement Study Working Paper*, no. 86, The World Bank.

Hardoy, J.E., Mitlin, D. and Satterthwaite, D. (1993), *Environmental Problems in Third World Cities*, Earthscan, London.

Hartlyn, J. and Morley, S.A. (1986), 'Bureaucratic-authoritarian Regimes in Comparative Perspective', in J. Hartlyn and S.A. Morley (eds), *Latin American Political Economy: Financial Crisis and Political Change*, Westview Press, Boulder, 38-53.

Hoselitz, B.F. (1957), 'Generative and Parasitic Cities', *Economic Development and Cultural Change*, vol. 3, pp. 278-94.

Huntington, S.P. (1991), *The Third Wave: Democratization in the Late Twentieth Century*, University of Oklahoma Press, Oklahoma City.

Kowarick, L. (ed.) (1988), *As lutas sociais e a cidade: São Paulo, passado e presente*, Paz e Terra, Sao Paulo.

Kusnetzoff, F. (1990) 'The State and Housing in Chile – Regime Types and Policy Choices', in G. Shidlo (ed.), *Housing Policy in Developing Countries*, Routledge, London, pp. 48-66.

Lerner, D. (1967), 'Comparative Analysis of Processes of Modernization', in H. Miner (ed.), *The City in Modern Africa*, Pall Mall, London, pp. 21-38.

Mainwaring, S. (1989), 'Grassroots Popular Movements and the Struggle for Democracy: Nova Iguaçu', in A. Stepan (ed.), *Democratizing Brazil: Problems of Transition and Consolidation*, Oxford University Press, New York, pp. 168-204.

Mattingly, M. (1994), 'Meaning of Urban Management', *Cities*, vol. 11, pp. 201-5.

Newman, P. and Kenworthy, J. (1999), *Sustainability and Cities: Overcoming Automobile Dependence*, Island Press, Washington.

Novaro, M. and Perelman, P. (1994), 'La provisión de agua en el Gran Buenos Aires', *Boletín Medio Ambiente y Urbanización*, vol. 49, pp. 3-15.

Nwaka, G.I. (1996), 'Planning Sustainable Cities in Africa', *Canadian Journal of Urban Research*, vol. 5, pp. 119-36.

O'Donnell, G. (1973), *Modernization and Bureaucratic Authoritarianism: Studies in South American Politics*, University of California Press, Berkeley.

Ogu, V.I. (1996-7), 'Enabling Strategies and Sustainable Infrastructure Development: Focus on Benin City, Nigeria', *Regional Development Strategies*, vol. 3, pp. 199-217.

Peck, J. and Tickell, A. (1994), 'Jungle Law Breaks Out: Neoliberalism and Global-local Disorder', *Area*, vol. 26, pp. 317-26.

Polèse, M. and Stren, R. (eds) (2000), *The Social Sustainability of Cities: Diversity and the Management of Change*, University of Toronto, Toronto.

Portes, A. (1972), 'Rationality in the Slum: An Essay in Interpretive Sociology', *Comparative Studies in Society and History*, vol. 14, pp. 268-86.

Portes, A. (1989), 'Latin American Urbanization During the Years of the Crisis', *Latin American Research Review*, vol. 25, pp. 7-44.

Punpuing, S. (2001), 'Commuting: The Human Side of Bangkok's Transport Problems', *Cities*, vol. 18, pp. 43-50.

Reed, D. (ed.) (1992), *Structural Adjustment and the Environment*, Earthscan, London.

Rees, W.E. (1992), 'Ecological Footprints and Appropriated Carrying Capacity: What Urban Economics Leaves Out', *Environment and Urbanization*, vol. 4, pp. 121-30.

Roberts, B. (1970), 'Urban Poverty and Political Behaviour in Guatemala', *Human Organization*, vol. 29, pp. 20-28.

Roth, G. (1987), *The Private Provision of Public Services in Developing Countries*, Oxford University Press, New York.

Satterthwaite, D. (1997), 'Sustainable Cities or Cities that Contribute to Sustainable Development', *Urban Studies*, vol. 34, pp. 1667-91.

Savedoff, W. and Spiller, W. (eds) (1999), *Spilled Water: Institutional Commitment in the Provision of Water Services*, Inter American Development Bank, Washington.

Schneider, C.L. (1995), *Shantytown Protest in Pinochet's Chile*, Temple University Press, Philadelphia.

Skidmore, T. and Smith, P. (1997), *Modern Latin America*, Oxford University Press, New York [fourth edition].

Tulchin, J.S. and Bland, G. (1995), *Peru in Crisis: Dictatorship or Democracy*, Lynne Rienner, Boulder.

UNCHS (United Nations Centre for Human Settlements) (1996), *An Urbanizing World: Global Report on Human Settlements 1996*, Oxford University Press, New York.

UNCHS (United Nations Centre for Human Settlements) (2001), *Cities in a Globalizing World: Global Report on Human Settlements 2001*, Oxford University Press, New York.

UNCRD (United Nations Centre for Regional Development) (1994), 'Enhancing the Management of Metropolitan Living Environments in Latin America', *UNCRD Research Report Series*, no. 1, Nagoya.

UNECLAC/UNCHS (2000), *From Rapid Urbanization to the Consolidation of Human Settlements in Latin America and the Caribbean: A Territorial Perspective*, Santiago.

UNEP (United Nations Environmental Programme) (1992), *Urban Air Pollution in Megacities of the World*, Blackwell, Oxford.

United Nations (1998), Revision of the World Population Estimates and Projections.

van Garderen, T. (1989), 'Collective Organization and Action in Squatter Settlements in Arequipa, Peru', in F. Schuurman and T. van Naerssen (eds), *Urban Social Movements in the Third World*, Routledge, London, pp. 105-23.

Walton, J. (1989), 'Debt, Protest, and the State in Latin America', in Eckstein (ed.), *Power and Popular Protest: Latin American Social Movements*, University of California Press, Berkeley, pp. 299-328.

Walton, J. (1998), 'Urban Conflict and Social Movements in Poor Countries: Theory and Evidence of Collective Action', *International Journal of Urban and Regional Research*, vol. 22, pp. 460-81.

White, R. and Whitney, J. (1992), 'Cities and Environment: An Overview', in R. Stren, R. White and J. Whitney (eds), *Sustainable Cities: Urbanization and the Environment in International Perspective*, Westview Press, Boulder, pp. 8-51.

World Bank (1991), *Urban Policy and Economic Development: An Agenda for the 1990s*, Washington.

World Bank (1992), *World Development Report 1992: Development and the Environment*, Oxford University Press, New York.

World Bank (1994), *World Development Report 1994: Infrastructure for Development*, Washington.

World Bank (1995), *Better Urban Services: Finding the Right Incentives*, Washington.

World Bank (1999), *Cities in Transition: World Bank Urban and Local Government Strategy*, The World Bank Infrastructure Group.

Chapter 3

Urban 'Unsustainability' and Environmental Conflict[1]

Joan Martinez-Alier

Introduction

Large cities are environmentally unsustainable. Their 'ecological footprints' are much larger than their own territories. They process large amounts of energy and materials, and they excrete different sorts of waste products. However, this article wishes to pose the following optimistic questions. Is it not true that cities are the main seats of eco-efficient technological innovation? Are there co-evolutionary trends in urban development which point towards environmental sustainability? As a consequence of the fast pace of world urbanization with massive energy and materials requirements, compounded by increasing urban sprawl, pessimistic answers are given to these questions (following Lewis Mumford rather than Peter Hall). Therefore, the article goes on to consider the ecological distribution conflicts caused by urban growth which are internal to the cities themselves (local conflicts regarding air, soil and water pollution, for instance), and also the conflicts which are 'exported' to the larger geographical scale. Where are the main actors of the environmental conflicts caused by urban growth? Are the outcomes of such conflicts the key to the improvement of urban 'unsustainability'? The article draws on examples mainly from Europe and India.

The Century of the Motor Car?

Among the interpretations of the twentieth century published during the last days of 1999, a seemingly incontrovertible one was that this was the century of the triumph of the automobile. First in the United States, then in Britain and continental western Europe, and also in Japan and Korea, automobile production was at different moments, and in some cases still is, the key economic sector.

In the twentieth century, the industrial working class in some countries, regimented on Taylorist lines during the working week, was able to buy cars and to enjoy using them over miles of new motorways leading to the parking lots of shopping malls or holiday resorts. In other words, modernity in the twentieth century meant the troika of Ford, Taylor and Le Corbusier. The number of private cars in the world exceeded 550 million in the year 2000, and in some countries there was a car for every two persons. Today, in the wealthy nations, this industrial working class seems to have vanished. Towards the end of the century we entered a 'post-Fordist' era. There was also a strong trend away from state regulation despite a new environmental awareness. Reliance on the unregulated market and environmental concern were reconciled by the belief that the economy could grow with increasingly diminished environmental impact, since the leading growth sectors of the New Economy were now information technology and many forms of services. Conventional wisdom was that we were moving into a 'dematerialized' economy due to the increasing weight of the service sector in terms of employment as well as in terms of economic added value. A British film such as *The Full Monty* captured the plight of unemployed post-Fordist, post-industrial workers in Sheffield who try to make a living in the entertainment industry. Was dematerialization a reality? True, incomes were increasingly earned not in factories but by providing services which directly required low energy and material inputs. Incomes might be obtained, for that matter, by trading immaterial financial derivatives at home on the Internet. One question was the increased consumption of electricity resulting from the use of computers as domestic appliances. Another more weighty question addressed the problem of how, on what items, would the increased incomes gained by economic growth be spent? Probably on well-heated and well-cooled houses, recreational travel, and computers and cars – indeed cars with computers.

Perhaps there was a permanent trend in the advanced economies towards relative 'de-linking', that is, the rate of growth of energy and material input was lower than that of GNP growth. 'De-linking' in absolute terms had not yet come about. Moreover, relative 'de-linking' was, to some extent, a consequence of a geographical displacement of energy sources and materials, and also of waste sinks (such as carbon dioxide emissions), an effect that was not correctly assessed in the statistics. Instead, in the coal age during the long nineteenth century and up until 1914, Europe and the United States had, by and large, both mined and consumed the coal they required *in situ*. Also, hydroelectricity rarely travelled outside the country of production. Now, oil and gas travelled long distances from the places of extraction. By the year 2000, even the United States was importing over half the oil it consumed. Moreover, though the twentieth century had seen coal decrease in importance as compared to oil and gas, five times more coal was mined in the world in 1990 than in 1900 (McNeill, 2000).

World population had grown fourfold in the twentieth century reaching six billion in the year 2000. It will perhaps grow to ten billion by 2050 though human demography is difficult to predict. Will a prosperous world then have a stock of five billion cars, almost ten times as many cars as in the year 2000? *Will the twenty-first century be the real century of the automobile?* Was the car to be considered, not economically but 'ecologically', a positional asset, a sign of oligarchic wealth which could not spread widely? In 2000, a new car cost at least ten times as much as a personal computer. Its construction and maintenance required an energy and material input, and also a labour input, far greater than the personal computer. The car remained, then, undoubtedly one main factor in economic growth. Although new techniques such as fuel cells able to reduce some forms of automobile pollution were promised, the fact that the automobile industry would remain a leading sector of the growing economy implied, without the need for much other research, that it would be the most difficult in which to decrease the inputs of energy and materials into the economy. What would be the implications of extending to the whole planet this gigantic technological lock-in, in terms of settlement patterns, energy consumption, air pollution, and climate change?

The car is then one important item of technological transferrals from rich to poor countries. As the environmental journalist Daryl D'Monte puts it, urban investment in a growing metropolis like Bombay (Mumbai) is determined by the 'nine per cent rule', for example, motorways and overpasses for the 9 per cent of car-owning families.

In most cities, policy-makers have endorsed the large-scale construction of overpasses and the widening of roads, ignoring the basic issues, namely, that more cars mean more pollution, and that unless the growth of vehicular traffic is checked, congestion and traffic jams will continue to be prominent features of urban India (Indian People's Tribunal on Environment and Human Rights, 2001).

This is not an article about energy nor is it primarily 'anti-automobile'. Due to population growth, the absolute number of traditional peasants and landless labourers in the world was greater in the year 2000 than in 1900. Their disappearance (there are nearly two billion, including their families) together with the disappearance of their agro-ecological wisdom and innovative capacity, is even more irreversible and possibly a more important trend that the diffusion of the motor car. Both trends go hand-in-hand, since the loss of agricultural population in the territory merges with a trend towards an urbanization pattern based on the automobile, which has not yet overwhelmed India, Indonesia, Africa or China at the beginning of the twenty-first century. This will probably be the century of irreversible urbanization. Many ecological distribution conflicts have nothing to do with cars. When oil and gas are not used as sources of energy, then either nuclear energy or hydroelectricity from large dams can come to the rescue – thus annoying the environmentalists, who are hard to please. Before the automobile age, there were strong environmental movements against sulphur dioxide in the nineteenth century. This problem has been solved in many places, but new conflicts arise. Today, despite computers and the Internet, there is an increasing use of paper in the world. This is one cause of increasing deforestation, and of new plantations of pines and eucalyptus. The environmentalists keep complaining. The economy is driven by consumption. In the United States, the year 1999 broke all records in the number of new cars and light trucks sold – over 19 million, many imported.

A Mexican government minister argued, early in 2000, that oil exports from Mexico to the US should increase against OPEC's restrictions and at the risk of lowering the price of oil, because car production, for the home and foreign markets, was becoming the driving force of the Mexican economy. Selling cheap oil was (he said) in Mexico's best interests. In the summer of 2000, there was some electoral debate in the US both regarding the increased greenhouse effect and the increased price of gasoline. Some politicians simultaneously declared themselves against both. Other politicians deconstructed the greenhouse effect out of the political agenda. In the winter of 2000-2001, green circles in Europe – pleased with the advances of eco-taxation – felt acutely embarrassed by the revolt of farmers, truck drivers, fishermen and ordinary citizens against the high price of oil.

Lewis Mumford's Relevant Views

Ecological economics assumes that there is a clash between economic growth and the environment. This cannot be made good by simply wishing for sustainable development, or by hoping for ecological modernization and increased eco-efficiency. One way of addressing the conflict consists in giving monetary values to negative (or positive) externalities. Another more comprehensive way is to consider money values and physical and social indicators of (un)sustainability at the same time, in a multi-criteria framework. This is the practice of ecological economics, which use indicators such as per capita water consumption, the production of sulphur dioxide, the production of carbon dioxide, the production of NO_x, VOC and particulates, the per capita expenditure of energy for transport, the per capita production of solid residues and their percentage recycling, etc. We observe contradictory trends in such indicators. We set targets for them, and we implement the (hopefully) most cost-effective policy in order to achieve such targets. We can also aggregate several indicators into composite indices of air quality, or the 'ecological footprint'.

This ecological view of cities, well-known today, has roots in nineteenth-century chemistry and physics, as when Liebig lamented the loss of nutrients in cities which did not return them to the soil. Before the Athens Charter and Le Corbusier's primacy, the ecological view was influential in urban planning, most significantly in Patrick Geddes's work, and later in the work of Lewis Mumford in the United States and Radhakamal Mukerjee, a self-described social ecologist, in India. Geddes was a biologist and urban planner. Writing to Mumford from Calcutta on 31 August 1918, he succinctly made one main point regarding ecological city planning. In his City Report for Indore, he wanted to break with the conventional drainage of 'all to the Sewer' substituting it with 'all to the Soil'. Shiv Visvanathan has powerfully asserted that if Gandhi were alive today, he would not be so uniquely concerned with the virtues of the rural village.

> Gandhi would ... make the scavenger the paradigmatic figure of modern urban India ... Gandhi would argue that waste has not been fully thought out by urban science ... rather than becoming a source of pollution sewage would become a source of life and work. The classic example of urban sewage use was Calcutta. This much-maligned city uses its sewage to grow the finest vegetables. By focusing on waste, today's urban sciences can recover an agricultural view of the world (Visvanathan, 1997, pp. 234-5).

One of the favourite indicators of urban (un)sustainability is Rees' and Wackernagel's 'ecological footprint' (1994) – a notion that was already to be found in H.T. Odum's works of the 1960s and 1970s. This is not merely a neutral index of the ecological (un)sustainability of a given territory, it also has a clear distributional content. Is there an inevitable conflict between cities and the environment? Or, on the contrary, are cities the seats of the institutions and the origins of the technologies which will drive the economy towards sustainability? Why has the Agenda 21 movement taken deeper roots at the urban level than at the regional, national or international levels? Who are the social agents active in cities in favour of or against sustainability? Are indicators of urban (un)sustainability also to be seen as indicators of (potential or actual) social conflict? Is there a new debate on 'de-urbanization', recalling that in Moscow around 1930, which was halted by Stalinism with the help of Le Corbusier (read his mocking letter to Moses Ginzburg, of 1930)? Or, on the contrary, is there new praise for cities? Indeed, the role of the city as the origin of technological and cultural innovation is the *leit motiv* of Peter Hall's *Cities in Civilization* (1998). Armed with a belief in the blissful kingdom of economic growth at compound interest as announced by Keynes, and in Kondratieff's long cycles of investment, Peter Hall produced a fascinating, dramatic book which culminates with the triumph of the 'new economy'. As with the initial cluster of car manufacturers in Detroit, and with personal computers, a local constellation of technical ability and 'garage' entrepreneurship develops into a new leading economic sector. Peter Hall pays lip-service to the notion of ecological sustainability, mentioning 'sustainable urbanism' (p. 965) and even 'sustainable urban development' (p. 620) whatever that may mean, but the main thrust of his book counters Lewis Mumford's pessimistic ecological view of large-scale urbanization.

There are two main questions to be addressed here: one is the increased urbanization of the world population, the second is the form adopted by cities, whether they are compact cities or whether, on the contrary, they sprawl. There was a close relation between the 'garden city' movement born from Ebezener Howard's proposals of 1900 for green belts to stop the growth of conurbations, and Mumford's regional planning of the 1920s against suburban overspill. (The term urban 'sprawl' was invented in 1956 by W.F. Whyte; it was not yet used by Mumford). Howard's 'garden city' idea, or rather his terminology, was often used for totally opposite goals, i.e. to justify private middle-class suburbs. Mumford wrote to Geddes on 9 July 1926, trying to find new words for Howard's approach:

> We are attempting to discard the word, Garden City. And Regional City is our present substitute, which must carry with it the notion of a balanced relation with the region, as well as a complete environment within the city for work, study, play, and domesticity (Mumford and Geddes, 1995).

Thirty years later, Mumford was still presenting a spirited defence of Howard's proposal to build relatively self-contained, balanced communities, supported by their local industry, with a permanent population of limited number and density on public land surrounded by a swath of open country dedicated to agriculture, recreation and rural occupation.

> Howard's proposal recognized the biological and social grounds, along with the psychological pressures, that underlay the current movement to suburbia ... The new kind of city he called the 'garden city', not so much because of its internal open spaces, which would approach a sound suburban standard, but rather because it was set in a permanent rural environment ... making the surrounding agricultural area an integral part of the city's form. *His invention of a ... green belt, immune to urban building, was a public device for limiting lateral growth and maintaining the urban-rural balance* (Mumford, 1956, pp. 395-6, emphasis added).

The Garden City approach was based on an ecological understanding of the city within its region. The ecological conflict over green belts is also an economic conflict regarding the appropriation of the potential differential rental income from the preserved green spaces as they are consumed by urban sprawl and soil sealing. When the economic conflict is solved in favour of realizing the potential rents by soil sealing and building over the greenbelt spaces, then unaccounted negative environmental effects arise. In Europe, 'over the past 20 years the extent of built-up area ... has increased by some 20 per cent and far exceeds the rate of population growth over the same period (six per cent)' (European Environment Agency, 2002, p. 109).

Mumford was the most universal and historically significant American ecological writer of his time because his subject was the ecology of cities – particularly New York – and the ecological critique of technology. He was in the vanguard of a new era, building on the work of authors such as George P. Marsh, Patrick Geddes and Ebenezer Howard who constitute a coherent line of ecological thought. Mumford also liked to acknowledge Kropotkin's influence. Mumford's moderate anarchistic sympathies and his eulogy of Kropotkin, and later his early opposition to nuclear power, isolated him from the political mainstreams of his time.

Although Mumford was indeed aware of Patrick Geddes' ecological view of the city as a centre for the gathering and dissipation of energy (and for the intensification of the materials' cycles), nevertheless Mumford did not develop Geddes' vision into an empirical energy analysis of cities (Bettini, 1998). This type of analysis had to wait until the 1970s when the study of 'urban metabolism' – by authors such as S. Boyden in his research on Hong-Kong (Boyden et al., 1981) – became an established field of study. When one looks at reality, one sees that the innovative cities, for instance Seattle, are also examples of car-based urban sprawl. And many other cities are not innovative. Large-scale urbanization is still before us. The largest cities are not yet to be found in India and China, they are Tokyo, New York, Sao Paulo, Mexico City. If the hierarchy of cities in China and India does not change, if their active agricultural population decreases to 20 per cent, conurbations of 40 or 60 million inhabitants will develop. As humanity becomes more and more urban, are we moving towards economies which use less energy and materials per capita? Certainly not.

Ruskin in Venice

Geddes died in Montpellier in 1932, the year of the Athens Charter when CIAM (the International Congress of Modern Architecture) under Le Corbusier, fresh from his polemics against the de-urbanization of Moscow, set out the principles of modern urban planning, totally contrary to the Garden City – Regional Planning ideas. Geddes', and Camillo Sitte's, romantic appreciation of historic city centres, crooked streets, small piazzas, as opposed to a rationalized grid pattern, had been anticipated in

Ruskin's *Stones of Venice*. Such a nostalgic outlook, based on cultural conservation and on the conviviality of small city life, makes amusing reading in retrospect. Almost all European cities have witnessed the increasing destruction of the old medieval street pattern. Instead, in Venice, the medieval layout has been preserved, as Ruskin wished, and many houses have been restored. Here again, the romantics proved more scientific than the 'rationalists'; they asked questions about urban ecology and they also posed the question of increased transport needs when cities became divided into zones of work, residence, recreation. We know that while the endosomatic energy consumption of a citizen is about 2,500 kcal per day, that is, a little over ten megajoules per day, or 3.65 gigajoules per year, the energy expenditure of one person during one year only in individual transport in an urban region characterized by urban sprawl such as Los Angeles, is about 40 gigajoules. In comparison, in compact cities, with metro or bus transport, one person will spend 4 gigajoules per year in urban transport. And, should the person travel on foot or by bicycle, then we have already included his/her energy expenditure in the endosomatic account.

Venice is still a pedestrian city, children walk to school or play in its piazzas without fear of being run over. Cars cannot come onto the island, because of the decision to maintain the canals. Ruskin wanted Venice to be a general model for so many medieval cities in Europe which still had the time to maintain their character. However, cities in Europe changed their patterns as early as the nineteenth century because of rationalist planning, and later as a result of the motor car and the bombs of World War II, as well as the Corbuserian rage. Venice is a singular exception in Europe. Rather than a model to be restored and copied, Venice now appears so quaint that large parts of it have become a European historic theme park, where, instead of Mickey Mouse, you may find Vivaldi's musicians in costume among the throngs of tourists.

Scale and Footprints

As conurbations sprawl into metropolitan regions, and as the throughput of energy and materials increases over the region, environmental indicators and indexes may show different trends at municipal and regional levels. This is a familiar phenomenon in Europe, where core areas improve their environmental quality (still with some exceptions, such as Palermo) while exporting pollution and importing environmentally costly materials and energy (Figure 3.1). There are many other cases in the world (Lima, for instance) where trends have been negative at all levels. Such phenomena are paralleled at the global level where metropolitan countries are able to displace environmental loads to the periphery.

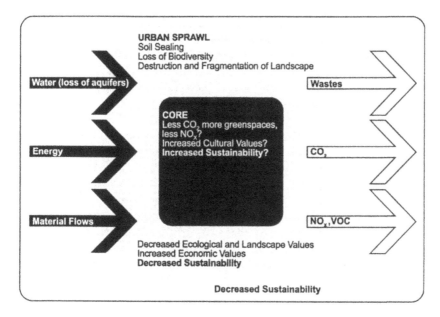

Figure 3.1   Urban (un)sustainability at different scales – European model

Barcelona is a nice city which, in the strictly administrative sense, occupies only 90 square km with a population of 1.5 million. The city is booming in economic and cultural values, the population has decreased in the strict municipal territory over the last ten years allowing a process of renewal and (partial) gentrification in the old city centre. Water consumption has also decreased, green spaces have increased (the new beaches in the Olympic Village, new parks), visits by tourists have increased. Are we then more sustainable, better adapted to increasing scarcities of energy and materials? Who has the power to favour one analytical point of view (the economic, the social, the environmental) at a chosen time-space scale? The conurbation is a half circle with a radius of about 30 km and a population of about four million people. This constitutes a single daily labour market. The improved private and public transport network facilitates travel. In fact, the largest Olympic investment in 1992 was the construction of a circular motorway which facilitates travel by car. This constitutes a familiar pattern of urban sprawl. While some environmental indicators have improved in the city itself, there are increases in the carbon dioxide produced in the conurbation. The agricultural green belt no longer exists. Water consumption is increasing, and Barcelona is contemplating importing water from the Ebro or the Rhone. The area utilizes oil and gas imported from Algeria and elsewhere, hydroelectricity from the Pyrenees, and nuclear power imported from three large stations in southern Catalonia, 160 km to the southwest of Barcelona. In February 2001, a strong local movement independent of political parties halted plans for the construction of another power station in this Ribera d'Ebre region. It was to have been a combined-cycle gas power station of 1,600 MW to be built by Enron. *At which scale(s) should (un)sustainability be assessed*? In contrast to the deterioration of some North-American city centres due to processes of urban sprawl, in Barcelona (as in many other European cities) urban sprawl has been compatible with increasing the economic and cultural values of the core of the conurbation. Tourism certainly helps. What are the main environmental conflicts? At which geographical scale should they be apprehended? Should we travel to the nuclear landscape of southern Catalonia, or should we go to Algeria and Morocco to see the gas pipeline? Should we trace the route of the CO_2 emissions from the Barcelona conurbation as they sink into the oceans or stay temporarily in the atmosphere, or should we travel around the outlying quarters of the conurbation and listen to complaints about noise from the motorways, against the threats of garbage incineration?

Energy and Evolution

In the 1880s, the views on biological evolution and on thermodynamics, which seemed to point in two opposite directions (evolutionary improvement or at least increasing complexity, and thermodynamic entropy) coalesced in Boltzmann's famous dictum, *the struggle for life is a struggle for available energy*. Lotka examined this in his book of 1925 on the physics of biology. Moving from biology into human affairs in some incidental passages, he asserted that Boltzmann's idea could be applied to nations which would gain a competitive advantage through the use of more energy. However, on second thoughts he also wrote that more efficient use of energy could also represent a competitive advantage. The study of energy (and materials) flows, taking into account the qualities of the different energy inputs, is indeed relevant for the study of human history, both rural and urban. Can one say that the increasing importance of a city is due to increasing net energy flows into the city? If both things happen at the same time, which is cause and which is effect?

We observe how cities and city centres concentrate energy flows. Such energy concentrations are a consequence, and not a cause, of the growth of cities, and depend on the affluence of their populations, transport systems, etc. Cities do not grow and 'outcompete' other cities because they have more energy available. Cities grow in size and political power, and therefore they are able to absorb more energy. And if they are not able to do so, they certainly cannot grow. The analysis of the social and economic causes of growth or failure to achieve growth must be combined with a physical analysis of energy and material inputs, and also the analysis of polluting emissions, in order to understand the social metabolism of cities.

H.T. Odum's interpretation of Lotka in terms of a so-called 'maximum power principle' (a principle of evolution) is of doubtful significance for the history of nations and cities or for the prescriptive analysis of urban ecology. If the throughput of energy in a given system (a nation, a city) is greater than in another system, are we going to say that the first system (nation, city) is better adapted? Or is it badly adapted? Is New York better than Calcutta or vice versa from an evolutionary viewpoint? We know that humans are able to use widely differing amounts of exosomatic energy, and therefore human ecology is a history of intra-human conflict. Can this be rephrased in terms of evolutionary adaptability and advancement? Is the information created by such energy throughput, able to compensate the extra expenditure of energy, thus reinforcing the system? Are we dealing with metaphors or with historical explanations? Does it matter what the content of the information is? Is the information contained in bio-diversity similar in quality to the information produced in cities, in its significance for ecosystem functions and complexity? What we can assert is that if a city grows today through cultural or technological competitive innovations, it will probably use more energy and materials. The same would occur if it grew through naked political power. Things were different in the distant past; technologies of energy and materials consumption were different in different places – this is clear in the ecology of historic Edo in Japan.

Urban 'Environmental Justice'

There is no spontaneous evolutionary trend linking ecological sustainability to the growth of cities; rather we can state the opposite. Nevertheless, social movements contesting some of the 'externalities' produced in cities which are not shifted elsewhere might help in the movement towards sustainability. The next section will offer some examples from India. However, some introductory remarks are needed on the Environmental Justice movement in the United States. In this country, we find a number of well-known popular movements under the heading of 'environmental justice' concerned with urban pollution issues (though this is not their exclusive concern, since they are also active in rural contexts). In 1987, the United Church of Christ Commission for Racial Justice published a study on the racial and socio-economic characteristics of communities with hazardous waste sites. Subsequent studies were said to confirm that African Americans, American Indians, Asian Americans, and Latinos were more likely than other groups to find themselves in proximity to hazardous waste facilities. Under the banner of fighting 'environmental racism', low-income groups, members of the working class, and minority groups set up a movement for environmental justice, which linked environmental issues to racial and gender inequality and to poverty (Bullard, 1993).

Many cases of local environmental activism in the United States sponsored by 'citizen-workers groups' (Gould et al., 1996) fall outside the organized Environmental Justice movement. Some have centuries-old roots in the many struggles for health and safety in mines and factories, perhaps in protests against pesticides in Southern cotton fields, and certainly in the struggle against toxic waste at Love Canal in upstate New York. This protest was led by Lois Gibbs who also led a nation-wide 'toxic-conflict' movement showing that poor communities would no longer tolerate being considered the dumping grounds for toxic waste (Gottlieb, 1993; Hofrichter, 1993). The 'official' Environmental Justice movement includes celebrated episodes of collective action against incinerators (due to the uncertain risk of dioxins) led by women. Cerrell Associates published a study in 1984 in California on the political difficulties facing the sitting of waste-to-energy conversion plants (such as incinerators of urban domestic waste), recommending areas of low environmental awareness and low capacity for mobilizing social opposition resources. There were surprises when opposition arose in unexpected areas, such as the movement led by Concerned Citizens of South Central Los Angeles in 1985. In the 1980s, other environmental conflicts gave rise to groups such as People for Community Recovery in South Chicago (Altgeld Gardens), led by Hazel Johnson, and the West Harlem Environmental Action (WHEACT) in New York led by Vernice Miller. The movement for Environmental Justice was successful in getting President Clinton to enact an Executive Order (11 February 1994) under which all federal agencies must flag and address any disproportionately high and adverse health or environmental effects of their policies and activities.

In many Third World cities we find conflicts regarding water distribution (Swyngedouw, 1997). In general many urban grassroots movements (Castells, 1983) can be interpreted as ecological distribution conflicts – meaning conflicts regarding a lack of equity in access to natural resources and in sustaining the burdens of pollution.

In many cities of the Third World, there is simultaneously growth of the city in the form of urban sprawl ('gated communities' with two cars per family), and 'peripherization' (a contrast suggested in conversation by the Brazilian authors Heloisa Costa and Roberto Monte-Mor). Peripherization takes the form of *favelas* or similar settlements which sometimes intrude into the interstices of the conurbations (internal green spaces and water basins, run-down central business districts) but quite often occupy fresh peripheral spaces. In Mexico City, for instance, urban sprawl takes places in Interlomas, peripherization in Chalco. The concept of periphery is not so much geographical as it is social and ecological. Urban sprawl can easily be compared to peripherization by means of economic and physical indicators such as income per capita, soil sealing (square metres per person), energy spent per person/year in urban transport, water consumption per person/day. In North-American sprawling cities, income per capita is on average larger in the suburbs than in the centre. But in the poor peripheries of many Third World cities (as also in Paris or Milan), income per capita is much lower than the urban average.

Today, the banner of 'Environmental Justice' (against so-called environmental racism) is also used in South Africa (McDonald, 2002) both in urban and rural situations. For instance, in the famous townships of Johannesburg (Alexandra or Soweto – i.e. south-west township), which house millions of people, a new social movement has asked for a 'free lifeline' of one kwh and 50 litres of water per person/day (to be seen as components of a 'basic income' in kind). In the sprawling white suburbs, the average consumption of electricity and water is ten times as much. Actually, in South Africa, the complaints against cuts in electricity and water services to the poor who cannot afford to pay the new rates established on the principle of 'full cost recovery' have given rise to a vigorous urban movement (as in Argentina and Bolivia) which questions the economic and energy model of the South African economy. They call this model the 'energy and mineral complex' and claim, with reason, that it is heavily subsidised. Furthermore, new metal smelters for exports are being planned. Thus, a livelihood struggle in urban peripheries motivated by neo-liberal tariff policies regarding municipal services questions the whole structure of water and electricity tariffs as well as the country's economic structure (Bond, 2002).

Pollution Conflict in India and Brimblecombe's Hypothesis

There is no strong movement against cars in most cities in the world. The environmental chemist and historian Peter Brimblecombe has argued that sulphur dioxide emissions usually provoke social reactions because they come from 'visible' single-point sources (coal power stations, smelters), while other forms of air pollution (NO_x and VOCs from cars, precursors of tropospheric ozone) are more dispersed and thus they tend to be more peaceably accepted (Brimblecombe and Pfister, 1990). Brimblecombe's hypothesis is particularly helpful in explaining movements against sulphur dioxide. Does this hypothesis also explain why nowhere has popular spontaneous environmentalism against cars come into being, even in the polluted cities of the South (including China) where most people have no cars? Is this a missed opportunity of environmentalism for the poor? Is this situation changing with the perception of the increasing incidence of infantile asthma in cities, and with the (successful) movements against leaded gasoline? Have we looked close enough?

Why is the reaction against 'London smog' usually stronger than against 'Los Angeles smog'? One answer is that London smog, largely sulphur dioxide, usually arises from easily identifiable sources. Hence for instance the 'chimney wars' in nineteenth-century Germany. Los Angeles smog is largely produced by the cars used throughout the city and so it is diffused.

In India, the colonial authorities enacted regulations in Bombay and Calcutta as early as the 1860s to curb air pollution. The problem was worse in Calcutta than in Bombay because of lack of wind during a good part of the year. Starting with the availability of Raniganj coal, Calcutta had witnessed a sudden change in its atmosphere. Anderson (1996) applies Brimblecombe's hypothesis to Calcutta. It was not so much that the aggregate levels of haze increased (such haze being due to the widespread burning of wood and dung in poor households across the city) but rather that there were now identifiable sources of black smoke from the industrial chimneys of the jute mills and from the ocean steamships. Opposition to these visible sources of pollution explains the reason for the new legislation promoted by the colonial powers and the general support it received. Nevertheless, such general support against industrial air pollution cannot be taken for granted. An environmental improvement, if achieved at the cost of decreasing economic distribution, might be opposed by the poor, as shown in Visvanathan's account (1999) of the conflict in Delhi.

Workers were faced with industrial shut-downs or displacement of industries outside Delhi limits as a result of Supreme Court decisions, especially under the 'green' judge Kuldip Singh, beginning in 1985 with the petition filed by the advocate M.C. Mehta against tanneries polluting the Ganga river. Foundries, fertilizer factories, steel mills, paper and pulp factories, and even textile mills were hit by the active role of the Court whose decisions were directed at visible industrial installations more than at diffuse sources of pollution. Compensation to the displaced labour force in Delhi was ordered, but tens of thousands of workers were not listed in the rolls because they were off-the-books, subcontracted workers.

A junior textile employee at Swatantra Bharat Mills complained about the displacement of this industry outside the so-called National Capital Region (NCR):

> Is this world the divide is between the rich and the poor? And it is the poor who have to die because they are cheaper! We will have to shift to Tonk (the new site) for the law is of the rich ... The management is powerful, the government is of the rich. This is an attempt to throw the poor out of the city. *Pollution in the city is vehicular, not industrial.* Does the government think about how a poor man will feed his wife and child? ... These wise legal thinkers Kuldip Singh and Saghir Ahmad have brought people to ruin ... What was the need of

leaving the NCR and going to Tonk, where there is nothing at the moment. With one stroke of the pen he wrote away the lives of thousands of people in difficult times (Vivanathan, 1999, p. 17).

Diffuse pollution due to traffic became now more visible than point-source pollution in the eyes of this textile employee and other workers like him in Delhi, contrary to Brimblecombe's hypothesis! The debate on asthma became more relevant politically than that regarding sulphur dioxide or water pollution! Figures from a combined pollution index show that in Delhi over 75 per cent of air pollution is vehicular (from private and public transport, with over three million vehicles including two-wheelers), 12 per cent domestic, 10 per cent industrial (of which two thermal power stations account for the major share) (Visvanathan, 1999). While official actions were directed at visible industrial installations, vehicular air pollution acquired a new social visibility in Delhi fuelled by the controversy on industrial dislocation and by a strong campaign from the Centre for Science and Environment led by Anil Agarwal.

Conclusion

Urbanization increases around the world because of a productivity increase in agriculture coupled with low income-elasticity of demand for agricultural produce as a whole. Thus agriculture expels the active population. The ecological critique is that increases in agricultural productivity (which today depend on increasing inputs into agriculture and on the externalization of environmental costs) are not well measured because they do not take into account the decreased energy-efficiency of modern agriculture, or the genetic erosion that takes place, along with the effluents produced. So, both the city and the countryside today tend to drive environmental problems to higher spatial and longer temporal scales. But, while it would be technically possible to return to a pattern of 'organic' agriculture, large prosperous cities are irremediably based on fossil fuels and on the externalization of environmental costs. Co-evolution, as used by Richard Norgaard in ecological economics, denotes a process in which human culture evolves, agriculture is invented, new varieties of plants are selected, new agrarian systems develop, all in a context of sustainability and (perhaps) increased complexity. There are no similar examples of technological change in cities on which one could construct a theory of 'sustainable' endogenous technical change. There is no spontaneous internal trend towards the use of sustainable forms of energy, for instance, or towards decreased production of material residues, because the internal complaints against 'externalities' in cities are often displaced elsewhere by changes in scale.

Do cities produce anything of commensurable or comparable value in return for the energy and materials they import, and for the residues they excrete? What are the internal environmental conflicts in cities, and are they sometimes successfully pushed outwards to larger geographical scales? These were the departure points for this article. Cities are not environmentally sustainable by definition; their territory is too densely populated with humans to be self-supporting. A world where urbanization is rapidly increasing, and moreover where urbanization is characterized by urban sprawl, becomes an ever more unsustainable world. Indicators of urban 'unsustainability' are also indicators of social conflict at different scales. However, at times, environmental decline is not socially visible. One may well ask in many Third World cities, why are there no movements by poor pedestrians and cyclists against private automobiles, not only because of the pollution they produce but also because of their disproportionate use of urban space? This in cities where most people are poor and have no cars, nor can expect to have cars in the short term. While the use of the bicycle is a 'post-materialist' luxury in rich cities, perhaps a Sunday pleasure for car-owning families, or a convenient and healthy means of transport for short distances in well-regulated European cities, everyday cycling to work in cities in India among the fumes and hazards of buses and private cars is the risky daily obligation of many people who in all likelihood cannot afford the small fee for public transport.

In a different cultural and economic context from that of India, in the United States, other urban ecological conflicts are considered under the heading of 'Environmental Justice'. Do such local conflicts in the US regarding the sitting of garbage incinerators or toxic waste dumps belong to a different system than the complaints against the foreseen location of nuclear waste in Yucca Mountain, Nevada shipped there from nuclear power stations that produce electricity for cities? Do the complaints by the Ogoni and the Ijaw in the Niger Delta against oil extraction belong to the same system as the cities in rich countries where the oil exported by Shell fuels cars, and indeed where Shell has its headquarters? When the carbon dioxide produced by urban sprawl in rich cities occupies world-wide carbon sinks and reservoirs, are there complaints? Where are the actors in urban environmental conflicts actually located? What are the true limits of the city? It would seem that the more prosperous a city, the more successful it is in solving internal environmental conflicts, and also in displacing environmental loads to larger geographical scales.

Note

1   My gratitude to two persons who gave me the stimulus to start writing about urban planning, Marta Giralt and Luigi Fusco Girard.

References

Anderson, M.R. (1996), 'The Conquest of Smoke: Legislation and Pollution in Colonial Calcutta', in D. Arnold and R. Guha (eds), *Nature, Culture and Imperialism. Essays on the Environmental History of South Asia*, Oxford University Press, Delhi, pp. 293-335.

Bettini V. (1998), *Elementos de ecologia urbana*, Trotta, Madrid [original edition: *Elementi di ecologia urbana*, Einaudi, Turin, 1996].

Bond, P. (2002), *Unsustainable South Africa*, Merlin Press, London.

Boyden, S., Millar, S., Newcombe, K. and O'Neill, B. (1981), *The Ecology of a City and Its People. The Case of Hong Kong*, Australian National University, Canberra.

Brimblecombe, P. and Pfister, C. (1990), *The Silent Countdown. Essays in European Environmental History*, Springer, Berlin.

Bullard, R. (1993), *Confronting Environmental Racism. Voices from the Grassroots*, South End Press, Boston.

Castells, M. (1983), *The City and the Grassroots*, University of California Press, Berkeley.

European Environment Agency (2002), *Environmental Signals 2002*, Copenhagen.

Gottlieb, R. (1993), *Forcing the Spring: The Transformation of the American Environmental Movement*, Island Press, Washington.

Gould, K.A., Schnaiberg, A. and Weinberg, A. (1996), *Local Environmental Struggles. Citizen Activism in the Treadmill of Production*, Cambridge University Press, New York.

Hall, P. (1998), *Cities in Civilization. Culture, Innovation, and Urban Order*, Weidenfeld and Nicholson, London.

Hofrichter, R. (ed.) (1993), *Toxic Struggles. The Theory and Practice of Environmental Justice*, foreword by Lois Gibbs, New Society Publishers, Philadelphia.

Indian People's Tribunal on Environment and Human Rights (2001), *An Enquiry into the Bandra Worli Sea Link Project*, Mumbai, July, (http://www.indiarights.org).

McDonald, D. (ed.) (2002), *Environmental Justice in South Africa*, Oxford University Press, Cape Town.

McNeill, J.R. (2000), *Something New under the Sun. An Environmental History of the Twentieth-Century World*, Norton, New York.

Mumford, L. (1956), 'The Natural History of Urbanization', in W.L. Thomas et al (eds), *Man's Role in Changing the Face of the Earth*, University of Chicago Press, Chicago, pp. 382-98.

Mumford, L. and Geddes, P. (1995), *The Correspondence*, edited and introduced by F.G. Novack Jr., Routledge, London and New York.

Rees, W. and Wackernagel, M. (1994), 'Ecological Footprints and Appropriated Carrying Capacity', in A.-M. Jansson, M. Hammer, C. Folke and R. Costanza (eds), *Investing in Natural Capital: The Ecological Economics Approach to Sustainability*, Island Press, Washington.

Swyngedouw, E. (1997), 'Power, Nature and the City: The Conquest of Water and the Political Ecology of Urbanization in Guayaquil, Ecuador', *Environment and Planning A*, vol. 29, pp. 311-32.

Visvanathan, Shiv (1997), *A Carnival for Science*, Oxford University Press, Delhi.

Visvanathan, Shiv (1999), unpublished paper on environmental pollution in Delhi, Carnegie Council Project on Environmental Values, New York.

Chapter 4

The Role of Intrinsic Values for Naturalization of the City

J. Baird Callicott

Introduction

Central to environmental philosophy has the been the problem of intrinsic value in nature. Immanual Kant grounded the intrinsic value of human beings in our rationality. 'Biocentric' environmental philosophers have substituted having interests for being rational as the intrinsic value-conferring property, thus providing intrinsic value for all organisms. This theory of intrinsic value in nature is theoretically problematic, because a fundamental assumption of modern Western philosophy is that all value is subjective, not objective. It is practically problematic, because it provides intrinsic value only for living organisms, not for the things environmentalists care most about – biodiversity, air, water, and soil. An alternative theory treats 'value' as a verb, and 'intrinsic' as an adverb, such that nature is intrinsically valuable. Why is it? Because nature is represented in ecology as a community – the 'biotic community' – to which we human beings belong, and we are evolved to value our communities intrinsically. But the city is an even more venerable and unequivocal human community. Therefore it too is, by parity of reasoning, intrinsically valuable. How then do we reconcile the intrinsic value of nature with the intrinsic value of the city? We try to integrate nature into the city and limit the city's incursion into nature.

What Is Environmental Philosophy?

Environmental philosophy has been less an 'applied' subdiscipline of philosophy than some of the other applied subdisciplines with which it is often lumped – biomedical ethics, business ethics, and engineering ethics, for example. Environmental philosophy has been more involved with reconstructing ethical theory than with applying standard, off-the-rack ethical theories to real-world environmental problems. In large part that is because standard ethical theory has been so resolutely – even militantly – anthropocentric that it seemed inadequate to deal with environmental problems. In scope and magnitude, contemporary human transformation of the environment is unprecedented.

We now recognize that the human transformation of nature has been going on for a long time. Two thousand five hundred years ago, even Plato, who was no environmentalist, deduced the anthropogenic wastage of his native Attica from the size of old roof beams on the acropolis, which could not have been made from the small trees then growing in the hills around Athens, and the existence of shrines that marked springs which no longer flowed. He observed that 'what now remains, compared with what then existed, is like the skeleton of a sick man, all the fat and soft earth having wasted away, and only the bare framework of the land being left'. Plato also hints at the cause – deforestation: 'There are some mountains which now have nothing but food for bees, but they had trees, no very long time ago, and the rafters from those felled there to roof the largest buildings are still sound'. Previously,

> ... there were many lofty trees ... and [the land] produced boundless pasturage for flocks. Moreover, it was enriched by the yearly rains from Zeus, which were not lost to it, as now, by flowing from the bare land into the sea; but the soil it had was deep, and therein it received the water, storing it up in the loamy retentive soil; and by drawing off into the hollows from the heights the water that was there absorbed, it provided all the various districts with abundant supplies of spring waters and streams, whereof the shrines which still remain even now, at the spots where the springs formerly existed, are signs which testify that our present description of the past landscape is true (Plato, 1929).

Urban Athens and its thirst for timber to build its temples and navies laid waste its countryside. But two and a half millennia ago, urbanization and dense concentrations of human population were confined to just a few regions of the Earth. Between then and now, cities are planted all over the world, and the human population has doubled many times, presently exceeding six billion. The impact of human activities on nonhuman nature has become almost ubiquitous in scope and unrelenting in intensity, so much so that by the mid-twentieth century, the existence of an environmental crisis was widely acknowledged.

And the contemporary environmental crisis seems morally charged. Presently, urban air and water pollution are a menace to public health – and in most cities, the poor and people of colour suffer from them disproportionately, in comparison with affluent and lighter-skinned people. This raises the moral questions of environmental justice and environmental racism. But the environmental crisis raises even deeper, more difficult and unprecedented ethical questions. For example, the current orgy of human-caused species extinction seems wrong – morally wrong – but not just because the extinction of many species might adversely affect human interests or human rights. A new subdiscipline of philosophy emerged in the 1970s to mount an ethical response to the environmental crisis.

Most first-generation environmental philosophers took the task of environmental ethics to be constructing a nonanthropocentric theory of ethics that would somehow morally enfranchise nonhuman natural entities and nature as a whole – directly, not merely indirectly to the extent that what human beings do in and to nature would affect human interests and human rights. This was the burden of Australian philosopher Richard Routley's 1973 paper, 'Is There a Need for a New, an Environmental Ethic?' presented to the Fifteenth World Congress of Philosophy in Varna, Bulgaria, the first discussion of environmental ethics by an academic philosopher (Sylvan, 2001). A similar task was set by Norwegian philosopher Arne Naess (1973) the same year in his paper, 'The Shallow and the Deep, Long-range Ecology Movements: A Summary'. In the first paper on environmental ethics by an American philosopher, Holmes Rolston III (1975) argued that the central task of environmental philosophy is to develop a 'primary', not a 'secondary', 'ecological ethic'. Animal rights theorist Tom Regan (1982) emphatically reiterated Rolston's understanding of the enterprise – that a proper environmental ethic was 'an ethic *of* the environment', not an 'ethic for the *use* of the environment', which he called a mere 'management ethic'.

Central to the theoretical challenge of developing a direct, a primary ethic *of* the environment is the problem of intrinsic value in nature. In this discussion, I summarize the progress to date that environmental philosophers have made in finding a solution to the theoretical problem of intrinsic value in nature. Then I indicate how one important theoretical construction of intrinsic value can be applied to humanized and built urban environments. In short, the central quest in environmental ethics has been to find a plausible and useful theory of intrinsic value *in nature*; and I think that a similar theory of intrinsic value *in the city* can be adapted from one such account.

Intrinsic Value

Although the early twentieth century English philosopher, G.E. Moore (1903) wrote much about intrinsic value, the modern classical concept of intrinsic value articulated by Immanuel Kant (1959) and the way it functioned in his ethics most influenced the thinking of contemporary environmental philosophers. Central to Kant's ethic is the precept that each person be treated as an end in him- or herself, not merely as a means.

Indeed, the second formulation of his categorical imperative is this: 'Act so that you treat humanity, whether in your own person or that of another, always an end and never as a means only' (Kant, 1959, p. 39). He justifies – or 'grounds', as he puts it – this precept by claiming that each person has intrinsic value. That claim, in turn, is justified by locating in each person an intrinsic value-conferring property, which Kant identified as reason. Thus, rational beings, according to Kant, have intrinsic value, and should therefore be treated as ends in themselves and never as means only.

This Kantian approach to ethics appears at first glance to be unpromising for developing a 'nonanthropocentric' environmental ethic, as Routley, Naess, Rolston, and Regan so unambiguously set forth the task. Why? Because Kant's intrinsic value-conferring property, reason or rationality, had long been regarded as a hallmark of human nature. At the dawn of Western philosophy, Aristotle declared that reason or rationality was the 'differentia' that distinguished 'man', as a species, from the other animals. *Anthropos* is the 'rational animal', according to Aristotle. Thus, Kant's approach to ethics appears to be a brief for anthropocentrism, and to foreclose the possibility of nonanthropocentrism. Indeed, Kant (1959, p. 46) goes out of his way to exclude non-human natural entities and nature as a whole from ethical enfranchisement: 'Beings whose existence does not depend on our will but on nature, if they are not rational beings, have only relative worth as means and are therefore called "things"; on the other hand, rational beings are designated "persons" because their nature indicates that they are ends in themselves, i.e. things which may not be used as a means'. For Kant, human beings are ends; beings whose existence depends on nature are means.

But look again. In the *Foundations of the Metaphysics of Morals*, Kant himself is quite careful to avoid speciesism – analogous to racism and sexism – the unjustified or ungrounded moral entitlement of one's own kind and the exclusion of other kinds. Not being human, but being 'rational' is that in virtue of which a human being has intrinsic value. And Kant consistently holds open the possibility that there may be other-than-human rational beings. He never more specifically identifies who such non-human rational beings may be. Some passages suggest Kant might be thinking of God and the heavenly host; others that he might be thinking of rational beings on other planets that inhabit very different bodies and therefore have very different desires and inclinations than do human beings. In the passage just quoted, he seems to hold open the possibility that there may be non-human rational beings found in terrestrial nature. It is in this orthodox Kantian moral climate that so much ethical significance was recently attached to proving that chimpanzees and gorillas could master rudimentary language skills, and could, via American Sign Language, express themselves creatively (Savage-Rumbaugh et al., 1988). For Descartes (1950) had insisted that the ability to use language creatively

– not merely by rote, as he believed parrots to do – was an indication of rationality.

Proving that chimpanzees and gorillas are minimally rational does undermine anthropocentrism, but only a little. It certainly does not take us very far in the direction of an expansive environmental ethic – however much it may help ethically rehabilitate our primate relatives and spare them the indignities and outrages of the zoo trade and biomedical research. Kant's conceptual distinction between humanity and rationality was, however, also exploited theoretically another way, which proved to be more powerful and transformative. Not all human beings are minimally rational. The so-called 'marginal cases' are not (Regan, 1979). Infants, the severely mentally handicapped, and the abjectly senile are the usual suspects. They are thus in the same boat with all the other '[b]eings whose existence ... depend[s] on nature ... i.e., things which may be used merely as a means', to quote Kant once more. Let us get specific; if we equitably applied Kant's ethical theory, we could justifiably perform the same painful and destructive biomedical experiments on unwanted non-rational infants that we inflict on non-rational nonhuman animals; we could open a hunting season on the severely mentally handicapped; and we could make pet food out of the abjectly senile.

Such abhorrent implications of Kant's moral philosophy provided nonanthropocentric theorists with an opportunity to propose retaining Kant's form of moral argument – which has, after all, been so compelling in Western ethical thought – but revising its specific conceptual contents, so as to include the marginal cases in the class of persons and rescue them from the class of things. The form or ethical architecture that was retained is Kant's close linkage of moral ends, intrinsic value, and a value-conferring property. Thus to be a moral end, and not a means only, you must have intrinsic value, but making rationality the value-conferring property, appears, in light of the 'Argument from Marginal Cases' to be too restrictive. Various alternatives to rationality have been proposed, selected to justify the theorist's personal ethical agenda. Regan (1983), who was content to limit 'moral considerability' to warm, furry animals, proposed being the 'subject of a life' as the intrinsic value-conferring property. Subjects of a life have a sense of self, remember a personal past, entertain hopes and fears about the future – in sum, enjoy a subjective state of being, which can be better or worse from their own point of view. Peter Singer (1977), who wanted to extend 'moral considerability' a bit more generously, proposed sentience, the capacity to experience pleasure and pain, as the intrinsic value-conferring property. That move reached a much wider spectrum of animals – how wide is not completely clear – but clearly left out the entire plant kingdom.

To reach out and touch all living beings with moral considerability, several theorists proposed having 'interests' as a plausible and defensible intrinsic value-conferring property. A living being – a tree, for example – can have interests in the absence of consciousness. This basic idea was variously expressed. A living being has a good of its own, whether or not it is good for anything else. Unlike complexly functioning machines, such as automobiles, whose ends or functions are determined or assigned them by their human designers to serve human ends, living beings have ends, goals, or purposes – *teloi*, in a word – of their own. They are, in the terminology of Paul Taylor (1986), 'teleological centres of life'. In that of Warwick Fox (1990), they are *autopoietic* – self-creating and self-renewing.

The problem, theoretically speaking, with biocentrism – as this modified or expanded Kantian approach to nonanthropocentric environmental ethics has come to be called – is that it seems to stop with individual organisms. At once biocentrism both too broadly *and* too narrowly distributes intrinsic value. As to the former, granting each and every organism moral considerability makes ethical space way too densely crowded, rendering our most routine and vital human actions ethically problematic. Surely, it is perfectly possible to refrain from ill-using our fellow primates as objects of amusement and subjects of medical experimentation, with little human inconvenience. Equally possible – and with only a little more mindfulness, sacrifice, and inconvenience – we might give up eating meat and using other products made from animals, our fellow sentient beings. But we have to eat something, slap mosquitoes and other annoying insects, rid ourselves and our domiciles of vermin, weed our flower gardens – all of which are morally questionable if every living being has intrinsic value and should be treated as an end in itself, not a means only. On the other hand, biocentrism too narrowly distributes intrinsic value in nature because it does not provide moral considerability for what environmentalists most care about. Frankly, environmentalists do not much care about the welfare of each and every shrub, bug, and grub. We care, rather, about preserving *species* of organisms, *populations* within species, *genes* within populations – in a word we care about preserving biodiversity. We care about preserving communities of organisms and ecosystems. We also care about *air* and *water* quality, *soil* stability, and the integrity of Earth's stratospheric *ozone membrane*. None of these things appear to have interests, goods of their own, ends, purposes, or goals, and thus none has intrinsic value, on this account.

Solutions to both biocentric distribution problems have been proposed. A solution to the too-broad distribution problem is to distribute intrinsic value unequally or differentially (Rolston, 1988). Grant all organisms base-line or minimal intrinsic value. Thus, when our own interests are not at stake, we should leave them alone to pursue their own ends, to realize their own *teloi*, each in its own way. Additional intrinsic value is distributed to sentient organisms, yet more to subject-of-a-life organisms, and more still to rational organisms. Thus, because we human beings, as rational, sentient subjects of a life, have the most intrinsic value, we are entitled to defend it and cater to it by doing bad things to other organisms with less intrinsic value – but only if we conscientiously deem it to be necessary. That seems plausible enough, although rather conventional, leaving us human beings at the top of the moral pyramid where we have always been. The difference is that in traditional Western ethics the pyramid was low and squat. Nonhuman organisms were mere things, with no intrinsic value at all. They were thus available for any human use at all, however fatuous. Differential biocentrism extends the moral pyramid's height and mass to much greater proportions, albeit leaving human beings at the pinnacle.

A solution to biocentrism's too-narrow distribution problem is less plausible. Lawrence Johnson (1991) has seized upon somewhat dated minority views in evolutionary biology and ecology to argue that species and ecosystems have interests. Some biologists have argued that species are not collections of organisms capable of interbreeding, but individuals that are protracted in space and time (Ghiselin, 1974; Hull, 1976). If so, we may convince ourselves they have interests, and therefore intrinsic value, and therefore moral considerability. And there is a long, albeit fading, tradition in ecology that conceives ecosystems to be superorganisms to which individual organisms are related as cells and species as organs (McIntosh, 1985). And if so, again, we may believe they have interests, and therefore intrinsic value, and therefore moral considerability. But these are big ifs. Rolston (1988) takes a different approach. He points out that the most fundamental end of most organisms is to realize their genetic potential, to represent their species and to reproduce it. They have a good of their own – *which is their genotype.* Thus does Rolston try to convince us that species per se may plausibly be said to have intrinsic value. For organisms to flourish, even to live at all, they must live in an ecological context or habitat. Thus does Rolston try to justify finding intrinsic value in biotic communities and ecosystems.

This mainstream line of argument in environmental ethics, which begins with a Kantian superstructure, works through animal liberation, and terminates in biocentrism, assumes that intrinsic value supervenes or piggybacks on some objective property. Thus intrinsic value, albeit supervenient, is itself an objective property in nature. Indeed, the adjective 'intrinsic' seems logically to require that intrinsic value, if it exists at all, exist as an objective property. It is intrinsic to the being that has it. Kant (1959, p. 46) himself appears to think that intrinsic value is something objective: 'Such beings [rational beings] are not merely subjective ends whose existence as a result of our action has a worth for us, but are objective ends, i.e., beings whose existence in itself is an end'. But the idea that value – or worth – of any kind can be objective seems to fly in the face of a shibboleth of modern Western philosophy: the division of the world into the *res extensa* and the *res cogito,* the subjective and objective domains, respectively, by Descartes (1950) and the ancillary distinction drawn by Hume (1960) between fact and value. All value is, from the most fundamental modern point of view, subjective.

Nevertheless, some nonanthropocentric environmental philosophers have argued that a robust account of intrinsic value in nature can be provided even within the severe constraints of the allied object-subject/fact-value distinctions. From a modern point of view, 'value' is first and foremost a verb. If so, 'instrumental' and 'intrinsic' may be regarded as adverbs, not adjectives. Thus one may value (verb transitive) some things instrumental*ly* – our houses, cars, computers, clothes, and such. Similarly, one may value (verb transitive) other things intrinsic*ally* – ourselves, our spouses, children, and other relatives. If we have learned our religion and moral philosophy well, we may intrinsically value all other human beings. Indeed, it is logically possible to value intrinsically anything under the sun – an old worn-out shoe, for example. But most of us value things intrinsically when we perceive them to be part of a community to which we also belong, because we evolved to do so (Darwin, 1871). 'Perceive' here is the key word, for perception can be trained and redirected. Much of the suasive environmental literature aims to train and redirect our perception of nature such that we see it as the wider community in which all our other communities are embedded. Aldo Leopold's *A Sand County Almanac* is an outstanding example. In the Foreword, Leopold (1949, p. viii) writes, 'We abuse land because we regard it as a commodity belonging to us. When we see land as a community to which we belong, we may begin to use it with love and respect'. Most of the remainder of the book is devoted to persuading us that ecology 'enlarges the boundaries of the community to include soils, waters, plants, and animals, or collectively the land' (Leopold, 1949, p. 204). When that happens, people will have 'love, respect, and admiration for land, and a high regard for its value ... [and b]y value I mean something far broader than mere economic value; I mean value in the philosophical sense' – intrinsic value, in other words (Leopold, 1949, p. 223). According to Leopold (1949, p. 223), 'a land ethic changes the role of Homo sapiens from conqueror of the land community to plain member and citizen of it. It implies respect for his fellow-members and also for the community as such'.

Of all the accounts of intrinsic value in nature this adverbial-subjectivist-communitarian account is the most transferable to the humanized urban environment. Indeed, this account of intrinsic value in nature reaches the natural environment via an analogy with the social environment – so it is more unequivocally applicable to the humanized urban environment than to the other-than-human natural environment. Let me explain more fully.

First, let me reiterate what 'intrinsic value' means in context of this adverbial-subjectivist-communitarian account. Practically by definition, the adjective 'intrinsic' entails that the character or property it modifies exists objectively in the entity to which it is attributed. Indeed, often the adjective 'intrinsic' means that the character or property it modifies is the very essence of the entity to which it is attributed. For example, transporting oxygen to tissues in organisms is intrinsic to haemoglobin; competition is intrinsic to sport; volatility is intrinsic to the gaseous state of matter. In environmental philosophy, however, 'intrinsic value' has also been consistently used as the antonym of 'instrumental value'. What value remains – if any does – after all something's instrumental value has been accounted for is its intrinsic value. Thus to value something intrinsically – as we shift from the adjectival to the adverbial form – is to value something for itself, as an end-in-itself (to reinvoke the Kantian mode of expression), not merely as a means to our own ends, not merely as an instrument. There is no objective property in entities to which the noun 'value' corresponds. Rather we subjects value objects in one or both of at least two ways – instrumentally or intrinsically.

What is it about some things, and not others, that moves us to value them intrinsically? Almost everyone values him or herself intrinsically. We might also wish to be productive members of society, useful to others, but when we are no longer of instrumental value to anyone, most of us consider our lives to be intrinsically valuable, if to no one else, at least to ourselves. Most of us also intrinsically value our closest relatives, especially our children. Children and other family members form the most primitive, venerable, and intimate societies to which each of us belongs. According to Charles Darwin (1871), we evolved to love and cherish members of our immediate and extended families and to value them intrinsically, in order that this most fundamental of human societies would be strongly united. For only in the midst of a well integrated social unit could human beings survive, flourish, successfully reproduce, and rear their offspring to sexual maturity.

Darwin (1871) also observed that as time went on extended families or clans merged to form larger more complex social units – tribes, nations, republics, and now, finally, meta-societies or communities for which we scarcely have names. What do we call the EC? – a 'meta-state', a 'confederacy'? We do have a name for the internet-cemented world community. We call it the 'global village'. With each stage in social development or evolution, Darwin traced a corresponding development or evolution of ethics. 'As man advances in civilization', Darwin (1871, pp. 100-1) wrote, 'as small tribes are united into larger communities, the simplest reason would tell each individual that he ought to extend his social instincts and sympathies to all the members of the same nation, though personally unknown to him. This point being once reached there is only an artificial barrier to prevent his sympathies being extended to the men of all nations and races'. The global-village stage of social-ethical evolution was only dimly envisionable to Darwin. But it is here, today at the dawn of the third millennium. The name of the corresponding ethic is 'universal human rights'. The emergence of the human-rights ethic for the global village was formalized by the General Assembly of the United Nations in 1948 when it adopted the Universal Declaration of Human Rights (Brownlie, 1981).

To create his justifiably famous 'land ethic', Aldo Leopold borrowed Darwin's account of the parallel evolution of society or community and added a new ecological element or developmental stage, that was more a matter of intellectual recognition than evolutionary accretion. Beginning early in the twentieth century, ecologists characterized the manner in which plants and animals were inter-dependent and united by way of a social metaphor (Elton, 1927). Plants and animals lived together in 'biotic communities'. Human beings were also, from an evolutionary-ecological point of view, 'plain members and citizens' of these biotic communities. Just as the universal-human-rights ethic crystallized with the emergence of a global village in human social evolution, so Leopold envisioned a land ethic to emerge with the broad recognition that we human beings are members of a biotic community, no less than we are members of a nested hierarchy of human communities. That we intrinsically value the biotic communities to which we belong and their members severally is central to the land ethic. In Leopold's words, once more: 'It is inconceivable to me that an ethical relation to land can exist without love, respect, and admiration for land, and a high regard for its value. By value, I of course mean something far broader than mere economic value; I mean value in the philosophical sense' or intrinsic value, as it is now called in academic environmental philosophy.

Intrinsic Value of the City

The biotic community is, however, only a metaphorical community; and the land ethic only an ethic by analogy. Human communities are paradigmatic communities, communities proper. If the reason we come to intrinsically value nature is because, through the lens of ecology, we perceive it to be a 'community' to which we belong – the metaphorical biotic community – then we have exactly the same reason to intrinsically value the human communities to which we belong. There are two such communities that almost all of us value intrinsically, without question. One is the family, the other the country or nation state. I remember going to a compulsory orientation meeting for new faculty members when I took my present job at the University of North Texas. Each of us was asked to introduce ourselves to the others and indicate what was important to us. Almost everyone said that most important was his or her family. Family per se was intrinsically valued. The other community which is intrinsically valued by almost all its members is the nation state or country. The moral sentiment for country is so palpable, widely experienced, and specific that it has a name of its own, 'patriotism'. The most memorable and oft-quoted thing that any twentieth-century American President ever said in his inaugural address was 'Ask not what your country can do for you, but what you can do for your country'. Feelings for family and country are so intense and special that they are sometimes blended together into a potent, and potentially dangerous amalgam. For Russians, Russia is the beloved 'motherland', for Germans, Germany is the 'fatherland'.

Between the family and the country lie many intermediate communities to which each of us also belongs. Among the oldest, and now among the most problematic, is the tribe or ethnic group. The United States is said to be a melting pot and many of its citizens are in fact multi-ethnic. The most famous is golfer Tiger Woods, whose mother is Asian and whose father claims African, European, and American-Indian ancestry. But most Americans today still identify themselves ethnically, with a hyphen – Italian-Americans, Irish-Americans, Japanese-Americans. While for most Americans, the national community transcends the ethnic in importance, for many people in southern and eastern Europe, the ethnic community seems to be, if not the most intrinsically valued, then second only to family. We could go on identifying the intrinsically valued communities lying between the family and the country, but let us go straight to the issue at hand. Prominent among those intermediate communities is the city. Does the city have intrinsic value? Yes, to the extent that its citizens value it intrinsically.

Armed with the philosophical analysis of intrinsic value developed here, that question was easy to answer. More difficult is another question. How do we reconcile the intrinsic value of the city with the intrinsic value of nature? For me, that question may be easier to answer than it is for others. A large part of the value I find in cities is the way they integrate or incorporate nature into themselves. The most moving memories I have of my native city, Memphis, Tennessee, are not her buildings – which are for the most part modest and nondescript – but her trees. Memphis is blessed with towering oaks, some so thick at the base that two grown men cannot encircle them with their arms. In my municipal reverie, I am seated on an iron chair beside an iron table on a mossy brick patio behind a graceful old Southern home, beneath an aged oak, whose roots have up-lifted the patio bricks near its trunk. Half-hidden among the garden plants are a shallow marble bird bath and a somewhat weathered and neglected piece of outdoor sculpture. I smell the sweet fragrance of a nearby gardenia and listen to the air-filling chorus of cicadas and the ever-new solitary song of a mockingbird, on a warm summer evening. I watch squirrels play chase in the security of their oaken aeries. The place I sit is in the heart of the old quarter of the city – revealingly called, 'the garden district' – but it is permeated and physically dominated by the natural environment. The biotic community and the municipal community coexist in what I experience as a perfect harmony of culture and nature.

My most painful memory of my native city is an experience I had in the early 1970s, after the advent of the environmental crisis, but before regulatory measures were enacted to remedy it. Memphis lies on the café-latté-coloured Mississippi River, which by then had become an open sewer. Tears welled in my eyes as I watched a black plume of municipal sewage and industrial waste run into the Mississippi from a grossly polluted tributary that skirted the city, while bits of some unknown white froth floated downstream from Cincinnati or St. Louis. As ecological city planner, Ian McHarg once remarked, we turn our municipal backsides, especially we Americans, to the rivers that flow past our cities (McHarg, 1969). A notable exception is San Antonio, Texas, the Venice of the American southwest. The San Antonio River runs through the centre of the city and has been lined with heavy hewn stones – and along its banks are hotels, restaurants, saloons, cafés, and shops. Compared with the mighty Mississippi, the San Antonio River is puny and runs below the level of the city streets like a watery subway system that is open to the sun and air. To reach the River Walk one descends stone stairways down about four meters from the street level. And as one does, it is as if one has walked through the looking glass and entered another, more intimate, more magical world. San Antonio is truly a beautiful city, and her river is no small part of that beauty, a beauty that wells up over the banks of the river itself.

It is one thing to bring nature into the city in perfect harmony. Just as important is to make sure that the city fits harmoniously into the biotic community in which it is embedded. We have made progress on this front. The Mississippi River is not as badly polluted by the cities on its banks, and the banks of its tributaries, as it once was. We need to do better than we are doing reducing the air pollution and the solid waste stream generated by cities. In the United States, one of the worst environmental offences of cities is urban sprawl. I love the way some European cities are compactly built and have hard edges, clear boundaries between the city and the countryside. In the US cities typically are shaped like this. The centre or arrondissement surrounding the centre is empty and desolate, as if it had been destroyed by aereal bombardment and never rebuilt. Then there is a dense urban core dominated by commercial and industrial buildings and low-income housing. Next comes the older, finer part of the city, consisting of expensive town houses and large single-family homes on small city lots. That is followed by ring after ring of suburbs, the older and more run-down surrounded by the newer, bigger, and better – on and on up to a radius of 100 kilometres in the cases of such cities as Atlanta, Houston, Dallas, and Chicago. The urban sprawl often gobbles up smaller, previously isolated towns. Farther from the city centre, the suburban pattern is erratic and the bedroom communities are often planted in the middle of farm and ranch lands, creating an incongruous mix.

While still prevailing, this trend is showing some signs in the US of giving way to another. Mainly because people are tired of the dullness of suburban living, and fed up with automobile commuting to everything – and the traffic jams that make commuting uncertain and aggravating – there is a revival of urbanism in America. Old warehouses in the city centre are being converted to tiny loft apartments; new townhouses and condos are going up on vacant blocks in the empty central spaces, along with pedestrian-scaled shopping, dining, and entertainment. While this shift may revitalize and beautify American cities, it will not, unfortunately, directly address the negative aesthetic and environmental consequences of ragged municipal edges. (Perhaps I should just move to Europe and forget it.)

I began with Plato and I will end with him. Plato loved the city, especially Athens. He valued it intrinsically. Almost all his dialogues are set in Athens and both his greatest work, *The Republic*, and his longest, *The Laws*, are focused on what in his day was the ultimate human polity. Between Plato's day and our own, meta-urban communities have evolved. In *The Republic*, Plato himself distinguishes war between Greek city-states from war between Greek and barbarian city-states, thereby implicitly anticipating the emergence of a then-unprecedented national community, a country, Greece. The community concept has been extended finally to nature, albeit metaphorically. Because we intrinsically value all the communities of which we are members, some more than others, one task we face is harmonizing such values when we can and reconciling them when we must. In my opinion, a key element in the beauty and liveability of any city is the extent to which it gracefully incorporates the biotic community into itself. And in my opinion as well, the city is a part of the larger biotic community, embedded in it, a corporate member of it. Thus, the city should be a responsible citizen of its biotic community and not spill its pollutants or sprawl its citizens into the surrounding countryside. Like the best and most beautiful European cities, and as ancient Greek wisdom recommended, the city should know its limits and keep to them.

References

Brownlie, I. (1981), *Basic Documents on Human Rights*, 2nd edition, Oxford University Clarendon Press, Oxford.

Darwin, C.R. (1871), *The Descent of Man and Selection in Relation to Sex*, J. Murray, London.

Descartes, R. (1950), *Discourse on Method*, Liberal Arts Press, New York [original edition: *Discours de la méthod*, Michaelem Soly, Paris, 1637].

Elton, C. (1927), *Animal Ecology*, Sidgewick and Jackson, London.

Fox, W. (1990), *Toward a Transpersonal Ecology*, Shambhala Publications, Boston.

Ghiselin, M.T. (1974), 'A Radical Solution to the Species Problem', *Systematic Zoology*, vol. 23, pp. 536-44.

Hull, D. (1976), 'Are Species Really Individuals?', *Systematic Zoology*, vol. 25, pp. 174-91.

Hume, D. (1960), *A Treatise of Human Nature*, Clarendon Press, Oxford [original edition: 1737].

Johnson, L.E. (1991), *A Morally Deep World: An Essay on Moral Significance and Environmental Ethics*, Cambridge University Press, Cambridge.

Kant, I. (1959), *Foundations of the Metaphysics of Morals*, Library of Liberal Arts, New York [original edition: *Grundlegung zur metaphysic der Sitten*, Felix Meiner, Leipzig, 1785].

Leopold, A. (1949), *A Sand County Almanac, and Sketches Here and There*, Oxford University Press, New York.

McHarg, I. (1969), *Design with Nature*, Natural History Press, Garden City.

McIntosh, R.P. (1985), *The Background of Ecology: Concept and Theory*, Cambridge University Press, Cambridge.

Moore, G.E. (1903), *Principia ethica*, Cambridge University Press, Cambridge.

Naess, A. (1973), 'The Shallow and the Deep, Long-range Ecology Movements: A Summary', *Inquiry*, vol. 16, pp. 95-100.

Plato (1929), 'Critias 111C-E', translation into English by R.G. Bury, in T.E. Page (ed.), *Loeb Classical Library: Plato*, William Heinemann Ltd, London, vol. VII, pp. 259-307.

Regan, T. (1979), 'An Examination and Defense of One Argument Concerning Animal Rights', *Inquiry*, vol. 22, pp. 189-219.

Regan, T. (1982), 'The Nature and Possibility of an Environmental Ethic', *Environmental Ethics*, no. 3, pp. 19-34.

Regan, T. (1983), *The Case for Animal Rights*, University of California Press, Berkeley.

Rolston, H. III. (1975), 'Is There an Ecological Ethic?', *Ethics*, no. 85, pp. 93-109.

Rolston, H. III. (1988), *Environmental Ethics: Duties to and Values in the Natural World*, Temple University Press, Philadelphia.

Savage-Rumbaugh, S., Shanker, S.G. and Taylor, T.J. (1998), *Kanzi: The Ape at the Brink of the Human Mind*, Oxford University Press, New York.

Singer, P. (1977), *Animal Liberation: A New Ethics for our Treatment of Animals*, Avon, New York.

Sylvan, R. (2001), 'Is There a Need for a New, an Environmental Ethic?', in M.E. Zimmerman, J.B. Callicott, G. Sessions, K.J. Warren and J. Clark (eds), *Environmental Philosophy*, 3rd edition, Prentice-Hall, Upper Saddle River, pp. 17-25.

Taylor, P.W. (1986), *Respect for Nature: A Theory of Environmental Ethics*, Princeton University Press, Princeton.

Chapter 5

Sustainable Development, the Struggle against Poverty and New Structures of Governance in the Era of Globalization

Stefano Zamagni

Introduction and Motivation

'Can philosophical ethics still offer a way out of the ecological crisis?' –
the German philosopher P. Kampits asked himself in 1978. Until today
environmental ethics, in its various forms (ecological, utilitarian, Rawlsian,
the ethics of rights), has demonstrated, with mixed results, how and why
humanity's relationship with the environment may reasonably be held to be
also a moral problem, a problem that implies the redefinition or extension
of the concepts of duty and responsibility, and an alteration in the very
image that humanity has of itself and of its relationship with nature. While
effective in dismantling the barrier of indifference that humankind has
placed between itself and nature until now, and breaking through the
limitations of a claustrophobic anthropocentric attitude deaf to the
problems of environmental integrity, environmental ethics remains
impotent in the sphere of establishing adequate criteria by which to choose
the priorities for concrete issues.[1] Indeed, if the ethical perspective does not
succeed in affecting the foundations of scientific economic thinking, not
much can be expected of it. It is not hard to see why. For good or ill, for at
least a couple of centuries, it has been economic thought – with its dual
function of representing reality and providing models of intervention to
change that reality – that has directed the choices of the various economic
actors, and guided decision-making in politics.

It must be recognized that the problem of ecology is first and foremost a
problem of public *ethos*, hard to solve without bringing into dispute certain
ways of organizing society without questioning ourselves regarding the
ways we live together and the values held in civil society. In this precise
sense, we should realize at once that economic theory is still quite
inadequate to deal fully with questions such as the environment. At the

heart of this inadequacy lies the formalistic concept, still prevalent in economic discourse, with its claim to be able to solve every conflict and controversy by separating form and content and by seeking laws and institutions that are 'neutral', i.e. that do not presume any adherence to values or cultural assumptions, and are thus acceptable to all actors independently of the historical context in which they operate.

But formalism is not this alone. It is also the idea that a society can find its cohesion and identity in efficient 'rules of the game' concerning the spheres of both income distribution and the formation of collective choices. One of the false necessities to which a certain tradition of thought has accustomed us is to see as alternatives the terms describing independence and belonging, efficiency and justice, self-interest and solidarity. A strengthening of the sense of belonging is seen as a reduction of the subject's independence; progress in efficiency is seen as a threat to justice; improvements in the individual's interest as a weakening of solidarity. These antinomies must be eliminated because they are false. It is remarkable, but not surprising, that it is precisely the subject of sustainable development that today forces the economist to rediscover the centrality of values in his/her scientific work. Work, note well, that is never merely an instrument to help us get to know reality, for if it is true, as I believe it is, that our beliefs concerning human nature contribute to the formation of human nature itself, and if it is likewise true that what we think of ourselves and our possibilities helps to determine what we aspire to become, then our economic theories regarding human behaviour lead to changes in the ways we behave, and hence contribute to a greater or lesser extent to modify reality itself.

In what follows, I shall first examine the way in which economics 'discovers' the environmental question. I shall then summarily trace the recent history of ecology as a problematic subject, starting from the Conference of the United Nations in Stockholm in 1972, up to the Conference in The Hague in November 2000. The aim of this rapid historic reconstruction is to indicate how the lack of a holistic approach to environmental matters explains the systematic alternation of the official positions so far taken, which has certainly not assisted in the development, over the last three decades, of adequate critical consciousness. Finally, I shall try to defend the thesis that the struggle against poverty and for sustainable development are two sides of the same coin. And this implies that any projects and strategies of intervention based on the separation of the issues of poverty and environmental quality are destined to fail. The essay closes with a proposal to set up a World Organization for the Environment, an agency I feel to be necessary to overcome the limitations of unilateral measures as well as the objective difficulties of implementing international treaties.

Economics 'Discovers' the Environment Issue

From its very beginnings as an independent scientific discipline, economics has focused on two central questions: how the social product is formed, and how it is distributed. The most important problems addressed by economics as a science over the last two centuries lead, directly or indirectly, back to these two central themes. The new phase of economic development, regarding the transition from an industrial to a post-industrial society, has led to the gradual emergence of new, more urgent and decisive problems. Among these, the most macroscopically obvious one we face today involves the ecological limitations that impinge on the production process which, until some decades ago, advanced substantially free from constraints. Nature was never actually presented as an absolute limitation although the scarcity of resources was of course a factor influencing the forms and rhythms of development. But the economic system, through its own mechanisms, managed to overcome scarcity (of fertile lands, of certain minerals, etc.), due to the intense flow of technological innovations that loosened the bonds of scarcity by means of increases in productivity. For this reason, if we look back at the industrialization process, we almost have the impression of a dizzy growth towards unlimited plenty, as if nature were not hostile and niggardly as the ancients thought.

The contemporary picture is completely different. Industrial growth involves 'external' effects on the environment. While they could be considered negligible at the beginning of the process (and indeed economists did neglect them almost completely), later developments showed them to be devastating. Some indispensable natural resources such as air and water have been altered to such an extent that we have cause to fear that the equilibrium of the biosphere itself may have been definitively modified by irreversible processes. We only need to think of the greenhouse effect, the holes in the ozone layer, the effects on climate of the disappearance of the rain forests, the modification of the chemical composition of the atmosphere, the fixation of solar energy and the conversion of raw materials. The important services continuously provided by our ecosystems for the normal functioning of natural systems, are today at risk.

It is not merely a question of decreasing returns, as some people insist on thinking. In the absence of more rigorous control of the effects of pollution caused by the general economic system, the human race is at risk of extinction. Starting from the second half of the twentieth century, humanity's capacity for destruction has become a 'biocide' (Vigna, 2001) in the sense that, for the first time, humanity sees itself as able to bend nature to its own ends, that is not just able to control it but to manipulate it. Now is the moment to recognize that an ever-increasing production of goods and services is incompatible (*given* the known productive techniques, the present organization of the economy and the rate of population growth) with the safeguarding of the natural and urban environment. Above all, now is the time to recognize that when humanity modifies the environment too rapidly (for example, by transforming the seas of oil under the Earth's crust into gas discharged into the atmosphere) a situation is created in which the speed of these changes is superior to the speed of the Earth's powers of adaptation to them.

What we should be asking ourselves today is whether the challenge of ecology is directing us not only towards a policy of restructuring our present methods of production, but above all towards a search for new ways of thought for a discipline – economics – that has been extraneous to this problematic field for too long. Indeed, when public awareness of the environmental question grew at the beginning of the 1960s – and the influence of Rachel Carson's *Silent Spring*, published in 1962, will certainly be remembered – economists felt they were able to face the issue by using their own specific ways of thought. However, the more influential subjects involved in the formation of public opinion were not quite up to focusing adequately on this, and hence passed on the idea that economics was synonymous with pollution and the destruction of nature. Economics and ecology were thus seen as alternatives, as opposite poles, despite the fact that the common root of the two words links respectively government (the economy) and knowledge (ecology) of what happens in an *oikos*, i.e. in a 'house', in a territory. Yet, since any form of good management must be based on knowledge, the conflict between the two disciplines should not be possible from a conceptual standpoint.

What are the reasons for misunderstandings of this kind? In my opinion, the most significant one lies in the fact that when the economists believed (starting from the end of the 1960s) that they should become involved in ecological problems, they thought they could make use of the instruments of analysis specifically designed for the branch of their discipline known as public economics, in turn born of the merging of the older welfare economics and the younger theory of social choice. What, economists reasoned, lies at the root of the environmental issue? Beyond the great variety of individual cases, some of the resources involved (land, air, water, animal species, forests) have some basic characteristics in common, regardless of the unit of measurement applied. To be precise, these resources: (1) can be regenerated naturally; (2) are often common property; (3) their over-use can lead to irreversible damage, in the sense of their total depletion; (4) the existing stocks of these resources, and not only their flows, directly influence people's well-being; (5) the impact of economic activities on these resources is often cumulative and can be seen only after a certain period of time; (6) the environmental consequences of economic activities are basically uncertain ('hard' uncertainty in the sense that, as Vercelli, 1994, shows, environmental uncertainty cannot be dealt with by using the tools of the familiar theory of probability).

Now, the handling of the problems in which resources of this kind appear at an analytical level, might be carried out – so economists thought – by starting from the two central notions of public economics: externality and public good. Thus, economists could conclude that the grave environmental damage caused by economic activities was, in the final analysis, to be attributed to typical 'market failure'. This means that, when dealing with environmental resources, market mechanisms no longer guarantee, on their own, the achievement of that result of allocative efficiency that, from Adam Smith on, had been considered their most important virtue. Hence the recommendation to intervene to remedy the need, through a suitable system of taxes and subsidies, as C. Pigou (the inventor of welfare economics) had suggested.

Of course, this translation of environmental problems into economic terms in no way did justice to the complexity of meanings and intentions that the emerging ecological movement was developing. Above all the conceptualization of the environmental problem into the terms of a problem of externalities concealed a serious theoretical gap, which may be briefly summed up as follows. The notion of externality, as the effect of the action of an economic agent on the welfare of other individuals that is not captured by the price system, is not a primitive notion. It depends, in fact, on the definition of the economic actor and on the existence of markets. For example, if two companies operate in such a way that one damages the other – a foundry that, through its emissions damages a nearby company – any merging of the two will mean that what before had been external effects now become an issue within the same decision-making unit: the externality is internalized.

The point is that we can speak of externality only after an explanation has been provided for the number of economic actors and markets in existence. And since the number of firms and markets depends on very precise economic factors (non-convexity of production sets, transaction costs, access to information, etc.), this means that only an analysis of the general equilibrium which, starting from market fundamentals determined endogenously the number of firms and markets, can be a conceptually satisfying way of dealing with the question of externalities. Which it is not, given that the two conditions that allow us to identify the existence of externality are put forward axiomatically. To give an extreme example, if only one firm existed in the economy, there could be no externality. And yet, if this firm polluted and destroyed the non-renewable resources, the integrity of the environment would turn out to be damaged in exactly the same way. Among other things, this simple consideration allows us to understand why, in the ex-Soviet nations, where no market economy existed, the destruction of the environment was certainly not lesser than in the western countries.

The conclusion must be that economic science should, at the level of its very foundations, rethink the relationship between humanity and nature, abandoning the idea of 'humanity without constraints' that leads us to believe that any devastation is legitimate, in reference to certain anthropomorphic myths of omnipotence.[2] Rather, what is needed is the recovery of the basic recognition that humanity is part of nature, is internal to it, and has a cognitive exchange with nature, which is its necessary term. The relationship here is of being born into it, and of orderly change, because humanity, as part of nature, changes it: this is inevitable and also useful. But this must not mean destruction. The ideology of 'man the predator', according to which knowledge is used only to produce more, and more quickly, must be eliminated from the cultural horizon of the economist.[3]

Fairness and Sustainable Development

I set out from the familiar idea of sustainable development – a notion, however, not without conceptual ambiguities. Where sustainability is a term that refers to the idea of conservation of a particular state, development is a term that implies the transformation of that state into one form or another. It is interesting to recall that the expression 'sustainable development' was originally chosen for reasons of political rhetoric. Today, it would be better to speak of intergenerational solidarity. Leaving aside questions of semantics, what I would like to point out here is that the plurality of meanings attributed to the notion of sustainable development is itself a symptom of profound conceptual unease. As is well known, it is in the famous Brundtland Report of 1987 that this notion received what we may call its official formulation. 'We mean by sustainable development a development capable of satisfying the needs of the present without compromising the capacity of the future generations to satisfy their own'. But just a few years afterwards, the Nobel prize-winner Robert Solow published an essay (1993) in which he claimed that sustainability is a generic moral obligation of the present generation to future ones. He writes: 'Insofar as it is a moral obligation, sustainability is a generic obligation, not a specific one. It is not an obligation to preserve this or that. It is rather the obligation to preserve the welfare capacity of those who come after us' (p. 187). From this, it can be deduced that the destruction of natural resources is acceptable insofar as it is compensated by investments capable of generating other goods or by services able to increase welfare. In fact, Solow's position dates back to 1974, the year in which this American economist, inserting a non-renewable resource into a standard model of inter-temporal growth, fixed a result that would later become a basic reference point for the entire literature on sustainable development. A level of sustainable consumption can be guaranteed, in principle, every time it turns out to be technologically possible to guarantee a sufficient degree of substitutability between natural resource and physical capital.

For other writers, on the other hand, sustainability concerns the property rights of future generations, an idea rendered by the phrase: 'We have not inherited the Earth from our parents; we are borrowing it from our children'. This emotional phrase is often attributed to Ralph Waldo Emerson, though in actual fact its origin is by no means clear (Keyes, 1992). At all events, this point of view is firmly shared by Howarth (1992) and Norgaard (1992) who, though accepting Solow's idea of sustainability as a question of equity between generations, do not accept its reduction to a problem of substitutability between natural resources and produced goods such as capital goods. They start from a consideration that is easy to share – that the fact that two goods are perfect substitutes for the present generation does not imply that they will be so for future generations also.

Again for other scholars, sustainability would not involve considerations about issues of distribution between generations, but considerably more traditionally, questions of economic efficiency. Starting from the premise that most environmental assets admit two alternative uses – one destructive, according to which the environment is converted into a private asset enjoyed by the present generation; and the other as a public asset, to be used also by future generations – Silvestre (1994) develops a model in which sustainability may be defined only in terms of the allocation of resources between generations. The interesting conclusion here is that, if the future generations are considered as part and parcel of present-day society, allocative efficiency would require that environmental resources be maintained in their state of nature for a considerable number of decades. And all this, ignoring the principle that the living should inherit the Earth from their parents, or that they borrow it from their children.

Whatever the approach one believes should be adopted, the relevance of sustainability to the wider question of the conflict between generations due to global environmental change will be obvious to everyone (Tiezzi, 1993). Indeed, if the scarcity of natural resources and environmental degradation did not, for one reason or another, constitute a serious threat to the well-being of future generations – as postulated by the notion of sustainability – economists could happily ignore questions of fairness among generations and concentrate their attention only on problems relating to the efficiency of inter-temporal allocations. The great flowering of scientific publications in the 1970s and 1980s on the subjects of externalities and, more in general, on the market failures caused by the presence of environmental assets owes its *raison d'être* precisely to that.

A radical change of perspective came about at the end of the 1980s, as awareness spread that environmental problems are global in scale, pervasive in their effects, and above all generators of important consequences for future generations. The global climatic changes, the reduction of the ozone in the atmosphere, and the irreversible damage to bio-diversity, present features that make even the quite elaborate approaches to sustainability postulated up until that moment useless. This was for the simple reason that today's actions determine potential costs for future generations that are inherently unpredictable, given the dynamics and complexity of ecological systems. For example, climatic change can jeopardize subsistence agriculture in many areas of the world, just as it may increase the frequency and the dangers of tropical storms. Again, the gaps in the ozone layer could noticeably increase the risk of skin cancer from exposure to ultraviolet rays, etc. Faced with perspectives of this kind, it makes no sense to speak of sustainability of development in terms of generic guarantees offered to future generations so that the latter can satisfy their needs.

Thus we are able to explain why, in recent years, it became obvious that the theoretical apparatus that environmental economics had set out with was inadequate to deal with 'new' questions. Not only is Solow's model, and before that Hotelling's famous model of 1931 (according to which competitive markets would be able to induce firms to administer the stocks of non-renewable resources in such a way as to maximize the present value of profits), based on the assumption of perfect foresight; but what is worse is that these models, as well as the literature on so-called optimal growth, do not address the question of the institutional mechanisms necessary to create a sustainable future. What institutions would be able to make private and social discount rates correspond so as to bring about Hotelling's equivalence result? More in general, what policies would be necessary to ensure that a path of sustainable development could be implemented? In addition, it is by now obvious that social and environmental problems are closely inter-linked. To be resolved satisfactorily, these problems must be dealt with together; so the assumption of *ceteris paribus* that characterizes the whole of the analysis of partial equilibrium turns out to be of very dubious utility (Norgaard, 1993).

This is the context of the on-going debate on sustainable development today, starting from a different perspective from that of the quite recent past. Some economists continue to believe that sustainability can be referred to adequately while remaining within the apparatus of cost-benefits analysis. In this case, the institutions needed to ensure the internalization of environmental externalities, the efficient management of common property resources and the efficient inter-temporal allocation of resources sufficient to guarantee the rights of future generations. But a moment's reflection is enough to convince us that this is not the proper way to consider these things.

Cost-benefit analysis is very useful when we need to identify potential Paretian improvements – opportunities to improve the welfare of all without worsening the welfare of anyone. But – as we know – the prices and shadow prices on which this kind of analysis is based depend on the initial endowments possessed by each agent. If these are assigned in a markedly distorted way, efficiency by no means guarantees the sustainability of development – it may even make it worse. The objective of sustainability, in other words, requires a good deal more than improvements in efficiency in the Paretian sense. It requires the implementation of policies that allow the transfer of goods and resources from one generation to another.

Two important consequences derive from this. In the first place, what makes the sustainability objective difficult are not just the famous market failures, but also, and above all, the various forms of distributive inequity. Secondly, the way out cannot derive from cost-benefit analysis, precisely because the latter possesses the tools for solving problems of efficiency but not of fairness. So the pursuit of an objective such as sustainable development also means taking into consideration political and ethical aspects. In other words, the horizon of efficiency is not wide enough to contain all the issues raised by sustainability, which is first and foremost a problem of defining the rights of different generations. A proposition of this kind involves a quite weighty problem that has hitherto not received the attention it deserves. Let me clarify.

The vast literature on the subject under discussion, aside from the differences between individual writers, is founded on a shared theoretical scheme that runs as follows. On the one hand, it is assumed that all individuals are egoists, having self-interested preferences; on the other hand, questions of fairness between generations are the concern of institutions or collective agents whose task is basically to operate transfers of resources from the present to future generations. However, a framework of this type contains a paradox. Since the social choice function, on whose basis decisions at a collective level are made, is rooted in individual preference, why should the public decision-maker, for example, a government, assume responsibility for the welfare of future generations if individuals (of which that government is the expression, and to which it answers from the electoral standpoint) care nothing at all? On the other hand, if the economic actors possessed solidarity preferences as regards future generations, what need would there be for the intervention of a government to carry out the transfer of resources to future generations?

As is well known, in economics, the traditional way to resolve paradoxes of this kind is to assume that the members of present and future generations are linked to each other by bonds of a family kind that guarantee the actual transfer of assets from 'parents' to their immediate descendants, i.e. their 'children' (Barro, 1974). This is true whenever the welfare of the children enters positively into the utility function of the parents. A resolution of this kind, however ingenious, is of little help when it comes to the problem of sustainable development – for an obvious reason. In the long term, that is in the temporal perspective needed to deal with the issue at stake, it is not particularly useful to consider only two consecutive generations. As Daly and Cobb wrote (1989, p. 39): 'Families last in time only by fusing and mixing their identities by means of sexual reproduction. They are thus not independent or clearly defined over the period of time embracing more than two generations. Your great great grandchildren will also be the great great grandchildren of 15 other people belonging to the present generation, whose identity is unknown. Presumably, the welfare of your great great grandchildren will depend on the inheritance of each of these 15 other individuals as much as on yours. This is why it does not make much sense that you worry overmuch about your descendants'.

As will be readily understood, the paradox addressed here cannot be resolved by Barros' suggestion, because it is inconceivable that the families of the present-day generation can be able to organize an adequate transfer of resources for the welfare of their children, who will, in their turn, set up families in the future. The simple reason for this is that the more important transfers between generations have to be carried through before the children have reached the stage of personal independence. It will thus be evident that the burden of guaranteeing to future generations everything necessary to satisfy their needs falls on society as a whole. And this is also the case where living individuals show altruistic preferences towards their distant descendants. Indeed, in circumstances of this kind, the welfare of future generations would take on the features of a public good and the individual transfers, in the absence of some kind of mechanism of a collective nature, might well generate sub-optimal, or even unfair, results for future generations, as Sen (1982) has persuasively demonstrated.

Generalizing for a moment, the argument sketched here exposes a very serious aporia in economic theory, which, while it busies itself *ad abundantiam* with individual behaviour and its consequences, shows no interest at all in the beliefs and motivations that underlay human action. This lacuna is sometimes concealed by the argument that, since in a market economy the consumer is sovereign and thus free to express any kind of preference, including altruistic ones, there is no reason to worry about the motivations behind his or her choices. (It should be noticed in passing that this is the most common justification in economics of consequentialism as an ethical doctrine.) That this is not the case is shown by the idea that caring for the needs of others (sympathy in Adam Smith's sense – the spirit of solidarity) is not an innate human virtue. It is rather the result of a slow and systematic process of education. This is why for sustainable development the argument regarding lifestyles that respect creation is so centrally important; in other words, the adoption by individuals of life practices that respect the environment.[4] As long as a culture founded on the models of a consumer society prevails, especially among the young, it is obvious that politics will be unable to do anything other than respond to this kind of signal and translate it into the choices that are its logical consequences: increasing productivity levels to diminish the prices of goods and services to further increase their production and consumption, etc. C.F. Weizsacher's words to the Seoul ecumenical assembly of 1990 are relevant here: 'I know some politicians who want to do the really necessary things, but who know that as soon as they do something reasonable they will lose the next elections. It is for this reason that I am against the idea that politicians are mainly responsible, the most guilty of all. No, it is we [citizens] who are the guilty ones'.[5]

The History of Official Declarations on the Subject of the Environment

Regarding institutional policies and international organizations, proper awareness of environmental issues is quite recent. If we exclude the *Octogesima Adveniens* of Paul VI (1971), where we find the first explicit stance on the relationship between humanity and the environment in an official document, its history commences in 1972 in Stockholm, where the Conference of the United Nations on the Human Environment took place. This is also the year of the publication of the famous Report of the Club of Rome, drafted for the latter by the System Dynamics Group at MIT (USA). The theory of the physical limits to economic growth finds its first rigorous formulation in this report. Natural resources are not endowed – as so many economists had thought from the end of the eighteenth century on – with such 'original and indestructible powers' as to make them unalterable, even in the long term, by man's economic activities. On the contrary, they constitute a finite stock, thus the thesis of unlimited growth loses all scientific foundation. Hence economic policy advice: we need to add a further constraint to the economic calculus to take into account the depletion of natural resources.

Only five more years were to pass before the Leontief Report came out in 1977. It was commissioned by the UN, and named after the Nobel prize-winner in economics who co-ordinated and led the whole research project. In that part of the Report which specifically addresses the environmental issue, the expression 'limits to growth' disappears. Rather the conviction is expressed that with the predisposition of adequate economic measures and well-designed incentive mechanisms, it would be possible to solve the environmental problem without imposing futile limits on the possibility of growth of the economic system.

We thus arrive at 1987, the year of the Brundtland Report, known also as *Our Common Future*. Two striking features emerge. For the first time the idea of sustainable development was introduced, even though this had previously been raised (without success) in 1980 in a declaration of the World Conservation Strategy of the International Union for the Conservation of Nature and Natural Resources. The Brundtland Report also explicitly opens to the ethical dimension in its treatment of the issue of the environment, starting precisely from the concepts of equity (both inter-generational and intra-generational) and the rights of future generations. I note in passing that this latter principle was to provoke a heated debate in the years immediately following in the field of the philosophy of right: how can the attribution of rights to people who do not yet exist (those belonging to future generations) be justified from an ethical standpoint?

To complicate the picture further, in 1991 came the 'Declaration of Peking/Beijing', signed by the representatives of the G77 countries (to the initial 77 developing countries another 30 were to be added). In this Declaration, not only was the ethical dimension of environmental issues completely ignored – in particular, no reference to the rights of future generations was made – but above all 'the rights of developing countries to growth' was strenuously asserted, indeed it was put forward as a priority, an objective to take precedence over environmental protection. Overall, the struggle to defend the environment was seen, by the more than one hundred developing countries that signed the Declaration, as a luxury for rich countries and as a tool of economic oppression.

The following year the well-known Conference was held in Rio de Janeiro. Organized by UNCED (United Nations Conference on Environment and Development), the similarly well known 'Agenda 21', the first important document outlining a program of environmental protection policies, concluded the conference. Three points are pertinent in the context of our present purposes. Firstly, the philosophical and political position of the Brundtland Report was reaffirmed, but with a particular slant: defence of the requirements of national sovereignty, also in environmental questions. Developing countries, especially, claimed recognition of the right to use their natural resources to accelerate growth without any external interference. Secondly, in the final document of the Rio Conference, the risk of keeping environmental and economic issues separate was expressly criticized. This was the risk of so-called 'eco-imperialism': environmentalist movements and defenders of protectionist policies in OECD countries collude to limit the access to western markets of products from developing countries. Thirdly, the project of the great transnational companies to gain acceptance for the principle that market instruments and economic growth offered the most valid guarantee to ensure sustainable development failed completely. Primarily the environmentalist groups of the North were afraid of the so-called 'pollution havens': i.e. the fear that the application of the rules of free trade sanctioned, at that time by GATT and today by the WTO, could overwhelm the measures for environmental protection.[6]

We thus arrive at the Kyoto Summit of 1997, where, quite unexpectedly, the logic of the separation of ecological and economic questions, abandoned by the Rio Conference, was reaffirmed. To be precise, the delegates to the 'Convention of the United Nations on Climatic Change' signed a Protocol committing the OECD industrialized nations (38 countries overall) to reduce their gas emissions affecting the greenhouse effect by 5.2 per cent, on average, compared to the 1990 levels, over the period 2008-2012. (The commitment for the EU, the USA and Japan is 8 per cent, 7 per cent, and 6 per cent, respectively.) The real novelty of the Kyoto Protocol was that, while the developing countries were not held to reducing their emissions, the advanced countries, to mitigate costs deriving from the implementation of the agreement, could utilize a certain number of flexible (market) mechanisms, in which the object of negotiations are 'emission permits': the country exceeding its agreed-to emissions could buy 'pollution permits' from those countries remaining below their established levels.[7]

The Hague Conference in November 2000, convened so that the Kyoto Protocol could begin to be applied in 2002, ended in sensational failure. The EU insisted on ratification, but the so-called 'umbrella group' (USA, Canada, Japan, and Australia) rejected ratification giving reasons only apparently of a technical nature.[8]

As will easily be understood from this rapid overview, the short but turbulent history of official positions on environmental issues is characterized by the almost systematic alternation of quite markedly different points of view and lines of action. It is a history of steps forward and steps back, of often apparently unmotivated swings from radical innovation to conservative retreat, as if the terms of what was at stake were not clear to everyone. The fact is that without a holistic vision of the environmental issue, that allows us to appreciate the fact that the environment is not simply a question of degradation or of depletion of resources, and without overcoming the limitations of scientific research that is too 'sector-oriented' and too little trans-disciplinary, the 'new alliance' between mankind and nature – to use the ichastic expression of I. Prigogine – will never be able to be achieved.

The Struggle against Poverty and Sustainable Development

Where do we begin if we wish to move beyond what is still the most common (dichotomous) way of facing the crucial issue of sustainable development? I would not hesitate to indicate the reduction of the welfare gap between the North and South of the world as the *primum movens* of a strategy of this kind. Let us see if we can clarify this.

As it is well known, there are three main causes of environmental degradation: the inefficient allocation of resources; their iniquitous distribution; the disproportion between population and the capacity of the environment to sustain it. While in rich countries the first of these causes is operative, poor countries are mainly afflicted by the other two causes. Through their structural characteristics, these countries tend to specialize in the production and exportation of goods with a high intensity of environmental degradation. Even today, two thirds of Latin America's exports are made up of natural resources – Africa's percentage is even higher – resources that are imported by and consumed in the countries of the North. This datum, though crude, is already sufficient to allow us to understand why the question of sustainable development cannot be separated from the reform of international trade regulations. When we discover that the South exports goods with a high degree of environmental degradation, though it is not true that the South possesses higher quantities of these goods compared to the North, we may understand why commercial policies based on the Ricardian principle of comparative advantage are a serious threat to sustainability.[9] If we then consider that most developing countries are located in the region known as the 'vital zone' characterized by a highly unstable ecological equilibrium and by a marked capacity to influence the atmosphere, we understand why, if we continue to force these countries to use their natural capital as a substitute for insufficient physical and human capital, environmental degradation will inevitably suffer rapid acceleration.

But there is still more. In a document published some years back (in 1992), the World Bank thoroughly detailed the relationship existing between some indicators of environmental quality and levels of GNP per capita. A relation emerged that could be shown through a curve in the form of an inverted U: environmental decay grows with the increase of average income when the latter is at low levels, whereas it decreases with the increase of average income when the latter exceeds a certain threshold. Basing their work on this rich empirical material, Grossman and Krueger (1994), through econometrics, find that the level of the critical threshold of average income, beyond which the above mentioned curve begins to decrease, stands at around $8,000 per capita annually (1985 dollars). The curve in question is known in the literature as the 'Environmental Kuznets Curve' (EKC) from the name of the Nobel prize-winner for economics who first studied its characteristics with reference to the relationship between levels of GNP per capita and variations in an indicator of the inequality of income within a specific population. The empirical evidence in support of the EKC is still today insufficiently robust to recommend its use for purposes of environmental policies. It is nevertheless possible to extract from the EKC the following broad indications: some indicators of environmental decay (CO_2 emissions; solid waste) increase, i.e. worsen, with the increase of pro-capita income; others (the lack of clean water;

hygiene indicators) diminish, i.e. improve, with the increase in per-capita income; still others (emissions of sulphur dioxide and nitrates) first increase and then diminish with the increase in per-capita income.[10]

What lessons can be learned from the EKC? Since Northern countries are located to the right of the critical threshold value mentioned above, whereas most Southern countries are still a long way from this goal, and since the environmental problems that today cause us the most concern are global ones, it is evident that we shall have to intervene as a matter of urgency regarding the rules of international economic activities. In particular, we must realize that in the context of an increasingly globalized economy, environmental regulation and commercial regulation should be integrated and harmonized – the exact opposite of what has occurred up to now in the WTO (World Trade Organization) (Pearson, 2000).

It is well known that international trade tends to separate production from consumption. An increase in demand for tropical wood in the North translates into a corresponding reduction in tropical forest in the Amazon. It is a fact that international trade throws a long, dark shadow over the environment. Without adequate rules and without forms of close co-operation between the agencies involved with trade and the environment, the growing volume of commercial exchanges (positive and a hopeful sign for the future) will translate into increases in environmental decay.

The second and more important message is that the problem of sustainable development, in present-day historical conditions, is intrinsically linked to the problem of poverty, both absolute and relative (Pasca di Magliano, 2000). It would be naive to imagine that we can solve the former problem separately from the second, or worse still, in opposition to it. Efforts to improve or preserve the quality of the environment in the North will be of very little use unless, at the same time, there is an urgent and comprehensive program to combat poverty to allow the countries of the South to move beyond the ECK critical threshold. Clearly, there is a need for a program of global redistribution, since policies on a national scale are no longer adequate for the purpose. If we stop and think for a moment, we find ourselves faced with a specific, yet remarkable, case in which the defence of justice also serves to improve efficiency (identified here with sustainable development) – so it is not always true that there is a trade-off between efficiency and justice!

Towards a World Organization of the Environment

S. Pastel wrote some years ago: 'The world economic system seems incapable of facing up to the problem of poverty and the protection of the environment. Seeking to cure the ecological ills of the Earth separately from the problems linked to situations of debt, commercial imbalances, gross inequalities in income levels and in patterns of consumption, is like trying to cure a heart disease without struggling against the obesity of the patient and his diet rich in cholesterol' (quoted in Brown, 1992). But to what do we ultimately impute this evident incapacity? To the fact that the very nature of the most important environmental assets is that of global public assets. While a single global economy does not yet exist – notwithstanding the great debate on globalization – we find ourselves dealing with a single climatic system, with a single ozone layer, etc. These are global public assets: their use by one country does not diminish the amount available to others; on the other hand, no country can be excluded from making use of them. (Clearly, the emissions of polluting substances are public global 'evils'.)

Now, as economic theory has realized for some time, public assets give rise to one irritating consequence, typical of all the situations known as 'the prisoner's dilemma'. And if the public good is global the terrible consequences will be global. In 1990, the Intergovernmental Panel on Climate Change showed that emissions of greenhouse gas led to an increase in average temperatures with all the well known consequences. And yet very few countries acted unilaterally to reduce emissions. Similarly, the European Union proposed the introduction of a carbon tax in Europe, but having seen that their example was not imitated by other countries (especially the USA) it changed its plans. It is precisely the two characteristics mentioned above, of the public good, that makes unilateral policies wrong as a strategy in environmental politics.

Even if negotiations were eventually to produce some form of agreement or international treaty, the problem of how to implement it would still need to be solved. We only have to think of the case of the Montreal Protocol for the regulation of the use of CFCs that destroy the ozone layer, and the already mentioned Kyoto Protocol on climatic change. Why was the former successful in producing the desired effects, whereas the latter did meet so many difficulties for its implementation? The answer is that the Montreal Protocol contains an incentive mechanism that encourages the active participation and adherence of all the signatory countries, a mechanism that implies that it is in the best interest of all countries to enforce the rules. The designers of the Kyoto Protocol were incapable of finding the right mechanism to ensure its self-enforcement (Barrett, 2001).

Where do these reflections lead? They suggest the urgent need to set up a World Environment Organization (WEO) along the lines of the World Trade Organization (WTO). The lack of institutions (not bureaucracies!) at global level makes so many problems of our age hard to solve, especially the environmental one. While markets become globalized, the transnational institutional landscape is still that of the immediate post-war world. But the Bretton Woods negotiators in 1944 could never have imagined what the environmental issue was to become. The objection will be raised that there is an adequate number of international treaties, or contracts at the domestic level to regulate relationships between individuals. The analogy is dangerously misleading, because contracts stipulated within a country can be enforced by that country's State; but there is no transnational authority empowered to enforce treaties between states. This is why a WEO is needed. On the whole, it is hard to see how the present state of affairs can continue; while the market, in its rich variety of forms, has by now become global, governance has remained basically national or at best international.

The two important tasks for this organization are as follows. First, by interacting with the WTO, such an agency must seek to make the rules of free trade compatible with those set out for environmental protection, and must also ensure that they are respected by all concerned. Secondly, WEO must intervene, in a supplementary role, in all those increasingly frequent cases in which price signals are unable to anticipate irreversible environmental loss. As we know, it is now proven that thresholds of environmental decay do exist, that to a certain extent economic activities do not block the environment's regenerative functions, but beyond that point irreversible changes can take place due to the level of economic activity which overwhelms the eco-system's capacity to assimilate it. In situations of this kind, market mechanisms become jammed: hence the need to support them through the intervention of an *ad hoc* agency.

In Lieu of a Conclusion

One question arises spontaneously: given the problems and the difficulties in solving them, should we perhaps resign ourselves and let the processes in progress today proceed according to their own internal logic? Thinking in this manner would be overwhelmingly irresponsible, because, in actual fact, there is no need, as some people suggest, to halt growth processes or those of globalization. What is really and urgently needed is to work for the establishment of an economic and social order founded on the plurality of power centres, i.e. on a 'polyarchy', which unlike pluralism, is not just a question of number, but above all of diversity both in modes of production and models of consumption.

The difficulties and risks inherent in the implementation of a strategy of this kind are obvious to everyone. It would be naive to think that the diversity of the interests involved does not mean high levels of conflict. But the task is unavoidable if we wish to overcome the affliction of rhetoric at all costs (rhetoric that often ends up appearing nihilistic), as well as the clear-eyed optimism of those who see in technical, scientific and economic progress a sort of triumphal march of humanity towards its fulfilment. The responsible person cannot become the victim of traps of this kind. Dante

Alighieri understood this very well when he closed the eighth canto of his *Paradiso* (139-44) as follows: '*Sempre natura, se fortuna trova / discorde a sè, come ogni altra semente / fuor di sua region, fa mala prova. / E, se il mondo laggiù ponesse mente / al fondamento che natura pone, / seguendo lui, avria buona la gente* [Always, if nature meets with fortune unsuited to it, like any kind of seed out of its own region, it has ill success, and if the world below gave its mind to the foundation that nature lays and followed it, it would be well for its people]'.

Notes

1 For an historical excursus into ethical thinking on environmental matters, and for a convincing defence of the thesis that the environment has to be included in the realm of ethics as such and not just insofar as it is a system of resources for humanity, see Vigna (2001).
2 See Stres (2000), for an excellent treatment of the specifically cultural roots of environmental questions.
3 An important line of philosophical and theological thinking on the subjects discussed here is Golser (2001). Referring to St. Bonaventura, Golser argues that the realities of creation were in the first place created for the glory of God and only secondly for humanity's benefit. Thus before being useful, they are good.
4 See A. Giordano's provocative text, 'La spiritualità e gli stili di vita sostenibili', mimeo, May 2001. The treatment of this subject in Keenan (2000) is quite effective.
5 Quoted in *One World* (Monthly Magazine of the World Council of Churches), no. 155, May 1990, p. 16.
6 For further detailed analysis see Vallega (1994).
7 Obviously there is much else that is new in the Kyoto Protocol, and the consequences of its eventual implementation have yet to be analyzed. To give just one example, there is the problem of the compatibility of environmental and commercial policies with policies of international investment. For a useful handling of this, see UNU/GEIC (1999).
8 It should be recalled that from December 1997 to the end of 2001, just over 30 Countries have ratified the Protocol, though more than 55 are needed for it to become effective. Of the countries that have ratified it, not one belongs to the so-called Annex I (i.e. the 38 more advanced countries, including those of Western Europe). See Victor (2001) and Carraro (2001). Only in late 2002, after the announcement of ratification by the part of China and Russia at the Johannesburg Conference, the implementation of the Kyoto Protocol has become effective.
9 See, on this point, the pungent analysis of Chichilnisky (1991).
10 A useful critical review of the more recent literature on the subject is to be found in Borghesi (1999).

References

Barrett, S. (2001), 'Can the Environment Survive Globalization?', SAISPHERE.
Barro, R. (1974), 'Are Government Bonds Net Wealth?', *Journal of Political Economy*, vol. 82, pp. 1095-117.

Borghesi, S. (1999), 'The Environmental Kuznets Curve: A Survey of the Literature', Fondazione Mattei, Milan.

Brown, L. (1992), *State of the World 1992*, Isedi, Milan.

Carraro, C. (2001), 'Non solo meno emissioni', *Equilibri*, no. 1.

Chichilnisky, G. (1991), 'Global Environment and North-South Trade', *WP 31*, Stanford University.

Daly, H.E. and Cobb, J.B. (1989), *For the Common Good. Redirecting the Economy toward Community, the Environment and a Sustainable Future*, Beacon Press, Boston.

Golser, K. (2001), 'Futuro della nostra terra. Responsabilità cristiana per il sociale, il lavoro, l'ambiente', mimeo, May 2001, Assisi.

Grossman, G.M. and Krueger A.B. (1994), 'Economic Growth and the Environment', *WP 4634*, NBER.

Howarth, R. (1992), 'Environmental Valuation under Sustainable Development', *American Economic Review*, vol. 82, pp. 473-7.

Keenan, M. (2000), *Care for Creation. Human Activity and the Environment*, Libreria Editrice Vaticana, Vatican City.

Keyes, R. (1992), *Nice Guys Finish Seventh: False Phrases, Spurious Sayings and Familiar Misquotations*, Harper Collins, New York.

Norgaard, R. (1992), 'Sustainability and the Economics of Assuring Assets for Future Generations', *WPS 832*, Asia Regional Office, The World Bank.

Norgaard, R. (1993), 'The Co-evolution of Economic and Environmental Systems and the Emergence of Unsustainability', in R.W. England (ed.), *Evolutionary Concepts in Contemporary Economics*, University of Michigan Press, Ann Arbor.

Pasca di Magliano, R. (2000), *Povertà e sviluppo*, Seam, Formello.

Pearson, C.S. (2000), *Economics and the Global Environment*, Cambridge University Press, Cambridge.

Sen, A.K. (1982), 'Approaches to the Choice of Discount Rates for Social Benefit-Cost Analysis', in R.C. Lind (ed.), *Discounting for Time and Risk in Energy Policy*, Resources of the Future, Washington.

Silvestre, J. (1994), 'An Efficiency Argument for Sustainable Use', *WP*, University of California, Davis.

Solow, R. (1993), 'Sustainability: An Economist's perspective', in R. Dorfman and N. Dorfman (eds), *Economics of the Environment*, Norton, New York.

Stres, A. (2000), 'Le radici antropologiche e culturali della crisi ecologica', *Notiziario*, April, CEI, Rome.

Tiezzi, E. (1993), 'Verso uno sviluppo sostenibile', in I. Musu (ed.), *Economia e ambiente*, Il Mulino, Bologna.

UNU/GEIC (1999), 'Global Climate Governance. Interlinkage between the Kyoto Protocol and Other Multilateral Regimes', Tokyo.

Vallega, A. (1994), *Geopolitica e sviluppo sostenibile*, Mursia, Milan.

Vercelli, A. (1994), 'Hard Uncertainty and the Environment', *WP 46*, Fondazione Mattei, Milan.

Victor, D. (2001), *The Collapse of the Kyoto Protocol and the Struggle to Slow Global Warming*, Princeton University Press, Princeton.

Vigna, C. (2001), 'Linee di un'etica dell'ambiente', in C. Vigna (ed.), *Introduzione all'etica*, Vita e Pensiero, Milano.

World Bank (1992), *World Development Report 1992: Development and the Environment*, The World Bank, Washington.

Chapter 6

Sustainable Urban Strategies for Developing Countries

Anil Laul

Introduction

> Our societies will never be great until our cities are great. There is the decay of
> the centre and despoiling of the suburbs. There is not enough housing for our
> people, nor enough transportation for our traffic. Open lands are vanishing and
> landmarks are being violated ... A few years ago we were concerned about the
> ugly country ... Today we must act to prevent an ugly city (Lyndon B. Johnson,
> President, USA, 1964).

That an urban crisis engulfing most parts of the 'civilized' world exists is
very obvious to everybody who lives and works in the urban areas. Indeed
the feeling of frustration is so strong that there are some who would like to
abandon the city altogether. The common bond of having to eke out a
living along with the desire to interact socially makes them perforce stay
together, but a relentless quest for greener pastures causes them to sever
their roots and leave their homes.

The basic perception of 'progress being synonymous with the city'
causes people to migrate to the metropolis, drawn like moths towards a
candle flame. To pursue the analogy, hopeful emigrants may often find
their wings clipped, if not singed, by being caught in the vicious trap of
inadequate shelter, encroachments, prohibitive land prices and inflation.

To curb man's innate desire for self-improvement in economic or other
terms is to stifle the human spirit which is constantly searching for
fulfilment. There is therefore a need to revamp and change the basic fabric
of day-to-day living to suit the needs and conditions of the people and the
times. It is time that all antiquated and inapplicable planning strategies (one
of the largest contributors to the ascending inflation scale) be re-evaluated.
With the population increasing drastically, we tend more and more to
concentrate on the already heavily populated areas. But unless we learn the
true meaning of planning, which is the introduction of diversity and variety

into a meaningful pattern, we will succeed in making our cities unliveable, unworkable places of infernal sameness, plagued by the discomforts arising from the shocking lack of the basic necessities of life – a fate which, in fantasy, is better known as hell!

The major protagonists of this unliveable hell are the homeless – their needs, their future and their financing which often become mere items for boardroom discussions or seminars. In urban India, as also in most developing nations, this problem of the homeless is most acutely felt in metropolitan areas.

Planners, administrators, sociologists and architects have attempted to grapple with the situation intermittently, but, like the Loch Ness monster, the problem has eluded them not only because of its gargantuan size, but because of the consequential complications. That the problem is man-made is apparent. The only way to tackle it is to understand it in full and above all, to utilize an holistic approach, which requires the backing of a team of people who know something about everything and everything about something. Most of all, we have much to learn from the past and the rationale of 'living with nature' as propagated in our ancient text, known as the *Vastu Vidya*. This text needs to be demystified and the reasoning behind the linking of human settlements to religion needs to be understood. These forms of guidelines for sustainable development, though mystified, exist in most developing countries.

Overview

An inadequate comprehension of the housing problem in its totality has resulted in a large proliferation of slums and unauthorized colonies on prime lands in the city. In addition to this, we must deal with the unemployed educated, the destitute, senior citizens and working women, who, when combined, comprise almost one third of Delhi's urban population (taken as a case in point). The same may be true in metropolises of other developing nations, whose extent may vary but whose problem areas remain similar. Though the government is spending vast sums on various programs for the benefit of these groups, demands are growing at a faster rate than the delivery system. Limited by their own resources, this vital segment of the population encroaches upon public land or resides in low rental areas which, for the most part, are devoid of all facilities and amenities. Such disorientation puts severe environmental constraints both upon the city as well as on city dwellers, and the basic constitutional right of 'living with dignity' is fast becoming a distant dream.

The government's efforts to resolve this problem, however, have further been aggravated by increasing investments made in urban areas, leading to inadvertent migration to these high density, unliveable pockets – 'a forced living option'. In Delhi around 600,000 such households for a total population of around three million (a figure on the increase), inhabit such shanties on prime public land, covering about 4,000 hectares. To use an analogy, this problem, with no apparent feasible solution in sight, seems to roll along like the veritable snowball, ever increasing in size. The failure of municipal bodies and government housing agencies regarding the needs of this strata of society is leading to public resentment and consequently to a break down in law and order.

There is little evidence of success in the popular slogan of 'one household – one house'. Although there is no dearth of various planning strategies, technological efforts, slum clearance and rehabilitation schemes in subsidized, standardized, unliveable, unaffordable housing units, with the government constantly ready with new solutions, the problems steadily outpace any solutions offered. Although the government has repeatedly emphasized its role as the 'great provider' at the policy level (for political gains or otherwise), it has frequently been found lacking in this aspect, with neither the resources nor the ability to carry out its plans. Surely it is time for the government to admit its limitations and face up to the reality of the situation?

Populist schemes such as the *Panchayati Raj,* professing 'power to the people' are formulated but they either stagnate at the discussion table or die a natural death at the implementation stage since they clash with other policies and schemes formulated on the principles of centralized decision-making processes. By the time some semblance of a solution is achieved, the problem is already out of hand and requires a totally different solution. It is therefore time that limitations in this role are accepted by the government. The *Panchayati Raj* typically depended on the wisdom of the five village elders to look after the day-to-day problems of the village, thereby dealing with problems in their initial stages. It was only the residual problems that were taken to the next level of decision-making where the individual representatives went to the decision-making body of the group of villages, following the principle that 'every action is best performed at the lowest level that it can be best performed'.

The city is what it is today principally as a result of the external factors (bureaucratic and political) influencing its planning strategies. One glaring misfortune is that the common man/woman seems to have almost no influence whatsoever on his/her life-style in terms of planning or decision-making. He/she is dependent, almost body and soul as it were, on the civil servant who is the major planner and decision-maker. This natural obeisance is a spillover from the days of the British Raj when the government servant was kingpin and service centres, administration offices, etc., revolved around him like satellites. Business centres had to move to the periphery, while at the hub of the city was the civil servant and his entourage of domestic help. When the British civil servant completed his term of office he was expected to return to his homeland. However even after his superannuation, the bureaucrat continues to provide sustenance for his entire entourage of domestic and office staff, who after retirement, are willing to stay on permanently in the metropolis that they once ruled. Wherever the bureaucrat takes up his residence initially, determines the pace and nature of development and eventually the fate of the city hinges on this.

Understanding the rationale as contained in the *Vastu Vidya* (India specific),[1] would have enabled one to understand the manner of exercising controls in human settlement patterns for a system that is sustainable, while at the same time respecting the social fabric of the citizens that the settlement was designed for. The other aspect of the forms of governance as being subservient to the *Vastu Vidya* and co-related and contained in the *Artha Shastra* (the text for the rules and forms of 'good governance')[2] must also be de-mystified and dovetailed into the understanding of providing sustainable human settlements. Careful examination shows that it is the tropical regions, the areas with the most fauna and flora, that are today considered as the developing nations. It is these regions that have the largest incidence of disease as well as the antidotes for those diseases. These regions are the most densely populated areas in the world, have the largest amount of produce from the land and are interdependent according to social and community values. These regions also abound in myths and religious beliefs which have been their mainstay in the past.

Similarly, traditional architecture in the Asian region, as also in most parts of the tropical regions of the Earth, was more than just a built-up form and its symbolism. The town planning methodologies, the mysticism linking it to religion, its symbolism and architecture all provided a total form of sustainable human settlement. Over years of rationalization, the past generations realized that most of the problems relating to sustainable human settlements were related to the immense human desire to leave an imprint on the sands of time. This aspiration to make an individual statement could best be met by the buildings man built. This would also be the single largest contributor to environmental degradation. The control of this aspiration was best exercised through the formulation of mystic codification propagated around religion. A sensible form of controls, in view of the fact that man has never before had to deal with the phenomenal level of land and building-related issues which confronts him today. The very existence of mankind seems to be at stake, but in spite of this, individualistic issue-based approaches are being explored, with each issue seeming larger than the previous one. A point worth pondering is that perhaps earlier generations realized that the single largest factor that could affect sustainable development was the built form and the city plan. What we today call 'behavioural sciences' was encompassed in the traditional building and planning strategies. Today what is known as architecture was in fact the most powerful tool devised through which the behavioural pattern of the entire society was controlled. Today, heated debate is in progress as to whether architecture is a science or an art, and no conclusions have as yet been reached. Architects and planners are today considered as a supportive profession to the engineers, but they continue to feel that it is the architectural profession that should be the guiding profession. Architects themselves do not realize that it is not the engineers that pose a threat to them, rather they are a threat to their own profession. If architects and planners are to command the respect they received in the past, then their endeavours should reflect the integration of the work of the architect, the engineer, the artist and the artisan. Though designated the leader of the team, the architect in the past worked in close co-operation with the religious head who was responsible for ensuring that social aspects were well integrated in the planning and implementation stages to cover sustainable development issues.

The endeavour to provide sustainable human settlements led man to mystify[3] the guidelines for social and value-based controls. This mystification ensured that the entire interdependent system of sustenance was respected. The forms of mystification gave rise to the various religious beliefs of the regions and the forms of governance which emerged are a derivative of both these aspects. A simple analogy of sustainable development becomes clear if religion is examined from one very interesting point of view. All religions are the same and only the manner of their explanation differs. All religions propagate sustenance through interdependence and most religions are based on the 'fatherhood' of God and the 'brotherhood' of Man, (e.g. the Commandments say so or the Holy Book says so), but religions or the manner of living in the tropical regions suggest the brotherhood of Man and thereby the fatherhood of God, i.e. in coexistence one can achieve salvation. These are two different ways of perceiving religion, one with a top-down approach and the other with a bottom-up approach, but both clearly propagate sustainability through interdependence. That is why it is often said that Hinduism is not a religion, but a way of life. It is also within the tropical regions that humankind worshipped or propagated myths around the elements or plants and even animals that gave sustenance. The Hindus in the Indian subcontinent, the First Nations in the Americas, the Africans, the Greeks, the Chinese and the entire so-called Orient, offer examples of this belief and form of worship.

Strangely, most of this system of planning with religion seems to be true within the tropical belt, but as one moves away from the tropics towards the poles, interdependency seems to drop considerably, until it is almost absent in those regions closest to the poles. It is within the tropics that society is interdependent and it also within this region that most of the values for survival are propagated around religion. Mysticism is a way of life and is the chord that holds society together. It was therefore the responsibility of the architect or the planner of human settlements to ensure that the principles of interdependency were respected as diffused by the religious doctrines and their propagators. The built-up form, being the most powerful manner of influencing the human mind, was thus utilized to full advantage. It was also within the tropical regions that most diseases were prevalent but the largest variety of plants and herbs also existed within this region. It was almost as if nature had provided the largest laboratory for man within this region, to explore, to appreciate and evolve the principles of co-existence. Today, the aspect of disease is being highlighted and is used as a tool for labelling this region as a developing region. The aspect of co-existence with nature and its other offshoots such as forms of human settlements, regional-specific customs, resultant forms of governance, traditional values, customs and cultures are being relegated to the realm of Romanticism only. So intense is this belief that the civilizations in the tropical regions are themselves convinced of their own shortcomings and aspire to mimic the so-called advanced nations without attempting to delve into their own past and understand their own values. It is not that the development of the so-called advanced nations must be ignored and wished away (this would be a grave error) but the rationale of the past must be dovetailed into present day developments without losing sight of coexistence. This is best understood by examining the rationale that governed the nature and patterns of human settlements and their inter-relationships.

So rapid was the transformation during the Industrial Revolution that all the wisdom and the rationale of the past was buried. The process of rationalization of the past took a back seat, and even reference to the traditional values of co-existence was considered archaic.

> ... we have the paradox of a world in which growing investment in education goes with the growing numbers of illiterates; growing investment in industry actually decreases jobs, and where fabulous unprecedented wealth co-exists with the highest of poverty and environmental destruction in recorded history (Ashok Khosla, Development Alternatives, India).

Land and Appropriate Planning

Evolving appropriate sustainable city strategies for developing requires, as well as developed countries, the re-examination of modern day frameworks of 'the city' as well as its components. The modern-day framework has, for over a century, ensured that cities have developed at the same pace as political and economic resources. In other words, this meant that as long as there was ample money to disburse as well as access to other resources, most modern cities could develop rapidly with little consideration being given to their natural environment and long-term sustainability.

Sustainability can be achieved as long as some very basic issues are examined, developed, and implemented. Prior to the Modernist movement, the majority of town planners, architects, engineers, artisans, etc., had a natural understanding of the relationship between built form and natural environment. One characteristic of the Modernists was the imposition of their rational concepts to make the Earth conform to their vision of man.

In order to achieve sustainability, smooth amalgamations of traditional (read context-specific) building practices and modern technologies can be developed and implemented. Of course, this is an arduous task, but at the same time there are some very basic guidelines and issues that, when viewed in the correct perspective, could form the foundations of sustainable development. Among other things, we would do well to deal with the issues of land, roads, water supply, water disposal and appropriate building materials.

Technologies appropriate at a national level must be segregated from those that are appropriate for local consumption. This would distinguish technologies that need to go into macro-industrial production from the micro-enterprise. Appropriate technologies are those that respond to the local environment, resources and economic needs.

Arousing public awareness regarding environmental and equity issues is indispensable for sustainable development. For the successful implementation of comprehensive and appropriate development issues, it is essential to educate the public, government, social and technical institutions and business groups as regards comprehensive sustainable development issues.

It is essential to ensure that future generations are constantly made aware of sustainable development issues in their decision-making processes. The subject must be introduced into the basic educational curriculum. Just as an individual understands the implications of his/her daily financial decisions, similarly he/she should be cognizant of the social and environmental implications of his/her actions.

Land Value and Credit Reforms

> We have not inherited the Earth from our forefathers, but borrowed it from our children (Chief Seattle, 1854).

Land is the basic matrix of life and all development activities generate on or from it. The other essential input for generating development activities is capital. In most developing countries, absolute value is based on land holdings. The fact that you can trade in land is in itself the core of the problem. Logically, it should be the asset *on* the land that can be bought and sold, and *not* the land itself. Most developing countries are suffering from the ill effects of unsustainable land and credit-related financial policies. The three areas that need critical examination are:

- the commodification of land, which is the largest contributor to inflation;
- credit against land as a mortgageable asset, which in turn leads to inequity;
- lack of access to credit due to land as the basis for credit and inequitable access to land.

The values attributed to a product frequently do not represent its real value as a result of the various market and credit systems. The manner in which land is valued is a typical example of this and it has far-reaching effects. In most Asian countries land has become a tradable commodity. Land values are often far greater than the produce of the land or the value of the asset on it. For instance, if the cost of a building is X, then typically in an Asian metropolis, the value of the land may be as high as 20X, or even up to 200X i.e., its value is magnified to a disproportionate extent.

This is mainly due to the banking system which lends against the value of the land in addition to the value of the existing or potential asset on it. The outcome is the production of inflationary effects on all products (since real estate value constitutes a major component of a product's value) and it leads to speculation that also fuels inflation without any real value/product/ asset, being created.

A possible remedy may lie in changing the financing system, so that lending agencies such as banks remove the land value from the project cost. Ideally, a project should be financed against the produce or value of the asset created on it. If land is valued, then it would be safe to assume that the entire Earth stands sold today. Is this an acceptable hypothesis?

A safe barometer for sustainable development would be that land values should not exceed the cost of construction more than fourfold, even when dealing with the most expensive metropolitan real estate. In other words, if the construction cost is X, then the land cost should not be more than 4X. Any increase in land cost over and above four times would result in the commodification of land that consequently leads to adverse effects on the quality of construction. For example, since the owner/builder has spent an exorbitant sum on the land alone, he will cut corners on the building itself. This is most often done by constructing thinner walls with more plinth area to save on construction, material and labour costs. Thus this leads to the use of inappropriate building materials and a complex process of problems is set in motion.

If we were to hypothetically subtract the value of land from the cost of an immovable asset, the entire economic face of financial as well as legal transactions would change. Approximately 70 per cent of the lawsuits in our courts are land-related. Land values and land ownership are considered synonymous with progress but this perspective needs to be re-examined. Traditional building practices, as well as the *Artha Shastra*, propagated a system that was very different from present day practices. Over the years, we have linked value to the land, making it a transaction commodity and assigning it an astronomical value.

While it may not be feasible to adopt the above strategy with immediate effect, we could work towards achieving this objective in an incremental manner by reducing the limits of the drawing capacity against land on a yearly basis until the objective of de-linking land from drawing power is achieved.

Land Use, Its Distribution and Management on a Sustainable Basis

National and state planning commissions deal largely with financial planning and resource management, which are divorced from land use planning. Land use planners are not involved in the process of formulating development strategies and plans for a region at a macro-level for sustainable human settlement design. Development strategies that are based on natural resource planning are often relegated to the background, and instead allow political considerations to dictate regional plans. This results in the misuse of land, inequitable growth and extensive degradation.

Today, there is widespread inequity regarding access to land in most Asian countries. Equitable distribution of land should be an integral part of the devolution of power. Access to land of itself is not sufficient unless micro-credit and other support services to generate produce from the land are provided.

Land – Flat versus Gradient

Besides the financial and legal aspects of land issues that require reformulation, the physical characteristics of land also need to be re-defined. There is a general misconception that it is more economical to build on flat land rather than on undulating terrain. Historically, urban centres that were built on higher ground were situated in this manner not only for militarily strategic reasons. Higher land lends itself to better drainage and more economical disposal systems owing to natural slopes. There are some pertinent lessons that we can learn from the past in order to achieve sustainable development in the present. If one respects the lay of the land and determines a city master plan on the basis of water supply systems and the disposal of waste, etc., there is a greater chance of developing a sustainable city environment. The micro plan can then be envisaged leading to comprehensive development plans.

Roads

The largest single contradiction in our present-day planning methodologies is the relationship between roads and drainage systems. Roads require minimal slope while drainage requires steep slopes and yet we choose to combine the two by placing our drainage systems alongside roads. If the performance criterion of roads and drainage is taken separately then possible solutions very different from present day planning practices emerge. If one were to de-link drainage from road networks on undulating land, then the obvious first step would be to establish drainage routes first. These routes should logically follow the shortest path to ensure maximum slopes and therefore emerge as straight lines placed within the lowest formation of the land to be developed. Roads should then wind across this path thus ensuring minimal road slopes, meandering across from one side to the other. Areas between the road and the drainage paths should be used as neighbourhood green areas or public recreational areas and development zones should therefore be located on the outer areas of the meanders created by the roads (Figures 6.1).

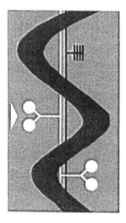 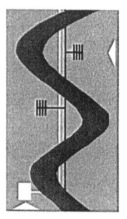

Figure 6.1   Road layout

In flat land areas, inappropriate and unsustainable road designs have become increasingly prevalent. The problems that arise stem from the fact that most roads, without proper drainage culverts, are built higher than adjacent lands. These roads act as mini-check dams, causing water logging and flooding (Figure 6.2). This problem is further compounded when houses are consequently built higher than the roads. Since developments on flat lands have inadequate slopes for natural drainage, deep waste and storm water drains have to be built, once again generating a complex series of problems.

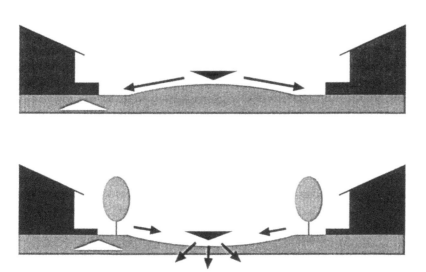

Figure 6.2   Drainage culverts: conventional approach and ideal situation

Water Supply

Sustainable and appropriate water supply systems are vital for any urban centre. At present, most water supply lines are placed underground. This is a primary cause of water-related disease problems, in more ways than one. Since the water supply in a centralized system, such as we have today, cannot be guaranteed around the clock, municipal authorities find it necessary to supply water only during specific times, forcing households to store water in receptacles which are often unhygienic. Shutting down water supply at intervals causes vacuums in the pipes resulting in their deterioration, thus contaminating the water with pollutants that are sucked in. One solution to this dilemma would be, wherever possible, to place water supply lines above ground level. This would reduce the amount of road digging undertaken by the municipal authorities whenever pipe repairs have to be performed. The above ground pipes could then be incorporated into decorative fencing along road boundaries. Where lines cross the road they may be taken underground by sloping the pipe at an inclination of not more than 45 degrees. Any leakage can be swiftly attended to and the pipes can also be used as low-level advertising spaces. With this type of water supply system, unauthorized connections can be impeded by residents' associations and by empowering neighbourhood associations.

Water Drainage

Traditionally sewage and kitchen and bath waste were never intermingled. Both were separated right at source. The night soil as well as the water that was used was disposed by allowing it to percolate into the soil. Whether this was done through localized pits or by physically lifting and disposing of it in pits at distant locations, the night soil was never disposed of in combination with the kitchen and bath waste. It is not that earlier generations were incapable of designing suitable drains to transport the combined effluent. Logical analysis shows that they chose not to adopt this system owing to their complete understanding of sustainable development. As stated earlier, human settlements in the past almost always developed on high ground, therefore disposal through drains was even easier, thus negating the argument of the non-availability of technology, which is often used as the main rationale. We acknowledge the advanced systems of planning adopted in the town planning strategies in Mohenjadaro and Harrappa and yet we fail to take cognizance of one of the strongest features of these developments. It is now acknowledged that the planning of the past provided for separate drainage systems for kitchen and bath wastes. They did recognize the fact that waste water does not necessarily mean contaminated water, as in the water used in disposal of night soil, and very simple methods were adopted to clean kitchen and bath waste. This was done at the first point, i.e. the house itself and the methods applied were extremely elementary, by disposal in the kitchen garden. The plants used here were papaya or banana, which are good digesters of grease which in turn is also a nutrient for these plants.

At present, kitchen and bath wastes are taken separately to the point of the first manhole and are then combined and discharged into a combined manhole. At this point, corrective action can be taken and both the effluents disposed off separately. Kitchen and bath wastes can be safely discharged into the open storm water drains that are presently provided outside every developed plot of land. This water must be allowed to absorb into these drains that often lie unutilized for the greater part of the year and are often blocked due to non-utilization. Lately, there has been a practice of plastering the inner surfaces of these drains thus preventing line percolation and ground water recharge. Some may argue that this is unhygienic, but any non-maintained service is unhygienic. The answer therefore lies in regular maintenance and not in its avoidance. The centralized system of city management is ill-equipped to perform this function effectively. This is where the issue of a decentralized system of city management down to the neighbourhood level would become important.

An area so far unexplored for waste percolation is the soling layer of the road. It seems that large parts of our roads lie underutilized. Natural slopes to enable wastewater flow are available because buildings are built with plinths higher than the road. Waste-water can therefore be allowed to flow under the roads into the soling layer, through leaking pipes, thus providing for wastewater disposal that is not exposed.

Some argue that the separation of kitchen and bath waste from the main sewage line leads to sewage disposal line obstructions owing to inadequate water. Here again it seems that the root of the problem is not being examined and a solution that leads to further complications is being relied upon. The first discrepancy in this argument is that it presupposes handling of the effluent through a centralized system. If the soil water was disposed off at the localized level, then the excess water required to carry it over large distances would be unnecessary. It may be seen that the civilizations of the past dealt with high densities within their fort precincts in this manner. Densities within urbanized areas or within the confines of the forts were often far higher than those we are unable to deal with today and yet we quote high densities as the main reason for our centralized municipal malfunctioning. However, localized disposal of soil water is only possible where the soil is absorptive and this is largely possible on the higher lands. The alluvial basin or flat land that we build on today is not as absorptive and is ideal for agriculture owing to its ability to retain water and it is in this context that the proper identification of land for human settlements assumes tremendous significance.

Today, as things stand, Delhi is on the brink of a major disaster. Water shortage has reached alarming proportions and the next elections may well be contested on the assurances that the political parties can give with regard to water. Our text, the *Vastu Vidya* stated that if a planner should design his/her human settlement around water, then he/she will live for 6,000 years. Today this seems truer than ever. This statement did not however mean that the *Sthapati* would never die, but implied that the settlement would be sustainable and would remain so for thousands of years, thus the *Sthapati* would be remembered. The question uppermost in everyone's mind is 'Has Delhi run dry' or 'Where has all Delhi's water disappeared to?' In a couple of years the essential appendages of a Delhite may well be a mobile phone in one hand and a bottle of suspect mineral water in the other. The cell phone and the computer may well be considered a mark of mobility and the rapid progress of information technology, but a bottle of mineral water can hardly be considered a sign of progress.

An area that requires critical examination is the flushing cistern that we use today. The earlier flushing cistern of the British Raj was of five gallons capacity. This has now been scaled down to 12 litres, based on the quantum of water required to flush down toilet paper. The traditional cistern was based on the water required to flush newspaper, which was used as toilet paper when the typical bottom on the throne was a British one. Most Indians wash and with the availability of the super satin variety, etc., even six litres is adequate. While it may not be possible to replace the almost four million cisterns of 12 litre capacity, a simple solution may suffice. Encourage people via the media to use approximately six litres of stones on the opposite side of the ball valve in the typical cistern. Even bottles filled with water and then sealed would reduce the capacity of the cistern to six litres. Considering an average of four flushings per person of the four million people owning them, there would be a savings of approximately 96 million litres of water per day in Delhi alone.

In Delhi there are over two million vehicles, requiring nearly 6,000 hectares of paved parking. The water falling on these vast paved areas also finds its way into the famous storm water drains. If one were to use the ferro-cement jaalis (the typical perforated concrete panels that one uses in toilets for ventilation) for the parking areas, and grow grass in the perforations, the result would be soft paved parking areas. The vehicles would not pressurize the roots of the grass and one could safely mow the lawn. A fringe benefit would be the reduction of heat build-up within the urbanized areas.

Coming back to my first point, never has land been traded more than in this century. Consequently, there has never been more discontent amongst people than in this century. Environmental degradation has reached new heights. Roads are designed on a 'universal standard' basis, without considering their multifarious functions and the natural lay of the land. Cities spring up on seemingly empty canvases, barely surviving their unnatural locations and consuming massive resources. Water is one of the Earth's greatest resources, and yet we have forgotten the numerous ways to replenish the Earth. Building materials are standardized to theoretically ensure consistency and uniformity, without considering the long term and humane effects of the manufacturing process and material usage.

The reason that developing countries seem to suffer from seemingly malfunctioning cities more than so-called 'developed' countries has more to do with the efficiency of the respective political and economic structures than anything else. High population densities, availability of resources, archaic dogmas, and modernization need not be stumbling blocks for sustainable development. We can learn from our historical past, immediate past and present to ensure sustainability through appropriate technologies, planning and thinking.

Sustainable Building Technologies and Appropriate Materials

Building activity and related industrial production in developing nations account for a large proportion of their Gross National Product (GNP). Within these societies, use of inappropriate building technologies and designs is the largest single contributor to environmental degradation, depletion of natural resources and inequitable distribution of wealth and opportunity. Developing nations must therefore focus on the use of appropriate technology in their building industry. At least 50 per cent of the entire developing nations' GNP goes into building and construction. Of this, 50 per cent - 60 per cent is for material consumption and 40 per cent is for labour. Therefore, in order to achieve sustainable development, it is imperative to identify the areas where macro-industry and micro-enterprise are required. If, as in the case of most macro-industries, the add-on is more than 40 per cent then there is unsustainable and inappropriate development.

Micro-Enterprise and Sustainable Consumption Patterns

Today, the developing nations are following the advanced nations' policy of achieving economic growth through macro-industrial production, which revolves around the concept of large-scale production and high-consumption patterns. The resulting impact on the environment is often overlooked. Large-scale production and consumption necessitate large distances for transportation of raw materials and end products, high marketing costs and other add-ons. Advanced nations today have 30 per cent actual production costs and 70 per cent add-on value to a product. Developing nations still have 70 per cent production costs and 30 per cent add-on value, but are rapidly following the unsustainable patterns of the developed nations.

Macro-production essentially leads to a centralized economy and unbalanced growth, while micro-production facilitates the distribution of wealth and power. There is a need to differentiate between products that need to go into the macro-enterprise and those that are appropriate for the micro-enterprise. A reliable barometer to evaluate products that should be in the micro-industry should be established. Broadly, if add-on costs exceed 40 per cent, then the product or the means of production must be re-examined for possible manufacture at the micro-industry level.

Building Materials

Misuse of building materials is probably the largest single factor that contributes to environmental degradation. In the last century, the largest amount of development in the construction industry came about in the realm of surfacing materials. Reinforced cement concrete (RCC) was clearly not the answer and it is to protect RCC that several surfacing materials have been developed, which also provide colour and texture.

A common misconception is that the life of a building depends on the strength of the building material. This is incorrect. If the soil-bearing capacity of Earth is 2-3 kg/sq cm then it would seem irrational to use building materials of 300-400 kg/sq cm. The strength of the material required is the direct consequence of its surface requirements. Surface engineered building materials require serious consideration.

Traditionally, considerable importance was placed on the choice of materials to ensure conservation of natural resources. It is the incorrect choice of materials that has resulted in the environmental degradation that we face today.

A closer look at brick and reinforced cement concrete, two of the most widely used materials in the industrial age, establishes the incorrect evaluation of the materials we choose to build with, reinforcing the efficacy of the mystical forms of establishing ecological balances. A lateral view opposing the mundane approach adopted for every component of a building is a revealing exercise.

To begin with, let us look at the most ubiquitous actor in the building drama – the 'burnt clay brick'. This tiny element of the building industry has, for centuries, been the most misunderstood. Today, the brick is considered a building material having universal application and standards. The sole determining factor is the crushing strength of the brick. However, the performance criterion around which the crushing strength has been formulated is often relegated to the background or has been long forgotten. Analyzing the established thumb rule for crushing strength brings to light a contradiction. Since the soil bearing capacity of most soils is a mere 2 kg/sq cm, then the reason for using bricks of crushing strengths of 150 to 200 kg/sq cm. is open to question. It seems highly illogical to use material of such high strength when the soil that the building is to rest on is of a lower crushing strength.

Yet the practice of achieving high crushing strengths for bricks is correct for an entirely different reason. The rationale is very simple: the strength determining factor for the brick is a direct consequence of its surface requirements. To ensure non-erodability, clay must be burnt adequately. Suitable non-erodability is achieved when there is a crushing strength of above 150 kg/sq cm. If the strength achieved is lower, then the brick wall would require additional surface treatment such as the application of cement plaster. In blocking off the natural porosity of the brick, one is confronted with the additional problem of having created a heat trap, apart from having used an unnecessarily expensive material.

Another aspect of the brick that requires rationalizing is its very size.

There is a basic error in standardizing the size of a brick at 3"×4.5"×9" for an entire country. The physical aspect of clay and its content varies from region to region. In attempting to standardize this building element we are actually trying to standardize the quality of clay that the Earth yields. This is clearly not possible and in order to obtain a standard product, set technological solutions such as 'high draft kilns' are invented. This further leads to consumption of coke that aggravates the fragile ecological balance. However, the bricks of yesteryear were of excellent quality in terms of strength and surface requirements. This was because the clay of the region determined the thickness of the brick and the final decision was that of the potter working in that area (Figure 6.3).

Figure 6.3   Thin bricks used for masonry

The brick seems to be the most widely used wall component and the most misunderstood. The fundamental error in crushing strengths of bricks was discussed with a view to rationalizing material use. Before going back to the brick and any possible alternatives, let us establish the criterion for good wall elements. It is a misnomer that wall elements require great strength. This first assumption is where the basic approach to materials really goes wrong. Wall elements must essentially be non-erodable and this must be the main criterion. Low thermal conductivity is the next priority together with the least amount of consumption of 'processed material'. Economy, colour and texture as intrinsic elements are other criteria that must be met.

The high benchmark of load-bearing capacity for brick was established to ensure its non-erodability. It is also an established fact that the denser the burnt clay brick, the greater the strength and non-erodability achieved. Conversely, greater density increases a brick's thermal conductivity. This results in higher internal temperatures resulting in the vicious cycle of expensive cooling systems. The essential criterion of a good walling material thus seems to be a non-erodable surface and a lean back-up material.

Figure 6.4 Surface-engineered interlocking blocks

Figure 6.5 Surface-engineered blocks

This brings us to the concept of surface engineering. This refers to the creation of a permanent, non-erodable surface diaphragm composed of waste material. Integration of this diaphragm with a lean back-up material like mud or fly ash enables a walling block with a non-erodable surface and a body with low thermal conductivity. This surface diaphragm can also be made in the form of a tile with a wedge that can be integrated with the body material in the mould while casting the walling block (Figure 6.4). Tiles can be used on both sides of blocks for a permanent finish on the interior and exterior (Figure 6.5).

Reinforced Cement Concrete

The second building material that dominates the building industry the world over is RCC: it is considered as the epitome of human achievement in the realm of building materials. It is pertinent to question our blind and misplaced faith in it as a magic formula. In order to evaluate RCC, it is necessary to briefly go into what may have been the reason for its development. In the past, stone was the most resilient material known to man. However, its transporting, handling and processing were cumbersome and required an immense amount of labour input. Besides, the available size of stone was a limitation in terms of design possibilities. With the rapid developments which came about during the Industrial Revolution and the invention of cement as a quick setting adhesive, it became possible to crush stone and remould it, thus making it pliable in the creation of a variety of forms. Pliability was, therefore, the main criterion and to this extent the invention and usage of concrete is justified.

RCC is an invention that forces natural materials to behave in the manner we wish them to behave. In the same way as stone has the inherent quality of being able to take considerable crushing loads, the derivative of stone (as used in concrete) has tremendous capabilities of resisting crushing loads. It is only when we try to use this material as flat slabs and push the material to respond against its natural properties, that we encounter a series of problems that constantly compound themselves. Instead of reflecting and examining where we may have gone wrong, we strive to find solutions without examining the base.

Typically, RCC consists of cement as an adhesive to bind sand and stone aggregate to create reconstituted stone. The coarse sand is the intermediate, used to fill voids, and the attempt is to obtain once again the strength of the stone we crushed in the beginning. The steel reinforcement is introduced in the lower regions of the RCC to neutralize the tension generated when RCC is used in a flat form. In the upper regions, when seen in the cross-section of the beam, concrete is behaving in compression and responding to its inherent qualities. Thus the problem is to be found in the lower part of the RCC, which is being made to withstand tension – against its natural behavioural capabilities.

It is not as if stone is incapable of withstanding tension. Flat stone slabs have been used in Hindu temples to roof considerable spans and the form of construction adopted was based on the inherent qualities of the material. For instance the flat stone slabs, in our traditional forms of construction, were used only where sedimentary stone existed. In areas where metamorphic or volcanic rock was available, compressive structures were built. Sedimentary rock is often capable of taking far more tensile stresses than RCC. Yet, the faith reposed in RCC is so great that it seems virtually impossible to convince the die-hards that there is a fundamental error in our perception of RCC.

We have fallen into the trap of using standard details the world over for foundations, walls, roofs and other building elements. Each successive generation of architects and builders mindlessly adopts the existing norm without rationalizing their advantages or examining alternative solutions. Only an extremely small percentage of professionals is involved in developing alternative technology and building materials.

Heritage-Art-Culture

These were not mere flights of fancy, as they seem to be today, but a way of living. Re-learning our heritage and history and imbibing what is relevant for us in today's world, making it a way of life – all this cannot be achieved at a moment's notice. A harmonious blend of the past with the present, of tradition and individual talent: that is what this paper seeks to illustrate and prove. The issues raised are not merely aimed at arousing awareness of the problems. Most of us are already aware of them, since we live with them. The intent here is to rationalize the problems with the single objective of arriving at workable solutions. In order to arrive at the solutions, it is necessary to link those solutions with the traditional wisdom of the past, with an open mind and some lateral thinking. It would seem that the best solutions are often so simple that they are disregarded just because of their simplicity.

Education, Training and Awareness for Sustainable Human Settlement Design

Although within the past few decades a number of institutions, research organizations and NGOs in India have worked in the field of sustainable development planning and appropriate building technologies and have made considerable headway, there has been no dynamic change in the mainstream planning and design of habitat. Two main problems exist in the current system.

The Challenge: To Create a Corps of Sustainable Design Implementers

The first and most important problem is a lack of integration of these efforts within the education system, since development as well as research in the field of sustainable human settlements and building systems is not linked with the academic institutions. Consequently, future architects and planners, who continue to absorb outdated, conventional methods, cannot apply their skills in the everyday working system. At best any change or development work continues to remain one of many pilot projects, or 'alternative' options. Their propagation at mass level is hindered by the lack of appropriately trained professionals within the profession, government agencies and amongst the educators themselves. This lack of awareness also exists amongst the general public who, furthermore, possess a woeful lack of information and expertise.

Currently there are over one hundred accredited schools of architecture and planning in India, with many more soon to receive government recognition. A central approving authority grants recognition to these institutions. The curriculum and syllabus for these schools are defined within a common framework laid out by the recognizing authority. As a result, education provided within this formal system functions on the principle of the lowest common denominator – institutions are thus unable to strive for excellence and further, regional response is lacking. In a system of this type, students are unable to develop skills to deal with sustainable design and technology issues. This is largely due to the following reasons:

- lack of awareness and exposure to sustainability issues in an holistic manner;
- lack of awareness and inability of the faculty to guide and support the students in these efforts.

Due to the requirements of working within the stipulated centralized syllabus, the educational institutions and faculty operating therein are required to function within the conventional framework. Frequently, despite attempts to search out options, the faculty does not respond to students even when they independently attempt to delve into such projects. In fact, at times they are even discouraged from stepping outside the established norms and approach.

Moreover, there is no organized feedback of research and developments in sustainable design into the institutions. Few students and faculty members return to encourage work in this area, hence we are left with single isolated efforts. The system remains static in the absence of a discerning coterie to advocate the changes necessary. Any significant change can only be effected through a cyclic link between agencies dealing with sustainable development and educational institutions, so that appropriate development methods become a mainstream concern as well as expertise.

The Need for More Holistic Planning and Research

The other problem is that to be truly sustainable, much of the research done in building technologies and planning should be carried out in a holistic manner. The research institutions, development agencies and other organizations address each issue individually and in a singular way. For instance, agencies involved with building technologies focus on specific technologies such as ferro-cement or soil blocks as isolated elements, while others deal with pollution, transport planning, environment or social issues. Co-ordination and cross-sectoral work among these agencies is lacking and thus development activities related to the design and management of human settlements does not take place in an holistic manner.

New Models for Educational Institutions and Curricula

The education, training and awareness for sustainable human settlement design should focus on training future professionals in the areas of appropriate building technologies and sustainable planning. Through such a program, a discerning group of trained personnel would be created to become future practitioners and educators within this field as well as in government and other institutions. In India, an example of such a new educational institution is the Academy for Sustainable Habitat Research and Action (ASHRA).[4]

Developing modules that become a part of the regular curriculum at school level should also be high on the educational agenda. Just as mathematics and other sciences are taught right from the primary level of the basic school curricula, the subject of sustainable development must be taught so as to become a part of the daily thought process.

Awareness Promotion and Diffusion of Technology

Aside from training, information dissemination is also a necessary objective. Awareness promotion, information and technical support will be provided to students of architecture and planning, to architecture and planning schools, as well as to architects, builders and developers, concerned citizens, institutions, business and industry in a comprehensive manner. Developing countries can set up academies similar to ASHRA, but which are suited to their zones and the programs can thus be location-specific. The process of rationalization and adaptation is much the same but if these academies interact on a continuing basis, the very fundamentals of sustainable development can be re-examined and definitive corrective actions initiated.

Conclusion

Human settlements are the basis of all development activities and the interaction of man with his environment. The building industry and other activities related to human settlements account for nearly half of the GNP in most developing countries. But it is also the single largest factor that contributes to environmental degradation and has a direct influence on finance, productivity and social behaviour. The design of human settlements encompasses a plethora of issues including land use strategies, watersheds and drainage systems, water supply, economic activity and resource generation, etc. A sustainable approach in an holistic manner is a powerful mechanism for promoting appropriate development.

These are just some of the issues pertaining to sustainable building technologies and appropriate building materials, and yet they form the core of sustainable development. Once the question of macro-industry versus micro-enterprise is addressed, it becomes obvious that there is more at stake than just simply building materials. To ensure consistent sustainable development at all levels, long-term strategies must envisage the processes of manufacturing, creating viable livelihoods, appropriate technologies and appropriate materials. Once these strategies are combined with the parameters set down, sustainable city strategies for developing countries can be implemented and a healthy future ensured.

Notes

1   The *Vastu Vidya* – the traditional Indian texts containing the fundamental principles of planning and building for human settlements – is the parallel of the *Feng Shui* in the Far East. Though propagated through myths and religion, if analyzed logically it is a complete builders' manual of dos and don'ts. These texts have a strong understanding of climatology, the behaviour of building materials and their appropriate application, respect for the natural elements and most importantly, the control of human aspirations. The texts are zone-specific and several versions exist, but the fundamental logic of living with nature is the common thread that binds all the versions together. These texts were revered by king and citizen alike and propagated by the religious heads through planners.

2   *Artha Shastra* is a Hindu text illustrating good governance and the rules that the king, the religious leaders and people must live by. Though mystified around religion the fundamentals are true and co-relate with the democracies that we are trying to develop today. There are various versions of this text written by several authors and translated into English. This document goes into various details such as the basis for town planning for good governance, defence strategies and the basis of tax and revenue generation.

3 Mystify, or mystification, is used in its sense of inducing a sense of the sacred. Thus mystifying planning controls would be to declare them as sacred and part of the spiritual and/or religious doctrine.

4 The word *Ashra* encompasses the concepts of home, security, support, refuge, and shelter. ASHRA is envisaged as a program to train future professionals in the areas of appropriate building technologies and sustainable planning strategies and develop a corps of sustainable habitat advocates within the mainstream. The primary target group consists of architectural and engineering students who are the future decision makers. The main focus will be to transfer sustainable practices from lab to land through a network of students with the Anangpur Building Centre as the catalyst. A website and over 11 films have been made and the site has been selected as the best educational site by Study Web. These resources will be used for lectures and online education. Students will be enrolled as members to the website; from this group of students the most motivated 30 students will be selected for hands-on training in live pilot projects at the ASHRA's base at Anangpur Building Center. After one year's training these students will go back to their colleges to complete their education and spread the know-how they have obtained among students and teachers alike. The objective of ASHRA is to facilitate the absorption and diffusion of sustainable planning and design practices and technologies into the mainstream and its propagation at a mass level. Through its partners in diverse countries facing similar problems it will foster exchange of knowledge and experiences. It will specifically look at the relevance of traditional wisdom in several areas of the world and dovetail it into the development practices of today. It will create links between agencies in sustainable development work and educational institutions in a cyclic self-sustaining manner. Typically it takes a few decades for a fresh approach and thinking to become part of the conventional education curriculum, but through the ASHRA process, hopefully the time taken for this is will be shortened.

Chapter 7

La Maison des Hommes:
Chandigarh as a Sustainable City

Sarbjeet Singh Sandhu

Introduction

Chandigarh was conceived immediately after India's independence in 1947, when Lahore, the historic capital of its Punjab province, was awarded to Pakistan. Besides the historic and status aspects of its design, Chandigarh also had its rationale as a 'city of convenience', planned to provide all basic physical and social infrastructure and a dignified existence even to the 'poorest of the poor'. With its theme of 'sun, space and green', it was to be *a capital city that would serve as a model in city planning for the nation, if not for the world*.

Fifty years later, as Chandigarh grows and expands both inwards and outwards, the 'model city' has also begun to face the all-too-familiar problems associated with the march of urbanization. Of the various issues that have surfaced during Chandigarh's evolution, the most compelling ones are: (1) the changed political scenario; (2) population growth (especially in the proliferating squatter colonies) and its attendant environmental problems; (3) the city's current status as a high-class regional locus of commerce, educational and medical facilities; (4) the development of new settlements in the periphery area placing a strain on the city's infrastructure.

The thrust of this paper is towards identifying the factors of growth and change that have emerged, and the threats that such changes pose to the city's original goal of sustainability. The paper will be based on a series of images of Chandigarh's urban reality, including both Le Corbusier's projects and other significant buildings as well as the state of recent urbanization.

Concept of the Sustainable City

Post-independence town planning practices in India have been largely influenced by British town planning, which had left its footprint in our cantonment and presidency towns. Since 1947 (when India became independent), three capital cities (besides other cities of lesser importance) in India have been planned to provide government headquarters, for the rehabilitation of refugees, for the generation of economic activity and for the provision of balanced regional growth and urbanization for the country. These new towns, as urban centres, have been planned to offer a high degree of liveability supported by sound physical and social infrastructure networks.

It was the pioneering work of Patrick Geddes, the Scottish biologist-planner, in India, that laid the foundation of institutions such as the Bombay Improvement Trust and the Calcutta Improvement Trust. The aim of these organizations was to provide clean, healthy habitats (to enhance the qualities of liveability) for the increasing population of the country. The Geddesian principles of 'folk, work and place' suggested that a sustainable living environment is possible/achieved only when a proper balance between living, working and care of body and spirit (all linked through a circulation system) is attained. In simple terms – a sustainable human settlement must ensure a balance between the natural and the built environment.

The Genesis of Chandigarh

The concept of the sustainable city was given a clear definition with the conceptualization of Chandigarh. Planned as a finite entity, which would harness its resources for the present and preserve its assets for future generations, Chandigarh has served as a role model for the development of new towns in India and abroad. A brainchild of the French architect, Le Corbusier and Jawaharlal Nehru (independent India's first Prime Minister) it represents the finest example of city planning, development and management in the world.

Chandigarh, which was to serve as the capital of East Punjab (since Lahore was awarded to Pakistan in 1947), was conceived during a period of political and social exigencies. The new capital was to be a finite-sized, self-contained entity. It was to be a new city 'unfettered by the traditions of the past, a symbol of India's new found freedom' – a step into the future. The city was planned with a definite goal – a government city – an administrative centre. It also had a social manifesto – the city which would offer all the amenities to all classes of people who would lead dignified lives. Based on Le Corbusier's Statute of the Land, the new city would create and promote the relationship between man and nature. The concept of sustainability did not end here. Since a city is akin to a living organism, it must continue to grow and change in response to its population's needs. The city had an agenda for its ordered growth and a set of regulatory measures to monitor its development to make it sustainable in the future as well as lend an environmental image to the city's urban form.

Attributes of the Sustainable Capital: Chandigarh

In order to actualize the sustainable city, the selection of its site was critically contemplated. As the built environment of the new capital on any existing city or as an extension to it would create enormous pressures on the parent city, selection of a virgin site became the starting point. Jawaharlal Nehru, the first Prime Minister of Independent India, wanted the new city to uplift the spirits of those refugees who suffered during the social trauma of partition. In the words of Pandit Nehru, 'The site chosen is free from the existing encumbrances of old towns and traditions. Let it be the first large expression of our creative genius flowering on our new found freedom'. The Chandigarh site was the most appropriate for ensuring the sustainability of the new city (Figure 7.1).

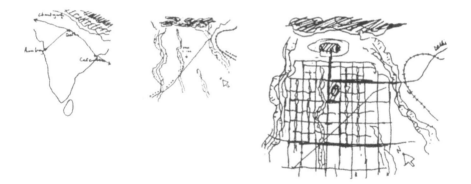

Figure 7.1   Chandigarh and its context as planned by Le Corbusier

The chosen site had the following attributes:

- stability of site (bearing capacity);
- favourable water supply conditions;
- favourable ground slope for an efficient drainage system;
- picturesque natural surroundings;
- favourable moderate climate, being in the foothills of the Shivaliks;

- close proximity to large-scale limestone deposits for setting up a cement factory;
- availability of an inexhaustible supply of building stone in the vicinity;
- reasonably safe distance from the neighbouring Pakistan border and good accessibility to nearby major settlements.

Growth Pattern for Chandigarh

The concept of a self-sustainable habitat was made feasible by deciding to build the city by the unit, wherein each unit was to be dedicated to a particular function – living, working, etc. – and each such unit was also to be self-sufficient. The master plan for the city was conceived by Le Corbusier, Maxwell Fry, Pierre Jeanneret and Jane B. Drew, along with an Indian team of trained engineers and architects who provided back-up support (Figure 7.2).

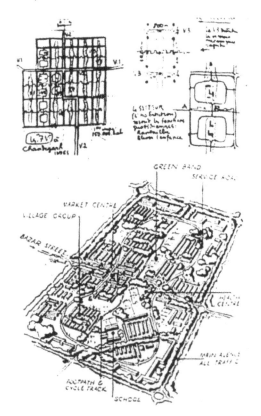

Figure 7.2   The 7 Vs and the Sector, according to Le Corbusier, and Sector 22, as it was developed

The city plan is biological in form, akin to an organism. The urbanism of Chandigarh emerged from the four functions listed in the *Athens Charter* of the CIAM (International Congress of Modern Architecture) Congress: living, working, circulation and care of the body and spirit. The force of this charter lies in giving the prime place to the dwelling – La Maison Des Hommes: this is the environment of the living – the family under the rule of '24 solar hours'. The second place is given to working – the human obligation; the third is the culture of the body on one hand, and intellectual leisure on the other. When all these functions received their definite containers and their rightful place, they were linked through a circulation efficient system. Furthermore, in order for the organism (city) to remain healthy, natural elements such as sun, space, and greenery were intrinsically deployed to generate the city mass. Thus indicators of a sustainable city habitat are reflected in the urban form of the city.

The City's Anatomy

Chandigarh has often been compared to a living organism. The city was planned on the analogy of the human being. The head – the think-tank that occupies the geographical top – is the North of the city, and contains the Capitol Complex (comprising legislative, judicial and executive bodies). All decisions for the state flow from here. The heart, pulsating with life, occupies a central location – represented by the city centre, the hub of all cultural and commercial activity. The limbs are represented by the University in the West and the industrial area in the East. The lungs are manifested in the north-south running leisure valley and the sector level greens. The arteries for circulation are depicted by the hierarchical road network.

Natural Denominations for the Sustainable City

The site selected for the city in the foothills of the Shivalik Hills was a gently rolling plain, ideal for drainage and contained within the natural confines of two seasonal rivulets – the Sukhna Choe to the East and the Patiali ki Rao to the West. The city was to grow southwards. To maintain constant contact between the city and nature, a six-meter-deep natural gorge traversing the site North South was retained in its natural state. Today, this linear central parkland – the Valley of Leisure – serves as a major recreational and green space for the city.

Situated on the 30° 50' N latitude and the 76° 48' longitude, Chandigarh has an altitude varying from 304.8 to 365.76 metres above sea level. Availability of elements such as an abundant natural groundwater supply, fertile soil, local building material – clay, sand, stone – paved the way for the city's development. Even climate has contributed as an element in the making of Chandigarh. Essentially, there are three seasons – a cold winter, a warm dry summer, intercepted by the humid inferno – the monsoon until winter sets in. It was the hot season, which defined the architectural design vocabulary of the city in the form of fenestration, parasols, louvers, projections, verandas, screens, and courtyards; these natural shading devices were used extensively to keep out the heat and to bring in the cool evening breeze. The city building budget was extremely modest and artificial mechanized means for construction were non-existent. A climate-responsive and site-sensitive approach was thus adopted for all building types in the making of Chandigarh – a sustainable city.

The Emerging Urban Form

The urban form of Chandigarh is a well-ordered matrix of built masses and urban spaces. The fabric of the city is made up of neighbourhood residential sectors, and a hierarchical circulation system resulting from Le Corbusier's 7V (*Les Sept Voies*). A rectangular grid of 800 m × 1,200 m, bordered by rapid traffic vehicular circulation V3 roads define each neighbourhood sector. The sector was envisaged as an introverted, self-sufficient unit making contact with the surrounding sectors at four specified points. No residential building could open directly on to V3. For reaching the houses, one has to move from a hierarchical V3 along V4, take the V5 loop within the sector and then a V6 street on which houses front. The sector was designed while keeping in mind the human scale and the safety of the pedestrian and the school-age child. The genesis of the sector lies in the studies made by Le Corbusier of Roman and Greek cities which were a checker-board pattern of grid-iron streets to make a mesh – the *cuadras*. The crossing points of *cuadras* were to paralyze vehicular circulation. This led to a valid regulation of automobile traffic. Within the Chandigarh sector, slow-moving vehicular traffic was permitted along the gently curved V4, the shopping street containing shops, etc., on the south-western side. Horizontal connections between adjoining sectors were made through the V4, whereas vertical connections came through the V5 network.

Yet another requisite which a sustainable habitat must fulfil is the appropriate use of locally available materials for construction as well as site-responsive building techniques (Figure 7.3). In the making of Chandigarh, the Punjab government sought the best of the Western skills and a good modern architect who would be capable of developing a new concept originating from the exigencies of the project itself. Furthermore, these needed to be suited to the Indian climate, to available materials and to the functions of the new capital. The constraints of a poor economy and a stringent budget also led to the use of low-cost construction materials and methods. The availability of cheap and plentiful manpower favoured manual labour which built the entire city. No machinery/mechanical means were utilized anywhere. In fact, a major decision which has determined the urban form and skyline of the city was to restrict buildings to four stories only. This was to do away with lifts/escalators which are energy-consuming (therefore diametrically opposed to the idea of sustainability). Very few buildings such as the Secretariat, a few earmarked sites in the city centre, etc., have provisions for lifts as they are more than four floors high.

Figure 7.3   A building type of Chandigarh

Bricks, which were cheap, were used extensively in the city for all building components (from load-bearing walls to reinforced roof beams, from boundary walls to fenestration, parapets to *brise-soleils*, and even built-in furniture). Human beings and animals were deployed to make and use bricks for different building components (made of eco-friendly clay) which has formulated an architectural design vocabulary typified as 'Chandigarh Architecture'. Since Chandigarh was a new city, it had to be built to meet demands of housing, employment, education, medical facilities, etc. The building types at Chandigarh, like any other town are multifarious. However, standardization of building components such as roof spans, lintel size, door and window openings, shutter/joinery sizes and designs ensured quality and cost control. Even the shuttering used in the Capitol has been reused in generating Chandigarh's huge government housing stock. Economy in building materials and techniques was achieved, and as a by-product, a vocabulary of Chandigarh architecture developed which in turn has generated the city's social patterns. Lower-income categories of housing shared open spaces, courtyards, privacy being provided by brick screens (which also act as sun-screens, parasols, etc.) (Figure 7.4).

Figure 7.4   A view of some significant buildings

The Current Scenario: Issues of Concern

Chandigarh was designed for a population of 150,000 persons to be accommodated in Phase I and 350,000 in Phase II, with an average density of 17 persons per acre in the former and 60 persons per acre in the latter. The current population is 800,000. The city and fringe areas contain pockets of habitations which include slums and squatter settlements crossing the 200,000 mark. Development pressure from the satellite townships of Mohali and Panchkula is creating heavy demand on the physical and social infrastructure of the city. Efforts to rehabilitate the squatter settlements under the minimum-needs program can barely match demand and is by no means stemming immigration into the city.

Chandigarh was originally conceived as the capital of one State, i.e. Punjab. It became the seat of Union Territory Administration, and also the capital of the States of Punjab and Haryana, which was carved out of Punjab in the year 1966. Today, Chandigarh, the seat of three governments, has a central location in the region and a sublime environment. Various government, and corporate magnets seek to locate their regional head offices in this city. The city, which was planned as a great experiment in urban planning, definitely offers a high degree of liveability aside from being self-contained and offering a high quality of urban infrastructure.

Figure 7.5   Chandigarh: La Maison des Hommes

Proposals to construct new townships in proximity to Chandigarh are on the books. One of the glaring consequences of this is traffic congestion. Inter-city as well as intra-city traffic on the city roads is bound to grow due to the dependence of the dormitory towns on the mother city Chandigarh. Even at the present time, during peak hours the existing traffic volumes are choking the main arteries of Chandigarh. Secondly, with the new townships, the growth along the urban corridors will lead to land speculation and unplanned growth. These developer-oriented dormitory suburbs will further pressurize the city's basic urban services.

The outskirts, which was envisaged to limit the city's size and provide agricultural backup, is rapidly being eaten away. The legislation promulgated in 1952, the Periphery Control Act was intended to safeguard the vulnerable peripheral lands around the planned city. Several townships – Panchkula, Mohali, etc. – have grown up in the periphery, due to the reorganization of Punjab, etc. As a result, not only has the peripheral green belt been depleted, but also the city infrastructure is under grave threat. Environmental pollution, population growth, traffic congestion are some of the problems faced by the city.

Four existing villages have been retained within Chandigarh. They are facing land speculation due to the absence of development controls or regulations. This is creating pressure on the city and adversely affecting the surrounding residential sectors.

Nevertheless, Chandigarh, as a harbinger of change, has ushered India into a new world of urbanism. It was planned as something unique in the annals of town planning and its place in India's history is invulnerable. It is a bold experiment in city planning with a moral and social commitment to improve living conditions. It did not ignore the compelling needs of Indian society and its cultural milieu seen as the contact between man and nature, despite freedom from the fetters of past traditions. It is a living city, whose original ideas have been translated into a spatial plan, which has been able to accommodate growth and manage change. Above all, it was and still continues to be the La Maison Des Hommes a living city – the Home of Man (Figure 7.5).

Chapter 8

Towards the Sustainable City: Planning and Urban Development for the Year 2000 World Exposition in Hanover, Germany

Jürgen Eppinger

Sustainability and Urban Development

The urban planning and the urban design professions have always been eager to incorporate innovative ideas into their current work.

The 1992 United Nations Conference on Environment and Development in Rio de Janeiro defined the general principle of sustainability as the most important new aspect for future development.

Agenda 21 – the outcome of the conference – postulates sustainability not only as the guiding principle for natural and physical development but, in following a very comprehensive approach, sustainability is declared to be a basic condition for activities in many fields of social and economic development as well.

To incorporate sustainability into planning, the main professional task will be to transform the general statements of Agenda 21 into a set of valid methodologies. This task must take into account the many scales and great variety of planning and building tasks.

In the highly multifaceted field of urban planning and development, this new concept will interact with many traditional ways of thinking. The functionalism of the Athens Charter, dating from the first half of the last century, defined a number of single – and frequently simplified – aspects of the complexity of human settlements. Housing, work, recreation and especially transportation were considered the basic functions of the city requiring regulation by planning. For many decades, this approach determined planners' educational and professional practice.

The incorporation of the principle of sustainability is not the discovery of one more function in this context but rather will become part of all the functions of planning. New and comprehensive strategies must take into account the great variety of natural, social and economic conditions in planning, design and management.

Development always brings about changes in existing conditions. The crucial issue will be the resulting overall quality emerging from the processes of change. There may be great value in protecting an existing situation; and there may be much greater value in improving a situation with the help of coordinated planning actions.

All scales of planning should be screened to identify appropriate fields for sustainable action. There is great necessity for, and value in, action on the small scale of the single building; there may be even greater value in the understanding and improvement of processes that govern large-scale natural, economic and social systems.

In most cases, planning will be able to effect only gradual change in the move towards sustainability. We will never create a totally sustainable city. However, there will be cities which, in comparison to others, fare better in this respect.

In real planning, this recognition may advocate the gradual introduction of sustainable principles with the help of very broad goals. Of practical help for immediate action may be a methodology for the development of alternative planning proposals and their evaluation according to specific sustainability criteria.

Planning for the EXPO 2000 World Exposition

Hanover was the host city for the EXPO 2000 World Exposition. The preparations for EXPO 2000 HANOVER, with its general theme of *Humankind-Nature-Technology*, offered a unique opportunity to develop new planning approaches and apply them to real conditions.

With respect to urban development, the planning for many of the previous universal expositions demonstrated the exact opposite of sustainable action. Unusable infrastructure, large tracts of unused developed land and many useless constructions exemplified the fundamental problem of temporary events confronting their host cities: the lack of long-term perspective marked these events.

There is general discussion among planners regarding the extent to which large events cause deformations in the regular course of development. In the sphere of local politics, it is obvious that planning for larger events tends to divert attention from other important fields of concern.

Understanding all this, strenuous efforts were made to draw maximum benefit for the long-term development of the city and region from EXPO 2000 HANOVER.

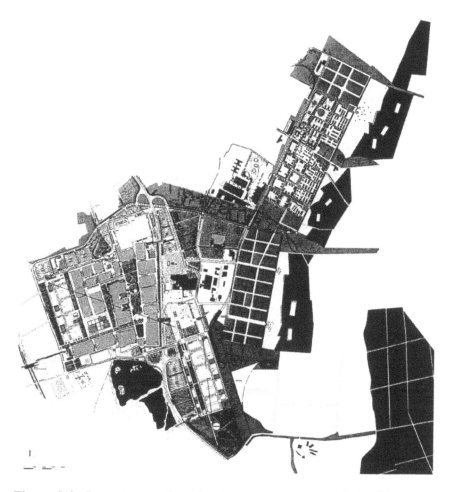

**Figure 8.1   Long-term urban development concept with the Hanover
Trade Fair grounds and the Kronsberg district**

From the beginning, in 1988, all planning connected with EXPO 2000 was
subsumed under two overall goals:

- to maximize the development effects for city and region and to avoid
  unusable investments;
- to organize a new type of universal exposition with an ambitious theme
  park as a new programmatic element.

The City of Hanover evaluated all the projects related to EXPO 2000 against the background of its set of long-term development aims (Figure 8.1).

The numerous planning processes for urban and regional development as well as for the majority of projects related to EXPO 2000 were guided by principles of sustainability.

Plans and projects included:

- regional and city-wide public rail transportation systems;
- revitalization of the existing Hanover Trade Fair grounds;
- full incorporation of the trade fair grounds within the area of EXPO 2000;
- new medium-scale development for institutional and commercial uses;
- development of the Kronsberg recreational and agricultural area;
- development of the Kronsberg housing district;
- external EXPO projects in the city and region.

Planning for the different elements demonstrates the value of the principle of sustainability in its application to very different fields and scales of development.

In the field of transportation planning, strong priority was placed on public rail transportation systems. For EXPO 2000, the Hanover Region obtained the rail systems for the year 2010.

The single elements include:

- a new mainline station close to the EXPO 2000 site suitable for high speed trains and regional rapid transit;
- re-modelling of the Central Hanover Station;
- regional rapid rail system (S-Bahn);
- extension of the local light rail network (U-Bahn);
- newly developed trains and cars for the different rail systems.

About 90 per cent of the funds for transportation improvement was spent on the public rail system improvements which will facilitate the future development of the city and the region.

In the area of planning for the EXPO 2000 site – also on a very large scale – sustainable principles were introduced as early as 1992, the year of the Rio Conference.

In order to incorporate sustainability principles, the planning competition was held very early on in the process, at land use planning level. The chosen competition area was very large and included the agricultural land surrounding the EXPO 2000 grounds. With the help of the advisory board for the competition, the idea of moderating, and compensating for, the necessary ecological impact on the area was elaborated.

Planning was governed by the following important goals:

- creation of a balanced and stable system of building land and open space for the 1,200-hectare Kronsberg development area;
- making maximum use of the Hanover Trade Fair grounds for the proposed exposition site;
- establishment of functional relations between public transportation and land uses;
- creation of a new kind of recreational and agricultural landscape on the edge of the city.

In the later planning process for the EXPO 2000 site, the winning scheme by the Arnaboldi, Cavadini and Hager planning team from Switzerland proved to be both very strong in its main structural elements and very flexible in relation to the developing and changing demands of a unique event with nearly 200 official participants. In addition, the scheme proved just as appropriate in terms of the long-term development of this part of the city.

The plans for the EXPO 2000 HANOVER site incorporated a number of distinctive elements unlike any used in earlier expositions of this kind.

The site included the following elements:

- accommodation for participants who did not intend to build their own pavilions in exhibition halls on the trade fair grounds;
- use of exhibition halls on the trade fair grounds for events;
- plots on the Pavilion Areas West and East for nations who wished to build their own pavilions;
- EXPO Plaza as the focal point comprising the Arena, the German Pavilion, and the World-wide Projects Building;
- the Theme Park sections in Halls 4-9 where the EXPO Corporation presented the major themes of the exposition.

The EXPO 2000 site had two distinct parts:

- the grounds of the Hanover Trade Fair – about 60 per cent of the total grounds;
- the newly developed areas east of the fair with the EXPO Plaza and the Pavilion Area East – about 40 per cent of the total grounds.

At the time of EXPO 2000 the trade fair portion received its new 'three pole structure', which now enables it to be used much more flexibly than in the past. Three main entrance areas served by public rail transportation make it possible to hold different fairs or other events simultaneously.

The whole area was subjected to an intensive renewal process. Six new exhibition halls of up to 30,000 square metres now provide state-of-the-art facilities in very spectacular structures.

Within the grounds, several large-scale open spaces give continuity and add amenities to the area. The most spectacular open space is the kilometre-long Boulevard of United Trees with about 400 different trees in four lines. The most spectacular structure built for EXPO 2000 was the 16,000 sq m umbrella-type wooden EXPO Roof.

The area to the east of the fair grounds was developed from scratch. For this part a plan was devised with a street structure and a technical infrastructure capable of serving both development phases: the EXPO period and post-EXPO uses.

Figure 8.2   Aerial view of the Pavilion Area East: permanent streets and utilities with the temporary exhibition pavilions

The EXPO Plaza, a ten-hectare development around a large square, during EXPO 2000 served as the central hub of the exposition. Most of the buildings in this area were built in advance and served temporary EXPO purposes.

The Pavilion Area East was planned to provide sites for pavilions that could be used after EXPO 2000 as well. Most of the participants in this area did not make use of this opportunity. After the exposition about 15 of the 30 participants in this area are planning to continue using, and are developing projects for this purpose (Figure 8.2).

Connecting design elements were the large public spaces and gardens laid out in this section of the site as well (Figure 8.3).

Figure 8.3   The Gardens of Change (by Kamel Louafi, Berlin): the permanent park in the Eastern Development Area

The results of the planning effort for the EXPO 2000 grounds have proved the value of planning procedures governed by principles of sustainability.

Kronsberg Housing District

Directly adjacent to the EXPO 2000 HANOVER site, between 1997 and 2000, the City of Hanover developed the first stage of the Kronsberg housing district.

Kronsberg in its final form will be home to about 15,000 people. At the start of EXPO 2000, about 3,000 of the planned 6,000 dwellings had been completed.

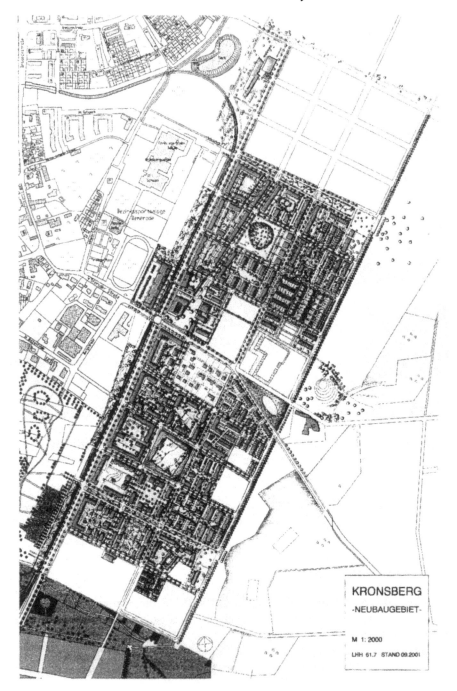

Figure 8.4   Kronsberg district: first development phase 1997-2000

The Kronsberg housing district – in addition to its quantitative function as the EXPO village for EXPO personnel and to serve the local housing market – was not solely designed to produce architectural highlights. The main aim was to combine consistent urban design principles with new environmental features of general practicability. The new principles were intended to be both applicable to the entire district and transferable to other communities.

Among the many qualities of the district today – besides its widely accepted natural and ecological features – are the great variety of housing and architecture, availability of all necessary public facilities, and a socially balanced population mix.

As long ago as the 1960s, there were initial proposals to develop new housing in the Kronsberg area which, during periods of stagnating population growth, were not pursued. Nevertheless, the continuing planning efforts in the mid-eighties resulted in a large-scale landscape plan and the first efforts towards its implementation.

In November 1992, the EXPO 2000 urban design and landscape planning competition marked the beginning of the planning process for this ambitious housing project.

The first competition was followed by an urban design competition in late 1993, which focused on the development of the Kronsberg housing district (Figure 8.4).

The winning scheme included a number of planning and urban design elements, which are part of sustainable planning on a general urban development scale (Figure 8.5). The most important are:

- public transportation – by means of a new tramline with stops at a maximum distance of 500 metres – to all housing;
- high residential densities, with an overall floor area ratio of 1.0;
- moderate building heights of 2-4 stories;
- encouragement of mixed-use development;
- a street network with special features to encourage use by pedestrians and cyclists;
- high-quality public and private open spaces within easy reach of all residents.

The winning scheme was further developed in close co-operation with the city's environment directorate. Some environmental features, summarized as 'ecological optimization', were incorporated into the planning process:

- energy use optimization with district heating systems;
- low-energy building standards;
- rainwater management;

CONSTRUCTION PRAXIS	SOCIO-CULTURAL CONSIDERATIONS	ENVIRONMENT
COMPACT LAYOUT	**SOCIAL MIX OF FUTURE RESIDENTS**	**ECOLOGICAL STANDARDS**
RESOURCE-EFFICIENT CONSTRUCTION	**CENTRAL FACILITIES**	**ENERGY**
MIXED USE: RESIDENTIAL AND COMMERCIAL	arts, community and advice centre	Energy use optimization
CONSULTATIVE PLANNING PROCEDURES	church and neighbourhood centre	district heating systems
TRAFFIC MINIMALIZATION CONCEPT	health centre	low energy buildings
tram route D		electricity saving measures
all amenities within easy walking distance	**SOCIAL INFRASTRUCTURE**	
cycle priority route	'kinderhouse' with community bakery	'Solar City'
	kindergartens	solar district heating system
parking space restrictions	primary school & middle/ secondary school	passive solar houses
	'FOKUS' housing project	fuel cell co-generation plant
OPEN SPACE QUALITY	'Habitat' international housing project	wind turbines
courtyards	decentralized support for senior citizens	photovoltaic cell technology
avenues	space allocation for community use	
neighbourhood parks	**NUTRITION**	**WATER**
green corridors	market	rainwater management concept
district park	Kronsberg Farm - 'Herrmannsdorfer Landwerkstätten am Kronsberg'	drinking water economy measures
		WASTE
		ecologically compatible buildings materials
		building waste concept
		domestic and commercial waste concept
		SOIL
		soil management
		inherited pollution - removal or containment
		LANDSCAPE
		ecological landscaping
		ecological farming
		ENVIRONMENTAL COMMUNICATIONS
		KUKA - Kronsberg Environmental Liaison Agency

Figure 8.5   The elements of sustainable community development

- soil management;
- ecological landscaping and farming;
- waste management.

These elements formed the 'Kronsberg standard', which was made obligatory for all public and private developers in the area.

To encourage the search for special architectural quality, the city drew up legally binding development plans which – somewhat different from earlier practice – contained only a few and very simple regulations regarding:

- range of possible land uses;
- building lines;
- height and bulk of buildings.

A special element of the development plans ensured that all the necessary environmental compensation measures (which according to German nature conservation laws needed to be taken into account) were provided within the area. This resulted in contributions to the quality of the local environment instead of merely fulfilling legal requirements.

The rigidity of the urban design concept called for a strong relationship between the public elements – streets, open spaces and public facilities – and the architecture of the housing sites.

Because the city council agreed to spend most of the income from property sales in the area on financing the local infrastructure, it was possible to achieve a very high level of service right from the very early stages of development.

A range of striking new landscape elements were designed – partly with the help of competitions or design workshops – and implemented:

- reforested areas on the crest of the Kronsberg hill;
- artificial hills containing the excavated soil from the development;
- boundary avenues and commons next to the forested areas;
- public open spaces between the districts of Bemerode and Kronsberg containing extensive rainwater retention areas;
- special hillside avenues with integrated watercourses;
- neighbourhood parks;
- a central square;
- tree-lined avenues;
- special rainwater retention and infiltration strips in the access streets.

The public facilities – elementary school, kindergartens and the KroKuS community centre on the central square – were conceived and designed very carefully (Figure 8.6). In addition, construction started very early on to provide the necessary services for the first new residents of the district.

The quality of the public buildings resulting from this design process demonstrates convincingly that operational standards developed under the heading of the general aim of sustainability do not preclude high architectural quality.

Figure 8.6   Public facilities: Kronsberg community centre KroKuS

Similar experiences emerged with the design and implementation process in the development of the housing areas. Before selling the building sites to developers, a tendering process with the aim of developing and enhancing the quality of the housing projects was organized. The main steps in this process were:

- application;
- selection of an architect;
- preparation of a preliminary project;
- review of the project with the help of the Kronsberg Advisory Board;
- agreement to the project;
- land sale contract including the obligation to implement the accepted project.

The review process with the help of the Kronsberg Advisory Board focused strongly on both urban design quality and the quality of the dwellings (Figure 8.7).

Figure 8.7   Kronsberg street design and housing architecture

Special features taken into account were:

- general urban design aspects;
- quality of the open spaces on the site;
- parking;
- semi-private path systems within the sites;
- private open spaces or terraces for each dwelling;
- spatial quality of the floor plans;

- general architectural quality;
- building materials.

The outcomes of all these efforts are:

- a great variety of architectural quality;
- a great variety of dwellings;
- above-average technical quality;
- several projects with special architectural, ecological or social features;
- high quality private open spaces.

In terms of the resulting product the Kronsberg district is regarded by all the different stakeholders – municipality, developers, building trades, architects and the citizens – as a successful prototype for future housing developments.

A number of social planning measures led to a social structure for the district that corresponds in most of its elements to the average city profile with two important exceptions: there are markedly fewer elderly people, but many more children compared to the city average. This fact emphasizes once more the importance of the provision of public facilities from the initial phases.

For the field of ecological optimization a special agency was set up: the Kronsberg Environmental Liaison Agency (KUKA), whose specific task was to provide services and promote a consensual spirit among the many participants in relation to the general aim of creating sustainable development. The activities of KUKA were directed to the property developers, architects and building trades as well as to district residents.

One example of KUKA activities was the training of building trades' workers in quality standards and final quality control. Another example is providing advice to residents on how to operate the technically advanced heating and ventilation systems in order to reduce energy consumption to the desired level.

In addition, the city also provided for a number of special services for the new residents to enable them to address their specific concerns.

Among these are:

- the KroKuS community centre with its great variety of cultural and social services for all groups;
- the 16 decentralized communal rooms for self-organized residents' activities;
- the District Coordinator, who deals with the various problems of the new district;
- the District Advocacy Planner, whose task is to organize the district's interests in the further development of the area.

Directly adjacent to the district, the 'dvg' data processing centre for the German public savings banks opened its office complex with about 2,000 employees in a spectacular building with a sweeping glass roof (Figure 8.8). Together with the adjacent building for the LBS state building society employing another 700 staff, this development has created a considerable number of employment opportunities.

Figure 8.8 'dvg' office development

It is foreseen that the housing and business developments will extend southwards and eventually connect with the new uses on the eastern part of the former EXPO 2000 site within range of the tram terminus at the EXPO Plaza.

Conclusions

For all participating professionals, the experience of developing and applying sustainable planning elements for the EXPO 2000 HANOVER and the Kronsberg housing district was a very rewarding experience.

This experience supports the following conclusions regarding urban planning, architecture and sustainability:

- sustainability as a planning principle is not an absolute goal but can be achieved gradually through a great number of single steps and actions on the many levels of planning, construction and practical use;
- sustainable planning principles can contribute considerably to the conservation, development and enhancement of the general quality of the environment and necessary urban development;
- sustainable planning principles should be made operational on the numerous different planning and design scales, from the regional down to the single building;
- the implementation of sustainable planning principles can encounter severe constraints regarding acceptance by existing economic, social and political conditions;
- new construction standards derived from and serving sustainable planning principles can encourage the search for, and the realization of, new architectural forms and qualities;
- implementation of sustainable planning principles demands very strong management initiatives and the 'invention' of many new strategies.

The experience in Hanover may well encourage those planners, architects and developers who are working on similar tasks elsewhere to look for a comparable and appropriate set of measures in relation to their own specific tasks.

In addition, there is the large task of introducing sustainable planning principles into renewal strategies for existing housing stock. Experimental approaches regarding new building can also provide practicable solutions for this new task as well.

Chapter 9

Strategic Policy Scenarios for Sustainable Mobility

Evgenia Dimitrakopoulou and Maria Giaoutzi

Introduction

Sustainable development is today a common policy goal and collective efforts have been devoted to reduce the impacts impeding this goal. One constraint in conceiving sustainability is formed by the complexity of the issue demanding an integrated approach. Integration in this respect concerns the various fields involved as well as the appropriate long-term horizons.

Transportation is one of the sectors in which sustainability acquires an increasingly crucial meaning, since it is one of the worst sources of environmental pollution causing multi-levelled impacts (including air quality, energy use, land use, waste production, health) from the local to the global level. Sustainable mobility in this context is one of the objectives serving the goal of sustainable development.

The focus of this paper will be an evaluation approach for a strategic policy analysis for sustainable mobility based on backcasting scenario building, supporting the assessment of a set of transport policies as regards their consistency and feasibility.

Evaluation contributing to the constructing of added values for sustainable development is of the utmost importance since it enables options to emerge and the possible results of alternative actions to be evaluated. The approach emphasizes targets simultaneously promoting economic efficiency and regional development, along with environmental issues. Based on these targets, future images (2020) were constructed.

The scenarios are explicitly policy-oriented and expert-based, supporting European and other decision-makers by providing strong evaluation tools, clearly presenting policy choices, in a monitored framework of impacts regarding several external factors.

An innovative process permitting the melding of different policy measures should become the means to achieve these targets, since individual policies alone cannot be expected to achieve sustainable mobility.

Combining transport and other related policies (e.g. regarding land use, development, taxation and technology) through the packaging of actions leads to a much greater probability of target achievement. In this respect, circuits were designed to explore at what point in time actions are required as well as to identify the responsible actors, along with the scale of implementation.

The Scenario Building Methodology[1]

The term *scenarios* in this context is used to describe the visions of possible future states which seem plausible under different sets of assumptions and which provide a background for policy assessments. Scenarios are thus distinct from forecasts, which are normally based on trend extrapolation.

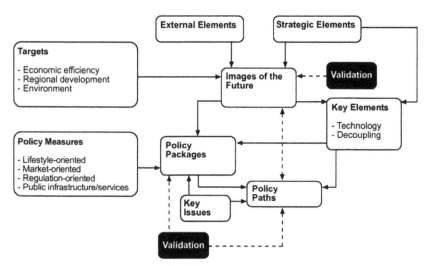

Figure 9.1   The POSSUM scenario building methodology

The present methodology for scenario construction is based on the *backcasting* technique. According to Robinson (1990), this particular type of scenario approach investigates how desirable futures can be attained being thus explicitly normative. This approach involves 'working backwards from a desirable future end-point to the present in order to determine the feasibility of that future and the policy measures which would be required to reach that point'.

The main components of the policy scenarios used in this approach are presented in Figure 9.1, and consist of:

- goals or targets set;
- external factors that are considered important; these are better defined as contextual elements as they form an essential part of the scenarios even though they may be transport-external factors (an element of the explorative scenario methodology, as a supplement to the backcasting approach);
- strategic elements that are mainly associated with each scenario.

These components are used to construct *Images of the Future*, which focus on the situation at the end of the study period (2020). Policy scenarios include the trajectory from the present state to a future image which encompasses *policy measures, paths and policy packages* such as to promote the desired developments.

Targets of Sustainable Mobility

The process of target design, generation and selection in such a context is based on the identification of sustainable development principles and the definition of the concept of sustainable mobility.

Table 9.1   POSSUM policy targets for 2020

Environmental targets
- 25% reduction of CO_2 emissions from 1995-2020
- 80% reduction of NO_x emissions from 1995-2020
- No degradation of specially protected areas
- Marginal increase of net infrastructure surface in Europe

Regional development targets
- Improve relative accessibility of peripheral regions (both internal and external). This general target includes cost and time, and allows for substitution of physical accessibility by telecommunications

Economic efficiency targets
- Full cost coverage (including external costs) of transport under market or equivalent conditions
- Reduce public subsidies to all forms of transport to zero, except where there are particular social equity objectives

The domains of *environmental protection, regional development* and *economic efficiency,* which reflect the three distinct objectives of the European Common Transport Policy, are of primary concern.

The targets are finally formed into an integrated outcome as shown in Table 9.1.

Strategic Elements

The strategic elements that were considered to have a crucial role in any given scenario were *technology* and *decoupling*; they will be analyzed in the following paragraphs.

Technology There is a substantial potential for reducing emissions and increasing energy efficiency within the transport sector through *vehicle technology* and *alternative fuels*. In order to assess their role in achieving the pursued targets, assumptions have been utilized regarding transport growth and have been conformed with assumptions regarding the impact of different technology implementations on emissions (Table 9.2).

The six cases presented in Table 9.2 illustrate possible changes in emissions that can occur as a result of the introduction of various technological and fuel efficiency measures up to 2020 (POSSUM, 1997). The assumed changes in transport volumes should be regarded as indicative since in this sphere much uncertainty exists.

It is worthwhile noting that even though, within the underlying assumptions, new technology and fuels play a very important role, target levels are not reached in any of the cases. This means that these measures alone are not sufficient.

Decoupling The constantly increasing mobility rate is currently overtaking the benefits offered by technological improvements and indicates that a technological solution alone is not sufficient for reaching sustainability targets. The rate of mobility growth should also be curbed.

Making travelling cheaper, more comfortable and/or faster, or increasing the possibility of reaching places with less effort, which are all targets/trends of the current transport system, generates an increased amount of transport, both passenger and freight.

However, the saturation levels of these trends are not expected to be reached in the near future, so transport volumes must be limited. On the other hand, not all types of transport can or should be limited to the same extent. *Decoupling transport growth (ton-kilometre or passenger-kilometre) from economic growth* is one solution to the conflict between the environmental, regional and efficiency objectives. It is a way to control the dynamics that have resulted in the very large increase in transport volumes over the last few decades.

Table 9.2   **Projected emissions as a result of various technological and fuel changes assumptions (1995-2020)**

Assumed changes in technology	Change in CO_2 emissions	Comparison to the POSSUM CO_2 target*	Change in NO_x emissions	Comparison to the POSSUM NO_x target*
1. Only fossil fuels with present average technology	+ 67%	+ 123%	+ 71 %	+ 754%
2. Only fossil fuels with high efficiency improvement	+ 24%	+ 65%	− 61%	+ 95%
3. Only fossil fuels with very high efficiency improvement	+ 11%	+ 47%	− 66%	+ 71%
4. Methanol introduced with very high efficiency improvement	− 7%	+ 24%	− 70%	+ 51%
5. Electric cars introduced with high efficiency improvement	+ 15%	+ 54%	− 63%	+ 87%
6. Electric cars and methanol introduced with very high efficiency improvement	− 14%	+ 15%	− 71%	+ 45%

*   The projected CO_2 and NO_x emissions are compared to the POSSUM targets (−25% for the CO_2 and −80% for the NO_x accordingly)

Source: POSSUM (1997)

Decoupling in this context promotes a decrease in transport intensity, measured as ton-kilometres and person-kilometres per unit of GDP. It is achieved when the growth rate of transport volumes is less than that of the GDP. During the period 1975 to 1995, the proportion between passenger transport and GDP growth – taken as an average of the 15 EU countries – was 1.4. For freight transport, the corresponding value was 1.0 and both results indicate that decoupling was not achieved.

Consumption patterns, production processes and *location decisions* are three factors that are likely to have an impact on decoupling, as will be indicated in the following section.

In many sectors, goods can be substituted by services. This applies to some products (leasing systems, joint use of durable consumer goods, repair systems) and mobility (i.e. car-sharing initiatives, public transport). The type of goods consumed also affects transport requirements. Bulk production with high material content is not a current trend, as opposed to high-tech products, with low material but high know-how content. This trend promotes the reduction of physical transport as well. Local demand, with a preference for locally produced goods, is another way to reduce the need for transport. Increased consumption of information technology (IT) services can be a substitute for goods and for travel in connection with shopping or even leisure.

In general, flexible specialization characterized by flexible technologies for specialized and segmented markets, small production series and flexible adjustment to changing consumer tastes, is more transport-efficient than global activities because the backward linkages of the production processes are regionalized. However, alternatives to globalization and flexible specialization – local production for local markets or a combination of global and local production, so called *glocal production* – can be even more transport-efficient. 'Glocal' production can be characterized by large network-firms that combine economies of scale and scope and maintain a network of local and global organizational units with close communication links. Information technology plays a key role. Transport needs can also be reduced by product design. Material flows can be reduced by the products' dematerialization/miniaturization, by their increased durability and design to make service and recycling easier.

The emerging opportunities of tele-working, tele-conferencing and so on would seem to generate a tendency towards a decrease in physical transport. On the other hand, they would constitute proximity to suppliers, buyers or public transport that are less important to location choices. This would also affect the significance of such spatial concepts as the 'compact city' and 'specialization and concentration' and their impacts, such as failing to reach the minimum volume of travel demand needed for public transport modes, would be evident. Governmental spatial policy should influence these locational choices.

Moreover, the structurally determined daily journeys for such purposes as work, services or shopping can potentially be reduced; for example, through increased doorstep delivery services and tele-working. Other journeys, especially leisure-time experience-oriented journeys, are more highly valued and thus have only small reduction potential.

In conclusion, the potential to decouple transport growth from economic growth should not only be based on trends, e.g. in production technology, IT and consumer values, but should also be supported by policy measures.

Future Images

Each scenario was designed to be relatively extreme but plausible so that the set of scenarios would cover a sufficiently wide range of possibilities. Reference year selection (2020) allows the assumption of quite radical changes while maintaining an aspect of the impacts of policy packages during this study period. A shorter time period might have reduced the possibilities of analyzing large shifts in technical and institutional environments, while a later time horizon might have limited the scenarios' policy relevancy. However, the description is maintained at a somewhat strategic level so that the impact of special features on transport systems in each country and city are not explicitly discussed.

The scenarios are designed by using different combinations of strategic and contextual elements thus requiring different policy alternatives.

The three Future Images investigated in the POSSUM context rely on different levels in the use of the strategic elements described above. Therefore,

Image 1: relies on a moderate pace of technological improvement combined with a considerable degree of decoupling (Technology+/ Decoupling+++).

Image 2: relies on rapid dissemination of cleaner technologies and fuels combined with moderate decoupling (Technology+++/ Decoupling+).

Image 3: relies on both rapid technological improvements and a considerable degree of decoupling (Technology++/Decoupling++, as for a Technology+++/Decoupling+++ case, the costs of achieving such far-reaching transformations in both dimensions would in all likelihood be too high).

In addition, the above Images are formulated by different combinations of contextual elements.

A successful approach to environmental protection would require agreement and cooperation outside the market either by political intervention or by 'grassroots' initiatives sponsored by those affected or by some combination of both. Hence, the level of cooperation in society will affect the possibilities of meeting the environmental targets. For the three Images, respectively, the following 'contextual framework' was selected:

- *local, regional and EU cooperation*, where policies are mainly driven by local and regional initiatives (bottom-up politics). Local and regional aspects have a political priority while global environmental issues are ensuing. Green values are pushed by 'grassroots' movements rather than by national or EU politicians, who try to follow the demands of the people. There is polarization at the global level, where the EU, the US and Japan take different stands on questions such as global warming, and tend to protect their own markets against outside competition;

- *global and EU cooperation*, with free trade and a striving for consensus on environmental issues. At local and regional levels the attitudes towards cooperation are more passive, as the political agenda is mainly driven by national and EU politicians. High-level problems (top-down politics) are more focused on. Politicians have a leading role and try to influence public opinion;
- *local-global cooperation* promotes an accord between local, regional and supranational initiatives and objectives – a kind of harmony between bottom-up and top-down politics. Green values are widespread with both local and international lifestyles.

The selected Images are outlined in Table 9.3, where the chosen combinations are the ones that seem better related and are highlighted accordingly.

Table 9.3   Future Images obtained from combining the two dimensions

Contextual Elements	Strategic Elements		
	T+/ D+++ *	T+++/ D+ *	T++/ D++ *
Local, Regional + EU Cooperation	*D1*	T1	TD1
Global + EU Cooperation	D2	*T2*	TD2
Local-Global Cooperation	D3	T3	*TD3*

*   Where T is Technology, D is Decoupling, and the number of + indicates the corresponding degree of advancement for each element

In Image I, the *EU Coordination of Active Citizens* is selected because radical decoupling demands behavioural changes (mode choice, choice of residential area, etc.) which in turn require 'grassroots' involvement and commitment.
    The main elements of the transport policy outlined for the Image are:

- measures intended to reduce structurally enforced travel, such as land use planning, promotion of tele-commuting, etc. (*decoupling*);
- measures such as standards and pricing, intended to achieve a shift of passengers from private cars to public transport and a shift from road freighting to train and ship (*modal shifts*);
- funding of research and development and promotion of market uptake by the creation, for example, of niche markets for novel systems (*cleaner technologies*);

- new transport network links to Central and Eastern European Countries (CEEC) and to some extent to other peripheral regions (*regional equity*).

In Image II, the *Global Cooperation for Sustainable Transport,* the general strategy emphasizes rapid technological evolution and dissemination which require global cooperation on such issues as the regulation of CO_2 emissions. The main elements of the transport policy that are outlined for the Image are:

- international agreements on CO_2 emissions and other regulations;
- internalizing transport externalities by means of taxation and feebates[2] (all modes should in principle pay their full costs);
- funding of research and development for cleaner technologies;
- promotion of new markets by the creation of niche status for novel systems;
- transport operations are largely privatized, but funding of new infrastructure is mainly public. Because of the political goal of regional equity, transport services to peripheral regions are subsidized where necessary.

Image III, finally, is the *Accord on Sustainability,* where a balanced strategy of rapid technological development and a considerable degree of decoupling are both supported.

In this Image, the solutions of Image I and Image II could be combined resulting in even better goal achievement (synergy effects), since the common attitude and the political climate at higher levels support this. However, financial constraints will influence what is attainable. European regions and municipalities largely choose their own ways to cope with local emissions, congestion, etc., while targets are agreed upon at higher levels.

The next step is to compare the three Images according to their priorities and their consequences, as well as their level of target achievement.

Policy Measures, Packages and Paths

For the identification of policy measures and subsequent policy packages and paths, as a *first stage,* key issues for future transport policy ('hotspots') are identified. This is necessary to ensure that the range of potential policy measures possesses the dynamics to deal with the key issues for future transport policy. As such, global environmental issues, urban pollution and congestion, freight transport (particularly at critical points such as the trans-Alpine region), the future of railways, as well as air transport growth (including issues concerning deregulation) are taken into consideration (POSSUM, 1998).

The *second stage* is a review of the different types of policy measures and their potential contribution to the achievement of the POSSUM targets. As such, policy measures affecting technology and new fuels, the role of passenger transport policies, the role of freight transport policies, as well as the role of organizational change are considered. In order to highlight the broad scope of action, these measures are examined under distinct basic policy orientations, namely lifestyle-oriented policies, market-oriented policies, regulation-oriented policies and public infrastructure/services.

Having identified the hotspots and the potential contribution of different policy measures to the achievement of the POSSUM targets, in the *third stage*, a comprehensive list of policy measures is constructed. The influence of these measures on each of the hotspots is indicated through a matrix, which is also used to identify (POSSUM, 1998):

- the influence of each measure on technology, passenger transport, freight transport and transport organization;
- the extent to which each of the policy measures might contribute to the three broad types of targets (environmental protection, regional development and economic efficiency);
- the policy orientation of each measure;
- the timescale of the effect of each policy measure – whether impacts are likely to be short-, medium- or long-term.

In a *fourth stage*, policy packages are developed which combine sets of policy measures that are likely to create synergies. Each of the policy packages is designed to relate to a specific Future Image. In particular, it must address a specific issue; it must give a convincing contribution to the solution of a perceived problem and it must demonstrate a balanced impact on different groups of stakeholders in order to be acceptable. The following policy packages can be outlined (POSSUM,1998):

- *Ecological tax reform.* The idea behind an ecological tax reform is the view that externalities, resources use and environmentally harmful activities are taxed too lightly, while labour is taxed too heavily.
- *Liveable cities.* This package aims at making cities more attractive by diminishing the dependence on car. Strategic measures are: increased accessibility by IT, more space and higher priority for walking, cycling and public transport combined with less space for cars and parking. Land-use planning in favour of decentralized concentration is also an important element.
- *Electric city vehicles.* This policy package aims at a better matching of transport demand with the type of vehicle used. This could significantly increase the efficient use of resources.

- *Long distance links – substituting for air travel.* This package is aimed at reducing long-distance passenger travels by substituting highly energy intensive modes with less energy intensive modes and other forms of communication. It also involves the reduction of travel distances.
- *Fair and efficient distribution of mobility – tradeable mobility credits.* All individuals and firms cannot equally compete, so some distributional mechanisms are necessary to ensure fair levels of accessibility.
- *Promoting subsidiarity in freight flows.* One basic strategy for decoupling freight transport from economic growth is to reduce the travel distance of goods.
- *Promoting dematerialization of the economy.* Reducing the material throughput of the economy can reduce the necessity for transport.
- *Minimizing specific emissions.* This package aims at a significant reduction of specific 'real world' emissions from road and air transport. It is in particular intended for Image II where the car has a strong position. In Image I transport volumes are lower, electric vehicles are more common and walking, cycling and public transport also have high shares in urban areas.
- *Resource efficient freight transport.* This policy package aims to increase the resource efficiency of freight transport and reduce haul distance.
- *Customer friendly transport services.* This package aims at making public transport and intermodal travel more convenient. It is mainly aimed at Image II which in part is due to its strong emphasis on technology. Furthermore, in Image I there are other strong measures contributing to competitiveness of public transport.

For each policy package, the construction logic, the possible variations according to the Images, the main policy measures, as well as impact on stakeholders, are explored (POSSUM, 1998).

The development of policy paths, by combining policy packages together, is the *fifth stage* of the process. Paths will contain a large number of policy measures that are needed to attain the image targets. Measures within a package and packages within a path should be interrelated.

The combinations of elements were chosen as shown in Figure 9.2.

The packages and supplementary measures that make up each path are outlined in Figure 9.3.

Finally, issues of acceptability and implications for the Images are considered.

	UNCERTAINTY: different futures	
	↓	↓
	Image I: focus on *decoupling*, bottom-up	Image II: focus on *technology*, top-down
Market and lifestyle orientation	Path 1.1	Path 2.1
Regulation and service orientation	Path 1.2	Path 2.2

CHOICE: → (Market and lifestyle orientation)

different → **strategies** (Regulation and service orientation)

Figure 9.2   The policy paths examined

Validation

Since the policy scenarios deal with complex systems and qualitative estimations and statements play an important role, validation is consequently significant. The involvement of a variety of actors is important for developing coherent scenarios and for identifying the key issues. At the same time the validation process was part of the dissemination strategy of the project results. Three aspects of the POSSUM project were distinguished for the validation stage:

- the framework, including the overall methodology and the Images;
- the policy paths including the technology and decoupling potentials;
- overall conclusions and recommendations.

Conclusions

The goal of this paper was to present an innovative methodology for investigating policy scenario building at the European level for the period 1995-2020, developed within the POSSUM project. Based on backcasting methodology, targets were established for the economic, regional development and environmental objectives set out in the EU Common Transport Policy. These targets were the basis of a framework for building Future Images.

Path 1.1	Path 2.1
• Ecological Tax Reform *(emphasis on shifting taxes from labour to resources)*	• Ecological Tax Reform *(emphasis on high taxes on energy, materials and emissions)*
• Fair and Efficient Distribution of Mobility – Tradeable Mobility Credits	• Customer-Friendly Transport Services
• Long-Distance Links – Substituting for Air Travel	• Minimizing Specific Emissions
• Promoting Subsidiarity in Freight Flows *(emphasis on price mechanisms)*	• Resource-Efficient Freight Transport *(emphasis on road pricing for freight)*
• Promoting Dematerialization of the Economy *(emphasis on tax policy)*	+ Facilitating IT accessibility for work, services and so on, in order to reduce travel
+ Facilitating IT accessibility for work, services and so on, in order to reduce travels	+ Tradeable permits or feebates according to fuel consumption of new cars and aircraft
	+ Feebates on new cars according to weight
	+ Introduction of methanol through economic incentives

Path 1.2	Path 2.2
• Liveable Cities	• Customer-Friendly Transport Services
• Electric City Vehicles	• Minimizing Specific Emissions
• Long-Distance Links – Substituting for Air Travel	• Resource-Efficient Freight Transport *(emphasis on new freight tracks and intermodal centres)*
• Promoting Subsidiarity in Freight Flows *(emphasis on information systems)*	+ CAFE standards or uniform reductions of average specific fuel consumption for cars and aircraft (e.g. 25% for all car manufacturers)
• Promoting Dematerialization of the Economy *(emphasis on stringent standard, recycling, etc.)*	+ Facilitating IT accessibility for work, services and so on, in order to reduce travels
	+ Introduction of methanol, for example combining R&D and through public procurement of methanol vehicles

Figure 9.3   Combination of policy packages and supplementary measures into paths

The policy scenarios for sustainable mobility represent possible alternatives, rather than policy options. However, they illustrate the range of available measures, packages and paths, as well as the scale of the required changes. Principles for implementation based on acceptability, lead-times, dynamic effects and adaptability were also developed within POSSUM, including comments on the role that the EU Commission can play, although they are not presented in this paper.

Some policy conclusions drawn from the Project and worth mentioning are set out below:

- for a more sustainable transport system, action is required as regards two main strategic elements: technology and decoupling. Although technology plays a key role, especially in the longer term, alone it cannot achieve sustainability in transport;
- required actions are not limited to the transport sector, but should be implemented in related sectors as well. Some of the latter are linked to structural social changes, macroeconomic policy interventions and the impact of technology;
- new policy actions should be set in hand immediately, otherwise the targets established will not be reached by 2020;
- EU policy priorities, which have not been analyzed in detail within the POSSUM policy scenarios, should be implemented with special care to ensure that actions in these priority areas do not result in a less sustainable mobility system;
- the packaging of policy actions is a means to promote successful implementation since it allows the application of principles of acceptability and adaptability;
- whatever elements may prevail in the future, it is important to implement certain common pertinent actions in several of the paths;
- the optimal solution to ensure sustainability in the longer term would be to introduce both strong decoupling and strong technology. This could be possible under particular conditions (POSSUM, 1998);
- transport must be more closely linked to other EU policy concerns. More emphasis should be placed on influencing economic, structural, agricultural, tourism and other policies for promoting the decoupling of transport growth from economic development.

Notes

1   POSSUM (Policy Scenarios for Sustainable Mobility), Strategic Research Task 13 in the 4th Framework Transport Program of the EU.
2   Feebates are a combination of charges (fees) and rebates, such as the charging of fees on inefficient, polluting cars and rebating the proceeds to efficient, clean cars (cf. von Weizsäcker and Jessinghaus, 1992).

References

POSSUM (1997), *POSSUM Deliverable 2. Development of Transport Policy Scenarios – The Images of the Future*, Deliverable submitted to the European Commission DGVII (Strategic Research), December 1997, Brussels.

POSSUM (1998), *POSSUM Final Report*, Deliverable submitted to the European Commission DGVII (Strategic Research), December 1998, Brussels.

Robinson, J. (1990), 'Futures under Glass: A Recipe for People Who Hate to Predict', *Futures*, October.

Weizsäcker von, E.U. and Jessinghaus, J. (1992), *Ecological Tax Reform: A Policy Proposal for Sustainable Development*, Zed Books, London.

PART II
AN INCLUSIVE APPROACH

Introduction to Part II

Maria Cerreta

An Inclusive City: Challenge or Paradigm?

Fighting social and urban exclusion is one of the greatest challenges that the city will face in the twenty-first century in order to guarantee that all citizens are able to participate in its social life, economy and politics. In general terms, exclusion means isolation from processes of social development, unemployment and distance from economic processes, marginalization, discrimination, lack of ties with cultural and political processes, vulnerability and lack of network connections (UNCHS, 2001a). In most cases, the laws of global economy have tended to establish the rule of inequality in terms of access both to resources and to rights, relegating the task of compensating its effects to social policy.

Therefore, the city is shaped like a paradox, by the fact that it exercises a tremendous power of attraction but, at the same time, creates segregation, helping to increase the dialectical process between exclusion and inclusion (Sassen, 1998).

The excluded are those who have been denied the benefits of urban life and its basic services; they are often forced to occupy the land in illegal ways and to live under conditions threatening health and safety. Exclusion is the result of physical, social and economic barriers that prevent participation in urban life, but it is also the consequence of the failure of local authorities who are unable to integrate the excluded in the decision-making process (UNCHS, 2001b). Ethnic, gender and religious differences are only a few of the factors that can determine exclusion and auto-exclusion, but they also contribute to the construction of processes of cultural integration, of sharing of values and trust in others, in governments and in politics. It should also be noted that urban and social exclusions are closely linked to housing exclusion (Cohen and Shabbir, 1992; World Bank, 1993; Hibou, 1998). To promote social inclusion means, indeed, taking into account both the individual and society, allowing the former access to housing, employment and services, the enjoyment of social mobility, the reduction of conditions of vulnerability, respect for human rights without discrimination, and the right to live in harmony with oneself and within the community in conditions of enabling and well-being. For society, it implies respect for human rights and fundamental liberties, for cultural and religious differences, for social justice, for norms and laws, as well as the satisfaction of the needs of the weak and democratic participation (UNCHS, 2001a).

The goal of creating inclusive cities was spelled out in the Habitat Agenda at the United Nations Istanbul City Summit (1996), and confirmed in the *Istanbul+5 Declaration* during the Special Session of the General Assembly meeting of the United Nations held in New York in June 2001, the aim being to ensure that all urban settlements have access to adequate housing and essential services within 2015.

The concept of the inclusive city constitutes the premise for a strategy aiming at social cohesion in order to improve the quality of life for those who experience discrimination and exclusion. Exclusion, after all, is not only a problem of minorities, families, communities or of some cities but is rather a problem of all cities, which are affected by it in different ways. Therefore, fighting exclusion means providing the opportunity for citizens to free themselves from economic insecurity, to satisfy their basic needs and to fully participate in the life of society. In many cases, traditional approaches to the reduction of urban poverty concentrate on the supply of services, allowing profit only for few and considering the poor as passive subjects. In reality, the creation of all-inclusive cities means giving voice to the poor and the emarginated through the mediation of civil society, community-based organizations, citizen groups and NGOs (Wakely and You, 2001). In fact, in the inclusive city, planning and urban management are much more effective if some responsibilities are delegated directly to the poor in recognition of the validity of transferring the decision-making process to the lowest possible levels (UNCHS, 2001b).

The inclusive city is one that fights poverty to activate a process of integration/inclusion of all its inhabitants. However, exclusion and poverty are not synonymous. Poverty refers to the lack of material goods, to the inability to satisfy elementary needs, while exclusion concerns the social process involving all the aspects of an overall condition of individuals and groups and makes it clear their expulsion from the same social system (Fayman and Santana, 2001). The poor are often excluded and different phenomena of exclusion can be the causes of poverty. In this sense, to adopt an inclusive approach to urban management requires, first and foremost, the identification of the root causes of poverty and exclusion, in the awareness that they are not unalterable states, but continuously evolving processes.

Therefore, it is necessary to develop a strategy that is simultaneously productive and inclusive, with the goal of reconstructing relationships and social bonds, granting the possibility to access fundamental rights and the decision-making process.

To build the inclusive city means to rebuild 'social capital', that, together with 'civic involvement' and 'governance', represents one of the principle corner stones of the Habitat Agenda. Social capital is the product of the construction of interpersonal networks, contacts, knowledge and human resources that individuals and the collectivity can utilize to counteract the negative effects of globalization. According to Coleman (1990), social capital is made up of social relationships which persist over time and which individuals in part possess and in part build up over the course of their lives. This form of capital is 'social' because it embodies the public good, insofar as people actively sustain and strengthen these structures of reciprocity not only producing benefits for themselves, but also for all components of society (Putnam, 1993a). Social capital can increase the benefits of investments in physical and in human capital, and represents what the philosopher Albert O. Hirschman defines as a 'moral resource' – that is a resource whose supply increases rather than decreases through use and which becomes depleted if not used (Putnam, 1993b). Therefore taking into account the positive role played by social capital means activating planning and management processes to create a more inclusive city. In this perspective, social capital represents the vital component of development and can foster the formulation of new intervention strategies. The strength of social capital can vary in function of different geographical and cultural contexts, but it represents the driving force in fighting exclusion and opposing spatial segregation, which can often reinforce disadvantages and the selfsame exclusion. In fact, urban and spatial segregation highlight socio-economic differences and express social fragmentation. In this sense, policies seeking to overcome these obstacles and the pursuit of occupational and financial goals should take into account such basic elements as the intensification of the informal sector, the activation of new forms of incentives, the public redistribution of finance. Reflecting upon these elements, we can identify three different ways to achieve the inclusive city: the informal sector can make an active contribution to the employment market (De Soto, 2001); decentralized finance can influence economic and social conditions at micro level, acting in an inductive (or 'bottom-up') way, and also open up possibilities for the poor (Baumann, 1999-2000); redistribution of the budget can follow a 'top-down' approach for the reduction or prevention of processes that produce or augment poverty. The inclusive city would then mean the 'city of solidarity' (Fayman and Santana, 2001); it would mean building upon recognized and shared values and upon the structural components of society, that make plain what is referred to as the 'sum of positive individual models' (Sen, 1999).

Green Agenda and Brown Agenda: Towards an Integrated Approach

A vision of the future was drafted at the Rio de Janeiro Conference (1992) – Agenda 21 – and a Global Action Plan in order to transform that 'vision' into reality. In particular, the importance of the role of local authorities and of the community for building a more sustainable future was emphasized, especially through the development of the Local Agenda 21, in accordance with the slogan 'think globally, act locally'. Agenda 21 delineates, therefore, the way forward to achieve sustainability on a local level with the broadest possible goal of improving the quality of life through the promotion of partnership, shared goals, decentralization, capacity-building and the construction of networks.

Subsequently, during the United Nations Conference on Human Settlements (Habitat II) (Istanbul, 1996), the Habitat Agenda was drafted; this emphasized the role of cities and urban sustainability, and recognized the importance of the land, housing and urban management for concrete actions to furnish *adequate shelter for all* and *sustainable human settlements in an urbanizing world*. It may be maintained that the Habitat Agenda in a certain sense maps out the principles and actions that can lead to sustainable human settlements, keeping in mind the bonds with the natural environment, with social development, with demographic trends and with populations at risk. It contains an overview of the objectives and the principles that should be adopted by governments along with the identification of implementation strategies.

The two Agendas help define the ties between the 'green' and the 'brown' perspectives (Allen and You, 2002; Cohen, 1991) bearing in mind the problems tied to urbanization, to the environment and to development. In specific terms, the 'Green Agenda' addresses long-term issues with global-level impacts (such as ecosystem loss, biodiversity risks, greenhouse effect, etc.) and which necessitate global cooperation; while, the 'Brown Agenda' refers to environmental issues with immediate impacts at the local level (such as air or water pollution, waste management, etc.) and which influence the quality of daily life (Wakely and You, 2001). Examining the relationships between the Habitat Agenda and the Agenda 21, it is possible to recognize a common 'blueprint for action' that has emerged in evident ways from their implementation over the past ten years. However, it is essential to ensure that the two Agendas are integrated within a coherent approach to guarantee policy, and concrete action for sustainable development. In particular, they share certain principles such as: the re-evaluation of the role of cities and the potential contribution that they can make to sustainable development; the need to face the issue of urban development bearing in mind social, environmental and economic performance, seeking an equilibrium among the goals of the fight against poverty; the improvement of environmental conditions in the short and long terms and the promotion of urban economic productivity; the recognition of the key role of local actors within the urban development process. Further, it is necessary to institutionalize this new approach within the sphere of urban planning and management processes placing them alongside participatory mechanisms to strengthen local governance. Essential to both is attention to the 'local' dimension based on ample community and stakeholder participation, as well as on an enabling approach and upon the subsidiarity principle, all supported by public policy through legislation and by the central government in favour of local initiatives. In this perspective, Local Agenda 21 is recognized as a process of integration to improve the political and social bases for development strategies, to underline the bond between the ecological and the social dimensions, and to mobilize different kinds of resources with attention to specific context. An important role is played by the decision-making process and by evaluation which verify coherence and transparency on all levels of economic planning, and urban planning and management, with the intent to reconcile 'goals' and 'values' (Haughton and Hunter, 1994).

The commitment of ICLEI, UN-Habitat's Best Practices and the Global Urban Observatory to the implementation of Local Agenda 21 stresses the importance of monitoring progress in different contexts, facing the obstacles that prevent its diffusion, and analyzing the implications on different scales. In particular, in the survey carried out by ICLEI (2002) on the occasion of the Johannesburg Summit, interesting data emerged regarding the diffusion and the realization of the processes of Local Agenda 21. The study states that, by December 2001, in 113 countries 6,416 local authorities had activated the process in concrete terms, while 73 per cent of the municipalities had formalized partnerships and the involvement of stakeholder groups; 59 per cent had integrated the process of Local Agenda 21 with its system of government. Furthermore, 61 per cent of the processes activated have reached the implementation phase of the Action Plan. So it can be deduced that the Local Agenda 21 process is spreading considerably especially in Europe and that, in comparison to the preceding investigation (ICLEI, 1998), it has increased with the adhesion of 49 additional countries. However, the study highlights differences in implementation levels in different specific contexts, depending upon the differences which characterize every community, from national policy regarding sustainable development on the local level to the funding activated. Despite concrete difficulties, over the last five years the number of the Local Agenda 21 processes implemented in developing countries has almost tripled and the type of processes underway demonstrates the incisive role played by the community and stakeholders involved in decision-making. It can be said, therefore, that the successes achieved, even in complex situations, testify to the validity of the Local Agenda 21 as a process of multi-stakeholder, participatory planning able to face important issues of global consequence through an integrated and local approach.

Ideas and Strategies for the Twenty-first Century

Examination of the concept of the inclusive city and how it can best become a reality through the application of the principles and the tools of the Habitat Agenda and of the Local Agenda 21 is represented in the essays selected for this part of the volume. The authors face complex issues regarding the future of the city and identify some possible strategies founded upon a 'human' vision of development.

What the city of the twenty-first century will be depends mainly upon the choices that will be made today as well as upon how, and to what extent, *past lessons* will be taken into account. As Üner Kirdar emphasizes, in light of past experience, it is essential to identify the ends and the means that will allow society to face the deep changes delineated for the future. A fundamental lesson, and an essential premise, concern the ensuring of peace, safety and liberty. However, the pursuit of these objectives requires wisdom, leadership, commitment and, above all, a *future vision*. Within the United Nations, Üner Kirdar has promoted an innovative thesis regarding the concept of development, according to which the peace, safety and prosperity of nations depend on a 'putting people first' policy based on a new paradigm founded on the trilogy of: *human rights, sustainable human development* and *human safety*. These three concepts are closely interwoven, indivisible, and complementary and can reinforce one another. As also emphasized in other writings (Kirdar, 1984; Kirdar and Haq, 1987; Kirdar, 1990; Kirdar, 1994; Kirdar and Silk, 1995; Kirdar, 1998), the attainment of this paradigm will involve not only economic growth, but will also allow equitable distribution of benefits, environmental regeneration and the empowerment of people while broadening the possibilities for choice and opportunity and fostering participation in decision-making processes. It is significant that the concept of sustainable human development has played a key role within United Nations programs since the mid-1980s. It is a *pro-people, pro-nature, pro-jobs, pro-women* development (Kirdar, 1998-1999), with the goal becoming the expression of the individual's freedom of choice, which is impossible without an open society, guaranteeing pluralism and reinforcing the democratic system with courageous leadership having a long-term perspective. The success or the failure of the 'put people first' political choices will depend on the quality of the 'human governance' which will need to emerge with a role of catalyst of development. Thus the challenge becomes the transformation of global threats into new opportunities for a safer, healthier, more human and more sustainable city, where the choice of the kind of governance represents one of the decisive elements if sustained by a project for the inclusive city. 'Good human governance' is proposed, therefore, as a new system of local-level government that can guarantee human rights, development and safety.

Kirdar's question of what we have learned from the past is placed side by side with the question that seems to underlie David Harvey's article: *who, as human beings, do we want to be in future?*

To reflect upon humankind and upon how we can change in order to alter our own destiny and the way in which we live is central to the reflection upon the city. Harvey underlines how the history of the city and the considerations developed over time regarding it have been periodically marked by attention to the human capacity for producing transformation and, in particular, transformation brought about by people comprising a community and social movements. He observes how the true sources of urban change are often brought about by civil society. *Humankind, community,* and *civil society* are recognized as the principal premises for 'humanizing' the quality of life in cities. According to Harvey, the distance between the reality of the transformations and the world of planning theories has often accentuated powerful separation, overcome in many cases by the role developed by different social urban movements in various historical and geographical contexts that show the effectiveness of 'bottom-up' action (Friedmann, 1987; Sandercock, 1998). This type of action can be associated with a theoretical structure that defines its principles and connections, clarifying the process that fosters the passage from *particularism* to a broad, collective and shared political vision, working towards an ever more inclusive city. In this perspective, it is essential to overcome the risk that 'community' and 'place' take on a negative meaning as obstacles to change, thus causing clear forms of exclusion. Furthermore, it underlines the need to transcend particularism to achieve global political concepts, analogous to what occurs in the relationship between the *universal* and the *particular*, where the one exists in relation to the other (Castells, 1996). On this subject, Harvey emphasizes the need for a common language that can overcome the fragmented heterogeneity of 'bottom-up' movements but that also imply respect for the 'other' and for difference. The possibility of attentive intervention upon the processes of transformation that concern humankind includes the importance of dialectical relationships, vital elements for the construction of a true democracy in contemporary urban scenarios.

The issue of humankind and the role it will play in the future of cities also reappears in Nicholas You's paper. In particular, *demographic growth, globalization* and *democratization* are three factors that have contributed to strengthening the role of cities as centres of production, consumption and political and social change, but also in delineating *new challenges.*

You recognizes that, after Chapter 28 of the Agenda 21 (UNCED, 1992) and the strategic lines of the Habitat Agenda (UNCHS, 1996), some conclusive factors have been identified that can render concrete the principles of sustainable development. The experiences contained in the UN-Habitat data bank selected within the Best Practices and Local

Leadership Program represent some tangible examples of how these strategies have produced significant results which could help improve the quality of life in cities in accord with sustainability principles. The *best practices* illustrated show how strategies and actions must be structured and implemented while taking into account certain key principles such as: local responsibility, participative democracy, partnership, decentralization, capacity-building, empowerment of local actors, construction of networks and access to information. It is clear that at the base of the intervention strategies, is an action on people – a process of self-awareness of their potential and that deriving from cooperation with others, where trust constitutes one of the essential elements upon which to found any kind of development process. Porto Alegre, Chengdu, Surat, Dar-es-Salam, Bangalore, Ahmedabad are only some examples. In addition, the bests practices attest to the validity of the strategic objectives of the Habitat Agenda as premises for achieving the Agenda 21 principles by making the link between sustainable urban development and 'good urban governance' explicit.

Some contributions make reference to the principles and actions of the Local Agenda 21 processes and demonstrate how, in different places in the world (India, Bangladesh, Lithuania, Italy, Great Britain), it is possible to pass from theoretical principles to practice. Kirtee Shah's essay is part of a broader research project commissioned by the International Council for Research and Innovation (CIB) concerning Asia, Africa and Latin America as part of the Action Plan for the CIB Agenda 21. With its complexity and differences, India provides a privileged point of view for this type of reflection; an attempt is made to understand whether or not the sustainable development model is a Utopia and if this Utopia can save the world from the risks posed by today's development model. Shah proposes a new paradigm whose principles follow those formulated by Gandhi and which could be based on the more measured application and more balanced distribution of natural resources, bearing in mind the evolution of local conditions and aspirations, the consideration of spiritual and religious components and the possibility of influencing existing institutional structures.

Rural India is still a good example of a sustainable model founded upon self-construction, self-management and self-financing, where respect for nature is an essential part of the culture and religion, and the protection of resources is a necessity and, at the same time, a tradition. The environmental sustainability of rural areas is, however, closely linked to urban development; Shah identifies a series of principles for rural settlements and sustainable construction according to a 'people centred' approach that considers the role of the social institutions, traditional knowledge, and the creativity and competences of each. The different points reiterate the key concepts of the Habitat Agenda, underlining the need to face both urban and rural poverty and, above all, the need for suitable housing that can influence degraded human capital in a decisive way. Indeed, lack of suitable housing is one of the principal causes of unsustainability. Housing is the centre of physical and social life, but also the *locus* of moral life and ethical choice (Cohen, 2000). If cities are considered 'the result of people living together', the dwelling – paraphrasing the words of David Harvey – becomes 'the space of hope' (Harvey, 2000). To re-establish the balance between urban and rural, but above all between strong and weak zones (Roncayolo, 1988), Shah identifies guidelines for sustainable construction, maintaining that the most noteworthy form of intervention must, first and foremost, concern a change in mentality.

The human dimension of sustainable development is also illustrated in the article by Mejbahuddin Ahmed who examines the town of Khulna, in Bangladesh. In particular, Ahmed proposes a critical evaluation of the role of the different agencies involved in Khulna's urban development, observing that citizen participation should be an integral part of the decision-making process, and of urban planning and management for a more human and programmatic approach to sustainable development. He examines the operations of two important agencies within the local administrative structure, taking into account such aspects as coordination, responsibility, models of intervention and the role of citizens in the planning process. The absence of monitoring and control structures, competencies and suitable organization negatively influences the selection of priority actions and planning and intervention choices. The author stresses the distance existing between citizens and government agencies, a distance which could be decreased by the implementation of a new model for local governance. It could be strengthened by active and integrated participation in a system of metropolitan-level governance and by decentralization of the decision-making process in accordance with the Habitat Agenda. Khulna's condition is analogous to that of the other great cities in Bangladesh and it necessitates solutions that address the issue of development in a sensitive and integrated way, according to a suitable planning model, conceived with a marked attention to people and to overcoming the gap between theoretical models and reality.

Olga Belous explores the possibility of applying the Habitat Agenda and Local Agenda 21 principles in such problematic contexts as Lithuania. The experience in Klaipeda illustrates the search for operationalizing sustainability principles with the economic difficulties of countries in transition (analogous to those of developing countries) and with the complexities of adopting the environmental management systems necessary for entering the European Union, besides creating the premises for sustainability. In this sense, the article points out the possibility of developing both methodological and international financial cooperation for the implementation of environmental policy, involving the different Local Agenda 21 processes already activated in the Baltic countries. In Klaipeda, an attempt was made to adopt a new approach within a Local Agenda 21 process with the intention of creating a consensus-based system for environmental management. This initiative can be considered an important example of environmental conservation and rehabilitation in which the principal objective was to influence a change in behaviour and the construction of a new awareness of the shortage of natural resources. The article focuses on the existence of numerous obstacles especially due to: lack of information and experience; contrast with local authority and unethical competition; elevated costs of new technologies.

Also of particular importance is the experience of Local Agenda 21 introduced by Keith Richardson, regarding the Earth Balance project in Wansbeck in northeast England. In a context characterized by serious economic and social problems, a proposal for environmental conservation was developed. The author states that the development process must be closely connected to the life of the people and must ensure that each individual can become an integral and active part of the process. In the process, some important difficulties emerged, above all due to the conflict between the demand to create real participation and the necessity to obtain short term results, due to the contrast between taking an holistic view of sustainability and traditional organizations that are distant from the logic of sustainability. An essential role is played by the participation of the community which perceived itself as part of the solution rather than part of the problem in a more equitable and more inclusive context. Following the Habitat Agenda principles, Earth Balance allowed equal opportunity for participation in the decision-making process within the context of good and democratic decentralized governance capable of enduring. Furthermore, choices and decisions were faced according to a 'joined-up thinking' approach rather than in a reductive way, developing the community capacity-building. Earth Balance has shown how it is possible to adopt the Habitat Agenda and the Local Agenda 21 in concrete terms, working with people and enhancing potential, showing how decentralization and empowerment can contribute to the creation of appropriate and professional know-how.

Another Local Agenda 21 experience – that of Venice – is recounted by Ignazio Musu, who examines the difficulties in activating sustainability processes in a complex context. Venice is an emblematic example of interaction between economy, society and environment, in which the urban and the natural framework determine a unique combination of cultural heritage and environmental context. The city's myriad problems were addressed during the process of Local Agenda 21, but they require political and structural transformations to bring about their incisive management. Unfortunately, after the identification of the issues and possible solutions, suitable action has not been forthcoming on the part of the institutions, which have proved to be incapable of organizing integrated interventions. According to Musu, Venice can be considered an example of the failure of an intervention model based on inter-institutional coordination. This stresses, therefore, the necessity to build a shared long-term vision on which to found concrete programs supported by inter-institutional coordination and legitimated by the social consensus of the different stakeholders involved in order to attribute a multidimensional value to the 'Venice-good' and to the lagoon ecosystem. The article observes how each Local Agenda 21 process should be able to combine local specificity with the issues preoccupying the national and international community, having institutions that can represent different expectations and emphasizing the need to follow a model of good governance, with respect for the equilibriums between needs, goals and tools, identified through social consensus.

One of the key elements that has determined the success of Local Agenda 21 is citizen participation. Bohuslav Blazek explores the role of participative methodologies in the construction of a 'bottom-up' process and in citizen involvement. Starting from a reflection upon the fact that the perception of the urban context depends upon the observer's point of view and how it changes over time based upon the city's urban structure, Blazek illustrates the importance of involving people and stimulating participation by teaching people to look, raising their awareness of a reality that they are not able to see or that they do not share. Within the framework of the theoretical constructs of social ecology, Blazek introduces a series of methods based upon the use of the photograph as a tool to express a personal point of view and to acquire awareness of context. A key characteristic of the proposed methods is the participative one, upon which to establish a complementary relationship between *observer* and *observed*, to stimulate action and reflection, to set up dialogue, and to seek to resolve specific problems. The different methods underline the importance of stimulating local participation and aiding people in expressing their personal world view. According to Blazek, in each method it is necessary to take into account the specific situation of each context of operation as well as its history.

The experiences of Local Agenda 21 and the models for soliciting community participation stimulate a series of ideas upon the role of the professionals that handle the construction of the city. In this perspective, Leonie Sandercock identifies the principal ingredients for a human sustainable city and what this means for urbanists. According to Sandercock, *difference, community* and *ecological sustainability* are the three prime issues of the contemporary city, a new paradigm and, at the same time, a challenge to build the sustainable city of the twenty-first century. In particular, difference is considered in its dual meaning: on the one hand, it is tied to the fear that has influenced the development of physical-spatial dynamics contributing to the realization of the city-fort; on the other, diversity is considered a catalyst that has influenced processes of re-urbanization, with the wealth of stimuli of urban life and with substantial changes of value. As also stated by David Harvey, the concept of community, and affiliation to it, can imply exclusion and non-affiliation, confusing the concept of community with that of homogeneity. It is necessary, therefore, to overcome the dichotomy between the sense of affiliation and exclusion, building places and community in which everyone can feel 'at home', recognizing the importance of difference and diversity (Young, 1990; Fincher and Jacobs, 1998). In addition, the change in paradigm from modernist to post-modern, cannot ignore the problem of language and how it influences transformations. For Sandercock, to work towards the sustainable city means to use a 'therapeutic planning' model that implies the organization of hope, the negotiation of fear, the mediation of memory, the facilitation of research and the transformation of a community's soul. Through the presentation of some telling case studies, a new approach to planning is delineated, involving confrontation, dialogue and negotiation among cultural differences, requiring a different kind of availability to know and to communicate based on the ability to listen, narrate and interpret body language. As the photo for Blazek, narration for Sandercock represents a useful tool in stimulating community involvement and building consensus. Therapeutic planning is represented as a process of collective learning, resulting in community growth and the realization of permanent transformations in values and in institutions, for a more inclusive base on which to found one's own vision of the future.

Concluding Remarks: Seeing the Potentials

The need for a new paradigm that refers to people and their values emerges clearly from the articles in this section (Kirdar, Harvey, Shah, Sandercock). This paradigm should guide the choices and the interventions aiming at a process of sustainability seeking an inclusive vision of the city. The concept of the inclusive city is one of the recurring themes both in the definition of the theoretical and methodological approaches as well as in the experiences. This concept stresses the need for a renewed and deeper attention to human beings, expressed through the different meanings of the human dimension of development.

From where we look and *from what we learn* represent the two components that allow the individual to build his/her own perception of the world, allowing him/her to find solutions to the new challenges that are rooted in his/her own culture, in social rules, traditions and in the value system. Attention to humankind implies the consideration of the local dimension and, in accord with the Agenda 21 and Habitat Agenda philosophies, the importance of participation and collective involvement in the process of seeking sustainability, understanding that success on a global scale will depend on the results achieved at local level.

The decision-making process takes on a key role in the construction of choices in complex environments, supported by an effective system of 'good human governance' in which the concepts of 'good governance' and of 'good urban governance' are integrated. The creation of such a system depends upon the sense of civic responsibility and on citizens' ability to become an active part of the decision-making process, with the goal of implementing policies of joint-decisions and joint-implementation to answer society's needs (UNCHS, 2001b).

Is a system of 'good human governance' able to produce an inclusive city? The answer, probably, calls for the re-examination of the complex concept of poverty, which changes if we are considering a stable or a destabilized system, and separating it from the phenomenon of exclusion. In addition, an approach not exclusively of the economic type is necessary to explore the notions of 'disaffiliation' (Castel, 1995) and 'urban despoilment' (Kowarick, 1994) which refer to ethical, cultural, historical and political values.

The cases of Local Agenda 21 and of Habitat Agenda in this volume show how, in different places in the world, the creation of the inclusive city implies, above all, the construction of awareness and the strengthening of such cooperative relationships as city-to-city and community-community which can guide the course of sustainability and stimulate active participation (Wakely and You, 2001). Participation is considered one of the key elements that can influence an urban future, reinforcing the bond between the citizen and local authority and coordinating the efforts of civil society and the private sector working for democracy in a local dimension. In this perspective, 'good human governance' constitutes an essential prerequisite for cohesion and for social inclusion that will encourage local authorities to focus on human and social capital, sustain citizens in urban activities, furnish the opportunity to foster the growth of civil society and consolidate the strength of weaker bonds (Granovetter, 1973).

The project for the inclusive city requires, however, the support of new planning models that are able to stimulate processes of enabling (Hall and Pfeiffer, 2000), of empowering and of capacity-building (Marcuse, 2001), recognizing the key role of the community. There is also a clear need for special communicative abilities that can transform planning language and utilize critical/evaluative models (Keeney, 1992) that help identify existing potential and bring about processes that are catalysts of broader transformations founded upon the recognition of shared values.

References

Allen, A. and You, N. (2002), *Sustainable Urbanisation. Bridging the Green and Brown Agendas*, The Development Planning Unit, University College London Press, London.
Baumann, E. (1999-2000), 'Société civile et micro-finance. Réflexions à partir d'exemples ouest-africains', *Rapport du Centre Walras*, Ed. Economica, Paris, pp. 291-304.
Castel, R. (1995), *Les métamorphoses de la question sociale. Une chronique du salariat*, Fayard, Paris.
Castells, M. (1996), *The Rise of the Network Society*, Blackwell Publishers Ltd, Oxford.
Cohen, M.A. (1991), 'Urban Policy and Economic Development: An Agenda for the 1990s', World Bank Policy Paper, Washington.
Cohen, M.A. (2000), 'Housing, Cities, and Development', Paper for *Urban 21 Global Conference on the Urban Future*, Berlin, Germany, 5 July 2000.
Cohen, M.A. and Shabbir, C. (1992), 'The New Agendas', in N. Harris (ed.), *Cities in the 90s. The Challenge for Developing Countries. Overseas Development Administration*, The Development Planning Unit, University College London Press, London, pp. 9-42.
Coleman, J.S. (1990), *Foundations of Social Theory*, Cambridge University Press, Cambridge.
de Soto, H. (2001), *The Mystery of Capital*, Daily Telegraph, London.
Fayman, S. and Santana, L. (2001), *Introductory Report on the Inclusive City*, Fourth International Forum on Urban Poverty, Marrakech, 16-19 October 2001.
Fincher, R. and Jacobs, J.M. (1998), *Cities of Difference*, The Guilford Press, New York.
Friedmann, J. (1987), *Planning in the Public Domain: From Knowledge to Action*, Princeton University Press, Princeton.
Granovetter, M. (1973), *The Strength of Weak Ties*, University of Chicago Press, Chicago.
Hall, P. and Pfeiffer, U. (2000), *Urban Future 21. A Global Agenda for Twenty-first Century Cities*, E and FN Spon, London.
Harvey, D. (2000), *Spaces of Hope*, Edinburgh University Press, Edinburgh.
Haughton, G. and Hunter, C. (1994), *Sustainable Cities*, Regional Policy and Development Series 7, Jessica Kingsley, London.
Hibou, B. (1998), 'Banque mondiale: les méfaits du catéchisme économique', *Les coopérations dans la nouvelle géopolitique. Politique Africaine*, Washington, no. 71, pp. 58-74.
ICLEI (International Council for Local Environmental Initiatives) (1998), 'Study on National Obstacles to Local Agenda 21', DESA/DSD, Background Paper no. 31.
ICLEI (International Council for Local Environmental Initiatives) (2002), 'Second Local Agenda 21 Survey', DESA/DSD, Background Paper no. 15.
Keeney, R.L. (1992), *Value Focused Thinking. A Path to Creative Decision making*, Harvard University Press, Cambridge.
Kirdar, Ü. (1984), 'Human Resources Development: Challenge for the 1980s', *Crisis of the '80s*, North-South Roundtable publication in collaboration with the UNDP Development Study Programme, New York, chapters 19 and 20.
Kirdar, Ü. (1990), *Human Development Report*, United Nations Development Programme, Oxford University Press, New York.
Kirdar, Ü. (1994), *Human Development Report*, United Nations Development Programme, Oxford University Press, New York.
Kirdar, Ü. (1998), *Integrating Human Rights with Sustainable Human Development*, United Nations Publications, New York.
Kirdar, Ü. (1998-1999), 'A Trilogy of Basic Human Concerns: Human Rights, Sustainable Human Development, Human Security', *Perceptions. Journal of International Affairs*,

vol. III (4), December 1998-February 1999.

Kirdar, Ü. and Haq, K. (eds) (1987), *Human Development: The Neglected Dimension*, United Nations Publications, New York.

Kirdar, Ü. and Silk, L. (eds) (1995), *People: From Impoverishment to Empowerment*, New York University Press, New York.

Kowarick, L. (ed.) (1994), *Social Struggles and the City. The Case of* Saõ *Paulo*, Monthly Review Press, New York.

Marcuse, P. (2001), 'A Sow's Ear or a Silk Purse?', Paper for Urbanizing World and UN Human Habitat II, Columbia University, New York.

Putnam, R.D. (1993a), 'The Prosperous Community Social Capital and Public Life', *The American Prospect*, vol. 4, no. 13, 21 March 1993.

Putnam, R.D. (1993b), *Making Democracy Work: Civic Traditions in Modern Italy*, Princeton University Press, Princeton.

Roncayolo, M. (1988), *La città. Storia e problemi della dimensione urbana*, Einaudi, Torino.

Sandercock, L. (1998), *Towards Cosmopolis*, John Wiley and Sons, Chichester.

Sassen, S. (1998), *Globalization and its Discontents*, The New Press, New York.

Sen, A. (1999), *Development as Freedom*, Alfred A. Knopf, New York.

UNCED (United Nations Commission on Environment and Development) (1992), *Agenda 21 and Rio Declaration*, Rio de Janeiro.

UNCHS (United Nations Centre on Human Settlements) (1996), *The Habitat Agenda and Istanbul Declaration*, Istanbul.

UNCHS (United Nations Centre for Human Settlements) (2001a), *The State of the World's Cities 2001*, UNCHS (Habitat), Nairobi.

UNCHS (United Nations Centre for Human Settlements) (2001b), *Cities in a Globalizing World. Global Report on Human Settlements 2001*, UNCHS (Habitat), Nairobi.

Wakely, P. and You, N. (2001), *Implementing The Habitat Agenda. In Search of Urban Sustainability*, The Development Planning Unit, University College London Press, London.

World Bank (1993), 'Housing: Enabling Markets to Work with Technical Supplements', World Bank Policy Paper, The World Bank, Washington.

Young, I.M. (1990), *Justice and the Politics of Difference*, Princeton University Press, Princeton.

Chapter 10

A Better and Stronger System of Humane Governance at the Turn of the Century[1]

Üner Kirdar

Introduction

When the twentieth century came to a close, the world celebrated not only the start of a new century but also the beginning of a new millennium. Left behind was a century that history will remember as an era in which humanity was confronted with two unprecedented and devastating armed conflicts and one political 'cold war' that succeeded in dividing the world for close on 50 years. Taken together, these three conflicts had a profound effect on the course and destiny of mankind.

During the Second World War alone, which lasted over three years in the Pacific, five years in Europe and close to eight years in China, the total number of military casualties exceeded 14 million, with over 45 million wounded, and millions of civilians either killed or missing. The result – numerous nations lost almost two future generations. The two World Wars not only took millions of lives but also caused untold sorrow.

The Cold War was, in its own way, equally as crushing and wasteful of human life. In the over 100 minor conflicts that occurred either directly as a result of super-power rivalry or were exacerbated by their efforts to gain ideological dominance, close to 20 million people were killed. Countless millions were forced to live in an environment of oppression and tyranny, and valuable resources that could have been used for the betterment of human existence were squandered as a result of the arms race.

Mankind's experiences during these turbulent times proved that global confrontations result not only in death and devastation, but upon their cessation, provide societies with the opportunity to affect profound changes in the ways in which they are organized. As history has so often shown, traumatic experiences such as war or political revolution cause people to rethink the premises upon which their lives are based, prompting them to envisage new ways of organizing their societies so as to prevent re-occurrence of such events.

The Second World War, in particular, taught us many valuable lessons. The ineffectiveness of the League of Nations in preventing such a devastating disaster pointed to the necessity of creating an international organization that had a different vision for ensuring international security. Hence when the United Nations was established on 24 October 1945, the Charter formulated was based explicitly on the notion that international peace can only be ensured if human security, rights and development are guaranteed for all.

The creation of the United Nations was indicative of the fact that, for the first time in its history, mankind recognized that economic and social problems were universal in nature, transcending national boundaries and affecting people all over the world. It is somewhat ironic that it was only towards the mid-twentieth century, when technology had advanced far enough to posses the means for destroying the world, that we realized that only through joint action could we hope to find solutions to the economic and social problems that collectively threaten us. Based, guided by, this vision the United Nations and its specialized agencies were created (including the Bretton-Woods institutions), the Marshall Plan was launched and the European Common Market initiated.

All the individuals involved in the creation of these institutions were undoubtedly guided by perceptions and visions shaped by their painful memories of the Great Depression and the Second World War. This is made abundantly clear by the fact that post-war economic arid social policies, both on the national and international levels, were guided by an overwhelming concern with ensuring the betterment of human life, full employment, and respect for human rights as a means of securing peace.

Looking back, it becomes evident that the first and most important lesson to be learned from the past century is that to ensure peace, we must, from time to time, re-evaluate and change the prevailing concept of security. While the concept of peace is easy to grasp, that of international security is more complex. During the Cold War, security was viewed primarily from a political perspective. This concept of security was shaped by the potential for armed conflict between the two adversary camps of East and West. For far too long, security was equated with threats to the borders of individual nation-states. These states relied on arms as the primary means for protecting their territorial security.

Recent events however, such as the conflict in Somalia, Rwanda, Bosnia, Kosovo, and Chechnya, show that, with increasing frequency, problems are more often than not to be found *within* nations, rather than between them. Their origins lie in growing socio-economic disparities, ethnic rivalries, human rights abuses, and deprivation. The United Nations was predominantly rendered powerless to deal with many of these crises because of selfish power policies followed both within the organization and by its member states, which rendered it unable to undertake the actions necessary.

Bearing these facts in mind, this essay argues that international peace in the twenty-first century can only be ensured only if we make a serious effort to fulfil the objectives of the United Nations Charter. We can only do this if we recognize, as the Charter does, that international security has many facets. It involves not only political but human security; the well-being of people is equally as important as national political security. The world cannot become a secure place unless people's security can be ensured in their homes, in their jobs, and in their communities. A better and more peaceful world can only be secured through the promotion of *higher standards of living, full employment* and *social progress*, all within the larger framework of *freedom for everyone*. This requires wisdom, leadership, commitment and, most important of all, vision.

New Perspectives and Challenges: Globalization

On the threshold of the new millennium, *all* countries are facing certain common problems and challenges that are affecting their people and require imminent and coherent policy actions that go far beyond the capacity and short term inward looking interest of each nation-state. There are therefore compelling reasons for countries to develop joint policy measures that will make each one of them more economically viable, politically peaceful and participatory, ecologically sustainable, and humanly and socially just.

During the last decade of the twentieth century, the world changed faster than ever before. In particular, changes occurred at a striking pace in three domains: economic globalization, information and communications technology, and politico-economic systems. These changes have shown not only that they can provide enormous opportunities for the betterment of human life but also represent serious threats to stable societies. Some strata of the population have risen to levels of unprecedented affluence while others have been thrust into substantial poverty, unemployment, social disintegration and racial and ethnic conflict. Despite (or perhaps even because of) this diversity in achievements, nations have become increasingly interdependent. This interdependency has been further complemented and reinforced by the new widespread personal mobility that is currently possible. The process of globalization has accelerated in direct proportion to these developments.

Much has been written and said recently about the globalization process. We know that it has become a reality and that it has both positive and negative aspects and impacts. Perhaps most important of all, we must realize that it is a one-way journey.

As a result of the globalization process, the world is currently confronted with issues that increasingly affect the entire human race. These issues represent the global challenges of the twenty-first century. They range from the economic requirements of finance, trade and monetary exchange to the social needs of communities, such as improved health, education, nutrition and employment possibilities, from the exchange of information to new discoveries in genetics and biotechnology. At the present time, the rate of growth in the importance of these issues and their dimensions transcend the capacity of individual states, self-determined national policies and classically defined sectoral disciplines.

The changes that we are currently experiencing also open up new horizons and present increasing possibilities for people to achieve their human, economic, social, political and spiritual aspirations. As never before, concerns for basic human rights, individual liberties, racial and ethnic equality, and economic opportunities are steering humanity.

The globalization process has shown us that developmental, humanitarian, economic, social and ecological problems cannot be solved by fragmented national and sectoral initiatives alone. Globalization has also accelerated growing interdependence between countries and people, as well as promoting interlinkages among different political, human, economic, social and ecological issues. We have learnt that peace, economy, the environment, social justice and democracy are all an integral part of the whole. Without peace human energies cannot be productively employed. Without economic growth there can be no sustained, broad-based improvement in material well-being or ecological balance. Without environmental protection the basics of human survival are jeopardized. Without social justice ever-increasing inequalities threaten social cohesion. And without political participation and freedom, development remains fragile and perpetually at risk.

In brief, we have learned that we are dependent upon one another and that a balance is needed between the democratic freedoms, economic growth, social progress and human and environmental development issues that are so essentially interlinked.

At present, unchecked urban growth, increasing poverty, environmental decline, unemployment, street children, homelessness, drug abuse and social disintegration are ills affecting all nations, whether of the East, West, North or South. Consequently, these concerns are becoming increasingly common concerns and it is in the interest of all countries to find shared solutions to these common problems.

Throughout history, sudden sharp changes in political and economic systems have had an inevitable impact on human values, ethics and beliefs. The same is true today. As a result of the globalization process, established social values and cultural traditions are undergoing radical changes. Hindsight and history alone will show whether these changes will prove beneficial or harmful to human progress; for the moment, it might suffice to say that societies all over the world are redefining their values.

Economic liberalism has created 'North' and 'South' polarization within individual nations. We see that a growing number of the affluent measure their happiness in terms of money and their ability to consume. Materialism and the emphasis on competition are eroding the more traditional emphasis on cooperation and collaboration. In this 'survival of the fittest' environment, a growing number of marginalized people are feeling increasingly alienated and are returning to spiritual values, giving rise to a new type of fundamentalism. In this search for a belief system, different religions and philosophies are acquiring new importance.

Also, today both governments and international organizations are no longer the sole actors on either the local or global stage. Helped by the remarkable advances in information and communications technology, transnational corporations, the media, local authorities, non-governmental and civic organizations, professional associations, foundations, etc., are playing an increasing and very dynamic role in shaping important global strategies according to their own rules, priorities and values.

The emergence of these new actors in global relations creates the need for the redefinition of the roles, functions, rights and obligations of each actor and for the establishment of appropriate partnerships between these actors in order to respond effectively to new global challenges.

Putting People First

At the United Nations, we have introduced a new concept, a new dimension to development. I feel proud to have played a pioneering leadership role in this undertaking. We have learned that development should no longer be evaluated in terms of the amount of growth but in terms of the type of growth. People should not be considered only as residual factors in growth but as the true objective of development. True development can be achieved only through a process that places people at the centre of all concerns. This process must develop human capacities and capabilities to help people release their human energies for the benefit of their own development and that of the societies they live in. Throughout the 1980s and 1990s, we became more aware that global peace and security could not be achieved unless governments learn to deal effectively with the threats stemming from failures in economic and social development and the lack of tangible human progress. Also, governments must prepare their people for the information age and the globalization age.

We have also learned that lasting peace, security and prosperity depend on policies that 'put people first' and that are based on a new paradigm – the trilogy of human concerns:

- human rights;
- human development;
- human security.

The achievement of this paradigm not only generates worldwide economic growth but also distributes its benefits equitably. It regenerates the environment instead of destroying it. It empowers people rather than marginalizing them. It widens people's choices and their opportunities and provides them with the chance to participate in the decision-making processes that affect their lives.

Human rights are recognized as the first basic human concern. The primary basis of today's activities at the United Nations and its member governments is to promote, protect and monitor human rights and the fundamental freedoms that derive from universal human rights law – the so-called International Bill of Human Rights that has evolved gradually over the years. The Bill is comprised of three documents:

- the Universal Declaration of Human Rights, adopted in 1948;
- the International Covenant on Economic, Social and Cultural Rights, espoused in 1966;
- the International Covenant on Civil and Political Rights, also launched in 1966.

To date, the International Covenant on Civil and Political Rights has been ratified by 144 countries and the International Covenant on Economic, Social and Cultural Rights has been ratified by 141 countries.

Taken together, these documents enshrine global human rights standards and have been the source of inspiration for more than 60 supplemental United Nations human rights conventions, declarations and legal instruments. Together, these have established the international rules, guidelines and other universally recognized principles that cover a wide range of human concerns, including – but by no means limited to – the right to development, women's rights, protection against racial and ethnic discrimination, protection of migrant workers and the rights of children. Through the years the full spectrum of this international human rights law has been designed to promote and protect the basic right of people to enjoy freedom, safety and healthy lives. The right to live a dignified life can never be attained unless all the basic necessities of life – work, food, housing, health care, education and culture – are adequately and equitably available to everybody.

The collective human rights outlined above are currently regarded as the common standard of achievement for all nations and all people. Similarly, they are viewed as indivisible, inalienable and universal. The emphasis on one aspect of human rights cannot be used to detract from the promotion and implementation of any other aspect. They are to be enjoyed equally by all, with no distinction as to race, ethnicity, sex, language, religion, political, national or social origin.

Humane Governance

In the twenty-first century the battle for sustainable development will be either won or lost in the cities. The quality of humane urban governance will make the difference between success and failure. Given these stakes and the limited resources available to meet the challenges, a catalyst is needed that will mobilize city residents to pursue a common goal for cities that provide benefits for all, not just for some. A better and stronger 'humane governance' will be that catalyst.

Modern history is the story of massive globalization and urbanization. A brief overview of the statistics reveals several important characteristics. First, an unprecedented demographic shift is taking place. In 1950, the number of people living in urban areas was 750 million. At the beginning of this millennium that figure is calculated at 2.9 billion, nearly 50 per cent of humanity. By 2020, some 4.4 billion people will be living in cities, that is nearly 60 per cent of world population.

The explosive growth of cities has been accompanied by the massive urbanization of poverty; UNDP estimates the total number of people living in poverty – defined as living on less than one dollar per day – to be 1.3 billion. An increasing proportion of the poor lives in urban areas. Current estimates place the number of urban poor at between 1.0 and 1.2 billion.

The new, emerging mega-cities will very likely experience enormous environmental and social strains that will push their inhabitants to the limits of their ability to sustain reasonable human life. Most cities will face common fundamental problems, including, but not limited to, polarization between the rich and poor, fewer employment possibilities with decreased earnings, inadequate housing and infrastructure services, traffic congestion and increasing social tensions and violence as well as severe environmental degradation such as air and water pollution.

At the start of the new millennium, these serious global problems affect most people and require urgent and coherent policy actions that go far beyond the short term interests of each nation-state. Thus there are compelling reasons for developing practical policy measures and options that will make the world's cities more economically viable, politically participatory, ecologically sustainable and humanely and socially just. The question then becomes how the global threats outlined above can be transformed into opportunities to make our habitats more liveable – to create cities that are safer, healthier, more humane and sustainable.

The trend towards urbanization appears irreversible. But in many countries national and local governments have a very limited capacity to cope with this transformation. Many urban residents have no access to clean water, sanitation or adequate shelter. Poverty and insecurity characterize a precarious urban existence. However, those cities that are properly planned and managed harbour the promise for human development and the protection of the world's natural resources through their ability to support large numbers of people, while limiting their impact on the natural environment. Major recent publications from UNEP, UNDP, the World Bank and Habitat all arrive independently at the same conclusion: in the face of current global trends the quality of governance will have a decisive impact on humanity's development. The testing ground is in the cities.

A new approach to 'humane' governance is emerging. It is one that supports the vision of what is termed the 'inclusive City'. This is a city where everyone, regardless of wealth, gender, age, race or religion, is enabled to participate productively and positively in the opportunities that cities have to offer. Inclusive decision-making processes are an essential means to achieve this end and are the normative foundation of the campaign. Local authorities are beginning to recognize and affirm their role as 'enablers' – encouraging civil society to contribute its resources to making cities successful. They are tapping into innovative strategies based on partnerships with the private sector and with civil society to deliver public goods and services in innovative ways.

The concept of governance is complex and controversial. Before one can say what is 'good' humane governance, one must be clear about what is meant by 'governance'. A starting point in this debate is UNDP's definition:

> The exercise of political, economic and administrative authority in the management of a country's affairs at all levels – local, national and international. It comprises the mechanisms, processes and institutions through which citizens and groups articulate their interests, exercise their legal rights, meet their obligations and mediate their differences.[2]

Three aspects of this definition are relevant to defining 'good humane governance'. First, governance is a neutral concept. Governance can manifest itself in many forms; tyrannical or benevolent, effective or incompetent. Second, governance is not government. Governance as a concept recognizes that power exists inside and outside the formal authority of government. In many formulations, governance includes government, the private sector and civil society. Third, governance emphasizes 'process'. It recognizes that decisions are made based on complex relationships between many actors with different priorities.

What is 'good humane governance'? Once the adjectives 'good' and 'humane' are added, the neutrality of governance disappears. UNDP defines 'good humane governance' as follows:

> Good humane governance is, among other things, participatory, transparent and accountable. It is also effective and equitable. And it promotes the rule of law.[3]

Thus, good humane governance is the new global governing system that ensures that the three basic human concerns referred to above are met. This system is based on the universal norms ratified by international legal instruments such as the Universal Declaration on Human Rights (1948), the Covenant on Civil and Political Rights (1966), the Covenant on Economic, Social and Cultural Rights (1966), the Convention on the Elimination of Discrimination Against Women (1979), and the Declaration on the Right to Development (1986). Among the promising areas drawn from these documents for connecting good humane governance to human rights are the following:

- legitimacy and accountability of government;
- freedom of association and participation;
- empowering people, especially women, as a key poverty eradication strategy;
- fair and legal frameworks for a predictable and secure living environment for citizens;
- availability and validity of information;
- efficient public sector management.

I strongly believe that the twenty-first century will be the century of 'putting people first' policies, as well as the era that will witness the advancement and realization of the new paradigm of the trilogy of basic human concerns detailed above. A better and stronger system of 'humane governance' will most certainly at last emerge. This new system will clearly define not only the rights, but also the obligations, of each actor and establish the appropriate relationship between them for the realization of this new paradigm.

Conclusion

From the above evaluation we may draw the following conclusions. At the start of the new millennium, humanity must face up to several pressing global challenges and neglected issues. These challenges and issues can be met and addressed only through multilateral and collective action. The most logical and legitimate place for such action is the United Nations. Paradoxically, there are currently many doubts as to whether the United

Nations is capable of meeting these challenges and dealing with these issues. Yet the ability of the United Nations to master these concerns depends largely on the political will and support of its Member States. It may be argued that we need a different type of United Nations – one that is restructured, revitalized and renewed. What is certain is that we can no longer operate on the basis of the short sighted and inward-looking selfish national policies that our shrinking planet has shown to be obsolete.

As a system, the United Nations and its related organizations should strengthen and coordinate their research policies and operational activities more vigorously to 'put people first' in all areas of its concern, namely peace-keeping and peace-building, economic, social, environmental and development cooperation, and human rights and humanitarian affairs.

Lastly, we must learn to live with a global perspective. The global issues that affect our lives must be the concern of all people and all nations and not only of a few. At the start of the new century, the world community has the ability, the means and the chance to turn the many threats of today into opportunities for human progress tomorrow. For that to occur, new vision, long-term perspectives and bold leadership will be required. Only then will a better and stronger system of 'humane governance' at last emerge.

Notes

1　This essay benefited from the ideas and argumentation presented by the author in several previous publications, such as: *Crisis of the 80's* (1984); *Human Development: The Neglected Dimension* (1986); *Development for People* (1989); *People: From Impoverishment to Empowerment* (1996), 'New Global Perspective at the Turn of the Century', *Perspective* (1998), vol. II, no. 2; 'A Trilogy of Basic Human Concerns', *Perspective* (1998), vol. III, no. 3.

2　UNDP (1997), *Governance for Sustainable Human Development*, New York.

3　Ibid.

Chapter 11

City and Justice:
Social Movements in the City

David Harvey

Introduction

The history of cities and of thinking about cities has periodically been
marked by intense interest in the transformative role of urban social
movements and communal action. Such movements get variously
interpreted, however, depending upon historical and geographical
conditions. The Christian reformism culminating in social control
arguments of Robert Park and the Chicago School of Urban Sociology
(evolved during the inter-war years in the United States and exported
around the world in the post-war period as standard fare for urban
sociologists) contrast, for example, with both the pluralist 'interest group'
model of urban governance favoured by Robert Dahl and the more radical
and revolutionary interpretations arrived at (mainly in Europe and Latin
America) during the 1960s and 1970s (culminating in Castells' magnum
opus on *The City and the Grassroots*, 1983).

In its most recent incarnations, interest has variously focussed upon
ideals of citizenship (Douglass and Friedmann, 1998), on the role of
religious and ethnic identities (communalism) or on a secular political
communitarianism, in the evident belief that the real sources of urban
change (no matter whether cast in a positive or negative light) lie (or ought
to lie) in civil society rather than in the 'official' spheres of the state
apparatus (Sandercock, 1998). In some instances and places, loss of
confidence in the state apparatus and political parties has resulted in the
coalescence of political thinking around ideals of local and people-based
action as the main means to humanize, ameliorate, transform or in some
instances even to revolutionize the qualities of urban life. A deep and
abiding faith in this latter path to social change even underpins that most
pervasive of all strategies for urban change, that of the so-called 'public-
private partnership'.

It is not my intention here to conduct any intensive critical or comparative review of this extensive literature. But what does strike me as curious is the way academic, intellectual and political interpretations of grass roots activism have ebbed, flowed and diverged without any clear or obvious relationship to the actual activities themselves. While the intensity and forms of the latter do vary, the attention paid to them in urban theorizing varies according to some other logic. Only at moments of intense turbulence or disruption do the two currents tend to flow together. But even then, events like the unrest in Los Angeles, the uprisings in Jakarta, the inter-communal violence in India or Sri Lanka, the riots in the suburbs of Paris and Lyon or even the extraordinary events in Prague and Berlin that saw the end of the Cold War, all too often catch urban theorists by surprise. Or, conversely, close observers of urban life find themselves perpetually surprised by the odd forms and manifestations of localized politics in the settings they trouble to study in any detail (Seabrook, 1996).

A crude but nevertheless fertile starting point to understand the roots of this disjunction lies in the ebb and flow of both the *sense of possibility* and the *desire* for change in political and intellectual circles (often expressed as utopian dreams of alternative city forms) on the one hand and the need to identify political agents – such as a proletariat or urban social movements – capable of realizing such dreams, on the other. The dialectical relation between these two currents of thought and action is of course important. The flood of student and activist believers into the neighbourhoods of Chicago or Paris in the late 1960s and early 1970s undoubtedly played an important role in infusing local social movements with global political ambitions. The subsequent retreat of such movements into what idealists construed as a rather ignoble and self-serving localism (degenerating into what many would regard as a reactionary 'not-in-my-back yard' or even actively exclusionary communal politics) played an important role in the political disillusionment and abandonment of left-wing utopianism that followed. On the other hand, those concerned to mobilize power – that, say, of Hindu revivalism – have largely done so by organizing and orchestrating communal movements in particular urban settings, impelling a completely different drift to urban transformations to that which the secular left would regard as healthy.

But this last example hardly appears as a simple example of a welling-up of grassroots sentiments. There is a great deal of orchestration from above. And this then raises the question as to the efficacy of grassroots activities in and for themselves of changing anything other than conditions in their own backyards. Sceptics, armed with a good deal of historical and geographical comparative information, might reasonably conclude that left to themselves such movements amount to nothing more than minor perturbations on the deeper currents of socio-ecological change. Yet even the most sceptical analyst would be forced to wonder why it is that again and again social theorists and political practioners turn to local grassroots movements as some sort of seedbed from which major social changes can arise. Is there, then, a more general way to understand the role of urban social movements that goes beyond mere episodic and particular constructions? I here explore a tentative theoretical framework to answer that question.

Militant Particularism and the Politics of Collectivities

The thesis of militant particularism to which I am strongly attached (Harvey, 1996, 2000) holds that all politics (of no matter what sort and no matter whether it is local, urban, regional, national or global in focus) have their origins in the collective development of a particular political vision on the part of particular persons in particular places at particular times. I presume that an undercurrent of grassroots ferment is omnipresent in all places and localities, though its interests, objectives and organizational forms are typically fragmented, multiple and of varying intensity. The only interesting question under this formulation is how and when such militant particularisms become internally coherent enough and ultimately embedded in or metamorphosed into a broader politics.

Collective grassroots politics often flow, of course, in constrained and predictable channels. As such, they often pass unremarked precisely because they seem more to be about business as usual than about social change. In the United States, for example, it is the homeowner associations, dedicated to protection of their property values, privileges and lifestyles, who dominate the urban/suburban scene (Davis, 1990). The violence and anger that greets any threat to individualized property rights and values – be it from the state or even from agents of capital accumulation like developers – is a powerful political force. It permeates religious institutions (I suspect it grounds much of the work of the Christian Coalition in the United States, for example) as well as much of what passes for active politics at the local, state and Federal levels.

Such collective movements preclude rather than promote the search for alternatives (no matter how ecologically wise or socially just). They tend to preserve the existing system, even as they deepen its internal contradictions, ecologically, politically and economically. For example, suburban separatism in the United States – based upon class and racial antagonisms – increases car dependency, generates greenhouse gasses, diminishes air quality and encourages the profligate use of land, fossil fuels and other agricultural and mineral resources. Militant particularism here functions as a seemingly immovable conservative force to guarantee the preservation of the existing order of things. Even when such a politics dresses up in democratic or radical clothing, its drift lies towards exclusionary and authoritarian practices. Etzioni (1997), a leading proponent of the new communitarianism in the United States (a movement that largely presents itself as progressive and antagonistic to market values), actively supports the principle of closed, exclusionary and gated communities. Collective institutions can also end up merely improving the competitive strength of territories in the high stakes game of the uneven geographical development of capitalism, as Putnam (1993) purports to show in the case of contrasting patterns of economic development in Italy. For the wealthy, therefore, 'community' often means securing and enhancing privileges already gained. For the marginalized it all too often means 'controlling their own slum'. Inequalities multiply rather than diminish. What appears as a just procedure, produces unjust consequences (a manifestation of the old adage that 'there is nothing more unequal than the equal treatment of unequals').

I cite these cases because high levels of local activism often signal strong barriers to progressive and juster forms of social change. Reformers interested in even such mildly transgressive objectives such as 'smart growth' and resource conservation in the United States, then have to confront or circumvent strong community-based powers if they are to make even the mildest headway with the policies they advocate. The greater equalization of well-being through spatial reorganizations faces formidable localist barriers.

But militant particularism is not *inherently* conserving and conservative. There are plenty of cases to show that this is not always or necessarily so. The militia or neo-fascist movements on the right (a fascinating form of insurgent politics), the movement towards religious communalism, the active forms of militant particularism that lead to inter-communal violence and ethnic cleansing, all illustrate how insurgent forms of politics can connect with grass-roots movements. Though these instances might be characterized as reactionary, the left has its own pantheon of examples to cite as well (the Paris Commune, the storming of the Winter Palace in St Petersburg, etc.). This evidence suggests that insurgent and transformative politics are constantly intermingling with local mobilizations. An understanding of how local solidarities and political cohesions are or can be constructed (particularly in today's unruly urban settings) is essential for thinking through how proposals for social change (particularly those emanating from ideological, political and intellectual circles) might become a reality.

All political movements have therefore to confront the issue of 'locality' and 'community' somehow. And in some instances, such as the turn to communitarianism (or even to a form of communalism inspired by religious or ecological beliefs) such concepts have become foundational rather than instrumental in the quest for alternative forms of social change. Articulating the place and gauging the significance of militant particularism – the coming together of individuals in local patterns of solidarity – within a broader frame of politics becomes, as many observers have noted, a crucial task for urban theory and practice.

'Community' must, however, be viewed as a process of coming together not as a thing. It is therefore important to understand the processes that produce, sustain and dissolve the contingent patterns of solidarity that lie at the basis of this 'thing' we call 'a community'. But it is also important to recognize the 'thing-like' qualities of what gets created. The dialectic of the 'process-thing' relationship (Harvey, 1996) is all too often ignored or forgotten in urban studies. Exactly how a structure of something called community gets precipitated out of the social process deserves careful attention. There is, for example, the tangible struggle to define its limits and range (sometimes even its distinctive territory) and its rules and conditionalities of membership and belonging (so crucial to identity formation). The social struggle to create and sustain its institutions (through social networks and collective powers such as the churches and other religious institutions, the unions, neighbourhood organizations, local governments, and the like) is often bitterly waged. Such struggles simultaneously shape community, the sense of a proper way to live and the identities of those within its sphere of influence. It is precisely within such struggles that we must look for hints and possibilities of insurgent forms of change and the quest for social and environmental justice.

But the re-making and re-imagining of 'community' works in more general directions only if it connects to and becomes embedded in a more broadly based politics that challenges the *status quo* in some way or other. The crystallization of a relatively permanent and coherent form of local organization, though not sufficient, is a necessary condition for broader kinds of political action. This means that systems of authority, consensus-formation and 'rules of belonging' must be set up and these inevitably become exclusionary in certain respects and even controlling of the social processes that grounded solidarities in the first instance. The dialectic between a free flow of processes involved in imagining and building something called 'community' and the stolid permanence of an institutionalized political presence lies at the contradictory heart of what militant particularism in general is about.

This points to a singular and important conclusion: although community 'in itself' has meaning as part of a broader politics, community 'for itself' almost invariably degenerates into regressive exclusions and fragmentations. The danger then exists that the institutionalized thing we call community will stifle the living processes that gave birth to it. Community organizations can become hollow at their core and liable to easy and almost instantaneous collapse when challenged or to easy manipulation by external political forces. If they are to function as meaningful agents of change, therefore, such movements must remain strongly nurtured by continuous processes of solidarity formation and reaffirmation. But one of the prime means whereby a community can remain alive to its constituents and resist the deadening effect of becoming 'for itself' is to be embedded in broader processes of social change. Militant particularist movements must either reach out across space and time to shape broader political-economic processes or, like the home-owner associations, become embedded in some more integrated and broad-based process of historical-geographical change. Militant particularism and local solidarities must be understood, therefore, as crucial 'mediators' between individual persons and a more general politics. Their liveliness and influence depends crucially upon how they play that mediating role. Understanding their situatedness in this way, locates their importance in terms of relations established inwards to the individuals that comprise them and outwards to the broader world of political economy.

The Dialectics of Particularity and Universality

Consider first the dialectical relation between grassroots movements and more general social processes. The critical problem for the vast existing array of localized and particularistic struggles is to transcend particularities and arrive at some conception of a more global if not universal politics. For oppositional movements (as opposed to those primarily dedicated to reinforcing the existing state of things) this means defining a general alternative to that social system which is the source of their difficulties. Grassroots movements only become interesting to the theorist or advocate of social change to the degree that they transcend such particularities. It is therefore important to understand how this transcendence can occur.

There is much to be learned in this regard from the study of the historical and geographical record of grassroots movements in general and urban social movements in particular as well as from the synthetic statements arrived at by someone like Raymond Williams (who first coined the phrase militant particularism and did much to unravel its problematics) or Castells. But I am looking for a more general and theoretical way to situate the problem.

Dialectics is here helpful. It teaches that universality always exists *in relation to* particularity: neither can be separated from the other even though they are distinctive moments within our conceptual operations and practical engagements. The notion of social justice, for example, acquires universality through a process of abstraction from particular instances and circumstances, but, once established as a generally accepted principle or norm, becomes particular again as it is actualized through particular actions in particular circumstances. But the orchestration of this process depends upon mediating institutions (those, for example, of language, law and custom within given territories or among specific social groups). These mediating institutions 'translate' between particularities and universals and (like the Supreme Court) become guardians of universal principles and arbiters of their application. They also become power centres in their own right. This is, very broadly, the structure set up under capitalism with the state and all of its institutions being fundamental as 'executive committees' of capitalism's systemic interests. Capitalism is replete with mechanisms for converting from the particular (even personal) to the universal and back again in a dynamic and iterative mode. Historically, of course, the primary mediator has been the nation state and all of its institutions including those that manage the circulation of money. And, as I have already argued, community and grassroots movements also play such a mediating role.

But this line of analysis points to a singular conclusion. No social order can evade the question of universals. The contemporary 'radical' critique of universalism is sadly misplaced. It should focus instead on the specific institutions of power that translate between particularity and universality rather than attack universalism per se. Clearly, such institutions favour certain particularities (such as the rights of ownership of means of production) over others (such as the rights of the direct producers) and promote a specific kind of universal. But there is another difficulty. The movement from particularity to universality entails a 'translation' from the concrete to the abstract. Since a violence attaches to abstraction, a tension always exists between particularity and universality in politics. This can be viewed either as a creative tension or, more often, as a destructive and immobilizing force in which inflexible mediating institutions come to dominate over particularities in the name of some universal principle.

But there always exists a creative tension within the dialectic of particularity-universality which is hard to repress, particularly under a social system like capitalism which demands change as a condition of its own survival. Mediating institutions, under such conditions, cannot afford to ossify. The optimal configuration that emerges is one of sufficient permanence of institutional and spatial forms (e.g. urban governance and physical infrastructures) to provide security and continuity, coupled with a dynamic negotiation between particularities and universals so as to force mediating institutions and their associated spatial structures to be as open as possible. At times, capitalism has worked in such a way (consider how, for example, the law gets reinterpreted to confront new socio-economic conditions and how new spatial structures and spatialities have been constructed).

Any alternative, if it is to succeed, must follow capitalism's example in this regard. It must find ways to negotiate between the security conferred by fixed institutions and spatial forms on the one hand and the need to be open and flexible in relation to new socio-spatial possibilities on the other. That process demands that grassroots movements be an integral part of any process of negotiating future trajectories of development. Without them, universals will remain empty and remote at best and authoritarian impositions at worst. Letting the dialectic work between the grassroots and mediating authorities becomes a vital strategy for pursuing social change of any sort (including that required to keep a capitalist dynamic in motion). If grassroots movements did not exist, then higher order power structures would have to invent, shape and implant them (as has often happened as political parties set up neighbourhood organizations or as religious institutions colonized spaces through conversions and congregation building). The dialectic between particularity and universality is a shadowy stalking horse for relations between different sources of power – local and more general. And it is often a biased relation that we are here contemplating in the sense that power is not necessarily evenly distributed at different scales. Grassroots politics become a focus of interest when they start to assume their own powers (by their own exertions or, as in the present circumstances, more by default) rather than simply deriving them instrumentally from some higher order power such as the nation state.

Institutions and Mediations

The formation of institutions that can mediate the dialectic between particularity and universality is, then, of crucial importance. Many of these institutions become centres of dominant discourse formation as well as centres for the exercise of power. In metropolitan areas, the offices of finance, the budget committees, the highways and transport committees, the public works departments, a wide range of non-governmental and civic organizations, as well as powerful individuals with particular interests, are all active in urban governance and operate in effect as mediators between particular localized interests and global social and political-economic relations.

Such institutions are often organized territorially and define a sphere of action at a particular spatial scale. The intermediate institutions typically take the militant particularism at work at the local grassroots level and use it or translate it, both theoretically and in terms of material action, to construct a workable spatial order facilitative of certain social processes operating at a quite different spatial scale (that, say, of the metropolis as a whole). In the process, they necessarily formulate universal principles (such as legally-binding zoning and land-use controls or, more informally, smart growth policies, philosophies of public/private partnership or urban entrepreneurialism) as guides to action. Decisions have to be made, of course, and arbitrary authority and power are invariably implicated in the process. Universal principles (of, say, urban planning and control and of neighbourhood organization) can then be imposed from on high. If the organization at the grassroots is fragmented, badly articulated and partially instrumentalized by a higher power, then that higher power can easily prevail. But then the danger exists of the hollowing out of local institutions by the gradual demise of processes of solidarity formation at their base.

No mediating institution is, however, free floating or outside of the process-thing dialectic of the social process as a whole. What we then identify are layers of mediating institutions, often organized into some rough hierarchy, operating as transmission centres through which social processes unevenly flow. Metropolitan governments, operating in a complex relationship to grassroots movements, for example, may be forced into economic competition with each other for investments or for support from some higher authority (such as the nation state or international agencies like the World Bank or European Union). Metropolitan governance 'precipitates out' as a distinctive institutional layering characterized by corporatist forms of organization and entrepreneurial modes of behaviour. It may then act predominantly as a mediator to impose upon grassroots movements a logic derived from, say, competitive globalization. That this has predominantly been the case in recent times does not mean, however, that metropolitan governance cannot also be organized as an oppositional rather than a compliant force in relation to, say, neoliberal market forces. It can functions as a 'protector' of localities from the ravages of neo-liberalism or, as in cases like Porto Alegre (Abers, 1998), become an active seedbed for some alternative at the grassroots scale.

Two conclusions then follow. First, the context in which to understand local social movements is set by a fluid but highly complex interaction between processes and institutions operating at a variety of quite different spatial scales (such as national, regional, metropolitan and local). If, as I believe to be the case, we have a very weak understanding of how relations and processes work across such different scales, then we have a very weak context in which to locate our understanding and interpretation of the dynamics of militant particularist movements. The danger then exists that the latter will either be fetishized as a form of political salvation or dismissed as totally irrelevant in relationship to powers and influences operating at an entirely different scale (e.g. national or global). Secondly, since all universal principles are filtered through these multiple layers and scalars of institutionalized discourses, the dialectics of universality and particularity can become refracted, distorted or even thoroughly opaque. These two conclusions are hardly startling in themselves but what is surprising is how easily thinking about them gets lost in our analytical frames.

The formulation of universal principles – like social and environmental justice – is consequently fraught and frequently contested (as one might properly expect) but on grounds that are not well understood. This condition is frequently reflected in arguments within planning theory as well as within the extraordinary diversity of formulations available concerning the role of social movements in urban life. Again, I cannot hope to summarize let alone resolve such conflicts here. But there is one particular difficulty to which I do want to pay some attention. This concerns how multiple militant particularisms may be brought into some kind of constructive relation to each other.

Translations

The fragmented heterogeneity of grassroots movements requires a common language, a coherent politicized discourse, if it is to coalesce into a broader movement with more universal impact. Of course, it is in this domain, as Foucault has again and again pointed out, that discourses of power, attached to distinctive mediating institutions (such as the state apparatus or, more informally, within the worlds of education, religion, knowledge production and the media), typically play their often overwhelming disciplinary and authoritarian role. Hegemony becomes the focus of political struggle. Imposing conceptions of the world and thereby limiting the ability to construe alternatives is always a central task for dominant institutions of power (consider how far and how deeply the ideology of free market individualism and liberalism has penetrated in recent times).

But if grassroots alliances are to emerge as an alternative political force (as they periodically do), then the problem of how to construct some sort of alternative hegemonic discourse out of multiple militant particularisms has to be confronted. The benevolent dictator who wishes to acquire a minimalist aura of legitimacy and consent must likewise negotiate a language through which to rule since, as Italo Calvino remarks, the only means of communication no Emperor – no matter how powerful – can ever control is language itself. And it is at this point that the question of translation moves to the fore as a means to codify a common political agenda. For James Boyd-White (1990, pp. 257-64) translation means:

> ... confronting unbridgeable discontinuities between texts, between languages, and between people. As such it has an ethical as well as an intellectual dimension. It recognizes the other – the composer of the original text – as a center of meaning apart from oneself. It requires one to discover both the value of the other's language and the limits of one's own. Good translation thus proceeds not by the motives of dominance and acquisition, but by respect. It is a word for a set of practices by which we learn to live with difference, with the fluidity of culture and with the instability of the self.
>
> We should not feel that respect for the other obliges us to erase ourselves, or our culture, as if all value lay out there and none here. As the traditions of the other are entitled to respect, despite their oddness to us, and sometimes despite

their inhumanities, so too our own tradition is entitled to respect as well. Our task is to be distinctively ourselves in a world of others: to create a frame that includes both self and other, neither dominant, in an image of fundamental equality.

This has, of course, a distinctively utopian ring and it is not hard to problematize it, as Said (1978) did so brilliantly in *Orientalism*, as the power of the translator (usually white male and bourgeois) to represent 'the other' in a manner that dominated subjects (orientals, blacks, women, etc.) are forced to internalize and accept. Rather more subtly, translation can alter political meanings and messages (sometimes even without knowing it) and thereby alter the whole dynamic of political beliefs and action. Benedict Anderson shows, for example, how the English rendering of the executed Philippine national poet Jose Rizal's work (originally written in Spanish in the late nineteenth century before the US occupation) destroys so much of the original meaning as to put an immense distance between the founding concept of national identity and its contemporary manifestations.

Such historical understandings themselves provide a hedge against the kinds of representational repressions and distortions that many feminist and post-colonial writers have recorded. Furthermore, as White points out, 'to attempt to "translate" is to experience a failure at once radical and felicitous: radical, for it throws into question our sense of ourselves, our languages, of others; felicitous, for it releases us momentarily from the prison of our own ways of thinking and being'. The act of translation offers a moment of liberatory as well as repressive possibility.

The importance of translation becomes even more obvious in the multicultural (and increasingly linguistically fragmented) settings that now prevail in many of the world's largest metropolitan areas. For translation offers a way to create common understandings without erasing differences. And there are two compelling reasons to push in this direction. First, as Zeldin (1995) remarks, we know a great deal about what divides people but nowhere near enough about what we have in common (the universals that bind us as a species). Secondly, without translation and the construction of some common language, collectivization of grassroots action becomes impossible. Armed with a common language that respects differences, grassroots movements can coalesce to re-imagine and reconstruct their social world. Translation is the hard work that has to be done in taking militant particularism and grassroots activism onto some broader terrain of struggle and mobilizing grassroots powers to some higher purpose.

But translation does not merely entail the exploration of the commonalities that lie within the diverse structures of feeling that characterize the materialities of social relations and social belonging. For language itself is a multilayered system in which powerful abstractions have their role to play. We have access, for example, to an important historical legacy of universal principles – liberty, freedom, justice, rewards for creative endeavours, responsiveness to needs, and the like. And part of what translation is about is giving tangible meaning to those abstractions (such as environmental or social justice, human rights, liberty and compassion) in particular settings and by so doing reaffirm the significance, power and meaning of such universal principles. Universal principles and truths are not free standing; they do not and cannot stand outside of us as abstract and absolute principles that descend from some ether of morality to regulate human affairs for all times and places. Once again we see that the processes of translation and conversion depend upon institutionalized practices and mediating institutions (such as those of education, religion, the media, the law, governments, etc.). But also, and in the final analysis, no universal principle holds good that is not connected to individuals and persons who act as conscious bearers of such principles. And it is at this point that we find ourselves forced to reflect upon the processes that nourish militant particularism and grassroots movements in the first place.

The Personal Is Political

Looked at through the other end of the analytical telescope, we see militant particularism and grassroots activism as a particular kind of collective expression of personal and individual needs, wants and desires. At this level we see a different kind of dialectic at work which helps us understand both its limitations and potentialities.

The beginning point is to understand how the personal is always political. Through changing our world we change ourselves. We cannot talk, therefore, about social change without at the same time being prepared, both mentally and physically, to change ourselves. Conversely, we cannot change ourselves without changing our world. That relation is not easy to negotiate. We encounter all manner of unintended consequences of our actions. And taking on struggles with some better organized external power at some larger scale (like the state apparatus) is a daunting enough task to be discouraging in itself.

But there is a more subtle problem to be confronted. Foucault (1984), for example, worried that the 'fascism that reigns in our heads' is far more insidious than anything that gets constructed outside. And it is important to understand what he might have meant by that and how it relates to the powers and limitations of grassroots activism.

Consider, then, the question of 'the person' as the irreducible moment for the grounding of all politics and social action. That person is not some absolute and immutable entity fixed in concrete but in some respects a social being open to influence and control. A relational conception of the person, for example, puts emphasis upon our porosity in relation to the world. But this then poses the key question. Does the collectivity shape the person or does the person shape the collectivity? This dialectic deserves some thought.

In the United States, to take the case with which I am most familiar, private property and inheritance, market exchange, commodification and monetization, the organization of economic security and social power, all place a premium upon personalized private property vested in the self (understood as a bounded entity, a non-porous individual), as well as in house, land, money, means of production, etc., as the elemental socio-spatial forms of political-economic life. The organization of production and consumption forges divisions of labour and of function upon us and constructs professionalized personas (the planner, the professor and the poet as well as the proletarian, all of whom, as Marx and Engels (1952) point out in *The Communist Manifesto*, 'have lost their halo' and become in some way or another paid agents of bourgeois power). We live, according to this argument, in a social world that converts all of us into fragments of people with particular attachments, skills, abilities integrated into those powerful and dynamic structures that we call a 'mode of production'. Furthermore, the fierce spatiotemporalities of contemporary daily life – driven by technologies that emphasize speed and rapid reductions in the friction of distance and of turnover times – preclude time to imagine or construct alternatives other than those forced unthinkingly upon us as we rush to perform our respective professional roles in the name of technological progress and endless capital accumulation. The material organization of production, exchange and consumption rests on and reinforces specific notions of rights and obligations and affects our feelings of alienation and of subordination, our conceptions of power and powerlessness. Even seemingly new avenues for self-expression (multiculturalism being a prime recent example) are captive to the forces of capital accumulation and the market (love of nature is made to equal eco-tourism and ethnicity is reduced to a matter of restaurants or authentic commodities for market, for example).

The net effect is to limit our vision of the possible. Our 'positionality' or 'situatedness' as beings is a social construct in exactly the same way that the mode of production is a social creation. And this 'positionality' defines who or what we are (at least for now). 'Where we see it from' within that process provides much of the grist for our consciousness and our imaginary. From the fund of our situated experience we draw certain conclusions as to possibilities and in that relation lies a limitation: we cannot see much further than the horizon broadly dictated by where we already are.

Even Adam Smith (cited in Marx, 1977, p. 483) considered that 'the understandings of the greater part of men are necessarily formed by their ordinary employments' and that 'the uniformity of (the labourer's) life naturally corrupts the courage of his mind'. If this is only partially true – as I am sure it is – it highlights how the struggle to think alternatives – to think and act differently – inevitably runs up against the circumstances of and the consciousness that derives from a localized daily life and the way the political person gets constructed. Where, then, is the courage of our minds to come from? The embeddedness of persons within larger collectivities (such as those of neighbourhood or community) then becomes a problem precisely because the norms of behaviour and of belonging that define social solidarities operate as constraints which, like our ordinary employments, can just as easily have the effect of limiting the courage of our minds rather than liberating them for more radical styles of action. The fierce social controls imposed by homeowner associations which tolerate very little deviance from social norms which are broadly internalized, accepted and even welcomed by most residents is a case in point. It is hard not to conclude with Paul Knox (*pace* Foucault) that such associations constituted 'a web of servitude regimes that regulate land use and mediate community affairs in what often amounts to a form of contracted fascism'.

But we can all of us individually desire, think and dream of difference. And we have available to us a wide array of resources for critique, resources from which to generate alternative visions as to what might be possible. Utopian schemas, for example, typically imagine entirely different systems of property rights, living and working arrangements, all manifest as entirely different spatial forms and temporal rhythms. This proposed re-organization (including its social relations, forms of reproductive work, its technologies, its forms of social provision) makes possible a radically different consciousness (of social relations, gender relations, of the relation to nature, as the case may be) together with the expression of entirely different rights, duties and obligations founded upon collective ways of living. 'Where we learn it from' can be just as important as 'where we see it from'. Communities and neighbourhoods are key sites within which explorations occur, both in terms of the learning and construction of new imaginaries of social life as well as their tangible realizations through material and social practices. The tension between conformism and deviation is writ large in the historical geography of community life.

But the deviations which form such a rich seedbed for social change and so often challenge the status-quo within the interstices of urban life are not without their internal contradictions either. Voluntary bonding and association to realize some common dreams is one thing but social pressure and the forcing that often occurs as solidarities are formed can sometimes veer towards coercions while charismatic and hierarchical leaderships forge structures of power, influence and control which can become highly centralized within localities. And when such structures become deeply embedded in the city they have their own fragmenting effect as local leaderships (even when not directly bought off by higher powers), depending crucially upon their positioning for their sense of identity, refuse to merge or submerge their particular interests into the framework of some broader movement. The United States is full of community activism of precisely this sort, the effect being to confine a militant grassroots politics within a straitjacket of self-imposed constraints with respect to larger social transformations. Here, too, the fascisms that reign in our heads as well as within our political practices take a toll upon the effectiveness of grassroots movements to radically alter the world.

Looking at matters from this micro-level tells us, however, how hard the practical work will be to get from where we are to somewhere else. To begin with, the chicken-and-egg relation of how to change ourselves through changing our world can at best be set slowly though persistently in motion as a project to alter the forces that construct the political person. This cannot occur as some radical revolutionary break (though traumatic events and social breakdowns – economic crises, uprisings, wars – have often opened a path to radically different conceptions). The perspective of a long revolution is necessary. To construct that revolution some sort of collectivization of the impulse and desire for change is necessary. No one can go it alone. And there are plenty of thinkers, armed with resources from, for example, political or utopian traditions who can act as subversive agents, fifth columnists inside of grassroots movements with all their limitations yet with one foot firmly planted en route to some alternative possibilities.

We cannot presume that *anything* personal makes for *good* politics. Nor is it possible to accept the thesis beloved in some radical alternative movements (such as deep ecology and some areas of feminism) that fundamental transformations in personal attitudes and behaviours are sufficient (rather than just necessary) for social change to occur. While social change may begin and end with the personal, therefore, there is much more at stake here than individualized personal growth or manifestations of personal commitment. In reflecting on how local solidarities form, it is of course vital to leave a space for the private and the personal (a space in which doubt, anger, anxiety and despair as well as certitude, altruism, hope and elation may flourish). And in bringing persons together into patterns of social and political solidarities there are as many traps and pitfalls as open paths to change.

Nevertheless, the construction of local solidarities and the definition of local collectivities and affinities is a crucial means whereby the person becomes more broadly political. The negotiation that always lies at the basis of militant particularism and grassroots activism is, therefore, between political persons seeking to change each other and the world as well as themselves. But what are they seeking to change themselves into and why? It is here that the perspective of what any 'long revolution' occurring through the long history of urbanization needs to be developed.

Species Being in the City

The urban sociologist Robert Park (1967, p. 3) once wrote (in a passage echoes Marx's observations on the labour process):

> ... the city and the urban environment represent man's most consistent and, on the whole, his most successful attempt to remake the world he lives in more after his heart's desire. But if the city is the world which man created, it is the world in which he is henceforth condemned to live. Thus, indirectly, and without any clear sense of the nature of his task, in making the city man has remade himself.

Many species, as Lewontin (1982) points out, adapt to the environments they alter and so initiate a long evolutionary process of dialectical transformations of selves and others. Human beings have proven particularly adept at such a process and the idea that 'Man Makes Himself' (to use Gordon Childe's title of long ago) also has a long and fertile history. We transform ourselves through transforming our world (as Marx insisted). We transform our species' capacities and powers through cultural, technological, political and social innovations which have wide-ranging ramifications for the kinds of environments to which we then have to adapt. And it is increasingly the environment defined by urbanization that becomes the central milieu within which this adaptive and transformative process occurs.

While it is plausible to argue for some kind of dialectical co-evolution between human biological characteristics and cultural forms over the long term, the explosion of cultural understandings and practices in the last few hundred years has left no time for biological adaptation. Nevertheless, there are basic possibilities and constraints derived from our species character. Elsewhere (Harvey, 2000) I have considered these under the headings of:

- competition and the struggle for existence;
- diversification and differentiation;
- collaboration, cooperation and mutual aid;
- environmental transformations (e.g. urbanization);
- the production and reconfiguration of space;
- the transformation of temporalities.

If these form a basic repertoire of capacities and powers, then the long term question is how to mobilize a particular mix of them to shape alternative urban forms with more humane consequences for social life. Cities are, after all, large scale collaborative enterprises incorporating competitive processes, diversifications (divisions of labour, of function of lifestyles and values), the production of built environments, of spaces and of divergent temporalities.

Can we reasonably aspire to consciously intervene in this process of 'remaking ourselves' through urbanization, even, perhaps, acquire some 'clear sense of the nature of (our) task?' It is at this point that commonalities and universal values enter back into the picture, for without discussion and debate upon them, we are left with nothing other than the cumulative effects of micro-actions, contingencies and chance as central to human evolution. Consideration of 'species being in the city' therefore appears just as important to the argument as any discussion of how the personal might be political. Indeed, the dialectic between particularity and universality here appears as fundamental to human affairs.

The Dialectics of the Grassroots

So how can this theoretical and somewhat abstract exploration be put to work to understand the limitations and possibilities of grassroots movements and militant particularism in relation to broader urban processes?

To begin with, it is immediately evident that urban social movements internalize effects (political, economic and ideological) from the broader social context (including species being) of which they are a part and that their character is heavily dependent upon this internalization. But the movements are not merely neutral mediators between, say, the personal on the one hand and broader political-economic and ideological forces (such as those that attach to, say, globalization or some nationalist developmental project) on the other. It is in and through this positioning that we have to interpret much of the complex historical geography of such movements in relation to broader currents of change and understand their future potentialities.

From the theoretical perspective I have constructed, it is entirely possible to understand urban social movements as predominantly socio-political reflections if not overt constructs of some broader politics or even biological imperatives. This entails mechanisms to procure tangible goods (material or psychic) for grassroots leaders that can be passed on as personal benefits to enough elements in the population to ensure adhesion to some collective politics. There are, in fact, many versions of this. The 'political machine' politics of many cities in the United States – a much maligned system of governance that often worked well for immigrants, the poor and even for certain elements of business (making Mayor Daley's

Chicago of the 1960s into 'the city that worked') – is a predominantly political version of this. While this is not usually referred to as an 'urban social movement' it forms, as it were, one polar extreme of localized collective action in the urban sphere. It overtly lacks that aspect of autonomy and voluntarism that is more often used to characterize urban social movements but there are strong theoretical grounds in any case for questioning the ideals of voluntarism and autonomy as vital values more generally. The homeowner associations in the United States are not orchestrated politically from above but in their acceptance of a dominant mode of a market economy characterized by individualism at one level and class, racial or ethnic interests at another they fall exactly into an ideological line that is just as politically repressive and homogenizing as any political system could construct. And the same could be said for much of the structuring of urban spaces that goes on through the powers of ethnicity, religion or cultural forms. To characterize religious communal movements as autonomous and voluntarist seems to go well beyond what they actually are, in exactly the same way that organized ethnic enclaves (such as the chinatowns that characterize many Western cities) can hardly be understood apart from the diasporic activities of ethnically based business elites that make use of such enclaves for broader purposes.

The central question to which this points is to identify the real relations internalized within *all* urban social movements of whatever stripe (and however autonomous and voluntarist they may claim to be or even appear). Only through such identifications is it possible to understand broader allegiances and potentialities for political action at both local and more general spatial scales. The actual 'how' of the internalization is of more than passing interest, however, since it defines direct as well as subtle ways in which a relative autonomy and relatively voluntarist forms of association can be part and parcel of a process of building political power. I have already alluded to the problem of community forms of organization that become hollow and thereby vulnerable and it is exactly at this point that the 'how' of the internalization of external influences and powers becomes an indicator of levels, strengths and persistence of local solidarities.

I emphasize the significance of these external relations for urban social movements because the latter flourish most and to greatest effect by drawing nourishment from broader resources (political, economic, ideological, religious, ethnic, cultural). Without such forms of nourishment (often structured by NGO's or other forms of organization such as religion or ethnic kinship structures) they quickly disintegrate or fade away. But putting such resource structures to the forefront as a long-term condition of survival of such movements also indicates something about their potentially insurgent qualities. Put simply, if local organizations do arise and find no broader resource field from which to procure nourishment, then they either have to create such a resource field through a broad based insurgent politics or by sheer strength and influence force their cooptation by existing powers (in the way that the Civil Rights movement in the United States in the early 1960s forced the Federal and then State governments into patterns of support for its actions and agendas).

While all of this may seem to propose a somewhat jaundiced or even negative view of urban social movements and militant particularism as sources of social change or even of urban life, I want to suggest that contextualizing them accurately in this way provides means to assess their extraordinary strengths and importance as mediating agents in the urban process. To begin with, ensuring the vitality of such movements becomes a crucial element in political participation more generally and vitality cannot be ensured by repressive and hierarchically structured forms of governance. If the Workers Party in Porto Alegre seeks more active political and economic participation of marginalized populations then it must set up structures (like the participatory budget process) to ensure relative autonomy and vitality at the grassroots and itself learn to adapt to what the grassroots are about. Dialectical relations of this sort are vital to the construction of any kind of viable democracy in contemporary urban settings. Even more important is the way in which general problems (of economic development, qualities of environment and of life) get recognized in grassroots settings and become politically sensitized as issues that must necessarily be addressed through a broader politics. The internalization of external forces at the local level frequently entails intense contradictions which demand resolutions at the local level which in turn place pressures upon external powers to change their ways (consider the classic case of capitalist developers being intensely resisted by bourgeois residents). Questions of environmental justice, of discrimination in land and housing markets, of discriminatory police violence, of social integration and education, have arisen in this way and been propagated through broader and broader circles from the felt needs of individuals willing and able to give expression to those needs through collective modes of action in local settings. The way in which the personal becomes political and translates back into broader political realms is, in the final analysis, just as important as the internalization of broader powers in local collective movements.

The essential point is to see urban social movements as mediators and militant particularism as a translation from the personal to a broader terrain of politics. Plainly, democratic procedures and governance in general as well as in urban settings already do rely and will continue to rely into the foreseeable future upon the mediating institutions of local action and the formation of local solidarities. Whether or not such mediating institutions will play a positive or negative role in relation to the democratization of urban governance remains, of course, to be seen. But broader political economic forces ignore this dimension to human action at their peril. Hollowed out local institutions are even more of a threat than a militant particularism characterized by relative autonomy and a charismatic vitality seeking broader scale reforms. The dialectics of the grassroots and the powers of militant particularism are vibrant forces in urban life in particular and socio-political life in general.

References

Abers, R. (1998), 'Learning Democratic Practice: Distributing Government Resources through Popular Participating in Porto Alegre, Brazil', in M. Douglass and J. Friedmann (eds), *Cities for Citizens: Planning and the Rise of Civil Society in a Global Age*, John Wiley, New York.

Boyd-White, J. (1990), *Justice as Translation*, Chicago University Press, Chicago.

Castells, M. (1983), *The City and the Grassroots*, University of California Press, Berkeley.

Davis, M. (1990), *City of Quartz: Excavating the Future in Los Angeles*, Verso, London.

Douglass, M. and Friedmann, J. (1998) (eds), *Cities for Citizens: Planning and the Rise of Civil Society in a Global Age*, John Wiley, New York.

Etzioni, A. (1997), 'Community Watch', *The Guardian*, 28 June, no. 9.

Foucault. M. (1984), 'Preface', in G. Deleuze and F. Guattari, *Anti-Oedipus: Capitalism and Schizophrenia*, Macmillan, London.

Harvey, D. (1996), *Justice, Nature and the Geography of Difference*, Basil Blackwell, Oxford.

Harvey, D. (2000), *Spaces of Hope*, Edinburgh University Press, Edinburgh.

Lewontin, R. (1982), 'Organism and Environment', in H. Plotkin (ed.), *Learning, Development and Culture*, Wiley, Chichester.

Marx, K. (1977 edition), *Capital*, Vintage Books, New York.

Marx, K. and Engels F. (1952 edition), *The Communist Manifesto*, Progress Publishers, Moscow.

Park, R. (1967), *On Collective Control and Social Behavior*, Chicago University Press, Chicago.

Putnam, R. (1993), *Making Democracy Work: Civic Traditions in Modern Italy*, Princeton University Press, Princeton.

Said, E. (1978), *Orientalism*, Pantheon Books, New York.

Sandercock, L. (1998), *Towards Cosmopolis*, John Wiley, New York.

Seabrook, J. (1996), *In the Cities of the South: Scenes from a Developing World*, Verso, London.

Zeldin, T. (1995), *An Intimate History of Humanity*, Harper Collins, New York.

Chapter 12

Challenges and Emerging Responses for Sustainable Development in an Urbanizing World

Nicholas You

Introduction

Since the adoption of Agenda 21 in 1992, several trends have emerged that are changing the equation and the search for sustainable development. Chief among these is the rapid transition to an urbanized world. Not only is half of the world's population now living in cities and urban settlements, but the other half is becoming increasingly dependent on cities and towns for its economic survival and livelihood. In the next 30 years, the population of the world's cities is projected to double to well over five billion with virtually all of this growth taking place in cities in developing country. Furthermore, projections anticipate that by 2015, there are likely to be 360 cities with populations greater than one million; 150 of these will be in Asia alone, and we shall also see some 30 mega-cities of 10 million or more, of which more than half are likely to be in Asia and Latin America. While this demographic shift was predictable in 1992, other factors such as globalization and democratization have reinforced the role of cities as centres of production and consumption and of social and political change.

These trends, significant in their own right, are also changing the way we view and approach sustainable development. In physical and spatial terms, while cities are already home to most of the global population, they occupy barely 2 per cent of the world's land area. The physical footprint of cities could allow planners and policy makers to envisage scenarios in which human society goes about its daily business with minimal impact on the surrounding territory. Unfortunately, cities also consume more than 75 per cent of the world's natural resources and generate an equally disproportionate amount of waste and pollution. Recent developments in ascertaining the 'ecological footprint of cities' show that the 21st-century metropolis is rapidly becoming a tentacle-like organism that draws its food, energy, water and other resources from further and further afield, and in such a way that its inhabitants are largely isolated from, and ignorant of, the global social, economic and environmental consequences generated.

In economic terms, cities are increasingly assuming a leading role in attracting investment and in harnessing human and technical resources for achieving unprecedented gains in productivity and competitiveness. At the same time, however, well over one third of the urban population in developing countries is living in extreme poverty, with little or no access to basic infrastructure and services. They are marginalized from the mainstream of the urban economy and society and have tenuous, if any, access to the political decision-making structures that could improve their lives and livelihoods. It is estimated that some 650 million urban dwellers live in life-threatening conditions of poverty and environmental degradation and that this number is expected to more than double by 2025. Thus, the global trend in urbanization implies, for the majority of the world's urban population, nothing less than the 'urbanization of poverty'. Unemployment combined with ineffective social services, misguided policies and increasing disparities resulting from globalization have, in many cities in developing countries, resulted in a high degree of social exclusion that is increasingly recognized as the principle cause of social dysfunction, crime and violence.

Cities are also witnessing major changes in their social, ethnic and cultural make-up. The liberalization of global trade and investment has also brought about considerable movement of people and the mixing of socio-cultural behaviour patterns. While this trend has contributed to the social capital and cultural diversity of cities, new challenges have also emerged in terms of social exclusion and intolerance.

Finally, trends in democratization and decentralization have provided cities with new roles and responsibilities. As the sphere of government closest to the people, representative democracy has, in many countries, strengthened the legitimate voice of cities and local authorities in the formulation of public policy. The often narrowly defined administrative competencies and outdated mandates of cities as 'lower tiers of government' and as local service providers remain, however, major barriers to the effective contribution of cities in forging more holistic and sustainable approaches to social and economic development and environmental management.

Some Emerging Responses

Chapter 28 of Agenda 21 recognizes the role of local authorities, stating 'because so many of the problems and solutions being addressed by Agenda 21 have their roots in local activities, the participation and cooperation of local authorities will be a determining factor in fulfilling sustainable development objectives'. The Habitat Agenda, adopted in Istanbul in 1996, further provided strategic guidelines for implementing 'sustainable human settlements development in an urbanizing world'. These include: partnerships and participation; decentralization and empowerment; capacity building and the use of information in decision-making. The following paragraphs provide some examples of how these strategies are being implemented in emerging metropolises of the developing world.

Local Accountability and Participatory Democracy

The Habitat Agenda not only recognizes the importance of effective partnerships in addressing the critical social, economic and environmental challenges of rapid urbanization and social change. By grouping the concept of partnership and participation, it implicitly endorses the fact that what is needed goes beyond representative democracy and the inclusion of 'beneficiaries' in the design and implementation of development projects. The Porto Alegre Participatory Budgeting initiative in Brazil is perhaps one of the better-known examples of how participatory democracy can effectively incorporate the population, and the urban poor in particular, in the decision-making, budgeting and planning process. Public resource allocation in the city has become a process in which citizens decide on municipal expenditures for public works and services. Through the formation of citizens' commissions to follow up the progress of projects, participatory budgeting has also become an efficient tool for monitoring the use of public funds and the implementation of public works. The system has contributed significantly to improving the level of transparency in city planning and management and in preventing the misuse of public funds. The benefits produced since its inception include:

- a high degree of consensus for public funds to be used in response to the most needy communities;
- the identification of priority works for the city in accordance with the vision that the population has developed for its city;
- the inclusion of previously excluded portions of the population in the decision-making process leading to their empowerment, self esteem and to the widespread exercise of democracy.

Additionally, participatory budgeting has decisively contributed to the health of City Hall's financial condition while allowing for a much more equitable distribution of funds, of urban infrastructure and in the delivery and improvement of basic urban services. Today, more than 70 cities in

Brazil and in Latin America have adopted the principles of participatory budgeting as a means of improving urban governance and in becoming more responsive to the needs of their respective citizens.[1]

Developing New Partnerships

Effective partnerships can also result in the mobilization of resources and the establishment of innovative financial and management mechanisms. In 1990 Chengdu, a metropolis of ten million located in the poorer western region, was one of the most severely polluted cities in China. Surrounded on four sides by two rivers (Fu and Nan), industrial effluent, raw sewage and the intensive use of freshwater deteriorated the rivers' waters and silted the rivers thus causing annual floods during the rainy season and leaving the rivers to run dry during the dry season. Slum and squatter settlements proliferated on the banks of both rivers, exacerbating the social, economic and environmental problems of the city. In 1993, in response to a petition by school children to the Mayor, Chengdu initiated a comprehensive revitalization plan. The goal of the plan was to harness and restore the ecological flow of the rivers, prevent future flooding, and improve water quality. To achieve this goal, however, several other steps had to be taken simultaneously, including:

- finding alternative housing solutions for the 100,000 inhabitants of the slum and squatter settlements bordering the rivers;
- relocating, retrofitting or closing down over 1,000 enterprises and factories to reduce or eliminate industrial effluent and emissions;
- implementing a comprehensive waste water collection and treatment system;
- adopting the necessary policies that would enable all of the above to be implemented in a transparent and accountable manner.

Owing to the capital investment required and the number of communities affected, the Municipal Government of Chengdu adopted a strategy of partnership and participation. This resulted in a substantial increase in environmental awareness and the mobilization of central and provincial governments, domestic and foreign investors and the general public. A gearing ratio of one-part central government finances to two parts local government resources to three parts civil society sector investment was established. Over 30,000 households previously located in the slums on both banks of the two rivers have been re-housed in new, fully equipped housing estates. The land area vacated has been used to create a continuous green space replete with parks, gardens, recreational and cultural facilities. The two rivers have been de-silted, widened and their ecological flow restored, thereby reducing flood vulnerability to a 200-year risk. A series of concomitant projects dealt with solid waste, sewage collection and treatment, industrial effluent, road infrastructure, transport and communications, and parks and gardens.[2]

Decentralization

The debate regarding decentralization in developing countries often focuses on the pervasive lack of autonomy of local authorities and the paucity of their revenue base. One of the ubiquitous arguments of central government for not devolving more powers to local government, whether at provincial or municipal level, is their poor performance. Surat, India, was, in many ways, a typical case in point. It captured the world's headlines in 1994 because of a frightening outbreak of the plague. Surat presented ideal conditions for the rapid spread of the plague due to its filthy environment and the extreme congestion of its slums. Prior to the outbreak, the Surat Municipal Council was a moribund and lethargic organization. Street cleaning covered barely 40 per cent of the city's area. Less than 50 per cent of solid waste was collected on a daily basis and the city accounted for 50 per cent of the mortality rate in water-borne and water-related public health diseases in Gujarat. Only 45 per cent of citizens had access to water supply and sewerage services. The maintenance of drains, street lighting, parks and gardens, roads and schools was, at best, erratic. With the support of the state government, a participatory planning effort was implemented and the municipal management system was completely overhauled. The key to the overhaul was decentralization. Whereas before all powers were concentrated in the hands of one commissioner, a new decentralized administrative structure devolved day-to-day responsibilities to ten 'commissioners' of equal decision-making and resource allocation powers. The newly formed team of 11 commissioners reached decisions on all matters of policy and met on a regular basis to co-ordinate their efforts and activities. Among the many actions taken, the most significant included:

- improving the working conditions and dignity of sanitation workers;
- widening and cleaning pathways, drains and streets in low-income neighbourhoods;
- informing citizens of their rights to quality and timely services and resolving 97 per cent of outstanding grievances;
- establishing an early warning system for environmental health risks;
- reforming the contracts and procurement system to improve accountability and transparency in contracts related to operations and maintenance.

The increased accountability, responsiveness and public awareness was successful in regaining citizens' support and in less that two years Surat was transformed from one of the filthiest cities in the country into the second cleanest city in India.[3]

Capacity-building and the Empowerment of Local Actors

Civil society organizations have proven in many cases to be highly effective agents for implementing and maintaining local development initiatives. When the City Council of Dar-es-Salaam, Tanzania, realized that it could not meet all its residents' demands for basic services, it established the Community Infrastructure Programme (CIP). The programme which initiated operations in 1996, works closely with communities to enhance community-based planning, implementation and monitoring activities. The key components of the CIP include:

- capacity building of community-based organizations (CBOs) including training, preparation of community profiles, preparation of community development plans, information pertaining to land ownership;
- Institutional Strengthening including the establishment of offices in each community, the establishment of a Steering Committee including representatives from all the partners and of formalized institutional links between the relevant partners and the CBOs through the signature of Memoranda of Understanding;
- Neighbourhood Infrastructure Upgrading including preparation of Terms of Reference pertaining to works and services to be undertaken, preparation of detailed engineering designs for the infrastructure to be upgraded (i.e. roads, drainage systems, sewerage, etc., technical sub-committees for monitoring and supervising the works and services and the establishment of community (locally managed) water systems.

The communities are running these water systems at cost – i.e. the community members buy the water and the money is ploughed back to run the systems. In the Tabata community, part of the money collected is used for solid waste collection. The water committee pays for the collection services and the community members are charged collection fees for the service. This ensures community responsibility and sustainability of the infrastructure provided. The CIP works closely with the City Council and donors to improve their ability to work together. In one notable example, one of the communities was unhappy with the standard of roads proposed by the World Bank. As a result of direct negotiations, the Bank agreed to finance a road with higher construction standards and lower maintenance costs in exchange for the community's commitment to increase their initial financial contribution. The strong sense of community responsibility for their own betterment, but also for the continued maintenance of infrastructure and basic services, has had a significant impact on the quality of life and is helping to ensure the programme's long-term sustainability.

Networking and Access to Information

Lasting improvements in the living conditions of the urban poor is often contingent upon access to information by the urban poor themselves and by those traditionally excluded from voicing their needs and demands, especially women. Prior to 1996, almost 80 per cent of the poor living in Ahmedabad did not have access to basic services. Moreover, poor women make up an estimated 70 per cent of the active voting population and 50 per cent of the users have little or no access to municipal services. Based on the successful implementation of the Report Card on urban services in Bangalore, the Foundation for Public Interest (FPI) modified the report card methodology to focus on how efficient service provision could make working conditions more productive for women residents in the poorest wards of the city. The subsequent project was carried out by the Self Employed Women's Association (SEWA) to enable the direct participation of poor women in carrying out performance assessment surveys. SEWA was able to implement the project rapidly owing to its extensive national network involving over 200,000 women from the informal sectors of the economy, of whom 40,000 were residing in Ahmedabad's poorest wards. The results of the survey confirmed the heavy reliance of poor women in Ahmedabad on crucial services such as water, sanitation and waste disposal, all of which were being provided on an irregular basis. However, one of the most significant findings was that only 6 per cent of the respondents had contacted the Municipal Corporation to voice their complaints and that the other 94 per cent were either unwilling or discouraged from expressing their grievances.

The Ahmedabad Municipal Corporation responded to the report card in a constructive manner and further analysis and feedback from municipal officers revealed the causal reasons for poor services' delivery, including misuse and abuse of services by the users themselves, political interference, and a marked propensity for new investments over maintenance. Consultations between all parties involved resulted in the implementation of citywide as well as ward-specific action plans. Lessons learned from the survey and the report card process were subsequently used by SEWA to develop training materials and evaluation instruments for its own operations (micro-credit for poor women) and were incorporated into Ahmedabad's Parvitan Slum Networking Programme. The knowledge, skills and expertise gained by all parties involved in the report card process, have since been shared among government agencies, NGOs and community-based organizations and have been applied in six other towns in Gujurat and adapted to enhance user participation and service performance improvements in such diverse areas as the street vendors of Radhampur Towns and recipients of malaria and cyclone relief services.[4]

Some Concluding Remarks

The examples quoted in this article were selected from over 1,600 *good* and *best practices* in improving living that have been documented and disseminated by UN-Habitat and its partners since the adoption of the Habitat Agenda in 1996. Together with the large and growing number of other initiatives in documenting innovations, best practices and lessons learned, they attest to the validity of the strategic objectives of the Habitat Agenda as entry points in forging more sustainable development and in implementing Agenda 21. As illustrated by the small selection of cases presented here, they substantiate the view that sustainable urban development is increasingly contingent upon good urban governance, namely a system and process of decision-making that is socially and economically just and inclusive.

Notes

1 Porto Alegre's initiative was recognized as a 'best practice' in 2000. See: www.bestpractices.org. The Best Practices and Local Leadership Programme is a global network of advocacy and capacity-building institutions dedicated to the identification, dissemination and transfer of lessons learned from 'good' and 'best' practices in improving the living environment. See: www.sustainabledevelopment.org/blp. UN-Habitat is the United Nations Human Settlements Programme, formerly known as the United Nations Centre for Human Settlements (Habitat). See: www.unhabitat.org. The Urban Secretariat is responsible for monitoring and assessing progress made in the implementation of the Habitat Agenda and produces the flagship publications of UN-Habitat.

2 Chengdu's initiative won the Dubai International Award for Best Practices in 2000.

3 Surat's initiative on Urban Governance in Environmental Health won the Dubai Award for Best Practices in 1998.

4 For Bangalore's Report Card and Ahmedabad's Innovative Urban Partnerships Programme, see: www.bestpractices.org; for Ahmedabad's Report Card see: www.sparcindia.org.

Chapter 13

Agenda 21 for Sustainable Construction in Developing Countries: The Indian Case[1]

Kirtee Shah

Introduction

This paper is part of one of the nine position papers commissioned (three each from Asia, Africa and Latin America) by the International Council for Research and Innovation (CIB) as part of the Action Plan for the Implementation of the CIB Agenda 21 on Sustainable Construction to further its proactive approach on the subject. The purpose is to bring to the forefront the special conditions, needs and perspectives of the developing countries to balance a developed world bias that had crept into an earlier effort. This paper attempts to present the Indian case.

With over a billion people in half a million villages and nearly 3,800 cities and towns, massive poverty, accelerated industrialization, rapid urbanization, growing economy, democratic polity, the special nature of the independence struggle under Gandhi's leadership (a champion of sustainable development and a committed practitioner of sustainable habits) and 40 years of socialist orientation and planned economy followed by a decade of economic liberalization, structural adjustment and globalization, India's choice of a development strategy, and its performance in this sphere, cannot fail to have great influence on the global sustainability concept. It is especially so because India has the strength of traditional wisdom, requirements posed by the size, diversity and complexity of its population, geography and society and a political philosophy and economic blueprint drawn up by Gandhi for an independent India. Having chosen the conventional and seemingly unsustainable development model, the question for India is: if a country such as India, with its conditions, history, heritage and leadership does not choose the alternative course, is the alternative development model an utopia? And can a utopia save the globe from the real danger posed by the current unsustainable development model?

The Indian construction industry, an integral part of the economy and a load bearer of a substantial part of its development investment, is not only on the brink of growth due to industrialization, urbanization, economic development and the people's rising expectations as to an improved quality of life. It is also bracing itself to face the challenges of modernization for improved productivity and a higher competitive edge. The challenge before it is: fast growth in response to increasing demand for goods and services; technological upgrade for speed, quality, cost reduction, and the substitution of manual labour; modern management practices leading to greater profitability and a 'modern', clean image; and technical skills, financial strength and organizational competence to meet domestic and international competition and capture a segment of the international market. The construction industry, steeped in tradition – in technology – and ways of working – largely informal in labour practices – has entered the race to change both its image and content.

Sustainable construction, admittedly, is neither the vision nor the immediate goal of its modernization thrust. It is looking at growth, efficiency, productivity, a greater market share and profit. Improved environmental performance, the reduction of pollution or substitution of high energy-consuming materials, or, as regards the human aspect, better tools and working conditions for the construction labour force, are mainly seen as a welcome by-product, useful in the sphere of public relations rhetoric, and nothing more. Nothing could better describe in graphic terms the mental block within construction practice than what recently occurred in a reconstruction project which took place in the wake of the January 2001 earthquake in Gujarat. In the reconstruction project of a village with 350 houses, to be constructed by a commercial contractor and funded jointly by four international humanitarian aid agencies, no provision whatsoever was made for some one hundred migrant, unskilled construction labourers, who would probably need to stay on site for over a year, in a remote place, under a blazing sun. No shelter, no toilets, no water, no child care facility. And this project is not even profit-making, it is charity!

The challenge of sustainable construction, therefore, implies more than changing tools, technology or energy-consuming materials; it means changing its mindset and attitude. Because the practitioner's world view is that the environment or labour safety and welfare is a luxury for the more affluent, more advanced, and more profitable. For the undeveloped, the starter, survival and growth rather than sustainability are the main issues. The prime concern is the price they pay. And questions such as ecological balance and saving the globe for future generations are for the intellectuals, philosophers and thinkers; not for a pragmatic material manufacturer or the worldly-wise contractor or estate developer!

Sustainable construction is a necessity if we want sustainable housing, sustainable settlements, sustainable cities and sustainable development. The environmental crisis is for real. The construction industry, which contributes so much to the damage side, must be prepared and equipped not only to mend its ways but also to make a positive contribution. Productivity and profits are essential. But these concepts should be broadened to include environmental and human aspects.

Sustainable construction is too vast and complex a matter to be addressed fully in its multiple backward and forward linkages. This paper, therefore, makes no claims to depth of treatment or comprehensiveness of coverage. It is selective and the omissions are both unintended and deliberate.

Sustainable Development, Settlements and Construction

Sustainable Development

The 'sustainable development' concept is perhaps one of the most significant gifts of the twentieth century to human kind in its search for peace, harmony and well-being. The World Commission on Environment and Development defined sustainable development as, 'Development that meets needs of the present without compromising the ability of the future generations to meet their own needs' and its successful pursuit on four interdependent principles related to meeting human needs, maintaining ecological integrity, attaining social sufficiency, and establishing social equity. This definition views development as much more than material progress. It links micro to macro, present to future, human to nature, and material to spiritual. It places a value on natural resources as social capital, indicates limits to growth, the finite nature of the globe's resources, and emphasizes the need for their judicious and responsible use, and equitable sharing. This concept puts ecological balance and environmental vulnerability in perspective as well as linking them with human activity. Sustainable development puts economic growth in the framework of enduring human happiness.

The sustainable development concept is not new to India. The ancient religions, whether Hinduism, Buddhism or Jainism, have deeply rooted respect for nature, restraint on want and material goods, sharing with others, caring for future generations, respect for all life forms and the promotion of economic pursuits in harmony with the environment. Principles of sustainable development are interwoven in the people's culture, tradition, behaviour, and life pattern. Vegetarianism preached by Jainism is based on respect for all life forms. Reverence for rivers (the river Ganges is mother to the Hindus) and cows reflect an understanding of ecosystemic interdependence. And a stand of trees taken by a local community as their deity and their 'puja' points not only to respect for the environment but also to a method for its preservation.

The most articulate advocate of sustainable development in a modern context in India was undoubtedly Mahatma Gandhi, not only a political leader in India's struggle for independence but also its spiritual leader. Gandhi had not only a vision for the development of an independent India, he also had a philosophy, a strategy and tools for achieving this goal. His vision of development was sustainable development.

Gandhi knew poverty at first hand. He recognized that 80 per cent of India's population was rural and that they faced problems of health, sanitation and survival. His plea was that development priorities should be focused on them and their villages. He asked Nehru, India's first Prime Minister:

> Why must India become industrial in the Western sense? Western civilization is largely urban. Small countries like England and Italy may be able to urbanize their societies. A big country like America cannot do otherwise. But one would think that a big country like India, with a teeming population and an ancient rural tradition that has hitherto answered its purpose need not – must not – copy the Western model. What is good for one nation is not necessarily good for another differently situated. One man's food is another man's poison.

If that is how Gandhi saw 'development' in the Indian context 80 years ago, critics of modern development see even more poison in how it is taking place and what it is now doing globally. The *Kauntaun Declaration*, 'Our cities, Our Homes: A Citizens' Agenda' adopted by a cross section of activists in the Asia Pacific Region says:

> This disturbing reality is in large part a legacy of the ideologies and institutions of the twentieth century, and in particular of the dominant neo-liberal economic development model of unfettered economic growth, unregulated markets, privatization of public assets and functions, and global economic integration that has become the guiding philosophy of our most powerful institutions. This model spawns projects that displace the poor to benefit those already better off, diverts resources to export production that might otherwise be used by the less advantaged to produce for their own needs, destroys livelihoods in the name of creating jobs, and legitimates policies that deprive persons in need of essential public services. The model advances institutional changes that shift the power to govern from people and governments to unaccountable global corporations and financial institutions devoted to a single goal: maximizing their own short-term financial gains. Its values honour a compassionless Darwinian struggle in which the strong consume the weak to capture wealth beyond reasonable need. It creates a system in which a few make decisions on behalf of the whole that

return to themselves great rewards while passing the costs to others. For them the system works and they see no need for change. The many who bear the burden have no meaningful voice.

E.P. Schumacher was one of the first economists to question the nature of economic growth taking place in the West. He asked, 'How can one argue that the American economy is efficient if it uses 40 per cent of the world's primary resources to support six per cent of the world's population without any observable improvement in the level of human happiness, well-being and peace?' Schumacher lobbied for a more holistic, people-centred view of economics. He felt that in trying to be scientific and quantitative, economists had ignored people's needs and motivations, cultural influences and spirituality.

Kamla Chowdhary in her essay *Economic Growth, Ethical and Ecological Concerns* has called for a new development paradigm. This would recognize that economic growth of itself is not development, nor are higher standards of living as measured by material goods. Catching up with the West, and therefore the Westernization of the world, is also not to be considered development. The new paradigm must be based on a more moderate demand on the Earth's resources and their more equitable distribution. Moving to a simpler lifestyle; evolving development strategies and processes that are the expression of local conditions, aspirations and control over resources; considering religious and spiritual issues when formulating the new paradigm; and changing existing institutional structures are some of her key observations.

Ever since independent India embarked on Prime Minister Nehru's path of economic development and social progress through centralized planning (borrowed from socialist Russia in the early 1950s) and capital-intensive industrialization in preference to Gandhi's model of economic growth through labour-intensive sustainable agricultural practices and village republics, debate on sustainable development has been a feature of public policy and academic dialogue. Following the liberalization, structural adjustment and global integration of the Indian economy in 1991, the debate is even more intense, with the privatized and globalized economy, environment and society providing arguments for and against the current model of development. While debate regarding options continues in the corridors of power, whether the ruling government is right-oriented BJP or socialist Congress or Marxist CPM, there is not much argument regarding direction. Fast and comprehensive economic reforms, greater privatization and globalization are the panaceas for further and higher growth and the speedy and effective alleviation of poverty. Turning back on the development model – whether it is sustainable or unsustainable – is considered neither practical nor wise.

Sustainable Settlements

Cities, we are told, are engines of economic growth. We have now learned that they not only produce growth, they are also produced by growth. The *quality* of growth (not only quantity), the *means* by which we achieve growth (whether in ecological harmony or in a polluting manner), the *nature* of growth (whether exploitative or just, whether creative or destructive), the *texture* of growth (whether equitable or unbalanced) and the *substance* of growth (whether leading to contentment, durable happiness and peace or greed, strife and violence) determine, to a great degree, the nature and quality of our cities.

Historically, cities are the products of many forces and influences. Whereas the industrialization that triggered urbanization in Western Europe and North America in the nineteenth and early twentieth centuries is still influencing urbanization processes in the developing world, there can be little doubt now that the most dominant influence shaping current urbanization trends and modern city development are the forces of economic globalization and its accompanying development model. Integration of global economy, characterized by an increase in trade in goods and services, an increase in investment by transnational corporations, and an explosion in financial and exchange rate transactions, while expanding choices by creating more goods and services for consumption, has a fundamental – and often negative – effect on the conditions of production and employment. The liberalization of national economies, their global integration, privatization, structural adjustment, the corporatization of business, and giving free rein to market forces undoubtedly spur economic growth, promote technological transformation and ensure high levels of prosperity and affluence for the chosen few. But we must also observe that they deepen poverty, widen inequality, causing exclusion and marginalization, promote wasteful consumerism, undermine national sovereignty, weaken state authority, destroy the environment and deplete natural resources, slanting the investment balance in favour of cities and mainly of big cities. This in turn leads to cultural alienation and seriously damages people's capacity to find solutions rooted in their culture, social norms, system of values and traditional wisdom. The way in which the developing world copes with these forces and factors will largely determine how humane, liveable and just its cities are.

When we quote statistics which establish that half of the world is now urban, we tend to ignore the fact that, by the same token, half of the world is still rural. In fact, it is more rural than urban in Asia and Africa where development challenges are the most difficult (70 per cent of India, for instance, is still rural; a staggering 700 million people!). In view of the growing trend towards urbanization, the increasing contribution of cities to national economic growth, and the complex problems of environmental management, resource mobilization, infrastructure provision and governance faced by the cities, this focus on cities is timely and unavoidable. However, we need to recognize clearly that poverty, lack of basic services, unemployment, under-employment, deficient infrastructure, paucity of investment resources, the declining contribution of agriculture to the GDP and the consequent marginalization of agriculture-dependent populations, inadequate housing, recurrent natural disasters, social and economic inequality and persistent forms of exploitation continue to afflict rural areas. Taken together, they constitute a formidable 'push factor' from rural to urban migration. Stable and economically viable rural settlements will ensure manageable urban growth. Viable and sustainable rural development strategies, therefore, should constitute an integral part of fashioning a new urban future. Villages cannot remain as the suppliers of food and raw materials and be relegated to the role of dumping grounds for rotting urban waste. They have a decisive role to play and should be allowed – and indeed helped – to play it.

The debate on sustainable settlements and cities, limited in nature and confined to special groups, is relatively recent and partly triggered by the Habitat II Conference in Istanbul and, to a certain extent, by its preparatory process. With over 700 million people in half a million dispersed and small villages, a high demographic growth rate, depressed rural economy, high incidence of poverty, unemployment, inadequate services, brain drain, migration, illiteracy, and lack of development in general, the question we must ask ourselves is: Can villages survive? Are they viable in the globalizing world? Can the quality of rural life be improved to a satisfactory level? The sustainability question in the rural context regards the inadequacy of 'development'.

In the urban context, it concerns the nature of development. With 300 million people in over 3,750 urban centres already, poverty-induced rural to urban migration, a rate of urban growth that would place almost half the country's population in cities and towns by 2025; a looming urban crisis due to the population explosion, growing consumerism, environmental degradation, strained services, urban poverty and weak governance, again, the question we must ask ourselves is: are cities sustainable? Fast growth and rapid deterioration in cities, some of which face a grave environmental crisis, are raising issues as to the sustainability of urbanization, the present form of urban growth and urban development, and posing questions on causes, remedies and the way forward.

Sustainable Construction

A broader, comprehensive and inclusive definition of sustainable construction must embrace much more than the mere process of constructing buildings and structures such as houses, bridges, roads, ports, silos and factories in a 'sustainable manner'. Both the process and the product must be viewed in the framework of its backward-forward linkages. Construction involves large investments. Its impact on the economy, productivity, employment, financial and property markets, therefore, is decisive. Construction occupies land and uses minerals, water, technology, chemical processes and energy in the production and use of building materials. Therefore its impact on the environment must be considered. A large labour force – both skilled and unskilled – is employed in construction work and users of the end product of the construction process are human societies. Therefore the social aspects of construction are important. The institutional framework governing the construction process and product has a substantial bearing on quality, output, and cost and, therefore, institutional factors are also important. Construction is a process and is made up of many parts. Therefore, sustainable construction should include sustainable design; sustainable planning; sustainable financing and investment; sustainable materials; sustainable tools, technology and methods; sustainable ownership and use; sustainable professional and labour practices; sustainable institutions and, of course, sustainable products. 'Sustainable' covers that which protects nature and the environment; reduces pollution; conserves resources and shares them equitably; saves energy; treats people fairly and in a just manner; respects knowledge and tradition.

Whose concern, if not priority, is sustainable construction in India? Who are the stakeholders and who, among them, are raising issues and working on alternative strategies for sustainable construction? Are the governments and public sector agencies, the biggest promoters and financiers of construction work aware, are they confronting issues or resistance, developing concepts, formulating policies, offering incentives, creating support institutions? Are private construction firms, both large and small, concerned, aware, active? Are professionals – architects, planners, engineers, supervisors – interested? Do the materials manufacturers, large and small, have an holistic perspective on sustainability? Are construction workers – skilled and unskilled – aware of the problem? What are research and academic institutions, social activists, environment and housing NGOs doing as regards sustainable construction?

To say that there is no awareness or action is simplistic. The stakeholders are active in many ways. Materials manufacturers are looking for energy-saving and cost-effective technologies. Environmentalists are highlighting environmental pollution and related issues. The national research establishments have research programs and budgets. Serious professionals are experimenting with alternative designs, materials and construction techniques. The governments are framing policies (to restrict the use of wood in construction, for instance), providing incentives to use industrial and other waste in material production and encouraging alternatives to non-renewable materials. NGOs are experimenting and demonstrating pilot projects. Things are happening. However, short term cost reduction rather than long term sustainability is the prime concern. Considering the large volume of investment in public and private construction; polluting and energy intensive methods of building materials production and use; low levels of technology development; the unorganized and untrained nature of the work force and potential for environmental damage by unsustainable technologies, materials and practices, interest and awareness as regards sustainable construction are limited, efforts are marginal and symbolic and impact is negligible. The issues related to the construction sector are many and complex. However, sustainable construction, as things stand today, is not seen as a priority concern or issue.

Vast diversity in the volume and nature of construction work, institutional arrangement, size of investment, and nature of construction practices suggest that the trends, issues and response in sustainable construction be examined separately for rural and urban sectors. Though part of the same whole and linked in multiple ways, the parameters guiding the construction industry, work, and practices in the urban and the rural sectors are so different that only a separate examination can ensure proper treatment. Agricultural versus industrial, dispersed versus centralized, small versus big, manual versus mechanized, informal versus formal, old versus new technology, low-cost versus high-cost, utilitarian versus trendy, uniform versus diverse, low versus high and community versus contractor are some of the characteristics of rural/urban differences in construction practice. The most significant difference, in the context of sustainability, is that while rural construction still retains a number of sustainable practices, the urban construction sector seems to be moving fast along the unsustainability track. While sustainable rural construction requires protection, preservation and upgrading (for quality and performance) of the existing system, in the urban sector the task is more difficult as it entails reversal of trends and systems transformation.

With the popular perception and image of the construction industry as unorganized and largely informal at the lower end, construction work as low status; construction practitioners (contractors) as unscrupulous and unethical; real estate developers as irresponsible and unaccountable; construction business as risky, sustainable construction, as defined in this article, is a far cry, an utopia. Before setting their sights on too high a goal of sustainable construction, concerned individuals would prefer greater emphasis on safe and quality construction, cost reduction, ethical practices, improved tools, technology and work conditions for the workers, and greater accountability to clients, financiers and users.

This paper attempts to do both, as they are inter-linked. Sustainable construction presupposes quality product, transparent process, and client accountability.

Profile of the Construction Sector in India

Construction is a vehicle for the growth of civilization. It builds structures that sustain a nation's economy. In India's plans for national development, construction constitutes 40 to 50 per cent of capital expenditure on projects in various sectors such as energy, transport, irrigation, communications, defence, the social sector, rural and urban infrastructure, etc. It contributes about 5 per cent to the GNP and is employment intensive.

Housing and construction render significant contributions to the economy in the form of enhancement of GDP, income and employment generation. Construction activity accounts for about 50 per cent of development outlay in India. A study by the Indian Institute of Management, Ahmedabad to evaluate the impact of investment in housing on GDP and employment ascertained that a unit increase in the final expenditure in construction generates national income five times as high and induces overall employment generation of nearly eight times the direct employment in construction. Over 32 million workers – unskilled, semi-skilled and skilled – are directly involved in construction work. Additionally, we must take into account secondary employment in ancillary industries, building materials supply, real estate development, fittings, furnishing, consumer goods, etc.

India's construction industry today faces enormous challenges posed by the massive scope of the country's plans, the need for project exports to countries who demand quality performance and a growing domestic consciousness regarding quality, speed and efficiency. The new liberalization and globalization policies are opening up construction activity to the private sector and this in turn heralds a new era of international competition within the country. With an average annual growth rate of around 6 per cent and focus on infrastructure development in support of industrial growth, the construction market shows fresh vitality. The growth of the domestic construction industry exceeds 10 per cent and is expected to show an upward trend.

Overseas business is almost three decades old for the Indian construction industry. With vast, technically well-trained and experienced manpower and managerial skills acquired through the execution of domestic projects, the industry has made its mark, especially in the Mid-Eastern/Far Eastern parts of the world.

The 1970s saw a boom in overseas construction and related activities involving deputation of technically qualified manpower, trading of construction materials produced in India, exportation of engineering services, and attractive employment opportunities for skilled construction workers (masons, carpenters, plumbers). With the slowing down of the oil boom, the volume of business in the Middle East dropped significantly. This loss of opportunity, however, has been compensated, to a certain extent, by the increased tempo of domestic work.

With the opening up of the Indian economy and as a result of major project funding by international development agencies, the institutional, legal and information barriers to the entry of foreign contractors have been removed. At the present time, there are over 75 construction companies of foreign origin operating in India. Such companies are mostly joint-venture companies or wholly owned subsidiaries of their foreign principals. Almost all the companies are engaged in core construction related to highway, power, petrol chemicals, fertilizers and other EPC contracts.

The strength of the industry rests on its substantial pool of qualified and experienced technical manpower and managerial personnel, abundant and inexpensive labour force, and well-established engineering practices. The weakness of the industry is due to limited access to the latest technologies, insufficient mechanization, inadequate system of construction financing and lack of suitable infrastructure and inadequate training facilities for the construction work force. At the lower end, construction and material production activities remain poorly organized and informal with the attendant disadvantages – absence of institutionalization, scarcity of capital, old tools and technology, untrained work force, unsafe and unhygienic working conditions, unstable employment and exploitative wages, and, of course, gender bias.

Despite the opening up of the economy, the public sector continues to be the largest employer in construction. Public housing, core industrial development, transportation, energy, power and other areas continue to be run and operated by the state, state owned companies, or the authorities established by the state. Private sector construction and engineering companies are therefore dependent on the state for their business. The scenario, however, is changing as several sectors have been opened to private sector participation. The mineral industries, traditionally under mixed control, have changed little. Greater participation of the private sector is aimed at attracting capital, entrepreneurship and managerial resources.

With economic liberalization, the private construction sector has been assigned an important role in nation building. Requirement for funds, the latest technology and greater efficiency have assumed importance. Roads and highways, docks and harbours, power plants and petrol chemical plants are now open to the private sector. Several projects on a Build, Own and Operate (BOO) or Build, Operate and Transfer (BOT) basis are under execution by the private sector, apart from full ownership basis. A majority of such projects are joint-venture business where partners of multi-country origin are involved. Housing and real estate development, however, is an area in which foreign participation is not permitted though the Indian private construction sector is actively involved.

With the general growth of the construction market, the repair and maintenance sector is also experiencing steady growth. Work, however, is executed by the respective owners and all too often is neglected. The need for professionalization and professional agencies is growing. Training of professionals in this specialized field is an area in which the Indian construction industry seeks to cooperate with foreign companies. With the present facilities, it is estimated that the total volume of work to be executed is in the region of US$ 300 million per year. Much of it requires specialized work. With the increasing costs of establishing new facilities, owners are paying careful attention to this aspect. The sector is on the brink of fast growth.

India has a large number of technically qualified engineering professionals and one of the largest pools of engineering companies specializing in various fields of construction. The majority of these companies are in the private sector. Some of the large ones are state-owned as well. The quality of the engineering services provided by these companies is rated high locally and internationally, though supplementary inputs are needed to make these services truly international in quality. During the past few years, a number of foreign engineering companies have started Indian operations, especially on EPC (Engineering, Procurement and Construction) projects. The strong point of these engineering companies is competitive costs, substantially lower than their overseas counterparts.

With a view to promote much-needed improvement in efficiency, quality, speed and economy in construction, a Working Group of the Planning Commission has recommended the setting up of an apex national body to take a balanced view on construction-related matters and evolve appropriate strategies. The Construction Industry Development Council (CIDC) is the response. It has been established to bring about systematic improvements which would minimize time and cost overruns, and achieve quality construction in projects. The CIDC functions as a nodal agency for the growth, development, modernization and professionalization of the construction industry as a whole. CIDC is designed to embrace all stakeholders including architects, engineers, contractors, consultant organizations, manufacturers of construction plant/equipment/materials and others involved in the planning and execution of construction projects. It is also assigned to evolve norms for the regulation/self-regulation of professional agencies. The Construction Workers Training Institute at Hyderabad established by CIDC and the National Academy of Construction are pursuing the mandate to extend training skills to labourers and professionals.

India has emerged as a new centre for construction activities and is attracting many international contractors and engineering companies. A rapidly growing economy, a rapidly expanding middle class (300 million) representing a vast consumer market, rapid urbanization and developing industry, housing and infrastructure are opening vast possibilities for sustained construction business. The existing resources comprising some 70 large construction companies, 28,000 small and medium size contracting companies and around 75 joint venture companies, employing about 32 million persons, are inadequate and need upgrading. Mechanization of works and modern construction techniques are required. The concerned construction companies are mobilizing their resources and are poised for a change in response.

Conventionally, construction workers are divided in two categories: the university-qualified managerial and supervisory man-power, and workers with on-site work experience but little or no formal education. For the training of the workers, the system in vogue is that of an informal Worker's Guild, where the master craftsman trains the apprentice worker under him, providing on-the-job-training, and with the passage of time, the individual acquires skills. This method of training skilled construction workers (especially masons and carpenters) is mainly hereditary, with the father training his son. The system has a strong caste basis as well. However, with the education system putting a premium on white collar jobs (a carpenter's son when he graduates from high school may well not know exactly what he wants to do for a living, but he usually knows very well what he does not want to do: that is he does not want to be a carpenter) and the guild system breaking down, the family tradition of training skilled construction workers is almost defunct. Moreover, in the present-day context the system is not fully relevant, since the average worker is required to be trained in specific disciplines not only at work-sites, but also with formal classroom education.

To fill the gap, many Industrial Training Institutes (ITIs) have been established by the government and industry over the past 20 years. The result is less than encouraging in the sense that neither in number nor in quality are these ITI products satisfactory. The declining workmanship standard is a serious concern. The Trade Training Program, conducted through a system of 'education at a distance', imparts training through audio-visual and written material while on the job. The reach and coverage, however, are limited and the quality of the product is not very satisfactory.

Construction financing is an area calling for attention. Inadequate institutional arrangements reflect on the efficiency, economy and overall performance of the sector. Large-scale infusion of black money at high interest rates, feared entry of funds from organized crime in land and construction and its impact on the overall image of the industry are cause for concern. A large portion – between 70 to 80 per cent of the total – of construction work is being executed by small contractors who lack the financial bases and therefore remain weak technologically and professionally and it is difficult to upgrade their image and overall performance.

The real estate business, popularly defined as the development and sale of residential and commercial properties (land, housing, in the form of bungalows, apartments, flats, row-houses, shops, offices, etc.) by the builder/promoter/contractor is going through one of its worst crises in the past 30 years. A crisis of confidence between supplier and consumer (resting on unprofessional and unethical practices: low quality, illegal, unauthorized and unsafe construction; black money transactions; time and cost over-runs; high cost; exploitative profit margin; lack of professionalism, etc.) characterizes the sector. In the past five years, both land and property prices have dropped dramatically (between 30 to 50 per cent), volume of business is stagnant, unsold properties and incomplete projects are causing stress and panic, investor confidence is low, and cash flow in the business has dried up. Though the climate is improving gradually and signs of recovery are evident, the mood in the market is one of crisis and stress.

The National Real Estate Development Council (NAREDCO) has been set up to improve the confidence level of investors and consumers in the real estate sector through self-regulation practices. NAREDCO has initiated measures to improve transparency in real estate transactions. A Code of Ethics has been drafted. An important initiative in enhancing the comfort level of consumers is the development of a rating system in association with CRISIL to facilitate prudent investment decisions in real estate ventures.

Recognizing the role of Building Centres as a potential grass-roots level mechanism for technology transfer, the Ministry of Urban Development and Poverty Alleviation, launched a program for the establishment of the National Network of Building Centres in 1988. The program – implemented with organizational and logistic support by HUDCO – envisages opening at least one building centre in every district of the country. The current number of Building Centres in the country is 575. Now HUDCO and the Ministry of Rural Development have teamed up to set up additional Building Centres in the district towns for rural areas.

The Building Centres are playing a key role in skill upgrading and training of artisans (masons, carpenters, bar-benders, plumbers, electricians); the production and marketing of various cost-effective components using local resources and sales outlets; employment generation through construction work using relevant technologies in housing and building programs; and housing guidance, information and counselling for the local population on cost-effective technologies.

The orientation of Building Centres in sustainable construction has the potential to spread the message far and wide; also to a diverse group consisting of workers, manufacturers and clients. Their role could be demonstration, education and propagation of the idea. Their heterogeneous activities – training, demonstration, material production construction – will provide the opportunity to function as a catalyst for sustainable construction practice.

The increasing volume of construction work is providing growth impetus to building materials production activity. Besides increased production capacity in core building materials – steel, cement, timber – a variety of new materials is entering the market. The projected demand for the period 2001-2006 for cement, steel, timber and bricks for the overall construction sector is 656 million tons (415 million tons for the period 1996-2001), 100 million tons (63 million tons in 1996-2001) and 1,350 billion units (857 billion for 1996-2001) respectively. For 2006-2011 the requirement for cement and finished steel will be up to 1,035 million tons and 159 tons respectively. Over 20 per cent of plastic production (1.8 million tons) in India is consumed for various building applications.

During 1996-2001, the residential building sector is estimated to have provided labour employment of 15 million man-years (10.30 urban and 4.70 rural). During this period in the urban areas, the residential building sector is estimated to have employed 3.60 million man-years of masons, 0.78 million man years of carpenters, 4.70 million man years of unskilled labour and 1.20 million man years of other types of construction labour. The projection for 2006-2011 is 23.78 million man years and 37.50 million man years respectively.

The share of the construction sector in Gross Domestic Capital Formation (GDCF) declined to 41 per cent in 1994-95 from 60 per cent during 1951-61. In 1994-95 residential, non-residential buildings and other forms of construction accounted for 10, 10.5 and 19.5 per cent of GDFC respectively. In 1994-95 whereas the share of non-residential buildings increased from 21 to 26 per cent (23 per cent in 1980-81) the share of other forms of construction declined from 56 to 49 per cent.

Due to an increase in the reduction in forest cover from 33 per cent at the time of independence to about 11 per cent at the present time, the central government, starting in 1993, issued instructions for the use of wood substitutes at least in government buildings. Demand for wood in the housing and furniture sector alone is about 25 per cent of the total wood requirement.

In recent years, aside from waste wood particles and flakes other ligno-cellulose materials such as rice husk, bagasse, cotton stalks, etc., are also being used as basic raw materials for making panel boards. Because of the advances in resin technology, a variety of boards made from the different types of raw materials mentioned above are available on the commercial market; they are bonded with different kinds of resins and have a wide range of applications.

Consumption of plastics in India increased from 450,000 tons in 1984-85 to 1.88 million tons in 1995-96 and is expected to reach 8.0 million tons in 2006-2007. The average consumption range of plastics in building applications for the period 1980-81 to 1995-96 is between 20 to 25 per cent. Per capita consumption increased almost five fold in the decade between 1984-85 to 1995-96, from 0.64 kg to 3.0 kg. By 2006-2007 it is estimated it will reach 10.0 kg/capita.

The housing finance sector has undertaken some major initiatives in the past two decades. The Housing and Urban Development Corporation (HUDCO), a public sector housing finance company, with a mandate to service mainly low income groups and the economically weaker classes through public agencies (Housing Board, Slum Clearance Board) also funds infrastructure projects and funds and promotes Building Centres. HUDCO was the lone player until the Housing Development Finance Corporation (HDFC) was set up in the private sector in the early 1980s. HDFC services the urban upper income bracket and retail clients. With the establishment of the National Housing Bank (NHB) in the 1990s, with a regulatory and refinancing role, banking sector funds are channelled to housing (earlier only life insurance and provident funds monies were available for housing finance). With HDFC in the lead, many housing finance companies have been set up in the private sector. Legal, regulatory and institutional changes, along with tax incentives, are strengthening the housing finance system. Access is still limited, especially for the low income brackets and costs are high.

These broad features of the construction industry show its changing character. Growth, mechanization, modernization, and professionalization trends are visible as is the trend towards quality improvement and productivity for a competitive edge. Consciousness regarding environmental and social issues, though marginal, is also visible. The industry's main thrust, however, is on the transition from the informal to formal and from the unorganized to organized.

Trends are not encouraging on the sustainability front. Due to preoccupation with mechanization, modernization, improved efficiency and higher profits at a faster pace and lower cost, long-term sustainability concerns and issues are not high on the list when selecting techniques, technology, materials or practice. The transition from informal to formal has a price in terms of sustainability. A changeover from slow manual practices to a middle-grade technology and higher speed mechanization has environmental and energy costs. Excessive profit expectations and the need to compete gravitate towards short-term gains, and even unsound, unethical practices. The construction industry in India today is primarily shaped by commercial considerations and governed by market forces. At this early stage of international competition in the domestic sector and the struggle to gain a foothold in the overseas market, productivity, quality and managerial improvement are certainly felt to be desirable but not many are mindful of the environmental, social or human dimensions involved. As someone once said, 'construction is a hard material business. Economic and pragmatic considerations are prime. Soft issues – social and human – are not for now'.

Sustainable Rural Settlements and Construction

Rural India, with over 700 million people scattered in half a million villages across the length and breath of the country, still provides a good example of sustainable settlements. Though tractors, hybrid seeds, chemical fertilizers, roads, electricity and television are transforming the panorama, energy consumption is low. 'Consumerism' compared to its urban counterpart is moderate. Waste is limited and recycled. Due to the absence or negligible presence of industrial activity, air-noise-water pollution is under control. Respect for nature is part of the local culture and religion and resource conversion is both a necessity due to scarcity and a tradition built on social norms. If India could find ways to improve the quality of rural life, especially that of the poor, without changing its character, it would be a winner in the sustainability race.

Things, however, are changing rather rapidly and probably for the worse. Part of the damage is due to urban development with its large 'footprint'. Water courses carry untreated urban and industrial affluent and sewage to pollute the rural water supply. Surface wells are drying up and the ground water table is dropping due to excessive pumping in urban centres. Forests are being rapidly depleted, primarily to sustain urban consumerism. The balance of the urban-rural hinterland relationship remains exploitative on the part of the cities. If villages seem more 'sustainable', under-development is possibly the price. The irony, however, is that despite paying that price, without seeing any improvement in their standard of living, villagers are forced to bear the burden of unsustainable urban development. Rural environmental sustainability is inextricably linked to the pattern of urban development.

Rural construction activity in India retains its unorganized and informal character. A portion of residential houses are self-built, self managed, self or community financed using local skilled workers and mud and brick, thatch or clay tiles. Relatively more affluent sections – rich farmers, teachers, shopkeepers cooperative managers, moneylenders – build pukka, r.c.c. roofed houses through small local contractors and occasionally use institutional finance with mud or brick, thatch or clay tiles. Infrastructure (roads, water works) and community buildings (school, dispensary, cooperative buildings) financed generally by the government and built mainly through developmental channels (including the Public Works Department) and the tendering system, are constructed by city-based small or medium contractors. Occasional industries in the public and private sector are built by large urban contractors. An informal system, small volume, traditional technology, local skills and materials, slow pace, small contractors, simple design, and moderate quality are other features. Material production – bricks, mud, tile – is almost always based on the small enterprise. For the industrialized materials such as cement steel, glass, asbestos sheets – the *taluka* or district town is the source. Local carpenters and masons are traditionally – as compared to formally – trained, with poor skills and usually handle other skilled jobs such as plumbing, bar-bending and even design. Trained architects or engineers are usually absent. Tools are conventional. This is a male-dominated job sector in which women provide unskilled labour. Due to a large number and a huge population base (700 million), investment is not small but its dispersed nature does not permit advantages in scale or in the forms of mechanism or modernization.

Though change is visible in the shelter sector as well, production and supply arrangements in rural housing still retain many of the practices which we can term sustainable. A large portion of the rural housing stock is self-built, self-managed and community-financed. Traditionally, the government, public agencies and the formal private sector have played a marginal role in the production and supply of rural housing. Unlike cities, neither a master plan to regulate development nor building bye laws to guide construction exist. Until recently, public or private housing finance agencies offering loan facilities for land acquisition or construction were not in the picture. No trained professionals – architects, engineers – or real estate developers or large contractors operate in rural areas. Houses in a typical Indian village are self-built (or self-managed) using locally available materials and skilled/unskilled labour; meant mainly for family use (not for rental purposes); and they are financed through family savings and informal credit. Rural housing in India is still primarily a 'people's process'.

National Housing Policy assesses the rural housing situation to be qualitatively different from the urban one. Absence of the commercial private sector in production and supply and the increasingly prominent role that the state sector programs and agencies play in social housing are the two main features of the current rural housing scene. Generally speaking, an underdeveloped housing and real estate market leaves a home builder in control of the production process: the household's level of access to housing components – land, finance, materials skills, technology and services – determine product quality. An owner-controlled rural house is typically incremental in nature, built within means and suitable to the family's functional needs, socio-cultural aspirations and aesthetic taste. A participatory 'social production process' involves family members in construction, observes community rules, respects neighbours' concerns and generally produces an environment-friendly, 'consensus' product. The contrast with a developer-built apartment in a large city is glaring!

A number of factors – economic, cultural and institutional – influence the production processes and product quality in rural housing. The main ones are as follows: a depressed agricultural economy; low income and high incidence of poverty; increasing commercialization and monetization of the rural economy; changing social relations affecting mutual-help/self-help practices; declining access to bio-mass materials; increasing alienation from traditional construction materials and practices; limited exposure and access to new building materials; exodus of skilled labour to the cities; underdeveloped housing credit system and institutions; tenure insecurity in land use; growing depletion in common property resources; scarce professional services; non-availability of credit for repair, upgrade and extensions; hierarchy system based on the feudal concept; caste system; suppressed status of women; continuing joint family tradition; migration; financially and administratively weak Panchayats (local self-government bodies); poor targeting of government subsidy; moderately successful land delivery interventions; limited industrial activity; and generally deficient environmental services and community amenities.

These factors determine the demand and supply equation in rural housing and show why land, real-estate and housing markets have not developed to a sufficient degree. They represent the contours of an underdeveloped housing delivery system and explain in part the reasons for the increasing state sector presence in rural housing. They also show why the rural housing construction system still shows 'sustainable' characteristics.

The new economic environment is changing this scene. Market forces are poised to take over. The 'developer', as we know him, is waiting on the sidelines. Can something be done to retain some of the positive features of the existing social production system? Can the people – owners and users – retain some control over the process and quality of their habitat? These questions are begging for an answer since a user-centred, decentralized delivery system appears more suited to the small and geographically scattered Indian villages.

The essential element of the rural housing challenge in India is the need to develop a self-sustaining delivery system. Lack of effective demand, a product of static income and low savings, and absence of housing credit systems are major constraints to its development. Rural economic growth, therefore, is a precondition for the development of a sustainable housing delivery system. In the new economic regime of structural adjustment and export-led growth, the rural sector could find itself marginalized. That is the first point at issue since a stagnant rural economy is not conducive to the development of the housing market or of a self-sustaining delivery system. The need for economic growth to take place in a sustainable manner is a crucial factor in ensuring sustainable rural housing and construction.

Considering its backward-forward linkages to the overall economy, it is essential that rural housing development is seen in the context of overall rural development and housing for the poor in the broader framework of rural poverty alleviation. The task of improving conditions of rural life, which must include job creation, providing physical infrastructure (roads, power, water, sanitation) and social services (school, dispensary, market, etc.) and upgrading/contracting houses has a major construction component with high employment potential. If investment is directed correctly (i.e. in a decentralized and labour-intensive manner; in such a manner that employment benefits reach the unemployed and poor local entrepreneurship is improved) not only will living conditions improve, but poverty will also decrease.

An agenda for sustainable rural settlements and construction should include the following:

- impetus to accelerated rural economic growth in a sustainable manner;
- 'people centred' approach that focuses full attention on people's social institutions, traditional knowledge, creativity and construction skills. A strategy to encourage, support and assist people's on-going, self-initiated housing actions;
- an economically viable and institutionally sustainable housing finance system, in tune with the people's economic and social systems;
- house design providing adequate shelter, an efficient work place, and an economic asset. Reducing poverty while improving housing conditions;
- settlement design that uses land optimally, is conducive to incremental growth, receptive to phased installation of services, considerate to traditional village forms and sensitive to the social aspects of rural living;
- an approach geared to creating new housing stock as well as improving/ upgrading/renewing existing housing stock;
- facilitator/enabler role for the government and its agencies;
- imaginative use of investments for the creation of short and long term employment opportunities for local communities;
- strategic, targeted and capacity-building subsidization;
- selection, promotion and development of building materials and construction technology bearing in mind the required elements of cost-reduction, maintenance, adaptability, employment generation and environmental preservation;
- a program to initiate new research and upgrade that underway regarding appropriate technology and cost effective, energy efficient, low cost and durable building materials. Also to ensure the passage of research from laboratory to market to people – especially, water resistant mud plaster, fire resistant thatch, and low cost sanitation. Emphasis on upgrading and

using indigenous technologies and local materials;

- a concept not of 'houses' alone but of adequately serviced settlements (water, sanitation, electricity, school, health care centre, community building, etc.);
- gender balance in decision making, ownership, employment and wages, and skill training;
- encouragement and support for the role of the private sector in land development, housing finance, infrastructure provision, material production, technology improvement, skill training, design and construction;
- gainful employment, tool improvement and skill upgrading for traditional skilled craftsmen;
- special rural orientation in professional training – architects, engineers, planers – nurturing the Worker's Guild and providing training for women in skilled construction jobs;
- small contractor development program;
- disaster-resistant technology introduction in a de-mystified, non-alienating and people-friendly manner;
- a role for the village Panchayat in decision-making, facilitation of construction and provision of services. Capacity building of Panchayat agencies for that purpose;
- major restructuring of Indira Avas Yojana and other state subsidy projects;
- an NGO role emphasizing advocacy, demonstration, participatory practice, innovation and sustainable construction.

Urban Sustainability

Urban Growth

In 1991, 846 million Indians lived in over half a million villages and 3,750 towns and cities. Though the country still remains predominantly rural, with 70 per cent of the population living in villages, population growth in the cities is rapid. In the short span of two decades, with even moderate growth rates of about 3.5 per cent per annum, India's urban population doubled from 109 million in 1971 to 217 million in 1991. By the turn of the century approximately 310 million Indians – 30 per cent of the total – are estimated to live in cities: a staggering four fold increase in 40 years and 600 per cent growth in the 50 years since independence! Currently India's urban population is the fourth largest in the world: next only to the USA, the former USSR and China. It is equal to India's total population at the time of independence.

Concentration

Though this growth is spread over a number of different sized urban settlements, a large share is concentrated in the metropolitan areas and other large cities. In 1991, 70 million people, one third of the country's urban population, lived in 23 metropolitan and other large cities. According to a UN projection, in the year 2001, of the 11 largest cities in the world, with population exceeding 13 million, three, i.e. Calcutta (16.53 million), Bombay (16.0 million) and Delhi (13.24 million), were in India. Today, India has six mega-cities (four million plus), 40 metropolitan cities, 300 large towns (0.1 million) and 3,400 medium and small towns.

Urban Productivity

Over the last three decades, the pattern of sectoral contribution to the national economy has changed substantially. In 1950-51, urban India contributed 29 per cent to India's GDP. This share increased to 47 per cent in 1980-81, 55 per cent in 1990-91 and is estimated to have crossed 60 per cent in 2001. The urban to rural productivity ratio is 7:2. With the structural adjustment program and liberalization and globalization of the Indian economy, the contribution of the urban sector to national output is expected to rise further, making the country's continued economic development heavily dependant on the efficiency of its urban sector.

Contrast

On the one hand, cities have become engines of economic growth and centres for culture, art, technology, education and entrepreneurship. On the other, as noted by the National Commission on Urbanization, set up by the late Prime Minister Rajiv Gandhi, 'these urban centres have also generated the most brutal and inhuman living conditions with large sections of citizens (almost half in Bombay and Delhi) living in slums and squatter settlements. The over-crowding in slums and desperate lack of water and sanitation lead not only to severe health problems but to the abject degradation of human life'.

Problems

The rapid and massive population growth in the urban centres coupled with severe resource constraints, weak governance, and managerial inefficiency have resulted in many problems, especially in big cities. Environmental decay in the form of water, noise and air pollution; housing shortages; rapid growth of slums and shanty-towns; quantitative shortage and qualitative deterioration in provision and access to municipal and other basic services (water, sanitation, garbage collection and disposal, education, health care, etc.); deficiencies in infrastructure (power, roads, transport, etc.); overcrowding; congestion; social tension; violence and poverty, to a varying degree, afflict many Indian cities.

Urban Poverty

While the incidence of poverty in rural areas is greater, the nature of poverty in the cities is different. The situation is particularly difficult in large cities where over one third of the city's population either lives on the sidewalks or in slums and squatter settlements. The most neglected sections among the urban poor are women and children who are excluded from the mainstream development process.

Services

The potable water supply is accessible to only 84 per cent of India's urban population, and it is too intermittent and of questionable quality. Sewer and sanitation services are absent or inadequate for close to 54 per cent of the urban population; 31 per cent of urban residents have no latrines. Waste collection and disposal is available to only 72 per cent of the population. And electricity has yet to be provided to close on 25 per cent of urban residents.

Resources for Infrastructure and Housing

The Rakesh Mohan Committee estimated that the total requirement for urban infrastructure development covering the backlog in service provisions, new investments and operation and maintenance, for the next ten years, is a mammoth Rs. 2,500,000 million (US$ 50 billion), a per annum requirement of Rs. 250,000 million (US$ 5 billion). Additionally, the urban housing sector requires an investment of Rs. 1,213,700 million (US$ 25 billion) during the next five years to meet the housing shortage of 7.57 million units, to upgrade 0.32 million semi-pukka units and meet an additional construction requirement of 8.67 million units. The overall funding requirement for the housing and urban infrastructure development for the cities stands at a figure of Rs. 3,713,710 million (US$ 75 billion). Against this mammoth figure, in the ninth plan Rs. 117,950 million for urban development, water supply and sanitation and Rs. 340,000 million for urban housing were budgeted. This implies that funding requirements for urban housing fell short by 3.5 times the requirement and for urban infrastructure development the shortfall was more then ten times the requirement.

Housing

The failure to provide adequate (in size and number), proper (in location and design), affordable (rental, hire purchase, or capital cost) new homes, neglect of the existing housing stock and inadequate services is manifested in many forms: over-crowding, congestion, dilapidation, slums and squatter settlements, sidewalk dwelling, and a sharp decline in the quality of the overall living environment. Rapid population growth; inadequate investment; low income and savings levels of the housing clients; poverty; an underdeveloped housing finance system; sluggish supply rate of new formal housing by public and private sector agencies due to legal and institutional constraints; inadequately organized real estate and construction sectors; high costs and a virtual freeze in land supply; declining investment in, and availability of, rental housing; deterioration in rental housing stock due to vacancy and poor maintenance; and active hostility to the informal housing and settlements built by the poor are some of the causes of the 'housing crisis' in Indian cities. The 1991 census projected an overall housing shortage of 23 million units: 8.20 million urban and 14.90 million rural.

Slums

The slum problem, due to its scale (number of people involved), diffusion (problem is confined not only to metro or large cities alone), persistence (no relief in sight, no sign of abatement), visibility (unmistakable landmarks on the urban landscape), socio-political implications (human degradation, suffering and waste of human resources), and limited success of the containment strategies and past fragmented responses, is begging for attention, fresh approaches and an holistic treatment. It is estimated that on the average, 30 to 35 per cent of citizens in large cities live in slums; 40 per cent of slum dwellers are without access to safe drinking water; and over 90 per cent are without access to adequate sanitation.

Considering the prevailing conditions and trends in Indian cities – large cities heading towards a crisis and rapid environmental degradation in the smaller ones – the obvious question is not so much long-term sustainability but the city's very survival. If cities are the future of the country, as indeed they are, the real concern is the immediate future in an existential sense rather than the abstract future of yet-to-be-born generations in a sustainability context. That is so because, while recognizing cities as engines of economic growth, centres of technology and innovation, crucibles of art, culture and knowledge, and also the last refuge of hope and livelihood for those trying to escape grinding rural poverty, it is difficult, even for a staunch optimist to draw a rosy picture of the Indian city. Not only because they are problematic – saddled with problems – but because there is not much evidence to suggest that a framework – which must include a vision for the future, political will, institutional preparedness, financial and human resources, and technological innovations – to address problems, respond to opportunities and shape the future, has evolved. The pace with which things are happening – and deteriorating – not a fire-fighting response but what Wally N'Dow, the Secretary General of Habitat II called a 'revolutionary approach to problem solving' is needed. That indeed is missing. And it is in this context that the urban sustainability concept must be examined.

Given the condition in cities and the alternative options its special situation offers, India is one country – there are many others in Asia and Africa – which can question the inevitability of urbanization, especially the inevitability of resource depleting, polluting, exploitative and in some ways dehumanizing urbanization. It is essential to recognize that the urbanization we experience and the cities we live in are products of the economic policies we pursue and the development models they promote. It is the result of the conscious choices we have made, it is not divinely ordained. If the policies and the model change, then urbanization trends and the cities will also change. There is nothing inevitable about it.

Action towards Sustainable Construction

Conservation of Existing Building Stock

Extending the working life of buildings is a step towards sustainability as it reduces the need to construct anew. Timely and regular maintenance, a much neglected aspect in Indian buildings, requires financial resources, tools, organizational infrastructure and skill. One of the more detrimental side effects of the Rent Control Act is the neglected maintenance of rental buildings. Frozen rents make it difficult for the owners to invest in maintenance. And renters tend to neglect maintenance too since they are not motivated. Deterioration of old buildings, especially in old city areas, even if owner-occupied, and of the rental properties due to poor maintenance and lack of timely repair necessitated a public response in Mumbai city. The Building Repairs and Maintenance Board, a public sector enterprise, was set up to repair and strengthen private buildings in poor conditions. Though this initiative has only achieved moderate success, the idea itself is sound and deserves replication in other cities. Proper legislative measures with proper orientation, equipment and tool support, an adequate capital base, institutional financing arrangements, trained professionals to provide design, structural engineering and management services, and contracting agencies will extend the life span of the buildings thereby conserving resources. Removing institutional constraints such as the Rent Control Act and ensuring a more ample role for the private sector are strongly recommended.

Preventive aspects of maintenance are good design, selection of durable building materials, proper detailing, and good workmanship. And these are not so much a function of cost as of attitude.

Disaster Mitigation Technologies

Protecting buildings from natural disasters is part of conserving the building stock and therefore a step in sustainable construction. About 1.5 million buildings are estimated to be destroyed or severely damaged by natural calamities every year. With about two thirds of the geographic area of the country disaster-prone – earthquake, flood, cyclone, land slides – both overall disaster preparedness as well as disaster resistant designs, detailing, technology and construction save lives and structures and prevents financial loss.

Publication of the Vulnerability Atlas by the Building Material Promotion and Technology Council (BMPTC) is an important step. Its proper use by concerned authorities, professionals, teaching and training institutions will help in disaster preparedness. The recent earthquake in Gujarat, which killed 18,000 people, destroyed or badly damaged over a million houses, public buildings and infrastructure, and caused an estimated loss of over US$ 3 billion, highlighting the flaws in the entire hierarchy of the construction system. Modification in building bye-laws and codes and review of the functioning of the building regulatory authorities; reorientation, training and education of design professionals (architects, structural designers, construction supervisors); greater quality control over construction work by the builders and contractors; greater interaction between research institutions, regulatory authorities and professionals; re-orientation, training and accountability procedures for the contracting agencies; training of skilled construction workers in disaster resistant construction; and comprehensive disaster preparedness plans and their implementation by the government including community awareness and education will reduce destruction and damage. Proper disaster preparedness and adequate management of disaster rehabilitation are steps in sustainable construction.

Land

Sustainable land use is a precondition for sustainable construction: land is scarce, non-elastic, expensive and one of the most critical components in construction activity. Thus land conservation, optimal and creative use, equitable distribution and re-cyclability are aspects of sustainable construction. A creative ownership and use policy is a key determinant in sustainable construction.

Some of the major distortions in urban development – high land values, scarcity and unequal distribution – are attributed to land ownership patterns and practices. The failure of India's rather bold legislative effort to correct them through the Urban Land Ceiling and Regulation Act of 1976, which sought to put a ceiling on land ownership, curb practices in excessive profiteering, land hoarding and speculation, and promote equitable distribution and balanced use, has proved a setback for sustainable land use and distribution. The UCLA's failure is attributed to its anti-market orientation rather than to inept and corrupt administration. With the advent of economic liberalization, privatization, globalization and greater emphasis on the role of the market, state intervention in the land market is no longer a viable policy orientation. With about one third of the urban population below the poverty line, even greater numbers in the low-income bracket, persisting income and wealth disparities and urban land's high asset, mortgage and speculative value, it appears almost impossible for the market alone to correct distortions in distribution.

With equitable land distribution being a critical precondition for sustainable construction, state intervention in urban land is inevitable. Giving secure land tenure to the urban poor and slum dwellers, though slow in implementation, is a correct orientation and direction. Granting land title to poor slum dwellers is a positive step forward in sustainable construction. It will motivate the slum population to invest in improving their houses and settlements.

Due to unaffordable land prices and low-income levels, even full coverage of the slum population under the secure land tenure scheme, a large segment of the urban population is out of the land market. A combination of measures including strategies to lower urban land prices by accelerated land development on urban peripheries; increasing the income and purchasing power of the lower income groups and access to credit for land purchase; upgrading the land-lease system; project level cross-subsidization through mixed – commercial, residential; low cost-high cost – use, would improve people's access to land.

Avoiding wasteful use through proper regulatory measures and planning is a step forward in the conservation of land resources and hence in sustainable construction. This stretches from rationalizing building bye-laws related to buffers to be left around buildings, to the relocation of activities from core city areas which use urban land unproductively (go-downs, jails, etc.) to releasing large land areas locked in by ailing industries and de-hoarding lands occupied by new industrial establishments.

Rethinking zoning regulations and planning practices which separate residential from commercial and industrial land, a direct influence of the western planning model, is also a step towards land conservation. In any planned settlement, roads occupy anywhere between 30 to 35 per cent of the land area. They also contribute to urban sprawl, adding to pollution by introducing motorized traffic and leading to productivity losses and fatigue due to time losses in covering distances. Segregation of industrial locations from the residential areas has also been seen as a license for air, water and noise pollution in the industrial areas. Coexistence of commercial and residential – a shop on the ground floor and residence on the upper floor – is a feature of traditional city planning in India.

Legislative tools, regulatory framework, support studies, reorientation of professionals and incentives in favour of low-rise-high-density construction is a step in the direction of sustainable construction. The most dense urban settlements – in terms of minimum land use per capita – are not high rise buildings, as generally believed, but low rise ground floor slums. In the sustainability framework ground story formal construction, however, is a luxury and represents a wasteful use of land; the low-rise, high-density construction – three to four story apartments – are preferred options. Compared to the high rise structures – which require heavy foundations and structural engineering, greater disaster resistance, high quality and expensive materials, high energy consumption in use and maintenance – low rise-high density buildings rate higher on the sustainability index.

Discouraging, by means of fiscal disincentives, higher taxation and social practices, single family bungalows and farmhouses, which cause urban sprawl, is also a step in optimal land use and therefore sustainable construction.

Selective densification strategies for sparsely-populated and underutilized city areas, which improve land use and efficiency of services are more sustainable.

Employment

A construction method or technique that internalizes employment benefits for users, especially the poor, is a sustainable construction practice. Coexistence of urban unemployment and inadequate urban infrastructure reflect planning and governance failure. A massive urban public works program, aimed at improving urban infrastructure and services – especially water supply, sanitation, roads, pavements, electrification, play areas, parks, school, dispensary, community centre, etc. – with a dominant construction component would deal simultaneously with the twin problems of unemployment/poverty and inadequate services. This, however, must be low cost and low investment in installation and maintenance; decentralized; community rather than contractor focused; and especially geared to enhance the generation of local employment. The contribution of construction activity in direct poverty alleviation and improving the quality of life through improved availability and quality of services form part of sustainability in construction.

Work Force

Productivity-enhancing mechanization and modernization, in the form of tool transition, technology upgrade and the modification of financing and management practices, in the sustainability context, must take into account environmental, macro-economic and social factors: conservation of natural resources; reduction of energy use and minimization of pollution (environment); labour intensive practices (macro-economy); and improving productivity, wages and welfare of construction workers (social). With a large population, massive poverty and high levels of unemployment and underdevelopment, it is vital that construction activity remains labour intensive without losing its competitive edge. This requires selective mechanization, skill upgrading, quality consciousness of the construction workers and improvement in their working conditions. A non-motivated, poorly paid and exploited construction worker with poor skills and low confidence – a normal sight on many construction sites – is a serious threat to sustainable construction.

Informal Housing

Awarding a place to informal housing and settlements in the urban landscape and recognizing the role of the peoples' processes in producing them are vital to the sustainability of cities and construction. Cities will be unsustainable if they negate, neglect or remain hostile to the resources, energy, creativity enterprise, and affirmative action of the poor. And construction activity will be unsustainable if it ignores the sustainability principle ingrained in this form of building activity.

Slums are produced by people – mostly by the poor – using scarce resources, construction skills, waste and recyclable materials, self-help and mutual aid practices with minimum land occupation. Considering its large volume of housing stock, its low-cost of production and high speed of construction, and the large size of the population living there, the slum is the most sustainable form of construction by any yardstick. Besides producing them in a sustainable way, these houses and settlements are sustainable in the sense that they are frugal in their use of water, electricity and other services. Slum settlements in the Indian cities, as elsewhere, represent both the solution and the problem. The process that produces an affordable shelter represents a potential, and even a solution (low cost, recycled materials, self help, easy and quick construction, fast supply rate, etc.). The illegal encroachment on public and private lands and unhealthy environmental conditions represent a problem.

Facilitating and supporting the self initiated housing action of the poor and providing assistance to improve quality of services and living is a step in sustainable construction. The key to success in housing the poor-both quantitatively and qualitatively – i.e. in sheltering the millions and providing need based, appropriate houses – lies in increasing their access to housing components: land, building materials, finance, and services. The state, taking responsibility for land supply; treating all city dwellers as equal in the matter of provision of basic environmental and social services and strengthening the resource base of the local bodies to ensure this; creating properly structured and staffed housing finance and housing development agencies which effectively reach out to and service the poor; making arrangements that accelerate production of low-cost building materials and increase the supply of reusable, recyclable materials are critical to increasing access to housing for the poor. Viewing the provision of housing and infrastructure in the context of poverty alleviation and designing delivery in a manner generating gainful employment are important as well. An inadequately sheltered citizen, whatever his degree of poverty and with all the implications in terms of productivity loss, poor health, social stress and human degradation is a cause of urban unsustainability.

Gender Equality

According women status as owners, recognizing their role as users and respecting their contribution as producers is a move towards sustainable construction, settlement and development.

Outside the agriculture, manufacturing and service sectors, which together employ more than 80 per cent of women workers, a significant and gradually increasing proportion of women workers are also engaged in the construction sector. Among the informal sector workers, women in the field of construction work are some of the worst victims of disorientation and deprivation. Working on construction sites is an arduous task. Unlike other industries where women are employed in semi-skilled or sometimes even in skilled jobs, in the building industry they are employed only as unskilled labourers. The job of an unskilled worker is more strenuous in the construction industry than in other manufacturing industries. As casual workers, women not only face insecurity but are paid lower wages compared to their male counterparts. Discrimination in wage structure is widespread. Minimum wage and other legislation are violated. Women face instability and insecurity in work, poor remuneration, discrimination in the payment of wages and the virtual absence of enforcement of protective labour legislation. Their work is regarded as unskilled but they are given no opportunity to acquire skills on the job. Men, on the other hand, learn and improve their construction skills while working.

To improve the working and living conditions of women construction workers, many legislative, organizational and attitudinal changes are needed. These include: stringent monitoring of the observance of existing laws; legal literacy; simplified judicial procedures for legal redress; government intervention in recruitment and registration of workers; improved tools, equipment and technology for greater safety and comfort, importing skills in masonry, carpentry, plumbing and other value added construction skills; and assistance on work sites for non-formal education, legal literacy, health care, childcare, etc. Gender equity is crucial to sustainable construction, settlements and development.

Improving the conditions of women working in construction, the work aspect, is one part. Making them owners – or co-owners – of the assets being created through subsidized land distribution and social housing projects is the second part. This type of provision included in massive urban and rural social housing programs – will improve their status in the family and society, increase resistance against family violence, and would prove to be an affirmative action in women's empowerment.

Professional Education

Awareness and concern as regards sustainability issues and ways to integrate them into personal life styles, living habits and one's economic pursuits need to be built in at all levels of education. Global-local interdependence is a cardinal principle of global sustainability. In achieving goals of sustainable environment, construction and development, the attitudes and actions of an individual, family, group and community are important. The basis for a sustainable economic and social global system is a sustainable individual and family system. Education prepares a person for life. Consciousness building and training regarding sustainability should start there: in the primary and secondary school, in college education, and in professional training programs.

Sustainable construction demands professionals with the knowledge and ability to integrate sustainable practices into their work. Properly trained planners, engineers, architects, supervisors, developers, utility specialists and manufacturers, who collectively shape the nature of construction activity, have a vital role to play in this matter.

Planning, architecture and engineering education and practice in India carry a holdover from the colonial past and from what is typically called 'western' influence. Despite a glorious past and a great tradition – displayed so eloquently in the planning of Jaipur or Jaisalmar, and architecture of a Bhunga in a Kutch village – the present system of planning and architectural education prepares professionals – admittedly there are exceptions – alienated from the local context: be it that of climate, lifestyle, tradition, economy or local needs and resources. The new urban landscape is partly the result of such alienating education, training and western influence. Land use, traffic and infrastructure development plans neglect land scarcity, interaction patterns, preponderance of non-motorized traffic – cycles, pedestrians – in cities, the space and service needs of the urban informal sector, general resource scarcity, water scarcity, and the reality of the poor. Multi story offices with full glass façades, a new status symbol of modern architecture in India, a direct import from the sun starved, cold and artificial energy sufficient West, neglects the reality of the bright sun, scarcity and high cost of energy, and generally poor record on maintenance. Engineering education – especially civil engineering – is probably more realistic but rather slack on the human side of professional preparation. Vastu Shastra, an ancient science of construction, is not part of the syllabus in architecture or engineering education.

Surprisingly, the professional training institutes are not too familiar with, or involved in, the innovative work being done by the non-government agencies (be it that of working with the poor and rural clients; use of non-conventional building materials and appropriate technology; people centred and participatory planning; cost effective, climate) conscious and tradition sensitive design and construction. This is a double disadvantage as young students and training professionals are denied an opportunity to see, learn from and become motivated by an alternative approach and effort. The NGO sector, usually in need of young, motivated and properly oriented professionals, remains starved of a critical human resource.

With the resource crunch and environmental crisis, the need to make education, especially professional education, more relevant was never as strongly felt as today. More than changing syllabi and teaching methods, much wider attitudinal reorientation and systemic change are needed.

The positive aspect is that the need for change is strongly felt and frequently articulated by different stakeholders. Some positive initiatives have been taken by educational and professional institutes but it is obvious that much still remains to be done in the reorientation of young students and the training of professionals.

With its broad reach and wide impact, it is critical for the present and the future, for the villages and cities, for the environment and human kind. The built environment, the abode of humans for their life pursuits, must be conducive to clean, healthy, comfortable, pleasant and aesthetic living. Green trees, clean air and water, birds and animals, gardens and open spaces are as much an integral part of the built environment as skyscrapers, bridges and roads. It is important that they co-exist in an harmonious manner.

Construction is a human activity. All kinds of actors – from the architect to the construction labourer to the manufacturer of an air conditioning unit, and factors – tools, technology, materials, bye-laws – influence the process and shape the product. It is important that the players, while pursuing their agendas and immediate goals – speed and profit, luxury and comfort, aesthetics and utility – remain sensitive to the broad picture and make conscious efforts to prevent damage to the environment and society.

India, just like every other country, is in a race to modernize, grow and develop. We, however, have learned – to our cost – that so-called development can also be destructive. Construction is a vehicle and also an expression of development. Unsustainable development cannot promote sustainable construction.

Unsustainable construction cannot produce sustainable cities and settlements. And unsustainable cities and settlements cannot lead to sustainable happiness – everyone's ultimate pursuit. We therefore must strive for sustainable construction, sustainable settlements and cities and sustainable development.

Note

1   The paper was prepared as part of the process for the Agenda 21 for Sustainable Construction in Developing Countries and a full copy of the latter report is available on www.sustainablesettlement.co.za.

Chapter 14

A Critical Evaluation of Approaches to Urban Development in Bangladesh: Case Study of Khulna

Mejbahuddin Ahmed

Introduction

Khulna is the third largest city in Bangladesh with a population of approximately one million people. The other two major cities in the country are Dhaka and Chittagong with populations of nine million and three million people respectively. The city of Khulna began its history as a small commercial centre; it was brought under a formal planning and development programme after the Khulna Development Authority Bill was passed in what was then the East Pakistan Lower Assembly in 1961. Development Authorities were established for other cities as well, such as the Dhaka Improvement Trust for the capital Dhaka and the Chittagong Development Authority for the port-city Chittagong. But the general development attitude was autocratic rather than humanistic. Only a few benefited from the so-called development activities of these agencies while the majority remained deprived. The primary reason underlying the crisis in the urban environment was a prevailing attitude by which the planning process ignored the common values of citizens. This paper seeks to critically evaluate the role and attitude of the different urban development agencies with a view to showing how participation by citizens in the decision-making process could be incorporated. To maintain the sustainability of urban growth and environment, there is no alternative to a humanistic planning approach. A set of guidelines for effective urban planning and management in such an approach will be outlined in this paper.

Khulna, the City

Khulna, the third largest city in Bangladesh, is located (Figure 14.1) in the south-west of the country (89° Longitude, 22.5° Latitude). Population is approximately one million and the city covers a land area of 70 square kilometres (Aqua-Sheltech Consortium, 1998).

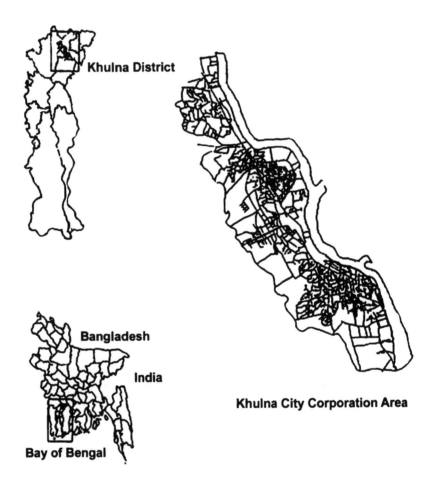

Figure 14.1 Location of Khulna City

Khan-E-Jahan (a warrior chief, popularly known as a Muslim saint) came with his followers to settle in this region in the fifteenth century. Some historians believe that even before the advent of Khan-E-Jahan, a rich civilization existed in the area near the present Sundarbans (the largest mangrove forest in the world, recently declared a UNESCO World Heritage Site). In the eighteenth century, under the rule of the British colonial administrators, Khulna developed as a salt trading centre. Khulna was declared a municipality in 1884. In 1947, Khulna's population was only 12,000. After the Second World War, the second sea port of the country was established in Chalna which was only 32 kilometres away from the city and Khulna became the major jute trading centre of what was then East Pakistan (Aqua-Sheltech Consortium, 1998). Very large quantities of jute bags were imported during the Korean War and Khulna enjoyed a golden period of commercial activity based mainly on jute exports. Nearby, some other heavy industries such as the Khulna Newsprint Mills, Khulna Hardboard Mills and Khulna Powerhouse began to operate. In fact, during this period Khulna emerged as an industrial city and eventually became the third largest city of what was then East Pakistan. After the liberation of Bangladesh in 1971, the introduction of artificial fibres all over the world led to the decline of the jute industry but growth of the city continued.

Today, the city's commercial activity depends on its export of frozen shrimp and port activities (now shifted to Mongla, 50 kilometres from Khulna). The connection of the port with the rest of the country through Khulna City is undergoing improvement. Moreover, the prospect of offering a goods-handling facility to the north-eastern provinces of India and Nepal through the port will create the possibility of tremendous urban growth in the near future. Simultaneously, a master plan for the city is being drafted. Therefore, now is the time to critically evaluate the city's development scenario. Fostering awareness in this field today might contribute to a pragmatic approach in the urban development process.

Contemporary Urban Development Institutions

Like other cities in the region, Khulna's development began in an indigenous way, reflecting social values and norms in urban management. The *mahalla* (indigenous neighbourhood) as the basic civic unit was managed by the *panchayet* (neighbourhood civic body). It was the *panchayet's* responsibility to meet the needs of the *mahalla* including spatial development and the maintenance of service facilities. In maintaining the urban environment, the moral obligation of the citizens to the civic bodies was the key (Mowla, 1997). The British colonial administrators introduced an administrative civic structure based on the municipality with provisions for limited public representation. At this time, responsibility for urban management began to shift from the traditional bodies to the administrative ones. In the 1960s, three separate development authorities were formed to manage planning and development in the three larger cities. They were the Dhaka Improvement Trust (DIT) in Dhaka, the Chittagong Development Authority (CDA) in Chittagong and the Khulna Development Authority (KDA) in Khulna. These organizations provided little scope for public representation and were instead run by appointed bureaucrats or army officials from the government. Ultimately, the citizens' moral obligation to the civic bodies was replaced by law enforcement carried out by government officials. Meanwhile, Khulna Municipality was renamed the Khulna Municipal Corporation and was later reshuffled to become the Khulna City Corporation in 1984. Since then, these two organizations have been the major agencies involved in the fulfilment of urban needs.

Khulna City Corporation

Khulna City Corporation (henceforth referred to as KCC) is the major stakeholder in urban development activity. The corporation was established under the provisions of the Khulna Municipal Corporation Ordinance, 1984. KCC is a local governmental body under the Ministry of Local Government, Rural Development and Co-operatives of the Government of the Peoples' Republic of Bangladesh. The members of this local governmental body are the commissioners and a mayor, elected by direct election on the basis of universal adult franchise (Aqua-Sheltech Consortium, 1998). The responsibilities of the corporation (according to the Khulna Municipal Corporation Ordinance, 1984) are:

• education;
• health, family planning and sanitation including drainage;
• town planning and improvement;
• public works and buildings;
• water and electricity;
• social welfare and community centres;
• trees, parks, gardens and forests, etc.

Major activities undertaken by Khulna City Corporation can be listed as (Khan, 2000):

• waste disposal and storm water drainage system development;
• construction and maintenance of community centres, mosques, auditoriums and conference facilities for citizens;
• construction and maintenance of children's parks and schools;
• management of the mobile hospital and immunization programme;
• maintenance of public toilets and slum clearance;
• the provision of sculptures and fountains in important locations.

The staffing organization chart of Khulna City Corporation is listed in Table 14.1.

Table 14.1 KCC Staff

No.	Name of Position (Class I)	Type of Appointment	No. of Position
1.	Mayor	Elected	1
2.	Deputy Mayor	Elected	1
3.	Ward Commissioners	Elected	31
4.	Chief Executive Officer	Bureaucrat appointed by the Government	1
5.	Secretary	Regular employee of KCC	1
6.	Chief Tax Officer	Regular employee of KCC	1
7.	Chief Engineer	Regular employee of KCC	1
8.	Chief Health Officer	Regular employee of KCC	1
9.	Magistrate ·	Appointed by the Government	1
10.	Executive Engineer	Regular employee of KCC	4
11.	Chief Planning Officer	None appointed	1
12.	Planner	Civil Engineer appointed	1
13.	Architect	Regular employee of KCC	1
14.	Assistant Engineer	Regular employee of KCC	5
15.	Health officer	Regular employee of KCC	1
16.	Medical Officer	Regular employee of KCC	2
17.	Budget Officer	Regular employee of KCC	1
18.	Tax Officer	Regular employee of KCC	1
19.	Legal Adviser	Regular employee of KCC	2
20.	Veterinary Surgeon	Regular employee of KCC	2
21.	Conservancy Officer	Regular employee of KCC	1
22.	Assistant Health Officer	Regular employee of KCC	1
23.	Water Supply Caretaker	Regular employee of KCC	1
	Total Class II positions		11
	Total Class III positions		509
	Total Class IV positions		589

Khulna Development Authority

The Khulna Development Authority (henceforth referred to as KDA) was established through an ordinance of 1961 to provide for development, improvement and expansion of the town of Khulna itself and of certain nearby areas by opening up congested areas and laying out or altering streets, by providing open spaces for ventilation or recreation purposes, by demolishing or constructing buildings, by acquiring land for such purposes and for the rehabilitation of persons displaced by the implementation of renewal schemes (The Khulna Development Authority Ordinance, 1961).

Table 14.2 KDA Staff

No.	Name of Position (Class I)	Type of Appointment	No. of Position
1.	Chairman	Appointed by the government (present chairman is a Brigadier General deputed from the Army)	1
2.	Secretary	Bureaucrat appointed by the Government	1
3.	Chief Engineer	Regular employee of KDA	1
4.	Executive Engineer	Regular employee of KDA	2
5.	Authorized Officer	Regular employee of KDA	1
6.	Planning Officer	Regular employee of KDA	1
7.	Accounts Officer	Regular employee of KDA	1
8.	Assistant Engineer	Regular employee of KDA	4
9.	Junior Architect	None Appointed	1
	Total Class II positions		4
	Total Class III positions		111
	Total Class IV positions		103

As per its constitution, KDA is an autonomous body supervised by the Ministry of Works of the Government of the Peoples Republic of Bangladesh. It is tasked with:

- formulating a master plan for Khulna City and its adjacent area;
- preparing detailed plans, zone plans, area development plans of areas under the master plan;
- preparing a five-year plan, annual development programme and perspective plan for development of the areas covered by the master plan;
- developing specific improvement schemes based on the five-year plan;
- implementing approved plans;
- approving building plans;
- developing control through rational and planned land use;
- according permission for the use of land in variance to master plan zoning;
- land allotment developed by the authority and realization of premiums;
- allotment of stalls in the markets constructed by the authority and collection of rents from the stall holders;
- public information on land zoning included in the master plan, etc.

Major works undertaken by the Khulna Development Authority are (Mahmud, 2000):

- roads (KDA Avenue, Majid Road, Mujgunni Main Road, etc.);
- markets (KDA New Market, Rupsha Market, etc.);
- housing (Sonadanga Residential Area, Neerala Residential Area, etc.).

By its nature, the KDA is a public autonomous body financed by both state revenues and development budgets. The organization chart of the Khulna Development Authority is listed in Table 14.2.

Other Agencies

Apart from the Khulna Development Authority and the Khulna City Corporation, the public sector agencies listed in Table 14.3 also work in the city area.

Table 14.3 Public sector agencies

Name of the Agency	Abbreviations	Activity Area
Bangladesh Railways	BR	Transportation
Department of Public Health and Engineering	DPHE	Health
Local Government Engineering Department	LGED	Infrastructure
Power Development Board	PDB	Electricity
Public Works Department	PWD	Buildings
Roads and Highways Department	RHD	Roads
Khulna Metropolitan Police	KMP	Law and Order
District Administration	DA	Administration
Directorate of Environment	DoE	Environment
Housing and Settlement Directorate	HSD	Housing
Bangladesh Telegraph and Telephone Board	BTTB	Communication

An Evaluation

It can be concluded from the above discussion that a number of government agencies are either involved in the urban development process or are working in the urban area. Their combined role in the urban development scenario will be discussed under the following headings.

Co-ordination

The governmental and semi-governmental organizations mentioned above are working under the supervision of different ministries located in Dhaka, the country's capital. KDA or KCC has no monitoring authority over other government agencies. Nor do KDA and KCC have any co-ordination between them. Generally, KDA is responsible for planning and development works while KCC performs project maintenance. But, as there is scope for KCC under the act to undertake development work as well, at times the work of these two organizations overlaps in comical ways. Recently, KCC constructed a road through residential lots earlier distributed by KDA (Alam, 2000). Later, KDA had to pay compensation for the same lots. Another frequently experienced sight is that of the Bangladesh Telegraph and Telephone Board (BTTB) digging up roads for the maintenance of its underground cable just after KCC has finished maintaining the road itself.

A vast tract (206 hectares) of Bangladesh Railway (BR) land is under-utilized – more precisely vacant – in the city heart. As there is no activity in the area, it has become a meeting point for the city hoodlums. Located in the interstices between the old Central Business District of the city 'The Barabazaar' and the new commercial area along KDA avenue, this area could provide the citizens with green space and other civic amenities. KCC is willing to develop the area in such a manner. KDA also is interested in the area and they have their own plan for it. But, the organizations involved are administered by three different ministries. So, nothing has come about so far except inter-ministerial land feuds.

Accountability

It was mentioned earlier that the Khulna Development Authority (KDA) was established in 1961. It was granted full authority to constitute and implement an urban master plan. But, ironically, there is little scope for public representation in this agency. So, the responsibility for urban development and future planning is left with bureaucrats, army officials and a few regular employees of KDA who cannot be ousted. That is why, even after being given the responsibility to provide ventilation and recreation spaces for the citizens, in the past 40 years KDA has not undertaken a single civic project. This has occurred because the people involved in KDA decision-making are not accountable to the people they are supposed to work for. In the past 40 years, KDA has laid roads in different places and sold the in-between land as residential lots to the social elite and thus has become more a state owned real-estate company than a civic organization. The Khulna City Corporation (KCC) has at least completed a few civic projects because the mayor and commissioners are re-elected at least once every four years.

Staffing

Both, KDA and KCC lack proper personnel for carrying out urban planning. KDA is supposed to do the planning for the city and has only one planner for a city of one million people. KCC has a post for a Chief Planning Officer but no one has been appointed. Another post meant for a planner is being held by a civil engineer. As a result, these organizations are dominated by civil engineers instead of planners. So, it is no wonder that roads rather than civic values and institutions are priority activities.

The procedure undertaken by the government at different times for appointing the chairman of KDA is also questionable. Either bureaucrats or senior army officers who have no experience in city planning and development are being appointed as chairman of KDA for three-year terms. They take a year to understand the city's problems and when they realize what to do, they are posted back to their original services. These organizations also lack vision for proper staffing to face the problems of the very near future. After the construction of the Rupsha Bridge, the urbanization rate will accelerate and is likely to spin out of control. In such situations, other cities in the country and region have faced serious environmental hazards. So, this is the time to take proper steps to avoid the environmental risks that often accompany urbanization. But ironically, KDA or KCC have no immediate plans to form environmental units to monitor the city's environmental aspects.

Master Plans, Patterns and Participation

Individual privacy and social harmony regulated by religious beliefs and physical parameters such as climate and topography are the elements that once dominated considerations of development patterns for settlements in this region. There was a certain spatial relationship that evolved from behavioural patterns within society. The sequence of spaces in the traditional city starts from *uthan* (courtyards) at the household level, then connects with the *goli* (lanes) at a community level, *morh* (roundabout) at a neighbourhood level and ultimately terminates in the *maidan* (square) at the urban scale (Figure 14.2).

The formal planning system such as master plans and housing areas developed by KDA were unsympathetic to traditional systems of spatial linkage. KDA's version of housing means acquiring land, laying perpendicular roads and then selling the remaining land after dividing it into rectangular plots (Figure 14.3). The traditional spaces for community interaction and identification are missing here. The rules and regulations imposed upon citizens by the building construction act enforced by KDA have no reference to the indigenous lifestyles either. The law encourages people to merely obtain access from the road to confine themselves to the plot of land they have been allotted. So, there is no space for the community and ultimately thousands of people live in a congested manner as individuals rather than as social beings.

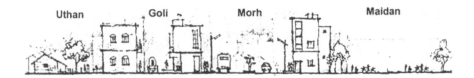

Figure 14.2 Sequence of traditional urban spaces

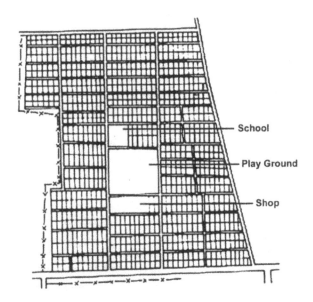

Figure 14.3 A typical KDA housing area

The master plans emphasize land-use, zoning, land subdivision and impose order upon the citizens from a birds-eye view. It is more inclined (the previous one of 1961) to sectoral development than traditional urban organization (Figure 14.4). It has been found that in the past, the master plans were not really down-to-earth solutions. Rather, they were overly optimistic and were never implemented. But, the citizens are also not very concerned about implementation because their participation in the decision-making process has not been taken into consideration. They do not feel at all involved in the urban development process. This trend began after the responsibility of civic development and maintenance had been shifted from the traditional bodies (*mahalla and panchayet*) to the administrative ones. As there is no scope for the citizens to participate in the planning process, it cannot be expected that they take responsibility for development and maintenance of the city.

Major Roads
River
Residential
Industrial
Commercial
Landuse not Assigned
Administration
Town Centre
Recreation
Low Land
Airport

Figure 14.4 Khulna Master Plan, 1961

Central Control

Under its constitution, the Khulna Development Authority is responsible for the development and planning of Khulna City and is mandated to work independently as an autonomous body. But, in effect, the Ministry of Works located in Dhaka monitors and controls every KDA project even if it is implemented directly by KDA funding. The ministerial bureaucrats have no understanding of the real needs of the city and continue discouraging projects that do not have direct monetary refunds. They also control other development authorities (DIT, which has recently been renamed RAJUK; the Dhaka Development Authority, the Chittagong Development Authority and the Rajshahi Development Authority) and in doing so, they outline a generalized policy for all the cities. Development of housing facilities is the priority. But this is a problem in Dhaka and not in Khulna. In Khulna only 25 per cent of the housing lots allotted by KDA/HSD have so far (in approximately 35 years) been utilized while the rest remain vacant. Dhaka's problem becomes the problem of the rest of the country perhaps because the ministries are located there and the bureaucrats live there as well. Thus, central control over regional planning and development organizations does not permit them to address specific regional issues; furthermore, generalized central solutions continue to be implemented, creating new problems for regional authorities. Though KDA is now busy drafting the Khulna Master Plan, lack of interest on the part of the bureaucrats to fund the civic portion of the planning may result in only partial development.

The idea of the city councils (such as the Khulna City Corporation) is to strengthen local governance by active participation of public representatives leading towards participatory administration. The mayor has been given ministerial status but his spectrum of work is limited. Important components of the city administration such as the Metropolitan Police and Civil Administration work separately under the direct supervision of the central government. For any development work within the city at any scale, the mayor has to seek land from the District Commissioner – a central government bureaucrat. Thus, the mayor's power has been restricted. In fact, the mayor himself is a politician and the central political leaders do not want to see the regional leaders become excessively powerful.

The Search for a Pragmatic Approach

Khulna is still in a situation where there is room for compensation through sensible and integrated development. The problems mentioned above are also common to the nation's other major cities. It is believed that Dhaka, the capital, is already dying with a population of nine million people because of its insensate growth. To avoid a similar situation, the following can provide a few first remedial steps for Khulna.

Effective Metropolitan Governance

The mayor is the supreme authority in the city because he/she is the person elected by the citizens to look after their well-being. The Khulna City Corporation should be strengthened to become the chief body of city governance. All the other organizations including KDA will work under the direct supervision of the elected mayor and commissioners. This will help solve the problem of co-ordination and accountability.

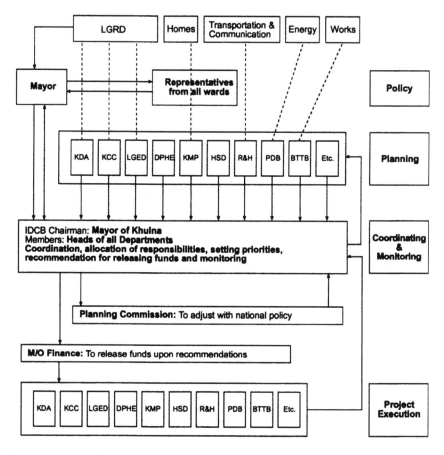

Source: adapted from Mowla (1997)

Figure 14.5 Interdepartmental Co-ordination Body

An Interdepartmental Co-ordination Body (IDCB) should be formed where the heads of all the departments will represent their organizations and the mayor will remain as chairman (Figure 14.5). The IDCB will scrutinize critically any development or maintenance activity (such as the formulation of the city's master plan) conceived by any organization.

Participation

A number of civic bodies (resembling the traditional *panchayet* system) can be formed in each ward and responsibility for co-ordinating these bodies can be left with the ward commissioners who will place the views of their area before the central body. Thus, the decision-making process will be decentralized and participation even from the grass-roots level will become possible. Community-based organizations can also play a very effective role in maintaining civic order and promoting cleanliness and services. A few community-based organizations and NGOs in the city have already proved their worth in urban waste disposal services which had become unmanageable for KCC.

Staffing

KDA and KCC must introduce dynamism in their staffing patterns. As the regular staff will form the core of the organization, it would be useful to review personnel organization charts. Planners, Architects, Environmentalists, Sociologists and Anthropologists should dominate the structure of agencies involved in urban development and there must be provision for them to be trained in contemporary urban problems, experiences and trends.

Concluding Remarks

Any type of development – be it rural or urban – is the result of a complex matrix. Maintaining the pattern and development strategies as natural and spontaneous as possible is perhaps the best solution. But in the case of urban development, size and population are sometimes too unmanageable without prior planning. It has also been observed that, in most cases, these planning and development strategies are the result of closed-door paper work, with no relation to the real situation. This makes the planning process inhuman and when this occurs, cities start to break down. Cities in other parts of the world have already undergone experiences like this. All those interviewed[1] during the research work for this article have acknowledged that only change in the planning and development attitude can keep the city liveable and sustainable. The goal of this paper is to lengthen this list with more and more people who believe that only humanistic development will sustain. And this is something that we must ensure for our future citizens.

Note

1   List of persons interviewed during the research work for this paper:
    - Advocate Sk. Tayebur Rahman, The Honourable Mayor of Khulna City Corporation;
    - Brigadier General Monzurul Alam, Chairman, Khulna Development Authority;
    - Mr. Akhter Hossain Chowdhury, Deputy Team Leader, Aqua-Sheltech Consortium Consultant Group for Khulna Master Plan Project;
    - Professor Qazi Azizul Mowla, Department of Architecture, Bangladesh University of Engineering and Technology;
    - Dr. Dilip Dutta, Head, Environmental Science Discipline, Khulna University;
    - Ms. Laila Arzumand Banu, Architect, Khulna City Corporation;
    - Mr. Mohammad Akhter Mahmud, Urban Planner, Khulna Master Plan Project, Khulna Development Authority Counterpart;
    - Ms. Kaniz Fatima, Formerly Urban Planner, Khulna Master Plan Project, Khulna Development Authority Counterpart.

References

Alam, M. (2000), *Personal communication*, Khulna Development Authority, Khulna.

Aqua-Sheltech Consortium (1998), *Preparation of Structure Plan, Master Plan and Detailed Area Plan*, Interim Report, vol. I, Khulna Development Authority, Khulna.

Khan, L.A. (2000), *Personal communication*, Khulna City Corporation, Khulna.

Mahmud, M.A. (2000), *Personal communication*, Khulna Development Authority Counterpart, Khulna Master Plan Project, Khulna.

Mowla, Q.A. (1997), 'Partners in Development: The Case of Dhaka City', *Partners in Development*, Glasgow.

The Khulna Development Authority Ordinance (1961), *Dhaka Gazette*, Government of the then East Pakistan, Dhaka.

The Khulna Municipal Corporation Ordinance (1984), *Ordinance no. LXXII of 1984*, Government of the Peoples Republic of Bangladesh, Dhaka.

Chapter 15

Lithuanian Business Environmental Management Based on Local Agenda 21 Principles

Olga Belous

Introduction

Background

Today, Lithuania, like other countries in transition, actively participates in the global environmental protection process and, with the support of its international partners, has begun to make preparations for a new approach to natural resource consumption, human needs and environmental management. People throughout Europe operate an active Habitat Agenda with the aim of providing good social, economic and natural conditions for present and future generations and compelling companies and organizations to act in more sustainable ways.

One of the most significant tools for managing sustainable businesses is the environmental management system ISO14000 series. However, there is a lack of experience and knowledge in this field in Lithuania. Not many individuals and groups in society appreciate the necessity for sustainable development. Today we should consider and discuss ways to motivate and involve our community in the Local Agenda 21 process as well as to prepare for the implementation of environmental management systems that are acceptable for enterprises.

Objectives

The main goal of this paper is to discover what is happening regarding sustainable management at local authority and business level, showing that some public and private organizations are adopting and utilizing environmental and social management procedures.

At the same time, this analysis might help show companies that there is an opportunity to move toward sustainable development and improve their eco-efficiency by implementing environmental management systems.

Resources

To be successful, future sustainable management depends on the correct identification of stakeholders, key people, groups or institutions who will be expected to get involved with or invest in specific environmental issues.

All resources mentioned in this study can be divided into three main groups. The first group regards human resources such as urban authorities, industrial and academic societies, non-governmental organizations (NGOs) and foreign assessors. Next are financial sources: company finances, state and local budgets, foreign and international organizations and funds. And the last group is made up of the methodological and informational support of Environmental and Economic Ministries, local and foreign Universities, and also includes best practice examples of other enterprises.

Methods

The fundamental yardstick for management is to create a collaborative atmosphere. Some well-known methods are: team building, conflict resolution, brainstorming, facilitation skills, majority rule and consensus.

Lithuanian, European Union (EU) and international environmental legislation and requirements guide the study. Qualitative and quantitative environmental aspects, ranking systems, and benchmarking are applied.

Processes

In order to promote LA21 and offer correct information to local businesses, authorities should be aware of the processes that are on offer for obliging industry to act in a sustainable way.

Some of the main processes are described during this study: staff training, local environmental policy formation and its influence on society's attitude to environmental quality, industrial enterprises' energy and material flows, key technological procedures and their impact on the environment.

Results

On the basis of an interdisciplinary holistic approach and practical applicability, the benefit of successful co-operation between local industry and academic institutions in the field of environmental management has been achieved.

General conclusions concerning the environmental performance of some companies in Klaipeda city were drawn and some elements of environmental management implementation were shown.

The final result obtained was the implementation of environmental management systems in some companies.

Lessons Learned

The following contributions regarding local business involvement in the sustainability process are:

- companies which successfully accept environmental management training change their environmental attitude towards sustainability;
- the number of organizations which would like to adopt ISO 14001 has already increased;
- the analysis of companies that adopted ISO 14001 shows that these organizations have increased their labour force as a result of the creation of new facilities for sorting and recycling waste, implementing information technology, providing better conditions for workers and improving quality of services.

Environmental Policy in the 1990s

In 1992 in Rio de Janeiro, the United Nations Conference on Environment and Development (UNCED) produced a joint agenda of actions to commit governments, industry and non-government organizations (NGOs) to sustainable development. Among six major items, such as public awareness and participation, sustainable energy use and others, it was held that sustainable industrial activities should focus on the application of clean technology, saving of natural resources, elimination of wastes, formulation of international base-line standards and monitoring programs (UNCED, 1992).

'Agenda 21', as the final UNCED document, has called upon local authorities the world over to develop their own strategies for implementing sustainable environmental policy. The International Council for Local Environmental Initiatives (ICLEI) in Europe has supported this call and played a major role in initiating the 'European Sustainable Cities and Towns Campaign' following the Aalborg Conference in 1994.

Many nations all over the world realize the value of environmental sustainability and as a result of environmental management implementation many organizations have adopted ISO 9000 and ISO 14000 standards.

Today humanity can learn from the many good examples of environmental management systems in enterprises, municipalities, and universities in developed countries (Federal Ministry for the Environment,

Nature Conservation and Nuclear Safety, 1999). But there are many developing and transition countries which need specific guidelines for putting ISO 14000 into practice under difficult economic conditions.

After Lithuania regained its independence from the Soviets, Klaipeda began active international cooperation in economic, environmental and cultural fields. The openness of the city is directly linked to its advantageous geographical location, convenient local and international transportation system and its well-developed infrastructure. It has an ice-free port, an international airport (located just 25 km far from the city), railways and a modern highway. The city occupies an area of 98.35 km^2 and has a population of 202,500. The service sector is the largest in the city. Attention is paid to the promotion of newly established enterprises, environmental protection, development of transportation, tourism and recreation. In this context, companies, with activities connected to all kinds of transportation, are the most active in environmental management.

The Need for Action in Transition Countries

All the Baltic countries are looking forward to becoming European Union (EU) members. Among the different economic, social and legal regulatory questions they must face are those concerning environmental rehabilitation and conservation. The problems regarding Baltic Sea eutrophication, soil contamination and remediation and waste disposal should be solved before joining the EU.

The EU policy for sustainability was first introduced in 1992 through the 5th Environmental Action Program and was later reinforced through the Amsterdam Treaty. In 1994, the Aalborg Charter emphasized the need to measure urban activities in the region and subsequently, the 1996 Lisbon Action Plan mentioned the use of sustainability indicators (Working Group on Measuring, Monitoring and Evaluation in Local Sustainability, 2000). *Sustainable management of the local authorities and local businesses was stressed* as one of ten in the first generation of European Common Indicators. Moreover, EU Directive 96/61 regarding Integrated Pollution Prevention and Control (Council Directive 96/61/EC) requirements should be mentioned as one of the necessary conditions for the achievement of sustainability. Another important reason for preparing for the adoption of environmental management systems is access to the European market.

Over and above these issues, it is necessary to emphasize the fact that the ways industries are using raw materials and the way products are being ultimately disposed of is very different from the management methods adopted in the traditional society and this causes fundamental problems (Andersson et al., 1999). Most of them could be partially solved by the implementation of innovative approaches and new prevention methods.

The Role of Local and International Cooperation

In 1992 in Rio de Janeiro, few Lithuanians were among the 173 representatives from different countries. When a representative of Klaipeda's local authority signed the Charter in Aalborg in 1994, the campaign for sustainable development began.

In 1998, under Klaipeda's municipal environmental policy, our citizens had an opportunity to participate in a 'Local Agenda 21' project. At the same time the first industrial enterprise 'Baltijos automobiliu technika' (BAT), announced its decision to adopt the Environmental Management and Audit Scheme (EMAS). It was the first organization in Lithuania to integrate environmental aspects in its overall enterprise management system. Together with the Natural Protection Department of Klaipeda municipality, BAT organized seminars and workshops on themes associated with environmental management. Local industry was prepared for a new understanding of the surrounding environment, raw material consumption, water, energy, emissions and waste recycling. In accordance with Local Agenda 21, the local government and public representatives conducted the following projects:

- the 'The Akmena-Dane river pollution reduction' action plan;
- the pilot project for biological treatment of domestic wastewater;
- the plan for a network of pedestrian and cycling paths;
- the environmental audit of four industrial state enterprises in Klaipeda, together with representatives of the Union of Baltic Cities (UBC);
- the city's biodiversity conservation program;
- the city's environmental quality monitoring program;
- environmental education work through media and annual environmental challenge seminars and workshops.

This list of environmental initiatives could be continued since many other local and international natural protection actions have been undertaken.

The strategic development plan of Klaipeda city was prepared two years ago. City strategy is based on five priorities (Klaipeda City Municipality, 2001):

- to create employment opportunities by offering investment and encouraging business development;
- to develop an infrastructure for improvement of businesses, as well as working and living conditions;
- to strengthen integration between the city and its port;
- to develop the housing stock and improve its quality;
- to develop the fields of education, science and culture.

Attention is focused on the eradication of poverty first of all through the creation of new working places in the marine complex, industry, tourism, etc.

The major activities of all five priorities are represented in the situation plan of Klaipeda city (Figure 15.1) in accordance with the strategic development plan of port city (Klaipeda City Municipality, 2001).

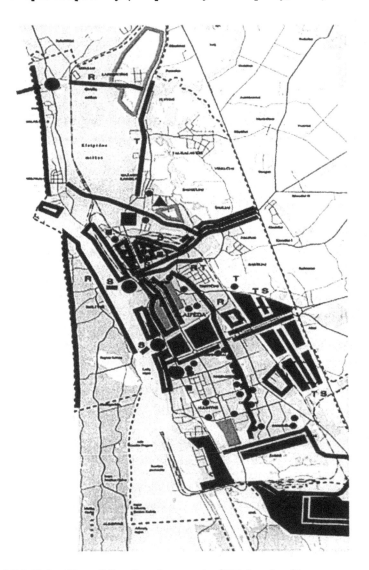

Figure 15.1 Priorities of the development of Klaipeda city

Environmental and resource protection benefit both the richer countries of the world as well as the poorer ones. In this regard, international cooperation is an essential feature for present world environmental policy.

One piece of evidence for putting international cooperation into practice is a number of Local Agenda 21 and other projects on sustainability in Baltic countries (Gronholm and Joas, 1999; Markowitz, 2000).

Maurice Strong, chair of the 1992 Earth Summit, estimated that: 'Development aid from the richer countries should be some US$ 150 billion per year, while internal investments in environmental protection by developing countries will need to be twice that amount' (Ryding, 1992).

Today, under these conditions, many Klaipeda city organizations are ready to start preparation for the introduction of sustainable management. Their position has received the support of Klaipeda University professors. On the basis of methodological and financial cooperation with Mid Sweden University the idea of ISO 14000 implementation has become a reality.

The Stimulus and Obstacles for Action

Modern society and the business world have changed their attitudes towards nature due to recognition of the fact that resources are limited and our activities can have a negative effect on the environment. Today human relationships with the natural environment are designed in accordance with environmental principles. This new approach is stimulated by some essential factors (Brorson and Larsson, 1999):

- increased environmental awareness among legislators, environmental groups, consumers, financial institutions, insurers, the company's own employees and, most of all, customers;
- an increasing number of national and international environmental schemes, laws and regulations, and a great commitment to their implementation;
- the use of economic sanctions such as taxes and penalties on emissions in order to encourage companies to consume fewer resources and emit fewer pollutants;
- the negative effects on the company's reputation resulting from a faulty environmental strategy including negative publicity, problems with customers and questions raised about the company's products.

But, nevertheless, many organizations have serious problems with environmental management performance and the approach to innovative technologies, prevention measures and safe and healthy working conditions.

The main barriers which arise in developing an overall company or organization management system, are limited information and a lack of experience, especially in developing countries.

Another major obstacle are local authority disagreements and incorrect forms of competition with other companies whose overall goals are to reap maximum profits in the shortest possible time.

The third group of barriers are the high costs of new technology (Gunningham and Sinclair, 1997).

Alongside these external causes are also some internal ones, such as preparation for pollution control according to environmental law requirements, the high cost of monitoring implementation, the lack of cooperation among company employees and workers. After regaining its independence, Lithuania began to build its community with the aim of meeting human needs, but the absence of trade unions in many organizations reduced the opportunity to defend workers' interests and they tend not to trust their companies' management. Moreover, the low level of environmental awareness of working personnel and an inert mid-staff attitude towards the company's negative environmental reputation might interrupt the sustainable development process.

Analysis of Some Industrial Companies' Environmental Issues and Strategy for Sustainable Management

Content of the Work-Study

After taking the 'Environmental Management in the Baltic' (Belous, 2000) training course, ten Klaipeda city organizations voluntarily participated in their enterprises' environmental work efficiency analysis. This investigation was divided into four stages:

- analysis of environmental policies;
- assessment of environmental aspects and their impact;
- evaluation of training, operation, and communication procedures;
- analysis of initial audit results.

The main characteristic of this evaluation was equal participation of company as well as Mid Sweden and Klaipeda University specialists. The academic representatives provided organizational, methodological and financial support. The opportunity to understand more about the environmental management system and its significance for sustainability was provided for everyone from industrial or other organizations, including Klaipeda University students. A chance to adopt ISO 14001 was given to medium and small organizations, which might not be able to afford the formation of a competent management system.

Objectives of the Study

The fundamental goals of the study were:

- to acquaint businesses with sustainable living and working styles;
- to help organizations conduct environmental work efficiently by providing structured and controllable methods.

The aims of the parts were:

- to give a summarized evaluation of companies' commitments and the consequences of different operations on nature;
- to stress significant companies' environmental issues;
- to investigate compliance with legislation;
- to integrate the target goal of sustainable development within enterprises and city authorities;
- to assess motivations and opportunities for the practical application of environmental management system;
- to evaluate the prospective movement towards sustainability.

The Short Characteristics of the Study Object

As the starting point of the study, the following Klaipeda city companies' environmental issues were investigated: timber plant, seaport authority, fabric company, cotton spinning company, company of wires sets (BAT), bakery, wood processing enterprise, city wastewater treatment plant, stevedoring company, shipbuilding yard.

Most of these enterprises are situated in the old part of the city centre or near the Curonian Lagoon. This means that company location has impact on both the urban city area and the coastal zone ecosystem.

Study Methods

Environmental management standards such as ISO 14000 series established requirements setting out how the system had to examine and provide management system structure and content.

Methods of effective collaboration such as team building, effective communication, brainstorming and others were suggested (Markowitz, 2000).

During the study, great attention was paid to national and international environmental legislation (Environmental protection law of the Republic of Lithuania, 1992).

Energy and substance balance methods based on chemical reactions and thermodynamic laws were used (Bonde and Annerud, 1999).

Elements of environmental impact and comparative risk assessment were applied (Colombo, 1992).

The method of benchmarking as a systematic assessment of a company's environmental performance was used (Andersen and Pettersen, 1996).

The basic principles of environmental management system creation at the company were described (Figure 15.2).

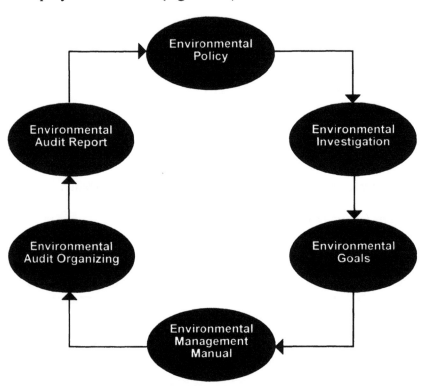

Figure 15.2 Basic principles of an environmental management system

Study Results and Discussions

Company environmental management performance evaluation included the following steps:

- Initial Environmental Review and Environmental Management Program (from choosing the main legal documents to preparing the environmental management program);
- Environmental Management System Manual (from preparing the company management system structure to establishing procedures for

recording training, review and audit results);
• Company Environmental Internal Audit (from working out the environmental management system audit's program to preparing the report on the audit results).

Working in the manner described, the industry representatives improved their theoretical and practical skills. A large database was created and a comprehensive analysis was carried out.

The general features of environmental policy for industrial enterprises were commitments to install modern technologies, reduce negative environmental impacts, avoid human injury and create favourable work conditions.

Company leaders were committed to educate, train and motivate employees to fulfil their duties in an environmentally responsible manner.

Special emphasis was placed on openness and objectivity. The main organizational players, including organization personnel, customers and other relevant parties were briefed on environmental issues.

Most environmental policies were in line with legal and other requirements and supposed continual improvement of environmental work.

The assets spent on environmental protection and production quality improvements were considered as a long-term investment in the context of company policy.

During the determination and evaluation of enterprises' environmental aspects, new assessment methods based on environmental impact were chosen or created. In this case the impact of the activities of each company on the environment was assessed in normal working conditions, in emergency situations and in the event of company closure. In addition, the original scale of environmental aspects according to their quantitative and qualitative characteristics was suggested.

The most significant environmental aspects examined were: air and water pollution, waste formation and inefficient use of raw materials and energy.

In order to draft an Environmental Management System Manual covering the training program, the communication system and the environment monitoring system, corrective or preventive actions were worked out.

Health and occupational safety issues were analyzed through national health protection requirements. Social conditions were improved by means such as an insurance program, disease prevention (vaccination) and transportation services.

During the last part of the investigation, the company environmental management system's internal audit was performed and the audit report was prepared. This task was fulfilled in accordance with ISO14010 (Guidelines for environmental auditing – General principles of environmental auditing) and ISO 14011 (Guidelines for environmental auditing – Audit procedures – Part 1: Auditing of environmental management systems).

The importance of the audit lay in the verification of how a company carried out its commitments and determined environmental management system performance. In this case, audit evidence was gathered using document examination, observation of conditions and activities, interviews, monitoring results, tests and others.

The companies' audit results showed that responsibilities were delegated to staff according to professional skills, but there were shortcomings in the procedures, working instructions and records explaining how to handle separate elements of the system. Many organizations did not have efficient internal communication systems. Also the staff training program was not always in line with modern legal, and other, requirements.

Nevertheless, most of the enterprises were able to recognize how far they were from ISO 14001 installations and what they had to do to achieve them. The majority of company ecologists contributed to environmental management system improvement. Together with industrial plant authorities, they were able to implement some elements of the environmental management system such as environmental policy, establishing objectives and targets of policy and action plan, identifying environmental aspects and evaluating their impact, structure and responsibilities, staff training, pollution and natural resources consumption monitoring and others.

The summarized overview of all environmental management system ISO 14001 element implementation is shown in Table 15.1.

Unfortunately, the Fabric company was unable to achieve any part of the environmental management system because of a change in company management.

BAT company has an ISO 14001 system installed since 1999. The company achieved an excellent result after three years of hard environmental work and participation in the study; this helped the company recognize the kinds of improvement strategies that should have been utilized.

At present, some of the companies, such as the seaport authority, stevedoring company, the shipbuilding yard and the wood processing company, which strongly influence the city environment, have announced their intention of managing their companies more effectively through ISO 14001 installations.

Table 15.1 Companies' environmental initiatives toward sustainability

Company	Implemented Elements of Environmental Management System ISO 14001.
Bakery	*Environmental policy, environmental aspects*: waste management action plan, nature pollution monitoring, communication and environmental information dissemination system.
Timber plant	*Environmental aspects*: noise reducing program, heat energy productions from waste, waste diminishing program, emergency preparedness plan, environmental legislation and other requirements dissemination inside the plant.
Wastewater treatment plant	*Environmental communication system, internal company audit, environmental aspects*: water-cleaning procedures applying, adding of training program.
Seaport authority	*Environmental aspects*: waste gathering and utilization action plan, contaminated soil disposal, policy, monitoring. *Preparation for ISO14001 installation.*
Wood processing company	*Environmental policy, environmental aspects:* waste management action plan, environmental monitoring, air pollution diminishing, storm water pollution control. *Preparation for ISO14001 installation.*
Cotton spinning company	*Environmental policy, environmental aspects*: waste of cotton yarn diminishing, reducing electricity consumption. *Structure and responsibility*: responsibility instruction for every member of the staff. *Communication*: system of exchange of internal information.
Stevedoring company	*Objectives and targets*: storm water pollution prevention measures, water pollution reducing plan. *Monitoring*: waste sorting, air pollution diminishing. *Non-conformance corrective and prevention action*: fertilizes loses, prevention means, implementation. *Preparation of ISO 14001 installation.*
Company of wires sets (BAT)	*ISO 14001 implementation, monitoring and measurement (continuous improvement)*: heating systems innovation in working places and administration building.
Shipbuilding yard	*Environmental policy, objectives and targets*: installation of cleaner heat production, storm water pollution reducing means, air pollution decrease. *Environmental aspects*: waste creation minimization program. *Communication*: introduction of new environmental information methods. *Preparation for ISO14001 installation.*

Conclusion

The most successful parts of the practical assignment were environmental review, policy and aspects resulting from the well-organized Lithuanian environmental protection system.

The most challenging part of the environmental management system was preparing the Manual, especially operation controls, because of poor understanding of the links between environmental aspects, procedures, training and control in practice.

In general, there was no major difference between the industrial companies' policy commitments and significant environmental aspects. The environmental pollution and safety work issues, taking into consideration the lack of implementation of pollution prevention measures, saving of natural resources and employee training, were common ones.

The evaluation of some industrial companies' environmental situation showed that the enterprises needed to install ISO 14001, but the shortage of funds available made this impossible.

Summarized audit results of some companies indicated that the environmental objectives and targets established were mostly realistic, though many organizations did not have efficient systems of internal communication or to improve staff environmental awareness.

The study highlighted the fact that Lithuanian industry was interested in local sustainability especially in preparation for the adoption of an ISO 14001 certification process.

References

Andersen, B. and Pettersen, P.G. (1996), *The Benchmarking Handbook. Step by Step Instruction*, Chapman and Hall, London.

Andersson, M., Migula, P. and Ryden, L. (1999), *Environmental Science for the Baltic Sea Basin*, A Baltic University Program Publication, Uppsala.

Belous, O. (2000), 'Environmental Management in the Baltic', Proceedings of the World Meeting *The Human Being and the City. Towards a Human and Sustainable Development*, University of Naples 'Federico II', 6-8 September 2000, Naples.

Bonde, H. and Annerud, J. (1999), *Compendium. Environmental Management in Lithuania*, Department of Ecotechnics, Mid Sweden University, Ostersund.

Brorson, T. and Larsson, G. (1999), *Environmental Management*, EMS AB, Stockholm.

Colombo, A.G. (1992), *Environmental Risk Assessment*, Kluwer Academic Publishers, London.

Council Directive 96/61/EC of 24 September 1996, concerning integrated pollution prevention and control, Official Journal L 257, 10 October 1996, pp. 26-40.

Environmental Protection Law of the Republic of Lithuania (1992), No I-2223, LRS, Vilnius.

Federal Ministry for the Environment, Nature Conservation and Nuclear Safety (1999), *Local Agenda 21: A European Comparison*, BMU, Bonn and UBA, Berlin.

Gronholm, B. and Joas, M. (1999), *Local Environmental Activities within and across Borders*, Abo Academy University and Union of the Baltic cities, Turku.

Gunningham, N. and Sinclair, D. (1997), *Barriers and Motivators to the Adoption of Cleaner Production Practices*, Australian Centre of Environmental Law, Canberra.

Klaipeda City Municipality, (2001), *The Strategic Development Plan of Klaipeda City*, Department of Economic and Finance of Klaipeda City and Municipal Enterprise 'Vilnius planas', Klaipeda.

Markowitz, P. (2000), *Guide to Implementing Local Environmental Action Programs in Central and Eastern Europe*, Institute for Sustainable Communities, Montpelier, Vermont and The Regional Environmental Center for Central and Eastern Europe, Szentendre.

Ryding, S.O. (1992), *Environmental Management Handbook. The Holistic Approach: from Problems to Strategies*, IOS Press, Amsterdam and Lewis Publishers, Boca Raton, Florida.

UNCED (United Nations Commission on Environment and Development) (1992), *Agenda 21 and Rio Declaration*, Rio de Janeiro.

Working Group on Measuring, Monitoring and Evaluation in Local Sustainability – Expert Group on the Urban Environment (2000), *Towards a Local Sustainability Profile: European Common Indicators. Technical Report*, Directorate-General Environment, European Commission and Third European Conference on Sustainable Cities and Towns, Hanover.

Chapter 16

Creating Neighbourhoods in Balance: Issues and Solutions

Keith Richardson

Introduction

The quest for sustainable development has assumed centre stage in policy making terms nationally and internationally since the Earth Summit in 1992. Tony Blair requested that all Local Authorities were to draw up their own Local Agenda 21 (LA21) strategy by 2000 (Blair, 1997). The government itself produced the White Paper *A Better Quality of Life* (DETR, 1999) which attempts to focus the governments attempts to create a sustainable Britain. English regions also have to produce a Regional Sustainable Development Framework, as well as an economic development strategy (One North East, 2000).

There can be no doubt that, whilst it may not yet be the number one policy issue for British governments, sustainable development is certainly now being taken very seriously. Indeed, whilst socialism may have become the S word that cannot be spoken, sustainability has become the S word that must be spoken.

National and international policy recognized that sustainability will not be achieved simply by the creation of government policy, important as that is. It also needs to be addressed at a local level. The Habitat Agenda recognizes the need for us all to participate in the process of sustainable development, 'the Habitat Agenda provides a framework to enable people to take responsibility for the promotion and creation of sustainable human settlements' (UNCHS, 1996).

Indeed, some authors have argued that what happens at the local level may be decisive. 'What will emerge as global success will be the aggregate of many separate advances taken locally, on the smallest scale' (Holdgate, 1996) and the most challenging. 'It is here that the tough choices associated with sustainable development are frequently cast into sharpest relief'. (Selman, 1998).

But when people talk about local, it becomes clear that, at least in

Britain, we may not all be speaking the same language. Policy makers and government may mean something quite different in scale to Holdgate and Selman or to individual citizens. Hence we have LA21 strategies for local authorities containing up to 600,000 people. To most people this is far from being 'local', and, as we shall see, is unlikely to result in the participation of all, as the Habitat Agenda, and many other policy documents, seem to feel is necessary.

As a result, in Britain there have been few examples of attempts to create sustainability at the local level in the type of communities most people live in. What examples there have been have been largely about single issues, such as recycling or environmental improvements.

One project that has attempted to look at how local sustainability can be achieved is Earth Balance. It was set up to show sustainability in practice on a demonstration site and in surrounding communities. In doing this, it achieved a considerable amount, but ultimately the charity managing the site went into liquidation in September 1999. However, the site is still functioning and the work done by the Earth Balance Trust with local people has continued through a new project, Community Balance.

Although Earth Balance was not a model many communities could adopt as their route to sustainability, it provides many important lessons that can be learned from. It was a rare practical example of trying to achieve local sustainability. It is therefore important that these lessons are not lost, particularly those that have implications for any local initiative trying to put LA21 and the Habitat Agenda into practice.

This chapter sets out what these are and how this experience is being used to inform the development of Community Balance.

Sustainability in Practice – The Earth Balance Experience

Earth Balance is located in the district of Wansbeck in the North East of England, north of Newcastle. It is an area that has been decimated by the decline of the coal industry. At its peak in 1960 there were 45 deep mines working, mostly in or close to the Wansbeck area, employing 45,000 people (Northumberland County Council, 1998). Now there is only one mine left employing 350 people.

The consequences of these closures have had a severe impact on local communities. Wansbeck has been ranked the 18th most deprived District in England in a preliminary analysis of deprivation in England by the government (DETR, 2000). It has the second highest level of teenage pregnancies Britain and high levels of long-term health problems (Northumberland Health Authority, 1999). The number of small businesses in Wansbeck is the lowest in Britain (HM Treasury, 2000). It has also not risen to the challenge sustainability with, for example, only 0.9 per cent of waste being recycled in Wansbeck, which compares to 36.6 per cent in the neighbouring district of Castle Morpeth (Audit Commission, 2000).

However, the area also has its strengths, crime levels are low compared to other similarly disadvantaged areas of Britain.

There is still a strong sense of community left over from the mining legacy. Social cohesion is therefore under stress, but has not yet collapsed. This cohesion was born from the way in which the mining communities were developed and run. Villages and small towns developed around the 'pit' (coal mine). It was not only as the principal source of economic activity, but also the focus for social provision through local initiatives, often funded by Unions, such as the Miners' Welfare (what would now be described as a community centre). This developed a strong sense that services and facilities should be provided locally. It has left a lasting legacy in former mining communities, where people do not understand the need to travel for work or other activities. Professionals traditionally see this as a problem, but in terms of sustainability it is clearly a strength.

Earth Balance evolved from a group of people living and working primarily in Northumberland. Its origins date back to before the Earth Summit when it was described as the Environmental Conservation Project. Following the impact of the Summit, the idea evolved into the creation of a sustainability centre. More and more people became involved in what was a very creative and open process. The site was identified in 1993 and plans were drawn up with the help of the Centre for Alternative Technology (CAT) in Wales.

However, whilst CAT was, and is, very much about demonstrating alternative technology in a rural idyll, the plans for Earth Balance took sustainability one step further. They looked at how a development could link into the lives of ordinary people and ensure that everyone was included in the development. Consequently, involvement became a high priority and local people, through the Friends of Earth Balance, normally had representatives on the Trust that governed Earth Balance. One of the first working groups to be set up was focussed on community participation. There were monthly meetings involving local people long before work on the site began. Indeed, the first facility opened on the site in 1996 a horticultural training resource for local people with disabilities.

Within a year of being officially opened in 1998 by the then Minister for Energy, John Battle MP, Earth Balance had achieved a great deal on its 260 acre site, including the following:

- created over 50 jobs and helped create seven new businesses, making it one of Northumberland's top ten job creators (Northumberland County Council, 1998);
- secured almost £2 million to develop the site;
- helped give Northumberland a national reputation for innovation, and

gave many local people in an area of high unemployment renewed confidence;

- developed one of the North East's first organic farms and the first organic garden centre;
- developed a highly successful Training Unit working with over 80 people with disabilities;
- obtained nearly £250,000 of funding from Europe, in conjunction with Northumberland College, to help people with disabilities create their own social firms;
- worked with local people to help them improve their communities through a £200,000 Lottery grant;
- set up youth clubs, kids clubs, hosted visits by dozens of schools, run playschemes and provided work placements which benefited hundreds of local young people;
- developed a visitor centre, organic bakery, crafts fair and shop which served local people and attracted thousands of visitors;
- created wildlife areas of national importance and planted miles of hedges and thousands of trees;
- developed its own integrated renewable energy system based on a wind turbine, hydro storage lake, solar panels, bio-mass combustion, bio-diesel and heat recovery;
- created its own vertical and horizontal reed bed sewage system that provided water to irrigate horticultural crops;
- informed people about how to live more sustainably and helped them put this into practice;
- secured contracts with two national supermarket chains to supply organic bread from a bakery using coppiced willow bio-mass as fuel for its specially designed ovens.

In essence with its low energy buildings, Earth Balance had become a vision of what a sustainable future might look like, a demonstration of the results of implementing LA21 and the Habitat Agenda. However, in September 1999, just as it was announced that the Director of Earth Balance had won the prestigious Schumaker Prize, Earth Balance went into liquidation with debts of over £200,000.

So why had it come to grief?

Although Earth Balance was not simply a visitor attraction, paying visitors were still a key aspect of the business plan. Due to difficulties in obtaining funding to develop and market visitor attractions, visitor numbers and income from them was far lower than predicted. In addition, rental income from on site businesses was also lower than it should have been. In some cases this was to allow for the lower number of visitors. More usually, however, it was to allow the new green businesses, often co-ops involving local people, the time they needed to establish themselves.

These losses were serious, but still manageable. It was an attempt to trade out of the problem that resulted in financial disaster.

Earth Balance's bakery was originally run by a co-op. After a year of trading and being on the verge of viability, it became the only one of the seven on-site businesses to fail in 1998. The Earth Balance Trust decided to re-open the bakery and run it directly through a trading company. It soon gained major orders to supply two national supermarket chains with organic bread.

However, as anyone knows who sets up a new business of this type, it is good news if they are breaking even at the end of their first year, and almost unheard of to be making a substantial profit. The bakery was to be no different. Rather than saving Earth Balance it became the final nail in the coffin. It lost substantial sums of money, over £100,000 in little over five months trading.

Practically Earth Balance Trust collapsed because income did not match expenditure. However, this was actually a symptom of far deeper problems within the organization and the environment it was operating in. Many of these were those that are ascribed to any business failure and are problems that can be found in many not for profit organization.

They included, lack of forward planning, poor financial monitoring, refusal to recognize looming disaster, some bad management decision, the problems of personality conflicts within a value led organization, poor internal and external communications and the unwillingness of one of the local authorities to lose control and so on. There is little point here in analyzing them any further. However, there were other reasons that had much more to do with the nature of the beast and the aims of the organization.

These reasons are perhaps of not only relevant to Earth Balance, but also to other organizations working towards sustainability and the realization of LA21 and the Habitat Agenda. We will therefore look into them in more detail and then go on to discuss how Community Balance will address them.

They are as follows:

- the conflict between creating real participation and short-term results;
- the complexity of addressing sustainability holistically;
- difficulties caused by working with conventional organizations, governmental structures and funding regimes that have not come to terms with sustainability.

We will now look at each of these issues in turn.

Participation and Short-term Results

Participation and the generation of ownership amongst the people affected by developments or using services have been found to be crucial in many spheres. It is rightly, as we have seen, a crucial element of the Habitat Agenda. They have both been embodied in international and national policy documents. For example, 'Community participation is a core element of HEALTH 21, the WHO strategy for health for all in the twenty-first century and of Local Agenda 21' (WHO, 1999). In Britain the government has issued guidance on regeneration funding requiring community participation (DETR, 1998).

Such policy directives are based on a clear evidence base. Effective regeneration programmes have been found to embody high levels of participation (Lowe, 1998). People have been found to be healthier in societies where there is greater equity and inclusiveness (Wilkinson, 2000). 'Societies that enable all their citizens to play a full and useful role in the social, economic and cultural life of their society will be healthier than those where people face insecurity, exclusion and deprivation' (Wilkinson and Marmot, 1998).

Thus, people who have a sense of ownership become part of the solution rather than the problem. They are less likely to become hooligans or agents of environmental destruction. As Holdgate (1996) stated in discussing how we will achieve sustainability 'unless people are informed, educated, motivated and led to feel their personal action matters, we will not get very far'.

However, despite the clear evidence of the benefits of participation, it is still the exception rather than the rule in Britain. This has not been helped by the growth in inequality in Britain which creates social exclusion, 'Britain had a greater increase in inequality during the 1980s than other developed market economies' (Wilkinson, 1997).

The reason why this is so are many and varied, it may be because professionals and elites do not wish to loss power. In some cases we all collude (and are often encouraged to do so) with this, we want to maintain a faith in experts such as Doctors or want 'them' to solve our problems.

As the example of Earth Balance will show, the reasons for this may also be born out of pragmatism. In the beginning Earth Balance appears to have been a very inclusive organization that encouraged participation. This led to a somewhat chaotic process at times, but it was one that was creative and enabled the organization to draw on the talents and skills of a huge variety of people. In this, it mirrored the aspirations of the Habitat Agenda 'where all people are encouraged and have an equal opportunity to participate in decision making and development' (UNCHS, 1996).

However, as it developed participation in the organization diminished. Indeed by 1999, although the Project took on staff to work with local communities, practically it had become very difficult even for senior staff and most directors of the Trust to influence its development, never mind local people.

So, as it neared the final crisis, no more than three or four people effectively made decisions. Rather than drawing people in, the overwhelming sense amongst all stakeholders, staff, local people, on site businesses, support organizations and local politicians was one of being excluded and marginalized.

Such exclusion is not unusual. However, for an organization of such complexity that depended on drawing in the skills and support of a wider variety of people, both practically and philosophically, it was fatal.

The personalities of those making decisions must have some impact on the development of such a situation. But so to can external pressures created, in part, by sources of funding (which will be discussed later) and the structures adopted to manage the organization.

Earth Balance was managed by a group of self selecting trustees chosen for their skills and abilities. There was no membership to elect them and no practical way others could influence decisions this group made. This structure had been chosen with the best of intentions. It was done to protect the embryonic organization from being taken over by cliques and local political faction. It was a conscious decision made after consideration of a more de-centralized and democratic structure. In the short-term it was successful and take over was avoided. It protected and allowed the organization to develop. But once the rationale for taking a centralized approach had passed, the structure remained. The means had in some ways become the ends, with disastrous results.

Burnheim (1985) looked at a number of factors that are needed for good and democratic governance relating to those making decisions, three of which are worth considering here. They are that they are that those making decisions are:

- competent and good at making decisions;
- directly affected by the decisions they make and that 'Nobody should have any input into decision making where they have no legitimate material interest';
- representative of the people on whose behalf the decisions are being made and therefore able to act in their best interest.

In terms of competence, the Trustees were experienced and skilled. There was a senior member of a bank, the environment manager for a large private utility, a director of a large voluntary organization, a senior political figure in the County Council. The Trustees had been selected for their skills and the positions they held, in doing this Earth Balance was following what some would describe as best practice.

However when it comes to the other two criteria, the failings of the Trustees as a body became more obvious. None of them lived in the area Earth Balance worked in and the majority had no direct stake in the organization. They did not benefit directly from Earth Balance's existence, as did site businesses, staff or local people who used the site. Such people included those with disabilities working in the garden centre, those coming for training and those using it simply for leisure activities. In a practical day to day sense, the lives of the Trustees would not be changed whether or not Earth Balance existed. The exceptions were the Director, who risked losing his livelihood and one of the Trustees. They were both regarded as the 'founding fathers' and both had committed huge amounts of time to the Project. The majority of Trustees, not surprisingly, did not have this level of commitment, or self interest.

Of course their political and professional standing were at stake and some represented organizations with a financial stake. However, the nature of such interests may well have made them act differently to others whose motives were more enmeshed in the site and its success.

Indeed, at the Trustees meeting which set in train the liquidation process, the dominant expressed motivation of most of the Trustees was their desire to protect creditors. This was under laid by understandable worries about the possibility of being found personally liable for the debts (if they could be shown to have traded recklessly) of the organization. A few did express their desire to strive to protect the local people, the staff, the on-site businesses and the trainees from closure. But such sentiments did not have much impact. Had more of the Trustees been aware of the consequences on these people, had they been one of these people themselves, then these arguments may have affected the decisions they took.

In terms of representativeness, it is difficult to judge in that there was no membership to be representative off. However, with regard to the stakeholders and, crucially, the local population, they were far from being representative. They were nearly all over 50, there was only one woman and they were all middle class. And, as mentioned before, they did not live near the site.

Earth Balance was attempting to do things in a holistic way and professed to deal with the complexities this created through a co-operative way of working. However, the structure it had adopted, of a traditionally run voluntary organization with a Board of Trustee, created a centralized hierarchy that was always at odds with this philosophical standpoint.

As a result rather than encourage participation and involvement it did the reverse; it created a them and us situation. None of the stakeholders in the organization, apart from the Trustees (some of whom represented funding organizations) and Director, had any formal role in decision making. This meant that increasingly staff, local people, site businesses and users felt that things were being done to them. They were not involved in making decisions and their knowledge and skills were not being called on.

Such a process is not only wasteful, it is also destructive. People began to feel increasingly dis-enfranchised, they were angry at what they saw as bad decisions. Most importantly, they felt they had no responsibility and their commitment dwindled. As one of the site businesses said, 'We are like mushrooms, kept in the dark and fed crap'. As things got worse, those involved felt increasingly powerless and helpless to do anything. Crucially, they could not see the point of making personal sacrifices for the sake of the common good when they neither understood the rationale for doing so nor had any faith in such actions making things better.

Attempts to re-kindle a shared direction petered out and their failures made matters worse. Burnheim's (1985) comments on 'a democracy that renders people impotent is no democracy', could have been written for Earth Balance.

The aims of Earth Balance were radical, but its structure did not mirror these aims and this inherent contradiction inevitably led to problems.

In many ways, what happened at Earth Balance is mirrored in British society. It is not one that encourages participation and over the last few years has exacerbated inequalities. Indeed, much of our structures, such as our welfare state and tax system, have the effect of limiting citizenship (Twine, 1994). Britain has also become one of the most centralized states in Europe (Hutton, 1993). As a consequence, Earth Balance's success at generating participation and social inclusion in its early phase was against the grain of British society. And this success cannot be underestimated. The creation of Earth Balance had involved the talents of hundreds of people, and for many people it became a valued part of their lives. For example, independent evaluations and funders of the services provided for people with disabilities made much of the fact that many organizations espoused the virtues of participation, but few had made it a reality as they felt Earth Balance had. Perhaps then, the real surprise was not the fact that ultimately Earth Balance began to revert to the norms of participation in Britain, but that it was able to maintain a participative and inclusive approach for so long.

The Problems of Holism

In Britain the term 'joined-up thinking' has become a mantra for the current government. Joined-up thinking, tackling issues as a whole rather than in a piecemeal reductionist way, is also an essential part of sustainability.

Thus in realizing sustainability each decision becomes more complex. Let us look at the issues one needs to consider in buying a can of paint. Most people would buy the paint in terms of its performance and cost.

Trying to ensure that the purchase is as sustainable as possible adds in a whole raft of other issues. For example, one also wants to buy it from a local producer, from a firm that treats its staff well and recruits them from economically disadvantaged groups. You want it to be made from local materials that are from a renewable, non-polluting source. These materials should be safe when applied, without any long-term health problems and be ultimately bio-degradable. Thus simply deciding which paint to buy becomes very complex.

The volume of decisions is also increased because sustainability and joined-up thinking mean one needs to address a wide range of issues. In LA21 and the Habitat Agenda it has been recognized that saving our environment cannot be done simply by tackling what could be regarded as purely environmental issues. Poverty, health, personal fulfilment and many other issues have to be tackled. It is not therefore enough to understand environmental issues to address sustainability, one also needs to know about social issues, health, community development, economics, business development and so on.

Thus at a policy level joined-up thinking makes obvious sense, at a practical level one soon realizes why few people carry it out.

The achievement of sustainability has implications for virtually every aspect of our lives and our societies. In the name of sustainability one can, and often should, be doing something about virtually every issue.

Such a situation can be intoxicating, the opportunity to have fingers in so many pies is exciting and means one has the potential to skip from one issue to another.

For the hierarchical centralized organization Earth Balance had become, the consequences of this was inevitably to create weak and unfocussed management.

It was not surprising, therefore, that, for example:

- it had not proved possible to get the renewable energy system to work;
- the training unit was starved of investment and the management time needed to build on its success;
- the site was not marketed properly nor proper interpretation facilities developed;
- cow barns were not built and there was nowhere to over-winter stock;
- a membership structure was not created;
- effective financial management systems were not developed.

Each of these areas require particular skills and, as we have seen, addressing them holistically, with an eye to sustainability, makes each of them far more complex. Of course, there were many other difficulties, many of them external and unnecessarily created by local bureaucracies, that exacerbated these problems. But the structure, as discussed previously, of the organization and the nature of what it was trying to achieve compounded these problems. It is hardly surprising that one group of Trustees and effectively two managers could not implement the apparently simple concept of joined-up thinking.

Even with the benefit of considerable local knowledge and links it proved difficult for a small traditionally structured organization working in a small area to deal with sustainability. This must, therefore, raise questions of the ability of larger organizations and government, which use equally old, hierarchical and centralized structures, to implement the Habitat Agenda in a comprehensive way.

Funding Regimes

Will Hutton (1993) identified the short-term nature of funding for British business as a major problem for the economy. It discourages taking a long-term view and forces businesses to demand short-term viability.

Short-termism equally affects local government, every autumn central government begins the process that determines each local authority's financial allocation for the next year. Funding from trusts and statutory bodies for voluntary organizations is similarly for short periods and rarely for more than three years. Indeed, local authorities, because their budgets are decided yearly, have problems committing funding for more than one year. The difficulties this creates has at last begun to be recognized and some small steps taken to address it. Some European funding is now available for up to five years and the government has introduced its New Deal for Communities, which lasts for seven years.

The public and voluntary sectors have to live with this reality and adopt strategies to deal with it. However, for projects dealing with sustainability short term funding poses additional difficulties because:

- of the complexity of the problem and the fact that not only are new things being done, but they are also being done in a different way;
- sustainability is inevitably a long term issue;
- being a holistic approach, funding needs to be available for a wide range of issues and needs to be compatible and synchronized.

In practice, these factors had the following impacts on Earth Balance.

Complexity and Newness

In attempting to do what it was doing, Earth Balance was breaking new ground in a huge variety of ways, from the creation of social firms run by people with disabilities, to the creation of energy efficient buildings. Many agencies and funding bodies recognized this. They supported and even encouraged it, particularly those agencies, such as the Local Authority's Social Services Department, with a greater degree of flexibility in providing funding, or, in their case, purchasing services. However, some did not.

For example, Earth Balance attempted to capitalize on its success in creating sustainable small businesses by setting up a green business support agency. Some funders in the public sector found it difficult to grasp why this was different from normal business support.

They did not recognize that green businesses were inherently different and were opening up new markets or their potential to create jobs, despite Earth Balance's proven track record. As such, conventional business advisors were of little use, they had little understanding of these new markets and the value driven nature of the businesses. Neither was there a recognition that developing new environmentally friendly production techniques, or developing new markets, is inevitably more costly and difficult.

They did not recognize the opportunity to make use of Earth Balance as both an inspiration and a magnet for people interested in developing green businesses. A fact demonstrated by the number of people who approached Earth Balance, on average one a month, for help in setting up a green business. These approaches were from people who did not even think of using traditional business support systems and in an area with the lowest level of business start ups in England.

Sustainability is Long-Term

Sustainability, as the saying goes, is about living like you mean to stay. It is about taking the long view and making decisions based on tens of years rather than one or two. As we have seen, many funding regimes do not recognize this.

It was relatively easy to obtain capital funding to develop the site. It proved much more difficult to gain revenue funding to support new developments until they were able to provide the return that was needed to make the site viable.

This resulted in a rush to get Earth Balance fully developed as fast as possible so that its full income generating potential, from visitor income to bakery sales could be realized. Whilst this was happening, however, a site conceived as a functioning whole had to be viable whilst incomplete.

Inevitably this created a sense of nothing ever being finished and completed before the next phase of development was begun. Thus:

- the site was opened to the public before it had been properly interpreted or any attractions developed that people would pay money to see;
- the renewable energy system, although almost complete, is still not functioning;
- the bakery was opened before the market had been properly assessed and means of drawing in more stable incomes, through, for example, training, developed.

Such factors caused further compromises to be made between involving users and local people and the need to get things done.

Development also became the only means of maintaining staff and a viable cashflow. Thus not only was there an imperative to get the site developed as fast as possible, development itself became a key revenue strategy. Earth Balance had to keep moving or it would quite literally sink. Earth Balance's development was therefore far too often dictated to by funding needs than the original business plan, which became increasingly irrelevant.

Holistic Funding?

In Britain, funding is largely uncoordinated with time scales and requirements that often do not match together. There are also areas for which it is difficult to obtain funding.

This causes problems for the not-for-profit sector as a whole, but they are exacerbated by an organization attempting to put sustainability into practice.

Thus, Earth Balance found it extremely hard to find any source of funding for marketing and creating visitor attractions. Indeed, this is why the site opened without the attractions or the marketing effort that the original business plan envisaged.

Whilst it was possible to gain funding to gain organic status for the site, plant and maintain hedging, it proved extremely difficult to fund the construction of the cow barns required to over-winter stock. Without these buildings the land was trampled in winter and it was not possible to collect the organic manure needed to fertilize crops.

As a consequence, funding was always being squeezed from areas for which it was relatively easy to gain to those for which it was difficult. Many successful organizations have to become adept at subverting funding at the margins to achieve their goals. This was true of Earth Balance, to such an extent that some funders were beginning to raise questions.

This, the other funding problems already mentioned, and the fact that Earth Balance inevitably drew in funding and income from a wide variety of sources, made managing the finances of the organization even more difficult and complicated. A further factor that, as already mentioned, contributed to the financial failure of the organization.

The Lessons for Community Balance

Of course, with hindsight better management, more supportive agencies and more luck, Earth Balance could have overcome many of the difficulties set out previously. However, because the Trust ultimately failed the test of financial viability, does not mean it was a failure. As has already been outlined it achieved a great deal and has left a lasting legacy.

Furthermore, the scale of the task set by the group that came together in 1990 to form what was to be Earth Balance should not be underestimated. It was not alone in wanting to set up a sustainability centre. At around the same time there were at least two other similar initiatives in the North East of England that received funding to develop their ideas. Despite involving some highly skilled and respected people, neither of them got beyond the feasibility stage.

However, lessons need to be learnt to ensure that progress to wards a sustainable society is made.

Community Balance is a development from Earth Balance carrying on the work it began helping local people create sustainable communities. As such in some ways its remit is more limited, in that it does not have responsibility for running the site, but in some ways much larger. Although Earth Balance was working with local communities, its ambitions were far more constrained than those of Community Balance by its focus on the site.

Although having a different focus, Community Balance is also attempting to show how we can live our everyday lives sustainably. Thus the particular issues that confronted Earth Balance in trying to achieve this are likely to affect us. So what are our plan to deal with these issues?

Participation

Earth Balance's experience indicates that participation is essential, Earth Balance worked best when it was present, and worst when it became marginalized as a victim of short term expediency.

At the outset, the urge to value people was seen as crucial and a hallmark of the organization. It provided people the opportunity (often in unconventional settings, such as Earth Balance walks around the countryside with over 20 people) and the security to contribute.

For Community Balance, the need to involve people and help them own the project and the process towards sustainability is, if anything, more vital than that of Earth Balance. Indeed, it has identified community capacity building as the first issue it needs to address.

Community Balance has begun to carry out a wide variety of pieces of work that aim to address this issue:

- it is supporting a group of local people to covert an old school along ecological lines that will promote community enterprise, particularly among young people. This will be a practical resource providing space for community action;
- setting up community environmental project led by local people. It will train unemployed people to carry out environmental improvements and look at the feasibility of developing community enterprises in organic food production and ecological landscape design;
- training a group of unemployed people in community work and employing them to work with community groups on topics of their choice and to develop community action plans. Those trained will, in the new jargon become effectively local social entrepreneurs. This will give local people the ability to gain relatively well paid work for which there is an increasing demand. They in turn will support the development of community groups and provide the catalysts around which the capacity of local communities to act can be built;
- building on Community Balance's success in setting up community arts groups and running community festivals through the creation of Creative Balance. It will help people consider issues of sustainability and health and develop creative abilities and self confidence.

These projects will help to improve participation locally in a wide variety of issues. But an equally important issue is the participation of local people in Community Balance itself.

The Sustainable Cities Research Institute of the University of Northumbria initially hosted the fledgling Community Balance after the demise of the Earth Balance Trust. During that year, with funding from the National Lottery's Community Fund, Community Balance developed its future work plan and strategy for helping local people achieve sustainability. It also began developing a membership and set up an advisory group made up of local people.

After the first year, and after three years funding had been secured from the Community Fund to implement its programme of work, Community Balance was launched as an independent organization. It became a Company Limited by guarantee and is currently in the process of applying for charitable status.

Practically, participation is a reality within Community Balance, with most of the above projects having been originally developed from the ideas of local people and community groups the organization works with.

However, structurally it is not yet that different from the former Earth

Balance, except for one important respect. All of Community Balance's management committee live in the area Community Balance operates in, as do all but one of the staff. They all, therefore, have a direct stake in its future success and have first hand knowledge of its impact. For example, one management committee member, who lives only 100 yards away from Community Balance's office, stated that her reason for joining the committee was to play a part in ensuring there was something positive in the area for her children and grandchildren.

Although still structured in a relatively traditional way, Community Balance plans to evolve into something quite unique. To avoid the problems faced by Earth Balance Community Balance proposes two developments. The first concerns Community Balances internal form of democracy.

Involvement in the political process in Britain is of a very low order and there is considerable talk of the 'democratic deficit'. Only 28.7 per cent of the electorate voted in the last round of local government elections in one of the wards near Earth Balance (Wansbeck District Council, 2000). Not surprisingly, it is areas like Wansbeck were the numbers of socially excluded people are greater that have the greatest democratic deficit.

Various efforts have been made to address this deficit, to make people more involved in elections and participate in the political process, but to little effect.

The value of involvement is increasingly being recognized in Britain and now citizenship is being addressed by the National Curriculum set by government for schools. However the challenge facing Community Balance to develop true participation is still great.

Developing good communications, by supporting people to participate, openness and a whole range of other factors, can increase participation. To this end, Community Balance produces a regular newsletter, has its own web site, has developed wide ranging partnerships with community and statutory groups and regularly sends out information on a variety of projects it is developing.

These can undoubtedly make a difference, but Burnheim (1985) suggests forcibly that it is the very form of democracy that we have decided to use that minimizes participation and maintains elites in power.

He believes that electing representatives to serve our interest is a fundamentally flawed process, as Community Balance members will effectively do. It can result in people making decisions about issues they have no concern about, un-representativeness and poor decision making.

To overcome this problem, he suggests decentralizing decision making and the creation of agencies that are localized and focus on specific issues. He also suggest that instead of elections to select representatives, we return to the democratic process people would have recognized 200 years ago, that is random selection of representatives from members or a community or group who will be affected by the decisions made. Such a process ensures people are genuinely representative and that people are making decisions about issues that affect them. It also means that their decisions are not affected by electoral pressures to be popular or to avoid contentious issues. It removes the possibility of cliques mounting take-overs and the development of power elites.

However, there does remain the issue of knowledge and ability to make decisions. Training and support can in part overcome this, so that individuals become knowledgeable about the issues they are making decisions about.

Such a system has been developed to select the majority of members of the Council for a social investment society, Shared Interest on an experimental basis. It proved very effective in bringing forward people who would not have stood for election and creating an effective representative group.

The government has also announced that it intends to use random selection for membership of Patients Forums which will monitor the National Health Service (Department of Health, 2000).

Of course such a system of selecting management committee members would be very radical and untried. As well as raising concerns about the knowledgeability and skills of people to make decisions, there is the additional issue that, as management committee members, such people would bear responsibility for the actions of the charity.

As a first step, it would therefore seem wise to use random selection to create a group of people to form a Council, as in the Shared Interest model. They would monitor and oversee the decision of a more traditionally selected management committee. From this they could develop in a number of different ways. They may take over the selection of the management committee or to set strategic objectives. The management committee and staff would then implement this strategy.

The second major difference concerns size and breaking away form a hierarchical management model to a more federal approach. As the organization develops, and it begins to address more issues it will set up projects such as those outlined above to develop local people's capacity to act.

However, it is not Community Balance's aim to retain direct control of all these projects or to become a large organization managing a wide range of project, as happened to Earth Balance. As with the example of the community enterprise centre, it will often be supporting local people and helping them to set up their own structures to develop new projects that are not controlled by Community Balance. Alternatively, as is planned with Creative Balance, it may well initially manage a new project with the understanding that this is a temporary situation.

Each new project would have its own advisory groups and their own

Councils made up of those directly effected by the project. As the project establishes itself, the advisory group will become the Management Committee with its own Council. How this will be done is described below.

A Holistic Approach

Compared to Earth Balance, Community Balance has the luxury of not having to get such a large critical mass of activity before it becomes viable to fund a large complicated site.

We can therefore adopt a more incremental approach. As has already been alluded to, this will mean developing a core that will develop and support new initiatives, some of which will be initially managed directly and some will be independent from the outset. We have developed plans after extensive consultation, for developments in a number of other areas from recycling to youth work, some of which have been outlined above.

It is our intention that we will develop projects in these areas that will eventually become separate autonomous projects. Such a process will result in a spider plant type of organization as envisaged by Gareth Morgan (1993). For example, Creative Balance will initially be directly managed by Community Balance, in partnership with other agencies. However, after its first three years, it is our intention that it should set up its own management structure but, if it sees fit, be part of the Community Balance federation.

Community Balance will then become a federation of organizations linked by a shared aim and mutual interdependence. It is planned that federated members will have a say in managing the core, Community Balance. To ensure that such a federation does not become unbalanced, it will be crucial that no one member organization becomes so powerful that it can dictate the direction of the whole or cause it to fragment.

In this way, the spider plant will begin to address as many issues as is deemed necessary. However, because each plantlet is autonomous, they will retain focus and flexibility. Furthermore, the failure of one of the plantlets, which is almost inevitable given the complexity and newness of what we are trying to do, will not bring down the whole.

Funding and Agencies

Here it will be more difficult to address directly the problem. We may be able to alter the approach of agencies locally; it is clearly beyond our reach to alter the behaviour of funding bodies or national organizations. Only in collaboration with other agencies can we hope to have any influence on them.

However, since Earth Balance was first envisaged, sustainability, as an issue, is of a much higher profile. Furthermore, as already discussed, funders are becoming more flexible and able to consider longer-term funding.

Because Community Balance does not have a site to develop, it will also be easier for us to develop activities for which funding is available and wait until it becomes available for others.

A more autonomous structure will make it easier to manage funding from a large number of sources, and to set up financial management systems that are workable.

Thus, although the problem will not go away, a different structure and the ability to be more flexible and responsive should help minimize its impact.

In Conclusion

Earth Balance showed that a sustainable approach, although not without difficulties, was possible to implement. It demonstrated that adopting the Habitat Agenda at a local level and the principles of LA21 can have a much greater impact than traditional approaches, even with relatively small amounts of funding.

We hope that we can learn from Earth Balance's experience and develop new methods of making sustainable communities a reality. Communities that will benefit the lives of all their members. Key to the promise of sustainability, and the holistic approach it requires, is developing new ways of people working together and valuing each other; ways that are decentralized and empowering so that we can truly engage the skills and talents of all in the drive to creating a sustainable society that reflects all their needs and wishes; ways that are therefore more able to deal with the complexities of sustainable development.

References

Audit Commission (2000), *Local Authority Performance Indicators, 1999-2000*, Audit Commission, London.

Blair, T. (1997), Speech given at the New York, UN General Assembly Special Session on the Environment, 23 June.

Burnheim, J. (1985), *Is Democracy Possible?*, Polity Press, Cambridge.

Department of Health (2000), *The NHS Plans*, London.

DETR (Department of the Environment, Transport and the Regions) (1998), *A Better Quality of Life*, HMSO, London.

DETR (Department of the Environment, Transport and the Regions) (1999), *SRB Challenge Fund Guidance Manual*, DETR, London.

DETR (Department of the Environment, Transport and the Regions) (2000), *Indication of*

Deprivation (draft), DETR, London.

HM Treasury (2000), quoted in 'North-South Divide Now Rekindled by Enterprise League', *Financial Times*, 29 September 2000, London.

Holdgate, M. (1996), *From Care to Action*, Earthscan, London.

Hutton, W. (1993), *The State We Are In*, Cape, London.

Lowe, J. (1998) *Regenerating Neighbourhoods: Creating Integrated and Sustainable Improvements*, Foundation Series, Joseph Rowntree Foundation, York.

Morgan, G. (1993), *Imaginization – The Art of Creative Management*, Sage, Newbury Park.

Northumberland County Council (1998), *Northumberland Economic Review*, Northumberland County Council, Morpeth.

Northumberland Health Authority (1999), *1999 Statistical Profile. Information for Primary Care Groups*, Northumberland Health Authority, Morpeth.

One North East (2000), *Regional Economic Strategy for the North East: Unlocking Our Potential*, One North East, Newcastle upon Tyne.

Selman, P (1998), *Local Sustainability – Managing and Planning Ecologically Sound Places*, Paul Chapman Publishing, London.

Twine, F (1994), *Citizenship and Social Rights – The Interdependence of Self and Society*, Sage, London.

UNCHS (United Nations Centre on Human Settlement) (1996), *The Habitat Agenda*, UNCHS, Nairobi.

Wansbeck District Council (2000), *Personal communication.*

Wilkinson, R.G. and Marmot, M.G. (eds) (1998), *Social Determinants of Health – The Solid Facts*, WHO Europe, Copenhagen.

Wilkinson, R (1997), 'Health Inequalities: Relative or Absolute Material Standards', *British Medical Journal*, no. 314, pp. 591-5.

Wilkinson, R (2000), 'Inequality and the Social Environment: A Reply to Lynch et al.', *J Epidemiol Community Health*, vol. 54, pp. 411-3.

Chapter 17

Agenda 21 and Sustainable Development in a Complex Environment: Venice and its Lagoon

Ignazio Musu

Introduction

The municipality of Venice has initiated a Local Agenda 21 process with the aim of identifying a sustainable development model on which general consensus could be achieved. A number of research projects have been promoted to support the whole process and to provide the basis of the attempt to understand the desired sustainable development model. This paper summarizes the results of this research effort.

The relevance of the 'Venice case' lies in its being an emblematic example of the complex interaction between economy, society and the environment. In the Venetian case, the problem of sustainability can be specifically defined as the problem of the relationship between economic development and the joint preservation of a unique combination of cultural heritage and an environmental asset represented by the city and the lagoon ecosystem.

The problem of the sustainability of development is embodied in the possibility of creating and maintaining a model of economic activity and human life which is structured in harmony with, and not in opposition to, this complex lagoon environment.

This paper will illustrate the complex net of interactions between physical, environmental, cultural heritage preservation and economic and social development. It will show that the difficulty of a fruitful approach in terms of public participation is increased by the number of institutions involved and by the fact that Venice and its lagoon are viewed as international public assets.

The Lagoon of Venice: A Complex Local Environmental and Social System

No other biological species can interact with the environment as can man, in whose hands lies the possibility to alter the balance between the evolution of the social system and that of the biological ecosystem. This capacity is at the root of the complex problems of interaction between economy, society and the environment. The 'Venice case' is an emblematic example of this type of complex interaction.

As a result of the historical evolution and of a debate that has been underway for years (Costa, 1993; Dorigo, 1972; UNESCO, 1969), an awareness has matured regarding the centrality of the problem of the relationship between development and the environment to the future of the city. In recent years, this awareness has taken on the form of the request for sustainable development. In this case, the problem of sustainability is specifically defined as the problem of the relationship between economic development and the lagoon ecosystem. Today, this relationship is facing a number of problems because of the transformation undergone by these two components.

Venice is a city made up not only of its historical centre, but also of a mainland portion, lagoon islands and a coastal zone. The lagoon is the unitary environmental reference context for urban Venice and the term of comparison to take into account in the analysis of the sustainability of local development. Although the historical, artistic and monumental assets of the historical centre take on particular importance, the peculiarity of the latter is still determined by the fact that it is built on the lagoon.

It would be mistaken to believe that without Venice the lagoon would be an ecosystem with greater quality and value than at the present time, since without Venice, but with an intense anthropization of the mainland, sediments would have caused the lagoon to disappear. Not only has the existence of Venice saved the lagoon, but it has transformed the lagoon into a wetland whose natural value is unique in the entire world, precisely because it not only contains a natural heritage but also a living city with a related and unique cultural heritage. The maintaining of this fragile equilibrium between a city, urban structure and environment is a specific objective of the sustainable development of Venice: it has been, and will always be, an 'unstable' equilibrium which is at one and the same time subject to dangers and open to opportunities.

The main reason for its instability derives from the characteristics of the lagoon environment (Rinaldo, 1998; UNESCO, 1995). Indeed, the lagoon is, by definition, an environment in a state of unstable equilibrium due to the combination of two groups of factors: those coming from the land and those from the sea. Their interaction allows the lagoon to exist and, at the same time, threatens its very existence. The rivers, carrying detritus and sediments, pose the threat of filling in the lagoon (countered by the Venetian Republic by the diversion of the rivers to the sea); but, if too much space is left to the excavating force of the sea's currents, the erosion processes threaten to turn the lagoon into open sea in the long-term.

Two further factors should be added which increase the relevance of the physical problems in the Venice lagoon: the action of subsidence and eustatism, that is the lowering of ground level and the rising of sea-level. The increase in the average ratio of sea level to ground level, which can be attributed mainly to subsidence (lowering of ground level) in the past, but also to eustatism (rise in sea-level), has caused an increase both in the average number of times which the historical city of Venice is called upon to face the phenomenon of high water as well as in the average level of the high tide itself. Erosion and flooding are the main consequences of the modifications in the hydrodynamic structure of the lagoon, which have taken place and which continue to occur as a result of human intervention (Rinaldo, 1998).

Venice has lived with the phenomenon of periodical flooding in the form of the so called 'high water' throughout the centuries but the city was also designed with the objective of reducing the impact of this phenomenon to a minimum. Subsidence in the past and the threat of eustatism in the future due to climatic changes have produced a crisis in the relationship between the city and high water. The likelihood of exceptional flooding will increase. This not only exacerbates the damage to the physical structures of the city, thereby increasing the need for very expensive maintenance and architectural restoration work, but will also create increasing problems in maintaining a normal lifestyle in the city. A solution to this problem involving some kind of separation of the lagoon from the sea, albeit temporary and flexible, would have some impact on economic activities and on the environment. The reduction of this impact to a minimum is one of the most important challenges for the sustainable development of Venice and its lagoon.

Throughout history, the criteria to be adopted for the preservation of the lagoon have been the subject of debates which obsessed and divided the ruling class of the Venetian Republic. The very objective of maintaining the lagoon has been subject to different interpretations for the last 400 years. However, until the 1800s, differing opinions had not yet caused the breakdown in the historical assignment of a dual function to the lagoon; i.e. of satisfying a civil function (the protection of Venice and also its military defence) at the same time as an economic one (the development of the Republic's commercial power).

Venice's entry into the industrial era, starting from the second half of the nineteen century, began to establish a distance between the objective of preserving the lagoon, a goal of a typically environmental and hydraulic nature, and the objectives of economic and social development. Today, the likelihood of possible conflict between the goals of maintaining the lagoon ecosystem and the goals of economic development is on the increase.

The modifications made in the morphology and, in particular, erosive processes have had an impact on the natural lagoon environment (Torricelli et al., 1998). The amount of the lagoon's surface area which is occupied by the valuable unique natural structures which correspond to the Venetian names *barene* (salt marshes), *ghebi* (little channels), and *velme* (shoals) has decreased from 20 per cent at the beginning of the twentieth century to less than 8 per cent. This reduction is linked to the above-mentioned effects of erosion, but also to past reclamation works in areas which are fortunately now undergoing natural restoration.

The load of general pollutants and nutrients discharged into the lagoon from the industrial area and the drainage basin has reached a level exceeding the lagoon's self-purification capacity. In the past, this led to an increase in the likelihood of the phenomenon of macroalgal bloom with the possible negative effects of anoxya in the water and of atmospheric pollution. Furthermore, it increased the level of stock pollutants in mud and sediments. Other aspects of the environmental decline of the lagoon are the existence of abandoned dumps and of high-risk industrial plants. The cumulative effects of past industrial waste disposal from Porto Marghera and solid urban waste also remain within the lagoon.

Some improvements which have taken place in the environmental situation of the lagoon are the result of increased concern on the part of the public and of institutions for the protection of the natural lagoon environment. However a comprehensive sustainable plan for the lagoon environment is still lacking. The fact that the lagoon is an anthropized wetland establishes a series of limits to a purely naturalistic protection plan. From another complementary perspective, the lagoon, as a protected natural area, can be considered a resource within a project for sustainable development. In the long term, the reduction in pressure on the lagoon environment resulting from human activities will be obtained by making changes in technology and in the production structure of the economic activities in Venice, in the lagoon and in the mainland drainage basin. The development of an appropriate production structure and technology is the essential core of the model of sustainable development for Venice.

Venice and the Industrial Society

Venice's entry into the industrial society produced a model of economic development which, from the second half of the nineteenth century to the first half the twentieth century, has been based upon material production. A crisis in this model came about in the 1980s with an overall reduction in employment almost entirely due to the material production sectors and, in particular, to the decline in the industrial pole of Porto Marghera. Industrial employment losses have continued in recent years.

Material production still bears some importance in the Venice municipality. However, international specialization together with high environmental and location costs make it unrealistic to predict an expansion of material production whether in the historical centre or in the coastal zone of the city. Some material production could play a role in the model of sustainable development in these parts of the city as well. Examples are the high quality agricultural activities existing on the islands, sustainable fishing, minor shipbuilding and ship-maintenance, building restoration and maintenance, traditional and high quality handicrafts, special traditional products such as Murano blown and handmade glass and lace-making in Burano.

The main problem concerns material production related to heavy industry concentrated at Marghera on the mainland portion of the city. In Marghera, compared to the 1960s, when the industrial area reached its employment peak, the workforce has more than halved: the number of workers has dropped from over 30 thousand to 13 thousand (Rispoli et al., 1998). Today Marghera is in a crucial transitional phase. The potential of activities connected to the post-industrial phase and to immaterial production is discernible in the project for a Science and Technology Park. Factors of location advantage for the activities of industrial transformation still persist as long as an adequate infrastructure system allows this area to act as a link between the sea and a broad international market in the mainland. Among the location factors at stake for the future of industry in Marghera, environmental constraint plays a central role. There can be no doubt that future investments will not be made in risky plants. Prospective plants will have to minimize their environmental impact and the areas available for location will be subjected to adequate environmental restoration work.

Conditions related to environmental impact and the level of risk to human health will play a particularly important role in the strategy relating to the chemical industry. Choices are not necessarily limited by decisions relating to the progressive elimination of oil traffic from the lagoon, since the chemical plants could also be supplied by pipeline. The significant decisions are related to the fact that existing plants are obsolete and high-risk. The alternative between decommissioning and radical (and obviously expensive) renewal is posited with increasing urgency. A decision seems to have been made in favour of the second line of action, that is restructuring with a highly acceptable level of environmental compatibility.

A further problem is determined by the fact that Marghera is an industrial area which would not be correct to define as coastal. Indeed, it is not directly located on the sea but on the lagoon; the real problem lies, therefore, in the future of the port as a lagoon port. With a viable commercial port, it would still be possible to conceive that Marghera could have an industrial function characterized by converted and clean production. However, if the port functions fail, there will be no future for Marghera as an industrial area.

The structural composition of the port functions has changed radically over the last ten years and will change again in the future. Future development will move towards increasing both the importance of the commercial side and passenger traffic, with the port section for passengers located in the historical centre. The main problems lie in the channels required to allow the ships passage through the lagoon. The experience with the *Canale dei Petroli* (Oil-Tanker Channel) shows that the excavation of channels entails the risk of increasing erosion. Moreover, the possible increase in the frequency and level of high water, within a global context of climatic change making a rise in sea-level increasingly likely, raises a number of problems which must be resolved to guarantee an adequate connection between the sea and the lagoon shoreline on which the commercial port is located. An important condition for sustainable development will be the compatibility between port activity, the preservation of the lagoon's hydro-geological equilibrium and the interventions aimed at protecting Venice from high water.

Towards Sustainable Tourism

Tourism is one of the economic activities recording the greatest growth at a global level both in terms of revenue and in terms of employment, even though it is characterized by seasonal peaks and by a production structure based on unstable contractual relationships. The growing tourist demand can, in turn, be linked to an increase in per capita income and to the international expansion of economic growth. An increasingly important sector of tourist demand is directed towards the cities of art and the historical centres within wider urban areas. Venice, a city of art that is unique in the world, is the natural recipient of this growing tourism demand. Furthermore, it is a demand which knows no limits since a visit to Venice is on the everyone's agenda, circumstances permitting.

It is, therefore, completely natural that tourism is the economic activity which has had the most success in Venice and which continues to develop with the favourable market drive. Furthermore, it is also equally evident that its historical centre is the feature which attracts an increasing number of tourists to Venice. The main concerns are focused precisely on the effects of the pressure of tourism on the historic centre. More than three million residential tourists and about six to seven million day-trippers annually visit Venice's historical centre.

Day-trippers to the historical centre can be classified in three categories

(Van der Borg and Russo, 1998): *traditional day-trippers* who visit Venice from their place of residence; *indirect day-trippers* who visit Venice starting from another location which is the real destination of their trip; false day-trippers or *commuter day-trippers*, that is, tourists who, for economic reasons, stay in areas on the outskirts of the historical centre, or even on the mainland in the same municipality of Venice, and restrict themselves to visiting the historical centre during the day.

The growth in the number of day-trippers belonging to the last two categories is a clear indicator for the expansion of the 'Venetian' area for accommodating tourists; i.e. of an area which allows commuter-trips to Venice's historical centre in only one day. This area already extends far beyond the boundaries of the municipality of Venice, above all along the littoral areas to the north and south of the lagoon.

The development of day-tripping tourism already prevails over the development of residential tourism in the Venetian historical centre. This structural transformation in tourist demand creates the majority of problems, both in relation to the city's economic development as well as in terms of policies for managing the tourist phenomenon.

The residential tourist has a greater impact in terms of spending than the day-tripper: the average daily spending in the historical centre of the former is almost double the latter's. In this sense, residential tourism is preferable to day-tripping. On the other hand, day-tripping is what causes the most negative effects of congestion, environmental pressure and wear and tear on monuments. In terms of day-trippers, the costs involved in the city's use are potentially greater than the benefits produced in terms of income, since day-tripping generates earnings which generally fall outside the area producing them.

In Venice's historic centre, a conflict has arisen between tourism and services for the resident population. Tourist demand makes the costs of these services very high and the growing amount of non-residential tourism makes their quality very low. The unchecked development of a spontaneous scenario characterized by the expansion of mass tourism and day-tripping could well become unsustainable in the sense that, in the long-term, it seriously threatens the survival of the monumental, artistic and environmental heritage which forms the very basis for producing the tourist demand. This threat to sustainability must be projected very far into the future and thus is not perceived by the producers of the tourist supply. Perception of the threat requires a very low rate of time preference over a very long period involving future generations and a much larger community at a global level.

The scenario for sustainable tourism development requires a policy for transforming tourist activities into an economic base which contributes to financing the maintenance of Venice's infrastructure, monumental, artistic and environmental capital. This is an important goal since it is becoming increasingly unlikely that the national and international community will make resources available for the maintenance of Venice's monuments and environment unless they perceive that there is a corresponding contribution from the earnings generated by the local exporting economic base; if they perceive that those who profit from this activity are the same as those who benefit from the results of efforts for maintaining the monumental, artistic and environmental capital without incurring any costs. Operators outside the municipality, and even outside the region, enjoy benefits from being located at an accessible distance from Venice's historic centre. For these operators, Venice constitutes a positive externality, hence they should contribute to the maintenance of Venice's cultural and environmental heritage.

Various instruments can be used to achieve the goals of sustainable tourism (Van der Borg and Russo, 1998). One important instrument is the regulation of flows. In Venice, the potential bottleneck created by the limited routes of access could be the instrument to work on in order to manage such flows: access routes are so well defined that they can be considered completely controllable. However, the historic centre of Venice is not, nor is it intended to be, a mere destination for tourist visitors or for people involved in tourist activities. Indeed, it is, and should remain, the centre of a differentiated set of economic activities and, therefore, a place of residence and access for people working in such activities. In these circumstances, the regulation of access of tourist flows cannot be managed along the same lines as visitor access to a natural park. Access control may be better achieved through the introduction of accommodation bookings and car-parks at the terminals and through incentives which guarantee the visitor a series of facilities and discounts on urban services ('multiservice card').

A second set of instruments should be aimed at upgrading supply to meet standards of higher quality in such a way as to solicit the demand for it. Included in this set of instruments are those designed to improve accommodations provided by the hotel structures, to improve the quality of the museum offer, and to organize artistic events, catering to different types of cultural demand, by planning and spreading them over a broader time period. To satisfy this cultural demand, Venice is already endowed with an artistic 'capital' which provides the required comparative advantages.

A Capital of the Information Society

The development of the tourist industry illustrates the most evident and natural way in which Venice's entry into the post-industrial era is taking place. In contrast to material production, its immaterial economy shows no signs of contraction in employment.

However, it is the mainland portion of the municipality, rather than the Venetian historic centre, that tends to integrate with the model for the immaterial economy's evolution in the whole metropolitan area. Some service activities which were traditionally located in the historic centre are strongly attracted towards the mainland: the headquarters of the public administration and the university, for example.

The most striking result of the macroscopic imbalances and contradictions produced by Venice's inclusion in industrial society is that it has led to the weakening of Venice's historic role as a capital city, which it was formerly assured by its cosmopolitan and inter-cultural dimension and by the use of the sea as a large communication network. From the 1920s to the 1950s, Venice's ruling economic class tried, initially with success, to transfer economic, entrepreneurial and financial resources into the venture for strengthening the connection between Venice and industrial society, availing themselves decisively of public support. In the post-war period, the plan for industrial expansion became a more explicitly public planning exercise but it came up against important changes in the international division of labour, the crisis in public enterprise due to increasing political corruption, and the emergence of heightened environmental awareness. The specific Venetian model entered into a period of crisis. The result was the 'passage from the long networks of the Venice-capital to the short networks of Venice-island' (Rullani and Micelli, 1998), tourist mono-specialization and a crisis in the large functions of exchange and services of the city.

In post-industrial economies it is, by definition, at least theoretically possible to develop large networks of production and exchange without also involving the movement of physical goods. The material content per unit of economic value produced is continuously reduced and there is a corresponding reduction in the use of the environment per unit of value produced. The immaterial economy is, structurally speaking, in greater harmony with the environment compared to the industrial economy.

Cities become the favoured places for the growth of the immaterial economy. Indeed, the role of large cities is closely connected to their capacity to play a leadership role in one or more functions which are typical of the post-industrial economy. In Venice these opportunities are especially open to the historic centre which is also provided with new means for escaping its inherently insular nature. In fact, the physical boundary formed by the lagoon is no longer as significant in terms of the criteria for communication networks in the immaterial economy as it was in the industrial era.

The growth of immaterial specialization can occur in many cities. This will cause much competition between cities for securing the role of 'capital' in the new post-industrial economy. It must be noted that entire cities – not just portions of cities – are in competition, and, even less so, just historic centres. Venice offers 'reference material' of cultural, artistic and environmental goods, which constitute a sum of location advantages for firms operating in immaterial production. These are important factors when selecting locations but their importance will not automatically guarantee that this choice of location will automatically come about.

A set of necessary conditions might cause a critical mass of operators and firms in a whole series of advanced sectors of immaterial production to 'elect' Venice as the capital city of that type of activity. This would require the functioning of a combination of different services, from transport services, to those relating to residence, financial services, telecommunications and services in the personal sector. Within a framework of co-operation with firms and of project financing, political intervention should promote an adequate 'infrastructuralization' of the city. This entails the provision of networks of infrastructure to allow the city to satisfy the requirements of developments in information and communications technology, but it also means that Venice will be able to supply services in the personal sector (education, health, culture) at required international standards of efficiency. Wealthy people who work in high value-added immaterial activities will be able to choose to live in Venice's centre even if this is relatively expensive. But to foster this, to the high costs of residence must correspond high quality services to support production activities and personal and family residential life.

The endeavour to attract activities involved in advanced immaterial production to the Venetian historical centre must overcome a further obstacle which tourism does not face. While for tourism Venice's uniqueness can be exploited in a positive manner (every person in the world wants to and, at least up to a certain point, is willing to pay to visit Venice, which means that potential tourist demand is practically infinite), for the location of high value added immaterial production, this same uniqueness can only be exploited in a relative way. Moreover, low quality tourist activity does not require particularly qualified 'human capital'; hence tourism can in principle more easily integrate with the features of the existing population than other more advanced immaterial activities, since it requires fewer adaptations in terms of mobility and changes in the qualifications of the resident population. Spontaneous specialization in tourism constitutes, of itself, a powerful incentive to avoid adapting the quality of services to the standards required by activities of high value added immaterial production. But a higher quality tourism will help to develop an advanced immaterial production in the Venetian centre specialized in the fields of production of cultural goods and environmental protection.

Actors and Institutions in the Agenda 21 Process for Venice

The complexity of Venice's problem is highlighted in the form of an overcrowded and dispersed network of actors: governance problems are addressed by a multiplicity of actors who do not form relationships of mutual co-operation as much as might be possible (Dente et al., 1998). The existence of composite structures for co-ordination (typically the Co-ordination and Control Committee that was set up with law 798/1984 and is known as the *Comitatone*) has not been successful in reducing the overcrowding of the network.

In similar situations in which formal participation is blended with a great deal of inexplicit pressure, the risk of overlapping veto powers which increase the probability of stalling in decision-making is quite natural. In this respect, the Venetian case represents, or has until now, an example of the failure of an intervention model based on inter-institutional co-ordination from above.

Two conclusions can be drawn regarding the institutional context required for the sustainable development of Venice (Dente et al., 1998). The first is that it is necessary to avoid overemphasizing the 'specialty' of Venice's problem. If the problems under discussion are perceived as problems only insofar as they arise in the Venetian context and insofar as they are specific to that context, it becomes increasingly difficult for a cooperative process between actors to emerge for achieving a shared and long-term vision on which to base programs of action. With a restricted and specific scope for defining the problems at stake, it is more than likely that each of the actors will believe that his/her particular interests are being unilaterally sacrificed in whichever comprehensive solution is proposed.

In reality, the factors of complexity in the Venetian problem arise from the impact on the specific situation of the global transformations currently in progress. These range from more general changes, such as the passage from an industrial to a post-industrial society, with the related consequences in terms of structure and production and market methods, to more specific changes, such as the effects of climatic change, new models of international sea borne transport and port organization, the change involved in the transformation of tourism into an activity of mass consumption, and the potential of new technology in immaterial production which is more beneficial to the environment.

Confronting the challenges posed by these epochal transformations makes it easier to escape the impasse of a zero-sum game, in which only a conflict of interests emerges, and to move on to a non-zero-sum game in which the possibility of mutual advantage in embracing the opportunities for change can be identified.

The second conclusion is of a more typically institutional nature. It results from the fact that inter-institutional co-ordination needs to find its own legitimization, not so much at an abstract level claiming to be complete and rational, but in the proof of the emergence of social consensus which involves all of the actors with interests and opinions to express regarding the problem of Venice. This can be achieved by giving a voice to all stakeholders in the process of Venice's sustainable development who have the right to be asked to assign a value, either for its use or its existence, to the 'Venice-good' and to the lagoon ecosystem in which it is incorporated. This is precisely what a Local Agenda 21 process is expected to do.

However the problem in Venice is rendered even more complex by the fact that, among the interested voices, we have not only the local community but also national and international stakeholders since the preservation of Venice and its lagoon takes on the properties of a 'global public-good'. Whether in terms of politics or of public opinion, the international community often makes its voice heard on the problem. This happens in an episodic way, regarding specific events, usually events considered dangerous and to be shunned, such as exceptional flooding. Whatever the occasion, this contribution is important because any expression of international public opinion helps local public opinion avoid an egocentric position by perceiving Venice's value for the whole world.

Any Local Agenda 21 process must take into account the need to combine points emerging from local debate and those deriving from the concerns of the national and international community. The institutional body bearing the responsibility for the decision-making process should include representatives of all these levels. It should also follow a methodology aimed at framing any specific decision within a more general scheme of sustainable development in order to preserve the consistency of the whole process of intervention in such a complex natural and social environment. This means that the coordinating institutional body must assume a true leadership role in the process, and be able to balance the need for decisions to implement projects, the need for transparency in information and procedures and the need for facilitating a social consensus regarding both the goals and the means of the eventually accepted sustainable development model.

References

Costa, P. (1993), *Venezia: economia e analisi urbana*, Etas Libri, Milan.
Dente, B., Griggio, C., Mariotto, A. and Pacchi, C. (1998), 'Governare lo sviluppo sostenibile di Venezia: elementi per un percorso di progettazione istituzionale', in I. Musu (ed.), *Venezia sostenibile: suggestioni dal futuro*, Il Mulino, Bologna, pp. 343-98.
Dorigo, W. (1972), *Una laguna di chiacchiere*, Emiliana, Venice.

Rinaldo, A. (1998), 'Equilibrio fisico e idrogeologico della laguna di Venezia', in I. Musu (ed.), *Venezia sostenibile: suggestioni dal futuro*, Il Mulino, Bologna, pp. 101-46.

Rispoli, M., Stocchetti, A. and Di Cesare, F. (1998), 'La produzione materiale nel Comune di Venezia', in I. Musu (ed.), *Venezia sostenibile: suggestioni dal futuro*, Il Mulino, Bologna, pp. 185-242.

Rullani, E. and Micelli, S. (1998), 'La produzione immateriale a Venezia: verso una economia del post-fordismo', in I. Musu (ed.), *Venezia sostenibile: suggestioni dal futuro*, Il Mulino, Bologna, pp. 299-342.

Torricelli, P., Bon, M., Mainardi, D. and Mizzan, L. (1998), 'La biodiversità nella laguna di Venezia alla base di un progetto di sostenibilità', in I. Musu (ed.), *Venezia sostenibile: suggestioni dal futuro*, Il Mulino, Bologna, pp. 47-100.

UNESCO (1969), *Rapporto su Venezia*, Mondadori, Milan.

UNESCO (1995), *La Laguna di Venezia*, UNESCO, Venice.

Van der Borg, I. and Russo, A.P. (1998), 'Per un turismo sostenibile a Venezia', in I. Musu (ed.), *Venezia sostenibile: suggestioni dal futuro*, Il Mulino, Bologna, pp. 243-98.

Chapter 18

Illegibility: A Milieu for Participation

Bohuslav Blazek

The Middle Ages, the Renaissance and Postmodernism: Three Landmarks of Legibility

The spatial organization of a European medieval town had a generally understandable logic (Wallis, 1967). In the centre, there were the spiritual and secular focal points, i.e. the church and the town hall. This hub was surrounded by the public space of the market place. The spokes of the main streets radiated outwards from this node towards a perimeter formed by the town wall with two or more gates located at an easy walking distance from the hub. Every radial street had its own unique atmosphere determined by the kind of artisans who worked and lived there. Each street offered peculiar services and goods, which generated typical sounds and smells. Visual signs played a subordinate role since the visual aspect was not the dominant one. Street names, if they existed at all, derived from the crafts or trades pursued in the neighbourhood or from the place's physical features (Blazek, 1995a). Something similar was also true of the artisan; it was not his shop sign but his reputation that led people to seek out his services.

The entire space was organized from the point of view of an observer at street level. The pedestrian or the horseman and their respective paces and points of view determined the street's scale. The passing of time was marked by the sound of bells from the cathedral or by cannon shots from the ramparts. Finding one's way in this centripetal town structure was not difficult: the town was easily legible both to its own inhabitants and to visitors from outside.

Since the Renaissance, understanding of what constitutes the legibility of town structures has been changing step-by-step (Blazek, 2000). Gradually, visual features were adopted as keys to a rational, noble and legible order. The lines, circles and right angles of elementary geometry guided the imagination of town builders. The bird's-eye view became the ultimate vantage point, because it was considered akin to the vantage point enjoyed by the Creator. It stood for a new view in which Man substituted himself for God and created his own world. Exalted high above a corruptible and never completely perfect reality was the Plan. The ideal city was identical to its representation on the plan.[1] Throughout Europe old towns were recast in new molds and new towns and castles built by would-be philosopher kings: modern-minded princes or former condottieri and generalissimos flush with new money and new power. To find his bearings in a modern town, the visitor needed a street map along with visual references to determine where on the map he was. Inevitably, the new geometrical order spilled over into the natural world as attested by the greatly imitated gardens of Versailles.

Towns, lacking the new 'optical logic' were considered barbarous, old-fashioned, irrational and, last but not least, illegible. The process of change reached one of its cataclysmic highpoints in Haussman's boulevards cutting straight wide swaths through the medieval body of old Paris. Le Corbusier's architectural dictates and the urban wasteland of La Défence are other sad triumphs of the same spirit.[2] Straight lines, right angles and wide thoroughfares paved the way for the onslaught of the Machines.

The de-sanctified, deformed, and alienated world was proclaimed to be objective reality. Only what we see really exists and the only part of reality that gives us satisfaction is something that is indiscernible from the Plan. Architectural photographs in professional journals are more or less devoid of people and traces of human life (Blazek, 1998a). Smells, sounds and tactile sensations, or such things as personal reputation attested by neighbours, are seen as anecdotal details having merely peripheral status in comparison with true Objective Reality. Deviations from this obvious perception are dismissed as childish and subjective, or branded as deriving from mental illness or antisocial attitudes.

A toddler exploring an attic, a hiker lost in a dark and pathless forest, a spelunker feeling his way through a cave after his light has gone out, or a blind man tap-tapping with his cane through an unfamiliar neighbourhood, all have something in common. They lack a spatial overview of their situation, every step forward or back can bring total surprise, and the direction in which they should proceed is not clear. They have no map, no central point of reference (except for their own body) and no sense of a periphery; there is no main road to which they can keep. In their situation, what they feel, smell, hear or intuit are valuable sources of information, although they are far from providing certainty.

Similar strategies of search – we could call them 'haptic' – are effective in our post modern world. You can forget about the bird's-eye overview in 'soft' social networks, in the suburbs of mega-cities, or on the Internet. If you evaluate these milieus through the optics of the orthogonal world you will find them extremely illegible and terrifying. However, if you accept them as legitimate phenomena you will find interaction with them most revealing.

Where Are We Now?

The present adult generation in Europe was born under the (declining) reign of an 'optical' spatial organization. Orthogonal architecture, enamoured of modules and repetitiveness, imposes habit: in fact, we become unable to perceive things as they are, and our concrete everyday world becomes psychologically invisible to us.

The more monotonous the man-made environment is, the stronger this slip into habit becomes. People living in beehive-like housing projects built during the communist era often fall prey to this perceptual disturbance. They have an impoverished, extremely unified and depersonalized perception of both the positive and the negative aspects of this environment. Thus, they have weak problem perception. Their eyes do not allow them to identify problems. Therefore they lack motives for conversation with their neighbour based on shared problems, a conversation which could well initiate the transformation of a haphazard agglomeration of people into a community.

More often than not, after a decision has been made to regenerate and 'humanize' such housing projects (in our country such decisions come mostly from far above), architects are unable to find a sufficient number of partners among local inhabitants. If you want to involve the local population, you must first open their eyes. Some may belong to the same political parties, but they are not aware of common interests rooted in the experience of their shared habitat.

As long as the fetishism of 'objective reality' still survives, a good stratagem consists in using a well-beloved instrument of this ideology, namely photography. The majority of people is still convinced that photographs show reality 'as it is'. The trick is to confront them with snapshots of local things which they have been unconsciously refusing to notice, pictures of suppressed phenomena. The best way to do this is in a group because of the group dynamics that come into play. In a group, people can help each other to liberate their latent creativity.

The situation in which some phenomena are suppressed is a dynamic one; 'dynamic' is used here in the sense common in psychoanalysis. In such a situation, when a person says that something is marginal, uncertain, illegible or even non-existent, it should be considered a symptom. What is stated, in fact, is that the person is bothered by it. A first hint regarding how to use eye-opening photographs: in a public space exhibit pictures of places and things in the town which the local people find illegible in this sense.

I have designed and tested a series of such methods for enhancing citizen participation, based on the use of photography. The theoretical basis for these methods was established by social ecology (Blazek, 1998b).

Methods for Social Ecology

Methods declaring themselves to be socio-ecological must be in accordance with the main experiences, insights, and principles of this discipline. Let us sum up the key features of these methods:

- participatory (taking into account the complementarity of the observer and the observed);
- enabling social intervention and, simultaneously, reflection about it;
- understandable to and, in principle, usable by lay people;
- harmless both for the observed and for the observers;
- using quantitative expressions only to structure the experience, but not for uncontrolled mathematical operations;
- dialogical (opening a dialogue within a group or a network of participants);
- problem-oriented, not academic;
- using scientists as partners;
- taking into account the target groups engaged in the procedure;
- contextual (adapted to a given environment);
- reflecting the tacit rules of the game;
- culture-bound and historical (born out of 'local' experience and tailor-made for a concrete set of historical circumstances rather than generic and automatically transferable anywhere);
- playful (closer to the mode of play rather than, for example, to the mode of work or struggle).

A first glance at this list will reveal that these methods are part and parcel of an *instrumentarium* of civic society. They imply that scientists and/or politicians may be respected and considered as partners but not deferred to as demigods.

In my view, social ecology should differentiate between three ideal types of context (which, as I understand are both system levels and phases in the evolution of the system itself), i.e. the 'countryside', the 'towns', and the 'world of media'. For a better understanding of the methods described below, it now suffices to say that the more the environment has the character of a countryside the more the methods should respect its typical face-to-face social structure, mixing kinship and neighbourhood. With more urban conditions you need more media intermediation, which is typical for the more formalized modes of communication between a vast number of people most of whom do not know each other personally.

Further Functions of Photography

Oddly enough, the representation of reality by photography has something in common with the representation of the population by elected politicians: in both cases there is an unfortunate tendency to consider the representative as more important than the entity represented, and to confuse him/it with reality itself.

Thus, civic society does not need photographs which people perceive as 'objective pictures' but photographs as counter-examples, undermining the unreflective popular theory of reality or helping citizens to doubt the paradigm (or, the social *a priori*), in which the invisible power is encoded. The angle from which these startling pictures were taken, is simply the angle from which the critical *Aha-Erlebnis* struck the photographer. Their aim is to make the viewer wonder: 'what on earth could this be?' These pictures are not intended as indicative statements but as interrogative, enigmatic 'ink blots' which, like a Rorschach test, elicit alternative answers, spouting from the perceiver's liberated unconscious. Thus, mere passive registration perception becomes participatory co-creation.

Such pictorial ideas do not purposely eschew text and are not meant to stand alone as 'pictures without words'. Neither are they mere illustrations of preconceived ideas. We are not dealing with a didactic approach that would lead pupils to the correct answers expected by their teacher. A symmetrical relationship of equal partners is a prerequisite for communication among mature citizens. 'Lecturers' and their monologues are not needed. There is even less need for the 'foreign experts' who arrive with methods designed in a context that is culturally and politically different, who are not interested in our Eastern reality, which they tend to consider a corrupted version of the brave Western world. Well-chosen, common-sense photographs of the local environment can help. That is, an urbanist can convince local inhabitants that he/she may be able to use his/her outsider position as a paradoxical vantage point for a fresh look at their daily reality.

Local photographs communicate to local citizens: we are aware that you already know what we are going to say; you just did not want to acknowledge it; you are the best expert regarding your own problems; your personal experience is crucial; every single one of you has a chance to make his or her personal contribution to the problem-solving process in your community.

This type of group or network experience is not tantamount to fabricated and manipulated consensus. People help one another to cast off conventions and say aloud that the king is naked. This liberating act creates a bond between people without making them into sectarians or fanatics. Creativity stimulated in this way does not produce ideas which are 'original at any price', but ideas which are subversive and, at the same time, socially constructive.

In this process, while the pictures help all participants to keep in touch with reality, verbal dialogue helps to avoid psychological blindness. The visual and the verbal code thus confront and fertilize one another.

Methods Based on the Use of Photography

The Strongest Oppositions

We begin with a well chosen set of photographs of local situations (we use 27 pictures of unique objects such as a church, of typical objects such as a farm, of psychologically invisible, and at the same time suppressed, 'ugly' phenomena, as well as pictures of what we call 'hidden beauties'). In a village or a small town neighbourhood, we then find about 15 local activists and ask them to select any one picture and find another picture which, in their opinion, is its strongest opposite. First, the numbers of these paired pictures (called dyads) are registered on a standardized form. Only then may brief verbal characteristics of the opposites be added (to avoid being 'locked in words alone').

We call the dyads which are repeatedly selected by the members of a group *strong opposites*. Typically, these strong opposites form thematically related chains or clusters. These provide an insight into the structure of the opposites shared by the local inhabitants, without the introduction of potentially misleading abstract terms.

Individual photographs can also be evaluated according to the verbal characteristics they elicit. You will find that some pictures are described only in positive terms (*symbols*), some elicit a uniformly negative response (*targets of criticism*), while others are ambivalent (*objects of debate*), or produce neutral reactions and purely descriptive terms (*grey zone*). It is a good idea to start a public dialogue with the ambivalent objects to initiate debate.

This method was used in more than ten Czech villages.

Problem Photographs

A wide selection of psychologically invisible problematic features of a town or a large town section (typically we use 60 pictures) is exhibited in a public hall, local library, etc. Under the pictures are brief critical comments, each covered by a piece of paper. Visitors are asked to think about why a picture was included in the exhibit before they uncover the texts. They are asked to comment on the texts which they find inspiring and add their name and address if they wish to collaborate with the planning team. Their comments can be used for a preliminary assessment of their possible contribution.

This method was applied in two Czech towns, Pribram (Blazek, 1995b) and Cheb (Blazek, 2001a), and on two large housing estates, Southern City in Prague and Scampia in Naples (Blazek et al., 1999).

Contrasting Milieus

In a 'foreign' milieu, e.g. in a village, a large set of pictures of typical local situations is made. This set is then halved randomly. The participating people are then separated into two subgroups, which are each given one subset of pictures. They are asked to study each photograph and identify features which they find 'foreign' to, or untypical of, their environment.

The spokesman of a subgroup would show one photograph and present the findings about it, then comes the other spokesman's turn, etc. Repetitive observations are weeded out.

This method was also used as a pedagogical tool in courses of social ecology (contrasting sets from villages in Estonia, France and Sweden).

Double Mirroring

In two comparable localities, pairs of thematically similar photos are made. Then, these dyads are presented to citizens of both localities in order to make their own place more visible to them by means of the similarities and differences in the paired pictures.

This method was use for Pribram versus Weimar (Blazek, 1995c).

Traces of Time

To the most invisible structures controlling our social life belongs the time order (Hall, 1984), or, rather a set of such orders (corresponding to historic periods).

To help uncover these hidden temporal phenomena, we again use dyads, triplets, etc., of thematically narrow pictures from two or three or more comparable localities.

This method was used in Copenhagen, Prague and Luxembourg City in connection with exhibitions in these places.

Anti-Guide

Group participants receive an explanation of the advantages of an approach that begins with the illegible aspects of their town (Blazek, 1999a, 1999b). Then, they are asked to set out in different directions on a short exploratory walk and make a note of every illegible thing they observe. In the course of a subsequent group presentation, various inherent elements of the illegibility (e.g. its fragmentary character, dysfunctionality, strangeness, absurdity, paradoxical message, etc.) are identified and discussed.

New photographs of the most intriguing things are made, complemented by short characterizations. They are then publicly presented as a sort of local anti-guide. This anti-guide can also be posted on the Internet.[3]

Coda

It would appear that the concept of citizen participation came to Central and Eastern European countries from the West after the fall of the Iron Curtain. Nevertheless older domestic traditions of citizen solidarity and civic involvement did exist. Only after the Communist coup d'état of 1948 were these home-grown traditions systematically rooted out, especially in the countryside.

When we look back on our recent history or even more deeply into our medieval one, we find many phenomena which can be interpreted as authentic strides toward the greater participation of citizens in the public sphere. First of all, we find the democratizing impetus of the Czech reformation with its stress on believers' right to full participation in worship (Hussite Utraquism). This led to an early translation of the Bible, the rapid development of the Czech language and uncommonly widespread literacy. In the Czech village, we find the deep-rooted traditions of communal solidarity that inspired Frantisek Cyril Kampelik's invention of mutual-help security banks for small farmers in 1861.[4] And we find a more recent instance in J. S. Machar's parallel invention of the psychodrama. The Czech writer Machar and the Austrian psychiatrist Moreno both lived in Vienna and apparently thought along the same lines although possibly they never met (Blazek, 2001b).

Paradoxically enough, apostles who bring participatory techniques from the West often do not reflect upon the fact that they are transplanting methods which are based on their own home-grown experience and traditions. Participatory ways, rather than simply culture-bound, are community-bound. There is no kind of citizen participation other than local participation. No-one else can represent your participation because it is an existential act. Moreover, participation is neither an individual nor a mass affair. Rather, citizen participation is community-based and is, in effect, the very way in which a community becomes a social subject. Thus, a community without its own participatory ways of seeing the world and coping with its challenges is not a real community at all.

It is no wonder that imported methods for enhancing citizen participation, appropriated and mechanically applied by local bureaucrats, tend to be perceived as artificial and foreign by local citizens. Some consider them a kind of service manual which can be absorbed and transformed into a routine (a most alienating exercise as you may well imagine).

In some Czech towns, there are mayors who, shortly after the democratic turnover, thankfully accepted the offer of a Western NGO and/or government, promising to set up planning weekends (*Partnership*, co-financed Western grant agencies), to facilitate public transactions of their planning documentation (*Agora*, a Dutch outfit), or to help draft regional strategic plans (*Centers for Communitary Work*, co-financed by *Open Society Fund*). After a promising initial period, the truly active local administrators usually found themselves disillusioned because no observable changes in the civic life of their towns had come about. Even worse, administrators who had ample reason to fear citizen participation discovered that they were completely safe, because the actual meetings, in their atmosphere not unlike the famous 'parties' organized by car dealers, were 'consummated' without leaving any trace on local public life.

Just one last example. The so called 'SWOT analysis' has been an obligatory part of bottom-up strategies promoted by the Czech Ministry of Agriculture and the Ministry of Local Development for SAPARD. This approach consisted in obtaining knowledge from local experts that was unavailable from official sources, concerning important facts and potentialities, both negative and positive. For a sensitive, creative procedure of this kind, participants must be chosen extremely carefully, since they need to be both genuine insiders and, at the same time, independent and open thinkers. The team should be an interdisciplinary one. During the sessions a free and open atmosphere is of the essence. This necessitates the exclusion of local authorities to eliminate a potential reason for self-censorship. In a country where real problems were systematically suppressed for four decades, one must proceed especially carefully. Otherwise the deeply ingrained habit of 'constructive criticism' asserts itself and the entire exercise becomes a farce.

My first objection is that, on a regional level, neither the number of participating experts nor their professional qualifications were revealed. Many of the anonymous texts resulting from the above mentioned process included half-truths parroted after the local media, and samples of wishful thinking by the local patriots and boosters. However, despite these biased ingredients, an imposing amount of voluntary work was performed and the first step towards genuine cooperation at regional level was taken.

Although criticism resulting from the aforementioned process was relatively harmless, it appeared unacceptable in the eyes of the ministers of the two resorts involved. Without any need to coordinate their action, they independently arrived at the same decision. They ordered their respective deputies to shred the arduously compiled, and often truly consensual, reports and to write (over one weekend!) a new synthesis, based on official 'theses' and 'documents'. The product of their weekend toil is taken off the shelf every year, slightly re-touched to show 'progress', and brazenly presented as the fruit of the vaunted bottom-up analysis. Needless to say, these digests have little to do with actual problems, and are unsoiled by any input from the grass roots. Amazingly, this act of superb arrogance has never been critically mentioned in the media (except for my own articles). I am sorry to report that the EU administrators were satisfied with this report, which was completed just-in-time. They did not notice that the 'bottom up' approach was only simulated. In my personal contacts with some of them, I always received the same answer to my queries as to whether they could apply a little pressure on our post-communist 'organs': 'It's your problem'.

It is hard to disagree. Nevertheless, should you decide to import SWOT analyses into a social environment in which public debate is still considered an uncouth difficulty that must be kept out of sight behind a Potemkin village, do not sit on your hands when the process is turned on its head.

This paper points out the existence of a thesaurus of original and home-grown participatory methods along with the theoretical tools for their evaluation in one Central Eastern European country, the Czech Republic. I dare to conclude with an appeal: *Dear Western colleagues, please stop and consider before you export participatory methods to us, that is those designed by and for people with a radically different historical experience. However well meant, sophisticated and lavishly financed by your governments and your grant agencies they may be, there is a good chance that they will not take root as transplants in the post-communist environment.*

Notes

1 For the very first regulatory plan drawn up for a town located to the North of the Alps, namely for Albrecht von Wallenstein's beloved Jicin, cf. Blazek (2001a).
2 More on the history of the reading of Paris see: Stierle (1998).
3 For the Czech town Jicin see (alas, in Czech only): www.jicinsko.cz/landscape/mamapapa/jicin-jinak-000.htm.
4 In parallel, Kampelik's idea was invented and popularized by the better known German reformer Raiffeisen.

References

Blazek, B. (1995a), 'Hlas ulice', *Kriticka Priloha Revolver Revue*, vol. 3, pp. 129-36.
Blazek, B. (1995b), *Vizualne zachytitelne problemy Pribrami*, EcoTerra, Praha.
Blazek, B. (1995c), *Vyznamova opozita v Pribrami a na pozadi srovnani s Vymarem. Socialne ekologicka studie*, EcoTerra, Praha.
Blazek, B. (1998a), 'Svet casopisu o bydleni', *Kriticka Priloha Revolver Revue*, vol. 10, pp. 122-5.
Blazek, B. (1998b), *Venkov/mesta/media*, Sociologicke nakladatelstvi, Praha.

Blazek, B. (1999a), 'Princip necitelnosti', *Souvislosti*, vol. 3-4, pp. 39-65.

Blazek, B. (1999b), 'Necitelnost mest', *Stavba*, vol. 7, p. 12.

Blazek, B. (2000), 'Skryty teror primky', *Kriticka Priloha Revolver Revue*, vol. 16, pp. 11-23.

Blazek, B. (2001a), 'Od renesancniho kondotiera k soudobemu urbanismu', *Kriticky sbornik*, vol. 20, pp. 49-53.

Blazek, B. (2001b), 'Urbanisticka prace jako socialni intervence', *Stavba*, vol. 5, pp. 10-3.

Blazek, B. (2001c), 'Participation: A Recent Phenomenon or a Tradition? Foreshadowing of Participation in Czech Past', in Proceedings of the Conference *EU Enlargement: Linking Civil Society, the Citizen and the State*, 21-24 November 2001, Berlin.

Blazek, B., Horky, I., and Mansfeldova, A. (1999), *Methods of Regeneration of Housing Estates. Final Report*, Czech Technical University and Foundation EcoTerra, Prague-Naples.

Hall, E.T. (1984), *Poza kultura*, PWN, Warszawa.

Stierle, K. (1998), *Der Mythos von Paris. Zeichen und Bewusstsein der Stadt*, Deutscher Taschenbuch Verlag, Muenchen.

Wallis, A. (1967), *Socjologia wielkiego miasta*, PWN, Warszawa.

Chapter 19

The Sustainable City and the Role of the City-Building Professions

Leonie Sandercock

Introduction

In this paper I develop a process-based rather than an institutionally-based approach to building the sustainable city. It is my belief that many of our institutions have failed us; that institutions are by definition always somewhat resistant to change; and that therefore we must look in other places for the inspiration for social transformation. Of course, institutional change is a very important question, but in our field it seems that the catalyst for institutional change is usually a challenge from the outside, from mobilized communities or committed individuals experimenting with new ways of doing things. This paper has three parts. First, I ask what are the main ingredients of a human sustainable city. Second, I ask what this means for the work of urbanists. Finally, I conclude with some remarks about the role of stories and storytelling in the work of the city and community building professions.

What Makes a Sustainable City?

I look around me, in my own city, and on my frequent travels, and what I sense is that people are searching for one or more of the following: diversity, community, and ecological sustainability. These contemporary urban quests are the sources of the positive energy that can build sustainable cities in the twenty-first century. I begin by discussing each of these quests and how they might reinforce each other.

The Search for Diversity

For the past 50 years, in British, North American and Australian cities, we have been deliberately, through planning and design practices, fragmenting our cities into homogeneous, isolated, self-contained spaces – suburbs, shopping malls, industrial parks. This tendency is also visible in European cities, from Paris to Rome and Naples, in the worst excesses of modernist city-building – the social housing projects on the periphery of these cities. Scampia, a peripheral neighbourhood of Naples, can serve as the local example of disastrous urban development, a dormitory mega-subdivision for 50 thousand people which Cerreta (2000, p. 5) describes as a 'nowhere land, the contradiction of the idea of a city... the expression of social fragmentation and insulation. Scampia is characterized by absences...'. One consequence of this kind of city-building is that most of us do not live the complexities of the city directly and physically, in where we walk or whom and what we see.

We insulate ourselves from encounters with those who are different, who are poor, or homeless, or recent immigrants. And then we fear them, because we fear what we do not see, what we do not know, what we have no way of understanding. So the people of Vomero, a residential area on the hill of Naples, fear the people of Scampia, without knowing them, and want to keep them out of their neighbourhoods. When such psycho-spatial dynamics develop in a city, it ceases to be sustainable and becomes a fortress city.

In my city, Melbourne, the metropolitan planning agency published a report on socio-demographic trends in 1998, titled, *From Donut City to Cafe Society*, which documented a reversal of locational preferences in the housing market which is beginning to have a significant impact on urban form. For the past decade, Melbourne has been undergoing a transformation of its urban fabric and a re-shaping of its pattern and direction of growth as a process of re-urbanization occurs. After 40 years of outward, low density suburban expansion, and the decline and hollowing out of the inner city (the Donut City effect), there are now significant counter-trends as young people (the 20-35 demographic) reject the suburban way of life in favour of the greater diversity of the inner city, while many of their parents are also selling up the family home in the suburbs once their children grow up, and are moving into inner city apartments, town houses, or historic housing stock which was built at medium density. Parts of the inner city which had been previously neglected, or abandoned, have suddenly been discovered as desirable places to live and have seen significant investment in renovation of older housing, conversion of industrial and office buildings to residential, and the building of new, high rise apartment buildings. A complicated mix of market forces, state policies, and individual preferences and social movements have driven this transformation, including the growing presence of immigrants and investors from East and Southeast Asian cities who prefer to live in more dense and lively neighbourhoods.

The shift in housing type and location preferences has been accompanied by two other changes: a boom in retailing, sporting, entertainment and cultural facilities in the inner city, and a vast improvement in the urban public realm as attention is paid to improving the quality of urban design of public space. While some urban analysts interpret this transformation with disapproval, as 'the city of spectacle' or the 'city of consumption', the reality is more complex. It is true that some of the people who have moved into the inner city are primarily focussed on a lifestyle of consumption. But it is also the case that the younger age groups want to live a different and less isolated lifestyle than that of their parents, and that this move back to the city embodies significant 'value shifts', including: the desire for a more convivial, sociable life than is lived in the privacy-obsessed suburbs; the desire to spend more time walking, cycling and using public transport than sitting in cars, which for some reflects a concern about sustainability issues; the desire to be among a greater variety of people, in terms of age, ethnicity, and income, than is possible in the essentially homogeneous suburbs; and that less tangible but nevertheless real attraction of urbanity, that enjoyment of the city as *oeuvre* (Lefebvre, 1996), the playfulness, surprise, unpredictability, spontaneity – yes, the spectacle – of urban life, especially the 'uncommodified pleasures' related to crowded streets, bright lights, energy, movement, the possibilities for anonymity as well as chance encounters, possibilities for learning just by looking and observing, the mixtures of stimulation and meditation.

This search for diversity and urbanity, expressed in the trends of re-urbanization and revitalization of downtowns and older inner city precincts, is not unique to Melbourne. It is happening in European and Canadian and some US cities and it contains within itself some conflicting desires. Some of the new apartment buildings are high security, vertical gated communities, whose occupants seem to be choosing to be in the city but not part of it, in terms of any sense of community. Others, however, become passionate defenders of the 'qualities of place' that attracted them there, including the history and memory embodied in the urban fabric, as well as advocates of the social, cultural and ethnic diversity of these neighbourhoods. And some have pursued this to its necessary public policy conclusion, for some form of state intervention to ensure that the property market does not completely dictate who can enjoy the newly discovered urbanity. The opportunity and the challenge exists to link this search for urbanity even more clearly with the other positive energies in the contemporary city, and to think about how to build more diversity into existing and future suburbs.

We need to know how to design 'border spaces', places where cross-border contacts between people from different walks of life are possible. I call these 'spaces of hope'. The major challenge to planners, as they assist in the re-urbanizing and re-vitalizing of inner cities, is to understand, and know how to consciously construct and protect, places where such interaction is possible.

The Search for Community

It was an interesting feature of late twentieth century urban life that there have been passionate struggles for the creation, recovery, or defence of community, world-wide. Even in the face of globalization, the life space of the local community has continued to assert itself and its claims.

In those cities which are the recipients of transnational or rural migrants, the membership of any one geographically defined community may change dramatically between one census period and the next, posing the challenge of creating and building community as well as defending it, and an increasingly important part of our work as urbanists/planners must be this work of community-building as well as city-building; that is, focussing on the social as well as the physical development of the city.

Now, community can mean 'my region or culture against yours'; my white Christian Australian/Italian/French culture against your (non-white, non-Christian) foreigners' culture; or my German or French culture against your Turkish or Algerian culture. Unfortunately, there is a long tradition of community-based movements which have been primarily inspired by exclusionary sentiments, whether based on race, ethnicity, religion or class (Sennett, 1970).

But there is more than one ideal of community, and Bell Hooks and Cornell West, as African Americans, offer an alternative to the exclusionary model in the American context:

> It is important to note the degree to which Black people in particular, and progressive people in general, are alienated and estranged from communities that would sustain and support us... We confront regularly the question: 'Where can I find a sense of home?' That sense of home can only be found in our construction of... communities of resistance... and the solidarity we can experience within them... As we go forward as Black progressives we must remember that community is not about homogeneity. Homogeneity is dogmatic imposition, pushing your way of life, your way of doing things onto somebody else. That is not what we mean by community... That sense of home that we are talking about and searching for is a place where we can find compassion, recognition of difference, of the importance of diversity (Hooks and West, 1991, p. 18).

Community, in the sustainable city, has to be inspired by the values expressed in Hooks' and West's writings; and by Mel King's work in Boston and beyond. For King, the whole purpose of our struggle, past, present, and future, is to 'create community', by which he means the human context in which people can live and feel nurtured, sustained, involved and stimulated. 'Community is the continual process of getting to know people, caring and sharing responsibility for the physical and spiritual condition of the living space' (King, 1981, p. 233). His work is informed by a vision of 'the city we can build together', but he also knows that moving towards this vision 'will entail some very uncomfortable experience as we root out our prejudices and confront our fears'. I am particularly interested in King's belief that 'we need, as individuals and as communities, to be about getting people to deal with the fears which immobilize us and bar us from our basic instincts towards growth, change, and harmony'. I will return to this idea that the search for community requires us to deal with fear, since the very attraction of community is its potential sense of belonging, and yet the dark side of that desire for belonging is its potential to exclude others who are deemed not to belong. The search for community is very much alive in the cities that we are all familiar with, but implicit within it are negative as well as positive energies. Our challenge is to recognize and work with the positive energies.

The Search for Sustainability

Part of that positive energy of creating community is the notion of caring about others, and sharing responsibility for the physical and spiritual condition of the living space. The search for ecological sustainability is becoming, and must become even more, a city-focussed quest. This case has been persuasively assembled by, among others, Peter Newman and Jeff Kenworthy (1999), who argue that a sustainable city must be a city of urban villages: that is, a compact city of far greater density than is the norm at present in Australia and North America, and it must be a city which has overcome its automobile-dependence. Step one, in their vision of the sustainable city, is the revitalization of the inner city, which is usually associated with community processes that have developed a new vision for an area. This vision is sometimes associated with strategies of housing rehabilitation, sometimes with historic buildings and streetscape preservation, street festivals and other community arts events, sometimes with the provision of low income housing to retain a mix of incomes, and investment in new businesses by innovative entrepreneurs. Finding the right spark for regeneration requires creativity and commitment by planners and urban managers, but it also, always, requires significant community input and effort, and is often triggered by community mobilization in defence of their life space.

Newman and Kenworthy note that while there are now strong market forces pushing inner city re-vitalization in some cities, that alone will not attract people back into the city if the streets are not safe and the schools are not satisfactory. Once begun, this kind of improvement in the urban public environment can become a signal and catalyst for broader regeneration. There are many inspiring examples of such efforts, from the well-known Brazilian city of Curitiba to European cities like Zurich, Stockholm, and Copenhagen, to Boulder and Portland in the US, and Toronto and Vancouver in Canada, examples which the authors describe as 'positive city-building processes rather than the city-destroying processes of dispersal, pollution, and community disturbance associated with automobile dependency'.

So far, I have outlined three components of the sustainable city. But I hope it is clear that this is not urban science fiction, in that the seeds of these changes have all been planted and there are enough demonstration projects in a wide range of cities and neighbourhoods to provide inspiration. The role of community mobilization has been critical in redefining a vision of the good city. The market is responding where it sees a profit to be made, most notably in inner city housing and consumption-based activities. But what of the role of planners and planning? What needs to change in professional practice?

Towards a Therapeutic Planning Practice

I have written elsewhere (Sandercock, 1998) of the need to shift from a modernist to a postmodern paradigm for the city-building professions. Here I want to focus on one aspect of that paradigm shift: the language we use as planners, and how that constrains the kind of work we might do to bring about transformations of values and institutions.

The language traditionally used in planning practice has been a rational discourse which explicitly avoids the realm of emotions – which is of course the stuff of storytelling. But surely it is bizarre to talk about diversity or urbanity without talking about memory, desire, spirit, playfulness, eroticism, fantasy. Or to talk about community without talking about longings and belongings, losses and fears, guilt and trauma, anger and betrayal. Or to talk about sustainability without talking about hostility and hope, compassion and caring, greed and nurturing. There is an ethics of city life and city death, a series of both everyday and long-term choices that get made and reproduced, and there is a corresponding ethical language in which to discuss such choices. There are desires and fears bound up in community building and a corresponding language of emotional acknowledgement. *I want to suggest that more and more of our work, if we want to work towards sustainable cities, will be bound up with organizing hope, negotiating fears, mediating memories, and facilitating community soul searching and transformation.* I would like to talk briefly about these activities – that is, about a more 'therapeutic planning practice' – for the remainder of this paper.

The Organization of Hope

Anastasia Loukaitou-Sideris (2000) and her students at UCLA recently concluded a participatory action research project in the Pico Union inner area of Los Angles, home now to large numbers of Mexican and Central American immigrants and refugees, an area which has experienced massive decline and disinvestment. Part of their approach was to research and record the multicultural social history of the area, and then to request a name change, from Pico Union to the Byzantine-Latino Quarter, as part of a process of creating a sense of identity, past, present, and future, to assist with community-building. This in itself is a very interesting approach. The name change begins a process of telling a new story about the neighbourhood, one which is redolent of pride in a diverse past, and hope for a sustainable future, which depends on the exercise of community-building. Their next step was to begin to work on the rehabilitation of small neglected public spaces which scarred the area, using the community's labour, and including children's involvement. Then they sought permission from and support of various public authorities whose own neglected spaces were contributing to the overall effect of neglect and abandonment. This is a story in progress, but it is also an example of turning around despair and passivity through community action.

Ken Reardon's work in East St. Louis is one of the most successful and inspiring models for the 'organization of hope'. Reardon (2000) tells the story of a ten-year university/community partnership, which has transformed one of the worst black ghettoes in the USA into an area which has attracted US$45 million of public and private investment in urban regeneration. This transformation process began ten years ago with one small action, namely the 'sweat', the labour of students and residents over one weekend to clean up two vacant, but trash-filled plots of land, and then to convert that space into a safe playground for children. Reardon gives us an old-fashioned story for a postmodern age: a story of heroism against impossible odds, with faith and quiet determination as the weapons, an inspirational story. Some of the lessons include the importance of participatory action research methods; of removing the fear of violence, which acts as a barrier to broader community participation; of securing the involvement of state and federal agencies; of ways of using the media strategically; and finally, of luring private sector investment back into the neighbourhood. But the overall lesson is that none of this would have happened without the faith, hope, and sweat of the quietly determined leaders and residents of East St. Louis. The result, a decade later, is that more than US$45 million in new public and private investment has come to this once-devastated neighbourhood and, in the process, more than 350 University of Illinois students have had a powerful, and for some, life-transforming, learning experience. This was a step-by-step approach to regeneration – what I have called 'a thousand tiny empowerments' (Sandercock, 1998). Some of the tools involved are technical: bubble charts, excel files, GIS, wall maps, interview schedules. But nothing would have happened if a trusting relationship had not been developed between the residents and students, which required openness and communicative skills on both sides. And the deeper meaning of the story is its inspirational quality, its description of a 'process of organizing hope'.

Negotiating Fear

Harvard Law Professor Gerard Frug argues in his book, *City Making*, that the single most important issue facing America's cities is fear, fear of strangers: and, yes, specifically, fear of the black stranger (Frug, 1999). Fear and hostility now also seem to be a pervasive feature of European cities which are experiencing significant immigration of people from different cultures. I have written about how the future of planning in polyethnic or multicultural societies requires a coming to terms with the existence of fear in the city, fear of the stranger/foreigner/outsider (Sandercock, 2000a, 2000b). The recent emphasis in the planning literature on more 'communicative approaches' for handling planning disputes (Innes, 1995; Healey, 1997), acknowledges the need for more process-based methods of conflict resolution, but their emphasis on rational discourse avoids the emotions at the heart of conflict, and thus often avoids the real issues at stake. I want to suggest a more therapeutic approach, which begins with an analysis and understanding of this 'fear of the other' and develops solutions which are processes for confronting these fears.

In a recently published paper I have discussed just such a case, in Sydney, Australia, where an apparently insoluble conflict between indigenous people and Anglo-Australian residents was eventually solved by an innovative practitioner who spent nine months creating the space in which these antagonistic residents could begin a conversation with each other, a conversation which ultimately led to greater understanding and the possibility of peaceful co-existence (Sandercock, 2000c).This kind of planning work, involving confrontation and dialogue and negotiation across the gulf of cultural difference, requires its practitioners to be fluent in a range of ways of knowing and communicating: from storytelling to listening to interpreting visual and body language. In such cases, in carefully designed public deliberative processes, the use of narrative, of people telling their own stories about how they perceive the situation, becomes a potential consensus-building tool for unearthing issues unapproachable in a solely rational manner. When the parties involved in a dispute have been at odds for generations, or come from disparate cultural traditions, or where there is a history of marginalization, something more than the usual tool-kit of negotiation and mediation is needed, some 'method' which complements but also transcends the highly rational processes typical of the communicative action model.

What also interests me about the philosophy underlying this therapeutic approach is the possibility of social transformation, of something beyond a merely workable trade-off, or a simple exercise in 'problem-solving'. Much of the negotiation and mediation literature, argues Forester (1999), remains economistic, more concerned with trading and exchange than with learning, more concerned with interest-based bargaining and 'getting to yes' than with the broader public welfare. But, just as in successful therapy there is breakthrough and individual growth becomes possible, so too with a successful therapeutically-oriented approach to managing our co-existence in the shared spaces of cities and regions, there is the capacity for collective growth. Or, to move from the language of therapy to that of politics, there is the possibility of social transformation, of a process of public learning which results in permanent shifts in values and institutions.

Mediating Memories

Another dimension of the work of building sustainable cities and communities involves a 'process of mediating memories'. All neighbourhoods have histories, and that accumulation of history is constitutive of local identity. Part of the work of community building involves invoking this history, these memories. But it should never be assumed that there is only one 'collective memory' of place. More likely, there are conflicting memories, and layers of history, some of which have been rendered invisible by whomever is the culturally dominant group. There is now some fine work being done by preservationist planners like Gail Dubrow (1998) and Dolores Hayden (1996) in exploring and acknowledging conflicting memories of place, and mediating those memories in community planning processes, in order to provide a more inclusive foundation for future community visioning.

An interesting example of recognition of the need to deal with memory in order for reconciliation, healing, and social transformation to occur, comes from Liverpool, England, a city which by the 1980s after two decades of economic decline, was on the brink of city death, with astronomical levels of unemployment, corresponding out-migration of young people, appalling race relations, and a hideously deteriorated and neglected built environment. How can a city regenerate from such despair and demoralization? There were, according to Newman and Kenworthy (1999, p. 328-9), apparently two catalysts. The first was a community mobilization around housing rehabilitation. The second was a major effort to combat racism, 'including removing this cancer from the police force...providing special opportunities for those from the black community...starting an arts anti-racist program; and perhaps of greatest spiritual and symbolic impact, opening the Museum of Slavery in the new Albert Dock tourism complex'. This award-winning museum shows how Liverpool was central to the slave trade. It graphically depicts the whole process of slavery, and names the many established Liverpool families who made their fortunes from slavery. 'The message for other cities caught up in inner city decline based on problems of race and dispirited neighbourhoods is encouraging. The implications for sustainability are obvious'. Here is a case where the telling of a buried story or stories provides some ground for healing a divided city, and in so doing, acts as a catalyst for regeneration and growth.

Stories and Language as Tools of Planning for Sustainability

I have argued that in working towards more sustainable cities we need new models of planning practice which focus on building communities and working with diverse communities to create the physical and socio-economic conditions for harmonious co-existence in the shared spaces of our cities and neighbourhoods. I have emphasized that such work demands, above all, communicative skills of a special kind: the skills of organizing hope, of negotiating fears, and of mediating memories (as well as the skills of design, of statistical analysis, and so on). This in turn requires a transformed language of planning, a language which acknowledges the emotional breadth and depth of the lived experience of cities: cities of desire, cities of memory, cities of play and celebration, cities of struggle. The tools of such a transformed language include the ability to listen to and to tell stories. We must be able to move back and forth in our planning work between critical/evaluative and narrative/receptive modes. We use stories as tools: to keep memory alive; to celebrate our history or identity; to derive lessons about how to act effectively; to inspire action; and, as tools of persuasion in policy debates.

I have provided some examples of this kind of planning work, from the US, Australia, and the UK. I have suggested that we can build the sustainable city by thinking of it as a process of a thousand tiny empowerments, each of which begins with apparently small interventions, but these interventions serve as catalysts which develop the momentum for a broader social transformation.

References

Cerreta, M. (2000), 'An Evaluative Approach for Promoting a Quality of Life-style According to Habitat Agenda and Local Agenda 21 Guidelines: The Experience of Scampia', paper presented to Chengdu International Conference on *Learning from Best Practices*, Chengdu, 16-18 October.

Dubrow, G. (1998), 'Feminist and Multicultural Perspectives on Preservation Planning', in L. Sandercock (ed.), *Making the Invisible Visible. A Multicultural Planning History*, UC Press, Berkeley.

Forester, J. (1999), *The Deliberative Practitioner*, MIT Press, Cambridge.

Frug, G. (1999), *City Making. Building Communities without Building Walls*, Princeton University Press, Princeton.

Hayden, D. (1996), *The Power of Place*, MIT Press, Cambridge.

Healey, P. (1997), *Collaborative Planning*, Macmillan, London.

Hooks, B. and West, C. (1991), *Breaking Bread: Insurgent Black Intellectual Life*, South End Press, Boston.

Innes, J. (1995), 'Planning Theory's Emerging Paradigm: Communicative Action and Interactive Practice', *Journal of Planning Education and Research*, vol. 14, pp. 183-90.

King, M. (1981), *Chain of Change*, South End Press, Boston.

Lefebvre, H. (1996), *Writings on Cities* [translated and edited by Eleonore Kofman and Elizabeth Lebas], Blackwell, London.

Loukaitou-Sideris, A. (2000), 'The Byzantine-Latino Quarter', *DISP* [Dokumente und Informationen zur Schweizerischen Orts-, Regional- und Landesplanung: Documents and Information on Swiss Local, Regional and State Planning], no. 140, January.

Newman, P. and Kenworthy, J. (1999), *Sustainability and Cities. Overcoming Automobile Dependence*, Island Press, Washington.

Reardon, K. (2000), 'Ceola's Vision', paper presented to *Planning as Storytelling Symposium*, Oberman Institute of Advanced Studies, University of Iowa, June.

Sandercock, L. (1998), *Towards Cosmopolis. Planning for Multicultural Cities*, John Wiley and Sons, Chichester.

Sandercock, L. (2000a), 'Negotiating Fear and Desire: The Future of Planning in Multicultural Societies', Keynote Paper, *Urban Futures Conference Proceedings*, Johannesburg, 14 July.

Sandercock, L. (2000b), 'Difference, Fear, and Habitus: A Reflection on Cities, Cultures, and Fear of Change', Keynote Paper, *Habitus Conference*, Perth, September.

Sandercock, L. (2000c), 'When Strangers Become Neighbours: Managing Cities of Difference', *Planning Theory and Practice*, vol. 1, pp. 13-30.

Sennett, R. (1970), *The Uses of Disorder*, Knopf, New York.

PART III
AN INTEGRATED APPROACH

Introduction to Part III

Fabiana Forte

Introduction

In ancient times, Aristotle believed that 10,000 was the optimum number of inhabitants for the 'ideal city'. Today, at a time when world population has reached about 6.1 billion people – and according to United Nations' forecasts, it will top 9.3 billion in 2050, more than two thirds of whom will be living in cities (United Nations, 2000) – cities such as Tokyo (with about 30 million inhabitants), Mexico City (18.1 million) or Bombay (about 18 million) show to what extent the phenomenon of 'urbanization' has assumed 'inhuman' dimensions.

How can these huge numbers of human beings live together in the same city? How, today, can a city be planned, improved and organized so as to guarantee a balanced and correct relationship between all the people who live in it and the physical/material environment which moulds it? How is it possible to reduce the widening gap between rich and poor, between 'up-scale' neighbourhoods and slums, between competitive areas and areas in crisis, within one city?

The articles which make up this third part of the volume attempt to provide some answers to a series of issues regarding human beings, the city, human and sustainable development.

As will be appreciated, these are complex subjects which can only be addressed and handled through an integrated approach that places the human being at centre stage.

Above all, it is the notion of 'human development' that we need to address (UNDP, 2001), paying greater attention to the way in which human beings live and the opportunities available to them, adopting a comprehensive view that embraces all aspects of life, including women and men, present and future generations, the people of the rich and disadvantaged countries, the strongest and the weakest, etc.

What is needed is a process of widening of opportunities to the benefit of all individuals and not just a 'favoured' few, so this means we are facing a problem of 'equity'.

Guaranteeing equal opportunities means allowing the participation of everyone in all areas of life: thus involving all human beings 'in depth' in economic, social, cultural and political processes. Therefore any act leading to exclusion, marginalization or discrimination is an obstacle to human development.

In this perspective, all human beings must be empowered to fully participate in productive processes, to access resources and a decent job, so that they can actively contribute to the improvement of the economic base of their city and country.

This naturally brings us to one of the core issues of our times: that of work, the need for job opportunities for all. And since the production aspect is important for every development policy, the fight against unemployment and hence poverty can remove one of the main barriers to development itself.

The concept outlined above was clearly expressed at the Copenhagen World Summit (1995) for Social Development, the first to have considered development as a global question, as a goal shared by all world societies.

The Declaration which resulted from this meeting, signed by 122 heads of government, identified *poverty, unemployment* and *social exclusion* as the three main signs of the serious imbalance produced by a development model which is not centred on the needs of all human beings. They are indeed three facets of a single phenomenon: inequitable access to opportunities – exclusion of large numbers of people from various aspects of social and economic life.

The exclusion of the majority of the world population is seen not only as the violation of rights but also as failure to tap into great potential for development. Poverty does not only concern those directly affected by it: it is actually an overall brake to the development of all.

Equity, productivity and participation are all relevant to human development and are inevitably interwoven with the notion of 'sustainable development' in its different dimensions (economic, social and cultural, environmental). In particular, equity, seen as the extension of opportunities to all human beings, concerns not only the present generations but also future generations who have an equal right to satisfy their needs and enjoy the same opportunities. Productivity, i.e. the growth of the economic system in which all human beings should have the right to participate, should come about through more efficient use of resources and respect of the natural ecosystem.

The ethics of responsibility (Jonas, 1990) on the part of human beings vis-à-vis their fellow humans and of humanity vis-à-vis Nature becomes the common denominator of human and sustainable development.

From a strictly technical viewpoint, we can no longer face the challenges of the different aspects/dimensions of development through partialized approaches, focused exclusively on economic, on environmental or on social factors. We must instead analyze and face these challenges through an 'integrated approach' enabling us to perfect new operational tools that can offer interdependent solutions.

And since the city has become the arena where these challenges are concentrated to the highest degree, we must begin with the city and the tools for its governance in order to change and improve this state of things.

Thus it is the theme of human beings and the city leads us to reflect on how and with what tools we can, today, in the third millennium, design a 'project' for an urban future that is both more human and more sustainable.

The City and Poverty: The Role of the Institutions

As we examine the wealth of figures, statistics and forecasts to be found in innumerable reports on various aspects of the quality of life in world cities, we are at once struck by the fact that a very large part of the population of our planet lives in exceeding poverty and degradation, stripped of all 'dignity' (United Nations, 1948, article 1).

But if we interpret dignity as the respect which each individual, conscious of his/her value, must feel for him/herself and translate into consequent behaviour, how can there be dignity where human beings do not even have the necessary tools for becoming aware of their own value and commit themselves to developing it?

Amartya Sen (1992, 1999) argues that poverty should be seen as an inability to realize the functions essential for human life: possessing an asset, or having the resources necessary to purchase it, is no guarantee of the capacity to utilize it in a beneficial manner. Affluence and its symmetrical term, poverty, cannot be described only in terms of having or not having, and are to be measured against what each individual manages to 'do' and 'be' – his/her 'capabilities' – the sum total of the alternative combinations of functions he/she is able to achieve. These functions range from the most elementary, such as procuring enough food and being free from avoidable diseases, to more complex personal activities or conditions, such as being able to participate in community life and possessing self respect.

The poverty affecting the numberless human beings who attempt to 'survive' in the city is certainly not the result of dignified behaviour by those who 'live in', 'reside in' and 'use' the cities, consuming their services, and reaping their benefits (Martinotti, 1993).

In the context of technological and economic globalization, it is by now a well-known fact that the growing marginalization of the so-called 'fourth world' is a phenomenon to be found in every large city, in its ghettos, in its slums, in its outlying areas prevalently inhabited by the unemployed, homeless, immigrants, etc. And they are destined to suffer increasing poverty, not only in terms of income deprivation but above all in terms of 'deprivation of capabilities', which only the local agencies, the cities themselves, can fight by rethinking and reconstructing the social and civil infrastructure of communal living from the 'bottom up'.

Making a 'commitment' to improve the living conditions of all human beings who are flocking to the cities in increasingly large numbers means placing the dignity of all in the forefront.

From its origins, the city was not created just to satisfy utilitarian needs but was rather the greatest material realization of the settled world. That is why monumental public and religious buildings were erected together with squares, boulevards and open spaces, embodying the concept of 'living together'. They were places binding *together* people and things (Leone, 1998).

Each city expresses an atmosphere through its architecture, its street plan and its monuments as well as a language of its own, in order to impart a specific character to the behaviour of its inhabitants. But the city is not only an artificial space of buildings, roads and services that moulds the life of its inhabitants. The city is also, and above all, what its inhabitants do with it and make of it; it is the behaviour of the community itself, its projects, aspirations and values.

And it is only by beginning with 'values', by coming back to explore them, and by attempting to de-codify them, that we can move towards a form of urban development that is both more human and more sustainable.

A primary role in this regard will be played by institutions, since we need common reference values in order to reduce inequalities, mediate conflicts, organize civil cohabitation and prevent marginalization.

Today, the different cities in the world must face a host of challenges: they must have a strong economy, be efficient from a functional point of view, be equitable in the social sphere, protect their cultural heritage, improve their possibilities of fruition, etc.

All these challenges can be met not through a single isolated act but through constant action, through a constant testing of the processes underway, a careful search for innovative solutions, a continuous effort of imagination, design and creation of an 'urban future' which blends the expectations of tomorrow with more immediate requirements.

The construction of a 'sustainable urban future' therefore requires a new project for the city (Hall and Pfeiffer, 2000), one that places emphasis on the role of civil society and its various forms of organization. It is highly unlikely that local authorities, business associations and individuals will manage to obtain significant results working alone.

Only a 'coalition' logic, founded on the joint selection of goals and the construction of shared tools for their pursuit, will make it possible to face the challenges outlined above. This will be possible through participatory mechanisms which take into account the needs and aspirations of all as well as diverse points of view, integrating them into the construction of collective shared choices aimed at tracing a course not *for* the city but *of* the city, seen metaphorically as a 'network of interacting subjects and collective players' (Camagni, 2000).

In this sense, tools such as the forums of Local Agenda 21 become indispensable since they are *processes of voluntary improvement promoted on the local level* through which it becomes possible to define, in a direct and participatory manner, the course to be followed *together* in order to concretely achieve a community's sustainable development, allowing all, including the weakest, the poorest and the most marginalized, to have their say.

All this naturally requires critical and interpretative capacity in order to make the most suitable choices – *a capacity for evaluation*. And that is why the evaluation process becomes essential: to evaluate means, indeed, to compare, ponder, define preferences, order values, assign priority. Evaluation is not only a technical tool for assisting decision-makers but also a means for promoting greater critical awareness of the course which a community wishes to follow (Fusco Girard, 2000).

A Global Call to Action

The requirement for implementing an integrated approach to the problems of sustainable human development was clearly expressed in the Habitat Agenda (UNCHS, 1996); in the introduction we read:

> We recognize the imperative need to improve the quality of human settlements, which profoundly affects the daily lives and well-being of our peoples. There is a sense of great opportunity and hope that a new world can be built, in which economic development, social development and environmental protection as interdependent and mutually reinforcing components of sustainable development can be realized through solidarity and cooperation [...] Human beings are at the centre of concerns for sustainable development, including adequate shelter for all and sustainable human settlements (§§ 1 and 2).

We should also note that, despite increasing worldwide urbanization – with all its attendant negative or positive consequences – the 'hope' of being able to construct a new world must be felt by the community.

Hope means faith in the possibility of achieving a good or a benefit. It is important to note that this faith that we can actually choose a more desirable direction – despite the many challenges which the city of the new millennium faces – is clearly expressed by the Habitat Agenda.

The Habitat Agenda is, in fact, a global appeal for action, which, within its framework of objectives, principles and commitments, offers a 'potentially' positive vision for sustainable human settlements. And it is here that the message of hope may be transformed into actions, in things to do, in commitments to be made, at various levels of governance.

The will to act, to make a commitment to improve the quality of life in the cities of the whole world expressed in this document, is even more compelling because it places human beings at the heart of the sustainable development issue – all human beings – without any distinction regarding race, colour, gender, age, religious beliefs, political orientation, etc.

Hence the attention paid especially to the weak, the poor, the homeless, the immigrants who must be offered equal opportunities for access to housing, work and spiritual, social and cultural growth; equal opportunities for participation in collective choices; equal rights and obligations regarding the protection of natural and cultural resources.

Adequate shelter for all and *sustainable human settlements* are two intertwined questions. They are also linked to goals of economic and social development and environmental protection – with the basic elements of sustainable development itself.

As to the technical tools necessary to solve the problems attendant on advancing urbanization, the Habitat Agenda, among other pleas, stresses the need to improve and rationalize urban planning and the evaluation of its outcomes, using adequate indicators in the light of 'best practices' (Fusco Girard, 2002).

In particular, the assessment of the impact of the various strategies adopted to achieve sustainable development plays a vital roll as a method of analysis, testing and appraisal of the results achieved in the implementation of the Habitat Agenda. This can best be done through a set of indicators which, while allowing for the specific conditions of different regions, are comparable and utilizable at different levels of governance.

This requirement becomes particularly significant in view of the need for a common base for a critical assessment of the effectiveness of the actions undertaken. But above all, a common set of indicators should enable us to create a benchmarking system and thus adopt an 'integrated approach' to the process of evaluation. Such a comprehensive approach, as opposed to a host of distinct technical procedures, each aimed at solving specific problems (project costs, real estate values, multicriteria/multidimensional assessments, etc.) would make it possible to evaluate economic, social and environmental impacts to improve spatial choices in human settlements.

The City and Sustainability: Different Approaches for a Common End

The need to meet the various challenges posed by increasing urbanization on a global scale is witnessed not only by a number of international charters and declarations but also, and above all, by a common awareness of the widespread 'unsustainability' of life in the various cities of the world, whether they be poor, still needing to satisfy primary needs, or affluent, whose problems – stemming from exclusive focus on economic development – while certainly different, are no less serious.

Beginning with a general awareness of the unsustainability of life in the various cities of the world, we can interpret the contributions in this part of the volume. The authors, each in his or her own specific sector of expertise (economists, planners, evaluators etc.), as 'technicians' dealing with the city and its future state, offer different replies to the many challenges which the problem of sustainable human development poses and which the cities of the third millennium are called upon to face.

In particular, these contributions focus on different issues which, while having the issue of sustainable development as their common ground, involve specific methods tested in different regions throughout the world.

A key feature is the greater focus on 'planning' and its associated 'evaluation'; a requirement highlighted by several authors in order to design urban strategies able to meet economic, social and environmental needs alike, and to provide durable solutions.

In particular, Nicole Rijkens-Klomp, Martin van de Lindt, Marjolein B.A. van Asselt and Jan Rotmans, when defining the quality of life in the city as social and cultural, economic and ecological quality, interpret the city itself as a dynamic system of *stocks* and *flows*, whose sustainability is described in terms of the interaction between economic, ecological and social capital. Based on this interpretation, the authors propose an innovative tool for planning the city, using an 'integrated approach' where participation of the various stakeholders takes a central role. The goal of this approach is not so much to search for the best solution, but rather to check the effectiveness of the various city management policies against the overall objective of improving the quality of urban life. This approach is well illustrated by the pilot project conducted in the city of Maastricht.

The need for appropriate evaluation methods able orient choices between different urban development strategies is expressed clearly in the paper by Peter Nijkamp and Francesca Medda. They stress the fact that in Europe, where cultural identity and the sense of locality have become crucial factors, cities are increasingly attempting to turn to account their cultural heritage through strategies blending conservation and development. But the choices regarding the conservation of our historical and architectural heritage are complex and necessarily require 'guidance'. The different evaluation techniques available for this purpose are not always comprehensive, and so it becomes necessary to develop new approaches. With this premise, the authors, stressing the requirement for more integrated use of the evaluation tools already available, propose an innovative approach based on a *combinatorial assessment methodology*. This is a procedure that combines several different methods (carefully chosen on the basis of the specific nature of the data and goals pertaining to each evaluation issue) highlighting their complementary nature, in order to improve the 'consistency' of the decision-making process. This procedure is illustrated by a comparative study of the evaluation of different urban renewal projects.

Also focusing on an integrated approach to the problems of urban planning, Nanne Engelbrektsson and Jan Rosvall present a detailed history of the Swedish planning system from the post-war period on. They show how, even in a country which saw one of the greatest expressions of its architectural culture in the 'functionalist' movement (with all that this implied in terms of standardization), the concept of *integrated conservation* evolved over time, until it included the entire built stock in its manifold dimensions, both tangible and intangible, quantitative and qualitative. The authors moreover highlight how, from the 1990s on, Sweden, which was the first country to raise the issue of sustainable development, has been able to resolve, over time, the dualism between the *conservation of nature* and the *conservation of culture* above all at local level, where Local Agenda 21 projects have launched a bottom-up, integrated approach to the problems of urban planning.

A real example of how the concept of conservation can be effectively interpreted in terms of the social, economic, cultural and environmental development of a millennial historical heritage is provided by Hassan Radoine. He describes the walled city of Fez, recognized by UNESCO as world heritage site and the subject of an international preservation campaign. This example illustrates very well how it is possible, through integrated conservation action, to harmonize human and sustainable development. Indeed, the project on the one hand covered structural, urban and environmental rehabilitation and restoration of the historical and architectural heritage, and on the other, supported the improvement of traditional economic activities, also through financial support from national and international institutions (in particular the World Bank). This strategy made it possible to face the challenge of poverty by tapping into the wisdom, skills and 'know-how' of the local community.

The conservation of cultural heritage is also addressed in the contribution by Guang-Jun Jin and Cong-xia Zhao, although they report from a country with a deeply different approach. Indeed, only over the last 20 years has China begun to address, in a coordinated manner, the problem of the conservation of its vast historical and cultural heritage, seriously threatened by the swift growth of the economy which has swept over the country since the 1980s. Increasing concern for the conservation of the historical and cultural heritage has led to the legislation of a set of rules. The authors illustrate some examples of projects implemented in various historical cities. However, they also stress that much is still to be done to achieve more efficient organization of conservation activities, to increase their funding and, above all, to raise awareness of the problem through participatory mechanisms.

Again, remaining in the sphere of conservation problems, Christian

Ost's paper illustrates the effectiveness of an economic approach in the appraisal of built cultural heritage and in decision-making processes covering associated recovery projects. In particular, he puts forward an interesting theoretical application based on the specific spatial indicators and their 'mapping' in order to identify five types of impact areas as a function of several project variables connected to the potential attractiveness of the built cultural heritage, its spin-off effect (in terms, for example, of tourist spillovers), its increased capacity to include alternative elements of attraction in the area. The author stresses the fact that it is the *competitive impact area* itself which poses the greatest difficulties regarding the economic dimension of built cultural heritage but it is also that in which integrated conservation, seen as improvement in the quality of urban life, must become the 'golden rule' in order to attract new investments.

The evaluation of the social and economic attractiveness of the urban environment is the subject of the article by Josep Roca Cladera, Malcolm C. Burns and Pilar García Almirall. Starting from the recognition of the limits of the techniques available for calculating the economic value of public assets and the importance of the social dimension, they demonstrate how it is possible to estimate the social use value of public urban space by identifying the different degree of attractiveness (residential, commercial, cultural, etc.) as perceived by the users based on subjective evaluation criteria, independent of market logic. Research carried out in Barcelona (through public opinion polls and statistical calculation) offers a clear example of this.

Finally, the article by Jack W. Scannell, Denise L. Scannell and Charlton D. McIlwain sees environmental protection as a crucial aspect for consideration in sustainable development policies. The authors, who make a scathing indictment of growing de-humanization in an increasingly technologically-oriented and fragmented context, make an urgent plea for a new relationship between Humanity and Nature. This can come about, they maintain, only through a 'new culture' of the environment which actively involves citizens, institutions, enterprises, the third sector, etc. In this regard, ECOSS, a non-profit organization founded in 1994 to support the community living in an industrial quarter on the outskirts of Seattle beset by a number of environmental problems, offers, with its many activities a concrete example of how it is possible to 're-humanize' technological development.

Conclusions

The many challenges which the cities of the world are called upon to face, the complexity of the way forward towards human and sustainable urban development, cannot prevent us from harbouring the 'hope' that something really can be done.

The articles presented bear clear witness to this fact since they highlight, in differing ways, the commitment to change and to the improvement of the relationship between people and the city through the use of adequate technical tools for meeting the new urban challenges.

Since there exists no single clear benchmark of urban sustainability and because it is not a product but an evolving process (Nijkamp and Pepping, 1999) with an extremely wide temporal horizon, we need a new approach that will make it possible to analyze the links between the many components (economic, social and environmental) and to find solutions that meet at once the requirements entailed by each of these components.

Urban planning is certainly a necessary tool for designing strategies for ensuring urban sustainability (Forte Fr., 1999). But in order to anticipate and forecast the future of the city through a plan, we also need to change our approach, focusing on greater 'responsibility' in the choices regarding land use and the transformation of 'space' that is increasingly called upon to integrate functions, flows, natural environment, cultural heritage, centre, outskirts, but above all, 'people' (of different races, income bracket, age, etc.) (Ellin, 2001).

Equally essential are evaluation techniques, since they help us learn/understand what choices are to be made along with being tools that support the decision-making process.

But if the shared paradigm of the different urban policies has become sustainability – i.e. the construction of a dynamic, co-evolutionary balance between a territory's different sub-systems, namely the economic, the social and the physical-environmental system – the pursuit of this balance still appears to be strongly conditioned by the economic dimension alone (Nijkamp and Medda, Roca Cladera et al., Ost, this volume).

Financial resources for intervention policies are still largely allocated and assigned on the basis of efficiency considerations, such as cost-benefit analysis, rather than effectiveness and social equity.

Thus, we need to implement an 'integrated approach' to the problem of sustainable development in which all phases of evaluation – ex-ante, on going and ex-post – are able to combine the manifold dimensions of the problem in question. Thanks to the vast range of evaluation procedures available to us (Fusco Girard and Nijkamp, 1997) we can overcome the problem of choosing the right technique, and adopt the required holistic approach (Fusco Girard, 1998).

'Integrated evaluation' (Rotmans, 1998; Rotmans and van Asselt, 2000), may be seen, therefore, as an inter-disciplinary and participatory process of interpretation, combination and communication of 'knowledge' leading to the better understanding and management of the complex and interacting phenomena involved in urban sustainability.

From a technical point of view, it is not only a question of identifying criteria and indicators to interpret and evaluate sustainability in its various forms. It is also necessary to set up an ongoing 'question-and-answer' process with the community. Thus, monitoring action – which in itself is a form of evaluation – becomes indispensable for attesting to the coherence between planned objectives and results achieved; it makes it possible for citizens to verify the correct behaviour of politicians regarding their commitments and allows planners to make the necessary adjustments to their work. Urban planning and evaluation are thus essential and closely interacting tools for building the scenario of an urban future that, in order to be sustainable, must be, first and foremost, 'responsibly' human.

References

Camagni, R.(2000), 'Processi di globalizzazione e sostenibilità urbana. Nuova governance urbana e nuovi strumenti per l'infrastrutturazione finanziaria', in L. Fusco Girard and B. Forte (eds), *Città sostenibile e sviluppo umano*, Angeli, Milan, pp. 296-322.

Ellin, N. (2001), 'Slash City', *Lotus International*, vol. 110, pp. 58-72.

Forte, Fr. (1999), 'Piano urbanistico e sostenibilità', in A. Dal Piaz and Fr. Forte (eds), *Pianificazione urbanistica ed ambientale*, Maggioli, Rimini

Fusco Girard, L. (1998), 'Legislazione urbanistica, sviluppo sostenibile del territorio e valutazioni' in Fr. Forte and L. Fusco Girard (eds), *Valutazioni per lo sviluppo sostenibile e perequazione urbanistica*, Clean, Naples.

Fusco Girard, L. (2000), 'Introduzione', in L. Fusco Girard and B. Forte (eds), *Città sostenibile e sviluppo umano*, Angeli, Milan, pp. 15-92.

Fusco Girard, L. (2002), 'Una riflessione sull'attuazione dell'Agenda Habitat: alcune "best practices"', in Various Authors, *Habitat Agenda/Agenda Habitat. Verso la sostenibilità urbana e territoriale*, Angeli, Milan, pp. 187-245.

Fusco Girard, L. and Nijkamp, P. (eds) (1997), *Le valutazioni per lo sviluppo sostenibile della città e del territorio*, Angeli, Milan.

Hall, P. and Pfeiffer, U. (2000), *Urban Future 21. A Global Agenda for Twenty-first Century Cities*, E. and F.N. Spon, London.

Jonas, H. (1990), *Il principio responsabilità*, Einaudi, Turin [original editition: *Das Prinzip Verantwortung*, Insel Verlag, Frankfurt am Main, 1979].

Leone, N.G. (1998), 'Il recupero e il senso della città', in C. Beguinot and A. Notarangelo (eds), *Habitat Recovery for the City in the XXI Century, Innovation and Cooperation*, DI.PI.S.T., Giannini, Naples.

Martinotti, G. (1993), *Metropoli, la nuova morfologia sociale della città*, il Mulino, Bologna.

Nijkamp, P. and Pepping, G.(1999), 'Una valutazione meta-analitica delle iniziative per la città sostenibile', in P. Lombardi and E. Micelli (eds), *Le misure del piano, temi e strumenti della valutazione nei nuovi piani*, Angeli, Milan.

Rotmans, J. (1998), 'Methods for Integrated Assessment: The Challenges and Opportunities Ahead', *Environmental Modelling and Assessment*, vol. 3, pp. 155-179.

Rotmans, J. and van Asselt, M.B.A. (2000), 'Towards an Integrated Approach for Sustainable City Planning', *Journal on Multi-Criteria Decision Analysis*, vol. 9, pp. 110-124.

Sen, A. (1992), *Inequality Reexamined*, Clarendon Press, Oxford.

Sen, A. (1999), *Development as Freedom*, Alfred A. Knopf, New York.

UNCHS (United Nations Centre on Human Settlements) (1996), *The Habitat Agenda and Istanbul Declaration,* Istanbul.

UNDP (United Nations Development Programme) (2001), *Human Development Report 2001*, Oxford University Press, New York.

United Nations (1948), *Universal Declaration on Human Rights*, New York.

United Nations (1995), *World Summit for Social Development*, Copenhagen.

United Nations (2000), *World Urbanization Prospects: The 1999 Revision*, New York.

Chapter 20

Integrative Policymaking for the Improvement of the Quality of Urban Life

Nicole Rijkens-Klomp, Martin van de Lindt,
Marjolein B.A. van Asselt and Jan Rotmans

Introduction

About 80 per cent of all citizens in the European Union live in cities with more than 10,000 inhabitants and half of them in cities with more than 50,000 inhabitants. Improving the quality of life in European cities while promoting sustainable development is an important common challenge in view of the societal aims of these cities. Quality of life can be defined as the social-cultural, economic and ecological quality of living in the city. In the case of social-cultural quality, the quality of the social structure, social cohesion, cultural heritage and the income level of the inhabitants are important indicators, for example. Economic quality involves economic competitiveness, job creation and infrastructure quality. And the ecological quality of a city is assessed by the quality of the green services, air quality and resource use such as water usage.

Cities are increasingly confronted with some relevant trends such as the emergence of clusters of cities, reshaping the economic structure, traffic congestion, waste and pollution issues, urban sprawl, growing social segregation, unemployment and deteriorating infrastructure (Rotmans and Van Asselt, 2000). Furthermore, cities are confronted with the influence of globalization. All these developments impact, positively or negatively, the quality of urban life, which in its turn is indicative of the city's level of sustainable development. However, this is a rather complex task as quality of life and sustainable development are multidimensional issues: they include socio-cultural, economic and ecological aspects of living in the city. Because the city's socio-cultural, economic and environmental dimensions have become increasingly intertwined and occur on different spatial and temporal scales, city management has become a complex undertaking. On the one hand, the city is an entity that consists of a mosaic of different neighbourhoods with different kinds of functions, qualities, opportunities, and problems. On the other hand, the city plays an increasingly major role in the region and, with the emergence of city networks, cities even play a role on the national and European scales. In this context, we can refer to the Deltametropolis situated in the Netherlands, an urban network consisting of the cities of Amsterdam, Rotterdam, The Hague and Utrecht and the area around these cities. This network can be seen as a metropolis competing with other metropolitan areas in Europe and even in the world.

Developments influencing the quality of life in cities can have different velocities. Some developments result in rapid changes, while others only cause slow changes, sometimes over a lifetime. For example, life-styles of human beings can change very rapidly, while changes in the economic or population structure, on the contrary, usually involve generations. In Dutch policies for greater cities (in Dutch: *Grotestedenbeleid*) it is recognized that cities face an enormous task in restructuring neighbourhoods. It is estimated that it directly concerns almost 800,000 dwellings, mostly built during the period from 1945 to 1970. In fact, this means that approximately one third of the housing stock built in this period has to be re-constructed in the coming decade. This operation is necessary because the existing housing stock no longer conforms to the relatively rapid change in housing preferences.

Stakeholders' participation and communication with the city population are indispensable in policy processes aiming at improvement of the quality of urban life and attaining sustainable development. Management of the city's capital is thus increasingly a multi-actor endeavour and therefore involves innovative and interactive styles of governance. In this context, participatory approaches should be applied to involve citizens and key stakeholders in the policy development phase.

From the above considerations, it is clear that the challenge for urban decision-making is to understand and manage the complex, and sometimes conflicting, interrelationships between environmental conditions and objectives, economic vitality, social cohesion, cultural identity and citizens' well-being as well as to take into account the interactions between spatial and temporal scale levels. As a result of this multidimensional character, stimulating the improvement of quality of life and enhancing sustainable development require the use of innovative, sophisticated planning tools able to take into account long term dynamics. These tools can assist in exploring the 'interrelatedness' of developments in the city and can be helpful in exploring developing integrated policies. One way to do this is to conceptualize the city as a system whose function is to satisfy the needs of its inhabitants and 'users', i.e. people that work, study, shop and recreate in the city. Improving the quality of life while promoting sustainable development as an ambition requires that this system should function so that the means of future generations are not compromised (intergenerational equity), and that the burdens are not externalized on a broader geographical level (intragenerational equity).

The City as a System

The SCENE-Model Approach

Thus, it can be concluded that cities aiming at improving the quality of life while promoting sustainable development should take into account the interactions between socio-cultural, economic and environmental developments, the interactions between spatial scale levels and the interaction between long-term and short-term developments. A system approach can be helpful in this context. This means that the city is seen as a dynamic system of stocks and flows, which is referred to as the SCENE-model (Social-Cultural, Environmental and Economic model) (Rotmans et al., 1999). The basic idea behind this model is that it describes the sustainability of the city in terms of economic capital, ecological capital and social capital and the interactions between these capital forms in a triangular form (Figure 20.1).

Capital forms consist of stocks that can be seen as entities changing in the long term. We can differentiate between economic stocks (for example, economic sectors and infrastructure), socio-cultural stocks (housing stock and population) and environmental stocks (for example, green areas and air quality). The flows in the model represent the interactions between the stocks; we differentiate between intra-flows and inter-flows. Intra-flows are flows between stocks that belong to the same capital domain. Inter-flows are flows between stocks of different capital domains. Flows can be tangible (material flows; for example, housing production) and non-tangible (for example, labour force participation). The dynamics of the city result from the interaction between long term (stocks) and short term (flows) developments (Figure 20.2).

Stocks can be described not only in terms of quantity, but also in terms of their function, spatial characteristics and quality. Furthermore, we distinguish renewable (for example, infrastructure) and non-renewable stocks, stocks that can be influenced directly (for example, green areas) and indirectly (for example, the labour market), and stocks that can be influenced in the short term (for example, public services) and in the long term (for example, the stock of cultural identity). The importance ascribed to the various stocks will be different for each city, thereby reflecting the city's unique identity.

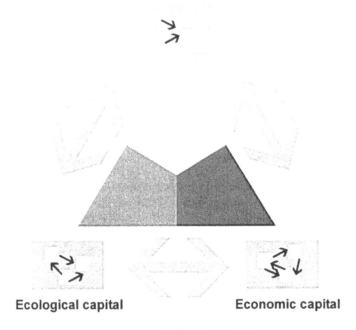

Figure 20.1 The principles of the SCENE-model

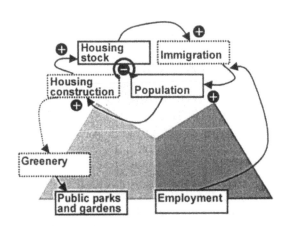

Figure 20.2 Examples of interaction

The surface of the triangle can be used as a qualitative indicator for developments in the total city capital in time; these developments can be weakening, substituting and strengthening (Figure 20.3). Weakening implies that there are losses in capital in all three domains. The notion of substitution can be used to describe the concept of weak sustainability with all its advantages and disadvantages. With substitution, one domain grows at the expense of another. An example is the growth of economic capital at the expense of natural capital. Next to weakening and substitution, strengthening is the third important development of the triangle. By the improvement of all three capital domains referred to as a win-win-win situation, the future ability to satisfy needs is improved. An example would be the successful creating of a natural reserve that could be exploited for recreation. The ecological domain benefits from the extension of natural area, in the economic domain employment and income are created and in the social domain, new recreational facilities are added.

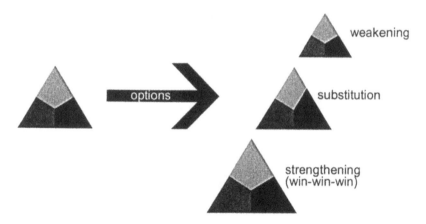

Figure 20.3 Weakening, substitution and strengthening

Sustainable City Management: Stock and Performance Management

Sustainable city management can be seen as strategic stock management: stocks need to be managed in order to improve the quality of urban life. In this respect it is important to note that each stock delivers a performance that not only depends on its quantity, but also on the quality, function and spatial component of the stock. Furthermore, the performance of stocks must be seen in relation to defined targets for the improvement of urban sustainability and the quality of urban life. These targets are not static, but can change over time through new insights or developments. For example, the transformation of neighbourhoods in the Dutch housing stock is a consequence of qualitative changes in demands on the Dutch housing market. Neither is the intrinsic performance of the stock static. Investments, maintenance or the lack of maintenance influences the performance itself (Figure 20.4). From this point of view sustainable city management implies strategic decisions about investments in, and maintenance of, stocks in relation to sustainability and quality of urban life targets.

Figure 20.4 Performance management of stocks

Stock and performance management should involve a participatory process. As stocks represent the societal capital of the city, it is not only the primacy of the local government which defines the targets for the stocks, judging their performance and managing them. In fact, citizens' and stakeholders' (such as firms, agencies, non-governmental organizations) perceptions, activities, choices and strategies also have a role to play; in many cases a stock can only be managed in collaboration with citizens and stakeholders. For example, management of the housing stock in the Netherlands is actually the responsibility/activity of housing corporations, real estate developers and private owners. Furthermore, it is important to include stock users in the management process as they have the relevant knowledge and expertise regarding the stocks themselves. Using this knowledge and expertise is necessary to make trade-offs between investments in the various stocks while aiming at a sustainable city management in order to improve the quality of urban life.

Integrated Assessment

The scientific paradigm underlying such a system and participating approach to cities as described above is that of Integrated Assessment (IA). Integrated Assessment is defined as a trans-disciplinary process of combining, interpreting and communicating knowledge from diverse sources (scientific knowledge, contextual and experiential knowledge) to allow a better understanding and management of complex problems. To that end, knowledge elements are structured in such a way that all relevant aspects of a complex problem are considered in their mutual coherence for the benefit of decision-making. Integrated Assessment thus involves interdisciplinary science and the participation of citizens, stakeholders and decision-makers in the process of knowledge production and management.

An Integrated Planning Tool to Assist Stock Management

In the previous paragraph, it was argued that a city can be seen as a system of stocks and flows and that stock management is crucial in improving the quality of life and sustainable development. In this paragraph it is explained that stock management requires the use of innovative, sophisticated planning tools that can assist in exploring the 'interrelatedness' of developments in a long term perspective. The basis of such planning tools is a conceptual model of the city, consisting of stocks and flows. This type of tool should be helpful in the complex process of stock and performance management. In policy making processes, it can play three roles:

- an agenda-setting and communication function;
- an integrating and structuring function by analyzing and evaluating changes in the major stocks and flows of the city to provide a flow of information to decision-makers;
- a monitoring function, to monitor the development of stock and flow indicators, in such a manner that the dynamic course of these core variables can be represented in time and in space to evaluate strategies.

These roles are related to phases in the policy cycle (Figure 20.5). Depending on its function, the planning instrument can be either a qualitative or a quantitative tool. In the *agenda-setting* phase, the city model especially has a structuring function with regard to the stocks and flows deemed important by policymakers, citizens and stakeholders. In this phase, support will be created for the common framework of stocks and flows that has been developed by the stakeholders. Furthermore, existing indicators will be analyzed and used as input for the city model. The framework can be used as a reference framework in the subsequent phases. In this way, the tool can also be seen as a communication instrument for the various stakeholders. It is important to note that the city model, in this phase also can be used as an instrument for analyzing the city system in a systematic way. In *the policy preparation phase* the planning tool can be used to explore different policy options with regard to their socio-cultural, economic and environmental consequences at different scale levels in time and space. The policy options will be explored by systematically analyzing their effects on the different stocks of the city. Thereafter the planning tool assists in developing long-term strategies for a sustainable city. In the *decision-making phase* the planning tool can be used to test the effectiveness together with the costs and benefits of the different policy strategies. In the implementation phase, the planning tool has a *monitoring function,* in that it makes it possible to check whether the targets set are actually reached by the policy strategies that have been implemented.

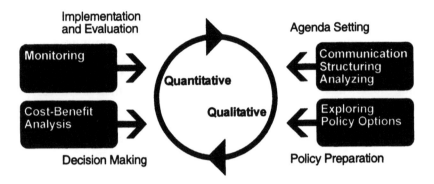

Figure 20.5 Planning tool and policy circle

The process of the use of the city model as a planning instrument is inherently subjective and beset with many uncertainties; it is proposed to organize a participatory process for developing and using the integrated city planning tool. In such a participatory process, all relevant stakeholders will be participating in an efficient way: city councillors, business-people, NGO-representatives, scientists, and citizens. Obviously, we need to differentiate between the different roles the various stakeholders play. Only a small core group of stakeholders can be actively involved as co-developers and co-users; then a larger group of stakeholders is constructed which acts in a more advisory mode, reflecting on different prototyping versions of the city planning instrument. If managed well, the resulting city planning tool reflects the interacting dialogue between the stakeholders in the form of a social discourse.

A Planning Tool for the City of Maastricht

To illustrate the proposed integrative approach a pilot project for the city of Maastricht, in the Netherlands, is described (Rotmans and Van Asselt, 2000). The city of Maastricht is situated in the southern region of the Netherlands and is the capital city of the province of Limburg, [1] one of the twelve Dutch provinces. Maastricht is the most southern city, directly adjacent to the border of Belgium and 30 kilometres from the German border. Maastricht claims to be the oldest city in the Netherlands and preserves its history by protecting the different historical sites. The city of Maastricht has currently approximately 121,000 inhabitants and a surface area of 6,000 hectares.

Over the last three decades, Maastricht has undergone remarkable changes. Partly due to the establishment of Maastricht University in the mid-seventies and the 'Maastricht' Treaty in 1991, it has been transformed from a provincial town into a medium-sized city with European aspirations. Furthermore, Maastricht now has the image of a rich city. However, if one studies the city more closely, one discovers that the city is also confronted with interrelated socio-cultural, economic and environmental problems. The city faces, for example, a high percentage of poorly educated people, an economic structure that is heavily dependent on traditional industries using low technology, and a high degree of soil pollution due to the industrial character of the city.

To tackle these problems, the city of Maastricht is currently developing a long-term vision for the year 2030. The aim of the city is to transform itself into a sustainable city in economic, environmental and socio-cultural terms. This vision will be developed with citizens and stakeholders and will be completed in two years. The Maastricht City Council decided to facilitate this visioning process with the aid of a planning tool based on the city model of stocks and flows. During the visioning process, the city-model will run through all phases of the policy circle as described above. Until now, the city model of stocks and flows has been used to analyze the state of the city in a systematic and integrative manner, in order to gain an understanding of important developments in the stocks of the city as a building block for the visioning process. This trend analysis will be described and summarized in the next paragraph.

Stocks and Flows Analysis of the City of Maastricht

Because the vision is meant to cover a period 30 years in the future, the stock and flow analysis focused on the period from 1970-2001. By looking 30 years back, insights were gained into the dynamics of the city in terms of autonomous trends, unexpected developments and the effects of political decisions.

First of all, the relevant stocks were identified for the city of Maastricht. This was done in close co-operation with a multi-sectoral group of policymakers of the city council of Maastricht. This process took about six months during which six meetings were organized where the stocks were analyzed thoroughly. The group found the stocks depicted in Figure 20.6 the most important for the city.

From the analysis of the history of Maastricht, we might conclude that the city has been confronted with some major switching points having a tremendous impact on the city. After World War II, Maastricht had the goal of becoming a city of 190,000 inhabitants in a short time period (Van de Venne, 1959). A consequence of this strategy was that rapid urban sprawl, reduction of the shortage of dwellings and demolition of some parts of the housing stock of low quality were emphasized. This resulted, as in the other greater cities in the Netherlands, in mass production of dwellings that today cannot compete with modern quality standards. In the period shortly after the war, the neighbourhoods in Maastricht were built in such a way that a network of neighbourhood facilities was provided. However, these facilities, especially facilities for young people, no longer meet present day demands.

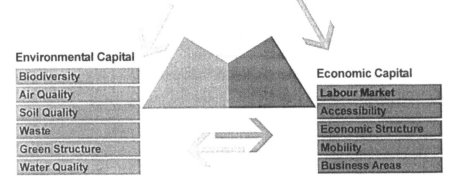

Social Cultural Capital
Cultural Identity
Population
Income Level
Housing Stock
Cultural Heritage
Services
Safety

Environmental Capital
Biodiversity
Air Quality
Soil Quality
Waste
Green Structure
Water Quality

Economic Capital
Labour Market
Accessibility
Economic Structure
Mobility
Business Areas

Figure 20.6 Relevant stocks of the city of Maastricht

At the end of the 1970s, Limburg province decided that Maastricht should not annex the surrounding villages to satisfy its ambitions for growth. In fact this meant the end of the expansion strategy of the city and the switch from an expanding city to a compact one (this meant that any expansion ambitions had to be fulfilled within the city borders). After this decision, population growth slowed appreciably due to emancipation, birth-control, individualization and the aging of the population. The consequence of the idea of the compact city was a growing pressure on the urban infrastructure and especially on the green infrastructure, which was partly compensated for by the beautiful cultural and historical landscape in which the city is situated. On the other hand, local authorities were forced by this development to pay special attention to the city as a whole and especially to the historical and cultural heritage.

An important moment for Maastricht was the establishment of Maastricht University which more or less compensated for the fact that the Dutch government had decided to close down the mines in the surrounding region (in the 1960s). From that time onwards, the city has developed from a small provincial town into one with large numbers of students in relation to the size of its population. In fact, it meant the beginning of the acceleration process for unlocking the traditional and Catholic city of Maastricht. Among other things, another acceleration of this unlocking process took place in 1991 with the 'Treaty of Maastricht'. Maastricht became a well-known city in the rest of Europe and even in the rest of the world. As a result, Maastricht, already a tourist city because of its famous historical and cultural heritage, was called upon to deal with mass tourism. In combination with such trends as globalization and internationalization, Maastricht was transformed from a Catholic introverted city to a extroverted city with European aspirations: it profiles itself as 'the Balcony of Europe' and as a complete and international city – a city in which the original inhabitants of Maastricht live together with the 'migrated citizens' of Maastricht.

Looking back over the past 30 years we can conclude that past developments have resulted in some rapidly changing stocks and others changing slowly. This difference in velocity caused a number of tensions between the stocks. These tensions might become problematic in the near or far future in Maastricht. The city's character and its population structure have changed rapidly. At this moment, a relatively large part of the population can be considered non-productive as it is composed of students or the elderly. Due to this structure, the birth-rate in Maastricht is relatively low, while the death-rate is relatively high. Maastricht's growth is totally dependent on its migration rate. Furthermore, the activities of Maastricht University rarely match the business activities in the city. This results in the migration of most of the students after graduating. Furthermore, the housing stock did not change as fast as the demands for housing by the people in the 30-40 year age bracket and this forces people out of the city into the surrounding villages to satisfy their housing demands. In other words, the city of Maastricht faces very selective migration due to the differences in velocity with which the various stocks are changing (Figure 20.7).

The economic capital of the city has not changed drastically over the last 30 years. In spite of the growth of the service industry, the role of traditional industry in terms of income for the city is rather substantial. This is due to the fact that industrial processes have been modernized. This has caused severe drops in employment in the industrial sector. As no substantial compensation for these losses had been organized, the city of Maastricht has been confronted with a rather high unemployment rate compared to other cities. Moreover, dependence on the old industry combined with the emigration of the students causes a rather low education level of the labour force. As a consequence, the labour market is quite unattractive for the more sophisticated branches in the business sector such as the ICT-sector. The old industry influenced the city capital also in another way: 90 per cent of the soil in the city has been polluted. Furthermore some problems exist with the quality of surface water and air. Environmental pollution has not only been caused by Maastricht's industry but also by traffic and cross border pollution from Belgium, Germany and even France.

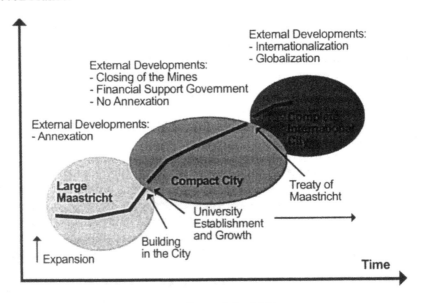

Figure 20.7 The transition to Maastricht 2001

Summarizing the analysis we might say that Maastricht is confronted with a number of interrelated problems:

- a high percentage of the elderly showing greater increases in comparison with the average trend in comparable cities. This has a significant impact on the social structure of the population;
- a high percentage of poorly educated people;
- the threat of the expansion of the number of districts where social problems such as low education level, low income and a relatively high percentage of unemployed accumulate;

- an economic structure, which is quite heavily dependent on the traditional industries using low technology;
- deterioration of accessibility for transport, due to traffic congestion;
- a high rate of environmental pollution due to the industrial character of the city and cross border pollution.

These problems have been caused by the tensions between the various stocks and capital forms, some examples of which are shown in Figure 20.8. These tensions influence negatively the sustainability of Maastricht and the quality of life of its inhabitants. To tackle these tensions and to improve the quality of life, the city of Maastricht has to view itself in an integrated way thereby focussing on the interrelations of socio-cultural, environmental and economic developments and take the following positive aspects into account:

- the historical and cultural heritage of the city centre and its atmosphere;
- the strong development of the consumer service sector;
- the geographic position of the city of Maastricht in relation to the growing importance of the European region.

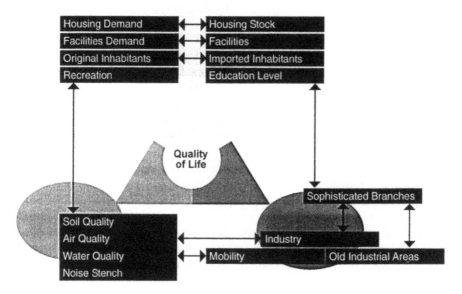

Figure 20.8 Examples of tensions

In summary, through the integrative stock and flow analysis, it has been possible to gain relevant insights into the strengths and weaknesses of the city in an systematic way. ICIS is currently working on a quantitative prototype of the Maastricht stock and flow model. At this moment, the planning instrument is being filled with stocks from the three domains. For example, the structure of the housing stock, population structure (socio-cultural domain), economic structure, labour force (economic domain), land use (environmental domain). Furthermore, relations have been defined between stocks. Examples of these are migration rates, labour participation rates and unemployment rates. The aim is to achieve a rather definitive prototype. This prototype will be applied in the visioning process as a policy support tool; it will be used to analyze the effects and consistency of various scenarios that could lead to a sustainable Maastricht in 2030.

Conclusions

In view of the growing complexity of managing rapidly evolving cities in Europe, there is a definite need for integrative approaches to assist city planners and councillors in their striving to achieve a sustainable city and hence a higher quality of urban life. Regarding the instrumental aspect, new sophisticated planning instruments are needed. These instruments no longer focus on the physical and economic infrastructure of cities, in particular on spatial planning, housing and transport, but also on the integration of the physical infrastructure, the socio-cultural infrastructure and the city economy and labour market. Such an integrated city planning tool can be helpful in decisions regarding trade-offs between investments in stocks and in the monitoring of current and future developments in relation to its targets. In order to use such an integrated city planning tool in the most effective and efficient way, it should be developed in a participatory manner, while taking into account the knowledge and expertise of the various stock users (stakeholders).

Ideally, the proposed integrated approach towards city planning aims to change the mental outlooks of city planners, councillors and other stakeholders, evolving into a more integrated culture. The interdisciplinary aspect of the integrated approach is a major difference from more traditional, often economic-based, approaches to city planning. The integrated approach does not look for optimal solutions, but aims at testing the effectiveness of various policy strategies, and estimating trade-offs among different policy options in relation to an improvement of the quality of urban life. The resulting integrated urban visions are not based on rigid quantification, but on a mix of qualitative, semi-quantitative and quantitative information, gathered from a process that combines participation with analysis. A city-planning tool is merely a means, and not a goal in itself. The ultimate goal is to improve strategic management aiming at a better quality of urban life through an improved understanding of the complexity of interrelated socio-cultural, economic and environmental problems that determine the current and future state of our cities.

Note

1 In 1999 a conceptual model with stocks and flows was developed for the Province; see also Rotmans et al. (1999).

References

Rotmans, J. and Van Asselt, M.B.A. (2000), 'Towards an Integrated Approach for Sustainable City Planning', *Journal of Multi-Criteria Decision Analysis*, vol. 9, pp. 110-24.

Rotmans, J., Van Asselt, M.B.A. and Rijkens, N. (1999), *A SCENE-model for POL* (in Dutch: *Een denkmodel voor POL*), Maastricht.

Van de Venne, J.J.J. (1959), *Maastricht a Vision of the Future* (in Dutch: *Maastricht, een visie op de toekomst*), Maastricht.

Chapter 21

Integrated Assessment of Urban Revitalization Projects

Peter Nijkamp and Francesca Medda

Setting the Scene

Cultural identity and sense of the local become central research and policy issues in an integrating European space. It is therefore no surprise that cities in Europe try to exploit the potential of their cultural heritage by developing intelligent strategies to combine the need for economic progress with the task of maintaining the socio-cultural assets in their locality. Nowadays we see far-reaching policy discrepancies emerging in the management of the built environment. A purely strict conservation strategy is incompatible with the need to reposition cities in the European space-economy, but a demolition of valuable architectural assets is also not acceptable. Hence, there is a need for a balanced perspective on maintenance and progress. This is once more a complicated task in urban socio-cultural policy for the built environment, as it is here that the market system does not offer reliable signals for proper policy development and assessment (Coccossis and Nijkamp, 1995).

There is a clear need for proper evaluation methods which can offer a trade-off between the various pros and cons of urban socio-cultural development strategies. In past years, we have witnessed the emergence of a variety of assessment techniques, such as cost-benefit analysis, community impact assessment, benchmark analysis, indicator systems, goal programming methods, and multi-criteria techniques. This has led to some fragmentation in evaluation analysis; there is a clear need for a more integrated use of the existing research apparatus in this field. This chapter aims to develop a new perspective by proposing a blend of various complementary assessment and evaluation methods as a framework for a more balanced policy analysis. These ideas will be clarified by means of an illustrative application to an urban revitalization project.

Combinatorial Assessment Methodology

Preservation of historical urban heritage in the presence of rapid urban growth is not an easy policy task. When addressing the problem of the assessment of urban revitalization projects the choice of the evaluation technique to be adopted plays a preponderant role for the selection of outcomes of projects. This choice affects the specific angle from which the decision-maker will examine and evaluate the project, as well as his/her perception of the problem. Consequently, in many choice situations – especially in those within the public domain – we observe a tendency to suppress straightforward optimization behaviour and instead to favour 'satisfying' or compromise modes of planning (Mintzberg, 1979; Simon, 1960). The role of the expert therefore shifts from that of a professional who knows best, to a moderator who scientifically guides a complex choice problem.

From this standpoint, our objective is to overcome the often mutually contrasting elements of different assessment techniques by proposing a synthesis framework. This suggested methodology embraces different assessment methods within the same framework in relation to a given evaluation problem. In the light of recent studies on the theoretical aspects of reasoning about data (Barwise and Moss, 1996; Pawlak, 1991), we assume that no single method is exhaustive and ideal per se; different assessment methods can be combined to overcome the limitations of the single methods with the aim of designing more flexible evaluation tools. We will call this assessment procedure a *combinatorial assessment methodology*.

In order to clarify our argument we use a general scheme (Figure 21.1) in which the characteristics of this method are illustrated. We notice here that the combinatorial assessment methodology offers a generic framework which, depending on the evaluation problem at hand, combines existing assessment methods that are well suited – both methodologically and functionally – for solving the evaluation problem. The following scheme describes the assessment process that will be discussed throughout our analysis. The assessment procedure is composed of five steps depicted by five diamond shapes, while the relevant assessment methodologies used here are identified by the three rectangles. It should be emphasized that this scheme is illustrative only for the type of synthesis that we are seeking. Instead of rough set analysis, one might, for example, also use another qualitative data method such as fuzzy set analysis, or instead of the Regime method, one might also use another pair comparison method such as a concordance method. Rather than adjusting the data set to the method chosen, in our approach we advocate the adjustment and selection of the assessment method in relation to the specific data and objectives of the evaluation exercise.

With this background the organization of the present chapter is as follows. We begin with an introduction of rough set analysis, Regime analysis and Flag model, respectively. We then demonstrate how these methods can be combined to obtain a useful result by means of an illustrative example, in which five different urban revitalization projects are to be assessed. This exercise will show the potency of the *combinatorial assessment methodology*.

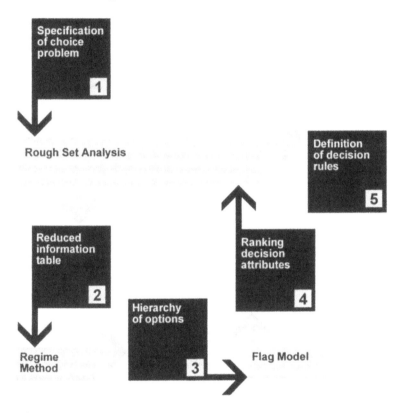

Figure 21.1 Schema of the combinatorial assessment methodology

Rough Set Analysis

The goal of rough set analysis is to recognize possible cause-effect relationships among the available data and to underline the importance and the strategic role of some data and the irrelevance of other data (Pawlak, 1991, 1992). This approach focuses on regularities in the data in order to identify and emphasize aspects and relationships which are less evident, but which can be useful in analysis and policy making.

Let us consider a finite universe of objects which we would like to examine and classify. For each object we can define a number n of attributes in order to create a significant basis for the required characterization of the object. If the attribute is quantitative, it will be easy to define its domain. If the attribute is qualitative, we divide its domain into distinct sub-intervals to obtain an accurate description of the object. In this way, we can classify our objects with the attributes, and thus with each object we associate a vector of attributes. The table containing all this organized information will be called the *information table*. From the table of information, we can immediately observe which objects share the same types of attributes. Two objects that are not the same object have an 'indiscernibility' relationship when they have the same descriptive attributes. Such a binary relationship is reflexive, symmetric and transitive.

Until now we have focused on the classification of uncertain data. Let us examine the case in which we wish to express a choice among different alternatives; this is best assured when we face an assessment problem. We referred above to the information table, and in this table we can, in the case of an assessment problem, identify two classes from the set of attributes: a class of condition attributes and a class of attributes called 'decision attributes' (essentially dependent variables determined by the condition attributes).

The class of condition attributes describes the relevant object following the procedure depicted above. The class of decision attributes is defined by all the attributes that the object must possess in order to be selected as an acceptable alternative. For instance, a set of objects can be described by the values of condition attributes, while classifications of experts are represented by values of decision attributes.

At this point we define a decision rule as an implication relationship between the description of a condition class and the description of a decision class. The decision rule can be exact or deterministic (namely, when the class of decision attributes is contained in the set of conditions), i.e., all decision attributes belong to the class of the condition attributes. We have an approximate rule when more than one value of the decision attributes corresponds to the same combination of values of the condition attributes. Therefore, an exact rule offers a sufficient condition of belonging to a decision class; an approximate rule admits the possibility of this membership.

The decision rules and the table of information are the basic elements needed to solve multi-attribute choice and ranking problems. The binary preference relations between the decision rules and the description of the objects by means of the condition attributes determine a set of potentially acceptable actions. In order to rank such alternatives, we need to conduct a final binary comparison among the potential actions. This procedure will define the most acceptable action or alternative.

Regime Analysis

The Regime analysis is a discrete qualitative multi-criteria method (Nijkamp et al., 1990). The fundamental framework of multi-criteria methods is based upon two kinds of input data: an evaluation matrix and a set of political or choice weights for the decision criteria. The evaluation matrix is composed of elements which measure the effect of each relevant alternative in relation to each criterion considered. The set of weights provides information regarding the relative importance of the criteria we wish to examine. Regime analysis is an ordinal generalization of pair-wise comparison methods and is able to deal with quantitative as well as qualitative data.

In Regime analysis, as in concordance analysis, we compare the alternatives in relation to all criteria in order to define the concordance index. Let us consider, for example, the comparison between alternative i and alternative j for all criteria. The concordance index will be the sum of the weights which are related to the criteria for which alternative i is better than alternative j. Let us call this sum, c_{ij}. Then we calculate the concordance index for the same alternatives, only by considering the criteria for which j is better than i, i.e., c_{ji}. After having calculated these two sums, we subtract these two values to obtain the index: $\mu_{ij} = c_{ij} - c_{ji}$. Because we have only ordinal information about the weights, our interest is in the sign of the index μ_{ij}. If the sign is positive, this will indicate that alternative i is more attractive than alternative j; if negative, it will imply the reverse. We will therefore be able to rank our alternatives. We notice that, due to the ordinal nature of the information, in the indicator μ no attention is given to the size of the difference between the alternatives; it is only the sign of the difference that is important.

We might nevertheless encounter another complication. We may not be able to determine an unambiguous result, i.e. a ranking of alternatives. This is because we confront the problem of ambiguity with the sign of the index μ. In order to solve such a problem, we introduce a certain probability p_{ij} for the dominance of criteria i with respect to criteria j as follows:

$$p_{ij} = prob(\mu_{ij} > 0)$$

and we define an aggregate probability measure which indicates the success score as follows:

$$p_i = \frac{1}{I-1} \sum_{j \neq i} p_{ij}$$

where I is the number of chosen alternatives.

The problem here is to assess the value of p_{ij} and of p_i. We will assume a specific probability distribution of the set of feasible weights. This assumption is based upon the criterion of Laplace in the case of decision-making under uncertainty. In the case of a probability distribution defined on qualitative information, it is sufficient to mention that, in principle the use of stochastic analysis, which is consistent with an originally ordinal data set, could help us overcome the methodological problem we may encounter by conducting a numerical operation on qualitative data.

The Regime method then identifies the feasible domain within which values of the feasible weights w_i must fall in order to be compatible with the condition imposed by the probability value. By means of a random generator, numerous values of weights can be calculated. This allows us finally to calculate the probability score (or success score) p_i for each alternative i. We can then determine an unambiguous solution and rank the alternatives.

Flag Model

In order to define a normative approach to the concept of sustainability, a framework of analysis and of expert judgment is needed that should be able to test actual and future states of the economy and the environment against a set of reference values. The Flag model has been defined to assess the degree of sustainability of values of policy alternatives (Nijkamp, 1995; Nijkamp and Ouwersloot, 1997). The model develops an operational description and definition of the concept of sustainable development. There are three important components of this model:

- identifying a set of measurable sustainability indicators;
- establishing a set of normative reference values;
- developing a practical methodology for assessing future development.

The input of the program is again an impact matrix with a number n of variables; the matrix is formed by the values that the variables assume for each scenario considered. Such values are defined by independent experts. The main purpose of the model is to analyze whether one or more scenarios can be classified as sustainable or not; this type of evaluation is based upon the values of the indicators used. The methodology therefore requires the identification and definition of indicators. Such indicators in the program have two formal attributes: class and type. There are often three main classes of relevant indicators which correspond to the main dimensions of the sustainability analysis: 1) environmental, 2) social, and 3) economic. The second attribute, type, relates to the point that some indicators, e.g., water quality, may have high scores (meaning a sustainable situation), while for others, such as the pollution indicator, we may have low scores which are sustainable as well. This difference is captured in the attribute type of the indicator; the first types are defined as 'benefit indicators', the second types are 'cost indicators'.

For each sustainable indicator we must now define critical threshold values which may not be exceeded. These values represent the reference system for judging actual states or future outcomes of scenario experiments. Since in certain areas and under certain circumstances experts and decision-makers may have conflicting views on the precise level of the acceptable threshold values, we estimate a band of values of the thresholds ranging from a maximum value (CTV_{max}) to a minimum value (CTV_{min}). This can be represented as in Figure 21.2).

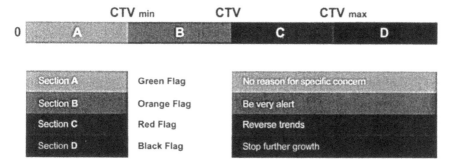

Figure 21.2 A representation in Flag form

The third component of the model, the impact assessment, provides a number of instruments for the analysis of the sustainability issue. This analysis can be carried out in two ways. The first is an inspection of a single strategy. The second is the comparison of two scenarios. In the former procedure we decide whether the scenario is sustainable or not. In the latter case, by comparing the scenarios, we decide which scenario scores best in case this question is centred on the sustainability issue. This option may be interpreted as a basic form of multi-criteria analysis.

In the sequel of this article we will now integrate the three methods (rough set analysis, Regime method and Flag model) in one combinatorial assessment procedure (Figure 21.1). This will be illustrated on the basis of an urban revitalization example in the next section.

Assessment of Urban Revitalization Projects: An Illustrative Case Study

In this section we illustrate an application of our *combinatorial assessment methodology* for urban revitalization projects. We assume here five different projects that are related to the renewal of a historical urban area. For each project we have five attributes which describe the characteristics of the projects to be evaluated. We observe that the information table contains numerical data, but they all represent qualitative rank order data (Table 21.1).

Table 21.1 Table of the assessment of urban revitalization projects

Options: Urban Revitalization Projects	Costs	Attributes			
		Integration of Historical City Centre	*Social Importance for Citizens*	*Economic Potential*	*Urban Image*
Project 1	1	2	1	3	1
Project 2	2	2	1	3	1
Project 3	1	2	3	2	3
Project 4	2	2	2	3	3
Project 5	3	3	3	1	2

The first step in the assessment methodology is the examination of the information table through a dissimilarity analysis. In the previous sections we have seen that rough set analysis can operate a dissimilarity analysis; therefore, we will first examine Table 21.1 from this perspective. For simplification of notation, we replace Table 21.1 by a coded information table where the values of attributes are coded in the following way:

$$V_{costs} = \{low[1] \Rightarrow (+), medium[2] \Rightarrow (0), high[3] \Rightarrow (-)\};$$

$$V_{integration} = \{poor[1] \Rightarrow (-), good[2] \Rightarrow (0), excellent[3] \Rightarrow (+)\};$$

$$V_{social\,imp} = \{poor[1] \Rightarrow (-), good[2] \Rightarrow (0), excellent[3] \Rightarrow (+)\};$$

$$V_{econ.potential} = \{low[1] \Rightarrow (-), medium[2] \Rightarrow (0), high[3] \Rightarrow (+)\};$$

$$V_{image} = \{poor[1] \Rightarrow (-), good[2] \Rightarrow (0), excellent[3] \Rightarrow (+)\}.$$

Table 1.1 can now be expressed in the reduced coded form (Table 21.2).

Clearly, in Table 21.2 *a* refers to Costs, *b* to Integration of Historical City Centre, *c* to Social Importance for Citizens, *d* to Economic Potential, and *e* to Urban Image.

Table 21.2   Coded information table

Options: Urban Revitalization Projects	Attributes				
	a	b	c	d	e
Project 1	+	0	−	+	−
Project 2	0	0	−	+	−
Project 3	+	0	+	0	+
Project 4	0	0	0	+	+
Project 5	−	+	+	−	0

The first noteworthy characteristic of Table 21.2 is that each row is different. This means that each project is identified by a unique set of the given features. By analyzing the information matrix, we can identify which of the features of the five revitalization projects are dependent on the other characteristics; we are therefore able to eliminate unnecessary attributes from the decision analysis. After five computations of the attribute reductions, we obtain the result that the core attributes are framed by the set $\{a, b\}$, and that the two sets of reduced attributes, i.e. $\{a, b, c\}$ and $\{a, b, e\}$, are consistent and independent. We can summarize our results in the following logical statements:

$$\{a, b, c\} \Rightarrow \{d, e\} \text{ and } \{a, b, e\} \Rightarrow \{d, c\}$$

These logic dependencies tell us that attributes a (Costs) and b (Integration of Historical City Centre) must always be considered when tackling this project evaluation problem. The attributes c (Social Importance for Citizens) and d (Economic Potential) can be mutually replaced, and attribute e (Urban Image) depends on the remaining set of attributes. We can use this information to observe that attributes a and b are more important than attributes c and d, and consequently of attribute e, since a and b must be considered in every evaluation, We can then determine a hierarchical relationship among the attributes.

We are now able to utilize this information about the dependency relations among the attributes, when we define the weights of the attributes in the Regime method. For instance, attributes a and b are considered more important than attributes c and d, but have equal weights, i.e. equal importance, when compared to each other. Attribute e is the least important of all attributes.

We now turn to the application of the above-described Regime method. A Regime method gives a quantitative performance score for each of the alternatives envisaged. When we run the Regime analysis, we obtain the final results, where the scores refer to the relative quantitative performance of each of the individual projects under consideration (the higher the better) (Table 21.3).

Table 21.3   Results from the Regime analysis

Rank 1	Project 3	0.873
Rank 2	Project 4	0.754
Rank 3	Project 1	0.435
Rank 4	Project 5	0.297
Rank 5	Project 2	0.103

The results of the Regime analysis tell us that revitalization project 3 is the most preferable in relation to the five characteristics and that the worst revitalization project is 2. The Regime analysis thus ranks the options of the choice from the best to the worst.

Finally, we will compare the previous analysis with the Flag model analysis (Nijkamp et al., 1998). The Flag model is a simple assessment method that can indicate the set of most suitable decisions according to the attributes of the options. It uses critical threshold values to eliminate inferior or less acceptable choice possibilities. In this case the Flag model gives us the same rank as the Regime method (Table 21.4), but in addition we can also subdivide the rank orders according to the Flag model into *accepted decisions*, *neutral decisions* and *rejected decisions*. These three clusters are defined within the methods by using critical threshold values. These values represent the reference system for judging the different decisions. We estimate a bandwidth of values of thresholds ranging from a maximum value (CTV_{max}) to a minimum value (CTV_{min}). We finally obtain the subdivision of our choice options on the basis of a screening analysis related to our combinatorial framework (Table 21.4).

Table 21.4   Results of the Regime analysis and the Flag model

Rank 1	Project 3	0.873	*Accepted*
Rank 2	Project 4	0.754	*Accepted*
Rank 3	Project 1	0.435	*Neutral*
Rank 4	Project 5	0.297	*Neutral*
Rank 5	Project 2	0.103	*Rejected*

We can broaden the results obtained by defining the decision rules related to decisions ranked by the Regime analysis and the Flag method. To do so we need to once more run the rough set analysis, which will now indicate the attributes and their values needed to reach the decisions. In Table 21.5 the decision attributes have been calculated by using the results of the

Regime method and Flag model as follows:

decision attribute = 1 implies that the alternative is *accepted*;

decision attribute = 2 implies that the alternative is *neutral*;

decision attribute = 3 implies that the alternative is *rejected*.

In the event that we obtain a neutral outcome of the decision attribute, we cannot express any judgment about the alternative; in other words, in that case the alternative can be either accepted or rejected. In order to avoid this neutral state in such a particular case, we need more precise specifications of the alternative and of the attributes. The information table can now be examined through rough set analysis (Table 21.5).

Table 21.5 Coded information table

Options: Urban Revitalization Projects	Costs	Integration of Historical City Centre	Attributes Social Importance for Citizens	Economic Potential	Urban Image	Decision Attribute
Project 1	1	2	1	3	1	2
Project 2	2	2	1	3	1	3
Project 3	1	2	3	2	3	1
Project 4	2	2	2	3	3	1
Project 5	3	3	3	1	2	2

We obtain now from our analysis that:

Rule 1 Attr.$_{Costs}$ = 1 Attr.$_{Social imp}$ = 3 $\Rightarrow$ decision 1;

Rule 2 Attr.$_{Integration}$ = 2 Attr.$_{Social imp}$ = 3 $\Rightarrow$ decision 1;

Rule 3 Attr.$_{Costs}$ = 1 $\Rightarrow$ decision 2;

Rule 4 Attr.$_{Costs}$ = 2 Attr.$_{Social imp}$ = 2 $\Rightarrow$ decision 2.

The simple algorithms in our result show the minimal set of attributes necessary for reaching the five decision rules, so that we indeed obtain the consistent decision process we set out to achieve.

In summary, in our case study we have demonstrated how the combination of three assessment methods (in this case, a data classification method, in the form of a rough set analysis, combined with the Regime analysis and the Flag model) can operate in a mutually complementary way, how it can consistently reduce the limitations of each method, and how it can reinforce the validity of the assessment procedure by improving the consistency of the process.

References

Barwise, J. and Moss, L. (1996), *Vicious Circles*, CSLI Publications, Stanford.

Coccossis, H. and Nijkamp, P. (eds) (1995), *Planning for Our Cultural Heritage*, Ashgate, Aldershot.

Mintzberg, H. (1979), *The Structuring of Organizations: A Synthesis of the Research*, Prentice Hall, New York.

Nijkamp, P. (1995), *Sustainability Analysis in Agriculture: A Decision Support Framework*, Report commissioned by FAO, Free University Amsterdam.

Nijkamp, P. and Ouwersloot, H. (1997), 'A Decision Support System for Regional Sustainable Development', *Tinbergen Paper*, no. 73/4, Tinbergen Institute, Amsterdam.

Nijkamp, P., Bal, F. and Medda, F. (1998), 'A Survey of Methods for Sustainable City Planning and Cultural Heritage Management', *Research Memoranda Series*, no. 50, Free University, Amsterdam.

Nijkamp, P., Rietveld, P. and Voogd, H. (1990), *Multicriteria Evaluation in Physical Planning*, Elsevier Science Publishers, Amsterdam.

Pawlak, Z. (1991), *Rough Sets: Theoretical Aspects of Reasoning about Data*, Kluwer Academic Publishers, Dordrecht.

Pawlak, Z. (1992), 'Rough Sets: Introduction', in R. Slowinski (ed.), *Intelligent Decision Support: Handbook of Applications and Advances of the Rough Sets Theory*, Kluwer Academic Publishers, Dordrecht.

Simon, H. (1960), *The New Science of Management Decision*, Harper and Row, New York.

Chapter 22

Integrated Conservation and Environmental Challenge: Reflections on the Swedish Case of Habitat

Nanne Engelbrektsson and Jan Rosvall

Introduction

The aim of this article is to provide a condensed overview of the modern and post-modern Swedish planning system, as a general basis for understanding the prerequisites of an emerging preservation movement with the objective of preparing for a sustainable future of habitat. A background of the 'Swedish middle way' is presented as an explanation to post-war development, with special regard to the huge housing programs and the large-scale anti-preservation and demolition of city centres. The opposition to this process among groups of concerned citizens and academics during the 1960s and 1970s, and the resulting initiatives are presented here; they include, for example, development of alternative planning instruments based on cross-disciplinary studies. General tendencies of urban restructuring in the context of the 'new economy' and the changed conditions of Swedish planning activities are outlined – since the late 1990s in a phase of ambiguity and reorientation – implying a more open attitude towards preservation aspects and humanities-oriented values and methods. Advantages and hindrances for implementation of a planning system, incorporating an 'integrated conservation' approach is discussed, the aim being increased awareness of human values of urban structures and ordinary built up environments.

Preservation Planning Focused on Social and Cultural Dimensions

'Integrated Conservation' – A Concept Used in Various Ways

During the last few decades the concept of 'integrated conservation' has primarily been used in research in connection with application-oriented and cross-disciplinary studies of urban conservation and architectural preservation. A joint statement for the use of this concept is an interpretation of the material cultural heritage in a broad sense, including architecture, generic buildings and urban areas, as well as 'ordinary landscape' (Meinig, 1979), and with respect to the manifold dimensions involved, such as intangible cultural values and symbolic meanings related to relevant historical, technical and socio-economic conditions. Thus, the subject of conservation is regarded as *im*-material, designated as 'socio-materia', closely related to human thought and also acting as a material resource of man, with respect to its economic, technical and functional significance. Consequently, the adoption of an outlook of this kind leads to a need for multidimensional professional care and maintenance of the cultural heritage and urban fabric. This concept however is used in somewhat varying ways, mostly as a labelling of a comprehensive multi-dimensional conservation *approach* and/or for the *methods* concerned, but also as a designation of a special kind of conservation *process,* where views and methods of this kind have been implemented (Appleyard, 1979; Engelbrektsson, 1987; Fusco Girard, 1993).

In order to avoid misunderstandings, 'integrated conservation' in this paper is used according to the definition and policy established by the *Amsterdam Declaration* (The Council of Europe, 1975). The overview approach, and its case studies as presented by Appleyard (1979), is, in our opinion, still valid as a benchmark, even if research on these phenomena has developed over the last years. In principle, this terminology follows the initial Italian conservation discourse (Brandi, 1963; Blomé, 1977; Marconi, 1984), which has laid the foundation for the modern international conservation movement, based on the *Charter of Venice* (ICOMOS, 1964). Obviously, this theoretical approach is, in principle, a humanities-based perspective of a genuinely trans- and multi-disciplinary nature, incorporating knowledge, methods and models from a broad range of relevant disciplines and professions, also including the natural sciences, technology and crafts.

The comprehensive concept of 'integrated conservation' – formulated and used in various scholarly-scientific contexts and planning situations, especially during the last decade – needs to be carefully examined and defined in relation to parallel heterogeneous conceptual frameworks. (As an example, the massive global use of this term on the web indicates strictly natural-science-based mechanisms applied to ecological programs of different kinds, primarily in developing regions.) Thus, there is a firm need for establishing generally accepted coherent definitions, formulas and processes concerning integrated conservation in connection with cultural heritage planning and its implementation in different kinds of situations (Zancheti, 1999). The important components are still to be delineated, defined and related to each other, as well as to a wider theoretical framework, directed to basic issues such as 'sustainable development', '(un)employment' and 'poverty eradication' (Fusco Girard and Forte, 2000).

Truly cross-disciplinary planning and research co-operation between town-planners, architects, economists, conservationists and scholars in these fields has only rarely been achieved and relates to explicitly formulated models characterized as 'integrated conservation'. Therefore there is an evident need for establishing an international network for research fellows to deal with empiric explorative studies in the field of integrated conservation planning, interpreting multifaceted problems in selected and specific kinds of urban spheres. Forming a common platform with a pronounced theoretical epistemology and subsequent comparative discussions of experiences and results, would in all probability be a very rewarding instrument for methodological development in this field. In relation to a pronounced sustainable planning formula – according to the Habitat Agenda (UNCHS, 1996) – discussions of this kind would imply possibilities of identifying complex social and cultural tendencies of urban habitat and new tendencies of spatial restructuring – of importance for concerned groups of inhabitants – not found in ordinary planning processes.

A Shift in Attitudes to Objects of Cultural Significance

A well-heeded comparative global interpretation of the structure and the constitution of cultural objects – officially legitimated as 'cultural heritage' – would probably offer a wide range of variety in different national and social contexts. This diverging phenomenon – related to scholarly typologies and constructions based on various ethics and epistemologies – is far from distinct, whether in a longitudinal or in a contemporary cross-cultural perspective. Since the cultural heritage systems and their objects are closely related to economic, social and cultural conditions in society, the decisive concept of cultural significance should always be explicitly defined with reference to its actual application (Rosvall et al., 1995/99). Whatever the types of 'cultural heritages', the selections can always be seen as expressions of specific national and social situations, and as components of the spirit of the age. Rather than being defined as static and objective entities representing 'intrinsic values', applicable for well-defined kinds of cultural objects, the heritage values should be used as 'instrumental tools' directly related to actual planning situations – not just arbitrarily and scholarly determined as a leftover factor referring to a long-vanished society. An explicitly defined theoretical framework on an operative level should be seen as a fundamental base to enable legitimate and consistent descriptions, interpretations and choices for local policy-making and interventions.

In Sweden – as in many other countries – the entire 'cultural heritage' in every region and municipality has, over the last decades, been surveyed and registered with its total amount of built environments. As a general outcome, this process has contributed to the awareness of new dimensions and often to the reconsideration of the preservation planning system. Among other effects, those broad and relatively systematical studies of the entire building stock and of cultural landscape have led to increased attention to *built-up structures* rather than *individual buildings* and *monuments*.

Focusing on fundamental social, cultural and democratic aspects of preservation planning in modern society, a consciousness regarding the 'heritage creating process' has implied a shift away from the traditional scholarly construction of cultural values – above all referring to classical Western characteristics of architecture and built environment based on professional morphological analyses. In a scholarly and professional context dominated by the history of art and architecture – which was very often the case in this field some decades ago – *style* and *aesthetic* aspects were naturally highlighted. In this context, qualities referring to *uniqueness* were the major indicators of selection, particularly those applying to age, authenticity, specific historic persons or situations, renowned architects, etc.

The concept of 'historical-cultural value' as an instrument for valorizing cultural heritage and selecting objects was subsequently scrutinized and re-defined in broader ways. Gradually, when scholars representing ethnology, social history and human geography took part in those investigations, *social, technical, economic* and *ecological* dimensions of the built environment were added, usually with a *process-oriented* approach. Thus, qualities of built environment considered as *representative* with respect to specific aspects were identified and interpreted (e.g. building traditions during special periods; life styles among particular groups of inhabitants or patterns of ecological adjustment to specific conditions in different regions). These kinds of interpretations, describing various national, regional or local processes – often clearly visible in building structures and the cultural landscape – have successively become one of the most important instruments of selection. Consequently, such qualities as *readability* have become more pronounced as have the *educational* aspects of cultural significance. As an effect of this somewhat modified professional outlook, working and industrial areas, as well as the building stock of the post-war period, have become of interest for heritage preservation, as described below.

New attitudes to preservation planning have also led to a direct need for collaboration between public cultural heritage bodies and local groups of concerned citizens. In this kind of project, the interpretations of *collective memory* and *local identity*, especially as connected to specific buildings, places or cultural landscapes, have a significant role to play. Approaches of this kind imply an anthropological/ethnological/sociological methodology based on a pronounced 'emic-perspective', referring to individuals and groups of concerned citizens. This field of study seems to be fruitful and necessary – but demands a consciously conceptualized methodological framing of questions, modelled to specific problems. Intrinsic qualitative studies of social resources and intangible communication in various urban structures of habitat (e.g. such as discriminated or endangered working-class districts in city centres, or peripheral industrial zones) have given evidence of richly varied and multifaceted resources of social networks, specific value systems and impressive local cultural patterns (Engelbrektsson, 1982, 1987; Rosvall, 1999).

Studies directed towards local urban lifestyles and cultural repertoires give insights of '...actual historical processes in the area' and '...a concern of equal dignity to be recognized, interpreted and valued, as the very buildings and their embracing environments – traditionally monitored professionally and scholarly explained' (Castells, 1989). In the same article, a request is presented for '...a firm political will and a clear planning policy based upon the principle that the existing city and its gradual development have to be preserved and managed as a collective use-value'.

In the inhabitants' perspective, residential areas can be regarded as vehicles of explicit and implicit intangible social and cultural meaning. Consequently, particular buildings or places can be ascribed specific *symbol values* – of great importance to the local inhabitants – values earlier often disregarded by professionals. In a planning strategy aiming at conservation, rehabilitation and maintenance, local analyses of social and cultural processes must be seen as important instruments for the protection of existing diversity in urban space.

Gradually, it has become evident that the field of heritage preservation can be recognized as politicized social processes, operating at all levels of society – rarely consciously and explicitly expressed in political or planning documents. Conservation perspectives and heritage planning thus need to be more evidently and openly incorporated within general political goals and regular planning processes – not operating on their own as an isolated phenomenon. This implies close cooperation with other relevant sectors of society, such as social, ecological and physical planning.

As an evident fact, the epistemological context of sustainability, based on Agenda 21 and Habitat Agenda, has strengthened preservation ideals and aspirations opening the way for maintenance and care economically feasible. From this perspective, urban space and its supportive tangible structures may be interpreted as a considerable material resource, also concerning relatively anonymous recent buildings and ambiences. As an outcome, we can note a tendency towards a comprehensive shift in attitudes, with attention being paid to all kinds of buildings and built environments, even if fairly modest, including ordinary social housing.

In a planning context of this kind, instruments for the *selection of cultural heritage* objects are not of the same vital importance as they once were. Of course, this fact does not compromise the obvious need to continue traditional monument-oriented procedures for outstanding examples of cultural heritage. In sum, this broad scope of surveying built-up environments implies that an integrated conservation approach has begun to be of interest for the continuing planning mechanism, especially at the municipal level.

The Swedish Middle Way

A Centralized Planning System[1] Based on Centuries of Peace

An evident background factor of the Swedish case is the seemingly unconscious leaning on a very long history without actions of war within its territory. Compared to most European, and other, countries, and certainly during the alarming periods of the nineteenth and twentieth centuries, resulting in massive military destruction, this development of Sweden has been peaceful. Therefore, there was no necessity for large scale schemes of post-war reconstruction or requirements regarding well-defined large-scale conservation policies, as was the case in many other countries (Ceschi, 1970).

When observing architectural and urban conservation in Sweden (Schönbeck, 1994), this dimension has to be further considered in relation to a more-or-less continuing national governmental core policy over several centuries. A heavily centralized public administration was in being until relatively recent times, originally based on the power of the crown and its strong impact on the planning system, even in many civic respects. From architectural, economic and socio-cultural points of view, this system has gradually entailed the introduction of certain relatively standardized characteristics, sometimes in conflict with the interests of local citizens. These aspects, as regards town-planning regulations, comprise fire protection, architectural features, regulation of technical methods of building construction and choice of materials as well as restrictions in the use of natural supplies.

During the mid-nineteenth century, when the liberal legal system was introduced in Sweden, this change involved the transfer of the planning monopoly in many different respects from governmental level to a structure of independent municipalities – at the time still divided into urban and rural administrations with strongly differing planning responsibilities related to building regulations, market restrictions, etc. (Nordström and Olsson, 1969). The rural districts had few legal requirements concerning land-use planning, building construction and other architectural dimensions. In general terms, this situation in many respects continued to exist until the 1950s and the 1970s, when major administrative reforms were introduced in Sweden, leading to the 'rationalization' of a few thousand towns and municipalities into less than three hundred administrative units. This reform also implied that the distinction between 'townships' and 'countryside' came to an end (Heineman, 1975), being replaced by the sole denominator of the 'municipality' (Swedish: *kommun*). This means that, since that time, big cities, metropolitan conurbations, small towns, villages and vast rural and natural countryside areas are, in principle, regulated by one common municipality act.

The Growth of the 'Swedish Model'

The functionalistic architectural movement, based on distinctly formulated ethic codes and an engineering spirit concerning the rational, social and hygienic aspects of society, constituted a platform for the gradually established Swedish 'middle-way' with its comprehensive welfare model for all citizens focusing on poverty eradication (Bergold, 1985). When observed over a period of some decades, the principal facts referred to above contributed to the 'take-over' in mentality by the Modern Movement, beginning programmatically in 1930 with the Stockholm Exhibition (Liedman, 1997). In addition to the gradual modification of democratic, political and social characteristics, this discourse was in many ways basically compatible with the age-old centralized elitist planning system, but compared to traditional standards it was revitalized by the introduction of new architectural design and spatial models. Introduced during the 1930s – and very much aiming at counteracting the recession phenomena of this period – this movement was interrupted by WW2 (Caldenby et al., 1998).

In the Swedish case, an evasive protective policy was generated concentrating on a neutral defence system, but resulting in a general lack of resources in civic society. This situation caused interruption of much debated proposals for large-scale implementation of the urban planning policies initiated in the cities of Stockholm, Göteborg and Malmö, as well as in smaller towns. It must be stressed that, in an international comparison, modernism in Sweden became a hegemonic bourgeois project of quite other dimensions than, for example, in Mediterranean societies, depending on different political circumstances as well as various forms of social and economic conditions (Leontidou, 1996; Ventura, 1995).

However, the fundamental social changes of the post-war period combined with the boom of the 1950s, led to a need for massive development in all respects, resulting in a lack of manpower and housing and requiring modern technical infrastructure, problems requiring urgent resolution. This development was engineered by the superior goals of stability and harmony, expanding economy and full employment, and might be subdivided into three main periods schematically characterized by (Holm, 1985):

- initial planning and policy (1945-60);
- large-scale implementation 1960-70/75);
- stagnation (1970/75-80).

The Swedish model was thus developed as an overarching national-level 'pact' between leading political parties, driven by the social democrats jointly with labour unions, industrial unions, important private corporations and other groups, comprising local communities all over the country. This very successful and dominating model, which governed Sweden and its planning system over a couple of post-war decades, was based on three paradoxes (Wohlin, 1985):

- a *mixed economy*, i.e. the combination of a liberal market economy and a socialist allocation policy;
- *economic balance*, i.e. maintaining full employment while keeping prices stable;
- a *'middle way'* in terms of consensus and equalization, implying harmony between partners in the labour market.

Post-War Housing Policy

The stable Swedish welfare policy proceeded from a collectivist planning model with the main guiding responsibility assigned to the municipalities. The power of initiatives in spatial planning, architectural design and other dimensions of material structures was transferred by legal means from private property owners to public agencies granted planning monopolies (Nilsson, 1996). Simultaneously a great deal of public research and strategic development was invested in the definition of high-quality standards for modern apartments, social institutions, constructions and technical infrastructure. This development was operated partly by national agencies, some of which were specially established for these purposes, partly by rapidly growing municipal social housing corporations, and partly by expanding and powerful nationwide cooperative housing associations.

These huge post-war escalating and standard-setting operations were marked by an important full scale demonstration facility (Norra Guldheden, Göteborg), soon to be followed by the internationally renowned satellite towns (for example, Vällingby in Stockholm; Baronbackarna in Örebro) in well-planned suburban districts (Caldenby et al., 1998).

Looking back historically at this planning process, much of the modelling was, in reality, based on further development of a mixture of earlier experiences. The background comprised a multitude of examples, such as the large housing blocks of the 1920s (e.g. Röda Bergen in Stockholm) inspired by municipal housing design in Vienna, the 1930s modern housing schemes (e.g. Ribersborg in Malmö) based on new industrialized construction methods (imported mainly from the USA) and the neighbourhood architectural tradition (deriving mainly from Great Britain).

At the same time, massive decay and destruction of downtown housing and small industry areas took place; this came about gradually and was caused by the massive relocation of dwellings and traditional business activities, and, in parallel, the construction of a new public transportation system in Stockholm (Johansson, 1997). These factors were reinforced by the combination of a legally prescribed system of fixed apartment rents and a lack of manpower for construction and financial resources for rehabilitation and conservation of existing buildings. This was especially evident in Stockholm, but also in Göteborg and Malmö, and elsewhere in regional centres such as Norrköping and Västerås (Lindahl, 1965, 1971).

Political awareness regarding the firm need to compensate for these considerable losses of housing capacity and the rising demands in living standards became apparent. Further, it was necessary to meet constantly escalating demands regarding new dwellings for expanding groups of citizens moving from their traditional residences to urban centres (Holm, 1985). A huge housing scheme, the so called 'one-million program' was implemented mainly during the 1960s, with approximately one million flats in multi-story apartment buildings and row houses (the total population of Sweden at that time was circa eight million inhabitants). Recently, this phase has been thoroughly reanalyzed with partly diverging results (Caldenby, 2000; Hall, 1999; Jörnmark, 1999, 2000; Wetterberg, 2000), leading to the conclusion that these areas today represent other qualities and are much more complex than was recognized in earlier more biased and critical studies.

During this planning period, great new interest arose regarding pollution of different kinds, such as the decay of nature and the environment (Carson, 1962). In Sweden this new movement was simultaneously initiated at universities, growing environmentalist organizations and in democratic and political arenas. Another internationally important milestone was the governmental report *Land and Water* (Hushållning, 1971), leading to considerable restructuring in the Swedish legal and administrative system at all public levels, especially concerning spatial planning both in urban and countryside areas. Soon, this began to impact any kind of structure and action by citizens and private enterprises, in industry, housing and transportation, energy production, waste treatment, etc. (En ny Plan-, 1997; Rosvall, 1988). The most challenging outcome perhaps was the UN Conference on the Human Environment (1972), concluding in the *Stockholm Declaration* and eventually leading to the UN *Brundtland Report* (WCED, 1987) and its continuing effects.

Reactions against Demolition of Urban Environments

Strong reactions gradually became apparent against the destruction and restructuring of large downtown areas and traditional habitats in the major cities (e.g. Stockholm, Göteborg, Lund and Uppsala), along with planning of new large-scale housing schemes and penetration by the new dominant networks of streets and freeways (Johansson, 1997; Lindahl, 1965, 1971; Schönbeck, 1994).

These events of the late 1960s and the 1970s paved the way for a multi-faceted approach to housing policies and increasing involvement of the citizens in democratic processes. A growing awareness of conservation aspects came to the fore, aiming at a comprehensive view of the entire habitat in all of its dimensions. Leading agents in this uncontrolled process were an *ad hoc* mix of conscientious citizens, evolving local grass-root groups and a small set of scholars-professionals, mainly based at the Royal Academy of Fine Arts (Stockholm), University departments of art history and ethnology (Göteborg, Lund, Uppsala), and schools of architecture (polytechnics in Göteborg and Lund). The public heritage bodies in this period – especially the dominant Central Board of National Antiquities, already established in the mid-seventeenth century – were still traditionally focused on important 'classical' isolated monuments, classified on the basis of their conventional archaeological, historical and architectural aspects, as discussed above (Janson, 1974; ICOMOS, 1981).

During this period however, a few towns had accomplished multi-dimensional and comprehensive inventories of an interdisciplinary nature. This kind of planning instrument, in the form of preservation plans, comprised entire townscapes also including heavily degraded areas, often with a mix of small enterprise working-zones, working-class housing districts, etc., e.g. in Lund and the Malmarna district in Stockholm. The outcome of this kind of initiative was manifold, leading to increased concern for the preservation of entire historic housing districts.

First the general public debate was startling – in the media, public meetings, democratic assemblies, publications, exhibitions and professional gatherings. At the Royal Academy of Fine Arts, promoted by Professor Göran Lindahl, a long-term project concerning renewal and planning conditions in middle-sized and small towns was carried out during the 1970s. A set of local studies, *The Scandinavian Wooden Town* (*Den Nordiska Trästaden*), led to increased interest and awareness of historic dimensions among a generation of young architects and students in arts subjects (Lindahl, 1965, 1971). Extra-mural academic cross-disciplinary courses, focused on conservation and urban rehabilitation, were initiated by the Italian-inspired conservation architect and scholar Börje Blomé, and consciously realized in several towns in Sweden (Blomé, 1977). Concerning these important innovative activities – in connection with research visits to conservation centres in Italy, France and other regions – a growing international network was established by these professional conservationist participants (Blomé, 1991). For example, the visits to Göteborg and Stockholm (1968 and later) by the renowned Italian conservation professionals Carlo Ceschi and Roberto Di Stefano had a great impact on the public debate concerning the contemporary 'blight' processes (McKean, 1977) in these cities (Blomé et al., 1972).

Second, a multitude of initiatives, such as the actions of local architectural conservation groups, took place in favour of processes oriented towards 'integrated conservation' (Paulsson, 1979). These activities were mainly focused on specific objectives such as the preservation and development of specific buildings and districts comprising intangible social and cultural qualities. Furthermore, a small number of devoted academic groups of advanced students and their mentors initiated research projects regarding stabilizing patterns of living, work and local commercial life in existing neighbourhoods. The aim was to develop instruments and analyses to meet such needs, including ethnological or sociological generative research models, focusing not only on previously surveyed environments, urban patterns and life styles, but also elaborating methods for typology, inventorying, registration, documentation and interpretation. Thus, new kinds of applied cross-disciplinary studies were carried out, considering historic and aesthetic aspects as well as the economic, social and cultural dimensions, aiming at 'diagnosing' often endangered urban districts of various kinds (Bjur and Wetterberg, 1990; Engelbrektsson, 1987). The purpose of these broad interpretations of specific urban areas was to raise awareness of, and place the focus on, important variations of different aspects as a necessary basis for modulated preservation planning '...each place, each city, will receive its actual social meaning from its location in the hierarchy of a network whose control and rhythm will escape from each place and even more from the people of each place' (Castells, 1989).

Third, these new trends of integrated conservation – coming from the media, citizens and concerned scholars-professionals – escalated coincidentally with a multitude of other social and political expectations, which developed in society during this crucial period.

In summary, these movements indicated a huge gap – on the one hand – between the centralized Swedish top-down planning system and its agents, protagonists and the firmly intertwined formal aspects of its operating mechanisms – and on the other – its individual end-users; for example different citizens' groups, local inhabitants or small entrepreneurs, who generally were unwilling to be treated as anonymous collective elements (Engelbrektsson, 1982; Schönbeck, 1994).

Urban Conservation Movements in the 1970s

The urban conservation movement during the 1960s and 1970s was, in principle, generated conceptually as a reaction against the seemingly necessary nullification of habitats and historic urban centres. Evidently this was a deliberate and politically permitted destruction of material history, lifestyles and local identity. Without any doubt, this was an automatically delivered effect of the Swedish housing scheme of the modern movement. The recession during the mid-1970s, dependent on the oil crisis, opened up possibilities for a more general understanding of the advantages of the conservation model, especially the integrated approach. Gradually, a growing number of supporters were found among politicians, planners and other professionals, and also, to some extent, among citizens at large. One effect of this was that many planning regulations, construction standards, housing policies, mortgage regulations and other kinds of administrative mechanisms were changed in favour of preservation and integrated conservation planning schemes.

New Urban Tendencies: Threats or Advantages for Cultural Heritage?

Transformation of Urban Space and Environments

The late post-industrial phase of urban development, firmly linked to globalization, migration and other changes in society, and with its roots in information technology and the 'new economy communication systems' (Sassen, 1994), has led to an immense transformation of urban space and environments (Castells, 1989; Mommaas, 1996; Soja, 1989; Städernas Europa, 1992). Paralleling the worldwide high-tech regions, these processes are also very dynamic in the Scandinavian countries – gradually or rapidly, depending on varying circumstances – and with somewhat heterogeneous identities in different sub-regions and conurbations (van Weesep, 1996). The global digitized economy is thus manifest in different ways throughout the urban landscape as a materialization of regional and local adaptation to the new markets and communication systems (Sassen 1994).

These processes of globalization and urban restructuring have been interpreted, either as the *continuity* of a post-war 'modernization', or as the *discontinuity* of 'post-modern(ization)'. In empirical terms, changes have often been shown to be more irregular, overlapping and ambivalent than protagonists of the post-modern theories seem willing to accept. Alternatively, these urban processes may be interpreted in a third way, as *transformational continuity* (Mommaas, 1996). This analytical approach seems reasonable and valid not least in the Scandinavian countries, characterized by an evident and ongoing dichotomy between the processes of stabilization and transformation.

A Nation Running into the Post(post)industrial Phase?

Throughout the entire post-war era, Sweden has been considered as the Scandinavian nation following most closely along the traces of the US in terms of life styles and culture, as well as material standards and fashion. This phenomenon is, in many respects, still valid. In Sweden, with its high rate of expansion regarding new electronic information systems (very high even regarding an international comparison on the competitive market), new socio-spatial tendencies are indeed evident, especially in multi-dimensional and specialized areas, as well as in the periphery of bigger cities. These so called 'non-places of super-modernity' in 'ordinary landscapes' are today beginning to take shape to such an extent that they can be identified, analyzed and understood. Studies of changes in the areas of urban peripheries indicate that these zones seem to constitute one of the most important potentials for urban development in the future (Bjur and Malmström, 1996). As an example, these fringe zones leave room for new technical systems such as recycling and traffic, with possibilities of stimulating the development of various kinds of activities; therefore they constitute a dynamic capacity to transform entire towns. As part of these processes, the disconnected housing areas dating from the 1960s might be revitalized and thus become an integral part of new activity spheres and constellations.

In the following points some evidently disparate – and partly contradictory – tendencies of urban space and urban life in the Scandinavia of today are outlined:

- *totally planned, conforming and dull cities*, lacking places for the eccentric and unexpected – where 'the old' in many cases has been replaced by pastiches and false historicism;
- *a digital and anonymous city*, designed in a global and finished style, to be seen as all large cities world-wide, released from regional and

national traditions;

- *segregated cities*, characterized by increasing gaps between inner-city areas with rising rents, and fringe zone suburbs, with a high quota of immigrants;
- *multiplex, heterogeneous inner city areas*, characterized by the meeting of different dimensions of time and visual expressions, of separate patterns of life and value systems;
- *the city as an arena for 'homo ludens'* – playing, non-working man, living in an increasing 'culture of events' – e.g. different kinds of festivals and large sporting events, periodically transforming the inner city, sometimes leaving architectural constructions of an *ad hoc* character, situated as weird urban islands in the townscape.

Towards New Critical Attitudes and Alternative Urban Policies

Planning Research – Paradigmatic Shifts during the Post-War Period

Longitudinal meta-level studies concerning aims and directions of research have indicated that paradigmatic shifts (with reference to Kuhn's classical observations), tend to take place as a result of general social changes and the displacement of its various components (Jevons, 1973). In the field of planning research, observed phenomena as well as other kinds of selected approach seem to vary over time in a corresponding way.

During 'normal' phases – for instance the post-war decades of modern planning in Sweden – much attention was paid to the relationship between theory and data (*empiricism*). In this situation interest was primarily focused on finding elaborate methods of calibrated precision and accuracy, as well as possibilities for explaining manifest and available data.

In phases of crisis and reconciliation – for example when traditional planning conditions no longer seemed to be valid, as occurred in Sweden in the late 1990s – an increasing interest in *values,* fundamental for planning activities, is generally developed (*criticism*). Subsequently, this kind of general rethinking and reconsideration concerning relevant interpretations and fields of study, is regularly followed by phases of *reorganization*, primarily focusing on the relationship between value and theory (*constructivism*), which seem to have been relevant during the last few years (Grahm, 1986).

A Planning System in a Phase of Ambiguity and Re-Orientation

The manifest homogenization and standardization of Swedish 'ordinary landscapes' and urban environments has, for decades, been criticized from a traditional conservationist standpoint – but only seldom systematically analyzed in these terms. Rather, intense public debate concerning the socio-spatial environment has taken place among groups of critical scholars and planners, social urban movements and neighbourhood organizations, as a continuation of the previously mentioned grass-roots and radical student movements of the 1960s and 1970s. Due to the transformed prerequisites for planning authorities, the institutional crisis in general, innovative cultural development and a more complex social situation during the 1980s, the discourse of the well-planned Swedish society, and the possibilities of creating the modern 'Good City', began progressively to lose credibility.

In the late 1990s, it became apparent that the centralist 'welfare-state' had been transformed into a more neo-liberal and market-oriented society, resulting in increased economic polarization and social gaps between different groups of inhabitants. In most cities, this social inequity was manifested in spatial terms, especially in districts where many immigrants live (van Weesep, 1996). Today, segregation tendencies are most evident in the suburbs of Stockholm, Göteborg and Malmö, but to a lesser degree even in medium-sized towns, especially in the degraded areas constructed during the 'one-million-program' period.

In today's complex situation, the well-established physical and social planning models, elaborated during the post-war modernist period, are suddenly being questioned (Nilsson, 1996). Furthermore, the green movement, and the public environmental planning-system at municipal level imperatively carried forward in the 1990s according to Agenda 21, pioneered re-evaluation and reflections on planning systems and methods, hitherto taken for granted. This phase of general ambiguity and reconciliation has evidently promoted a new openness towards a preservation and conservation discourse among planning professionals in the context of 'sustainable urban development' (Fusco Girard, 1993; Nilsson 1996).

Referring to Sweden, as an illustrative example of the general transformations of modern society – ultimately depending on global economic conditions, as well as changes in industry and commercial life at a national level – new critical attitudes have developed among citizens, not least during the last decade (Bertilsdotter et al., 2000; Schoonbrodt, 1997). It is obvious then, that traditional policies for full employment, poverty eradication, social welfare and well-organized housing during the post-war era have had to be reduced or replaced in many aspects. However, these significant changes – in many respects negative for exposed groups – have created a broad range of diverging discourses and social movements, based on a strongly growing concern for environmental quality, urban policies and the living conditions of citizens. This collective critique of everyday life has often been interpreted in terms of deterioration of the quality of life and an explicit demand for the respect of humanistic and historic values. In connection with urban planning, these ethical considerations and collective movements of criticism can be summarized as an obvious need for a vision and the formulation of an integrated conservation plan for the entire habitat.

Attitudes to Preservation Planning in the 1990s

In reality, however, the conservation model became more widely accepted in the 1990s. The reasons for this are evident. Macro-economic factors, such as energy pricing, bank interest, fashion trends and migration movements at national levels and in broader contexts, obviously also set the standard for conservation, especially for the low budgets of elementary integrated conservation. Now, decades later, in an engineering country such as Sweden with its taken-for-granted welfare state model, the long-term effects of the early education of conservation professionals and mid-career and volunteer training courses for vocational groups are evident. Likewise, the consequences of small, but continuing, research activities, formulating a theoretical discourse regarding 'conservation discipline', gradually became obvious, along with the results of application-oriented themes of a multi-disciplinary nature, bridging humanities and social and natural sciences including tera-technology as well as high-tech.

The outcome is evident. Society at large, including market-based private companies and consortia, demand these services, since it has become evident that there is a tremendous need for awareness of the human dimensions of the city, making it 'liveable'. This refers not only to technical specifications, but also to delicate qualities, e.g. 'human well-being', which by definition cannot be constructed, but only conscientiously cared for and continuously cultivated in a well-cured atmosphere.

Towards a Sustainable Society

Dichotomy between Conservation of 'Nature' versus 'Culture'?

In the Scandinavian region, especially in Sweden, the relationship between the conservation of 'nature' and of 'culture' jointly comprising almost any environmental dimension, has long since developed into an assimilation process moving towards an integrated approach. In Sweden, this implies various kinds of policy action, legislative measures, funding and sponsoring initiatives at national and lower levels, as well as administrative and educational mechanisms, which together foster and promote a relatively well-organized co-operative effort between 'the two sides'.

On a national level, this has gradually been organized through close co-operation between the governmental agencies for the protection of nature and the environment (*Naturvårdsverket*), conservation of cultural heritage (*Riksantikvarieämbetet*), and physical planning/building/housing (*Bover-*

ket). At a local level, especially in municipalities, solutions are many and varied, but the legally prescribed Local Agenda 21 formula is intertwined at all levels. This provides a mandatory requirement for the planning of a sustainable future, necessarily implying an integrated relationship between spatial planning, habitat, industry and commercial life, commodities of citizens, transport systems, environmental issues and cultural heritage. In this way, the traditional paradigm with conflicts between the 'two cultures' (according to C.P. Snow) is gradually merging into a process of assimilation with cultural assets with, for example, built environment as its focus.

The Ecological Movement in Sweden

When looking for traces and practices that have led to the situation described above, the ecological movement in Sweden might be singled out as a distinct line of qualified opinions, studies and actions in the Linnéan tradition, already more or less expressed a century ago. This gave rise to growing environmental concerns and conservation measures, providing a platform for expanding policy making and planning underpinned by applied research. In the post-war period from the 1960s on, this has become even more evident.

In this respect, Swedish ecological consciousness, giving support to the conceptual framework presented during the first UN Conference on the Environment (Stockholm, 1972), eventually gave birth also to a rapidly widening discourse regarding cultural heritage conservation. In the first phase, this was primarily related to cultural landscape preservation and an evolving concern for a comprehensive approach to the environmental conservation of entire settings, such as traditional villages with modest vernacular architecture integrated with representative landscape typologies.

This planning process is, to some extent, dependent on a strong archaeological tradition in Scandinavia, a tradition which places emphasis on available traces of prehistoric and historic landscapes forming the living structure of the present modern environment in Sweden. Linked to discourses also deriving from ethnology and human geography, with emphasis on sources of non-verbal communication (NVC), this process deviated from traditional conservation practice, based in the realm of objects of art history, architecture and town planning, with its accent on 'classical monuments' in the continental European Beaux-Arts tradition. As presented above, a first step to integrated conservation planning in Sweden was initiated during the same period, partly in city centres in metropolitan areas, partly in small towns constructed in wood. Results, depending on a series of factors, varied but even if many historic districts and city centres were demolished, these growing movements nevertheless paved the way for general criticism of existing urban policies, expressing the need for an integrated conservation approach to built environments.

During the period following the 1970s, this chain of events fostered a mentality in the administrative system and among quite a number of groups of citizens and their political representatives, leading to the introduction of a set of legal planning instruments at all levels of society. In this context, it might be sufficient to mention some of these public models of great importance for the establishment of environmental and integrated conservation planning in Sweden.

Instruments for a Sustainable Society

A new comprehensive law (NRL – *Naturresurslagen*) was introduced during the 1980s which furnished the instrument to control all natural resources in Sweden – comprising the entire system of land, water and air, their components and their implications for the built infrastructure available to private and public landowners, to be controlled by planning authorities at all levels. This legal instrument automatically included all relevant ground-fixed cultural resources and sites, thus implying that heritage conservation planning had become an accepted part of an integrated view within the natural resource context.

As a consequence of the UN Rio-Conference in 1992, Sweden has developed a general and mandatory operating system for a sustainable society, based on the Agenda 21 formula, legally prepared for implementation at all planning levels ranging from national governmental responsibility down to the local municipalities (close to 300 separate administrative units). In practice, this means that each municipality is responsible for the management and control of a sustained future within its limits and ability.

At the same time, this provides a planning instrument covering vital social sectors, for example components of fundamental importance to conservation planning. In a long-term perspective, it is expected that this model will gradually involve critical sectors and components, which, in practice, are expected to offer good possibilities for a truly integrated conservation of the built environment, especially habitat, and also including defined cultural heritage. As part of the continuously revised editions of these local/regional/national environmental, planning, monitoring and controlling guidelines, public offices for cultural heritage and conservation are automatically incorporated in this cross-professional process, both as contributors as well as actors responsible for the inclusion of environmental requirements and cultural assets.

In parallel, a new legal planning system (PBL – *Plan- och Bygglagen*) was established by parliament during the same period. The objective was to give executive power to municipalities for the spatial and physical planning of the entire Swedish territory – to municipalities in urban regions as well as conurbations of any kind of ground with or without buildings and other types of man-made structures. This legal instrument provides for the right of a landowner to control such structures and their equivalents, if for some reason they are eliminated. But this system, on behalf of its planning authorities, also offers the right of society to restrict changes to such existing buildings and other spatial structures, under the heading 'continuing use of the land'. In practice, this system can be interpreted as an initial step towards administrative development for establishing a model for general and continuous integrated conservation planning of a generic nature, applicable to any kind of building and function, independent of its position, age, typology, character, use, values, users and inhabitants.

As part of the national monitoring of all habitat available to the entire Swedish population (Swedish: *bostadsförsörjningsprogram*), well-developed statistics were produced as a means for decision-making on all levels regarding numbers of dwellings of all kinds, their sizes, standards and technical equipment, but also including estimations of other specific characteristics, such as related cultural value.

Up-grading of Post-War Residential Areas

During the last few years, the Swedish governmental planning bodies responsible for cultural heritage (headed by *Riksantikvarieämbetet*, the National Board of Antiquities) have developed a new approach to recent residential areas, notably typical post-war social constructions, with standardized multilevel concrete blocks mostly to be found in distant peripheral areas in the metropolitan regions of Stockholm, Göteborg and Malmö, but also elsewhere in smaller towns. This *Storstadens arkitektur och kulturmiljö* project (National Heritage Board, 2001), is contributing to a reappraisal of post-war residential areas and their typical architectural characteristics, more varied and in some cases of considerable quality, especially as compared to former prejudices.

Incorporated into the research and policymaking of this national project, strong emphasis is placed on different aspects of communication. Establishing contacts with the residents and other actors in the areas under study and understanding their opinions and multifaceted knowledge about these resources is thus an explicit goal of the project. Another aim is to make the results accessible to wider circles of citizens, in similar areas, but also to those who do not have direct experience or information regarding these phenomena. This approach is based on a fundamental idea of integrated conservation, aiming at these environments in various respects. One further goal is to pave the way towards the abandonment of earlier general attitudes of deeming such areas as more or less 'hopeless', and gradually interject and stimulate visions concerning their specific values and potential for a new phase of appreciated development.

The changed Swedish cultural heritage policy for social housing representing 'modern movement architecture' reflects a general international tendency to gradually incorporate recent 'monuments' (e.g. according to proposals from ICOMOS-Documomo), and also to widen the range of types of objects acceptable for inclusion within the cultural heritage sector (e.g. industrial archaeology). Aside from this strong tendency to widen the traditional scope of cultural heritage to include new dimensions and new kinds of objects – even incorporating contemporary examples – the principal factor of change contributed by the Swedish public cultural administration, is to focus on the *entire environment* in all its possible aspects, notably social and cultural dimensions and multi-faceted residential demands from the local population. The reason for this change in professional direction is based partly on democratic demands, partly on the interdisciplinary organization of relevant knowledge, and partly on long-term economic considerations of optimum management and development (Scholz, 2001).

Rehabilitation of Residential Areas from the 1970s

Hjällbo and Gårdsten, two typical residential areas dating from the 1970s on the outskirts of Göteborg, are examples of the new way of applying the Swedish welfare model, now that the classical 'middle way' in many respects has come to an end. These projects have developed in response to considerably changed conditions, including the combined formula of a vision regarding environmental planning for a sustainable society, poverty eradication, creation of new employment, supporting social equity and striving for the inclusion of discriminated groups, e.g. new groups of immigrants. This scenario, from Hjällbo and Gårdsten, may be seen as a progressively evolving model for integrated preservation planning in its widest application directed towards residential areas with multi-factor problems. In this case, initiative did not come from the cultural heritage sector, but from a publicly owned social housing company, according to ambitious political indications. The Hjällbo and Gårdsten programs, planned as part of a joint venture experiment partly with co-financing from the European Union, were sharing experiences with similar partners from France, Germany, the Netherlands and the UK.

These Swedish cases have established a model potentially suitable for adaptation to other circumstances, also abroad. The social approach, organizing a local network between area residents, not manifest in advance, provides the fundamental platform for opening different kinds of communication between inhabitants from many countries (hardly any Swedes). The new immigrants represent many ethnic groups, cultural habits and different languages ($n \approx 80$), all of which imply latent causes of conflict related to the complicated communications situation, both in spoken language and certainly in NVC dimensions.

The material rehabilitation – combined with enhanced technical infra-structure and technical improvement of all amenities (both in private flats and in common spaces such as micro-gardens and well equipped laundry facilities) – has resulted in valuable upgrading in all respects. For economic reasons, an effective and efficient energy system with district heating, solar energy collectors, considerable thermal insulation and sophisticated monitoring devices in each flat for energy consumption control were also installed in the Gårdsten project. This investment further includes the reorganization of new installations important for social health and quality of life on a general level, such as 're-inventing' the commercial services which have disappeared such as shops, banks, post-offices, enhanced public transport, reliable security systems, introduction of local offices, production facilities, etc., all aiming at offering not only services, but new jobs.

An important factor within these programs is the intentional reorganization of service-oriented and highly appreciated local wardens and repair staff for on-going surveying and preventive interventions. Their overtly noticeable pro-active contacts with the local inhabitants, especially children, young people and mothers, offer a base for fostering a positive atmosphere, overriding practical problems of many kinds, such as communication obstacles and negative attitudes. One decisive factor in these districts seems to be the manifest intent to programmatically establish a plan for growing employment opportunities for local inhabitants. This objective serves to inspire enhancement of language capacity as a critical personal factor, promoting enterprising initiatives and slowly developing a positive local economic spiral. Obviously the intention is for this process to become a stimulating factor for finding one's way in the surrounding world, and thereby reducing poverty, inactivity, isolation and discrimination.

It is obvious that this kind of rehabilitation program for social housing districts was not defined in terms of 'integrated conservation' and it is not composed of traditional cultural heritage components. Nevertheless, there can be no doubt that in practical terms the intent and over-all effects reach the objectives of the integrated conservation policy, albeit in a new and unforeseen manner.

Industrial Environmental Actions Benefiting Conservation

Along with the integrated conservation approach, directed at the specific local built environment, the ecological movement also requires preventive and/or pro-active programs as part of the underlying infrastructure and on the general system level. Because industry has been one of the heaviest polluters in history, it constitutes one of the principal targets for environmental criticism (Rosvall, 1988). For many reasons, including company good will, as well as strong economic incentives, certain forward-looking industries increasingly strive to avoid environmental pollution, energy losses and other kinds of negative ecological effects. Some Swedish examples can illustrate this dimension of great importance at all levels, locally as well as globally. The automotive industry has always been one of the typical large polluters. With this in mind, it is evident that the Swedish Volvo Corporation was well aware of its negative impact on society and nature thus compromising its ambition to be recognized as a leading company with an environmental-friendly and security-conscious image.

One important negative impact observed during the 1980s was the evident corrosion produced by atmospheric car traffic pollution on the surfaces of valuable monuments, for example in Rome, but also elsewhere in the world especially in big cities. This has led to support for scientific research in the area of cultural heritage conservation, providing results indicating strictly non-controversial reasons to eliminate or reduce generation of SO_2 and NO_x (Rosvall, 1988).

The immediate scientific/technical conclusion and decision from Volvo was to introduce catalytic converters in its new cars. At the same time this action illustrates the overall environmental policy of the industry concerned with promoting cultural preservation as an indirect but consciously intended side effect.

A policy of this kind is based on the goal of reducing negative environmental impacts, especially when this process promotes a general positive tendency among other industries, as well as a consciousness-raising trend in society at large. This policy includes three phases, each requiring parallel elimination (or reduction) of relevance (noises, gases, particles, solid wastes, gases, etc.) on the ground, in the atmosphere, or in the seas:

- reduction/elimination of environmental effects related to *production* and *distribution,* also among e.g. suppliers;
- reduction/elimination of environmental effects related to *consumers* and the *use period* of the product;
- reduction/elimination of environmental effects related to the *residue of the product,* after the end of its intended or actual use.

When an explicit environmental policy of this kind is formulated by a relatively small corporation like Volvo, it has manifold international impacts, e.g. on the surroundings of its industrial plants, not only in Göteborg, but also elsewhere globally among subsidiaries and suppliers, in the general traffic system and otherwise in interfacing with urban ambience as in city centres. This kind of development requires considerable fundamental research guided by a meta-modelling approach (van Gigch, 1991).

It is evident that some concerned industrial corporations have come to appreciate their responsibilities for environmental development benefiting a sustainable society. The growing cooperation concerning such future-oriented programs – between industry, public agencies and scientific research – has reached a situation where truly high calibre interdisciplinary activity promotes an improved environment, and ultimately enhances economic results. In this respect, the conservation of material cultural assets has been approached in a serious way, paralleling the general promotion of a gradually more liveable habitat.

District Heating Supporting Conservation Objectives

Another evident example of important environmental impacts for the built environment and its preservation, is the modern type of district heating developed in metropolitan areas as Göteborg, a typical medium-sized conurbation in a moderately cold region. The majority of its buildings in residential areas, commercial centres and industrial zones are linked by a pipeline system providing hot water during the winter season, and for offices also chilled air during the summer. Under normal conditions, the necessary energy is derived from the super-efficient combustion of consumer-produced garbage. In peak periods this is supplemented by some more costly additional raw materials, but continuously from excess energy – otherwise left in nature as pollutants from industrial plants, for example heat from petroleum refineries or heat exchangers in the hydro-purification plants of the wastewater system.

This system, producing consumer and environmentally friendly energy at reasonable prices, comes at the same time from an effective use of wastes and surplus energy, which would otherwise cause heavy environmental, sanitary, economic and comfort problems. The combustion at this kind of district heating central plants, in Göteborg is without ($\approx 100\%$) any polluting effects, but still however produces CO_2 since the 'greenhouse problem' has still to find a solution. However, recent scientific reports (National Agency for Protection of Nature) firmly indicate that the level of carbon dioxide in Sweden is also progressing to a level strictly below target.

The district heating energy system evidently solves a whole set of practical problems in the urbanized regions of the cold hemisphere. This kind of system leaves metropolitan areas unpolluted and releases them from much unnecessary transport of energy (oil, etc.), reducing the numbers of trucks in the streets, in turn leading to lesser impact on the external world (minimum consumption of carbon, petroleum products and electricity). At the same time, it also means minimizing installations with only minor impact of disturbing technical interventions on the authentic material structure of the buildings, most notably the cultural heritage.

Green Zones as an Environmental Conservation Model

The final illustration of this set of examples of environmental impacts on cultural heritage and development factors, promoting, on a general level, integrated conservation processes, refers to vegetation areas as an interfacing environmental phenomenon related both to *nature* and *culture*.

Sweden's capital, Stockholm, has established a municipal planning system protecting the plentiful amount of 'green zones', partly conceptualized as parks or as distinctly planned vegetation belts, partly well preserved remains of scattered zones of 'original' nature, stretching from outside the suburban periphery to the very urban core of the city. The green zones are made up of vegetation, seawater surfaces, intersected by, or intersecting into, habitat from all periods, of all kinds of built environment typical of a modern metropolitan area with historic origins, with its complicated traditional and recent technical infrastructure.

Within Stockholm's system of green zones, based on a local decision by the City Council, a large area with many valuable characteristics has been designated a National Park according to Swedish legislation on nature conservation. This was the very first example of its kind of an 'urban national park' including various components of 'nature'-oriented bio-topes, as well as cultural parks, other kinds of cultivated vegetation as well as the built environment. These green zones of all kinds – ranging from royal gardens and strict baroque parks, to small green pastoral meadows and productive pine forests – are cared for in accordance with an ambitious environmental preservation plan. Thus, it is implementing preventive anti-pollution measures on a general regional level with a pro-active conservation policy regarding continuing relations between green zones and the interfacing built environment and its dynamic commercial or private activities, with precise instructions for relevant interventions and cure of all these very varied types of bio-topes.

In fact, in this way the green zones are organized as a huge environmental quality-of-life indicator verifying the salubrious living conditions of the Stockholm area and its population. At the same time it is providing real-time proof that *nature* can be maintained in a decent way, fully integrated with *culture* in a complex and high-tech oriented modern conurbation. Most of all, this conservation model demonstrates in a fruitful way that in modern society it is possible to combine ecological objectives with integrated conservation planning, to the benefit of nature, the cultural heritage and citizens, providing a high quality habitat (Dahlqvist and Snickars, 1998).

Towards an Holistic and Humanities-Oriented Planning Approach

In a planning situation such as the one under consideration, characterized by reorientation and reconciliation, fruitful cooperation between planners and conservation professionals is beginning to come about. Awareness of sustainable dimensions at all planning levels in society has also led to increasing attention to hitherto neglected qualities and values of architectural heritage and ordinary built-up environments, as well as threatened urban social networks and local economic life (Fusco Girard, 1997; Rosvall, 1999).

Unfortunately, diverging educational and professional backgrounds among the planning staff, implying different terminology and bodies of knowledge, have tended to hinder rather than promote the creation of new solutions and methods. This dysfunctional situation has further been reinforced by a still rather segmented and sector-oriented planning-system organized in separate administrative areas, such as physical, social and ecological planning – normally isolated from the preservation planning of cultural heritage, which in turn has generally been carried out by museums and landmarks commissions. In addition, the university system in Sweden has, until recently, been run in accordance with a centralized administrative model, and is still strictly divided between humanities, social and natural sciences and other areas. In a reference framework of formal educational conditions of this kind, it has been possible only in a few cases to create genuinely cross-disciplinary educational programs at undergraduate and graduate level for humanities-oriented planners and conservationists (Engelbrektsson, 1999; Rosvall *et al*, 1995/99).[2]

In sum then, the new tendencies of general openness and reorientation among planning professionals may be seen as a great advantage and a challenge for humanities-oriented conservation planning. The post-war planning discourse, extremely oriented towards quantitative and technical conceptions and methods (which during several decades was taken for granted), gradually seems to be opening up to non-measurable qualitative dimensions. Increasing interest in 'integrated conservation planning' is evident, and it also includes anthropological, ethnological and historical studies of complex, intangible dimensions, such as those related to life-styles, 'identity' of built environment, and the values and needs of the inhabitants and actors, which form the entire habitat.

Notes

1   *Spatial development* in Sweden is divided between *Physical planning* and *Regional planning*, managed by separately organized professional competencies, traditionally carried out on different levels respectively by municipalities and by state agencies.

2   The only comprehensive Master program and Ph.D. program is available in the Discipline of Conservation at Göteborg University, with specialization in *Integrated Conservation of Built Environments.*

References

Appleyard, D. (1979), *The Conservation of European Cities,* Cambridge and London.
Bergold, C.E. (1985), *Bostadsbyggande i Uppsala 1900-1950. En aspekt på Folkhemmets framväxt,* Acta Universitatis Upsaliensis, Ars Suetica, no. 8, Uppsala.
Bertilsdotter, M. et al. (2000), *Det framtida Stockholm – Den högteknologiska stadens resurser.* Stiftelsen Vetenskapsstaden, Programrådet för Det framtida Stockholm – En hållbar Storstadsregion, Stockholm.
Bjur, H. and Malmström, B. (1996), 'Periferins gestalt', *Arkitektur,* no. 8.
Bjur, H. and Wetterberg, O. (1990), *Kulturmiljö och planering. Om historia för framtiden,* Byggforskningsrådet, Stockholm.
Blomé, B. (1977), *Kyrkorestaurering i teori och praxis. Den italienska restaureringsdoktrinen och dess tillämpning vid restaurering av tre svenska kyrkor 1966-77,* Ph.D. Dissertation, Konstvetenskapliga Institutionen, Göteborgs Universitet, Göteborg.
Blomé, B. (1991), 'Venedigdokumentet 1964 och dess betydelse och tillämpning i Sverige', *Kulturmiljövård,* no. 1, pp. 3-6.
Blomé, B., Holst, A. and Löwe, A. (1972), *Låt stå! Om bevarande av stadsmiljön,* Lund.
Brandi, C. (1963), *Teoria del restauro,* Einaudi, Turin.
Caldenby, C. (2000), 'Inte bara betong. Miljonprogrammet sett ur ett annat perspektiv', Göteborgs-Posten.
Caldenby, C., Lindwall, J. and Wang, W. (1998), *Sweden. 20th Century Architecture,* Prestel, München and New York.
Carson, R. (1962), *Silent Spring,* Houghton Mifflin, Boston.
Castells, M. (1989), *The Informational City. Information Technology, Restructuring, and the Urban-Regional Processes,* Basil Blackwell, Oxford.
Ceschi, C. (1970), *Teoria e storia del restauro,* Bulzoni, Rome.
Dahlqvist, M. and Snickars, F. (ed.) (1998), *Det framtida Stockholm - En hållbar storstadsregion. (Future Stockholm – a sustainable metropolis)*, Stiftelsen Vetenskapsstaden, Programrådet för Det framtida Stockholm – en hållbar stadsvision. Stockholm.
Engelbrektsson, N. (1982), *Landala – stadsdel och livsform som försvann,* Etnologiska institutionen, Göteborgs universitet, Lokalhistorisk identitet, no. 4, Göteborg.
Engelbrektsson, N. (1987), *Integrated Conservation –Research and Student Projects in Swedish Communities,* in Proceedings of the Third International Congress on Architectural Conservation and Town Planning, Heritage Trust, London.
Engelbrektsson, N. (1999), *Magisterutbildningar i Kulturvård,* Reports from the Institute of Conservation, Göteborg University, Göteborg.
Fusco Girard, L., (ed.) (1993), *Estimo ed economia ambientale: le nuove frontiere nel campo della valutazione. Studi in onore di Carlo Forte,* Angeli, Milan.
Fusco Girard, L. and Forte, B. (eds) (2000), *Città sostenibile e sviluppo umano,* Angeli, Milan.
Fusco Girard, L. and Nijkamp, P. (1997), *Le valutazioni per lo sviluppo sostenibile della città e del territorio,* Angeli, Milan.
Grahm, L. (1986), 'Nyorientering i regionalpolitiken ställer nya förväntningar på

forskningen', *Plan*, no. 3.

Hall, T. (ed.) (1999), *Rekordåren. En epok i svenskt bostadsbyggande*, Boverket, Stockholm.

Heineman, H.E. (ed.) (1975), *New Towns and Old. Housing and Services in Sweden*, The Swedish Institute, Stockholm.

Holm, P. (1985), 'Swedish Planning 1945-1985: Ideology, Methods and Results', *Plan International*, pp. 9-20.

ICOMOS (1964), *The Charter of Venice*, International Charter for the Conservation and Restoration of Monuments and Sites, Venice.

ICOMOS (1981), 'The Cultural Heritage in Sweden', *ICOMOS Bulletin*, no. 6.

Janson, S. (1974), *Kulturvård och samhällsbildning*, Nordiska Museets Handlingar, no. 83, Stockholm.

Jevons. F.R. (1973), *Science Observed. Science as a Social and Intellectual Activity*, London.

Johansson, B.O.H. (1997), *Den stora stadsomvandlingen. Erfarenheter från ett kulturmord*, Kulturdepartementet/Fritzes, Stockholm.

Jörnmark, J. (1999), 'Vägen till miljonprogrammet', Paper presented to the Stockholm School of Economics.

Jörnmark, J. (2000), 'Miljonprogrammet', article in the Swedish *National Encyklopedien*, vol. 22.

Leontidou, L. (1996), 'Alternatives to Modernism in (Southern) Urban Theory: Exploring in-between Spaces', *International Journal of Urban and Regional Research*, vol. 20, p. 2.

Liedman, S.-E. (1997), *I skuggan av framtiden. Modernitetens idéhistoria*, Bonnier Alba, Stockholm.

Lindahl, G. (1965), 'Omvandlingen i städernas mitt', *Arkitektur*, vol. 5, pp. 152-159.

Lindahl, G. (1971), 'Centrumkvarterens öde: återblick på 50 – och 60-talen i svenska städer', *Arkitektur*, vol. 5, p. 26.

Marconi, P. (1984), *Arte e cultura della manutenzione dei monumenti*, Laterza, Rome.

McKean, C. (1977), *Fight Blight. A Practical Guide to the Causes of Urban Demolition and What People Can Do about It*, Kaye and Ward, London.

Meinig, D.W. (1979), *The Interpretation of Ordinary Landscapes. Geographical Essays*, Oxford University Press, Oxford-New York.

Mommaas, H. (1996), 'Modernity, Postmodernity and the Crisis of Social Modernization: A Case Study in Urban Fragmentation', *International Journal of Urban and Regional Research*, vol. 20, pp. 196-216.

National Heritage Board/Riksantikvarieämbetet (2001), *The Cultural Heritage in Society*, [On line] available: http://www.raa.se.

Nilsson, J.E. (1996), Framväxten av samhällsplaneringen. Nordplan. Nordiska Institutet för Samhällsplanering, Stockholm.

Nordström, L. and Olsson, R. (1969), 'Hur landet är indelat', *Det moderna Sverige*, Samhället, Bonniers, Stockholm, pp. 214-47.

Paulsson, T. (1979), *Den nya staden?, Natur och Kultur*, Stockholm.

Rosvall, J. (ed.) (1988), Air Pollution and Conservation. Safeguarding Our Heritage. Elsevier Science Publishers, Amsterdam-New York-Tokyo.

Rosvall. J. (1999), 'Göteborg, an Example of Integrated Conservation in European Historic City Centres', *Restauro*, no. 149, pp. 66-96.

Rosvall, J., Engelbrektsson, N., Lagerqvist, B. and van Gigch, J. P. (1995/99), 'International Perspectives on Strategic Planning for Research and Education in Conservation', Paper presented to the International Meeting: *La cultura del restauro, tutela e conservazione delle opere d'arte*, Bergamo 9-11 March, *Bolletino d'Arte*, supp. no. 98, pp. 177-188.

Sassen, S. (1994), *Cities in a World Economy*, Pine Forge Press, Thousand Oaks.

Scholz, R.W., (ed.) (2001), 'Lundby on the Move. Mobility and Sustainable Urban Development. Gothenburg Case Study 2002', GMV – Centre for Environment and Sustainability, Göteborg University and Chalmers University of Technology, Göteborg.

Schönbeck, B. (1994), *Stad i förvandling. Uppbyggnadsepoker och rivningar i svenska städer från industrialismens början till idag*, Byggforskningsrådet, Stockholm.

Schoonbrodt, R. (1997), 'The SMEs and the Revitalization of the European Cities', *Perceive, Conceive, Achieve. The Sustainable City*, II, CEC.

Soja, E.W. (1989), 'The Historical Geography of Urban and Regional Restructuring', in *Postmodern Geographies. The Reassertion of Space in Critical Social Theory*, Verso, London and New York, pp. 157-89.

Städernas Europa (1992), *Gemenskapsåtgärder i stadsmiljö*, Europeiska Kommissionen, Luxembourg.

The Council of Europe (1975), *The Amsterdam Declaration*, Amsterdam.

UNCHS (Habitat) – United Nations Centre for Human Settlements (1996), *The Habitat Agenda*, Istanbul.

van Gigch, J. (1991), *System Design Modeling and Metamodeling*, Plenum, New York.

van Weesep, J. (1996), 'Urban Restructuring and Equity', Nordplan, Nordiska Institutet för Samhällsplanering, Meddelande, no. 4, Stockholm.

Ventura, P. (1995), *Town Planning, Design and Conservation in Italy*, Faculty of Architecture, University of Florence, Florence.

WCED (World Commission on Environment and Development) (1987), *Our Common Future* (The Brundtland Report), Oxford University Press, Oxford.

Wetterberg, O. (ed.) (2000), *Det nya stadslandskapet. Texter om kultur, arkitektur, planering*, Chalmers Tekniska Högskola, Göteborg.

Wohlin, H. (1985), 'The People's Home as an Information Society', *Plan International*, pp. 142-7.

Zancheti, S.M. (ed.) (1999), *Conservation and Urban Sustainable Development. A Theoretical Framework*, CECI – Centro de Conservaçao Integrada Urbana e Territorial, Federal University of Pernambuco, Pernambuco.

Chapter 23

Conservation-Based Cultural, Environmental, and Economic Development: The Case of the Walled City of Fez

Hassan Radoine

Introduction

When dealing with 'conservation' one has to realize that heritage, which has endured over centuries, can be neither grasped nor discerned all at once, within the limits of time and place. Furthermore, the legacy of centuries of innovation, development, human experience, mutation, and change requires an holistic vision to unveil its true dimensions. This holistic vision cannot be achieved easily, and unfortunately it is often subsumed by assumptions and attempts toward preordained conclusions and syntheses through self-projection and foreknowledge.

Indeed, this vision is the key to the puzzle that permits us to understand the essence of the past and shape sound strategies for the future. Conservation is a double-edged sword. On the one hand, it reveals the 'positivity' of the past and its value that is worthy of consideration and cultivation and on the other hand, it restrains and imprisons the future in its own realm. Thus, the present can oscillate between the readiness of the past, which tends to preserve itself as it was and the projected future, which drives it forward.

The historic site is now identifiable and has its own undeniable integrity and it is due to its very 'energy' that many cities have been improved. On the contrary, regarding the site as an open-air museum piece has been a cause of its neglect and abandonment. The position regarding the historic site as a determined and invariable entity is derived from lack of dialogue and understanding. It renders it merely a sacrosanct object. The extreme respect for this sacrosanct object leads to its abandonment not as a negative reaction but for fear of dealing with it, or for the anguish of monotonous submission.

This is not, by any means, a generalizing conclusion. Rather, it is drawing lessons and assessing the conservation policy-making of one of the greatest world heritage sites, Fez. Since Fez was declared a world heritage site in 1981, it has become a hub for national and international researchers and experts for the study of the conservation of a city which is still living beneath the shade of the past even while in the twentieth century. It is home to approximately 160,000 people, covers an area of 375 hectares and encompasses 13,385 buildings.[1] This immense historic urban site still preserves all the features of a medieval city ranging from its water system, urban facilities, dwelt houses, markets (*souks*), to working neighbourhoods. Together with its blank and austere facades, its network of winding pedestrian streets has never been altered. In addition to its intact physical environment, the walled city remains the hub of the local economy and the core of Morocco's spiritual and cultural legacy.

Setting up a conservation policy for Fez has required more than three decades of sound research, experimentation, and implementation of pilot projects in order to crystallize a practical strategy for approaching this complex and intricate urban site. The local expertise that each historic site needs to develop was considered necessary to maintain the course of action, the harmony of the whole, ensure a grass roots approach, and avoid applying imported 'ready-magic' strategies. Those 'magic' strategies, often immature, which have been duplicated and which do not stem from the site itself, were behind the failure of many previous conservation efforts. Whereas the effectiveness of a specific type of imported expertise can be better obtained through interaction with the locally developed one. In order to further clarify this idea, it is of the utmost importance to examine how the concept of 'conservation' evolved in the case of Fez.

Evolution and Mutation of the Concept of 'Conservation'

It is noteworthy to mention that this paper represents a brief overview of conservation through a broad historical study. The space here does not permit us to explore all its ramifications.

Pre-colonial Period (before 1912)

Why and how has Fez been preserved over the centuries since its founding by Idriss II in 808 A.D.?

Since the days of the *Idrissid* dynasty which ruled Morocco in the ninth century, successive rulers in different dynasties have respected the tradition of 'sultan-builders'. Without destroying their predecessors' achievements, each dynasty had to compete with them and erect new works. Be it a mosque, *madrassa*, *founduk*, hospital, palace or gateway, Fez is a 'portfolio' filled with traces of each historic period.[2] In addition to these landmarks, the sustainability of the city is deeply related to the societal development and the community institutions that have played an important role in keeping its heart beating without stopping.

The balance between the institution of the sultan and that of the community was a major factor in the development of urban life. The former was concerned with the strategic features of the city such as guaranteeing its defence by building walls and fortifications, providing the city with water via aqueducts, supervising and preserving the main urban patterns, i.e. main thoroughfares, gateways, etc. This sultan institution was composed of the sultan, the chief judge, the guild trustees, the Muslim scholars (*ulama'e*), and neighbourhood representatives. The latter supervised the daily life of the different self-organized neighbourhoods. Each neighbourhood had a centre that catered to daily needs such as a small mosque (*Masjid*), bakery (*Ferran*), Turkish bath (*hammam*), public fountain (*sequaya*), and grocery stores (*dakkakin*). Those public services were joined through a node upon which all dead-end alleys belonging to that neighbourhood converged. This spatial unity could not be achieved without the neighbourhood institution which was composed of local judges, scholars (*ulama'e*), *Muhtassib*, trustees of local guilds (*Umanae*), and local saints' brotherhoods (*Zawaya*). Furthermore, these neighbourhood institutions had moulded the most complex organic urban body through embodying the spirit of the community as a honeycomb.

These two institutions developed the city, preserving its unity. This unity is demonstrated by the harmony of the whole structure that appears as one single neighbourhood. It is worth mentioning that the change over time and space was based on adaptation and innovation rather than on destruction. From the ninth to the nineteenth century, the city evolved and grew without any major or sudden change that might have altered its integrity. Therefore, conservation was not displayed as a separate concern since the language, the tools, and the values of change had been respected. The example here is of the different interventions upon the medina over centuries in order to restore a monument, improve the sewage network, or expand the wall for protection purposes as a result of the growth of the city, etc. The medina has kept its strength as a sustainable city through the strong relationship created between the manmade environment and the spirit of man himself. Conservation was not seen as a precise technical action but rather as an imbued state of mind embodied in a style of living.

Colonial Period (1912-1956)

When one compares Morocco where the cultural heritage is still physically well-preserved with other countries colonized by France, one might ask the question, why and how did the French avoid erasing historic sites? Why did the French use conservation as an alibi?

Once Lyautey was assigned to fill the position of General Resident of Morocco, he kept in mind the mistakes and destructive policies of French colonial policy in previously occupied countries such as Algeria[3] and Madagascar. Having accumulated experience in colonization tactics, Lyautey came to Morocco with a new policy for enhancing France's presence in this land. As Lyautey himself stated: 'They [the Moroccans] still do not know us well. We frighten them. They still remain rather withdrawn, but they are easy to win over when one shows them intelligent sympathy, especially when they feel that they are appreciated. For the secret is a welcoming hand, and not a condescending one, a loyal man-to-man handshake, made in order to understand one another...' (Scham, 1970, p. 89). His policy consisted of first understanding the cultural context and then shaping the cultural tools for French intervention in Morocco.

To reach this end, he called upon pioneers of different disciplines, most particularly planners, to explore the country.[4] Among those planners, Prost appears to be the man who made Lyautey's dreams come true.[5] Both Lyautey and Prost claimed a 'culturalist' approach toward dealing with colonization issues. Prost, as a leader among his peers in his time, had drawn up the most significant urban colonial policies and territorial management strategies in Morocco. Those policies took into consideration two positions. The first was to show to the 'indigenous' people that the French were aware of the importance of their cultural heritage sites. Therefore they would distinguish them from the French colonial centres and would conserve them in order to avoid their opposition.

> Lyautey himself was responsible for the practice whereby the French in Morocco (unlike those in Algeria) built their own cities outside Arab cities; he wished to preserve the character and the charm of the Arab cities. But this separation also accentuated the French tendency to look upon the Moroccans as the 'natives', holding lower position in the social and class structure. (Scham, 1970, p. 192).

The second position was that, instead of relying only on military power and destructive means, as applied elsewhere, Lyautey tried to gain the core of the country by understanding its spheres of influence, i.e. its ruling institutions and the main sources of leadership in its local communities. Thus, he was able to shift the lever of power from powerfully historic large urban sites such as Fez, Marrakech, Mekness, and southern *Kasabas* to newly designed colonial urban settlements that were erected in their precinct not far away from the French military camps. This shift was achieved through four main actions:

- land acquisition for expanding the colonial urban centres;
- substituting local institutions through the creation of new modern ones;
- military presence for eventual intervention and control;
- evolving economic strategies based on taxation and the decentralization of local wealth to new geographically designed rich and powerful centres.

This centre consisted in the newly created capital of Rabat instead of Fez,[6] the port of Casablanca from which wealth was exported to France, and Kenitra, a newly created colonial city which was primarily a military one. With the implementation of this type of policy, the historic urban settlements remained physically intact but were deprived of their economic, institutional, spiritual, intellectual, and social strengths. They were transformed into poor, overpopulated 'dormitories' for the large number of immigrants from the countryside who were brought in to provide labour for the colonial industrial units. These historic urban settlements were not considered real cities, to be developed, but rather were treated as 'exotic indigenous' hubs to be sought out by tourists. That was the role of the Beaux-Arts, which consisted in restoring single monuments and displaying them as museum artefacts.

Post-Colonial Period

The tradition of building historic cities contrasts with the rise of new colonial cities, which was followed – after independence – by new policies dealing with this urban duality. As a result, Moroccan cities are complex urban entities, consisting in the historic *medina*,[7] a colonial *ville nouvelle*, contemporary urban extensions, and shantytowns *(bidonvilles)*. The shift from the tradition of developing the *medinas* to the expansion of the colonial precinct, together with the housing crisis, transformed the historic *medinas* into areas of many kinds of disorder and irregularity.

Since the Protectorate period, the term 'conservation' has been used in what might be called an ironic way. For the sake of mere preservation, the historic urban settlements were dealt with as if they were dead artefacts rather than living entities that require development and adaptation to contemporary needs without the loss of their authentic integrity and their historic memory. Government agencies have reached a chaotic stage in dealing with the intricate issues of both historic and modern urban forms. Therefore, the gap between policy-making and the actual manner in which cities are growing is continuously widening.

Since the 1970s, all urban documents and master plans designated the medinas as 'preservation zones', but without providing any defined guidelines or norms. The most striking case is that of Fez. Indiscriminate preservation of such a large and complex unit has condemned it to decay.

Experts have hesitated to tackle its challenges since it has been regarded as an untouchable site under the label of an undefined 'preservation'. Thus it has suffered for decades from neglect and intense decay, and the sustainability of its socio-economic and cultural networks, which are in fact its *raison-d'être*, has been disregarded.

Launching the National and International Fez Conservation Program in 1981

By the end of the nineteenth century, the population of the historic city of Fez was about 90,000 and due to the above-mentioned neglect, together with the many years of drought in Morocco, the population of Fez had reached 180,000 inhabitants in the 1980s. This increased population density, the result of continuous rural immigration, had accelerated the city's physical decay and weakened its socio-economic conditions. These accumulated issues and the lack of responsible actions by the government for solving the growing problems at the right time in an efficient manner had rendered Fez little more than a 'ghetto'. Until that point in time, it is sad to note, policies were of two kinds: catastrophe and prevention. It seems that the policies of catastrophe were more applied in this case since problems were not faced at the right time or could have been avoided if their causes had been eradicated with minimum cost and effort by following a preventive approach.

Based on the GIS of ADER-Fès (*l'Agence pour la Dedensification et le Rehabilitation de la médina de Fès*), which provides us with detailed data about the Fez medina there are 13,385 buildings, of which 11,601 are historic ones. Their physical condition can be proportioned as follows: 49 per cent of these buildings are in a medium physical state (neither excessive decay, nor excessive preservation); 41 per cent are decayed ones; 8 per cent are in danger of collapse; and 1.5 per cent are actual ruins. The population density is around 800 to 1,200 people per hectare. In addition to these significant numbers, the medina was a favourable place to locate semi-industrial or industrial activities, which took the place of palaces and magnificent historic buildings. Those industrial activities had a negative impact on both the buildings' structures and the city's infrastructure, which was not designed to accommodate industrial waste, either chemical or physical. Thus, pollution had become a major issue. The medina's critical state had led concerned international institutions to take urgent measures in order to save this historic city from disappearance. UNESCO launched an international protection campaign for Fez and listed it as a world heritage city in 1981. As the former Director General of UNESCO, Amadou-Mahtar M'Bow, stated:

The changes had become so important during the last decades that Fez risks, under demographic, social, and economic pressures without equivalent in its history, losing its profound originality of being one of the purest jewels of Islamic culture... Nevertheless, it is by its very nature a campaign without precedent in the activities of UNESCO. It is the first campaign to be undertaken on behalf of an Islamic city. The operation to be carried out exemplifies, by virtue of its scope, one of the major challenges to which humanity must rise if it is to preserve and enrich its cultural heritage in the face of the constraints imposed on us by the process of accelerated modernization and industrialization. This challenge is of a nature to tax man's capacities and imagination to the full.[8]

Among the incentives for launching the national and international campaign to safeguard Fez was the expression of the will of the late king Hassan II through his letter addressed to the Moroccan government on 21 July 1980. He asked the government to place the project of safeguarding Fez among its most urgent priorities and give it particular attention.

Setting up the Institutional, Financial, and Legal Framework

In 1982, the government created a commission for the safeguarding of Fez. Its mission was to implement the protection program. Since its creation, this delegation had undertaken such actions as:

- establishing the necessary studies covering all areas of expertise in order to set up a sound data base;
- coordinating the implementation of experimental pilot projects related to the above program;
- offering technical assistance to concerned public services and private sectors interested in restoration and rehabilitation;
- sensitizing the population of Fez as to the importance of cultural heritage and enhancing public participation;
- promoting the safeguarding of Fez at national and international levels.

As a delegation, the group had neither clear legal guidelines nor the financial resources to cover the immense task that it was assigned yet a larger amount of field studies and pilot projects were undertaken via donations. This caused the government to create a new efficient and operational structure. Moving away from the public administrative style of agency, which relied only on public financial resources, which are often insufficient for undertaking large actions, a new semi-private institution was created in 1989, ADER-Fès. The main role assigned to this institution was to implement conservation programs in the historic city, which gained funding from the government-supported private projects implemented outside the medina (cash flow operations). This agency has an administrative council with representatives from all ministries – since all of them are involved and conservation is no longer limited to artists and poets and it is seen as a national duty – NGOs, and local municipalities. This institutional, legal, and financial structure has enabled the Fez project to move forward and launch its major implementations.

In addition to the operational agency, ADER-Fes, the medina of Fez has had its own Municipality and authority headquarters (*Prefecture*) since 1985. This has transformed it into a real city requiring care and administration and not just an isolated district belonging to the *ville nouvelle*. The Municipality and the *Prefecture* have had a great impact on the development of the medina through the introduction of needed urban facilities and services, and its adaptation to contemporary requirements. Together with ADER-Fes, introduction and adaptation are made following the norms of an historic site.

Meanings and Dimensions of Conservation in Fez

As stated in the introduction, Fez has been a locus of national and international expertise. This has enabled its project, which has lasted more than three decades, to reach a high degree of maturity compared to other similar cases where complexity can be perplexing. Starting from the first seeds of trying to gain understanding, conservation could not be viewed without bearing in mind the ingenuity of those who had built the city with craftsmanship and dexterity. Layers of experience and dynamic historic evolution that never ceased to add new layers of innovation have sustained the whole city as a human body that requires all its organs and inner energy to remain alive. To import conservation techniques or borrow sophisticated chemicals and high tech will not be the right way to rescue Fez from death, since the people who built it are still there. If you were to talk with *maalem* Abdellah or *maalem* Larbi about restoration techniques they would wonder whether you are from Fez or if you are a foreigner tourist! Simply and politely, they are proving to you that they are doing their duty of building, restoring, teaching others, etc., as their fathers and grandfathers did before them. A trained professional might be shocked but will gradually learn to adapt to those who were able to shape a whole city with modest tools and centuries of practice. Conservation has a whole new meaning in Fez.

The example of the craftsmen is just one among many others in the city and thus the way conservation is perceived should develop with the spirit of the site itself (Figure 23.1). This spirit resides in understanding the different hidden energies and synergies that need to be explored so they can flourish anew. New ideas are not precluded, rather, they are needed and they should act as catalysts to enliven an existing energy or as tools to innovate a new effective process of intervention. This was proved in many restoration projects in Fez, which were learning processes. Therefore, restoration is a way of integrating and not a way of dismantling. By acting in this way, one is preserving *the whole in the part* and *vice-versa*.

The same criteria for the conservation of a building can be applied to the whole city by trying to understand its main organs and their different dynamic inter-relations. To reach this understanding all concerned disciplines are asked to interact, in order to reach a comprehensive strategy that can be translated into practical tactics to deal with the related issues of the historic site. I cannot apply the concept of 'multidisciplinarity' that seems to be often used. The only reason why is that multidisciplinarity could not reconstitute the whole past since this past is 'encyclopaedic' and was not generated or built-up by a limited number of specialized disciplines whose methods and, even *raison-d'être*, differ from one another.

Figure 23.1 Example of the craftsmen

In order to crystallize these ideas, we should recall the initial period of the Fez conservation program when specialists hesitated to venture into exploring the medina and few of them showed interest and willingness to learn from the site and acquire appropriate skills in complementing their knowledge. Among those specialists were planners, engineers, architects, economists, sociologists, historians, chemists, archaeologists, etc. It might be noteworthy here to state that the *terrain suggests the goal and the method.*

To overcome the lack of appropriate expertise, to rebuild the community's trust in its heritage, to bring the master-builders back to their original work, to involve more public and private sectors in investing in the historic city, and so on, a common ground has been established and a training environment has been set up for the simple citizen as well as the craftsman, technician, politician, stakeholder, businessman, intellectual, etc. By doing so, Fez has succeeded in making conservation a common concern and all parties are required to act and participate. It has taken a long time to reach this stage of consciousness regarding conservation issues in the city, which are not, by any means, limited to one institution.

The Fez conservation program, in developing such dimensions, is internationally considered a model in undertaking the challenge of not only restoring its monuments but also of crafting its future. Development, culture, and environment are the framework upon which these conservation efforts are based. Moreover, one of major factors of sustainability in Fez is that of its dynamic community. If Fez is still intact, it is not because of its monuments but rather it is because of its people. Over its history, the population of Fez was self-organized. The inherent qualities of this city need several abilities so as to be grasped properly.

Conservation Planning and Management

Since the launching of the Fez conservation program, documentation and data building related to the site of the medina is seen as being of the utmost importance. No action or project can be built without know-how and expertise. Therefore, efforts have been made to set up a core of national experts who would develop the first conservation team. Most Moroccan professionals have been trained in France without knowledge of their own country; to work on heritage for them seemed just an escapade. It was the growing national interest and the importance of these issues that led them to take on the responsibility of such a huge task.

The integrity of the project and the soundness of its objectives was the main concern of this conservation team that started up under the auspices of the Ministry of Housing (*l'Habitat*) in 1978 and moved to that of the Ministry of the Interior in 1981. Thus, the tools to conserve such a city cannot be found anywhere but within the city itself. Acting in this way is to guarantee a sustainable line of action while trying to build a general sense of liability among the ones to whom this heritage belongs in the first place. The challenge to know what to do and how to do it was among our top priorities. The meagre financial resources allocated to the project prevented the team from tackling the city's 'macro-urgencies'. However, efforts were made to push and implement the population density decreasing programs, infrastructure rehabilitation, transfer of polluting activities, the establishing up of emergency street networks, etc. These macro-urgencies were the key actions for slowing down the rapid decay process and for upgrading the quality of life within the medina.

The First Fez Master Plan

The local conservation team started in 1976-1978 by establishing the first comprehensive master plan (*Schema directeur*)[9] for Fez. This master plan was unprecedented in terms of its scope and ambitions. Instead of dealing with the issues of the medina as an isolated entity, it focused on the global development of the whole city of Fez. This was aimed at bringing the historic hub to the forefront first by centralizing it in the city's urban fabric and second by revitalizing its key social, economic, cultural, and environmental functions. This attempt to integrate the medina with the rest of the city failed. As a consequence of this failure, the eastbound expansion of the city was partially replaced by westbound expansion because of the continuous pressure of the Colonial centre (*Dar Dbibagh*), *Ville Nouvelle*.

Furthermore, because of the housing crisis, since 1970 this zone has been a main hub for immigrants and the needy. Massive efforts have been made, over the last five or six years, to improve it and bring it up to the average urban norms. Besides, the walled city was at the centre of this *extra-muros* critical situation since the problems of the eastern zone were the result of its explosion. In the 1980s, 40 per cent of medina inhabitants were immigrants from rural areas. This shift in the social structure enhanced the disparity between the *ville nouvelle* and the medina. The former encompassed more than 70 per cent of urban facilities and infrastructure and so municipal investment was notably slanted to one side. This clearly demonstrates the social and spatial segregation that started gaining ground.

In spite of its consistency and its sound findings, this master plan was not respected. The pressure of other parameters prevented the adoption of its guidelines in the whole urban agglomeration of Fez. Nevertheless, those guidelines regarding the medina were taken into consideration and provided insightful orientations for the successful operations undertaken in the walled city.

The Rehabilitation Plan

It is important to ask the question: how can an historic city be managed through a plan? It is true that no plan can embody the complexities and intricacies that characterize an historic city. At the same time, it is regrettable to halt the urban development of an historic site with potentials for adaptation and upgrading because of the lack of a definition of what exactly is 'historic'. Moreover, it is inappropriate to carry on random interventions without guidelines or regulations. A rehabilitation plan is a necessity and its main purpose is the establishment of technical guidelines based on legal considerations. Due to the lack of urban documents and technical guidelines, many historic sites in Morocco have been mistreated. This absence has led to a lack of control and therefore, these sites have been turned into places where illegal and random interventions were commonplace.

The rehabilitation plan of the Fez medina was launched in 1995 by the ADER-Fez team. It was the first national urban plan for an historic city. It was followed by many other cities in view of its positive impact on the preservation and development of Fez. The rehabilitation plan was not by any means limited to the design process and pencil sketches, but was developed by a team of professionals from different disciplines. The emphasis was on understanding the dynamics of the past and on how to find the synergies provided by the city itself. Fez by its nature is a complete and coherent historic city where neighbourhoods are still intact with their functional centres. Its linear markets (*souks*) are the busiest in the whole city. Thus, the main goal achieved by the team was to define the city as a dynamic entity. The inhabitants contributed to the evolution of the city and have been the driving force behind its extension and continuity. The question of evolution is a central one, since the attachment of people to their heritage is not stagnant but evolving. It is by understanding this fact that we can evaluate the limits and capacity for change to be integrated within a historic area. But if these changes, are not measured properly the existing harmony will be disrupted and the city will cease to function normally.

The first step was to find the limits of all neighbourhoods – residential, commercial, scientific, or productive. We focused on the real limits and not on the administrative ones, which did not reflect the true spatial urban organization. The second step was to delimit all key historic areas following a hierarchy of historical and archaeological values. The third step was to identify all the buildings and monuments of great architectural value. The fourth step was to define the environmental features of the entire city, starting from its internal green areas and moving on to the green belt surrounding its exterior walls. The fifth step was to locate all linear or nodal commercial and production activities. The sixth step was to locate infrastructure, and so forth. This set of dynamic layers permitted the building of a plan or plans with a certain depth. This depth was translated through district plans at the scale of 1:500 and in some cases 1:200 since the rehabilitation plan cannot go beyond the spatial limits of 1:2000. In this district plan, a detailed urban orientation was provided by giving the nature of precise interventions in every building in the district and potential development that may result. However, this is a short description that may not reveal the intricacy of the process that took years of reflection and research.

In addition to spatial analysis, the legal guidelines were developed in parallel considering that regulations should facilitate the initiatives of the inhabitants and not hinder their innovation or their intervention. This rehabilitation plan was presented to the community and feedback was recorded and taken into consideration. This process culminated in the establishment of coherent urban documents that are now one of the main tools for managing the medina space. This plan is now supervised by the *Agence Urbaine de Fès*, a local agency whose main role is the implementation and the follow-up of urban documents in the city in coordination with all concerned institutions. It is essential to note that the plan is not an end in itself and there are possibilities of large numbers of cases that may occur in the site due to its very complex nature. Therefore, an interdisciplinary and inter-institutional committee is reviewing and scrutinizing any innovative effort that may not be covered by documents in a proposed private or public initiative.

The Geographical Information System (GIS)

The GIS of Fez is a planning and management tool. It is an active database covering, in an exhaustive manner, all its 13,385 buildings with a minimum of 30 items of information for each one and all its infrastructure, sewage, springs, rivers, and electricity networks. The idea of developing a GIS for the Fez medina stemmed from the growing concern for managing the subtleties of such a complex site. The medina's tiny interlaced alleys and its dense overlapped urban fabric cannot be dismantled without the computer capacity for recording small details.

The digital map of the medina in Microstation™ and its database in Oracle™ provides a grounding for the planning processes in different scales with an unlimited number of layers. This flexibility of moving up and down avoids the errors that can occur due to the manual manipulation of information and cartographic documents. The GIS provides the cartographic support for the rehabilitation plan, as mentioned above, and is used to manage projects within the medina. In addition, it is the tool used for designing and managing all future urban and architectural projects

(Figure 23.2). The information provided by the GIS on the whole medina ranges from the nature of the buildings (traditional, neo-traditional, transformed, or modern), ownership status, occupation status by levels, infrastructure (sewage, water, and electricity), cultural value (architectural, archaeological, social, urban, and artistic value) to the action to be undertaken in the building (restoration, rehabilitation, renewal, or emergency intervention through consolidation or demolition).

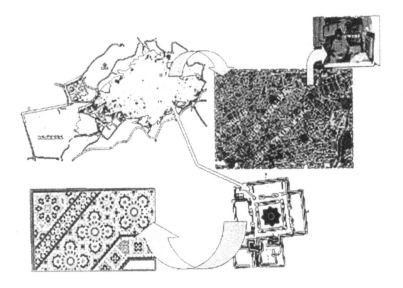

Figure 23.2 The GIS of Fez

Examples of Conservation Implementations in Fez

The experimental operations undertaken in Fez between 1985 and 1989 proved that the conservation of the medina is possible. In spite of the limited financial resources available, these operations have covered many areas such as monument restoration, residential rehabilitation, emergency interventions in unsound buildings in danger of collapse, rehabilitation of the sewage and river networks, restructuring of artisan activities, and insertion of urban facilities within the medina (schools, administrative services, institutes, etc.). All these operations were funded by private donors and ADER-Fes.

The restoration of the *fonduk* Nejjarine (caravanserai) dating back to the seventeenth century was a true training ground for artisans and technicians. The restoration was not limited to one building but covered the whole

Nejjarine complex, composed of the carpenters' market (*souk* Nejjarine), four houses above the market, a mosque, a public square, and a fountain. This example of restoration showed that restoration in Fez cannot be achieved without the rejuvenation of the built environment surrounding a monument. This project was funded by the Foundation Karim Lamrani (Figure 23.3).

Figure 23.3 Examples of restoration

The ongoing rehabilitation of houses started as an experimental operation and is now a successful action, undertaken by the inhabitants and supported by ADER-Fes and the Municipality. This rehabilitation consists mainly in assisting owners in refurbishing their houses by introducing sanitary services and maintenance works. It is not a restoration per se but respects the traditional residential typology.

The Emergency Interventions program has been developed by ADER-Fez in coordination with the Municipality of Fes-medina in order to protect human lives from the threat of collapsing unsound buildings and structures. More than 200 houses were included in that program.

The restoration of historic walls consists in consolidating and reconstructing the missing parts. Most of the walls were built with the ancestral method of rammed earth or *pise*. *The Banque Populaire* funded the first restoration project of the Bab Mahrouk gateway (Figure 23.4).

Among the priorities of the conservation program was the rehabilitation of the river and sewage networks. ADER-Fez has intervened in 7 km of canals below the medina. It is important to mention that the medina's decrepit water system was the main cause of building collapse (Figure 23.5).

Figure 23.4 Restoration of historic walls

Figure 23.5 An effect of the medina's decrepit water system

The World Bank Loan to Fez – An Unprecedented Step

Since its participation in the Second International Colloquium of World Heritage Cities held in Fez in 1993, the World Bank has shown interest in beginning the adventure of rehabilitating historic cities. Though it was a new trend for the Bank to face cultural heritage issues, the colloquium had great impact on international financial institutions. The main purpose of this successful colloquium was to bring these financial institutions together so that they could become concerned and persuaded about the importance of cultural heritage in the economy. In addition, another goal was to overcome the usual image that heritage is the domain only of artists, archaeologists and architects and hence the scarcity of financial resources which heritage conservation has suffered for years due to the narrow perception and ignorance of its potential in local sustainable developments.

The first thing that comes to mind when dealing with the financial component of heritage is tourism. Unfortunately, this remains the only criterion to prove the economic benefit of heritage on the national level and, thus, it is the only investment that can be made. Consequently, many places with great archaeological and historical value are now nothing more than a zoo for tourists to visit, yet one should not ignore the success of a very few cases for which this phenomenon was under control. Consequently the original inhabitants have been, replaced by bazaars and *Ali Baba*'s adventures to build up a new façade based on 'extraordinary' or exotic scenes.[10] This has resulted in the reduction of the value of the living heritage as a sustainable economic potential for the local population. Undoubtedly, this potential, if promoted properly, will maintain the intrinsic values of a historic site and protect them from the loss since they are reflecting its originality and *raison d'être*.

Again to talk about economics in heritage is a dilemma in itself. Our economists are not trained to think beyond the equation of cost-benefit analysis. Many elements, such as the socio-cultural values as perceived by local communities, cannot be equated or assigned an economic value *per se*. The assessment of heritage assets from the point of view of this equation raised another complicated issue: 'poverty'. When thinking about intervening in multifaceted cases where the site reflects certain complexity regarding its social mosaic vis-à-vis the urban fabric in particular for the case of developing countries, poverty is one of the labels easily applied to the problem at hand.

It would, however, seem more logical to perform a comprehensive inquiry into the 'micro-mechanisms' that could generate sustainability of the proposed action. Hence, when 'poverty' label is solely magnified, historic areas are subject to 'charity'. No one can deny the importance of donations for the needy everywhere but how can we find out catalysts for a continuous process of self reliance and set up a local sustainable development?

Tackling the social, cultural, physical, economic, and environmental issues with the 'yardstick' of poverty alone will not solve the problem of poverty itself, which is seen to be treatable in its own realm. By treating only the consequences and symptoms of poverty rather than its causes, the problem is left intact, since its roots are not investigated.

The first missions of World Bank experts to Fez were of the utmost importance, but at the same time subtle, since their visions were different from those of the local team. It took more than three years to reach the conclusion that cultural heritage issues are different from the case studies and projects undertaken by the Bank elsewhere. This project developed between the Bank, ADER-Fez, the Municipality of Fes-medina, and the

Moroccan government was an unprecedented one. Firstly, because of its ingenious institutional and legal set-ups and secondly due to its well-woven components that were made to complement the local line of action and sustain local energy. The project was not tailored as a package but aimed to generate and stimulate the local culture and economy through its future impact. The rate of returns for public investment is in the order of 10-20 per cent and will remain consistently at ten per cent after ten years.

The components of the World Bank loan for the Fez conservation project are the following:

- community development which consists of rehabilitating the unsound buildings and following the ADER-Fez emergency actions which showed a great impact on the population by protecting their lives from the danger of the crumbling and dilapidated structures. This component also includes the removal from ruins of polluting wrecks and rubble, the rehabilitation of public services, and improvement of domestic urban environments through neighbourhoods;
- improvement of accessibility by setting up an emergency street network to facilitate access to the inaccessible parts of the medina for medical and fire emergencies. It is to be noted that this is not aimed at destroying the existing fabric but at improving large existing pedestrian accesses;
- improvement of the urban environment by clustering and organizing non-polluting activities inside the medina. In addition, this component is encompassing the improvement and management of solid waste collection and treatment of public spaces;
- rehabilitation of the physical heritage, including monuments and improving existing tourist circuits with different themes (walls and fortifications, Andalusian gardens and palaces, craftsmanship, monuments and *souks*, and the Andalous historic district);
- institutional development improves the managerial capacities of the institutions involved with the conservation projects such as the Municipality of Fes-medina, ADER-Fes, and so on. Its main objective is to reduce the gap between those institutions and to set up a coordination ground that will, without doubt, affect the efficiency of the project.

This project is a model for other historic cities to follow and learn how to 'avoid mistakes' to save time and as it was assessed by the World Bank in its *Quality at Entry Assessment*:

After a careful assessment of project components, including review of project documents and meetings with key members of the project appraisal team, peer reviewers, Bank managers, as well as with Mr. Mohamed Kabbaj, former

Minister of Finance and Foreign Investments of Morocco, and Professor François Vigier of Harvard University, the panel finds the project *fully satisfactory*, and wishes to congratulate the task team on the novel and replicable approach adopted for the rehabilitation of Fez. This is an important 'first' project in a possible series of similar projects in other Medinas of Morocco, and it may serve as a reference as a learning ground for planning rehabilitation projects of other historic cities in the region and elsewhere in the world ... The Fez Medina Rehabilitation Project has been also successful in raising consciousness concerning cultural heritage issues both in the [World] Bank and in Morocco due to the attention it has received from the highest authorities of Morocco, as well as from Executive Management of UNESCO and the senior management of the Bank...[11]

Finally, it is important to mention that the Word Bank loan for Fez does not cover all the needs of the conservation program, which is supported by other financial resources from other national and international institutions. National and international donors have played a prominent role in raising interest regarding heritage conservation at national and international level. The FADES (the Arab Fund for Social and Economic Development) contributed with its funding to the restoration of more than seven km of water networks and public fountains. And last but not least, UNESCO has been of great support for Fez in informing the world community about the importance of this mankind's shared legacy.

Notes

1 Based on ADER-Fès GIS. The population of the whole city of Fez is one million.
2 Ibn Khaldûn (1332-1406) stated in his *Muqaddimah* that very large monuments are not built by one dynasty alone: 'The reason for this is the aforementioned need for cooperation and multiplication of human strength in any building activity. Sometimes buildings are so large that they are too much for (human) strength, whether it is on its own or multiplied by machines ... Therefore, the repeated application of similar strength is required over successive periods, until (the building) materializes. One (ruler) starts the construction. He is followed by another (the second by) a third. Each of them does all he can to bring workers together in a common effort. Finally, (the building) materializes, as it was planned, and then stands before our eyes ... we find that (later) dynasties are unable to tear down and destroy many great architectural monuments, even though destruction is much easier than construction, because destruction is return to the origin, which is non-existence, while construction is the opposite of that' (Ibn Khaldûn, 1958, vol. 2, pp. 241-242).
3 'La conquête de l'Algérie a été faite par le soldat de France; soldat de métier, il est vrai, vigoureux et ardent, fils du soldat de l'époque napoléonienne, mais non adapté à la vie coloniale, ignorant tout du pays où il allait lutter, de l'adversaire qu'il allait rencontrer, de sa langue, de sa manière de combattre, de ses mœurs et des mobiles divers qui animaient son âme de guerrier. La pacification du Maroc, au contraire, est exclusivement conduite avec des troupes indigènes, musulmanes, puisées dans l'Afrique

du Nord...' (Dugard, 1918, p. 235).

4   'De fait, Lyautey eut la chance d'être porté par son époque, de disposer d'une pléiade de jeunes et remarquables architectes-urbanistes et d'être averti par la déplorable expérience algérienne'. (Rivet, 1999, p. 228).

5   'Les principes suivis par l'architecte, par l'urbaniste, par l'artiste plutôt qu'est M. Prost, restaurateur de Sainte-Sophie et auteur déjà du plan d'agrandissement d'Anvers, sont les suivants: séparation totale des anciennes villes indigènes et des villes européennes nouvelles...' (Dugard, 1918, p. 123).

6   'Fès était véritablement et est restée la métropole indigène du nord; tandis que Marrakech était semblablement et est demeure le centre indigène du sud. Pourquoi choisir Rabat, et non l'une des trois villes [la troisième c'est Casablanca]. M.Mareschal, dans son article de France-Maroc du 15 septembre 1917 sur Rabat-Résidence, nous dit quelle fut la raison qui inspira le choix du Général Lyautey à ce moment: La situation militaire exigeait que notre grand chef fût à même d'agir à la fois sur Marrakech et sur Fès, sur le sud et sur le nord du Maroc. Pour être le maître des deux capitales indigènes, il ne fallait s'établir dans aucune, mais accourir dans chacune d'elles toute les fois que les événements l'exigeraient. Il suffit de regarder une carte du Maroc pour voir que c'est sur la côte de l'Atlantique, vers Rabat et Casablanca, que se trouve le point de départ, le lieu géométrique des grands axes, des voies de pénétration économiques et militaires de notre Maroc...' (Dugard, 1918, p. 132).

7   The term *medina* means the historic walled city and is used nowadays to distinguish this entity from the *Ville nouvelle*, or new town. First used by French while they were in Morocco.

8   Amadou-Mahtar M'Bow, ex-Director General of UNESCO, appeal for the Safeguard of Fez on the 9 April 1980 at Fez.

9   This master plan was funded by UNDP with a global sum of US$ 672,000.

10   I was amazed going through an article written by Mona Serageldin in which she states the following: '...This is a challenge, because Fez is not particularly tourist-friendly environment. The population is very conservative, and their absorptive capacity for foreign visitors is quite limited. Moreover, tourists find the physical environment intimidating, with its dark shadows and tiny alleyways, which architects and designers find breathtaking. Tourists tend to go to Marrakech, completely bypassing Fez'. (Serageldin, 2001, pp 238-239)
     It is indeed striking to have such a view in the twenty-first century that sounds as an Orientalist writing or drawing in a canvas this dark shadows and tiny alleys of the Arab city in eighteen century. It may be deduced that this medina is totally unsecure and still is a place of Moor pirates. Moreover, it is the visitors themselves who find this physical environment breathtaking which has lead to approximately more than 15 European and American families to purchase houses in the midst of this medina who they enjoy the warmth of its community, and not architects who fled for ages to design their nice glass and aluminium facades. So then please what do you propose to make it more welcoming? Is it to bring more serpent charmers and make people dance for tourists and rely on their coins so as to have nice economic indicators or maybe take away and demolish all these shadowed alleys? This is not by any means an emotional reaction nor a refutation of tourists that are welcome to discover their own world heritage but it is only a way of conveying that a tourist education should be initiated to know how to deal with different peculiarities of different cultural sites they visit and not ask too much from people who they live as they live. It is to be believed that each historic site attracts its own visitors such as Fez.

11   The World Bank: Quality at Entry Assessment, Morocco-Fez Rehabilitation Project.

References

Dugard, H. (1918), *Le Maroc de 1918*, Payot & Cie, Paris.

Ibn Khaldûn, I (1958), *The Muqaddimah, an Introduction to History*, Translated from the Arabic by Franz Rosental, Pantheon Books, New York.

Rivet, D. (1999), *Le Maroc de Lyautey à Mohammed V, le double visage du Protectorat*, Denoël, Paris.

Scham, A. (1970), *Lyautey in Morocco*, University of California.

Sergeldin, M. (2001), 'Preserving a Historic City: Economic and Social Transformations of Fez', *Historic Cities and Sacred Sites*, Washington.

Chapter 24

Cultural Heritage Conservation in China: Some Significant Good Practices

Guang-Jun Jin and Cong-xia Zhao

Introduction

China, with its long history, has many cultural heritages. Its historic cities number are almost 2000, and the diversity of their historic features is famous worldwide. With their beautiful natural environment, historic heritage and buildings, the cities reflect the brilliant historic culture of the Chinese nation.

Since the early 1980s, with rapid urban economic development, urban development and redevelopment activities became active. Because there was no law regarding conservation, most of the old cities, historic buildings and their surroundings were modified. So it is important for us to realize the problem of cultural heritage conservation.

With the increasing recognition of the problem, the new concept of 'historic cultural city' was established and research work on their conservation began. Historic cultural heritage conservation has become a new concern for urban construction. Through 20 years of hard work, China has achieved unprecedented results in historic cultural conservation.

Development Phases

We can divide the development process of cultural heritage conservation in China into two phases over two decades. The first phase runs from 1982 to 1994. During this period, the first law regarding cultural historic conservation was issued – the Law of Cultural Historic Conservation of the Peoples' Republic of China. Soon the concept of the 'historic cultural city' was established. Since then, the double conservation system has been introduced: on the one hand, cultural historic conservation, on the other the historic cultural city.

The second phase started in 1994 and runs to the present day. The different levels of the conservation system were implemented. The

Document of the Ministry of Building Construction pointed out that: 'The historic district is the most important part of our cultural heritage conservation program. It includes three levels: historic buildings and heritage, historic cultural districts and historic cultural cities. They form an integrated historic cultural conservation system and are one of our major works in historic conservation'.

At the same time, the criteria for the historic cultural city and requirement for urban conservation planning were clearly defined.

The Level and Organization of Conservation

The level of conservation consists of three parts: historic cultural cities, historic cultural districts, historic buildings and heritage.

The historic cultural district is divided into two types: cultural heritage site and historic district.

The historic building and heritage category includes three types:

- historic buildings, including ancient buildings, historic monumental buildings, buildings and structures with cultural values and which are important in urban development, important modern buildings and structures;
- ancient cultural heritage, including relics, traces, and so on;
- ancient gardens, scenic spots, old trees and distinctive plants.

Conservation organization in China is made up of two parts: The first – an academic organization – is the Research Group of the Chinese Cultural Heritage City sponsored by the Architectural Society of China. The other – an administrative organization – is the Committee of Chinese Historic Cultural Heritage Cities sponsored by the city government of historic cultural heritage cities.

Furthermore, we find an Expert Board of Conservation Planning in most cultural heritage cities, established by the local government.

The Guiding Ideology

Goals of Cultural Heritage Conservation

The relationship of conservation and development should be well coordinated in order to pursue the goal of sustainable development in urban physical construction. Conservation activity could provide great developing potential for the urban physical environment. And in the meanwhile, funds can be obtained for conservation through development activity.

Principles of Cultural Heritage Conservation

Historic cultural cities should be preserved with an eye to aspects of the natural environment (geography and ecology), the man-made environment (city pattern, historic buildings, streets and plazas), and the human environment (local culture, traditional customs).

Historic cultural districts should be preserved regarding general style and features, while improving their infrastructure, and the quality of the environment.

Historic buildings and heritage should be preserved regarding their state of preservation, that is preserving not only the building itself but also its surroundings.

Experience in the Country

Historic Cities

The State Council of China has named 'National Historic Cultural Cities' three times since 1982 (in 1982, 1986 and 1994). A total of 99 cities was highlighted as National Historic Cultural Cities. They were divided into seven types: Ancient Capital City, Traditional City, Historic Scenic Sports City, National Feature City, Modern Historic City, Special Function City and Other Historic City.

Any city that is included in the list of the National Historic Cultural Cities must add historic heritage conservation planning to its general city planning.

Beijing Beijing, 3,000 years old, the Capital City of China, is a world famous historic cultural city.

The layout of the old city is a reflection of the traditional Chinese hierarchy of religious and civil power. The Imperial Palace is the heart of the city and forms the city's gravely formal north-south axis. The old city walls dating from the Ming and Qing dynasties are still visible today, and form the preservation area of the city (Figure 24.1).

The concepts of urban preservation are:

- controlling the old city and planning new urban development outside the area;
- controlling building height in the preserved area.

Figure 24.1 Qing dynasty plan, Beijing

Figure 24.2 Streetscape of Pingyao city

Pingyao Pingyao, 2,000 years old, is located near Taiyuan City, Shanxi Province. It was first built during the Zhou dynasty. The present well preserved wall and moat were rebuilt during the early Ming dynasty (Figure 24.2).

The strategy for 'Overall Preservation' was carried out in the city of Pingyao. The city was well preserved through the use of the tools of city planning, law and administration. In 1997, Pingyao city was listed in the UNESCO Inventory of World Cultural Heritage.

Historic Districts

There are locally designed historic districts in almost all old cities and towns in China. The majority of these districts are residential, commercial or mixed-use in character. These districts are preserved on the basis of conservation laws, and are usually designated through survey, analysis and research. Once a historic district is designated as such, a special committee or board, appointed by the city government, reviews the proposed changes within the district boundaries.

Figure 24.3 The old street in Tunxi town

The Old Street in Tunxi Town Tunxi town belongs to Huangshan city, Anhui Province. The Old Street in Tunxi town, 800 metres long and six metres wide, is the oldest, most characteristic, attractive and vital traditional commercial street. Along the street are two story-high shops with a unique environmental structure and traditional street grid (Figure 24.3).

To preserve the street and integrate water, mountain and town, three levels of preservation area were declared. They are the core of the preservation area, the control area and the harmonizing area.

Baita Temple Block in Beijing Baita Temple, the biggest Buddhist Pagoda in China, was built during the Jin dynasty and is a symbolic monument in Beijing.

In the Baita Temple Block rehabilitation project, unique alleys and their life, the traditional feudal courtyard houses and street space were emphasized and preserved. The heights and styles of new buildings were managed to harmonize with the old (Figure 24.4).

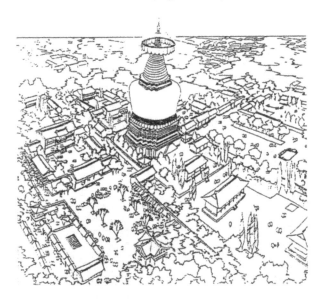

Figure 24.4 Baita Temple Block

Good Examples in Harbin

The city of Harbin is one of the largest cities in north-eastern China. We call it 'the winter-city' or 'eastern Moscow' because of its cold climate and its unique foreign cultural influence.

The geographic position of Harbin, the capital city of Heilongjiang province, is 45 degree north latitude, with approximately 190 below freezing days each year. So we have *The Ice and Snow Festival* every year with an ice lantern competition, snow sculpture exhibition, skiing and sightseeing.

The city of Harbin was financed and developed during the construction of the China Eastern Railroad sponsored by Tsarist Russia. As the central city of the project, Harbin developed rapidly under European cultural influence.

Now Harbin is one of the most famous and distinguished cities in China with one central city, five sub-central cities and several small towns. The total population of the central city is 2.3 million.

Overall City Historic Conservation

Harbin's first general city plan was drawn up in 1906. Since then, the plan has been revised several times. In the 1994 version, Harbin was approved as a 'National Historic Cultural City'. According to the national requirement for historic cultural city planning, the city's first special conservation plan was implemented. This plan included seven parts:

- the evaluation of the city's historic culture;
- the balance between preservation and new construction;
- the domain and distribution of historic cultural districts;
- the preservation of historic buildings (preservation area and control area);
- four historic cultural conservation districts were determined;
- research on sub-preservation planning and urban design;
- implementation methods and technologies.

Historic District Conservation

There are 5 historic districts in Harbin: Central Street District, Russian Garden Housing District, Nangang Temple and Church District, and Daowai Market District.

Of these districts, two have been rehabilitated in recent years. One is Central Street, while the other is Nangang Temple and Church District.

The Central Street District The Central Street, which is 1,460 metres long and 22 metres wide, was funded in 1902. Along the street are three-four story-high dwellings and shops with many kinds of Europe architectural styles and stone paving. The streetscape is well proportioned, with positive definition and providing support for vital activities.

The construction along the central street and within Central Street

District has been controlled for quite a long time. In 1997, the city government decided to improve the street for pedestrian use only as a shopping mall.

Vehicles were banned from the street. New parking lots were planned and built. Signage and illumination were redesigned for night shoppers.

Figure 24.5 Harbin central street and its stone pavement

Stone paving, the street walls and building styles ware preserved (Figure 24.5). Some old buildings were restored, and some new buildings required to be redesigned to harmonize with old street buildings.

Five plazas were built with stages, benches, tables, green areas, fountains and so on for people to relax and enjoy city life.

Historic Building Conservation

In 1983, the city government organized the Evaluation Committee of Harbin Historic Architecture. Through examination and evaluation, many historic buildings were designated as preserved buildings, totalling 75 buildings in the first group. They were divided into three degrees with different conservation methods. Meanwhile, the Historic Building Preservation Ordinance was issued. It stipulated clearly: 'All the new projects and restoration projects come under strict control, all changes to preserved buildings are prohibited'. In particular:

- *First degree preservation buildings*: All building activities in these buildings are prohibited. Their surroundings should be controlled also. These kinds of buildings should be city landmarks and scenic spots of the city.
- *Second degree preservation buildings*: All building activities on the exteriors of these buildings are prohibited. Some restoration activities are permitted.
- *Third degree preservation buildings*: These buildings should be appropriately preserved and rehabilitated.

In the past religious buildings played an important role in Harbin's urban development. They were city landmarks and dominant skyline elements. Now they are still the main works in Harbin historic building conservation.

The following cases are the three conservation projects for historic churches and their surroundings.

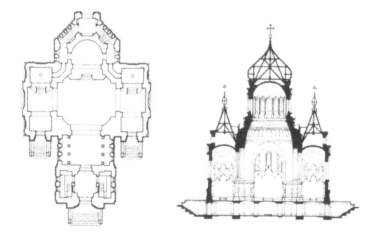

Figure 24.6 Church of S. Sophia, plan and section

The Conservation of S. Sophia Church and Its Surroundings The S. Sophia Church, in a Russian architectural style, was built in 1923 and designed by a Russian architect. Before 1989, the church was used as a warehouse for a department store and was surrounded by other buildings (Figure 24.6). In 1989, the city government began to rehabilitate the church and improve its surroundings (Figure 24.7). Now, the church is altered to be the Harbin Architectural Plaza with exhibitions inside the church and an open space around it. It is the most attractive point and a symbolic place in city of Harbin.

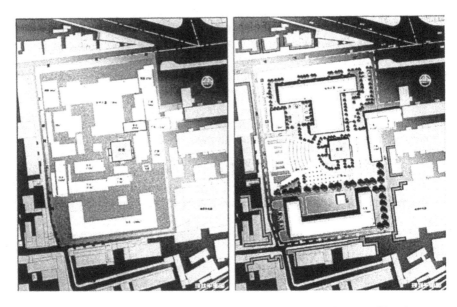

**Figure 24.7 The conservation plan: existing plan and rehabilitation
        plan**

*The Research on the Conservation of S. Ibervel Church and Its
Surroundings* The S. Ibervel Church, also in a Russian architectural style,
was built in 1907 and designed by a Russian architect. At the present time,
the church is surrounded by buildings and is used as a factory workshop. So
the church is seriously compromised.

The research project began with the investigation and analysis of the
church and its surroundings (Figure 24.8). Through public hearings and
participation and discussions with the office of city planning, we obtained
the following concept for the conservation of the church building and its
surroundings:

- to move the workshop, restore the church and reuse it as a community
  centre;
- to demolish some buildings that influence the church and form a public
  open space for the community;
- to enhance the visual importance of the church, to make the church a
  landmark of the area;
- to create a special incentive policy for implementation.

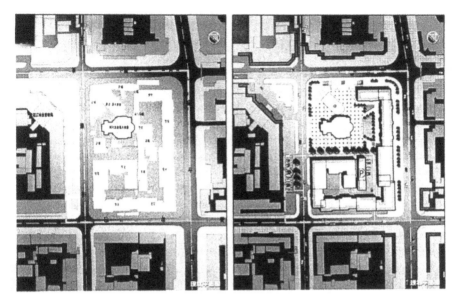

Figure 24.8 The conservation plan: existing plan and rehabilitation plan

The Research on Conservation of S. Aleksejev Church and Its Surroundings
The S. Aleksejev Church also in a Russian architectural style, was built in 1935 and designed by a Russian architect. The church is a first degree preservation building in Harbin.

The church is located within the city's commercial area and is well preserved. At the present time, the church is used for religious purposes.

The research project began with the investigation and analysis regarding the church and its surroundings. Through public hearings and participation and discussions with the office of city planning, we obtained the following concept for the conservation of the church building and its surroundings:

- to restore the church and maintain its religious use;
- to demolish some buildings that influence the church, forming a public open space for city life;
- to enhance the visual importance of the church and make the church a landmark of the commercial area;
- to make special incentive policy for implementation.

Conclusions

Although we have made great strides in cultural heritage conservation over the past two decades, we still have many problems to solve and much work to do.

In conclusion, I would like to make four points that are of vital importance for conservation projects to be implemented in China:

- firstly, we must address the organization of conservation (the special administrative office within the city government and special research institutions for the conservation);
- second, we need to consider the funding of conservation (the foundation for research, the incentive policy to encourage conservation projects and city investment for conservation);
- third, we must arouse consciousness in the sphere of conservation (public participation, education regarding historic cultural heritage conservation and inventory of city heritage);
- fourth, we need legal guarantees (including legislation and implementation of the law).

Historic cultural heritage conservation cannot, and should not, stand alone. Only when the above aspects work together, will conservation become truly effective.

Chapter 25

Can Economics Help Preserve and Conserve Heritage? And if so, Can Economics Help to Improve Quality of Life and of the Environment?

Christian Ost

Introduction

Tools developed by economics as a science address a vast array of human activities, insofar as they are characterized as the satisfaction of needs satisfied by the use of resources.

The consciousness that the resources necessary to satisfy these growing needs are not inexhaustible has led to increasing awareness that future well-being will depend on their careful use – rationally planned and optimally designed. Hence the rediscovery of healthy economic principles regarding the overall problem of resource monitoring and the emergence of a new body of literature regarding the subject of efficient allocation in fields hitherto not approached.

Attributing an economic value to things has become increasingly important as allocation and efficiency problems develop (thus implying the need to address the sensitive subject of a choice between feasible options). Limited in the past to problems easily transformed into figures, the field of economics has now extended to matters in which not only quantitative but also qualitative data are used for interpretation purposes. The perception that objective evaluation is not always possible and that qualitative factors are important features of the world surrounding us has given rise to a growing use of carefully balanced qualitative statements in economics.

This opening to qualitative matters has highlighted a whole new field of research for economists, now able to tackle questions such as the efficiency of health or transport systems, of museum or justice management. Cultural activities and, among them, the conservation of cultural heritage, belong to these new research fields.

Efficiency in resource allocation is one problem. Equity and the equal access of all to major resources is another. In a world where market forces are predominant, the debate between supporters of profit-oriented (private) and government-supported cultural institutions is far from being exhausted. Indeed, public intervention is common in the case of culture, as its collective dimension implies collective responsibility, endorsed (to a certain extent) by community representatives.

Cultural activities have a price, but the agent paying that price (private or public?) and the extent to which their price covers the expenses incurred is an intricate matter. Financial constraints as well as management and sponsoring in cultural fields are currently being investigated.

The Background: An Historical Perspective on Cultural Economics

Cultural economics or 'economics of the arts' are a relatively recent branch of economic thought, initiated in the US at the end of the 1960s. One of the first books on the subject of cultural economics was a compilation of articles by M. Blaug revealing the diversity of research undertaken and the growing interest in using the cultural field as a test for the concrete application of fundamental economic tools. This work is also representative of the goal envisioned by economists for their discipline:

> Economics is indeed more than a collection of techniques for investigating the workings of an economic system. It is a way of looking at the world, being a special case of a much more general logic of rational action. For that reason, economists experience little difficulty in appraising activities which appear, at first glance, to have nothing to do with economic ends; their apparatus will not always be equally illuminating but in a surprising number of instances, it yields immediate, dramatic insight.

Cultural economics deal with the entire cultural spectrum: performances (opera, ballet, concerts, theatres), cultural industries (editing, television, cinema, records), museums, art galleries, festivals, exhibitions, visual arts (painting, sculptures), and cultural built heritage.

Cultural built heritage, in short CBH, represents only a fraction of the contributions mentioned: there are few literary references, as the economic analysis of CBH appears to be a recent subject. The first publications date back to 1983-84 and they stressed the economic effects of conservation and rehabilitation, often with a strong financial bias. Since then, important contributions have been made to tackle the different aspects of conservation in the theoretical light of economic theory.[1]

The assumptions that economic forces are becoming increasingly prevalent in contemporary society, and that these forces literally shape the possibilities of conservation are at the core of a double postulate:

- culture needs economics, and if conservation fields want to be heard and their projects financed, they will have to come to terms with the power and influence of the economic approach;
- economists dealing with culture, heritage and the arts in general must be willing to examine the limits of traditional economic thinking and the potential contribution of other disciplines.

The Foreground: Basic Principles and Objectives

The goals of economics applied to conservation should be:

- to elaborate and update a survey of all activities in economics of conservation;
- to communicate the main contributions to non-economists;
- to survey and monitor on-site analyses and expertise;
- to list priorities for further economic research (field analysis and theoretical approach).

This should include seven kinds of principles: (1) focus on measuring impact; (2) the role of economics of conservation; (3) definition of Cultural Built Heritage (CBH); (4) public intervention and market situation; (5) financing; (6) research data; (7) tools and methods.

Focus on Measuring Impacts

As economists never tire of repeating, resources are scarce and choices have to be made between alternative uses. This is also true in the case of conservation projects. What can be done to make choices easier? How can we measure/evaluate the multiple values of heritage? Impacts of conservation projects are numerous at multiple levels. What techniques have been developed to measure them in order to capture the values of cultural heritage? Impact analysis, cost-benefit analysis, willingness-to-pay and contingent valuation studies, referenda, etc., all are designed to facilitate a choice between alternative options.

'To measure is to know' might be the motto of economic investigation into the valuation of cultural heritage, although in the absence of effective markets, *measurement remains a tricky business*, as the Getty Institute puts it.[2]

The Role of Economics of Conservation

On one hand, the role of economics in conservation can be conceived to mean measuring the economic impact of tourism, pricing movable heritage in art markets and identifying means of financing conservation, all matters that it would be more accurate to call the 'business' concerns of conservation. Yet economic issues of conservation run much deeper and require a good deal of conceptual clarification. In this view, cultural economists should be encouraged in their ongoing work of discussing conceptual issues and assumptions that could be briefly evoked in this regard.

Further research on such topics as the links between cultural projects and urban planning, cultural capital, the role of culture in sustainable development, the role of the third (non-profit) sector, decision-making processes of the involved agents, and cultural indicators should provide a rich fund of ideas on which conservation professionals and policy makers could draw as alternatives to measuring the value of heritage simply in terms of price.[3]

Definition of the Cultural Built Heritage (CBH)

The notion of CBH is a difficult one, its meaning varying in time and space according to culture and tradition. The problem of the exact definition of CBH is extremely complex. If once CBH was composed only of buildings exceptional for their aesthetic qualities, for their originality, and above all for their age (conferring their 'historicity' to cathedrals, abbeys, town halls, palaces and antique ruins), this is no longer the case today. Indeed, the notion of CBH has been enlarged to include typology, age, artistic and historic significance, the consequences being that the number of recognized 'monuments' has considerably increased, that their role in everyday life has been fundamentally modified and that the economic significance of CBH has taken on a whole new dimension. Now, peculiarities of CBH (in other words economic a-typical characteristics) could affect the validity of economic analysis. The peculiar aspects of CBH as an object of analysis are addressed in the following scheme.[4]

Public Intervention and Market Situation

The image of CBH that emerges from these characteristics is the image of a commodity/service inadequately taken into account by market mechanisms in the strict sense, including a dimension of collective utility justifying public intervention.

The presence of externalities (such as option, prestige, education values) unaccounted for by the market is one major argument in favour of subsidization. Other analysts advocate national or regional prestige, 'endowment' reasons to 'protect' CBH, while the induced effects of the conservation of CBH and its nature as an international resource constitute two more arguments of a more prospective nature. The public character of

CBH means that, whereas conservation is undertaken for the benefit of a broad community (not only residents, but tourists and even future generations), the costs are localized on the owners, occupiers and local community. It would therefore appear equitable for the public authority to intervene to reduce this gap.[5]

Financing

Nevertheless, and particularly in times of tight budgetary constraints, private partnership is sought as a complementary source of financing.

In this case, the authorities attempt to draft measures inducing the private sector to become involved in the rehabilitation of CBH. They can do this in two ways:

- adopting a dynamic approach to create a favourable political and legal framework encouraging the private sector to invest in restoration projects (by supporting urban planning, handling cooperative projects efficiently, etc.)
- using a financial approach, namely through tax exemptions.

Research Data

The range of possible economic impacts attributable to CBH is wide. Measuring them requires a survey of all potential flows generated by CBH. This must be done on site, bearing in mind that impacts can be both quantitative and qualitative, and it is important to avoid thinking of them as opposites, hierarchically ranked, and mutually exclusive – we should rather view qualitative analysis as a step toward quantitative analysis. From a qualitative point of view, impacts are either ordinal (more, less, etc.), binary (yes/no), or nominal (classified by names). Quantitative measures can be commensurable (measurable) or incommensurable (they do not have a measure that is translatable in figures), monetary or non monetary (e.g. number of employees).

The 'incommensurable' is an effect that can be noted but not quantified quite simply because research has not yet led us that far, while intangibles are not logically capable of being measured. For instance, intangibles often attributed to preservation projects include improved aesthetics, reduction in density, neighbourhood cohesiveness (stronger neighbourhood associations), reinforcement of community cohesiveness.

Tools and Methods

How to express in monetary terms (when and if possible) the values of CBH is a difficult question economists have so far attempted to answer in various ways. Depending on what they are trying to assess, they have essentially two possibilities:

- analysis of the costs and benefits generated by the presence and/or utilization of CBH in its current state is usually labelled impact analysis or value assessment of current CBH. A distinctive feature of this type of analysis is that it involves no decisional process, as there is no rehabilitation project at stake. Referring to a single moment in the long life of the CBH, it simply assesses the weight of the CBH in socio-economic life, and involves a cross-section description of a flow of resources over a given period of time;
- unlike impact analysis, project evaluation involves a decision-making process, while looking at the costs and benefits that will eventually be generated by the rehabilitation/restoration of CBH over a given time period. Project evaluation aims at distinguishing, among the impacts listed for a project, the main costs and benefits emanating from the project, for all economic agents concerned. It allows integration of long term investment for a given collectivity and takes into account not only financial but also social benefits.

Broadening of scope could also be achieved through the ever-improving multi-criteria analyses and multi-objective decision models. The latter are beginning to receive much attention and seem to offer a new opportunity for the achievement of a balanced analysis of all facets of modern planning problems, particularly because many intangibles such as social effects and environmental repercussions can be worked into the equation.

Both impact analysis and project evaluation rely on techniques aiming at identifying actions, perceptions or attitudes on the site and around the site. This implies a description of economic flows in the impact area, an evaluation of direct, indirect and induced effects, and a differentiation of economic actors.

Moreover, spatial indicators and mapping can help to visualize the impact of decisions. As far as the economic dimension of CBH is concerned, we suggest four project variables which need to be identified: potential attractivity of CBH, tourist spill-overs, inclusiveness considering alternative sources of attractivity, directionality (efficient management of internal flows) or connectivity (integration in international networks) in the area.

When project effects are treated in their own dimensions, the obvious problem arises of how to weigh the various project effects against each other. Clearly, this type of weighing procedure depends on the relative priorities attached to the various decision criteria for the plan concerned. These methods are, therefore, also called multi-criteria methods. Examples of these methods are benchmarking, spider models, meta-regression analysis, Regime analysis, Flag model, and rough set analysis.

The theory of the so-called 'tourism multiplier' shows that various levels of impact created in the economy can be subdivided into three distinct categories:

- *direct effects*: the amount of income (employment, output, etc.) created in the sector as a direct result of the change in tourist expenditure, e.g. wages, salaries and distributed profits in hotels, restaurants and tour companies;
- *indirect effects*: the amount of income created by the increased expenditure of the tourist sectors on goods and services from their suppliers in the domestic economy (which may, or may not, be directly related to the tourist sectors). The indirect effects also include that of the increased demand created by tourist sector suppliers to their own suppliers;
- *induced effects*: as income levels increase throughout the economy, as a result of the direct and indirect effects of a change in tourist expenditure, some of this additional income will be re-cycled within the domestic economy. This repercussion effect on the demand for domestically produced goods and services will in turn increase income, output, employment, etc.

Economics as the Interdisciplinary Driver: An Applied Theory

The idea is to apply the concepts, originally developed for the tourism industry, to the particular case of CBH, starting with the location of poles, axes, and impact areas.

We need to stress at the outset that the immobility of CBH makes it a magnet: it is because people move towards an interesting historic site or building (in order to visit it, to live or to work in it) that we can speak of commercial spill-overs and multiplier effect. It is the attractiveness of the site that creates the flows of revenues that we would like to measure, and this explains why CBH can be viewed as an 'attraction pole'. Clearly, the sequence is as follows: (no) pole, (no) attractiveness, (no) spill-overs. The presence of a symbolic value is then the necessary prerequisite for an economic analysis of the multiplier effect generated by the CBH.

The concept of a pole is envisaged in relative terms: some monuments represent a pole in opposition to others which do not. Moreover, the attractiveness of a pole is not necessarily connected to its architectural value: more people can be attracted to places which are comparatively poor from an architectural point of view.

Priority here is given to attractiveness (by reason of the important economic spill-overs it generates through the numbers of CBH users attracted) rather than to architectural and artistic value.

Preservation projects are also said to be acting as magnets: they create new businesses and stabilize old ones by bringing people into a particular area in great numbers. The term 'pole' is generally associated with tourist businesses, but there is a more extensive sense to the word when we think of the new businesses located around CBH. Magnet effects can be measured in terms of greater-than-average business formation rates on the one hand and lower failure rates in the case of existing business on the other. This allows a separation of the income generated by existing business and the income generated by those who are drawn to the area to make investments. Determination of the poles is, then, the first step in any economic analysis of CBH.

CBH can be approached in terms of an architectural site. The site can be identical to the pole: this is the case with an isolated monument; its structure is then said to be unipolar. The site can also consist of a group of poles in a multipolar structure. Or again, a site may contain historic buildings with various CBH-related uses: the predominance of one particular use does not hinder analysis, but orientates it in a particular direction (for example, a predominating residential use induces a cadastral survey analysis, in a ground rent approach, whereas a predominating commercial use implies a study of the percentage of turn-over generated by the tourist flows).

The axes frame the site by relating the different poles, and can be extended outside the site, reaching into what we shall call the 'impact area' of the CBH. Axes are the obliged ways through which visitors of the site have to pass: streets, avenues, squares in urban sites; roads, by-roads, communication nodes in larger impact areas.

We can detect three types of axes:

- *Polar axes*: the pole is constituted by one or more axes. This is often the case in urban historic centres, where the architectural monuments are integrated within the city (for instance, the Champs Elysées).
- *Joining axes*: axes that interrelate different poles, through which people must pass when circulating from one pole to another. These are often commercial axes, gathering together commercial activities related to tourism attractiveness.
- *Axes giving access to poles*, from outside the site.

Isolating the axes facilitates the analysis of economic costs and benefits generated by the CBH, as each axis can be treated separately.

The impact area is the limited zone in which significant economic spill-overs can be detected. Outside this area, these spill-overs can be ignored: it is superfluous to stress the fact that careful investigation will be necessary in order to determine this frame of analysis. A convenient analogy would be with the economic hinterland or zone coming under the economic and commercial influence of an urban, industrial or commercial centre (in our terminology 'the pole'). An architectural hinterland around CBH will be known as the 'direct impact area' around CBH.

There is no absolute rule when tracing it: economic impacts do not necessarily propagate in concentric circles with decreasing intensity; they might well diffuse further and in other directions than previously thought.

Four elements can help us detect impact areas of CBH:

- *Ground configuration*: impact areas must be drawn differently according to the geographic situation of the CBH (in open ground, in the mountains, in an urban region, at the seaside, etc.). Impact areas follow the geography of the site, according to natural obstacles, and account for the development steps of a town or region.
- *Road connections*: if the CBH is located along an important communication node, the impact area will propagate along this particular axis, following the visitors' movements. If it is situated at the far end of a difficult road, the impact area will probably move away from the site itself, to a more convenient place. The presence of a nearby airport or railway station can also influence the aspect of the area.
- *Commercial equipment*: the presence or absence of trades and shops around the pole is an essential determinant of the shape of the impact area. Commercial equipment does not necessarily coincide with road connections, even if trade opportunities develop more easily along these tourist communication axes. The impact area must therefore account for the visitors' easy access to the site and for the possible detours that they would make in order to purchase 'souvenirs'.
- *Methodological requirements*: in some cases, if the elements of analysis mentioned so far reveal themselves as inoperative or incoherent, we will have to dismember the impact area for a better 'reading' of the CBH. It would then be justifiable to follow a more arbitrary procedure, aiming at maximum clarity.

As to the shape of the impact area, various hypotheses are possible: concentric around the site, eccentric as to the site, directional (along one or more axes), or star-shaped.

Spatial indicators and mapping can help visualize the impact of decisions. As far as the economic dimension of CBH is concerned, we suggest that four project variables need to be identified: potential attractivity of CBH, tourist spill-overs, inclusiveness considering alternative sources of attractivity, directionality (efficient management of internal flows) or connectivity (integration in international networks) in the area. These variables should be described separately on specific maps.

Overlaying the maps would then provide us with information as to the type of impact area.

When spatial indicators have been gathered, a typology summarizes the information relevant to CBH. Using the project variables, five types of impact areas can be detected: (1) tourism-intensive impact area; (2) multiple functions impact area; (3) multipolar impact area; (4) decentralized impact area; (5) competitive impact area.

Area 1: Tourism-Intensive Impact Area

These areas include a large number of monuments, none of which are isolated. Although some of the monuments have outstanding cultural value, the interest for this heritage is derived from the homogeneity of the monuments, buildings or groups of buildings and from their integration in the local environment. Historic centres are the best example.

Tourism is the major source of economic flow. Souvenir shops, hotels and restaurants are located on the site and provide food, accommodation and commercial services almost exclusively to tourists. Because of the tourism-intensive activities, most of the original urban functions are sized down, if not forced to migrate out of the cultural area.

These 'museum-oriented' areas bring about a huge amount of economic benefits, while simultaneously facing a deterioration of their monuments due to an excessive flow of tourists.

Area 2: Multiple Functions Impact Area

These areas include groups of buildings of architectural interest but very few outstanding monuments. Tourist attractiveness is rather low and the economic flows of revenues are mainly due to urban activities (commercial, administrative, housing).

A main feature of this type of area is an intricate urban system where many functions are intermingled. Urban planning requirements have contributed to develop many activities over time, giving a truly systemic dimension to this area and providing a mix of activities as a result of both public regulation and private markets.

Large and densified urban areas illustrate this type of situation. Even in a large city with outstanding CBH, the complexity and size of the city make the economic flows from culture less obvious, because the relative share of tourist revenues over the total amount of urban resources is low.

Area 3: Multipolar Impact Area

These areas present the multipolar structure described above. Rather than being homogeneous, CBH is distributed among several locations over the site. The attractive poles are linked together by either tourist or commercial flows. In a multipolar structure, monuments can compete with each other in terms of attractiveness or can be integrated in a common scheme (guided tours, single entrance fee to several monuments, etc.).

Such areas are in fact the subdivision of a larger area. Depending on the size of the site, we could separate a homogeneous area into several sections of cultural interest with specific flows of economic revenues. Bearing in mind the fact that the total amount of benefits generated by the heritage exceeds the sum of the partial benefits of each section, we could still rely on this method as a proxy of the revenues of the heritage as a whole.

Area 4: Decentralized Impact Area

These areas can be identified as flows of revenues geographically separated from their cultural source. A monument located on an island or isolated from any urban area will generate flows of revenues far away from the site itself. In this regard, mobility is a key-word because the physical links between the CBH and its impact area (roads, mass-transportation, parking lots, etc.) will be a pre-requisite for any economic benefit.

Monuments or historic sites must eventually be of outstanding interest. Their attractiveness must be so powerful as to generate impacts far away from the site. It should be noted that this situation does not imply a tourism-intensive area, for the decentralized impact can provide many activities other than tourist-related ones.

Area 5: Competitive Impact Area

These areas constitute the most difficult issue of the economic dimension of CBH. Many studies have shown the complexity of consumer behaviour concerning leisure activities. Most of the visitors to monuments take their journey in the form of a 'package' (of which the visit is just a part), and people who live in an historic district enjoy looking at the monuments just by passing-by. Therefore, indirect or induced effects from the heritage are difficult to determine.

To the extent that more appropriate methods can be effective, it is important to detect and describe this type of situation. Great cities often rely on that type of area: poles are not just architectural in kind, not even cultural ones. Conflicts that could arise between different functions (housing versus offices, industrial versus environmental-friendly activities, administrative versus private use, etc.) or between different actors, could also arise with leisure activities. As an example, tourists are eager to go to Greece for their vacation not just because of the cultural heritage.

Competitive areas are situations where integrated conservation must be the rule. History shows that urban development was partly the result of socio-economic and physical factors: intersection of two roads, intersection of a road and a river, access to the sea, the vicinity of raw materials or a source of energy, cheap labour force. Competition between urban centres or regions for attracting new investors was mainly based on objective elements. Today, it seems that both globalization and the surge of new technologies imply a new kind of competition. The production of economic wealth is no longer related to fixed assets but to moveable resources.

In this regard, quality of life plays a key-role in modern development and architectural or cultural poles become new assets for attracting investment. Accordingly, competitive areas can be defined as an internal competitive market (on-site competition between all sectors improving quality of life) and external competition (off-site competition between cities or regions).

Notes

1 Part of this contribution to the reflection on the economics of conservation has been made by fellow economists gathered in an International Economics Committee, set up inside ICOMOS. This is an opportunity to underline the major work contributed by the first Chairman of the ICOMOS economics committee, Professor Emeritus of the London School of Economics, Nathaniel Lichfield. Under his supervision, many reflections were brought together and a major leap forward was made in the evidence that economic tools could provide a better understanding of conservation and help the decision-making process in that field. Today, the ICOMOS Committee on Economics of Conservation is acting as a follow-up of the work of these pioneers. A core of fellow members is indebted in the task of writing a *Chart of Economic Principles and Methods for Conservation*. This work will be submitted in the coming months to a larger group of national representatives.

2 To the question 'how can the economist contribute to a valuation of the cultural element in CBH?', all authors agree on the answer that he can register 'signals on value', i.e. what buyers are prepared to give up for the utility from the goods and services which are exchanged, or the cost of achieving this utility. From this, his particular contribution will be to establish the nature of costs and benefits either to all or to particular sectors of the community which will experience them, and to assess the relationship between such costs and benefits in order to advise, basing his suggestions on particular economic criteria, whether the expenditure of resources on that particular outlet will be worthwhile in terms of viability, and whether it will represent 'value for money' compared with expenditure on other outlets. But, while the necessity of attributing an economic value to things can be justified, we must not forget that, particularly in the case of CBH, the economic view is complementary to the others, and its role is only that of a contribution to the global picture of CBH.

3 Whereas economic analysis can be justified by the necessary congruence of limited resources with the multiple possible uses of these resources, the final choice is not the economist's, but rather has to be made by the agent in charge – be it an individual (policy-maker, occupier, owner, etc.), a firm or a collectivity. The role of the economist is merely to illustrate economic conditions and the consequences of various decisions concerning the uses of CBH but he should leave a set of options open and he should not become involved in aesthetic, artistic or historic debates.

4 We need to agree on a set of characteristics of CBH that will shape our analysis:
   - immobility, heterogeneity, non-reproducibility, lack of substitutes;
   - predominance of supply aspects;
   - price formation and CBH-related values;
   - evaluation of demand and willingness to pay in cultural economics;
   - mobilization of supply of CBH;
   - 'market' or 'markets' for CBH?
   - collective good providing individual and collective services;
   - longer life cycle than any other economic good;
   - induced effects, notably in terms of employment;
   - international resource, opportunity for local development.
5 Public intervention essentially takes place at four levels:
   - public authorities can provide cultural services directly, by managing the monuments themselves;
   - they can subsidize them (directly or through intermediaries);
   - they can provide incentives for preservation projects (e.g. contribution to maintenance works, tax deduction or exemption, repayable loans at favourable interest rates);
   - they can use regulations and rules (listing, prohibiting demolition).

Chapter 26

The Social and Economic Attractiveness of the Urban Environment: An Exercise in the Valuation of Public Space in Barcelona[1]

Josep Roca Cladera, Malcolm C. Burns and Pilar García Almirall

Introduction

The valuation of a city's public space, of its streets and squares, of its parks and gardens, continues to be a topic of heated debate. Its essential characteristic of being a public good, over which it is not possible to exercise restrictions of use, represents the principal difficulty when attempting to establish its value with any degree of precision. Despite its clearly having an economic and social value, the discipline of property valuations, understood as the valuation of the 'exchange value' of urban goods, comes to a halt when confronting the challenge of attempting to quantify the value of public space.

What is the value of a street, or a square, or an urban garden? Is it the sum of the value of the surrounding private property? Is it the aggregated economic wellbeing of the users, direct or indirect, of the urban space? The theory of the value of the public goods, with regard to 'externalities', is an attempt to resolve the problem raised here. From this perspective the value of such goods, excluded from the market, would manifest itself through its impact on the price of the surrounding private goods, in this case, of the neighbouring properties benefiting from its presence. However, frequently one finds that the market does not internalize the totality of the benefits generated by public urban space. For this motive, *cost-benefit analysis* has attempted to generalize the socio-economic value of these types of public goods. It would mean, from this viewpoint, valuing the average social value, not only of its positive (or negative) effects in the value of private goods (externalities), but also the totality of its repercussion on the wellbeing of the citizens. Cost-benefit analysis has its starting point in the premise that the direct and indirect users of a determined good, can be identified, as well as valuing economically, the costs and benefits generated therefrom, representing the value of the said good and the capitalization of the corresponding cash-flows.

The valuation of intangible goods, therefore, represents one of the key factors for the resolution of the problem set out here. Specialized literature has made some effort to identify the totality of the aspects that shape the value of public goods, excluded by nature from the market. Together with the value of direct use, resulting from the utility of the use and its enjoyment, notions have emerged such as the indirect use value (Pearce and Moran, 1994), the option value (Weisbrod, 1964), and the existence value (Krutilla, 1967). Similarly the inheritance value (Pearce and Turner, 1990) has set out the problem of the legacy for future generations. The sum of all these values would represent the *total economic value* of the public goods.

All these comprehensive approaches to determining the social value of public goods have come up against the problem of the limitations relating to current valuation methodologies. To the intrinsic limitation of the method of market comparison, it is necessary to add the equally unsatisfactory character of the rest of the valuation techniques: hedonic prices, transport costs (Clawson, 1959) and the contingent valuation methods.[2] The problem at the heart of the insufficiency of these previous methodologies, over and above the practical difficulties of their concrete development, lies in the doubt as to whether or not the overall economic value represents a gross simplification of the 'real' value of the public goods. Can all the value be measured in the simple terms of 'wellbeing'? How can the dimension of the seemingly individual structure of economic value be overcome, in order to generalize a social conception of value?

From this critical perspective, some authors have defended a 'dual' conception of value. For example, Lutz and Lux (1979), highlight the fact that consumers' preferences are not uni-dimensional. Etzioni (1988) has strongly defended the existence of two sources of value: together with that resulting from utility, the corresponding 'ethical' value; and the 'citizen' value together with that of the 'consumer'. Some authors have defended the need to overcome the paradigm of economic value, with regard to the single and exclusive quantification of the value of human goods, in order to refer to 'complex social value' (Fusco Girard and Nijkamp, 1997). This would include the first, although it would not be limited to it alone: there exists an irreducibly non-economic dimension in the valuation performed by people through perception. The limitation of the traditional concepts of value, as well as the intrinsic insufficiency in the usual methods of valuation, lie at the same root in the determination of the value of public urban spaces. However, at the same time, the valuation of these spaces emphasizes the non-existence of alternative procedures of valuation that highlight the complex nature of the social value of such spaces. This chapter attempts to make a contribution to this complex field of valuing urban spaces of a public nature.

Methodology

What is the value of a street? What is the value of the streets, understood as spaces of public use, of a city such as Barcelona? A first approach could identify the value of such spaces with regard to the sum of the value of the totality of the land parcels and properties that surround them. Such a quantification has been undertaken on various occasions. Since 1984, the *Centre de Política de Sòl i Valoracions* (CPSV), of the *Universitat Politècnica de Catalunya*, has been monitoring the evolution of Barcelona's property market. In 1995 the CPSV established a public database of principally residential property values, in collaboration with Barcelona City Council. In addition to continued monitoring and the introduction of some 20,000 new entries to this database on an annual basis, the database has enabled detailed modelling of the spatial formation of urban (exchange) values across the city.

However, as indicated in the previous section, such quantification does not seem wholly satisfactory. The irreducibly social dimension, of a not exclusively economic nature, of such urban spaces is not accurately reflected by the exchange values of private property. Alternatively, a system of valuation based upon the *contingent valuation methodology* could be conceived. From this perspective, the value of the streets could be quantified as a function of the sum that the users would be prepared to pay for the continuing benefit of their use. Conversely it could be expressed as the sum that the same users would be willing to accept as compensation in the case of the disappearance of the said streets. Such an approach, however, lacks all logic in the case of public roads, as does their privatization (not even the restriction of their use[3]), and their loss for public use and enjoyment (and their sale to third parties). The contingent valuation methodology is therefore not considered an efficient mechanism for the valuation of public urban space.[4]

Given the difficulties of the conventional methodologies of valuation, this chapter seeks to make an advance in the valuation of public space, from *quantifying it through the intensity of the use as well as from the degree of attractiveness that such spaces hold for the users of the city*. The users here are understood to be those individuals who use it in a direct form, whether in their capacity as residents, or by virtue of the type of use carried out therein (for employment, shopping, recreation, tourism, walking, etc.). The research therefore had two objectives:

- to quantify the intensity of use of the public ways, on the hypothesis that a space with a higher use reflects a higher social value than another space characterized by a less accentuated use, unless there exist restrictions in people's mobility; and

- to ascertain the degree of attractiveness, in different terms (residential, commercial, employment, recreational, cultural, etc.) that the public spaces offer their urban users.

For purposes of data collection, a questionnaire was administered by a group of largely post-graduate students, working in pairs, over an eight-month period between November 1998 and July 1999. The questionnaire sought to determine the subjective attractiveness of different parts of the city. It also sought to identify justification for the respondents' valuation, as well as their opinion concerning specific aspects of the immediate environment. These aspects covered architecture and urban design, civic and cultural vitality, the availability of community services and facilities, access to public transport, and key aspects of traditional urban environmental management, and a profile of the use of the public space with regard to predominant land uses. A copy of the questionnaire is contained in the Annex.

The municipal boundary of Barcelona has an area of just under 100 km² and is divided into ten districts.[5] These ten districts are in turn sub-divided into 38 zones and 245 micro-zones. Accordingly, some 275 data collection points were selected across the city, as shown in Figure 26.1. A previous study carried out earlier in 1998 over a central area of the city, comprising some 65 street blocks in Barcelona (CPSV, 1998; García et al., 1999) drew upon a similar methodology and served as a pilot study for this more spatially extended research. In the pilot study, information was gathered through a questionnaire, at four strategic locations on two dates (a mid-week day and a Saturday), at five different times throughout the day, over a period of one hour. As well as administering the questionnaire, a count was taken of the number of people passing the particular location. This provided a key as to the parts of the day with the highest numbers of passers-by.

On the basis of the results of the pilot study, the questionnaire used for the second more extensive study was amended and two key times were identified for its administration. Ideally the same day should have been chosen for the administration of the questionnaire across the 275 points of the city, but for logistical reasons it was not possible to achieve this. As a consequence the information was gathered through the questionnaire and the counting of the passers by, from Monday to Thursday, between 13.30-14.30h and 19.30-20.30h over the eight-month period. In order to maximize the uniformity of data collection, Fridays, weekends and public holidays were avoided, as were the extended Christmas/New Year period and days on which there were adverse weather conditions. As a result, some 3,500 responses were gathered together with the corresponding data on numbers of passers-by at each of the 275 locations.

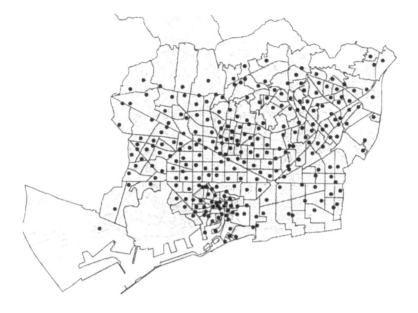

Figure 26.1 Data collection points

The research, therefore, sought to determine the social value of Barcelona's public space, by virtue of the *psychological estimation of the multiple dimensions of urban attractiveness*. Such an approach, based upon subjectivity, clearly has its drawbacks, especially those deriving from the 'non-contrasted' character of the opinions revealed by those questioned. It reflected the state of opinion, at a given moment, by virtue of the different criteria of evaluation of the users of the city. While differing to a certain extent from the objective value represented by market value,[6] it had the virtue of evaluating aspects of the urban reality intrinsically outside the market and where methodologies based upon exchange value are simply not applicable.

Analysis of the Results

As can be seen from Table 26.1, the principal results of the analysis indicate that the attractiveness of the city's public space scores highly in the minds of people in Barcelona. Average attractiveness reached a value of 65.75 per cent. This attractiveness varied from a minimum of 54.36 per cent in District 3 (*Sants-Montjüc*), to a maximum of 71.22 per cent in

District 4 (*Les Corts*). Figure 26.2 illustrates the different values of the perceived attractiveness at the scale of the microzone.

Table 26.1 Respondents' (resident and non-resident) values for the perceived attractiveness of the respective districts of Barcelona

District	Average value	Minimum value	Maximum value
Ciutat Vella	67.04	30.00	83.21
Eixample	68.08	48.82	81.20
Sants-Montjüic	54.37	1.00	76.67
Les Corts	71.22	61.19	91.67
Sarrià-Sant Gervasi	69.41	57.14	84.00
Gràcia	70.56	60.94	89.17
Horta-Guinardó	63.73	45.00	75.06
Nou Barris	58.15	40.71	76.25
Sant Andreu	64.77	32.10	77.42
Sant Martí	67.73	46.11	86.00
Total	*65.75*	*1.00*	*91.67*

With regard to the *non-resident users* in the zones where the questionnaire was administered, the average attractiveness reached a score of 62.27 per cent (Table 26.2), which contrasted with the higher score of 68.93 per cent for the *residents*. Similarly in all of the ten districts, the resident respondents valued attractiveness more highly than the non-resident respondents.

Looking first at the attractiveness of the different areas for different activities, in terms of the *residential attractiveness*, the average score for the city (on a scale of 10) was 6.21. With regard to the *attractiveness for employment purposes*, the average score for the city was 6.01. Turning to the *attractiveness for shopping purposes*, the city as a whole obtained an average score of 6.07. The *attractiveness for recreation* obtained an average score notably lower across the whole city (5.22).

Turning to what can be considered as the 'negative' aspects associated with the public space (4.c. xi-xv of the questionnaire), the question of *security* scored 5.95 across the city. Again with the level of *noise* the central district of the *Eixample* scored the highest (7.37) exceeding the average for the city of 6.48. In terms of atmospheric contamination, the average score for the city was 6.35, with the central zone of the *Eixample* again obtaining the poorest valuation (7.40).

Figure 26.2 Perceived 'attractiveness' of Barcelona's public space

Table 26.2 Resident respondents' values for the attractiveness of the respective districts of Barcelona

District	Average value	Minimum value	Maximum value
Ciutat Vella	69.08	30.00	92.50
Eixample	71.36	48.13	92.50
Sants-Montjüic	64.76	47.33	83.75
Les Corts	77.63	66.00	100.00
Sarrià-Sant Gervasi	74.36	50.00	93.00
Gràcia	73.15	50.00	94.50
Horta-Guinardó	67.27	42.13	90.00
Nou Barris	58.36	39.17	75.00
Sant Andreu	66.59	34.56	83.63
Sant Martí	67.73	41.25	100.00
Total	*68.93*	*30.00*	*100.00*

The aspect of *traffic congestion* scored 6.41 for the whole city. In terms of *street litter* Barcelona's historic core, comprising the *Ciutat Vella* district scored most poorly, with a value of 6.60.

The foregoing provides an *analysis of the principal components* in order to synthesize the information obtained with regard to the attractiveness of the public space of Barcelona. This analysis revealed the existence of two principal factors, which explained 60.36 per cent of the variation of the 16 variables under investigation, as contained within the questionnaire.

The first factor, 'commercial', was found to have a positive correlation with attractiveness for shopping (R=0.79), attractiveness for employment (R=0.67), attractiveness for recreation (R=0.67), public transport links (R=0.70), and street vitality (R=0.79). However this factor includes several negative externalities, such as the presence of noise (R=0.85), atmospheric contamination (R=0.89), traffic congestion (R=0.83), street litter (R=0.63), as well as the lack of green open space (R= −0.57).

A second 'residential' factor presented a high correlation with the overall attractiveness (R=0.83), residential attractiveness (R=0.86), quality of the architecture (R=0.72) and the quality of urban design (R=0.64). It also had an equally positive correlation with the security of the public ways (R=0.66), as well as a negative correlation with the presence of street litter (R= −0.41).

The analysis for the *intensity of the use of the public space* of Barcelona, i.e. incidence of passers-by, indicated an average value for the city of 854 persons/hour per data collection point. However this average figure was well exceeded for two of the city's districts: the *Ciutat Vella* historic core, which scored some 1,437 persons/hour per data collection point; and the central *Eixample* district, with an average of 1,217 persons/hour at each data collection point.

On the other hand the *aggregated global attractiveness*, i.e. the product of the average attractiveness for each data collection point with the intensity of use of each point, presented the closest image to that which could be deduced as the 'social value' of Barcelona's public space. This is significantly removed from the traditional images of the city obtained from property values. The *Ciutat Vella* historic core, normally considered as an urban space in the process of urban deterioration, demonstrates the highest aggregated attractiveness of the city, some 83 per cent above the average. This is clearly indicative of its central situation combined with the strong sense of cultural identity to be found in this area. Certainly it is an area that has been the subject of inner city urban regeneration initiatives, aimed at improving social conditions and the physical fabric, experiencing similar types of social and environmental problems as other western European inner city areas. In contrast, the urban fabric of the *Eixample* area, planned and developed in the latter half of the nineteenth century, is characterized by wide streets and a uniform grid iron street pattern. The area conserves a privileged role in collective appreciation with regard to the social value of public space, with an aggregated value some 52 per cent above the average of Barcelona. Faced with these two unique districts, the rest of the city denoted an aggregated attractiveness clearly below the average for the city, especially in the case of the most peripheral districts located in the north of Barcelona (*Horta-Ginardó* and *Nou Barris*).

Conclusions

The research described here sought to achieve progress in the complex field of the social value of public urban space. To this end, three basic indicators were constructed:

- the (subjective) attractiveness that the city holds for the users of the public space;
- the (objective) intensity of the use of the same space;
- the aggregate attractiveness resulting from the product of the two previous indicators.

In several aspects the results obtained differ from the traditional image of the city. Spaces which from the perspective of the private property market, do not seem to have a relevant value, at least not in their residential component, acquire an unexpected interest in the light of this study. The case of the historic core of *Ciutat Vella*, in this regard, is significant, as can be observed from Figure 26.3. In other cases, such as the *Eixample*, the research confirms the pronounced social attractiveness anticipated by planning studies.

The city appears segmented, with regard to the values of use of the public space, in two types of differentiated spaces: the city characterized by a strong component of *residential attractiveness*, and the city of *commerce, employment and recreation*. The first carries with it a significant valuation of the quality of the built stock, of the architectural values and of the urban design, the open spaces and the citizens' security. The second carries with it significant values related to ease of accessibility, employment, commercial and recreational opportunities, as well as the civic and cultural vitality found within the public domain. However at the same time it involves significant negative externalities linked to traffic congestion, atmospheric contamination, noise and litter within the public space.

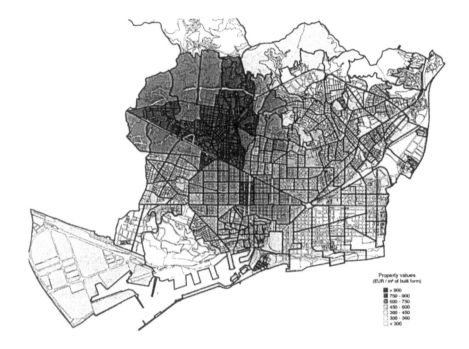

Property values
(EUR / m² of built form)

- ■ > 900
- ■ 750 - 900
- ▨ 600 - 750
- ▨ 450 - 600
- ▢ 360 - 450
- ▢ 300 - 360
- ▢ < 300

Figure 26.3 Residential property values (Euros/m² of built form)

Nevertheless, in the light of research undertaken to date, there does not appear to be a significant correlation between the ('subjective') attractiveness detected and the ('objective') value resulting from the private property market (relating to the value per square meter of residential property). The positive correlation (R=0.50) with the factor of 'residential' attractiveness is clearly inferior to that which might have reasonably been expected. Similarly the property values denote a negative correlation, albeit of little significance, with the 'commercial' attractiveness of the urban space (R= –0.15). Further work is clearly necessary in this field to achieve deeper understanding of the apparent paradoxes indicated by these results.

Notes

1   The authors gratefully acknowledge the funding provided by the Spanish *Comisión Interministerial de Ciencia y Tecnologia* (CICYT) (AMB98-0641) for this research project.
2   There is a long tradition of such techniques, for example travel cost and contingency valuation methods, being used for the valuation of public monuments, and buildings of

historic and cultural interest, as well as public parks and protected open space.

3 Although often, whether it be for environmental reasons (atmospheric contamination), or for traffic congestion, traffic circulation restrictions are produced.

4 Here reference is made to the public roadways. Contingent valuation can be useful in certain cases, for example in the valuation of urban parks and gardens.

5 *Ciutat Vella, Eixample, Sants-Montjüic, Les Corts, Sarrià-Sant Gervasi, Gràcia, Horta-Guinardó, Nou Barris, Sant Andreu* and *Sant Martí.*

6 Although in essence, the market value is also a subjective value, depending upon the opinion of the purchasers of the urban good, there is also a basic component of objectivity, stemming from the contrast of the purchase value with the sales value, reflecting the overall value the market assigns to each urban area. By contrast, the 'value' obtained in the research does not have a contrasting value in the public arena, corresponding to the degree of subjectivity of attractiveness of the public space for each user of the city.

References

Clawson, M. (1959), 'Methods for Measuring the Demand and Value of Outdoor Recreation', *Resource for the Future*, no. 10.

CPSV (1998), *Elaboració d'un sistema d'avaluació econòmica de la ciutat en base a factors medi ambientals*, CPSV, UPC, Barcelona.

Etzioni, A. (1988), *The Moral Dimension, Towards a New Economics*, The Free Press, New York.

Fusco Girard, L. and Nijkamp, P. (1997), *Le valutazioni per lo sviluppo sostenibile della città e del territorio*, Angeli, Milan.

García Almirall, P., Burns, M.C. and Roca Cladera, J. (1999), 'An Economic Evaluation Model of the Environmental Quality of the City', Paper presented at the Sixth European Real Estate Society (ERES) Conference, Athens, 23-25 June 1999.

Krutilla, J.V. (1967), 'Conservation Reconsidered', *American Economic Review*, vol. 57.

Lutz, M. and Lux, K. (1979), *The Challenge of Humanistic Economics*, Benjamin-Cummings Publishing Co., Menlo Park.

Pearce D.W. and Moran D. (1994), *The Economic Value of Biodiversity*, Earthscan, London.

Pearce, D.W. and Turner, K. (1990), *Economics of Natural Resources and the Environment*, Harvester Weathsheaf, New York.

Weisbrod, B.A. (1964), 'Collective Consumption Services of Individual Consumption Goods', *Quarterly of Journal of Economics*, no. 78.

Annex

Copy of the questionnaire used to collect data.

Questionnaire   REF.Date_____Time_____Place_____
Sex: Male/ Female
Age: under 25; 25-45; 45-65; 65+

This study is being carried out by the *Universidad Politécnica de Catalunya* in order to evaluate the attractiveness of different urban areas of Barcelona.

1. How regularly do you visit this part of the city?

Once a day	Several times a day
Once a week	Several times a week
Once a month	Less than once a month

2. a) What mode of transport have you used to come to this area?

On foot	Private car
Bicycle	Bus
Metro	Train
Motorcycle	Taxi
Other	

   b) How long does it take to reach here from your home?

   _____

3. What are the principal activities you normally carry out in this area? For example related with: (mark with a cross the activities with the corresponding frequency.)

	Regularly	Sometimes	Occasionally
Residential			
Work			
Studies			
Routine shopping			
Specialized shopping (clothing, etc.)			
Personal business transactions (banking, etc.)			
Visiting / Walking			
Cinema			
Recreation / Culture			
Others_____			

4. a) What do you consider to be the level of 'attractiveness' of the area? (1 – 100)

_____

    b) Why? _____

_____

    c) How would you rate on a scale of 1-10, (1 = very low, and 10 = very high) the following aspects of the area?

    i)   the quality of the architecture (of the buildings, etc.)   _|_

    ii)   the street vitality   _|_

    iii) the quality of the urban design (squares, landscaping, street furniture, footpaths, etc.)   _|_

    iv) links to public transport (metro, bus, train)   _|_

    v)   the services and community facilities of the area (schools, health services, parking facilities, post offices, etc.)   _|_

    vi) the level of open space, parks and gardens   _|_

    vii) the attractiveness of the area for residential purposes   _|_

    viii) the attractiveness of the area for employment purposes   _|_

    ix) the attractiveness of the area for commercial purposes   _|_

    x)   the attractiveness of the area for cultural and recreational purposes   _|_

    xi) the security of the area   _|_

    xii) noise levels   _|_

    xiii) level of atmospheric contamination   _|_

    xiv) level of traffic congestion   _|_

    xv) level of street litter   _|_

5. a) In which municipality do you live?_____

    b) In the case of a resident of Barcelona, please state the street intersection at which you live: _____

    c) In the case of a tourist, please state the country of origin: _____

Chapter 27

Re-Humanizing an Environmental Protection Culture: A Case Study of Integrating Multiple Perspectives in Achieving Environmental Behaviour Change in a Regulated Industry Sector

Jack W. Scannell, Denise L. Scannell and Charlton D. McIlwain

Introduction

For the past few decades, private citizens from all cultural and economic backgrounds across the globe have become increasingly concerned with the environmental conditions of their lives. Many worry about the relationship between man and nature, forewarning the consequences of using technology to solve environmental issues, and suggesting that there be a more humane approach to improving and sustaining liveable environmental spaces. While many describe recent civilizational fluctuations as a product of the postmodern era, information age, the age of science and technology, etc., there is one label whose absence has been conspicuous, yet is most accurate with regard to the human condition: dehumanization. The concept of dehumanization, influenced by Marxist humanism, is a complex issue with several specific communication concerns, such as alienation, the fragmentation of science and philosophy, and the division of subject and object (Marx as cited in Kovaly, 1974).

Marxism suggests that the economic and historical dimensions of society, along with the abolition of private property, are the initial cause of the unsettling quandary between man and society. The paradox: modernity is the unsettled solution. One cannot celebrate the technological advancement of civilization without celebrating the alienation from oneself, other humans and nature. 'Modern life has departmentalized, specialized, and thereby fragmented the being of man. We now face the problem of putting the fragments together into a whole' (Barrett, 1963, p. 89). This paper seeks to propose what can be viewed as a more 'humane' approach within the environmental protection culture and means by which governmental enforcement agencies, non-government agencies, and other entities might approach the task of environmental protection in a way that reconnects human citizens with the natural world. We begin with a theory of cultural transformation which helps us understand our contemporary predicament regarding our relationship with the natural environment.

Theoretical

Jean Gebser's (1985) theory of culture and consciousness delineates the essence of, or the necessary conditions for cultural expression, as well as how such expressions have manifested themselves throughout human history. Gebser's idea of cultural evolution is built on the concept of 'plus mutation', which entails that humans, while constantly gaining new qualities which allow them to interact with the natural and social environment, do not lose the old qualities in order to adapt. Rather, at any given point in time all forms of conscious awareness are present within human consciousness. While certain characteristics are, at a given period of time, dominant, other latent characteristics are still present and are evident in cultural experience. According to Gebser, all cultural expression presents a unique awareness of space and time. While magical awareness is spaceless and timeless, signalling no differentiation between man and nature, mythic awareness expresses the beginnings of human awareness as separate from nature. The present manifestation of our awareness of space and time is perspectival. The perspectival world, which is mental-rational, signalled a new psychic awareness of space, objectified or externalized from the psyche out into the world. As well, there begins to be a visualization of time in quantifiable, spatial character (the clock).

Perspectival consciousness inaugurated a realistic, individualistic, and rational understanding of nature. The mental rationality of perspectival awareness is characterized by directedness and perspectivity, together with unavoidable sectoral partitioning. There is calculation. It is this dominant, perspectival awareness, with its focus on pure rationality, measurement, and intense individualism, that expresses itself in a variety of communication modalities characterized in Kramer's theory of dimensional accrual/dissociation. The theory of dimensional accrual/dissociation (Kramer, 2000) seeks to explain the varieties of cultural expression that exists in the world. Kramer claims that this theory of social interaction/ communication 'can be used to explain any social behaviour/ communication including other theoretical artifacts, even the bewildering array of other conflicting theories of communication...' (p. xiii.). Kramer bases this theory on the definition of culture as expression and space and time as necessary conditions for such expression. Thus, civilizational variations in spatio-temporal articulation accounts for the myriad of differences of cultural expression across the globe. According to Kramer, these various spatio-temporal articulations are evident in all contingent expressions. Space-time is the pre-condition that allows for various forms of articulation and expression of space-time.

The theory, which follows from Gebser, the present dominant perspectival/signalic-codal mode of communication expresses extreme dissociation in that an arbitrary relationship between expression and expressed exists. As such, there is a severe loss of emotional attachment. Everything, in effect, becomes the same. Because of its dissociative nature, everything is open to manipulation. Perspectival consciousness locates the 'I' making individual identity the centre of concern; further removed from the clan or other objects in our symbolic environment.

Globalizing the Environment

Globalization refers to the 'rapidly developing processes of complex interconnections between societies, cultures, institutions, and individuals world-wide' (Monge, 1998). It is a process that influences and is influenced by many aspects of modern society, such as politics, economics, technology, and culture. Globalization theory is not a new concept. In 1968, Marshall McLuhan made reference to the world becoming a single harmonious place, the 'global village'. However, several important changes that have occurred over the past few decades contradict his predictions of this emerging village lifestyle that was to be a consequence of new communication technologies. The ability to obtain information without the constraints of time or space, along with the greater level of information exchange occurring between cultures is evoking a global city, not a village. The global city is driven by the capitalist commodification of culture. This is to say, it is the drive towards seamless financial transactions, economic policies, and environmental management.

An imminent criterion for living among the global society is to be 'plugged in'. Lacking the financial or technological resources (satellites, computers, television, cell phones, etc.) to plug into the world information system is problematic for many people. Consequently, the unified world that McLuhan predicted is fragmented by technology and isolation, what Meyrowitz (1985) calls 'no sense of place', and what Kramer (2000) refers to as 'the aggregate of competing individuals'. Kramer argues, in opposition to McLuhan, that the world is not 'retribalizing' or getting closer as a result of global communications. The ability to obtain information without the constraints of time and space, along with the greater level of information exchange occurring between cultures is constructing a 'cosmopolitan nobody' as identities, ethnicities, and cultures are blurring into sameness. This sameness is nowhere more apparent than in the city. Cities are places were homogeny is created and recreated. The dissociated massification of sameness is simultaneously decreasing the unique individual while encouraging apathy and intolerance for cultural differences. 'Life in the city holds the possibility of crushing the vitality of humanity by atomizing individuals' (Worth, 2000, p. 111); compromising humanity at any level can lead to dehumanization.

Dehumanization

Montagu and Matson (1983) argue that the modern world, generated systematically by industrial society and technological intelligence, has severed the balancing attributes of human nature (i.e. feeling, thought, consciousness, etc.) – in other words, being human. The concept of dehumanization is expressed in extreme anxiety; on the one hand, man is thought to be disinherited from his senses (Montagu and Matson, 1983) and his identity (Kramer, 1997); on the other, humanization is pertinent to solving man's fundamental communication issues (Kovaly, 1974). Modern human beings long to return to a magic consciousness where there is intense human connection. Kovaly refers to this connection as 'rehumanization'. 'As people seek to humanize nature, technology; they search for ways to humanize their environment, society, and all social relations...they are concerned with humanizing man himself' (Kovaly, 1974, p. 7). Unfortunately, modern humans have torn themselves from their roots, and can never return (Heidegger as cited in Barrett, 1963).

Dehumanization and its effects are nowhere more evident than those found in our attempts to globalize the environment and sustain development in underdeveloped states. The driving force towards international environmental policy and agenda-setting stems from the shift in the value of the environment: protect and preserve for future use. Yet, how can the environment be successfully governed without a unified government? The establishment of governance at the most basic level involves sets of rules, decision-making procedures, and programs that serve to define social practices, such as language, traditions, and gender roles. Organizations of the West (government agencies, non-profit agencies) have attempted to resolve social conflict, generate solutions, and promote cooperation among diverse peoples of the world. However, environmental management is exercised through the use of organizations, which possess characteristics of the imperialist system of the western world. There are some cases where adopted global policy prohibits indigenous people from using their own environmental space: natural resources, food, work, play, and livelihoods. This space is where they socially interact and construct their identity. The policy, for their own good or for the good of the 'shared environment', makes no difference to the immediate or latent consequences of their lives.

By disregarding the cultural diversity of other people, we run the risk of dissociating them from their world. They have no true ownership of reality therefore it becomes alien. Unfortunately, 'deep dehumanization of man is reached through enormous limitations of basic human rights and liberties, [brought about by some type of] unlimited power of the ruling political organization and the state' (Kovaly, 1974, p. 27). Consequently, the rhetoric of environmental protection and the resulting policy initiatives put into place by nations, government officials, and environmental non-governmental organizations are cultural expressions dominated by Western perspective.

Because there is little real emotional attachment between man and the natural environment and everything is interchangeable, talk of the environment is often politicized, subsumed into the capital market and used as an impetus for power and control. However, the rising concerns for dehumanization along with the exigency of cultural diversity is redefining the methods used to protect and preserve natural resources and the ecosystem. Thus, evoking a 'new culture' of environmentalism. Any social approach to governing, as it relates to environmental policy, needs to be inclusive of various perspectives and empower a wide range of citizens and organizations to build an 'environmental protection culture' and solve environmental problems without reducing valuable human resources to mere objects, stripping the knowledge and wisdom one may have.

Small Businesses and Environmental Protection Issues in the United States

In the United States of America, there are currently 25 million small businesses with less than 500 employees operating throughout the 50 states. There are also thousands of large businesses that have well over that number of employees. Regardless of size or industry sector, most businesses are regulated to some degree by 34 separate federal agencies, authorized with various mandates, including compliance monitoring and enforcement of the regulations. Of these national agencies, one with far-reaching authority in the business world is the US Environmental Protection Agency (EPA). In addition, separate state and local government agencies have the authority to impose regulations more stringent than those of the federal government, if deemed necessary by that entity.

Interfacing and complying with this myriad of formal organizations and bureaucratic rhetoric is no easy task for businesses, especially the small business owner (SBO). In a recent Small Business Administration report to the Congress, it was noted, 'Too often, enforcement and compliance activities have bewildered, frustrated, and angered small business owners who struggle to comply' (The National Ombudsman's 2000 Report to

Congress, 2000, p. 6). Since large businesses have expertise and systems in place for dealing with the various regulations and agencies, the individuals assigned this function are not personally subjected to the dehumanizing/ dissociating effects caused by the actions of governmental organizations. However, the SBO is subjected to a wide range of negative emotions based upon their perceptions of a variety of injustices from agencies with a 'gotcha' mentality that often have far-reaching consequences on their businesses and personal lives.

Nearly all periods in the history of mankind have recorded these kinds of perceptions and complaints as anecdotal evidence of the need for change in the ways that government organizations operate, especially in the infamous area of tax collection. In the past, upper management in charge of these powerful agencies would have simply dismissed the complaints as coming from 'cranks', or whining violators and subsequently directed their staff to continue with policy and behaviour as usual. But, in the last several decades of the twentieth century, things began to change in western countries, such as America, with regard to what the public was willing to tolerate in that regard. There were several high profile 'whistleblower' court cases where organization insiders came forward to reveal confidential organization policies and/or strategies that deliberately misled the public, often resulting in putting the consumer's very health at risk (i.e. tobacco, etc.). Whistle blowing on organizations is not confined to the private sector, but also is alleged to be widespread in government. In the environmental field, where immediate public health as well as the future of our planet is increasingly considered to be at risk, whistleblowers have raised concern over the manipulation of public opinion by various agencies, including the US Environmental Protection Agency (EPA).

To finally determine and document the validity and widespread nature of the perceptions of complaining SBOs concerning the 34 United States agencies, in 1996 Congress authorized the Small Business Administration to create the impartial Regulatory Fairness Program. This program had several important participatory facets, but the most important was the yearly report to Congress summarizing the results of SBO hearings and representative information from the nation's 25 million small businesses in all 50 states concerning their experiences with agencies such as the US EPA. The results of collecting this broad base of information from the hearings, appraisal forms and daily interactions between Fairness board members and SBOs, identified the following four common recurring themes (The National Ombudsman's First Annual Report to Congress, 1997):

- agencies change the rules in the middle of the game;
- agencies disregard the economic or other consequences of their actions on small businesses;

- small businesses often get ensnared in conflicting regulatory requirements when two federal agencies' jurisdictions overlap;
- small businesses fear agency retaliation.

In 1998, a significant complaint was that the tones conveyed in the enforcement activities are too adversarial and confrontational. Other complaints included, agency enforcement practices too frequently have 'draconian' effects; too many compliance and enforcement officials utilize a broad-brush approach; agencies often fail to communicate their own procedures and standards. (The National Ombudsman's 1999 Report to Congress, 1999).

It should be noted that the issue of retaliation was specifically addressed with respect to the EPA, and as a result the EPA agreed to develop and issue a formal, unambiguous anti-retaliation policy by March 1999. By the end of 1999, the significant common themes reported were:

> Many small businesses conclude that agencies do not understand their industry, the impact of agency requirements, or worse, that they do not care about the repercussions. Businesses believe that agencies too often focus on the process as opposed to the goal, which in many instances makes it more difficult and expensive for small businesses to achieve compliance. Small businesses often feel that an agency's only mission is to try to catch violations and penalize the companies; some agency staff that perform inspections or compliance audits are not well-trained, and sometimes are not familiar with the industries they inspect, much less the operations of those industries (The National Ombudsman's 2000 Report to Congress, 2000, p. 20).

It was pointed out in the 2000 report that a major goal and continuing theme for the RegFair Program was to encourage Federal agencies to create a friendlier, non-punitive regulatory environment for the nation's 25 million small businesses. While success in this area was achieved by some agencies, i.e. the IRS, it did not alter the SBOs perceptions of other agencies, such as the EPA.

New Environmental Protection Organization Model

Finally, in the United States, ample documented and verifiable information was gathered by the government itself to support the claim that various agencies have been interacting with their stakeholders and the general public in ways ranging from non-responsive to abusive. Therefore, it is our opinion that some of these ways have fostered accompanying feelings in the individuals involved in these sectors ranging from distrust to dehumanization and victimization by certain government organizations.

While some government organizations, such as the EPA, may have been non-responsive to humane needs in the past, and are likely to be rendered even more ineffective in addressing these needs in the future (Scannell et al., 2001), this does not mean government regulatory agency roles should be abandoned. There will always be a need for a formal management structure to administer responsible compliance monitoring and enforcement of just laws/policies to safeguard public resources and interests, such as the environment. However, in a similar way that significant changes have taken place in many parts of modern society, government organizations must also undergo a meaningful transformation from their traditional state and behaviour to one that is both contemporary and humane in nature. The means for accomplishing such a transformation can be easily identified. Organizational cultures of the west have several common systems elements necessary for a long-term, effective operating lifetime:

- *common interest/purpose*: managing the environment;
- *people*: interested public, stakeholders, scientists, regulators, etc.;
- *participation*: employees, small business owners, activists, interested public, industrial stakeholders, etc.;
- *communication – internal and external*: accountability, credibility, goals, etc.

In some organizations, these elements are applied very successfully and the group is able to carry out its mission with good performance and credibility. In others, the elements are applied in dysfunctional ways, especially for communications. The inherent malfunction of the western organizational culture is that it tends to mirror the capitalist system, therefore enhancing certain dysfunctional effects, such as dehumanization/ dissociation throughout the globe. For the new model proposed in this paper, a general discussion of some of the above elements and proposed insights in terms of developing an organization for environmental management that meets the stated goals of the environmental culture can be found in Scannell et al., 2000.

At a minimum, the new organizational structure should be capable of confronting and regulating the relentless global economic forces, while operating in humane ways that protect the planet and its sustainable growth, and include the participation of all population sectors in our communities. If large government organizations are to be transformed into a structure that is humane, includes representative diversity, and is responsive to the needs of today's society, where and how is such a significant change accomplished? Appreciating the difficulty of achieving a change in 'worldview' necessary for such a transformation, suggests that it must begin at the community level and expand upward in all cities (Winter, 2000). From communities, cities, states, and regions, such change within government must eventually reach the national level if there is to be credible interaction with international forces.

A General Approach

A general approach proposed for addressing the consequences of dehumanization is to construct an organization with a humane image based on solidarity among humans and between them and nature. Such an image embodies relevant environmental values like freedom, equity, and justice. One concern with this approach is on a very practical and operational level, emanating from a perspective of significant direct experience working within the various groups often at odds over the responsibility and culpability for the current state of affairs, including government agencies, non-profit agencies, and private industry. From that vantage point, the authors of this paper suggest that creation of such a humane image will require both a fundamental change in the behaviour and structure of the organizations empowered with the means to embark upon and maintain the new path, as well as similar kinds of change in the behaviour of the individuals making and remaking the city. In other words, it will require a cultural change of enormous magnitude.

The envisioned cultural change will take the involvement and participation of the whole community to accomplish such a lofty goal, every business and most citizens, not just a chosen few. In a utopia, achieving such an image is probable. However, given the embedded dissonance over ecological values and beliefs, it may only be achieved in contemporary society from a dedicated and non-selfish top-down and bottom-up effort; some would refer to a change of this magnitude as an environmental revolution. As the term 'community' suggests, (communi)cation – which entails participation by all individuals and groups sharing a common interest – will be a necessary part of such a model. The bottom-up effort will naturally require enlistment and representation from all population segments, including the 'prisoners of the enlarging circle of poverty' (i.e. the ghettos, the poor quarters of unemployed and the homeless). The mechanisms for accomplishing the goals in this significant bottom-up effort are not considered here, however, the cultural concept proposed accounts for the presence of that sector.

The top-down effort includes government agencies, non-government organizations (NGOs) and other pertinent organizations concerned with sustained development. All must creatively address the participatory challenges and opportunities in the community if establishing the image with the desired values of freedom, equity and justice is to be accomplished. Especially for the area of environmental justice where one of the most important aspects for providing a community with a safe, clean and accessible environment is the issue of participation. The emphasis on the participatory nature of top-down change in behaviour and perception implies a basic change in the structure, operating policy and environmental rhetoric of organizations involved with sustainable development.

Specific Changes in Government Environmental Protection Organizations

The overall approach to the new environmental protection organization model proposed here consists of changes in basic functional elements generally accepted as affecting the policies, operations and behaviours of the system. However, even these important changes will not guarantee the desired humane and all-inclusive nature considered necessary for transforming an agency, such as the US EPA, into an organization that is truly responsive to citizen and business needs at the local community level in all cities. For that level of transformation, a more radical change has to be included in the approach. Considering the limited scope and outreach efforts used for contacting and recruiting some . members of these populations, widespread participation by the general public has been more nominal than true and active involvement by diverse communities.

As a solution to this challenging problem, the new model proposes a unique dedicated effort at building collaboration across very large and diverse populations, engaging, involving, and assembling members until there is a common path in which people can move together (Senge et al., 1994). The larger the scale of collaboration the more accurately the organization will reflect the shared vision of the community as a whole. With such participation, the potential for open communications and networking between members will offer great opportunities for an 'ongoing organization-wide collaborative learning process' (Senge et al., 1994, p. 123). While this basic aspect is not unusual, the means proposed for accomplishment may be revolutionary.

As an important structural element for the ideal model, it is proposed that a special oversight coalition of non-government employees be created to serve and operate with equal status within government organizations, such as the US EPA. The coalition would consist of a diverse membership representative of that typically found in all cities, including members from the business community, citizen/residential community and environmental community. This group would also provide the multiple perspectives component that always should be considered prior to any policy implementation or changes by the agency. It is necessary that this coalition be independently funded, but established to operate within the bureaucracy to perform functions that include reviewing, advising and approving of policies and behaviour of the organization. If the organization is modelled as a 'learning organization', then it is expected that participant training will be an ongoing process, where each committed coalition member is given the tools and opportunity to develop their full potential for making a contribution. While the current focus of this proposal is on the national level, the same business/citizen coalition approach also can be applied to state and local government levels in all communities.

A Transition Model

It is acknowledged that changing from the status quo, represented by an organization such as the US EPA in the United States, to an environmental protection model as radical as the one proposed here would be impossible without a suitable transition model to act as a demonstration vehicle and to enlist important governmental support. Furthermore, the transition model must have certain characteristics to ensure future success. Based upon the information presented in other parts of this paper and elsewhere, the transition model selected for implementation will have several important characteristics including:

- establishment of the organization as a federally recognized non-profit coalition, based in a community with both residential and industrial segments;
- organization administration is by a Board of Directors consisting of voluntary members representing the local business community, residential community, regulatory community and environmental community;
- an operating staff capable of interacting with, and providing various free environmental services to, all members of the local business community, residential community, regulatory community and environmental community;
- the coalition will have the capability for interaction with all relevant government agencies for various purposes, including community information outreach and clarification, communications intermediary, and accessing information for providing assistance to referrals;
- treatment of all community member information as proprietary, confidential and anonymous by the coalition;
- development of a non-aligned, credible and humane relationship with the various served community segments and government agencies;
- the capability of the model to be replicated in selected communities/ cultures in other locations.

Finally, the transition model should be capable of demonstrating the key principles over a reasonable period of time, be non-threatening to government entities, and eventually be recognized and accepted by these entities as having sufficient value to consider experimentation with the ideal model.

The Environmental Coalition of South Seattle

A new organizational model, founded in 1994 to assist both the residential community and local businesses located in a residential-industrial neighbourhood with serious environmental issues, was legally established as a non-profit environmental services organization, located in Seattle, Washington, USA, as the Environmental Coalition of South Seattle (ECOSS).[1] While not intentionally designed to satisfy the stated characteristics of the transition model previously described, this model was recognized in 1999 as meeting the basic requirements. When nationally compared to other similar non-profit organizations, ECOSS was discovered to be especially unique in one very important respect: government regulatory agency staff are organization members and regularly serve on the Board of Directors responsible for ECOSS administration. After approximately eight years of successfully operating in a South Seattle residential-industrial neighbourhood, ECOSS has earned a reputation for equally serving all local stakeholders for the benefit of the environment. These stakeholders represent the members of the residential community, business community, government regulatory community and the environmental community.

Transition Model Case Study: Assisting the Auto Recycling Industry Sector

The auto recycling facility Affordable Auto Wrecking (AAW), located in Seattle, Washington, USA, has been continuously operating in the same location for over 15 years. AAW uses a business model that combines sales of salvageable used parts with materials recycling, typically crushing 150-200 vehicles per week prior to sending the hulks to a metal recycler. The facility is located on a rectangular-shaped site of less than five acres and has been used by automobile wrecking/salvage yard businesses for over 50 years. On the basis of a complaint in May 2000, AAW was inspected by the Washington State Department of Ecology (DOE) after being referred to this location:

> ...with the request that we inspect it for environmental problems such as venting CFC's into the atmosphere, allowing oil, antifreeze, and other automobile fluids to collect on the ground and be washed away by storm water run off, etc. (Washington State Department of Ecology Report, 2000).

The results of this inspection revealed numerous problems, including those identified in the referral and some associated with 'general housekeeping'. The owner of AAW was officially notified of all items of non-compliance requiring corrective action within specified timeframes.

In addition to the notice of violation status associated with the DOE letter, the potential of significant monetary penalties due to the various violations was a realistic concern for the company. Given the seriousness of the identified environmental problems, the relatively brief time frame required to accomplish some tasks and management's unfamiliarity with the regulations involved, this company needed environmental technical guidance on a level that they could not afford, i.e. a professional engineering consultant. While seeking advice from the local chapter of Automobile Recyclers of Washington (AROW), the owner of AAW was encouraged to contact the free, local non-profit environmental technical services provider known as the Environmental Coalition of South Seattle (ECOSS). Staff from DOE familiar with the reputation of ECOSS also suggested the use of this organization for assistance. When AAW finally initiated a working relationship with ECOSS in July 2000, they had been given a 30-day deadline for taking corrective action in some of the selected areas known to have the most serious environmental impact.

As a consequence of the long history for this type of industrial activity on the site, there was a high probability that soil contamination was present. However, because the current owner had the property capped with a concrete layer, ranging in thickness from 8' to 18', the potential for direct groundwater contamination from current and future operations was virtually eliminated. Therefore, storm water contamination was the primary concern for this media. At the time of the first inspection of the facility, the thick layer of dirt and debris covering the ground made it impossible to see that concrete, indicating a high probability that storm water pollution was occurring on a regular basis, and suggested that general housekeeping was an obvious major facility problem area. In addition, several different hazardous materials specifically associated with the automobile recycling industry were expected to be identified as potential site pollutants, including oils, greases and cooling fluids from various vehicle systems; fuels from gasoline and diesel engines; battery acid; and core metals including lead and mercury.

Assisting businesses with environmental compliance is a process consisting of several discrete phases, including site assessment, process/ operations review, waste stream analysis, improvement planning and implementation. The AAW owner and staff provided enthusiastic support and full cooperation with ECOSS during all phases of the program established with the company.[2] General ECOSS staff activities during the program consisted of the following:

* information review and analysis;
* plan/schedule development, resource coordination, i.e. consultants,

testing labs, etc., coordination of agency regulatory visits, coordination of equipment vendors;
• implementation assistance for appropriate record keeping and other formal documentation.

Assessment

During the site assessment phase, environmental problems associated with the high probability for polluting both air and storm water were identified in several process areas. As anticipated, all of the materials associated with this type of business as potential pollutants were found in various locations on the site. The problems identified were of sufficient magnitude to result in citations from different regulatory agencies, if not immediately corrected. The general problems found for each environmental medium at various locations around the facility are generally described in terms of their potential for having an environmental impact.

First, with respect to storm water, there was a high potential for pollution from sediments containing various materials dropped on the ground from incoming vehicles and improperly stored parts removed from vehicles. Also, there was a high potential for pollution from various contaminating materials during improper fluid recovery processes performed on those same parts, and their subsequent storage. Gasoline was specifically identified as a major potential contaminant as a result of spills occurring while being removed from the vehicles.

Second, there was a significant potential for local air pollution from gasoline vapours emitted during the gas recovery process performed on vehicles. In addition, there was a significant risk of stratospheric pollution from CFCs (chlorofluorocarbons) and non-CFC refrigerant gas releases during the vehicle incoming inspection process and the vehicle crushing operation. For the refrigerant gases, there was no established system for tracking the gas recovery and disposition.

Finally, there was no established system/schedule for maintaining the facility grounds free of storm water contaminating materials dropped from vehicles during parts removal by customers. In addition, there was no established system/schedule for general facility housekeeping, or environmental management, i.e. Best Management Practices (BMPs).

Following the facility assessment phase, a thorough review was performed of the operation's flow and individual processes involved in the vehicle recycling activity. The industrial process activities performed on this site were evaluated for their potential as sources of pollution.[3] As a result of the identification of potential pollutants performed in the Assessment phase and the details of all process steps associated with the Process/Operations Review phase, the analysis of the waste stream was essentially completed and plans for recommended changes were made.

Process/Operations Review

Subsequent to the facility assessment phase, a thorough review was performed of the operations flow and individual processes involved in the vehicle recycling activity. The industrial process activities performed on this site were evaluated for their potential as sources of pollution. These activities were performed in the following areas and are listed essentially in the order of the normal incoming vehicle flow through the operations:

- vehicle inspection and holding area;
- fluid removal and general process area;
- vehicle storage area with customer access;
- parts storage areas;
- fuel removal area;
- crushing area;
- waste storage areas.

Specific potential pollution issues associated with each of these areas were addressed by ECOSS and AAW.

Company Commitment

Prior to implementing any of the improvements, it was necessary for the business to demonstrate a commitment to the program. One essential element for demonstration and commitment to this support was to identify/designate a company team responsible for the overall pollution prevention program. That team was named by the AAW owner with the operations general manager being assigned as the team lead to work with ECOSS for accomplishing the necessary tasks. Based on AAWs agreement to work with ECOSS and the progress made during the first 30-day period to correct the major problems, the WA DOE extended the deadline for accomplishing the additional changes.

Accomplishments

Details of the various tasks performed towards correcting all of the compliance issues, record keeping, general housekeeping and implementation of BMPs in all process areas of the facility are found at the ECOSS website. Highlights of this activity include environmentally approved recovery and handling of all hazardous fluids, especially gasoline and the CFCs. In November 2000, the Washington State Department of Ecology and other local agencies toured the AAW facility to inspect for compliance, view the progress accomplished by company staff over recent months and determine AAWs commitment for maintaining their environmental management system on a long term basis. A thorough review of newly implemented weekly checklists, records related to recovered refrigerant storage, disposition, and disposal of hazardous waste materials confirmed that all required corrective action was completed on schedule, and the facility was in compliance in these specific areas. Additionally, a comprehensive approach to implementing appropriate site-specific BMPs as part of their environmental management system was now part of the company's standard operating policy (SOP).

The favourable finding by the regulatory agencies allowed AAW to continue to operate without restrictions. In addition, the business model was under review by the owner as part of a long-range plan to stop unsupervised parts removal activities by the general public. Finally, the company was being viewed by the AROW organization and other auto recycling businesses as an example to others in the industry for changing behaviours. The prior negative image that the company once had to contend with in their interactions with the public was also changed to an image of being a more responsible environmental steward. A detailed report of this project also can be found at the website for the International Society for Industry Ecology (Scannell, 2001).

General Case Study Results

This case study of typical environmental compliance problems of small businesses, targeted for complex violation issues by various government regulatory agencies, has been reported to demonstrate the need and usefulness for a new organizational model, such as the transition model described earlier in this paper. With the humane approach to guidance and assistance provided by ECOSS, the owner, employees and customers of AAW were able to conduct daily operations with a minimum impact. During this period, the company learned and implemented the behaviour changes necessary to achieve compliance and improved stewardship.

Case Study Results from Multiple Perspectives: Lessons Learned

The case study reported in this paper provides an example of how environmental behaviour change can be accomplished by businesses when the interaction with the model for environmental protection is humane in nature. However, it is also a good example of the importance of an environmental protection culture capable of taking into account various other perspectives, beyond the obvious environmental perspective. By combining the knowledge, background and experience of all concerned, or involved with this project, ECOSS was able to consider and utilize the insight associated with these different perspectives. As a result, several important lessons learned are noted and apply to all participants, including those from the residential, business, government regulatory and environmental communities. These lessons will be discussed in terms of several perspectives of importance, including *environmental management, land use management, infrastructure management, economic development, environmental justice* and *urban governance.*

Environmental Management Representing the local trade association for the industry sector, the Automobile Recyclers of Washington (AROW), recognized in 1999 that the sector, was going to be inspected and scrutinized to a much higher degree than in the past and attempted to alert their members of their potential liabilities and the need to begin to comply with the environmental regulations. Representing the company, the owner of AAW was made aware that continuing to operate in the new atmosphere of tighter environmental regulation would require implementation of a comprehensive system for monitoring and managing facility activities identified as having a potential impact on the environment. As a result of the ECOSS-guided activity, a custom, site-specific, environmental management system was developed and implemented to satisfy the needs of AAW and the regulatory agencies. The primary lesson learned by both participants during this activity was that, with humane assistance from an organization such as ECOSS, small business owners in this sector could be motivated to voluntarily make positive environmental behaviour changes. In the context of developing a more humane culture of environmental protection, the primary lesson learned by the agencies was that positive environmental behaviour change, i.e. compliance and long term stewardship, could be achieved by taking a more humane approach with small businesses and viewing their problems in the context of economic sustainability.

Land Use Management This perspective was well understood by ECOSS due to direct experience with the ongoing community Brownfields program activities. As a participant in the EPA/King County Brownfields Showcase Community activities, ECOSS identifies abandoned land parcels previously contaminated during industrial use. After identifying such parcels and the possibility for remediation, ECOSS then attempts to locate new business candidates to consider re-development of the property. Therefore, preventing the processes leading to business closure and subsequent abandonment was an important element for realistic and practical land use management. If AAW had been unwilling to engage in implementing the required operating changes and corrective actions, it is likely that the regulatory violation penalties would have triggered the process leading to that business closure. Based on the long history of auto wrecking businesses operating on that site, it was virtually certain that contamination at levels meeting the Brownfield criteria would be found, and redevelopment of that land would have become a major problem for the county. In the situation with AAW, therefore, if the agencies had simply followed the available legal path for assigning penalties, this action would very likely have resulted in the removal of economically valuable land from viable use. The land use lesson learned during this case study was that, rather than following the penalty path, it was more practical and productive for agencies to provide businesses with effective compliance assistance services that facilitate their continued successful business operations.

Infrastructure Management   This perspective is related to a problem associated with the auto recycling industry in general and the AAW business in King County, in particular. For many years, a common urban problem in large, American cities has been the timely removal of abandoned, or derelict vehicles from the streets of urban neighbourhoods. Left on neighbourhood streets for extended periods, these vehicles have the potential for causing a serious negative community impact in several different ways. From an environmental perspective, there is a potential pollution impact due to the likelihood of hazardous fluid leaks onto the ground that could ultimately end up in the storm or ground water. Some of these leaks are the direct result of parts scavenging taking place over a period of time while the vehicles are unattended. In the City of Seattle, the police may have these vehicles towed to a recycling facility, such as AAW, once identified as meeting the abandoned/derelict criteria. Since AAW is one of the few locations that are in close proximity to the City, many end up at that facility. If AAW was not available, due to business closure, towing to the next nearest location would be cost prohibitive for the City, and the vehicles may have to remain on the street for a much longer period to time. Thus, the lesson learned and appreciated by all during this activity was that AAW was a valuable local resource for neighbourhood infrastructure management, and their economic sustainability was important to community quality of life and the environment.

Economic Development   AAW had a relatively small staff and, therefore, only had a minor impact on the economy when compared to larger organizations. However, their employment policies assisted the community in a unique way. They hired, and in many cases, gave a 'last chance' opportunity to, workers who could not otherwise find gainful employment. These individuals often had employment, or personal history problems that prevented them from being fairly considered by more traditional/ mainstream types of businesses. Thus, in the context of poverty eradication, the lesson learned here is that a business such as AAW is a valuable community resource for employing and assisting marginal populations.

Urban Governance In terms of the urban governance perspective, there are several important issues that require comment. It was previously discussed that both top-down and bottom-up changes would be necessary for the kind of revolution needed to accomplish a re-humanizing of the environmental protection culture and for government agencies to 'address the challenges and opportunities in the community'. The authors believe that the reported case study here qualifies as an indicator that both types of voluntary behaviour change are possible. The top-down change in a government organization was evident by the willingness of the regulatory agencies for referring ECOSS to assist, and participate with, the small business owner in humane ways to accomplish the goals for compliance. The only alternative to their action was to pursue a legal and dehumanizing path that may have resulted in the business being bankrupted and closed. The bottom-up change was evident by the willingness of the small business owner to voluntarily work with ECOSS to make several costly and permanent changes in the facility in order to become better environmental stewards, as well as compliant with the regulations.

Since re-humanization was a primary goal for this new approach to urban governance, an important lesson learned by the authors was that ECOSS, the vehicle selected as the organization model for this work, was successful as the transition model for the general concept. A quotation from a letter by the owner of AAW is submitted to support that assertion. From the owner's perspective:

> ...with ECOSS's oversight and monitoring, we were able to implement changes in operations and management that by November had resolved all of Ecology's concerns. To us, Ecology's requirements appeared to be overwhelming until ECOSS provided us with technical assistance and a plan to address our environmental problems. It is quite possible that without this assistance, we would not be able to continue providing the city with the outlet for abandoned and derelict vehicles that it seriously needs (Setergren, 2001).

Environmental Justice   The location for the AAW facility is in a residential-commercial-light industrial area with lower housing costs for residents than in other neighbourhoods of the city. Typically, those who reside in this community are from low income and immigrant minority populations lacking the financial means for living elsewhere. In the vicinity of AAW, compared to living in a purely residential area, there also is a higher risk for residents to be exposed to a greater amount of pollution. Thus, the surrounding neighbourhoods meet the general US EPA criteria for consideration as environmental justice communities. Any reduction in pollution in these areas may have a positive impact on local residents' health and life expectancy. Of special importance in this regard were the gasoline vapour air emissions that occasionally occurred during the process of removal from the vehicles at AAW. Major changes made by AAW for eliminating these emissions resulted in a significant potential improvement in local air quality. The lesson learned by all involved in the program, including nearby residents, was that providing small businesses with the proper community resources can reduce pollution experienced by the surrounding population, while giving the business an opportunity to become a better neighbour and environmental steward for the benefit of the community and city.

Conclusion

Concerns for the environment have spawned new areas of consideration for scholars in a variety of disciplines. This is especially true given the fact that 'environmental protection' and other issues have been linked together with the idea of 'global communication' and other aspects of globalization. The idea of globalization, an outgrowth of modernity, has not produced a 'global village' of sorts, but rather has manifested itself through increased dissociation and dehumanization. The twin phenomenon of dissociation and dehumanization has reduced the environment to simply an object with use-value and those who work in the area of environmental protection to mere cogs in a wheel in an imperialistic hierarchy with narrow vision and calculated purposes. In contrast to the utopia of a shared global space, environmental rhetoric contains indications of power struggles between nation-states, including government enforcement agencies; non-governmental organizations, private industry and citizens, giving rise to a variety of communication concerns. As researchers, we believe that sustainable development and environmental policy, which seek to protect and preserve the environment, must be approached through a multiple perspective cultural model that includes a large and diverse group of citizens, that channels communication flow equally throughout the current environmental protection culture, that fosters voluntary environmental behaviour change and gives people at all levels of involvement some control over the environmental outcomes that impact all of our lives.

Notes

1   Detailed history and operational information about this organization is available online on the ECOSS website (www.ecoss.org).
2   Details of the phases and an overview of the improvements implemented at AAW during this assistance program are described on the ECOSS website.
3   These activities were performed in the various process areas and are listed in detail as part of a publication link from the Pollution Prevention page located on the ECOSS website.

References

Barrett, W. (1963), *Irrational Man*, Doubleday, New York.

Gebser, J. (1985), *The Ever-present Origin* [translated by Noel Barstad and Algis Mickunas], Ohio University Press, Ohio.

Kovaly, P. (1974), *Rehumanization or Dehumanization?*, Branden Press, Boston.

Kramer, E.M. (1997), *Gebser and Culture: An Introduction to the Thought of Jean Gebser*, Greenwood Press, Connecticut.

Kramer, E.M. (2000), 'Cultural fusion and the Defense of Difference', in J.E. Min (ed.), *African-American and Korean-American Relations*, University Press of America, New York.

Meyrowitz, J. (1985), *No Sense of Place: The Impact of Electronic Media on Social Behaviour*, Oxford University Press, London.

Monge, P.R. (1998), 'Communication Theory in a Globalizing World', in J.S. Trent (ed.), *Communication: Views From the Helm for the 21st Century*, Allyn and Bacon, Boston.

Montagu, A. and Matson, F. (1983), *The Dehumanization of Man*, McGraw-Hill, New York.

Scannell, J., (2001), *Unique Non-Profit Assists Auto Recycler with Environmental Compliance*, International Society for Industrial Ecology, [On-line] available: http://www.yale.edu/is4ie/.

Scannell, J., Scannell, D. and McIlwain, C. (2000), 'Creating a Humane Environmental Protection Institution', Proceedings of the World Meeting *The Human Being and the City. Towards a Human and Sustainable Development*, University of Naples 'Federico II', 6-8 September 2000, Naples.

Scannell, J., Scannell, D. and McIlwain, C. (2001), 'Environmental Governing as Cultural Expression: (Re)Humanizing Man and Nature by Fostering a New Culture of Environmental Protection', *Plurimondi*, Milan.

Senge, P., Kleiner, A., Roberts, C., Ross, R. and Smith, B. (1994), *The Fifth Discipline Fieldbook*, Doubleday, New York.

Setergren, R. (2001), *Private correspondence*.

The National Ombudsman's 1999 Report to Congress on Regulatory Fairness, (1999), [On-line] available: http://www.sba.gov/regfair/report/.

The National Ombudsman's 2000 Report to Congress (2000), 'Building Small Business-Agency Partnerships', [On-line] available: http://www.sba.gov/regfair/report/.

The National Ombudsman's First Annual Report to Congress on the Regulatory Fairness Program (1997), [On-line] available: http://www.sba.gov/regfair/report.

Washington State Department of Ecology Report, 2000.

Winter, D. (2000), 'Some Big Ideas for Some Big Problems', *American Psychologist*, vol. 55, p. 519.

Worth, D.S. (2000), 'Expression of Modernity: New York as Perspectival Rationality', *Integrative Explorations Journal of Culture and Consciousness*, vol. 6, pp. 101-11.

An Open Conclusion

Bruno Forte

An ethical question is implicit in the whole set of issues addressed by the various authors in this book. Reflecting on an era of profound changes, marked by the swift advancement of rampant economic and financial globalization and widespread urbanization, all the authors recognize the future of humanity itself in the need to rediscover ethical foundations of our common life. People need a new reason, open to the ultimate horizon of life and history, to live together in true human dignity. Over the course of the last two centuries – the so called 'modern era' – 'reason' has been the decisive protagonist: it lies at the very heart of the parable which sees both its apex and decline in the twentieth century. Opening with the triumph of the Enlightenment's 'strong reason', modernity has lead to a widespread experience of the fragmentation and the non-sense typical of the 'weak reason' which has flourished since the fall of ideologies. Succeeding the 'long' century, which began with the French Revolution and ended with the outbreak of the Great War (World War I) the so-called 'short twentieth century' (Hobsbawm, 1994) was marked by the affirmation of the extreme fruits of the totalitarianism of ideological models, which ultimately led to their collapse (1989).

The process is described by Max Horkheimer and Theodor W. Adorno in a powerful metaphor at the beginning of their *Dialectic of Enlightenment*: 'The fully enlightened earth radiates disaster triumphant'. (1973, p. 3). The aim of enlightenment – understood in its broadest philosophical sense as a continuous process – was to rid men and women of all fear and to grant them complete control of their destinies, thanks to boundless faith in the possibility of reason. Its extreme outcome – fulfilled through the dramas of the two world wars and the elevated costs of totalitarianism – can be recognized in the condition of renunciation, in the denial of the question of meaning and the search for the foundation, which is the condition of the so-called post-modern 'weak thought'. Three stages can be identified in this process lying at the origin of the crisis of the Western consciousness on the threshold of the third millennium; and can be expressed respectively through metaphors of light, night and dawn.

The first stage is characterized by the metaphor of *light*, which expresses the inspiration underlying modernity, the pretext of adult reason to be able to understand and illuminate every thing. According to this pretext, the ability of reason to embrace the world makes people the master of their own identities. Emancipation is the dream that pervades all the great processes of transformation in the modern era. The presumption to triumph over obscurity through the use of reason is expressed in the total visions of the world – the ideologies. Ideology seeks to impose the order of reason on the whole of reality, going so far as establishing a complete equation between the ideal and the real. It excludes any form of diversity and is, by its very nature, violent. The dream of totality becomes inexorably totalitarian. It is neither by chance, nor is it an accident, that all forms of modern ideology resulted in totalitarian and violent systems. Indeed, it is precisely the historical experience of the violence of totalitarian ideologies that has produced the crisis surrounding the absolute causes of 'enlightened' reason.

If the 'adult reason' of modernity sought to give a sense to everything, the 'weak thought' of the post-modern condition does not recognize any sense in anything. It is a condition that could be expressed by the metaphor of *night*: it is a time of ruin and failure, of darkness and uncertainty, and is, above all, marked by indifference. For many people, the rejection of the strong and total horizons offered by ideology bears the inability to pose the question regarding sense: this has led to the loss of any interest in seeking out the ultimate reasons for human life and death. The extreme face of the epoch-making crisis of the Western consciousness can be associated with the idea of 'decadence'. This means loss of value, since there is no longer interest in comparing or measuring the options of life to anything. It is in this way, then, that the passion for the truth has become less evident. The 'strong culture' of ideology shatters into fragments of 'weak cultures' in which the loss of hope folds people in on themselves and reduces every goal to a narrow horizon of the individual's own particular viewpoint. In this way, the collapse of ideologies appears as a pallid predecessor to the advent of the idol, that is the total relativism of those who no longer have any faith in the power of the truth and seem unable to pass from phenomenon to foundation. This is the extreme face of the crisis surrounding Western culture at the close of the 'short twentieth century'.

In the analysis of the process, passing from the triumph of modern reason to the decadence, we cannot exclude some signs of change and hope, to which we will associate the metaphor of the *dawn*. There is 'nostalgia for a perfect and consumed justice' (Horkheimer, 1970), which will enable us to recognize a sort of *search for lost sense*. We are not talking about '*une recherche du temps perdu*' – that is an operation based in the past, but rather, we refer to an attempt to rediscover the meaning beyond ruin and failure that enables people to discern a horizon that inspires and moves them towards an ultimate goal and meaning. We should characterize this search as *a rediscovery of the other*, witnessed by a growing awareness of the need for solidarity at an interpersonal level, as well as at social and international levels. We can also see a sort of emerging 'nostalgia for the totally other' (Max Horkheimer), a rediscovery of the ultimate questions and of the ultimate horizon. It outlines the need for a *new consensus about ethical values*, to motivate moral involvement, not in light of the benefits that arise from it, but rather in light of the good it arouses in itself. The nostalgia evident in the crisis of our present time has, therefore, the face of other, not only the face that is close at hand and immediate, but also of the Other, that is the transcendent foundation of life and of living together. Thus we can say that there are, in fact, some signs of a return to a reason that is open to transcending itself and to seeking out the Other.

We need the others: that is why there will be no improvement in the quality of life for everyone unless we set in motion processes for the humanization of our common life at all levels. We need new forms of city which would be images of the future promised City of God. From the point of view of ethics, one of the main issues at stake is the construction of a 'people-friendly' city, a form of sustainable human development, of urban cohabitation that can overcome the inequalities stemming from injustice, of fostering respect and rehabilitation not only of our historical and cultural heritage but also of our environment.

The ethical basis for this action might well be linked to Saint Augustine's inspired reflection in an historical moment no less dramatic and complex than our own, during the decline and fall of the Roman Empire. Replying to those blaming Christianity for that appalling collapse, the African Bishop did not hesitate to expose the true reasons for the crisis. The impact of the Barbarian hordes was, in his view, only a concurrent element, which could even have had some positive consequences such as infusing new lymph into a civilization by then in its death throes. The true, deep cause of the crisis of Rome was a moral one for Augustine. It was the widespread mentality (supported by the ruling class, but also espoused by the commoners) which led Rome to prefer *vanitas* to *veritas*. The two concepts were the expression of opposing logics: vanity is linked to appearing, to the triumph of the mask which hides self-interest and immediate prospects behind pompous words. Truth, on the other hand, means measuring choices against enduring ethical values, and thus against the inalienable dignity of the human being in the face of his temporal and eternal destiny. A passage from the *De Civitate Dei* (The City of God) may help us appreciate the difference as it was understood by Augustine: to the world 'that is corrupted and is falling into ruins' (*tabescenti ac labenti mundo*) he opposes the hand of God, which gathers together with family to create His eternal glorious city 'whose glory rests not on the acclamations of vanity, but on the judgment of truth' (*non plausu vanitatis, sed iudicio veritatis*: II, 18, 2). This intuition seems to me extraordinarily relevant in our times: faced with a civilization of appearances, which pursues the myths of exasperated consumerism and rampant hedonism, we might see the emergence of an alternative vision constructed on the truth of things and the primacy of values which no one is entitled to deny. And what is this truth? What are these values? I should like to attempt to identify them by comparing *vanitas* to *veritas* in the five main problematic areas the various authors have touched upon.

First, *the arena of politics and institutions*: the dehumanization of the city we so often face stems from a type of governance which divorces the wielding of power from moral responsibility, and democratic representation from true concern with the needs and interests of citizens. Where the administrator or politician pursues solely his or her own interests, focusing on public image and seeking consensus through favouritism and the support of lobbies, we find the triumph of *vanitas* over *veritas*. The role played by the media in this process is quite obvious, as is the role which they might play by exposing and criticizing. The primacy of truth in this sense requires that policy-makers and administrators be engaged in a disinterested quest for the common good, open to citizens' needs, rights, proposals and potential for achievement. The ideal of so-called *good governance* has a strong ethical element: it requires the participation of all stakeholders in decision-making and seeks to serve the community rather than taking advantage of it in order to build consensus.

A similar form of dialectics is to be found on the *level of cultural models and spiritual resources*: *vanitas* triumphs where the search for the ephemeral is favoured, uprooting all efforts for the achievement of the common good – and their precious traces left in works of art and invention – from the collective memory. A community whose memory has been eradicated is not only without identity but is also vulnerable to perverse exploitation. In this regard, upholding *veritas* means respecting and recovering the cultural, artistic and religious heritage of the collectivity as a basis for recognizing its true needs and priorities. Widespread education, sustained by an efficient teaching and scientific research system, is essential for the conservation of cultural and environmental assets. Any vision of the city separated from its ethical and spiritual roots will inevitably be ephemeral and inconsistent. Only respect for our past will make it possible to create a future on a human dimension and to improve the quality of life for all.

A third sphere in which we can put Augustine's dialectics to the test is *urban planning*. Here we may consider products of *vanitas* all those ideological approaches that impose on reality function-oriented logic based on ready-made models, disconnected to the analysis and respect for territory, for ecology, for human resources and spiritual components. Conversely, a 'truthful' approach to urban planning places the dignity of the human being at the centre and heart of each action, and aims at creating a community geared to human needs, where interpersonal relationships are enhanced and promoted. This approach involves social and political actions seeking to overcome social inequalities, targeting, in particular, the weaker groups and their rights as individuals and citizens. While *vanitas* makes efficiency an absolute requirement, *veritas* chooses the primacy of equity, both regarding the distribution of resources and the programming and the active involvement of recipients.

The *economic arena* is no less subject to the opposition of *vanitas* and *veritas*: if the former inspires economic action based exclusively on profit and private interest, the second seeks an integrated economy that targets not only maximization of profit but also the participation of all in assets, involvement of disadvantaged groups, empowerment of youth, women, senior citizens, and minorities. It is an economic model based on communality. Some of its goals are putting resources at the disposal of all, respect for nature, collective participation in profits, targeted re-investment for social purposes and responsibility towards future generations. It can be a truly significant model for a change of direction in the economy. The city of the future cannot be planned and managed based on an exclusively utilitarian logic: either it will stem from an integrated economy that harmonizes public interest with compatible private interests in a 'civil economy' that can enhance the role of all players and promote collective growth, or it will run the risk of increasing processes of fragmentation leading to the de-humanization and degradation of human communities.

Finally, we should consider Augustine's enduring relevance in terms of modern *ethics*. We must oppose an individualistic and utilitarian moral stance, aimed exclusively at promoting the interests of the individual or the few with the ethics of truth open to values founded on common humanity and the transcendent dignity of the human being. This form of ethics will be marked by the primacy of responsibility towards others, towards ourselves and towards the environment, by the consequent requirement for solidarity, which places in the forefront the rights of the weak, the single individual, groups, peoples or whole countries. Consider, for example, the debt of Third World countries and the need to cancel it, also as a form of reparation for the ecological damage caused by over-development of the rich countries. This form of ethics is open to spiritual values which range from respect for cultural and artistic heritage, to religious liberty, to respect and promotion for religious quest, devotion and preaching. On their part, believers should feel called upon to collaborate to the greatest extent possible in achieving the humanization of the future city through active and responsible participation in processes of sustainable human development.

The *Naples Declaration* which closes this volume was adopted by all attendees at the World Meeting "The Human Being and the City. Towards a Human and Sustainable Development" (Naples, 6-8 September 2000). It seems to take a stance in favour of the ethics of truth. Its various sections uphold the logic of sharing and service against the logic of *vanitas* (the ephemeral, the apparent, the self-serving). In this sense, it is a manifesto serving the cause of improving the quality of life for all with the convinced and responsible involvement of each individual notwithstanding differences in political orientation or religious creed.

The fact that the ethics of *veritas* finds its confirmation, and most profound inspiration, in biblical tradition in no way limits its universal applicability. On the contrary, it proves – if there were any need of further proof – that the 'great codex', the Bible, contains the potential for justice and peace from which the whole of humanity has drawn, and will continue to draw, inspiration with no fear of sectarianism or oppression. This affirmation with reference to a congress held in the Jubilee year is a reason for hope that involves us all – believers and non-believers – insofar as we truly desire the creation of a city of the future less dissimilar to the City of God, desired and hoped for by the Lord of history for the whole family of humankind.

References

Hobsbawm, E. (1994), *The Age of Extremes: The Short Twentieth Century 1914-1991*, Penguin, London.

Horkheimer, M. (1970), *Die Sehnsucht nach dem ganz Anderen*, Fursche Verlag, Hamburg.

Horkheimer, M. and Adorno, T.W (1973), *Dialectic of Enlightenment*, translated by John Cumming, Allen Lane, London.

Naples Declaration

Preamble

We, the participants in the World Meeting *The Human Being and The City: Towards a Human and Sustainable Development*, held in Naples, 6-8 September 2000:

- In recognition of the pivotal role that cities play in economic development and job creation, in promoting cultural creativity and technological and organizational innovation;
- Concerned with the social, economic, and environmental impacts of urbanization, globalization and social change; and
- Noting the potential contribution that cities can make in promoting more sustainable forms of development and improving the quality of life;

hereby declare:

1. Justice for a more Humane City

A more humane city must be based on the principles of social and environmental justice. It must respect and promote the dignity of every person, and ensure the right of self-expression by diverse cultures. Urban problems, such as poverty, unemployment and underemployment, lack of adequate shelter, secure tenure and basic services, and social and ethnic exclusion are not inevitable evils. Rather, they are a scandal, too often resulting from a lack of political will and good governance. Particularly in developing countries, foreign debt and environmental degradation are closely linked. The 'global common good' of a more humane city cannot be achieved without reducing inequalities of all kinds and at all levels.

2. Good Governance

The challenge of more humane and sustainable urban development cannot be met without good governance. Good governance requires the participation of all humankind – women and men of all ages – in public choices at all levels of decision-making.

3. Towards a New Integrated Economic Vision

There is a need to build a new paradigm for economic development based on inherent human and environmental values, recognizing the contribution of the 'civil economy'. This expression, inspired by the Neapolitan economist Antonio Genovesi (1713-1769), means an economy that incorporates the wealth, added value produced by the family, community, non-profit, voluntary, LETS (Local Exchange Trade System), micro and ethical financing, fair trade and mutual and self-help activities, as well as the critical unaccounted use of natural resources. Such an economy requires adequate indicators, not only economic but environmental, not only aggregate but also distributional, not only material but also spiritual.

4. The Role of Integrated and Participatory Planning

Integrated and participatory planning should provide the basis for more sustainable urban development strategies. Such planning should strengthen civil society; build social capital; promote community-based development; and stimulate local enterprise (particularly among women and the young) and cultural vitality.

5. The Principle of Subsidiarity and the Promotion of Sustainable Communities

The Habitat Agenda and Local Agenda 21 are important instruments recognizing the critical contribution of partnerships, participation, capacity-building and decentralization based on the principle of subsidiarity. They should be widely applied by governments at all levels, and involve the active participation of religious, social, economic, cultural and professional associations, academic and research institutions, and grassroots organizations.

6. The Importance of Collective Memory and the Culture of the City

Cities are increasingly multiethnic and multi-cultural. The right to the city must be broad-based and all-encompassing. Nevertheless, the historical and cultural heritage, representing the collective memory of the city, its specificity and identity, must be preserved and promoted as a key contribution to the humanization of our cities.

7. Technology

Scientific and technological advancement is an essential component of sustainable development. In the past, however, it has too often accentuated inequality and harmed the environment. From now on, new forms of technology should directly address the needs of the poor and abide by the precautionary principle.

8. The Cultural and Educational Dimension

The cultural and educational dimensions have a strategic role to play in providing the human and social capital with more sustainable forms of development. These dimensions must be promoted together with spiritual, aesthetic and relational ones within more comprehensive and holistic educational systems. A particular responsibility lies with the media. New Information and Communication Technologies should be put to work to promote the education necessary to achieve social and environmental justice.

9. Towards a New Global Ethics

Our norms and ethics of behaviour for the twenty-first century should be based on a shared recognition of our common humanity and our shared eco-systems, to enable the non-violent resolution of conflicts and differences and the recognition of the ' common global good'. These ethics and norms must keep the human being and human relationships at the centre of all decision-making, thus going beyond the narrow logic of economic development to include the concern for social and environmental justice.

10. The Importance of the Spiritual Dimension

The spiritual dimension in its broadest sense is essential to sustainable human development. It strengthens justice, solidarity, reciprocity and aesthetic values. Every city should preserve and promote this dimension as an essential aspect of the well-being of its people.

Index

For Product Safety Concerns and Information please contact our EU
representative GPSR@taylorandfrancis.com
Taylor & Francis Verlag GmbH, Kaufingerstraße 24, 80331 München, Germany